# New Perspectives on

# Microsoft® Offic Access 2003

D1311919

## Comprehensive

**THOMSON** ™

**COURSE TECHNOLOGY**

Australia • Canada • Mexico • Singapore • Spain • United Kingdom • United States

# What does this logo mean?

It means this courseware has been approved by the Microsoft® Office Specialist Program to be among the finest available for learning Microsoft Office Word 2003, Microsoft Office Excel 2003, Microsoft Office Access 2003, and Microsoft Office PowerPoint® 2003. It also means that upon completion of this courseware, you may be prepared to take an exam for Microsoft Office Specialist qualification.

This text will prepare students for Microsoft Office Specialist certification for Microsoft Office Access 2003.

# What is a Microsoft Office Specialist?

A Microsoft Office Specialist is an individual who has passed exams for certifying his or her skills in one or more of the Microsoft Office desktop applications such as Microsoft Word, Microsoft Excel, Microsoft PowerPoint, Microsoft Outlook®, Microsoft Access, or Microsoft Project. The Microsoft Office Specialist Program is the only program in the world approved by Microsoft for testing proficiency in Microsoft Office desktop applications and Microsoft Project.* This testing program can be a valuable asset in any job search or career advancement.

# More Information:

To learn more about becoming a Microsoft Office Specialist, visit  www.microsoft.com/officespecialist

To learn about other Microsoft Office Specialist approved courseware from Course Technology, visit **www.course.com/newperspectives/teacherslounge**

**www.course.com/NewPerspectives**

# New Perspectives on

# Microsoft® Office Access 2003

## Comprehensive

**Joseph J. Adamski**
Grand Valley State University

**Kathleen T. Finnegan**

**THOMSON**
**COURSE TECHNOLOGY** ™

Australia • Canada • Mexico • Singapore • Spain • United Kingdom • United States

**THOMSON**

**COURSE TECHNOLOGY**

**New Perspectives on Microsoft® Office Access 2003—Comprehensive**
is published by Course Technology.

**Managing Editor:**
Rachel Goldberg

**Senior Product Manager:**
Kathy Finnegan

**Senior Technology Product Manager:**
Amanda Young Shelton

**Product Manager:**
Karen Stevens

**Product Manager:**
Brianna Germain

**Editorial Assistant:**
Abigail Z. Reider

**Senior Marketing Manager:**
Rachel Stephens

**Associate Marketing Manager:**
Caitlin Wight

**Developmental Editor:**
Lisa Ruffolo

**Production Editor:**
Summer Hughes

**Composition:**
GEX Publishing Services

**Text Designer:**
Steve Deschene

**Cover Designer:**
Nancy Goulet

# Preface

Real, Thought-Provoking, Engaging, Dynamic, Interactive—these are just a few of the words that are used to describe the New Perspectives Series' approach to learning and building computer skills.

Without our critical-thinking and problem-solving methodology, computer skills could be learned but not retained. By teaching with a case-based approach, the New Perspectives Series challenges students to apply what they've learned to real-life situations.

Our ever-growing community of users understands why they're learning what they're learning. Now you can too!

**See what instructors and students are saying about the best-selling New Perspectives Series:**

> "I have used books from the New Perspectives series for about ten years now. I haven't been able to find anything else that approaches their quality when it comes to covering intermediate and advanced software application topics."
> — Karleen Nordquist, College of St. Benedict & St. John's University

**...and about New Perspectives on Microsoft Office Access 2003:**

> "The author's approach to databases is unique. Students learn the importance of databases in the real world through the completion of hands-on tutorials and each case study. This book is highly recommended among college faculty as well as database users."
> — Amal Rowezak, Alfred State College

> "One of the greatest strengths of this text is the detailed explanations that accompany the step-by-step instructions. Too many textbooks focus solely on the step-by-step instructions leaving out important concepts of how and why the techniques work."
> — Dwight Clayton, Northern Maine Community College

> "I believe this book is an excellent choice to take individuals from little knowledge to having a strong background in typical business use of Access as a business manager or entry-level database support person."
> — Daniel J. Moseler, Harrisburg Area Community College

> "I love the New Perspective series. I have used them for years and we plan to continue to use New Perspectives in the future. I think this book lives up to its reputation, and I would highly recommend it."
> — Sandra Brown, Finger Lakes Community College

**www.course.com/NewPerspectives**

# Why *New Perspectives* will work for you

**Context**

Each tutorial begins with a problem presented in a "real-world" case that is meaningful to students. The case sets the scene to help students understand what they will do in the tutorial.

**Hands-on Approach**

Each tutorial is divided into manageable sessions that combine reading and hands-on, step-by-step work. Screenshots—now 20% larger for enhanced readability—help guide students through the steps. **Trouble?** tips anticipate common mistakes or problems to help students stay on track and continue with the tutorial.

Review

**Review**

In New Perspectives, retention is a key component to learning. At the end of each session, a series of Quick Check questions helps students test their understanding of the concepts before moving on. And now each tutorial contains an end-of-tutorial summary and a list of key terms for further reinforcement.

Apply

**Assessment**

Engaging and challenging Review Assignments and Case Problems have always been a hallmark feature of the New Perspectives Series. Now we've added new features to make them more accessible! Colorful icons and brief descriptions accompany the exercises, making it easy to understand, at a glance, both the goal and level of challenge a particular assignment holds.

Reference Window

Task Reference

**Reference**

While contextual learning is excellent for retention, there are times when students will want a high-level understanding of how to accomplish a task. Within each tutorial, Reference Windows appear before a set of steps to provide a succinct summary and preview of how to perform a task. In addition, a complete Task Reference at the back of the book provides quick access to information on how to carry out common tasks. Finally, each book includes a combination Glossary/Index to promote easy reference of material.

Reinforce

**Lab Assignments**

Certain tutorials in this book contain Lab Assignments, which provide additional reinforcement of important skills in a simulated environment. These labs have been hailed by students and teachers alike for years as the most comprehensive and accurate on the market. Great for pre-work or remediation, the labs help students learn concepts and skills in a structured environment.

**Student Online Companion**

This book has an accompanying online companion Web site designed to enhance learning. This Web site includes:

- Internet Assignments and Lab Assignments for selected tutorials
- Student Data Files and PowerPoint presentations
- Microsoft Office Specialist Certification Grids

**Certification**

This logo on the front of this book means that this book has been independently reviewed and approved by ProCert Labs. If you are interested in acquiring Microsoft Office Specialist certification, you may use this book as courseware in your preparation. For more information on this certification, go to www.microsoft.com/officespecialist.

**www.course.com/NewPerspectives**

# *New Perspectives* offers an entire system of instruction

The New Perspectives Series is more than just a handful of books. It's a complete system of offerings:

### New Perspectives catalog
Our online catalog is never out of date! Go to the catalog link on our Web site to check out our available titles, request a desk copy, download a book preview, or locate online files.

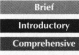

### Coverage to meet your needs!
Whether you're looking for just a small amount of coverage or enough to fill a semester-long class, we can provide you with a textbook that meets your needs.

- Brief books typically cover the essential skills in just 2 to 4 tutorials.
- Introductory books build and expand on those skills and contain an average of 5 to 8 tutorials.
- Comprehensive books are great for a full-semester class, and contain 9 to 12+ tutorials.
- Power Users or Advanced books are perfect for a highly accelerated introductory class or a second course in a given topic.

So if the book you're holding does not provide the right amount of coverage for you, there's probably another offering available. Go to our Web site or contact your Course Technology sales representative to find out what else we offer.

### Instructor Resources
We offer more than just a book. We have all the tools you need to enhance your lectures, check students' work, and generate exams in a new, easier-to-use and completely revised package. This book's Instructor's Manual, ExamView testbank, PowerPoint presentations, data files, solution files, figure files, and a sample syllabus are all available on a single CD-ROM or for downloading at www.course.com.

### How will your students master Microsoft Office?
SAM (Skills Assessment Manager) 2003 helps you energize your class exams and training assignments by allowing students to learn and test important computer skills in an active, hands-on environment. With SAM 2003, you create powerful interactive exams on critical Microsoft Office 2003 applications, including Word, Excel, Access, and PowerPoint. The exams simulate the application environment, allowing your students to demonstrate their knowledge and to think through the skills by performing real-world tasks. Designed to be used with the New Perspectives Series, SAM 2003 includes built-in page references so students can create study guides that match the New Perspectives textbooks you use in class. Powerful administrative options allow you to schedule exams and assignments, secure your tests, and run reports with almost limitless flexibility. Find out more about SAM 2003 by going to www.course.com or speaking with your Course Technology sales representative.

### Distance Learning
Enhance your course with any of our online learning platforms. Go to www.course.com or speak with your Course Technology sales representative to find the platform or the content that's right for you.

**www.course.com/NewPerspectives**

# About This Book

This book provides comprehensive instruction of Microsoft Access 2003, from essential database concepts through advanced topics such as macros and VBA.

- Updated for the new software! Includes coverage of the new Property Update Options button; the new Object Dependencies feature; and the new Property Propagation feature.
- This edition has been expanded into 12 tutorials and reorganized to provide focused attention on queries, forms, and reports. New features include guidelines for designing forms and reports and lists of common macros and common events.
- Tutorials 1–4 introduce students to fundamental database concepts. Students create a database from scratch and use Wizards to create simple forms, queries, and reports. Now includes coverage of setting field captions.
- Tutorials 5–7 have been reorganized for greater focus: Tutorial 5 concentrates on queries; coverage of forms has been consolidated into Tutorial 6; and Tutorial 7 offers expanded coverage of reports. T8 continues to focus on integration with the Web and other Microsoft Office applications.
- Tutorials 9–12 offer in-depth coverage of action queries; relationships; macro creation and switchboards; and managing and securing a database.
- In response to customer feedback, the tutorial on VBA has been updated to introduce a data validation function.
- The Relational Databases and Database Design appendix has been revised to include surrogate keys and database naming conventions.
- By popular demand, this book now includes a new tutorial on file management.
- This book meets certification requirements for the Microsoft Office Access 2003 exam.

New to this edition!

- Larger screenshots!
- Sequential page numbering!
- New end-of-tutorial material provides additional conceptual review in the form of key terms and a tutorial summary.
- New labels and descriptions for the end-of-tutorial exercises make it easy for you to select the right exercises for your students.

# Acknowledgments

I would like to thank the following reviewers for their helpful and thorough feedback: Sandra Brown, Finger Lakes Community College; Dwight Clayton, Northern Maine Community College; Shui-lien Huang, Mt. San Antonio College; Glen Johansson, Spokane Community College; Daniel Moseler, Harrisburg Area Community College; Amal Rowezak, Alfred State College; and Kathy Winters, The University of Tennessee at Chattanooga. Many thanks to all the Course Technology staff, especially Rachel Goldberg for her inspiring leadership and unwavering support; Karen Stevens, whose outstanding product management and good humor kept us focused and energized; Abbey Reider for her many contributions along the way; Summer Hughes for her excellent management of the production process; John Bosco, John Freitas, Ashlee Welz, Marc Spoto, and Marianne Snow for ensuring the quality and accuracy of this text; and Rebekah Tidwell, Steven Freund, and Dave Nuscher for their work on the Instructor Resources. Special thanks to Lisa Ruffolo for her exceptional editorial skills and careful attention to detail, and for always being there to help just when I needed it most. As always, I'm grateful to Joe Adamski for his continued guidance and expertise. This book is dedicated with love to my two incredible sons, Connor and Devon, who make me proud in some way, every day.
— Kathleen T. Finnegan

Thank you to all the people who contributed to planning, developing, and completing this book, with special thanks to Kathy Finnegan, Lisa Ruffolo, and Karen Stevens. I was one of the few authors of a Microsoft Access 1.1 book approximately ten years ago, so I would like to take this anniversary occasion to especially thank the students and instructors who have used the New Perspectives Microsoft Access books and have provided positive and constructive feedback over the years.
— Joseph J. Adamski

# Brief Contents

## Access—Level III Tutorials — AC 441

# Table of Contents

## Access
**Level II Tutorials** . . . . . . . . . . . . . . . . . . . . . . . **AC 169**

## Tutorial 5        AC 171

### Enhancing a Table's Design and Creating Advanced Queries . . . . . . . **AC 171**

## Tutorial 6        AC 221

### Creating Custom Forms . . . . . . . . . . **AC 221**

## Tutorial 10        AC 489

### Automating Tasks with Macros . . . . AC 489

Creating a User Interface for the
Overseas Database   . . . . . . . . . . . . . . . .AC 489

# New Perspectives on
# Managing Your Files

Creating and Working with Files
and Folders in Windows XP

FM 3

# Read This Before You Begin

## To the Student

### Data Files

To complete the Managing Your Files (FM) tutorial, you need the starting student Data Files. Your instructor will either provide you with these Data Files or ask you to obtain them yourself.

The Managing Your Files tutorial requires the folder named "FM" to complete the Tutorial, Review Assignments, and Case Problems. You will need to copy this folder from a file server, a standalone computer, or the Web to the drive and folder where you will be storing your Data Files. Your instructor will tell you which computer, drive letter, and folder(s) contain the files you need. You can also download the files by going to www.course.com; see the inside back or front cover for more information on downloading the files, or ask your instructor or technical support person for assistance.

If you are storing your Data Files on floppy disks, you will need **two** blank, formatted, high-density disks for this tutorial. Label your disks as shown, and place on them the folders indicated.

▼**FM Data Disk 1: Tutorial**
    FM\Tutorial folder
▼**FM Data Disk 2: Exercises**
    FM\Review folder
    FM\Cases folder

When you begin this tutorial, refer to the Student Data Files section at the bottom of the tutorial opener page, which indicates which folders and files you need for the tutorial. Each end-of-tutorial exercise also indicates the files you need to complete that exercise

### Course Labs

The Managing Your Files tutorial features an interactive Course Lab to help you understand file management concepts. There are Lab Assignments at the end of the tutorial that relate to this lab. Contact your instructor or technical support person for assistance in accessing the labs.

## To the Instructor

The Data Files and Course Labs are available on the Instructor Resources CD for this title. Follow the instructions in the Help file on the CD to install the programs to your network or standalone computer. See the "To the Student" section above for information on how to set up the Data Files that accompany this text.

You are granted a license to copy the Data Files and Course Labs to any computer or computer network used by students who have purchased this book.

## System Requirements

**If you are going to work through this book using your own computer, you need:**

• **Computer System** This tutorial assumes a typical installation of Microsoft Windows XP Professional (although the Microsoft Windows XP Home version is acceptable as well).

• **Data Files** You will not be able to complete the tutorials or exercises in this book using your own computer until you have the necessary starting Data Files.

• **Course Labs** See your instructor or technical support person to obtain the Course Lab software for use on your own computer.

## Objectives

- Develop file management strategies
- Explore files and folders
- Create, name, copy, move, and delete folders
- Name, copy, move, and delete files
- Work with compressed files

# Managing Your Files

*Creating and Working with Files and Folders in Windows XP*

## Case

### Distance Learning Company

The Distance Learning Company specializes in distance learning courses for individuals who want to participate in college-level classes to work toward a degree or for personal enrichment. Distance learning is formalized education that typically takes place using a computer and the Internet, replacing normal classroom interaction with modern communications technology. The company's goal is to help students gain new skills and stay competitive in the job market. The head of the Customer Service Department, Shannon Connell, interacts with the Distance Learning Company's clients on the phone and from her computer. Shannon, like all other employees, is required to learn the basics of managing files on her computer.

In this tutorial, you'll help Shannon devise a strategy for managing files. You'll learn how Windows XP organizes files and folders, and you'll examine Windows XP file management tools. You'll create folders and organize files within them. You'll also explore options for working with compressed files.

## Lab

**Using Files**

## Student Data Files

**▼FM folder**

▽ **Tutorial folder**

Agenda.doc
Holiday.bmp
New Logo.bmp
Proposal.doc
Resume.doc
Salinas members.eml
Stationery.bmp
Vinca.bmp

▽ **Review folder**

Billing Worksheet.wk4
Car Savings Plan.xls
Commissions.xls
Contracts.xls
Customer Accounts.xls
Filenames.pps
Personal Loan.doc
Speech.wav
Water lilies.jpg

▽ **Cases folder**

Invoice Feb.xls
Invoice Jan.xls
Invoice March.xls
Painting Class -
  Agenda.doc
Painting Class -
  Questionnaire.doc
Painting Class - Teaching
  Manual.doc
Paris.jpg
Vegetables.jpg

**Using Files**

# Organizing Files and Folders

Knowing how to save, locate, and organize computer files makes you more productive when you are working with a computer. A **file**, often referred to as a **document**, is a collection of data that has a name and is stored in a computer. Once you create a file, you can open it, edit its contents, print it, and save it again—usually using the same program you used to create it. You organize files by storing them in **folders**, which are containers for your files. You need to organize files so you can find them easily and work efficiently.

A file cabinet is a common metaphor for computer file organization. A computer is like a file cabinet that has two or more drawers—each drawer is a storage device, or **disk**. Each disk contains folders that hold documents, or files. To make it easy to retrieve files, you arrange them logically into folders. For example, one folder might contain financial data, another might contain your creative work, and another could contain information you're collecting for an upcoming vacation.

A computer can store folders and files on different types of disks, ranging from removable media such as **floppy disks**, **Zip disks**, and **compact discs (CDs)** to **hard disks**, or fixed disks, which are permanently stored in a computer. Hard disks are the most popular type of computer storage because they can contain many gigabytes of data—millions of times more data than a floppy disk—and are economical.

To have your computer access a removable disk, you must insert the disk into a **drive**, which is a computer device that can retrieve and sometimes record data on a disk. See Figure 1. A hard disk is already contained in a drive, so you don't need to insert it each time you use the computer.

**Figure 1** ▶ **Computer drives and disks**

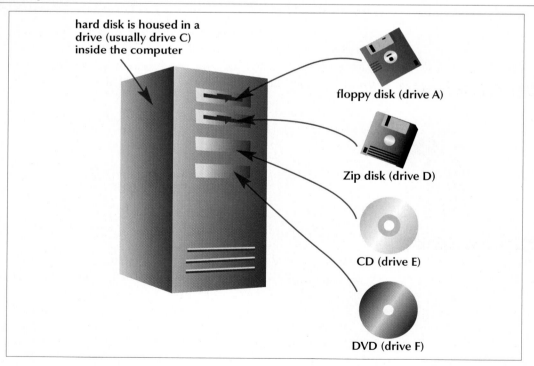

hard disk is housed in a
drive (usually drive C)
inside the computer

floppy disk (drive A)

Zip disk (drive D)

CD (drive E)

DVD (drive F)

A computer distinguishes one drive from another by assigning each a drive letter. The floppy disk drive is drive A. (Most computers have only one floppy disk drive—if your computer has two, the second one is called drive B.) The hard disk is usually assigned to drive C. The remaining drives can have any other letters, but are usually assigned in the order that the drives were installed on the computer—so your CD drive might be drive D or drive F.

# Understanding the Need for Organizing Files and Folders

Windows XP stores thousands of files in many folders on the hard disk of your computer. These are system files that Windows XP needs to display the desktop, use drives, and perform other operating system tasks. To ensure system stability and find files quickly, Windows organizes the folders and files in a hierarchy, or **file system**. At the top of the hierarchy, Windows stores folders and important files that it needs when you turn on the computer. This location is called the **root directory**, and is usually drive C (the hard disk). The term "root" refers to another popular metaphor for visualizing a file system—an upside-down tree, which reflects the file hierarchy that Windows uses. In Figure 2, the tree trunk corresponds to the root directory, the branches to the folders, and the leaves to files.

**Windows file hierarchy**  Figure 2

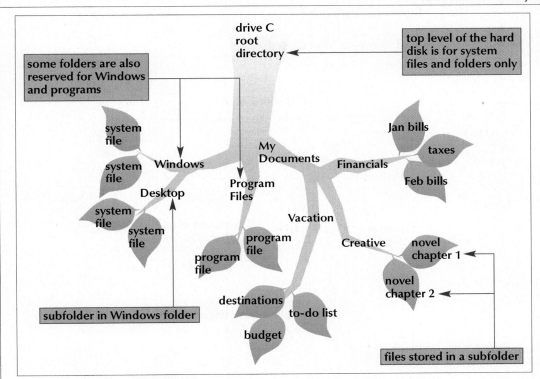

Note that some folders contain other folders. An effectively organized computer contains a few folders in the root directory, and those folders contain other folders, also called **subfolders**.

The root directory, or top level, of the hard disk is for system files and folders only—you should not store your own work here because it could interfere with Windows or a program. (If you are working in a computer lab, you might not be allowed to access the root directory.)

Do not delete or move any files or folders from the root directory of the hard disk—doing so could mean that you cannot run or start the computer. In fact, you should not reorganize or change any folder that contains installed software, because Windows XP expects to find the files for specific programs within certain folders. If you reorganize or change these folders, Windows XP cannot locate and start the programs stored in that folder. Likewise, you should not make changes to the folder that contains the Windows XP operating system (usually named Windows or Winnt).

Because the top level of the hard disk is off limits for your files—the ones that you create, open, and save on the hard disk—you must store your files in subfolders. If you are working on your own computer, you should store your files within the My Documents folder. If you are working in a computer lab, you will probably use a different location that your instructor specifies. If you simply store all your files in one folder, however, you will soon have trouble finding the ones you want. Instead, you should create folders within a main folder to separate files in a way that makes sense for you.

Likewise, if you store most of your files on a removable disk, such as a Zip disk, you need to organize those files into folders and subfolders. Before you start creating folders, whether on a hard disk or removable disk, you should plan the organization you will use.

## Developing Strategies for Organizing Files and Folders

The type of disk you use to store files determines how you organize those files. Figure 3 shows how you could organize your files on a hard disk if you were taking a full semester of distance learning classes. To duplicate this organization, you would open the main folder for your documents, create four folders—one each for the Basic Accounting, Computer Concepts, Management Skills II, and Professional Writing courses—and then store the writing assignments you complete in the Professional Writing folder.

**Figure 3** ▶ **Organizing folders and files on a hard disk**

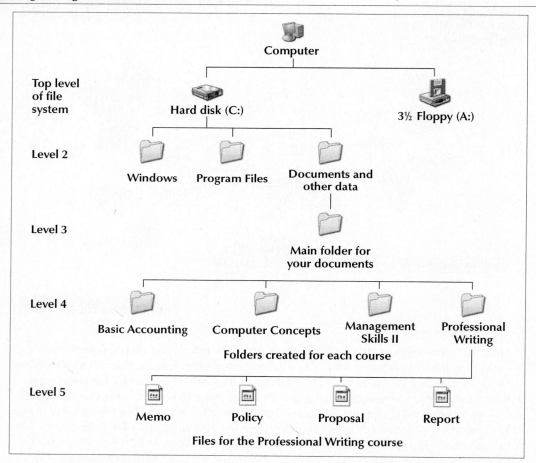

If you store your files on removable media, such as a floppy disk, Zip disk, or rewritable CD, you can use a simpler organization because you do not have to account for system files. In general, the larger the medium, the more levels of folders you should use because large media can store more files, and therefore need better organization. For example, you could organize your files on a 100 MB Zip disk. In the top level of the Zip disk, you could create folders for each general category of documents you store—one each for Courses, Creative, Financials, and Vacation. The Courses folder could then include one folder for each course, and each of those folders could contain the appropriate files.

You could organize these files on 1.44 MB floppy disks. Because the storage capacity of a floppy disk is much less than that of a Zip disk, you would probably use one floppy disk for your courses, another for creative work, and so on. If you had to create large documents for your courses, you could use one floppy disk for each course.

If you work on two computers, such as one computer at an office or school and another computer at home, you can duplicate the folders you use on both computers to simplify transferring files from one computer to another. For example, if you have four folders in your My Documents folder on your work computer, you would create these same four folders on your removable media as well as in the My Documents folder of your home computer. If you change a file on the hard disk of your home computer, you can copy the most recent version of the file to the corresponding folder on your removable media so that it is available when you are at work. You also then have a **backup**, or duplicate copy, of important files that you need.

## Planning Your Organization

Now that you've explored the basics of organizing files on a computer, you can plan the organization of your files for this book by writing in your answers to the following questions:

1. How do you obtain the files for this book (on a floppy disk from your instructor, for example)? _____

   _____

2. On what drive do you store your files for this book (drive A, C, D, for example)? _____

   _____

3. Do you use a particular folder on this drive? If so, which folder do you use? _____

   _____

4. Is this folder contained within another folder? If so, what is the name of that main folder?

   _____

5. On what type of disk do you save your files for this book (hard disk, floppy disk, Zip disk, CD, or network drive, for example)? _____

   If you cannot answer any of these questions, ask your instructor for help.

## Exploring Files and Folders

Windows XP provides two tools for exploring the files and folders on your computer—Windows Explorer and My Computer. Both display the contents of your computer, using icons to represent drives, folders, and files. However, by default, each presents a different view of your computer. **Windows Explorer** shows the files, folders, and drives on your computer, making it easy to navigate, or move from one location to another within the file hierarchy. **My Computer** shows the drives on your computer and makes it easy to perform system tasks, such as viewing system information.

The Windows Explorer window is divided into two sections, called **panes**. The left pane, also called the **Explorer bar** or **Folders pane**, shows the hierarchy of the folders and other locations on your computer. The right pane lists the contents of these folders and other locations. If you select a folder in the left pane, for example, the files stored in that folder appear in the right pane. The My Computer window is also divided into panes—the left pane, called the task pane, lists tasks related to the items displayed in the right pane.

If the Folders pane in Windows Explorer showed all the folders on your computer at once, it could be a very long list. Instead, Windows Explorer allows you to open drives and folders only when you want to see what they contain. If a folder contains subfolders, an expand icon ⊞ appears to the left of the folder icon. (The same is true for drives.) To view the folders contained in an object, you click the expand icon. A collapse icon ⊟ then appears next to the folder icon; click the collapse icon to close the folder. To view the files contained in a folder, you click the folder icon, and the files appear in the right pane. See Figure 4.

**Figure 4**  **Viewing folder contents in Windows Explorer**

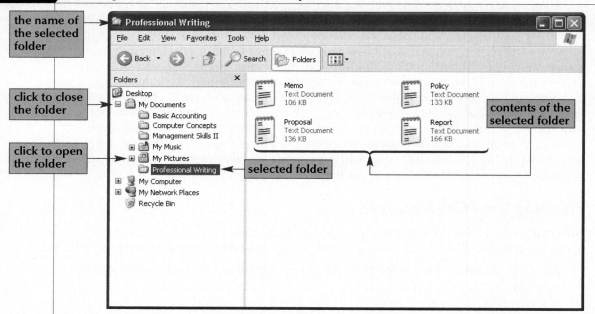

Using the Folders pane helps you navigate your computer and orients you to your current location. As you move, copy, delete, and perform other tasks with the files in the right pane of Windows Explorer, you can refer to the Folders pane to see how your changes affect the overall organization.

Like Windows Explorer, My Computer also lets you view, organize, and access the drives, folders, and files on your computer. Instead of using the Folders pane, however, you can navigate your computer in four other ways:

- **Opening drives and folders in the right pane:** To view the contents of a drive or folder, double-click the drive or folder icon in the right pane of the My Computer window. For example, to view the contents of the Professional Writing folder as shown in Figure 5, you open the My Documents folder and then the Professional Writing folder.
- **Using the Standard Buttons toolbar:** Click the buttons on the Standard Buttons toolbar to navigate the hierarchy of drives, folders, subfolders, and other objects in your computer.
- **Using the Address bar:** By clicking the Address bar list arrow, you can view a list of drives, folders, and other locations on your computer. This gives you a quick way of moving to an upper level of the Windows XP file system without navigating the intermediate levels.
- **Using the task pane:** The Other Places area of the My Computer task pane lists links you can click to quickly open folders or navigate to other useful places.

By default, when you first open My Computer, it shows all the drives available on your computer, whereas Windows Explorer shows the files, folders, and drives on your computer. However, by changing window settings, you can make the two tools interchangeable. You can change settings in the My Computer window to show the Folders pane instead of the task pane. If you do, you have the same setup as Windows Explorer. Likewise, if you close the Folders pane in the Windows Explorer window, the task pane opens, giving you the same setup as in the My Computer window.

Viewing folder contents in My Computer | **Figure 5**

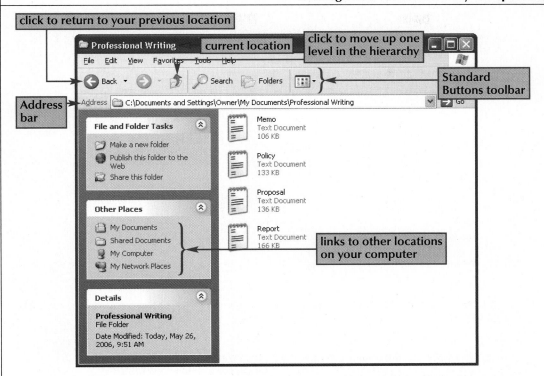

Shannon prefers to use Windows Explorer to manage her files. You'll use Windows Explorer to manage files in the rest of this tutorial.

## Using Windows Explorer

Windows XP also provides a folder for your documents—the **My Documents folder**, which is designed to store the files and folders you work with regularly. On your own computer, this is where you can keep your data files—the memos, videos, graphics, music, and other files that you create, edit, and manipulate in a program. If you are working in a computer lab, you might not be able to access the My Documents folder, or you might be able to store files there only temporarily because that folder is emptied every night. Instead, you might permanently store your Data Files on removable media or in a different folder on your computer or network.

When you start Windows Explorer, it opens to the My Documents folder by default. If you cannot access the My Documents folder, the screens you see as you perform the following steps will differ. However, you can still perform the steps accurately.

**To examine the organization of your computer using Windows Explorer:**

▶ 1. Click the **Start** button on the taskbar, point to **All Programs**, point to **Accessories**, and then click **Windows Explorer**. The Windows Explorer window opens.

▶ 2. Click the **expand** icon ＋ next to the My Computer icon. The drives and other useful locations on your computer appear under the My Computer icon, as shown in Figure 6. The contents of your computer will differ.

| Figure 6 | Viewing the contents of your computer |
| --- | --- |

3. Click the **expand** icon + next to the Local Disk (C:) icon. The contents of your hard disk appear under the Local Disk (C:) icon.

**Trouble?** If you do not have permission to access drive C, skip Step 3 and read but do not perform the remaining steps.

My Documents is still the selected folder. To view the contents of an object in the right pane, you can click the object's icon in the Folders pane.

4. Click **Documents and Settings** in the Folders pane. Its contents appear in the right pane. Documents and Settings is a built-in Windows XP folder that contains a folder for each user installed on the system.

You've already mastered the basics of navigating your computer with Windows Explorer. You click expand icons in the left pane until you find the folder that you want. Then you click the folder icon in the left pane to view the files it contains in the right pane.

## Navigating to Your Data Files

The **file path** is a notation that indicates a file's location on your computer. The file path leads you through the Windows file system to your file. For example, the Holiday file is stored in the Tutorial subfolder of the FM folder. If you are working on a floppy disk, for example, the path to this file is as follows:

**A:\FM\Tutorial\Holiday.bmp**

This path has four parts, and each part is separated by a backslash ( \ ):

- **A:** The drive name; as you've learned, drive A is the name for the floppy disk. If this file were stored on the hard disk, the drive name would be C.
- **FM:** The top-level folder on drive A.
- **Tutorial:** A subfolder in the FM folder.
- **Holiday.bmp:** The full filename with the file extension.

If someone tells you to find the file A:\FM\Tutorial\Holiday.bmp, you know you must navigate to your floppy disk drive, open the FM folder, and then open the Tutorial folder to find the Holiday file. My Computer and Windows Explorer can display the full file path in their Address bars so you can keep track of your current location as you navigate.

You can use Windows Explorer to navigate to the Data Files you need for the rest of this tutorial. Refer back to the information you provided in the "Planning Your Organization" section and note the drive on your system that contains your Data Files. In the following steps, this is drive A, the floppy disk drive. If necessary, substitute the appropriate drive on your system when you perform the steps.

### To navigate to your Data Files:

1. Make sure your computer can access your Data Files for this tutorial. For example, if you are using a floppy disk, insert the disk into the floppy disk drive.

   **Trouble?** If you don't have the Data Files, you need to get them before you can proceed. Your instructor will either give you the Data Files or ask you to obtain them from a specified location (such as a network drive). In either case, be sure that you make a backup copy of your Data Files before you start using them, so that the original files will be available on your copied disk in case you need to start over because of an error or problem. If you have any questions about the Data Files, see your instructor or technical support person for assistance.

2. In the Windows Explorer window, click the **expand** icon ⊞ next to the drive containing your Data Files, such as 3½ Floppy (A:). A list of the folders on that drive appears.

3. If the list of folders does not include the FM folder, continue clicking the **expand** icon ⊞ to navigate to the folder that contains the FM folder.

4. Click the **FM** folder. Its contents appear in the Folders pane and in the right pane of the Windows Explorer window. The FM folder contains the Cases, Review, and Tutorial folders, as shown in Figure 7. The other folders on your system might vary.

**Navigating to the FM folder**   **Figure 7**

5. In the left pane, click the **Tutorial** folder. The files it contains appear in the right pane. You want to view them as a list.

6. Click the **Views** button ⊞ on the Standard Buttons toolbar, and then click **List**. The files appear in List view in the Windows Explorer window. See Figure 8.

Figure 8 ▶   **Files in the Tutorial folder in List view**

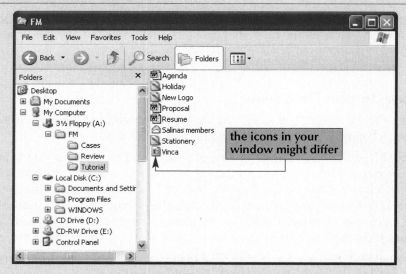

The file icons in your window depend on the programs installed on your computer, so they might be different from the ones shown in Figure 8.

Leave the Windows Explorer window open so you can work with the files in the Tutorial folder.

## Working with Folders and Files

After you devise a plan for storing your files, you are ready to get organized by creating folders that will hold your files. You can do so using My Computer or Windows Explorer. For this tutorial, you'll create folders in the Tutorial folder. When you are working on your own computer, you will usually create folders within the My Documents folder.

Examine the files shown in Figure 8 again and determine which files seem to belong together. Holiday, New Logo, and Vinca are all graphics files containing pictures or photographs. The Resume and Stationery files were created for a summer job hunt. The other files were created for the Salinas neighborhood association project to update a playground.

One way to organize these files is to create three folders—one for graphics, one for the job hunt files, and another for the Salinas files. When you create a folder, you give it a name, preferably one that describes its contents. A folder name can have up to 255 characters, except / \ : * ? " < > or |. With these guidelines in mind, you could create three folders as follows:

- **Graphics folder**: Holiday, New Logo, and Vinca files
- **Job Hunt folder**: Resume and Stationery files
- **Playground folder**: Agenda, Proposal, and Salinas members files

Shannon asks you to create three new folders. Then you'll move the files to the appropriate subfolder.

## Creating Folders

You've already seen folder icons in the windows you've examined. Now, you'll create folders in the Tutorial folder using the Windows Explorer menu bar.

## Creating a Folder Using Windows Explorer

- In the left pane, click the drive or folder where you want to create a folder.
- Click File on the menu bar, point to New, and then click Folder (*or* right-click a blank area in the folder window, point to New, and then click Folder).
- Type a name for the folder, and then press the Enter key.

Now you can create three folders in your Tutorial folder as you planned—the Graphics, Job Hunt, and Playground folders. The Windows Explorer window should show the contents of the Tutorial folder in List view.

### To create folders using Windows Explorer:

1. Click **File** on the menu bar, point to **New** to display the submenu, and then click **Folder**. A folder icon with the label "New Folder" appears in the right pane, and the expand icon appears next to the Tutorial folder because it now contains a subfolder. See Figure 9.

**Creating a folder in the Tutorial folder**  **Figure 9**

**Trouble?** If the "New Folder" name is not selected, right-click the new folder, click Rename, and then continue with Step 2.

Windows uses "New Folder" as a placeholder, and selects the text so that you can replace it with the name you want.

2. Type **Graphics** as the folder name, and then press the **Enter** key. The new folder is named "Graphics" and is the selected item in the right pane.

You are ready to create a second folder. This time you'll use a shortcut menu to create a folder.

3. Right-click a blank area next to the Graphics folder, point to **New** on the shortcut menu, and then click **Folder**. A folder icon with the label "New Folder" appears in the right pane with the "New Folder" text selected.

4. Type **Job Hunt** as the name of the new folder, and then press the **Enter** key.

5. Using the menu bar or the shortcut menu, create a folder named **Playground**. The Tutorial folder contains three new subfolders.

Now that you've created three folders, you're ready to organize your files by moving them into the appropriate folders.

## Moving and Copying Files and Folders

If you want to place a file into a folder from another location, you can either move the file or copy it. **Moving** a file removes it from its current location and places it in a new location you specify. **Copying** places the file in both locations. Windows XP provides several techniques for moving and copying files. The same principles apply to folders—you can move and copy folders using a variety of methods.

Reference Window

### Moving a File or Folder in Windows Explorer or My Computer

- Right-click and drag the file you want to move to the destination folder.
- Click Move Here on the shortcut menu.

*or*

- Click the file you want to move, and then click Move this file in the File and Folder Tasks area.
- In the Move Items dialog box, navigate to the destination folder, and then click the Move button.

Shannon suggests that you continue to work in List view so you can see all the files in the Tutorial folder, and then move some files from the Tutorial folder to the appropriate subfolders. You'll start by moving the Agenda, Proposal, and Salinas members files to the Playground folder.

### To move a file using the right mouse button:

1. Point to the **Agenda** file in the right pane, and then press and hold the *right* mouse button.

2. With the right mouse button still pressed down, drag the **Agenda** file to the **Playground** folder. When the Playground folder icon is highlighted, release the button. A shortcut menu opens.

3. With the left mouse button, click **Move Here** on the shortcut menu. The Agenda file is removed from the main Tutorial folder and stored in the Playground subfolder.

   **Trouble?** If you release the mouse button before dragging the Agenda file to the Playground folder, the shortcut menu opens, letting you move the file to a different folder. Press the Esc key to close the shortcut menu without moving the file, and then repeat Steps 1 through 3.

4. In the right pane, double-click the **Playground** folder. The Agenda file is in the Playground folder.

5. In the left pane, click the **Tutorial** folder to see its contents. The Tutorial folder no longer contains the Agenda file.

The advantage of moving a file or folder by dragging with the right mouse button is that you can efficiently complete your work with one action. However, this technique requires polished mouse skills so that you can drag the file comfortably. Another way to move files and folders is to use the File and Folder Tasks links in the task pane of the Windows Explorer or My Computer window. Although using the File and Folder Tasks links takes more steps, some users find it easier than dragging with the right mouse button.

You'll move the Resume file to the Job Hunt folder next. First, you'll close the Folders pane so that the task pane replaces it.

### To move files using the File and Folder Tasks area:

▶ **1.** Click the **Folders** button on the Standard Buttons toolbar. The task pane replaces the Folders pane, so that this window now resembles the My Computer window. Switch to List view, if necessary.

▶ **2.** Click the **Resume** file to select it. The task pane links change so that they are appropriate for working with files.

▶ **3.** In the File and Folder Tasks area, click **Move this file**. The Move Items dialog box opens. See Figure 10.

**Move Items dialog box**  ◀  **Figure 10**

use the expand and collapse icons to navigate your computer

▶ **4.** Click the **expand** icon ⊞ next to the drive containing your Data Files. Continue clicking **expand** icons ⊞ to navigate to the Tutorial folder provided with your Data Files.

▶ **5.** Click the **Job Hunt** folder.

▶ **6.** Click the **Move** button. The Move Items dialog box closes; Windows moves the Resume file to the Job Hunt folder, and then displays the contents of the Tutorial folder, which no longer contains the Resume file.

You'll move the Stationery file from the Tutorial folder to the Job Hunt folder.

▶ **7.** Click the **Stationery** file in the Tutorial window, and then click **Move this file** in the File and Folder Tasks area. The Move Items dialog box opens again, with the Job Hunt folder already selected for you.

▶ **8.** Click the **Move** button.

You can also copy a file using the same techniques as when you move a file—by dragging with the right mouse button or by using the File and Folder Tasks links. Another easy way to copy a file is to use the file's shortcut menu. You can copy more than one file at the same time by selecting all the files you want to copy, and then clicking them as a group. To select files that are listed together in a window, click the first file in the list, hold down the Shift key, click the last file in the list, and then release the Shift key. To select files that are not listed together, click one file, hold down the Ctrl key, click the other files, and then release the Ctrl key.

| Reference Window | **Copying a File or Folder in Windows Explorer or My Computer** |
| --- | --- |

- Click the file or folder you want to copy, and then click Copy this file or Copy this folder in the File and Folder Tasks area.
- In the Copy Items dialog box, navigate to the destination folder, and then click the Copy button.

*or*

- Right-click the file or folder you want to copy, and then click Copy on the shortcut menu.
- Navigate to the destination folder.
- Right-click a blank area of the destination folder window, and then click Paste on the shortcut menu.

You'll copy the three graphics files from the Tutorial folder to the Graphics folder now. It's easiest to select multiple files in List view or Details view.

### To copy files using the shortcut menu:

▶ **1.** In the Tutorial window, switch to List view, if necessary, and then click the **Holiday** file.

▶ **2.** Hold down the **Ctrl** key, click the **New Logo** file, click the **Vinca** file, and then release the **Ctrl** key. Three files are selected in the Tutorial window.

▶ **3.** Right-click a selected file, and then click **Copy** on the shortcut menu.

▶ **4.** In the right pane, double-click the **Graphics** folder to open it.

▶ **5.** Right-click the background of the Graphics folder, and then click **Paste** on the shortcut menu. Windows copies the three files to the Graphics folder.

▶ **6.** Switch to List view, if necessary.

Now that you are familiar with two ways to copy files, you can use the technique you prefer to copy the Proposal and Salinas members files to the Playground folder.

### To copy the two files:

▶ **1.** In the Graphics folder window, click the **Back** button on the Standard Buttons toolbar to return to the Tutorial folder.

▶ **2.** Use any technique you've learned to copy the **Proposal** and **Salinas members** files from the Tutorial folder to the Playground folder.

You can move and copy folders in the same way that you move and copy files. When you do, you move or copy all the files contained in the folder. You'll practice moving and copying folders in the Case Problems at the end of this tutorial.

## Naming and Renaming Files

As you work with files, pay attention to **filenames**—they provide important information about the file, including its contents and purpose. A filename such as Car Sales.doc has three parts:

- **Main part of the filename:** The name you provide when you create a file, and the name you associate with a file
- **Dot:** The period ( . ) that separates the main part of the filename from the file extension
- **File extension:** Usually three characters that follow the dot in the filename

The main part of a filename can have up to 255 characters—this gives you plenty of room to name your file accurately enough so that you'll know the contents of the file just by looking at the filename. You can use spaces and certain punctuation symbols in your filenames. Like folder names, however, filenames cannot contain the symbols \ / ? : * " < > | because these characters have special meaning in Windows XP.

A filename might display an **extension**—three or more characters following a dot—that identifies the file's type and indicates the program in which the file was created. For example, in the filename Car Sales.doc, the extension "doc" identifies the file as one created by Microsoft Word, a word-processing program. You might also have a file called Car Sales.xls—the "xls" extension identifies the file as one created in Microsoft Excel, a spreadsheet program. Though the main parts of these filenames are identical, their extensions distinguish them as different files. You usually do not need to add extensions to your filenames because the program that you use to create the file adds the file extension automatically. Also, although Windows XP keeps track of extensions, not all computers are set to display them.

Be sure to give your files and folders meaningful names that will help you remember their purpose and contents. You can easily rename a file or folder by using the Rename command on the file's shortcut menu.

Shannon recommends that you rename the Agenda file in the Playground folder to give it a more descriptive filename—that file could contain the agenda for any meeting. The Agenda file was originally created to store a list of topics to discuss at a meeting of the Salinas neighborhood association. You'll rename the file "Salinas Meeting Agenda."

### To rename the Agenda file:

1. Click **Tutorial** in the Other Places menu, and then double-click the **Playground** folder.

2. In the Playground window, right-click the **Agenda** file, and then click **Rename** on the shortcut menu. The filename is highlighted and a box appears around it.

3. Type **Salinas Meeting Agenda**, and then press the **Enter** key. The file now appears with the new name.

   **Trouble?** If you make a mistake while typing and you haven't pressed the Enter key yet, press the Backspace key until you delete the mistake, and then complete Step 3. If you've already pressed the Enter key, repeat Steps 1 through 3 to rename the file again.

   **Trouble?** If your computer is set to display file extensions, a message might appear asking if you are sure you want to change the file extension. Click the No button, right-click the Agenda file, click Rename on the shortcut menu, type "Salinas Meeting Agenda.doc", and then press the Enter key.

All the files that originally appeared in the Tutorial folder are now stored in appropriate subfolders. Shannon mentions that you can streamline the organization of the Tutorial folder by deleting the files you no longer need.

## Deleting Files and Folders

You should periodically delete files and folders you no longer need so that your main folders and disks don't get cluttered. In My Computer or Windows Explorer, you delete a file or folder by deleting its icon. Be careful when you delete a folder, because you also delete all the files it contains. When you delete a file from a hard disk, Windows XP removes the filename from the folder, but stores the file contents in the Recycle Bin. The **Recycle Bin** is an area on your hard disk that holds deleted files until you remove them permanently; an icon on the desktop allows you easy access to the Recycle Bin. If you change your mind and want to retrieve a file deleted from your hard disk, you can use the Recycle Bin to recover it or return it to its original location. However, after you empty the Recycle Bin, you can no longer recover the files that were in it.

When you delete a file from a floppy disk or another disk on your network, it does not go into the Recycle Bin. Instead, it is deleted as soon as its icon disappears—and you cannot recover it.

Shannon reminds you that because you copied the Holiday, New Logo, Proposal, Salinas members, and Vinca files to the Graphics and Playground folders, you can safely delete the original files in the Tutorial folder. As with moving, copying, and renaming files and folders, you can delete a file or folder in many ways, including using a shortcut menu or the File and Folder Tasks menu.

### To delete files in the Tutorial folder:

▶  **1.** Use any technique you've learned to navigate to and open the **Tutorial** folder.

▶  **2.** Switch to List view (if necessary), click **Holiday** (the first file in the file list), hold down the **Shift** key, click **Vinca** (the last file in the file list), and then release the **Shift** key. All the files in the Tutorial folder are now selected. None of the subfolders should be selected.

▶  **3.** Right-click the selected files, and then click **Delete** on the shortcut menu. Windows XP asks if you're sure you want to delete these files.

▶  **4.** Click the **Yes** button.

So far, you've worked with files using Windows Explorer and My Computer, but you haven't viewed any of their contents. To view file contents, you open the file. When you double-click a file in Windows Explorer or My Computer, Windows XP starts the appropriate program and opens the file.

# Working with Compressed Files

If you transfer files from one location to another, such as from your hard disk to a removable disk or vice versa, or from one computer to another via e-mail, you can store the files in a **compressed (zipped) folder** so that they take up less disk space. You can then transfer the files more quickly. When you create a compressed folder, Windows XP displays a zipper on the folder icon.

You compress a folder so that the files it contains use less space on the disk. Compare two folders—a folder named My Pictures that contains about 8.6 MB of files and a compressed folder containing the same files, but requiring only 6.5 MB of disk space. In this case, the compressed files use about 25 percent less disk space than the uncompressed files.

You can create a compressed folder using the Compressed (zipped) Folder command on the New submenu of the File menu or shortcut menu in Windows Explorer or My Computer. Then you can compress files or other folders by dragging them into the compressed folder. You can open files directly from a compressed folder, or you can extract the files first. When you **extract** a file, you create an uncompressed copy of the file and folder in a folder you specify. The original file remains in the compressed folder.

If a different compression program has been installed on your computer, such as WinZip or PKZip, the Compressed (zipped) Folder command does not appear on the New submenu. Instead, it is replaced by the name of your compression program. In this case, refer to your compression program's Help system for instructions on working with compressed files.

Shannon suggests you compress the files and folders in the Tutorial folder so you can more quickly transfer them to another location.

## To compress the folders and files in the Tutorial folder:

▶ **1.** In Windows Explorer, navigate to the Tutorial folder.

▶ **2.** Right-click a blank area of the right pane, point to **New** on the shortcut menu, and then click **Compressed (zipped) Folder**. A new compressed folder with a zipper icon appears in the Tutorial window. See Figure 11. Your window might appear in a different view.

**Creating a compressed folder** ◀ **Figure 11**

**Trouble?** If the Compressed (zipped) Folder command does not appear on the New sub-menu, a different compression program is probably installed on your computer. Click a blank area of the Tutorial window to close the shortcut menu, and then read but do not perform the remaining steps.

▶ **3.** Type **Final Tutorial files**, and then press the **Enter** key. Windows XP creates the compressed folder in the Tutorial folder.

▶ **4.** Click the **Graphics** folder in the right pane, hold down the **Shift** key, click the **Playground** folder in the right pane, and then release the **Shift** key. Three folders are selected in the Tutorial window.

▶ **5.** Drag the three folders to the **Final Tutorial files** compressed folder. Windows XP copies the files to the folder, compressing them to save space.

You open a compressed folder by double-clicking it. You can then move and copy files and folders in a compressed folder, though you cannot rename them. If you want to open, edit, and save files in a compressed folder, you should first extract them. When you do, Windows XP uncompresses the files and copies them to a location that you specify, preserving them in their folders as appropriate.

## To extract the compressed files:

▶ **1.** Right-click the **Final Tutorial files** compressed folder, and then click **Extract All** on the shortcut menu. The Extraction Wizard starts and opens the Welcome to the Compressed (zipped) Folders Extraction Wizard dialog box.

▶ **2.** Click the **Next** button. The Select a Destination dialog box opens.

**3.** Press the **End** key to deselect the path in the text box, press the **Backspace** key as many times as necessary to delete "Final Tutorial files," and then type **Extracted**. The last three parts of the path in the text box should be "\FM\Tutorial\Extracted." See Figure 12.

**Figure 12** ▶ **Select a Destination dialog box**

**4.** Click the **Next** button. The Extraction Complete dialog box opens, indicating that your files have been successfully extracted to the specified folder.

**5.** Make sure the **Show extracted files** check box is checked, and then click the **Finish** button. The Extracted folder opens, showing the Graphics, Job Hunt, and Playground folders.

**6.** Open each folder to make sure it contains the files you worked with in this tutorial.

**7.** Close all open windows.

Shannon says you have successfully completed basic Windows XP file management tasks, and are ready to use Windows XP to organize your files.

**Review**

# Quick Check

**1.** What is the term for a collection of data that has a name and is stored on a disk or other storage medium?

**2.** If you have only one floppy disk drive on your computer, it is usually identified by the letter _____ .

**3.** The letter C is typically used for the _____ drive of a computer.

**4.** What are the two tools that Windows XP provides for exploring the files and folders on your computer?

**5.** What is the notation you can use to indicate a file's location on your computer?

**6.** True or False: The advantage of moving a file or folder by dragging with the right mouse button is that you can efficiently complete your work with one action.

**7.** In a filename, the _____ identifies the file's type and indicates the program in which the file was created.

**8.** True or False: When you extract a file, the original file is deleted from the compressed folder.

# Tutorial Summary

In this tutorial, you examined Windows XP file organization, noting that you need to organize files and folders to work efficiently. You learned about typical file management strategies, whether you are working on a hard disk or a removable disk. Then you applied these strategies to organizing files and folders by creating folders, moving and copying files, and renaming and deleting files. You also learned how to copy files to a compressed (zipped) folder, and then extract files from a compressed folder.

# Key Terms

| | | |
|---|---|---|
| backup | extract | move |
| compact disc (CD) | file | My Computer |
| compressed (zipped) folder | file path | My Documents folder |
| copy | file system | pane |
| disk | filename | Recycle Bin |
| document | floppy disk | root directory |
| drive | folder | subfolder |
| Explorer bar | Folders pane | Windows Explorer |
| extension | hard disk | Zip disk |

# Review Assignments

**Data Files needed for the Review Assignments: Commissions.xls, Contracts.xls, Customer Accounts.xls, Billing Worksheet.wk4, Car Savings Plan.xls, Personal Loan.doc, Speech.wav, Filenames.pps, Water lilies.jpg**

Complete the following steps, recording your answers to any questions in the spaces provided:

1. Use My Computer or Windows Explorer as necessary to record the following information:
   - Where are you supposed to store the files you use in the Review Assignments for this tutorial? _____
   - Describe the method you will use to navigate to the location where you save your files for this book. _____

   - Do you need to follow any special guidelines or conventions when naming the files your save for this book? For example, should all the filenames start with your course number or tutorial number? If so, describe the conventions. _____

   - When you are instructed to open a file for this book, what location are you supposed to use? _____
   - Describe the method you will use to navigate to this location. _____

2. Use My Computer or Windows Explorer to navigate to and open the FM\Review folder provided with your Data Files.
3. Examine the nine files in the Review folder included with your Data Files, and then answer the following questions:
   - How will you organize these files? _____

   - What folders will you create? _____

- Which files will you store in these folders? _____

_____

- Will you use any built-in Windows folders? If so, which ones? For which files?

_____

4. In the Review folder, create three folders: Business, Personal Finances, and Project Media.
5. Move the **Commissions**, **Contracts**, **Customer Accounts**, and **Billing Worksheet** files from the Review folder to the Business folder.
6. Move the **Car Savings Plan** and **Personal Loan** files to the Personal Finances folder.
7. Copy the remaining files to the Project Media folder.
8. Delete the files in the Review folder (do *not* delete any folders).
9. Rename the **Speech** file in the Project Media folder to **Ask Not**.
10. Create a compressed (zipped) folder in the Review folder named **Final Review files** that contains all the files and folders in the Review folder.
11. Extract the contents of the Final Review files folder to a new folder named **Extracted**. (*Hint:* The file path will end with "\FM\Review\Extracted.")
12. Use Windows Explorer or My Computer to locate all copies of the **Personal Loan** file in the subfolders of the Review folder. In which locations did you find this file?

_____

13. Close all open windows.

**Apply**

*Use the skills you learned in the tutorial to manage files and folders for an arts organization.*

# Case Problem 1

**Data Files needed for this Case Problem: Invoice Jan.xls, Invoice Feb.xls, Invoice March.xls, Painting Class – Agenda.doc, Painting Class – Questionnaire.doc, Painting Class – Teaching Manual.doc, Paris.jpg, Vegetables.jpg**

*Jefferson Street Fine Arts Center* Rae Wysnewski owns the Jefferson Street Fine Arts Center (JSFAC) in Pittsburgh, and offers classes and gallery, studio, and practice space for aspiring and fledgling artists, musicians, and dancers. Rae opened JSFAC two years ago, and this year the center has a record enrollment in its classes. Knowing you are multitalented, she hires you to teach a painting class for three months and to show her how to manage her files on her new Windows XP computer. Complete the following steps:

1. In the FM\Cases folder provided with your Data Files, create two folders: Invoices and Painting Class.
2. Move the **Invoice Jan**, **Invoice Feb**, and **Invoice March** files from the Cases folder to the Invoices folder.
3. Rename the three files in the Invoices folder to remove "Invoice" from each name.
4. Move the three text documents from the Cases folder to the Painting Class folder. Rename the three documents, using shorter but still descriptive names.
5. Copy the remaining files to the Painting Class folder.

**Explore**

6. Using My Computer or Windows Explorer, switch to Details view and then answer the following questions:
   a. What is the largest file in the Painting Class folder? _____
   b. How many files (don't include folders) are in the Cases folder? _____
   c. How many word-processed documents are in the Cases folder and its subfolders? ____
   d. How many files in the Painting Class folder are JPEG images? (*Hint:* Look in the Type column to identify JPEG images.) _____
7. Delete the **Paris** and **Vegetables** files from the Painting Class folder.

8. Open the Recycle Bin folder by double-clicking the Recycle Bin icon on the desktop. Do the Paris and Vegetables files appear in the Recycle Bin folder? Explain why or why not. _____

9. Copy the Painting Class folder to the Cases folder. The name of the duplicate folder appears as "Copy of Painting Class." Rename the "Copy of Painting Class" folder as "Graphics."

10. Create a new folder in the Cases folder named "JSFAC." Move the Invoices, Painting Class, and Graphics folders to the JSFAC folder.

## Case Problem 2

**Challenge**

*Extend what you've learned to discover other methods of managing files for a social service organization.*

**There are no Data Files needed for this Case Problem.**

***First Call Outreach***   Victor Crillo is the director of a social service organization named First Call Outreach in Toledo, Ohio. Its mission is to connect people who need help from local and state agencies to the appropriate service. Victor has a dedicated staff, but they are all relatively new to Windows XP. In particular, they have trouble finding files that they have saved on their hard disks. He asks you to demonstrate how to find files in Windows XP. Complete the following:

**Explore**

1. Windows XP Help and Support includes topics that explain how to search for files on a disk without looking through all the folders. Click the Start button and then click Help and Support to start Windows Help and Support. Use one of the following methods to locate topics on searching for files.
   - On the Home page, click the Windows Basics link. On the Windows Basics page, click the Finding and organizing files link, and then click the Searching for files or folders topic. In the article, click the Related Topics link, and then click Search for a file or folder.
   - On the Index page, type "files" (no quotation marks) in the Type in the keyword to find text box. In the list of entries for "files," double-click "searching for." In the Topics found dialog box, double-click "Searching for files or folders."
   - In the Search box, type "searching for files," and then click Search. Click the Searching for files or folders link.

**Explore**

2. Read the topic and click the Related Topics link at the end of the topic, if necessary, to provide the following information:
   a. To display the Search dialog box, you must click the _____ button, point to _____ from the menu, and finally click _____ from the submenu.
   b. Do you need to type in the entire filename to find the file? _____
   c. Name three file characteristics you can use as search options. _____

**Explore**

3. Use the Index page in Windows XP Help and Support to locate topics related to managing files and folders. Write out two procedures for managing files and folders that were not covered in the tutorial. _____

**Assess**

## SAM Assessment and Training

If you have a SAM user profile, you may have access to hands-on instruction, practice, and assessment of the skills covered in this tutorial. Log in to your SAM account and go to your assignments page to see what your instructor has assigned.

**Reinforce**

Using Files

## Lab Assignments

The New Perspectives Labs are designed to help you master some of the key concepts and skills presented in this text. The steps for completing this Lab are located on the Course Technology Web site. Log on to the Internet and use your Web browser to go to the Student Online Companion for New Perspectives Office 2003 site at **www.course.com/np/office2003**. Click the Lab Assignments link, and then navigate to the assignments for this tutorial.

**Review**

## Quick Check Answers

1. file
2. A
3. hard disk
4. Windows Explorer and My Computer
5. file path
6. true
7. extension
8. false

New Perspectives on

# Using Common Features of Microsoft® Office 2003

Preparing Promotional Materials      OFF 3

# Read This Before You Begin

## To the Student

### Data Files

To complete the Using Common Features of Microsoft Office 2003 tutorial, you need the starting student Data Files. Your instructor will either provide you with these Data Files or ask you to obtain them yourself.

The Using Common Features of Microsoft Office 2003 tutorial requires the folder named "OFF" to complete the Tutorial, Review Assignments, and Case Problems. You will need to copy this folder from a file server, a stand-alone computer, or the Web to the drive and folder where you will be storing your Data Files. Your instructor will tell you which computer, drive letter, and folder(s) contain the files you need. You can also download the files by going to www.course.com; see the inside back or front cover for more information on downloading the files, or ask your instructor or technical support person for assistance.

If you are storing your Data Files on floppy disks, you will need one blank, formatted, high-density disk for this tutorial. Label your disk as shown, and place on it the folder indicated.

▼**Common Features of Office: Data Disk**
 OFF folder

When you begin this tutorial, refer to the Student Data Files section at the bottom of the tutorial opener page, which indicates which folders and files you need for the tutorial. Each end-of-tutorial exercise also indicates the files you need to complete that exercise.

## To the Instructor

The Data Files are available on the Instructor Resources CD for this title. Follow the instructions in the Help file on the CD to install the programs to your network or standalone computer. See the "To the Student" section above for information on how to set up the Data Files that accompany this text.

You are granted a license to copy the Data Files to any computer or computer network used by students who have purchased this book.

## System Requirements

**If you are going to work through this book using your own computer, you need:**

• **Computer System** Microsoft Windows 2000 or Windows XP Professional or higher must be installed on your computer. This tutorial assumes a typical installation of Microsoft Office 2003. Additionally, to complete the steps for accessing Microsoft's Online Help for Office, an Internet connection and a Web browser are required.

• **Data Files** You will not be able to complete the tutorials or exercises in this book using your own computer until you have the necessary starting Data Files.

**www.course.com/NewPerspectives**

## Objectives

- Explore the programs that comprise Microsoft Office
- Start programs and switch between them
- Explore common window elements
- Minimize, maximize, and restore windows
- Use personalized menus and toolbars
- Work with task panes
- Create, save, close, and open a file
- Use the Help system
- Print a file
- Exit programs

# Using Common Features of Microsoft Office 2003

*Preparing Promotional Materials*

## Case

## Delmar Office Supplies

Delmar Office Supplies, a company in Wisconsin founded by Jake Alexander in 1996, sells recycled office supplies to businesses and home-based offices around the world. The demand for quality recycled papers, reconditioned toner cartridges, and renovated office furniture has been growing each year. Jake and all his employees use Microsoft Office 2003, which provides everyone in the company the power and flexibility to store a variety of information, create consistent files, and share data. In this tutorial, you'll review how the company's employees use Microsoft Office 2003.

## Student Data Files

▼**OFF folder**

▽ **Tutorial folder**

    (no starting Data Files)

▽ **Review folder**

    Finances.xls

    Letter.doc

# Exploring Microsoft Office 2003

**Microsoft Office 2003**, or simply **Office**, is a collection of the most popular Microsoft programs: Word, Excel, PowerPoint, Access, and Outlook. Each Office program contains valuable tools to help you accomplish many tasks, such as composing reports, analyzing data, preparing presentations, compiling information, sending e-mail, and planning schedules.

**Microsoft Word 2003**, or simply **Word**, is a word-processing program you use to create text documents. The files you create in Word are called **documents**. Word offers many special features that help you compose and update all types of documents, ranging from letters and newsletters to reports, brochures, faxes, and even books—all in attractive and readable formats. You can also use Word to create, insert, and position figures, tables, and other graphics to enhance the look of your documents. The Delmar Office Supplies sales representatives create their business letters using Word.

**Microsoft Excel 2003**, or simply **Excel**, is a spreadsheet program you use to display, organize, and analyze numerical data. You can do some of this in Word with tables, but Excel provides many more tools for recording and formatting numbers as well as performing calculations. The graphics capabilities in Excel also enable you to display data visually. You might, for example, generate a pie chart or a bar chart to help readers quickly see the significance of and the connections between information. The files you create in Excel are called **workbooks**. The Delmar Office Supplies operations department uses a line chart in an Excel workbook to visually track the company's financial performance.

**Microsoft Access 2003**, or simply **Access**, is a database program you use to enter, organize, display, and retrieve related information. The files you create in Access are called **databases**. With Access you can create data entry forms to make data entry easier, and you can create professional reports to improve the readability of your data. The Delmar Office Supplies operations department tracks the company's inventory in a table in an Access database.

**Microsoft PowerPoint 2003**, or simply **PowerPoint**, is a presentation graphics program you use to create a collection of slides that can contain text, charts, pictures, and so on. The files you create in PowerPoint are called **presentations**. You can show these presentations on your computer monitor, project them onto a screen as a slide show, print them, share them over the Internet, or display them on the World Wide Web. You can also use PowerPoint to generate presentation-related documents such as audience handouts, outlines, and speakers' notes. The Delmar Office Supplies sales department has created an effective slide presentation with PowerPoint to promote the company's latest product line.

**Microsoft Outlook 2003**, or simply **Outlook**, is an information management program you use to send, receive, and organize e-mail; plan your schedule; arrange meetings; organize contacts; create a to-do list; and jot down notes. You can also use Outlook to print schedules, task lists, phone directories, and other documents. Jake Alexander uses Outlook to send and receive e-mail, plan his schedule, and create a to-do list.

Although each Office program individually is a strong tool, their potential is even greater when used together.

## Integrating Office Programs

One of the main advantages of Office is **integration**, the ability to share information between programs. Integration ensures consistency and accuracy, and it saves time because you don't have to re-enter the same information in several Office programs. The staff at Delmar Office Supplies uses the integration features of Office daily, including the following examples:

- The accounting department created an Excel bar chart on the previous two years' fourth-quarter results, which they inserted into the quarterly financial report created in Word. They included a hyperlink in the Word report that employees can click to open the Excel workbook and view the original data.
- The operations department included an Excel pie chart of sales percentages by divisions of Delmar Office Supplies on a PowerPoint slide, which is part of a presentation to stockholders.
- The marketing department produced a mailing to promote the company's newest products by combining a form letter created in Word with an Access database that stores the names and addresses of customers.
- A sales representative wrote a letter in Word about a sales incentive program and merged the letter with an Outlook contact list containing the names and addresses of his customers.

These are just a few examples of how you can take information from one Office program and integrate it into another.

# Starting Office Programs

You can start any Office program by clicking the Start button on the Windows taskbar, and then selecting the program you want from the All Programs menu. Once the program starts, you can immediately begin to create new files or work with existing ones. If you or another user has recently used one of the Office programs, then that program might appear on the most frequently used programs list on the left side of the Start menu. You can click the program name to start the program.

Reference Window

### Starting Office Programs

- Click the Start button on the taskbar.
- Point to All Programs.
- Point to Microsoft Office.
- Click the name of the program you want to start.

*or*

- Click the name of the program you want to start on the most frequently used programs list on the left side of the Start menu.

You'll start Excel using the Start button.

## To start Excel and open a new, blank workbook:

1. Make sure your computer is on and the Windows desktop appears on your screen.

   **Trouble?** If your screen varies slightly from those shown in the figures, then your computer might be set up differently. The figures in this book were created while running Windows XP in its default settings, but how your screen looks depends on a variety of things, including the version of Windows, background settings, and so forth.

2. Click the **Start** button on the taskbar, and then point to **All Programs** to display the All Programs menu.

3. Point to **Microsoft Office** on the All Programs menu, and then point to **Microsoft Office Excel 2003**. See Figure 1. Depending on how your computer is set up, your desktop and menu might contain different icons and commands.

| Figure 1 | Start menu with All Programs submenu displayed |
| --- | --- |

**Trouble?** If you don't see Microsoft Office on the All Programs menu, point to Microsoft Office Excel 2003. If you still don't see Microsoft Office Excel 2003, ask your instructor or technical support person for help.

4. Click **Microsoft Office Excel 2003** to start Excel and open a new, blank workbook. See Figure 2.

New, blank Excel workbook ◀ **Figure 2**

**Trouble?** If the Excel window doesn't fill your entire screen, the window is not maximized, or expanded to its full size. You'll maximize the window shortly.

You can have more than one Office program open at once. You'll use this same method to start Word and open a new, blank document.

### To start Word and open a new, blank document:

▶ **1.** Click the **Start** button on the taskbar.

▶ **2.** Point to **All Programs** to display the All Programs menu.

▶ **3.** Point to **Microsoft Office** on the All Programs menu.

**Trouble?** If you don't see Microsoft Office on the All Programs menu, point to Microsoft Office Word 2003. If you still don't see Microsoft Office Word 2003, ask your instructor or technical support person for help.

▶ **4.** Click **Microsoft Office Word 2003**. Word opens with a new, blank document. See Figure 3.

**Figure 3**    New, blank document in Word

**Trouble?** If the Word window doesn't fill your entire screen, the window is not maximized. You'll maximize the window shortly.

When you have more than one program or file open at a time, you can switch between them.

## Switching Between Open Programs and Files

Two programs are running at the same time—Excel and Word. The taskbar contains buttons for both programs. When you have two or more programs running, or two files within the same program open, you can use the taskbar buttons to switch from one program or file to another. The employees at Delmar Office Supplies often work in several programs at once.

**To switch between Word and Excel:**

1. Click the **Microsoft Excel – Book1** button on the taskbar to switch from Word to Excel. See Figure 4.

Excel and Word programs opened simultaneously ◄ **Figure 4**

2. Click the **Document1 – Microsoft Word** button on the taskbar to return to Word.

As you can see, you can start multiple programs and switch between them in seconds.

# Exploring Common Window Elements

The Office programs consist of windows that have many similar features. As you can see in Figures 2 and 3, many of the elements you see in both the Excel program window and the Word program window are the same. In fact, all the Office programs have these same elements. Figure 5 describes some of the most common window elements.

Common window elements ◄ **Figure 5**

| Element | Description |
|---|---|
| Title bar | A bar at the top of the window that contains the filename of the open file, the program name, and the program window sizing buttons |
| Menu bar | A collection of menus for commonly used commands |
| Toolbars | Collections of buttons that are shortcuts to commonly used menu commands |
| Sizing buttons | Buttons that resize and close the program window or the file window |
| Task pane | A window that provides access to commands for common tasks you'll perform in Office programs |
| Status bar | An area at the bottom of the program window that contains information about the open file or the current task on which you are working |

Because these elements are the same in each program, once you've learned one program, it's easy to learn the others. The next sections explore the primary common features—the window sizing buttons, the menus and toolbars, and the task panes.

# Using the Window Sizing Buttons

There are two sets of sizing buttons. The top set controls the program window and the bottom set controls the file window. There are three different sizing buttons. The Minimize button, which is the left button, hides a window so that only its program button is visible on the taskbar. The middle button changes name and function depending on the status of the window—the Maximize button expands the window to the full screen size or to the program window size, and the Restore button returns the window to a predefined size. The right button, the Close button, exits the program or closes the file.

Most often you'll want to maximize the program and file windows as you work to take advantage of the full screen size you have available. If you have several files open, you might want to restore the files so that you can see more than one window at a time or you might want to minimize the programs with which you are not working at the moment. You'll try minimizing, maximizing, and restoring windows now.

### To resize windows:

▶ **1.** Click the **Minimize** button ⬛ on the Word title bar to reduce the Word program window to a taskbar button. The Excel window is visible again.

▶ **2.** If necessary, click the **Maximize** button ⬛ on the Excel title bar. The Excel program window expands to fill the screen.

▶ **3.** Click the **Restore Window** button ⬛ on the Excel menu bar. The file window, referred to as the workbook window in Excel, resizes smaller than the full program window. See Figure 6.

| Figure 6 | Resized Excel windows |
|---|---|

file window sizing buttons

program window sizing buttons

maximized program window

restored workbook window (yours might be a different size or shape)

drag to resize window to a custom size

▶ **4.** Click the **Maximize** button ⬛ on the Excel workbook window title bar. The Excel workbook window expands to fill the program window.

**5.** Click the **Document1 - Microsoft Word** button on the taskbar. The Word program window returns to its previous size.

**6.** If necessary, click the **Maximize** button ▣ on the Word title bar. The Word program window expands to fill the screen.

The sizing buttons give you the flexibility to arrange the program and file windows on your screen to best fit your needs.

## Using Menus and Toolbars

In each Office program, you can perform tasks using a menu command, a toolbar button, or a keyboard shortcut. A **menu command** is a word on a menu that you click to execute a task; a **menu** is a group of related commands. For example, the File menu contains commands for managing files, such as the Open command and the Save command. The File, Edit, View, Insert, Format, Tools, Window, and Help menus appear on the menu bar in all the Office programs, although some of the commands they include differ from program to  program. Other menus are program specific, such as the Table menu in Word and the Data menu in Excel.

A **toolbar** is a collection of buttons that correspond to commonly used menu commands. For example, the Standard toolbar contains an Open button and a Save button. The Standard and Formatting toolbars (as well as other toolbars) appear in all the Office programs, although some of the buttons they include differ from program to program. The Standard toolbar has buttons related to working with files. The Formatting toolbar has buttons related to changing the appearance of content. Each program also has program-specific toolbars, such as the Tables and Borders toolbar in Word for working with tables and the Chart toolbar in Excel for working with graphs and charts.

A **keyboard shortcut** is a combination of keys you press to perform a command. For example, Ctrl+S is the keyboard shortcut for the Save command (you hold down the Ctrl key while you press the S key). Keyboard shortcuts appear to the right of many menu commands.

### Viewing Personalized Menus and Toolbars

When you first use a newly installed Office program, the menus and toolbars display only the basic and most commonly used commands and buttons, streamlining the program window. The other commands and buttons are available, but you have to click an extra button to see them (the Expand button on a menu and the Toolbar Options button on a toolbar). As you select commands and click buttons, the ones you use often are put on the short, personalized menu and on the visible part of the toolbars. The ones you don't use remain available on the full menus and toolbars. This means that the Office menus and toolbars might display different commands and buttons on each person's computer.

**To view a personalized and full menu:**

**1.** Click **Insert** on the Word menu bar to display the short, personalized menu. See Figure 7. The Bookmark command, for example, does not appear on the short menu.

**Figure 7** ▶ **Short, personalized menu**

**Trouble?** If the Insert menu displays different commands than those shown in Figure 7, you need to reset the menus. Click Tools on the menu bar, click Customize (you might need to pause until the full menu appears to see the command), and then click the Options tab in the Customize dialog box. Click the Always show full menus check box to remove the check mark, if necessary, and then click the Show full menus after a short delay check box to insert a check mark, if necessary. Click the Reset menu and toolbar usage data button, and then click the Yes button to confirm that you want to reset the commands. Click the Close button. Repeat Step 1.

You can display the full menu in one of three ways: (1) pause until the full menu appears, which might happen as you read this; (2) click the Expand button at the bottom of the menu; or (3) double-click the menu name on the menu bar.

▶ **2.** Pause until the full Insert menu appears, as shown in Figure 8. The Bookmark command and other commands are now visible.

**Figure 8** ▶ **Full, expanded menu**

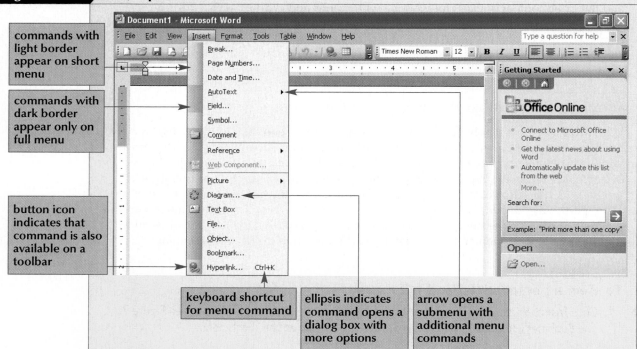

▶ **3.** Click the **Bookmark** command. A dialog box opens when you click a command whose name is followed by an ellipsis (...). In this case, the Bookmark dialog box opens.

▶ **4.** Click the **Cancel** button to close the Bookmark dialog box.

▶ **5.** Click **Insert** on the menu bar again to display the short, personalized menu. The Bookmark command appears on the short, personalized menu because you have recently used it.

▶ **6.** Press the **Esc** key on the keyboard twice to close the menu.

As you can see, the menu changed based on your actions. Over time, only the commands you use frequently will appear on the personalized menu. The toolbars work similarly.

### To use the personalized toolbars:

▶ **1.** Observe that the Standard and Formatting toolbars appear side by side below the menu bar.

**Trouble?** If the toolbars appear on two rows, you need to reset them to their default state. Click Tools on the menu bar, click Customize, and then click the Options tab in the Customize dialog box. Click the Show Standard and Formatting toolbars on two rows check box to remove the check mark. Click the Reset menu and toolbar usage data button, and then click the Yes button to confirm you want to reset the commands. Click the Close button. Repeat Step 1.

▶ **2.** Click the **Toolbar Options** button ⯆ on the Standard toolbar. See Figure 9.

**Toolbar Options palette** ◀ **Figure 9**

**Trouble?** If you see different buttons on the Toolbar Options palette, your side-by-side toolbars might be sized differently than the ones shown in Figure 9. Continue with Step 3.

▶ **3.** Click the **Show/Hide ¶** button ¶ on the Toolbar Options palette to display the nonprinting screen characters. The Show/Hide ¶ button moves to the visible part of the Standard toolbar, and another button may be moved onto the Toolbar Options palette to make room for the new button.

**Trouble?** If the Show/Hide ¶ button already appears on the Standard toolbar, click another button on the Toolbar Options palette. Then click that same button again in Step 4 to turn off that formatting, if necessary.

Some buttons, like the Show/Hide ¶ button, act as a toggle switch—one click turns on the feature and a second click turns it off.

▶ **4.** Click the **Show/Hide ¶** button ¶ on the Standard toolbar again to hide the nonprinting screen characters.

Some people like that the menus and toolbars change to meet their work habits. Others prefer to see all the menu commands or to display the default toolbars on two rows so that all the buttons are always visible. You'll change the toolbar setting now.

**To turn off the personalized toolbars:**

1. Click the **Toolbar Options** button ⬚ on the right side of the Standard toolbar.
2. Click the **Show Buttons on Two Rows** command. The toolbars move to separate rows (the Standard toolbar on top) and you can see all the buttons on each toolbar.

You can easily access any button on the Standard and Formatting toolbars with one mouse click. The drawback is that when the toolbars are displayed on two rows, they take up more space in the program window, limiting the space you have to work.

## Using Task Panes

A **task pane** is a window that provides access to commands for common tasks you'll perform in Office programs. For example, the Getting Started task pane, which opens when you first start any Office program, enables you to create new files and open existing ones. Task panes also help you navigate through more complex, multi-step procedures. All the Office programs include the task panes described in Figure 10. The other available task panes vary by program.

**Figure 10** ▶ **Common task panes**

| Task pane | Description |
|---|---|
| Getting Started | The home task pane; allows you to create new files, open existing files, search the online and offline Help system by keyword, and access Office online |
| Help | Allows you to search the online and offline Help system by keyword or table of contents, and access Microsoft Office Online |
| Search Results | Displays available Help topics related to entered keyword and enables you to initiate a new search |
| New | Allows you to create new files; name changes to New Document in Word, New Workbook in Excel, New File in Access, and New Presentation in PowerPoint |
| Clip Art | Allows you to search for all types of media clips (pictures, sound, video) and insert clips from the results |
| Clipboard | Allows you to paste some or all of the items that have been cut or copied from any Office program during the current work session |
| Research | Allows you to search a variety of reference material and other resources from within a file |

No matter what their purpose, you use the same processes to open, close, and navigate between the task panes.

## Opening and Closing Task Panes

When you first start any Office program, the Getting Started task pane opens by default along the right edge of the program window. You can resize or move the task pane to suit your work habits. You can also close the task pane to display the open file in the full available program window. For example, you might want to close the task pane when you are typing the body of a letter in Word or entering a lot of data in Excel.

You will open and close the task pane.

**To open and close the task pane:**

1. If necessary, click **View** on the menu bar, and then click **Task Pane**. The most recently viewed task pane opens on the right side of the screen. See Figure 11.

Getting Started task pane ◄ **Figure 11**

**Trouble?** If you do not see the task pane, you probably closed the open task pane in Step 1. Repeat Step 1 to reopen the task pane.

**Trouble?** If a different task pane than the Getting Started task pane opens, then another task pane was the most recently viewed task pane. You'll learn how to open different task panes in the next section; continue with Step 2.

2. Click the **Close** button ☒ on the task pane title bar. The task pane closes, leaving more room on the screen for the open file.

3. Click **View** on the menu bar, and then click **Task Pane**. The task pane reopens.

There are several ways to display different task panes.

## Navigating Among Task Panes

Once the task pane is open, you can display different task panes to suit the task you are trying to complete. For example, you can display the New task pane when you want to create a new file from a template. The name of the New task pane varies, depending on the program you are using: Word has the New Document task pane, Excel has the New Workbook task pane, PowerPoint has the New Presentation task pane, and Access has the New File task pane.

One of the quickest ways to display a task pane is to use the Other Task Panes button. When you point to the name of the open task pane in the task pane title bar, it becomes the Other Task Panes button. When you click the Other Task Panes button, all the available task panes for that Office program are listed. Just click the name of the task pane you want to display to switch to that task pane.

There are three navigation buttons at the top of the task pane. The Back and Forward buttons enable you to scroll backward and forward through the task panes you have opened during your current work session. The Back button becomes available when you display two or more task panes. The Forward button becomes available after you click the Back button to return to a previously viewed task pane. The Home button returns you to the Getting Started task pane no matter which task pane is currently displayed.

You'll use each of these methods to navigate among the task panes.

### To navigate among task panes:

1. Point to **Getting Started** in the task pane title bar. The title bar becomes the Other Task Panes button.

2. Click the **Other Task Panes** button. A list of the available task panes for Word is displayed. The check mark before Getting Started indicates that this is the currently displayed task pane.

3. Click **New Document**. The New Document task pane appears and the Back button is available.

4. Click the **Back** button ⊕ in the task pane. The Getting Started task pane reappears and the Forward button is available.

5. Click the **Forward** button ⊕ in the task pane. The New Document task pane reappears and the Back button is available.

6. Click the **Home** button 🏠 in the task pane. The Getting Started task pane reappears.

## Using the Research Task Pane

The Research task pane allows you to search a variety of reference materials and other resources to find specific information while you are working on a file. You can insert the information you find directly into your open file. The thesaurus and language translation tools are installed with Office and therefore are stored locally on your computer. If you are connected to the Internet, you can also use the Research task pane to access a dictionary, an encyclopedia, research sites, as well as business and financial sources. Some of the sites that appear in the search results are fee-based, meaning that you'll need to pay to access information on that site.

To use the Research task pane, you type a keyword or phrase into the Search for text box and then select whether you want to search all the books, sites, and sources; one category; or a specific source. The search results appear in the Research task pane. Some of the results appear as links, which you can click to open your browser window and display that information. If you are using Internet Explorer 5.01 or later as your Web browser, the Research task pane is tiled (appears side by side) with your document. If you are using another Web browser, you'll need to return to the task pane in your open file to click another link.

The Research task pane functions independently in each file. So you can open multiple files and perform a different search in each. In addition, each Research task pane stores the results of up to 10 searches, so you can quickly return to the results from any of your most recent searches. To move among the saved searches, click the Back and Forward buttons in the task pane.

## Using the Research Task Pane

- Type a keyword or phrase into the Search for text box.
- Select a search category, individual source, or all references.
- If necessary, click a link in the search results to display more information.
- Copy and paste selected content from the task pane into your file.

Jake plans to send a copy of the next quarter's sales report to the office in France. You'll use the bilingual dictionaries in the Research task pane to begin entering labels in French into an Excel workbook for the sales report.

### To use the bilingual dictionaries in the Research task pane:

▶ 1. Click the **Microsoft Excel – Book1** button on the taskbar to switch to the Excel window.

▶ 2. Click the **Other Task Panes** button on the Getting Started task pane, and then click **Research**. The Research task pane opens.

▶ 3. Click in the **Search for** text box, and then type **paper**.

▶ 4. Click the **Search for** list arrow and then click **Translation**. The bilingual dictionary opens in the Research task pane. You can choose from among 12 languages to translate to and from, including Japanese, Russian, Spanish, Dutch, German, and French.

  **Trouble?** If a dialog box opens stating the translation feature is not installed, click the Yes button to install it.

▶ 5. If necessary, click the **To** list arrow, and then click **French (France)**. See Figure 12.

Research task pane ◀ Figure 12

▶ 6. Scroll to read the different translations of "paper" in French.

After you locate specific information, you can quickly insert it into your open file. The information can be inserted by copying the selected content you want to insert, and then pasting it in the appropriate location in your file. In some instances, such as MSN Money Stock Quotes, a button appears enabling you to quickly insert the indicated information in your file at the location of the insertion point. Otherwise, you can use the standard Copy and Paste commands.

You'll copy the translation for "paper" into the Excel workbook.

### To copy information from the Research task pane into a file:

▶ 1. Select **papier** in the Research task pane. This is the word you want to copy to the workbook.

▶ 2. Right-click the selected text, and then click **Copy** on the shortcut menu. The text is duplicated on the Office Clipboard.

▶ 3. Right-click cell **A1**, and then click **Paste**. The word "papier" is entered into the cell. See Figure 13.

**Figure 13** ▶ **Translation copied into Excel**

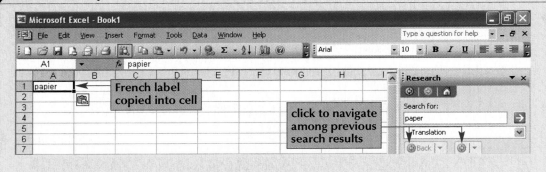

You'll repeat this process to look up the translation for "furniture" and copy it into cell A2.

### To translate and copy another word into Excel:

▶ 1. Double-click **paper** in the Search for text box to select the text, type **furniture**, and then click the **Start searching** button in the Research task pane.

▶ 2. Verify that you're translating from English (U.S) to French (France).

▶ 3. Select **meubles** in the translation results, right-click the selected text, and then click **Copy**.

▶ 4. Right-click cell **A2**, and then click **Paste**. The second label appears in the cell.

The Research task pane works similarly in all the Office programs. You'll use other task panes later in this tutorial to perform specific tasks, including opening a file and getting assistance.

# Working with Files

The most common tasks you'll perform in any Office program are to create, open, save, and close files. The processes for each of these tasks are the same in all the Office programs. In addition, there are several methods for performing most tasks in Office. This flexibility enables you to use Office in a way that fits how you like to work.

## Creating a File

To begin working in a program, you need to create a new file or open an existing file. When you start Word, Excel, or PowerPoint, the program opens along with a blank file— ready for you to begin working on a new document, workbook, or presentation. When you start Access, the Getting Started task pane opens, displaying options for opening a new database or an existing one.

Jake has asked you to start working on the agenda for the stockholder meeting, which he suggests you create using Word. You enter text in a Word document by typing.

### To enter text in a document:

▶ **1.** Click the **Document1 – Microsoft Word** button on the taskbar to activate the Word program window.

▶ **2.** Type **Delmar Office Supplies**, and then press the **Enter** key. The text you typed appears on one line in the Word document.

   **Trouble?** If you make a typing error, press the Backspace key to delete the incorrect letters, and then retype the text.

▶ **3.** Type **Stockholder Meeting Agenda**, and then press the **Enter** key. The text you typed appears on the second line.

Next, you'll save the file.

## Saving a File

As you create and modify Office files, your work is stored only in the computer's temporary memory, not on a hard disk. If you were to exit the programs, turn off your computer, or experience a power failure, your work would be lost. To prevent losing work, save your file to a disk frequently—at least every 10 minutes. You can save files to the hard disk located inside your computer or to portable storage disks, such as floppy disks, Zip disks, or read-write CD-ROMs.

The first time you save a file, you need to name it. This name is called a **filename**. When you choose a filename, select a descriptive one that accurately reflects the content of the document, workbook, presentation, or database, such as "Shipping Options Letter" or "Fourth Quarter Financial Analysis." Filenames can include a maximum of 255 letters, numbers, hyphens, and spaces in any combination. Office appends a **file extension** to the filename, which identifies the program in which that file was created. The file extensions are .doc for Word, .xls for Excel, .ppt for PowerPoint, and .mdb for Access. Whether you see file extensions depends on how Windows is set up on your computer.

You also need to decide where to save the file—on which disk and in what folder. A **folder** is a container for your files. Just as you organize paper documents within folders stored in a filing cabinet, you can organize your files within folders stored on your computer's hard disk or a removable disk. Store each file in a logical location that you will remember whenever you want to use the file again.

Reference Window | **Saving a File**

- Click the Save button on the Standard toolbar (*or* click File on the menu bar, and then click Save or Save As).
- In the Save As dialog box, click the Save in list arrow, and then navigate to the location where you want to save the file.
- Type a filename in the File name text box.
- Click the Save button.
- To resave the named file to the same location, click the Save button on the Standard toolbar (*or* click File on the menu bar, and then click Save).

The two lines of text you typed are not yet saved on disk. You'll do that now.

### To save a file for the first time:

1. Click the **Save** button 🖫 on the Standard toolbar. The Save As dialog box opens. The first few words of the first line appear in the File name text box, as a suggested filename. You'll replace this with a more descriptive filename.

2. Click the **Save in** list arrow, and then click the location that contains your Data Files.

   **Trouble?** If you don't have the Common Office Features Data Files, you need to get them before you can proceed. Your instructor will either give you the Data Files or ask you to obtain them from a specified location (such as a network drive). In either case, be sure that you make a backup copy of your Data Files before you start using them, so that the original files will be available on your copied disk in case you need to start over because of an error or problem. If you have any questions about the Data Files, see your instructor or technical support person for assistance.

3. Double-click the **OFF** folder in the list box, and then double-click the **Tutorial** folder. This is the location where you want to save the document. See Figure 14.

4. Type **Stockholder Meeting Agenda** in the File name text box.

**Figure 14** ▶ Completed Save As dialog box

location where file will be saved;
click list arrow to choose another location

list of folders and other Word files already in the save in location would appear here

shortcuts to locations on your computer

new filename

click to save file

**Trouble?** If the .doc file extension appears after the filename, then your computer is configured to show file extensions. Continue with Step 5.

▶ 5. Click the **Save** button. The Save As dialog box closes, and the name of your file appears in the program window title bar.

The saved file includes everything in the document at the time you last saved it. Any edits or additions you then make to the document exist only in the computer's memory and are not saved in the file on the disk. As you work, remember to save frequently so that the file is updated to reflect the latest content of the document.

Because you already named the document and selected a storage location, the second and subsequent times you save, the Save As dialog box doesn't open. If you wanted to save a copy of the file with a different filename or to a different location, you would reopen the Save As dialog box by clicking File on the menu bar, and then clicking Save As. The previous version of the file remains on your disk as well.

You need to add your name to the agenda. Then you'll save your changes.

**To modify and save a file:**

▶ 1. Type your name, and then press the **Enter** key. The text you typed appears on the next line.

▶ 2. Click the **Save** button 🖫 on the Standard toolbar to save your changes.

When you're done with a file, you can close it.

## Closing a File

Although you can keep multiple files open at one time, you should close any file you are no longer working on to conserve system resources as well as to ensure that you don't inadvertently make changes to the file. You can close a file by clicking the Close command on the File menu or by clicking the Close Window button in the upper-right corner of the menu bar.

As a standard practice, you should save your file before closing it. If you're unsure whether the file is saved, it cannot hurt to save it again. However, Office has an added safeguard: If you attempt to close a file or exit a program without saving your changes, a dialog box opens asking whether you want to save the file. Click the Yes button to save the changes to the file before closing the file and program. Click the No button to close the file and program without saving changes. Click the Cancel button to return to the program window without saving changes or closing the file and program. This feature helps to ensure that you always save the most current version of any file.

You'll add the date to the agenda. Then, you'll attempt to close the document without saving.

**To modify and close a file:**

▶ 1. Type the date, and then press the **Enter** key. The text you typed appears under your name in the document.

▶ 2. Click the **Close Window** button ✕ on the Word menu bar to close the document. A dialog box opens, asking whether you want to save the changes you made to the document.

▶ **3.** Click the **Yes** button. The current version of the document is saved to the file, and then the document closes, and Word is still running.

   **Trouble?** If Word is not running, then you closed the program in Step 2. Start Word, click the Close Window button on the menu bar to close the blank document.

Once you have a program open, you can create additional new files for the open program or you can open previously created and saved files.

## Opening a File

When you want to open a blank document, workbook, presentation, or database, you create a new file. When you want to work on a previously created file, you must first open it. Opening a file transfers a copy of the file from the storage disk (either a hard disk or a portable disk) to the computer's memory and displays it on your screen. The file is then in your computer's memory and on the disk.

---

| Reference Window | **Opening an Existing or a New File** |

- Click the Open button on the Standard toolbar (*or* click File on the menu bar, and then click Open *or* click the More link in the Open section of the Getting Started task pane).
- In the Open dialog box, click the Look in list arrow, and then navigate to the storage location of the file you want to open.
- Click the filename of the file you want to open.
- Click the Open button.

*or*

- Click the New button on the Standard toolbar (*or* click File on the menu bar, click New, and then (depending on the program) click the Blank document, Blank workbook, Blank presentation, or Blank database link in the New task pane).

---

Jake asks you to print the agenda. To do that, you'll reopen the file. You'll use the Open button on the Standard toolbar.

### To open an existing file:

▶ **1.** Click the **Open** button 📂 on the Standard toolbar. The Open dialog box, which works similarly to the Save As dialog box, opens.

▶ **2.** Click the **Look in** list arrow, and then navigate to the **OFF\Tutorial** folder included with your Data Files. This is the location where you saved the agenda document.

▶ **3.** Click **Stockholder Meeting Agenda** in the file list. See Figure 15.

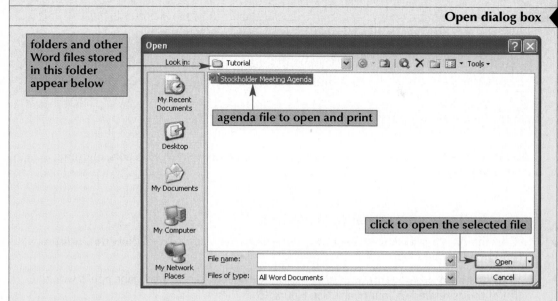

**Open dialog box** ◀ **Figure 15**

folders and other Word files stored in this folder appear below

agenda file to open and print

click to open the selected file

▶ **4.** Click the **Open** button. The file containing the agenda opens in the Word program window.

Next, you'll get information about printing files in Word.

# Getting Help

If you don't know how to perform a task or want more information about a feature, you can turn to Office itself for information on how to use it. This information, referred to simply as **Help**, is like a huge encyclopedia available from your desktop. You can access Help in a variety of ways, including ScreenTips, the Type a question for help box, the Help task pane, and Microsoft Office Online.

## Using ScreenTips

ScreenTips are a fast and simple method you can use to get help about objects you see on the screen. A **ScreenTip** is a yellow box with the button's name. Just position the mouse pointer over a toolbar button to view its ScreenTip.

## Using the Type a Question for Help Box

For answers to specific questions, you can use the **Type a question for help box**, located on the menu bar of every Office program, to find information in the Help system. You simply type a question using everyday language about a task you want to perform or a topic you need help with, and then press the Enter key to search the Help system. The Search Results task pane opens with a list of Help topics related to your query. You click a topic to open a Help window with step-by-step instructions that guide you through a specific procedure and explanations of difficult concepts in clear, easy-to-understand language. For example, you might ask how to format a cell in an Excel worksheet; a list of Help topics related to the words you typed will appear.

| Reference Window | **Getting Help from the Type a Question for Help Box** |

- Click the Type a question for help box on the menu bar.
- Type your question, and then press the Enter key.
- Click a Help topic in the Search Results task pane.
- Read the information in the Help window. For more information, click other topics or links.
- Click the Close button on the Help window title bar.

You'll use the Type a question for help box to obtain more information about printing a document in Word.

### To use the Type a question for help box:

1. Click the **Type a question for help box** on the menu bar, and then type **How do I print a document?**

2. Press the **Enter** key to retrieve a list of topics. The Search Results task pane opens with a list of topics related to your query. See Figure 16.

| Figure 16 | **Search Results task pane displaying Help topics** |

**Trouble?** If your search results list differs from the one shown in Figure 16, your computer is not connected to the Internet or Microsoft has updated the list of available Help topics since this book was published. Continue with Step 3.

3. Scroll through the list to review the Help topics.

4. Click **Print a document** to open the Help window and learn more about the various ways to print a document. See Figure 17.

**Print a document Help window** | **Figure 17**

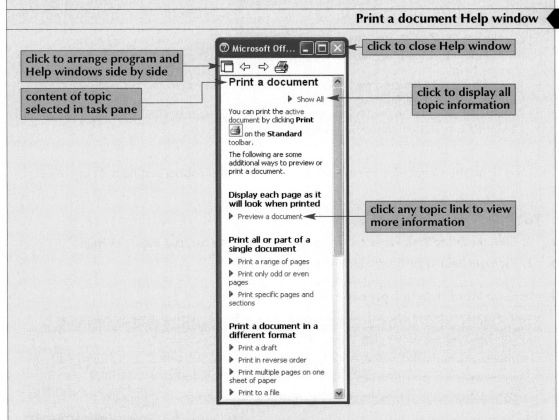

Trouble? If the Word program window and the Help window do not appear side by side, then you need to tile the windows. Click the Auto Tile button on the toolbar in the Help window.

5. Read the information, and then when you're done, click the **Close** button ☒ on the Help window title bar to close the Help window.

The Help task pane works similarly.

## Using the Help Task Pane

For more in-depth help, you can use the **Help task pane**, a task pane that enables you to search the Help system using keywords or phrases. You type a specific word or phrase in the Search for text box, and then click the Start searching button. The Search Results task pane opens with a list of topics related to the keyword or phrase you entered. If your computer is connected to the Internet, you might see more search results because some Help topics are stored only online and not locally on your computer. The task pane also has a Table of Contents link that organizes the Help system by subjects and topics, like in a book. You click main subject links to display related topic links.

Reference Window

## Getting Help from the Help Task Pane

- Click the Other Task Panes button on the task pane title bar, and then click Help (*or* click Help on the menu bar, and then click Microsoft Word/Excel/PowerPoint/Access/Outlook Help).
- Type a keyword or phrase in the Search for text box, and then click the Start searching button.
- Click a Help topic in the Search Results task pane.
- Read the information in the Help window. For more information, click other topics or links.
- Click the Close button on the Help window title bar.

You'll use the Help task pane to obtain more information about getting help in Office.

### To use the Help task pane:

▶ 1. Click the **Other Task Panes** button on the task pane title bar, and then click **Help**.

▶ 2. Type **get help** in the Search for text box. See Figure 18.

Figure 18

**Microsoft Word Help task pane with keyword**

▶ 3. Click the **Start searching** button. The Search Results task pane opens with a list of topics related to your keywords.

▶ 4. Scroll through the list to review the Help topics.

▶ 5. Click **About getting help while you work** to open the Microsoft Word Help window and learn more about the various ways to obtain help in Word. See Figure 19.

About getting help while you work Help window ◄ **Figure 19**

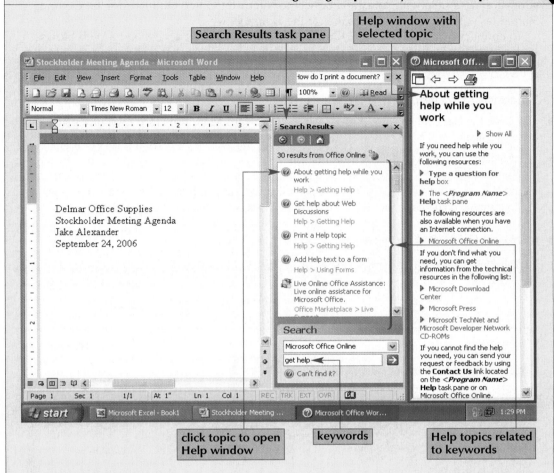

Search Results task pane

Help window with selected topic

click topic to open Help window

keywords

Help topics related to keywords

**Trouble?** If your search results list differs from the one shown in Figure 19, your computer is not connected to the Internet or Microsoft has updated the list of available Help topics since this book was published. Continue with Step 6.

**Trouble?** If the Word program window and the Help window do not appear side by side, then you need to tile the windows. Click the Auto Tile button on the toolbar in the Help window.

6. Click **Microsoft Office Online** in the right pane to display information about that topic. Read the information.

7. Click the other links about this feature and read the information.

8. When you're done, click the **Close** button ☒ on the Help window title bar to close the Help window. The task pane remains open.

If your computer has a connection to the Internet, you can get more help information from Microsoft Office Online.

## Using Microsoft Office Online

**Microsoft Office Online** is a Web site maintained by Microsoft that provides access to additional Help resources. For example, you can access current Help topics, read how-to articles, and find tips for using Office. You can search all or part of a site to find information about tasks you want to perform, features you want to use, or anything else you want more help with. You can connect to Microsoft Office Online from the Getting Started task pane, the Help task pane, or the Help menu.

To connect to Microsoft Office Online, you'll need Internet access and a Web browser such as Internet Explorer.

### To connect to Microsoft Office Online:

1. Click the **Back** button 🔵 in the Search Results task pane. The Word Help task pane reappears.

2. Click the **Connect to Microsoft Office Online** link in the task pane. Internet Explorer starts and the Microsoft Office Online home page opens. See Figure 20. This Web page offers links to Web pages focusing on getting help and for accessing additional Office resources, such as additional galleries of clip art, software downloads, and training opportunities.

| Figure 20 | Microsoft Office Online home page |

**Trouble?** If the content you see on the Microsoft Office Online home page differs from the figure, the site has been updated since this book was published. Continue with Step 3.

3. Click the **Assistance** link. The Assistance page opens. From this page, you browse for help in each of the different Office programs. You can also enter a keyword or phrase pertaining to a particular topic you wish to search for information on using the Search box in the upper-right corner of the window.

4. Click the **Close** button ☒ on the Internet Explorer title bar to close the browser.

The Help features enable the staff at Delmar Office Supplies to get answers to questions they have about any task or procedure when they need it. The more you practice getting information from the Help system, the more effective you will be at using Office to its full potential.

# Printing a File

At times, you'll want a paper copy of your Office file. The first time you print during each session at the computer, you should use the Print menu command to open the Print dialog box so you can verify or adjust the printing settings. You can select a printer, the number of copies to print, the portion of the file to print, and so forth; the printing settings vary slightly from program to program. For subsequent print jobs, you can use the Print button to print without opening the dialog box, if you want to use the same default settings.

Reference Window

## Printing a File

- Click File on the menu bar, and then click Print.
- Verify the print settings in the Print dialog box.
- Click the OK button.

*or*

- Click the Print button on the Standard toolbar.

Now that you know how to print, you'll print the agenda for Jake.

### To print a file:

▶ **1.** Make sure your printer is turned on and contains paper.

▶ **2.** Click **File** on the menu bar, and then click **Print**. The Print dialog box opens. See Figure 21.

**Print dialog box** ◀ **Figure 21**

▶ **3.** Verify that the correct printer appears in the Name list box in the Printer area. If the wrong printer appears, click the **Name** list arrow, and then click the correct printer from the list of available printers.

▶ **4.** Verify that **1** appears in the Number of copies text box.

▶ **5.** Click the **OK** button to print the document.

**Trouble?** If the document does not print, see your instructor or technical support person for help.

Now that you have printed the agenda, you can close Word and Excel.

# Exiting Programs

Whenever you finish working with a program, you should exit it. As with many other aspects of Office, you can exit programs with a button or from a menu. You'll use both methods to close Word and Excel. You can use the Exit command to exit a program and close an open file in one step. If you haven't saved the final version of the open file, a dialog box opens, asking whether you want to save your changes. Clicking the Yes button saves the open file, closes the file, and then exits the program.

### To exit a program:

▶ **1.** Click the **Close** button ⊠ on the Word title bar to exit Word. The Word document closes and the Word program exits. The Excel window is visible again on your screen.

**Trouble?** If a dialog box opens, asking whether you want to save the document, you may have inadvertently made a change to the document. Click the No button.

▶ **2.** Click **File** on the Excel menu bar, and then click **Exit**. A dialog box opens asking whether you want to save the changes you made to the workbook.

▶ **3.** Click the **Yes** button. The Save As dialog box opens.

▶ **4.** Save the workbook in the **OFF\Tutorial** folder with the filename **French Sales Report**. The workbook closes, saving a copy to the location you specified, and the Excel program exits.

Exiting programs after you are done using them keeps your Windows desktop unclut-tered for the next person using the computer, frees up your system's resources, and prevents data from being lost accidentally.

Review

## Quick Check

1. List the five programs included in Office.
2. How do you start an Office program?
3. Explain the difference between Save As and Save.
4. What is one method for opening an existing Office file?
5. What happens if you attempt to close a file or exit a program without saving the current version of the open file?
6. What are four ways to get help?

Review

## Tutorial Summary

You have learned how to use features common to all the programs included in Microsoft Office 2003, including starting and exiting programs; resizing windows; using menus and toolbars; working with task panes; saving, opening, closing, and printing files; and getting help.

## Key Terms

| | | |
|---|---|---|
| Access | menu | Outlook |
| database | menu bar | PowerPoint |
| document | menu command | presentation |
| Excel | Microsoft Access 2003 | ScreenTip |
| file extension | Microsoft Excel 2003 | task pane |
| filename | Microsoft Office 2003 | toolbar |
| folder | Microsoft Office Online | Type a question for help box |
| Help | Microsoft Outlook 2003 | Word |
| Help task pane | Microsoft PowerPoint 2003 | workbook |
| integration | Microsoft Word 2003 | |
| keyboard shortcut | Office | |

Practice

## Review Assignments

*Practice the skills you learned in the tutorial using the same case scenario.*

**Data Files needed for the Review Assignments: Finances.xls, Letter.doc**

Before the stockholders meeting at Delmar Office Supplies, you'll open and print documents for the upcoming presentation. Complete the following steps:

1. Start PowerPoint.
2. Use the Help task pane to learn how to change the toolbar buttons from small to large, and then do it. Use the same procedure to change the buttons back to regular size. Close the Help window when you're done.
3. Start Excel.
4. Switch to the PowerPoint window using the taskbar, and then close the presentation but leave open the PowerPoint program. (*Hint:* Click the Close Window button on the menu bar.)
5. Open a new, blank PowerPoint presentation from the Getting Started task pane. (*Hint:* Click Create a new presentation in the Open section of the Getting Started task pane.)
6. Close the PowerPoint presentation and program using the Close button on the PowerPoint title bar; do not save changes if asked.

7. Open the **Finances** workbook located in the **OFF\Review** folder included with your Data Files using the Open button on the Standard toolbar in Excel.

8. Use the Save As command to save the workbook as **Delmar Finances** in the **OFF\Review** folder.

9. Type your name, press the Enter key to insert your name at the top of the worksheet, and then save the workbook.

10. Print one copy of the worksheet using the Print command on the File menu.

11. Exit Excel using the File menu.

12. Start Word, and then use the Getting Started task pane to open the **Letter** document located in the **OFF\Review** folder included with your Data Files. (*Hint:* Click the More link in the Getting Started task pane to open the Open dialog box.)

13. Use the Save As command to save the document with the filename **Delmar Letter** in the **OFF\Review** folder.

14. Press and hold the Ctrl key, press the End key, and then release both keys to move the insertion point to the end of the letter, and then type your name.

15. Use the Save button on the Standard toolbar to save the change to the Delmar Letter document.

16. Print one copy of the document, and then close the document.

17. Exit the Word program using the Close button on the title bar.

**Assess**

## SAM Assessment and Training

If you have a SAM user profile, you may have access to hands-on instruction, practice, and assessment of the skills covered in this tutorial. Log in to your SAM account and go to your assignments page to see what your instructor has assigned.

**Review**

## Quick Check Answers

1. Word, Excel, PowerPoint, Access, Outlook
2. Click the Start button on the taskbar, point to All Programs, point to Microsoft Office, and then click the name of the program you want to open.
3. Save As enables you to change the filename and storage location of a file. Save updates a file to reflect its latest contents using its current filename and location.
4. Either click the Open button on the Standard toolbar or click the More link in the Getting Started task pane to open the Open dialog box.
5. A dialog box opens asking whether you want to save the changes to the file.
6. ScreenTips, Type a question for help box, Help task pane, Microsoft Office Online

# New Perspectives on
# Microsoft® Office Access 2003

# Read This Before You Begin: Tutorials 1–4

## To the Student

### Data Files

To complete the Level I Access Tutorials (Tutorials 1 through 4), you need the starting student Data Files. Your instructor will either provide you with these Data Files or ask you to obtain them yourself.

The Level I Access tutorials require the folders shown to complete the Tutorials, Review Assignments, and Case Problems. You will need to copy these folders from a file server, a standalone computer, or the Web to the drive and folder where you will be storing your Data Files. Your instructor will tell you which computer, drive letter, and folder(s) contain the files you need. You can also download the files by going to www.course.com; see the inside back or front cover for more information on downloading the files, or ask your instructor or technical support person for assistance.

If you are storing your Data Files on floppy disks, you will need six blank, formatted, high-density disks for these tutorials. Label your disks as shown, and place the folders indicated below on the relevant disk.

Access 2003: Data Disk 1 - Brief\Tutorial folder
Access 2003: Data Disk 2 - Brief\Review folder
Access 2003: Data Disk 3 - Brief\Case1 folder
Access 2003: Data Disk 4 - Brief\Case2 folder
Access 2003: Data Disk 5 - Brief\Case3 folder
Access 2003: Data Disk 6 - Brief\Case4 folder

The Data Files you work with in each tutorial in Level I build on the work you did in the previous tutorial. Thus when you begin Tutorial 3, you will use the Data Files that resulted after you completed the steps in Tutorial 2, the Tutorial 2 Review Assignments, and the Tutorial 2 Case Problems.

### Course Labs

The Level I Access tutorials feature an interactive Course Lab to help you understand database concepts. There is a Lab Assignment at the end of Tutorial 1 that relates to this lab. Contact your instructor or technical support person for assistance in accessing the lab.

## To the Instructor

The Data Files and Course Labs are available on the Instructor Resources CD for this title. Follow the instructions in the Help file on the CD to install the programs to your network or standalone computer. See the "To the Student" section above for information on how to set up the Data Files that accompany this text.

You are granted a license to copy the Data Files and Course Labs to any computer or computer network used by students who have purchased this book.

## System Requirements

**If you are going to work through this book using your own computer, you need:**

- **Computer System**  PC with Pentium 133-MHz or higher processor; Pentium III recommended. Microsoft Windows 2000 operating system with Service Pack 3 or later, Windows XP recommended. These tutorials assume a typical installation of Microsoft Access 2003.

- **Data Files**  You will not be able to complete the tutorials or exercises in this book using your own computer until you have the necessary starting Data Files.

- **Course Labs**  See your instructor or technical support person to obtain the Course Lab software for use on your own computer.

## Objectives

**Session 1.1**
- Define the terms field, record, table, relational database, primary key, and foreign key
- Open an existing database
- Identify the components of the Access and Database windows
- Open and navigate a table
- Learn how Access saves a database

**Session 1.2**
- Open an existing query, and create, sort, and navigate a new query
- Create and navigate a form
- Create, preview, and navigate a report
- Learn how to manage a database by backing up, restoring, compacting, and converting a database

## Lab

**Databases**

## Student Data Files

# Introduction to Microsoft Access 2003

*Viewing and Working with a Table Containing Employer Data*

## Case

## Northeast Seasonal Jobs International (NSJI)

During her high school and college years, Elsa Jensen spent her summers working as a lifeguard for some of the most popular beaches on Cape Cod, Massachusetts. Throughout those years, Elsa met many foreign students who had come to the United States to work for the summer, both at the beaches and at other seasonal businesses, such as restaurants and hotels. Elsa formed friendships with several students and kept in contact with them beyond college. Through discussions with her friends, Elsa realized that foreign students often have a difficult time finding appropriate seasonal work, relying mainly on "word-of-mouth" references to locate jobs. Elsa became convinced that there must be an easier way.

Several years ago, Elsa founded Northeast Seasonal Jobs, a small firm located in Boston that served as a job broker between foreign students seeking part-time, seasonal work and resort businesses located in New England. Recently Elsa expanded her business to include resorts in the eastern provinces of Canada, and consequently she changed her company's name to Northeast Seasonal Jobs International (NSJI). At first the company focused mainly on summer employment, but as the business continued to grow, Elsa increased the scope of operations to include all types of seasonal opportunities, including foliage tour companies in the fall and ski resorts in the winter.

Elsa depends on computers to help her manage all areas of NSJI's operations, including financial management, sales, and information management. Several months ago the company upgraded to Microsoft Windows and **Microsoft Office Access 2003** (or simply **Access**), a computer program used to enter, maintain, and retrieve related data in a format known as a database. Elsa and her staff use Access to

▼ **Brief**

| ▽ **Tutorial folder** | ▽ **Review folder** | ▽ **Case1 folder** |
|---|---|---|
| Seasonal.mdb | Seasons.mdb | Videos.mdb |
| ▽ **Case2 folder** | ▽ **Case3 folder** | ▽ **Case4 folder** |
| Meals.mdb | Redwood.mdb | Trips.mdb |

maintain data such as information about employers, positions they have available for seasonal work, and foreign students seeking employment. Elsa recently created a database
named Seasonal to track the company's employer customers and data about their available positions. She asks for your help in completing and maintaining this database.

# Session 1.1

**Databases**

# Introduction to Database Concepts

Before you begin working on Elsa's database and using Access, you need to understand a
few key terms and concepts associated with databases.

## Organizing Data

Data is a valuable resource to any business. At NSJI, for example, important data includes
employers' names and addresses, and available positions and wages. Organizing, storing,
maintaining, retrieving, and sorting this type of data are critical activities that enable a
business to find and use information effectively. Before storing data on a computer, however, you must organize the data.

Your first step in organizing data is to identify the individual fields. A **field** is a single
characteristic or attribute of a person, place, object, event, or idea. For example, some of
the many fields that NSJI tracks are employer ID, employer name, employer address,
employer phone number, position, wage, and start date.

Next, you group related fields together into tables. A **table** is a collection of fields that
describe a person, place, object, event, or idea. Figure 1-1 shows an example of an
Employer table consisting of four fields: EmployerID, EmployerName, EmployerAddress,
and PhoneNumber.

| Figure 1-1 | Data organization for a table of employers |
| --- | --- |

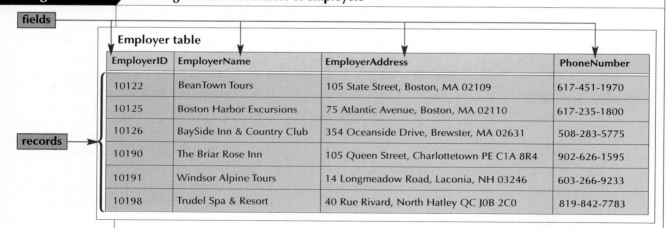

**fields**

**Employer table**

| EmployerID | EmployerName | EmployerAddress | PhoneNumber |
| --- | --- | --- | --- |
| 10122 | BeanTown Tours | 105 State Street, Boston, MA 02109 | 617-451-1970 |
| 10125 | Boston Harbor Excursions | 75 Atlantic Avenue, Boston, MA 02110 | 617-235-1800 |
| 10126 | BaySide Inn & Country Club | 354 Oceanside Drive, Brewster, MA 02631 | 508-283-5775 |
| 10190 | The Briar Rose Inn | 105 Queen Street, Charlottetown PE C1A 8R4 | 902-626-1595 |
| 10191 | Windsor Alpine Tours | 14 Longmeadow Road, Laconia, NH 03246 | 603-266-9233 |
| 10198 | Trudel Spa & Resort | 40 Rue Rivard, North Hatley QC J0B 2C0 | 819-842-7783 |

**records**

The specific value, or content, of a field is called the **field value**. In Figure 1-1, the first
set of field values for EmployerID, EmployerName, EmployerAddress, and PhoneNumber
are, respectively: 10122; BeanTown Tours; 105 State Street, Boston, MA 02109; and
617-451-1970. This set of field values is called a **record**. In the Employer table, the data
for each employer is stored as a separate record. Figure 1-1 shows six records; each row
of field values is a record.

## Databases and Relationships

A collection of related tables is called a **database**, or a **relational database**. NSJI's Seasonal database contains two related tables: the Employer and NAICS tables, which Elsa created. (The NAICS table contains North American Industry Classification System codes, which are used to classify businesses according to their activities.) In Tutorial 2, you will create a Position table to store information about the available positions at NSJI's employer clients.

Sometimes you might want information about employers and their available positions. To obtain this information, you must have a way to connect records in the Employer table to records in the Position table. You connect the records in the separate tables through a **common field** that appears in both tables.

In the sample database shown in Figure 1-2, each record in the Employer table has a field named EmployerID, which is also a field in the Position table. For example, BaySide Inn & Country Club is the third employer in the Employer table and has an EmployerID field value of 10126. This same EmployerID field value, 10126, appears in three records in the Position table. Therefore, BaySide Inn & Country Club is the employer with these three positions available.

**Database relationship between tables for employers and positions** | **Figure 1-2**

Each EmployerID value in the Employer table must be unique, so that you can distinguish one employer from another and identify the employer's specific positions available in the Position table. The EmployerID field is referred to as the primary key of the Employer table. A **primary key** is a field, or a collection of fields, whose values uniquely identify each record in a table. In the Position table, PositionID is the primary key.

When you include the primary key from one table as a field in a second table to form a relationship between the two tables, it is called a **foreign key** in the second table, as shown in Figure 1-2. For example, EmployerID is the primary key in the Employer table and a foreign key in the Position table. Although the primary key EmployerID has unique values in the Employer table, the same field as a foreign key in the Position table does not necessarily have unique values. The EmployerID value 10126, for example, appears three times in the Position table because the BaySide Inn & Country Club has three available positions. Each foreign key value, however, must match one of the field values for the primary key in the other table. In the example shown in Figure 1-2, each EmployerID value in the Position table must match an EmployerID value in the Employer table. The two tables are related, enabling users to connect the facts about employers with the facts about their employment positions.

## Relational Database Management Systems

To manage its databases, a company purchases a database management system. A **database management system (DBMS)** is a software program that lets you create databases and then manipulate data in them. Most of today's database management systems, including Access, are called relational database management systems. In a **relational database management system**, data is organized as a collection of tables. As stated earlier, a relationship between two tables in a relational DBMS is formed through a common field.

A relational DBMS controls the storage of databases on disk and facilitates the creation, manipulation, and reporting of data, as illustrated in Figure 1-3. Specifically, a relational DBMS provides the following functions:

- It allows you to create database structures containing fields, tables, and table relationships.
- It lets you easily add new records, change field values in existing records, and delete records.
- It contains a built-in query language, which lets you obtain immediate answers to the questions you ask about your data.
- It contains a built-in report generator, which lets you produce professional-looking, formatted reports from your data.
- It protects databases through security, control, and recovery facilities.

**Figure 1-3** **Relational database management system**

A company such as NSJI benefits from a relational DBMS because it allows users working in different departments to share the same data. More than one user can enter data into a database, and more than one user can retrieve and analyze data that was entered by others. For example, NSJI will store only one copy of the Employer table, and all employees will be able to use it to meet their specific requests for employer information.

Finally, unlike other software programs, such as spreadsheets, a DBMS can handle massive amounts of data and can easily form relationships among multiple tables. Each Access database, for example, can be up to two gigabytes in size and can contain up to 32,768 objects (tables, queries, and so on).

# Opening an Existing Database

Now that you've learned some database terms and concepts, you're ready to start Access and open the Seasonal database.

## To start Access:

1. Click the **Start** button on the taskbar, point to **All Programs**, point to **Microsoft Office**, and then click **Microsoft Office Access 2003**. The Access window opens. See Figure 1-4.

   **Trouble?** If you don't see the Microsoft Office Access 2003 option on the Microsoft Office submenu, look for it on a different submenu or as an option on the All Programs menu. If you still cannot find the Microsoft Office Access 2003 option, ask your instructor or technical support person for help.

**Microsoft Access window**  ◄  **Figure 1-4**

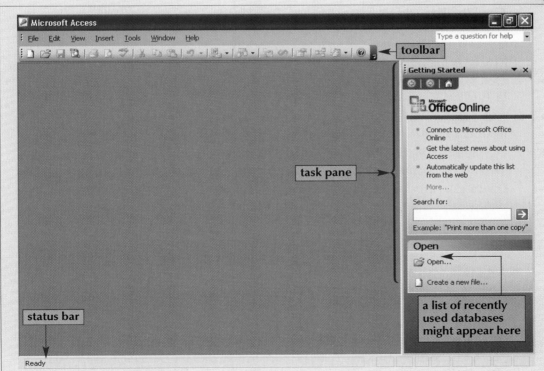

**Trouble?** If the Access program window on your computer is not maximized, click the Maximize button on the program window title bar.

When you start Access, the Access window contains the Getting Started task pane, which allows you to create a new database or to open an existing database. The "Create a new file" option in the task pane provides options for you to create a new database on your own, or to use one of the available online templates and let Access guide you through the steps for creating one of the standard databases provided by Microsoft.

In this case you need to open an existing database, the Seasonal database, which Elsa already created. To open an existing database, you can select the name of a database in the list of recently opened databases (if the list appears), or select a database in the Open dialog box. You need to open an existing database—the Seasonal database included with your Data Files.

### To open the Seasonal database:

1. Make sure you have created your copy of the Access Data Files, and that your computer can access them. For example, if you are using a removable disk, place the disk in the appropriate disk drive.

   **Trouble?** If you don't have the Access Data Files, you need to get them before you can proceed. Your instructor will either give you the Data Files or ask you to obtain them from a specified location (such as a network drive). In either case, be sure that you make a backup copy of your Data Files before you start using them, so that the original files will be available on your copied disk in case you need to start over because of an error or problem. If you have any questions about the Data Files, see your instructor or technical support staff for assistance.

2. In the Open section of the task pane, click the **Open** option. The Open dialog box is displayed.

   **Trouble?** If your task pane doesn't provide an Open option, click the More option to display the Open dialog box.

3. Click the **Look in** list arrow, and then click the drive that contains your Data Files.

   **Trouble?** If you do not know where your Data Files are located, consult with your instructor about where to open and save your Data Files. Note that Access slows noticeably if you are working with a database stored on a 3 ½-inch floppy disk, and might not be able to perform some tasks, such as compacting and converting a database.

4. Click **Brief** in the list box (if necessary), and then click the **Open** button to display the contents of the Brief folder.

5. Click **Tutorial** in the list box, and then click the **Open** button to display a list of the files in the Tutorial folder.

6. Click **Seasonal** in the list box, and then click the **Open** button. The task pane closes, and the Seasonal database opens in the Access window. See Figure 1-5.

   **Trouble?** If a dialog box opens with a message about installing the Microsoft Jet Service Pack, see your instructor or technical support person for assistance. You must have the appropriate Service Pack installed in order to open and work with Access databases safely.

   **Trouble?** If a dialog box opens, warning you that the Seasonal database may not be safe, click the Open button. Your security level is set to Medium, which is the security setting that lets you choose whether or not to open a database that contains macros, VBA, or certain types of queries. The Seasonal database does not contain objects that will harm your computer, so you can safely open the database.

   **Trouble?** If a dialog box opens, warning you that Access can't open the Seasonal database due to security restrictions, click the OK button, click Tools on the menu bar, point to Macro, click Security, click the Medium option button, click the OK button, restart your computer if you're requested to do so, and then repeat Steps 1–6. Your security level was set to High, which is the security setting that lets you open a database that contains macros, VBA, or certain types of queries only from trusted sources. Because the Seasonal database does not contain objects that will harm your computer, you need to change the security setting to Medium and then safely open the Seasonal database.

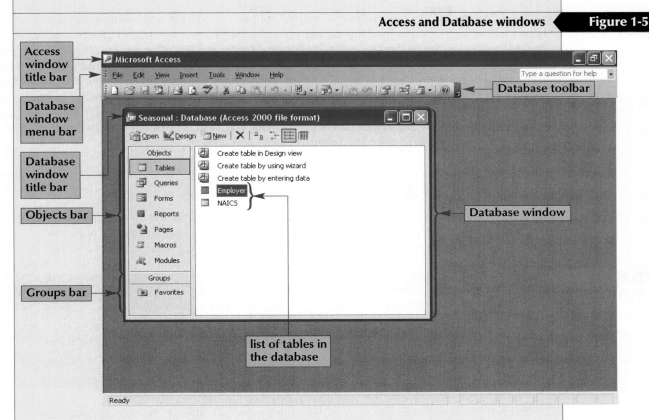

**Trouble?** The filename on your screen might be Seasonal.mdb instead of Seasonal, depending on your computer's default settings. The extension ".mdb" identifies the file as a Microsoft Access database.

**Trouble?** If Tables is not selected in the Objects bar of the Database window, click it to display the list of tables in the database.

Before you can begin working with the database, you need to become familiar with the components of the Access and Database windows.

## Exploring the Access and Database Windows

The **Access window** is the program window that appears when you start the program. The **Database window** appears when you open a database; this window is the main control center for working with an open Access database. Except for the Access window title bar, all window components now on your screen are associated with the Database window (see Figure 1-5). Most of these window components—including the title bars, window sizing buttons, menu bar, toolbar, and status bar—are the same as the components in other Windows programs.

Notice that the Database window title bar includes the notation "(Access 2000 file format)." By default, databases that you create in Access 2003 use the Access 2000 database file format. This feature ensures that you can use and share databases originally created in Access 2003 without converting them to a format for an earlier version of Access, and vice versa. (You'll learn more about database file formats and converting databases later in this tutorial.)

The Database window provides a variety of options for viewing and manipulating database objects. Each item in the **Objects bar** controls one of the major object groups—such as tables, queries, forms, and reports—in an Access database. The **Groups bar** allows you to organize different types of database objects into groups, with shortcuts to those objects, so that you can work with them more easily. The Database window also provides buttons for quickly creating, opening, and managing objects, as well as shortcut options for some of these tasks.

Recall that Elsa has already created the Employer and NAICS tables in the Seasonal database. She asks you to open the Employer table and view its contents.

## Opening an Access Table

As noted earlier, tables contain all the data in a database. Tables are the fundamental objects for your work in Access. To view, add, change, or delete data in a table, you first open the table. You can open any Access object by using the Open button in the Database window.

**Reference Window**

### Opening an Access Object

- In the Objects bar of the Database window, click the type of object you want to open.
- If necessary, scroll the object list box until the object name appears, and then click the object name.
- Click the Open button in the Database window.

You need to open the Employer table, which is one of two tables in the Seasonal database.

### To open the Employer table:

1. In the Database window, click **Employer** to select it (if necessary).
2. Click the **Open** button in the Database window. The Employer table opens in Datasheet view on top of the Database and Access windows. See Figure 1-6.

Employer table displayed in Datasheet view ◄ **Figure 1-6**

**Datasheet view** shows a table's contents as a **datasheet** in rows and columns, similar to a table or spreadsheet. Each row is a separate record in the table, and each column contains the field values for one field in the table. Each column is headed by a field name inside a field selector, and each row has a record selector to its left. Notice that the field names are displayed with spaces between words—such as "Employer ID" instead of "EmployerID" and "Employer Name" instead of "EmployerName." (You'll learn how to change the display of field names later in this text.) Clicking a **field selector** or a **record selector** selects that entire column or row (respectively), which you then can manipulate. A field selector is also called a **column selector**, and a record selector is also called a **row selector**.

## Navigating an Access Datasheet

When you first open a datasheet, Access selects the first field value in the first record. Notice that this field value is highlighted and that a darkened triangle symbol, called the current record symbol, appears in the record selector to the left of the first record. The **current record symbol** identifies the currently selected record. Clicking a record selector or field value in another row moves the current record symbol to that row. You can also move the pointer over the data on the screen and click one of the field values to position the insertion point.

The Employer table currently has 13 fields and 45 records. To view fields or records not currently visible in the datasheet, you can use the horizontal and vertical scroll bars shown in Figure 1-6 to navigate the data. The **navigation buttons**, also shown in Figure 1-6, provide another way to move vertically through the records. Figure 1-7 shows which record becomes the current record when you click each navigation button. The **record number box**, which appears between the two sets of navigation buttons, displays the current record number. The total number of records in the table appears to the right of the navigation buttons.

**Figure 1-7** ▶ **Navigation buttons**

| Navigation Button | Record Selected | Navigation Button | Record Selected |
|---|---|---|---|
| ⏮ | First record | ⏭ | Last record |
| ◀ | Previous record | ▶✳ | New record |
| ▶ | Next record | | |

Elsa suggests that you use the various navigation techniques to move through the Employer table and become familiar with its contents.

### To navigate the Employer datasheet:

▶ **1.** Click the right scroll arrow in the horizontal scroll bar a few times to scroll to the right and view the remaining fields in the Employer table.

▶ **2.** Drag the scroll box in the horizontal scroll bar all the way to the left to return to the previous display of the datasheet.

▶ **3.** Click the **Next Record** navigation button ▶ . The second record is now the current record, as indicated by the current record symbol in the second record selector. Also, notice that the second record's value for the EmployerID field is highlighted, and "2" (for record number 2) appears in the record number box.

▶ **4.** Click the **Last Record** navigation button ⏭ . The last record in the table, record 45, is now the current record.

▶ **5.** Click the **Previous Record** navigation button ◀ . Record 44 is now the current record.

▶ **6.** Click the **First Record** navigation button ⏮ . The first record is now the current record.

## Printing a Datasheet

At times you might want a printed copy of the records in a table. You can use the Print button 🖨 on the Table Datasheet toolbar to print the contents of a table. You can also use the Print command on the File menu to display the Print dialog box and select various options for printing.

Reference Window | **Printing a Datasheet**

- Open the table datasheet you want to print.
- Click the Print button on the Table Datasheet toolbar to print the table with default settings; or click File on the menu bar, and then click Print to display the Print dialog box and select the options you want for printing the datasheet.

Elsa does not want a printed copy of the Employer table, so you do not need to print the datasheet at this time.

## Saving a Database

Notice the Save button 💾 on the Table Datasheet toolbar. Unlike the Save buttons in other Office programs, this Save button does not save the active document (database) to your disk. Instead, you use the Save button to save the design of an Access object, such as a table, or to save datasheet format changes. Access does not have a button or option you can use to save the active database. Similarly, you cannot use the Save As option on the File menu to save the active database file with a new name, as you can with other Office programs.

Access saves changes to the active database to your disk automatically, when a record is changed or added and when you close the database. If your database is stored on a removable disk, such as a floppy disk, *you should never remove the disk while the database file is open*. If you remove the disk, Access will encounter problems when it tries to save the database, which might damage the database.

You're done working with the Employer table for now, so you can close it.

**To close the Employer table:**

▸ **1.** Click the **Close** button ☒ on the Employer Table window to close the table. You return to the Database window.

Now that you've become familiar with database concepts and Access, opened the Seasonal database that Elsa created, and navigated an Access table, Elsa wants you to work with the data stored in the Seasonal database and to create database objects including a query, form, and report. You will complete these tasks in Session 1.2.

## Session 1.1 Quick Check

1. A(n) _____ is a single characteristic of a person, place, object, event, or idea.
2. You connect the records in two separate tables through a(n) _____ that appears in both tables.
3. The _____, whose values uniquely identify each record in a table, is called a(n) _____ when it is placed in a second table to form a relationship between the two tables.
4. In a table, the rows are also called _____, and the columns are also called _____.
5. The _____ identifies the selected record in an Access table.
6. Describe two methods for navigating a table.
7. Explain how the saving process in Access is different from saving in other Office programs.

# Session 1.2

## Working with Queries

A **query** is a question you ask about the data stored in a database. In response to a query, Access displays the specific records and fields that answer your question. When you create a query, you tell Access which fields you need and what criteria Access should use to select the records. Then Access displays only the information you want, so you don't have to navigate through the entire database for the information. In the Seasonal database, for example, Elsa might create a query to display only those records for employers located in Boston.

Before creating a new query, you will open a query that Elsa created recently so that she could view information in the Employer table in a different way.

# Opening an Existing Query

Queries that you create and save appear in the Queries list of the Database window. To see the results of a query, you open, or run, the query. Elsa created and saved a query named Contacts in the Seasonal database. This query shows all the fields from the Employer table, but in a different order. Elsa suggests that you open this query to see its results.

### To open the Contacts query:

1. If you took a break after the previous session, make sure that Access is running and that the Seasonal database is open.

2. Click **Queries** in the Objects bar of the Database window to display the Queries list. The Queries list box contains one object—the Contacts query. See Figure 1-8.

| Figure 1-8 | List of queries in the Seasonal database |

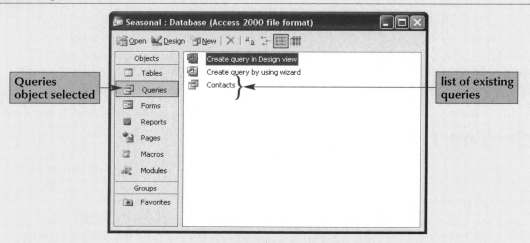

Now you will run the Contacts query by opening it.

3. Click **Contacts** to select it, and then click the **Open** button in the Database window. Access displays the results of the query in Datasheet view. See Figure 1-9.

| Figure 1-9 | Results of running the Contacts query |

Query window title bar

| Employer ID | Employer Name | Contact First Name | Contact Last Name | Phone | Positi |
|---|---|---|---|---|---|
| 10122 | BeanTown Tours | Sarah | Tasker | 617-451-1970 | Office Manag |
| 10125 | Boston Harbor Excursions | Beth | Petr | 617-235-1800 | Office Manag |
| 10126 | BaySide Inn & Country Club | Jeffrey | Hersha | 508-283-5775 | General Man: |
| 10130 | Seaview Restaurant | Donald | Bouwman | 508-776-8593 | Manager |
| 10131 | Claire's Cottages | Claire | Markovicz | 508-822-1328 | Manager |
| 10133 | The Inn at Plum Hill | Michele | Yasenak | 508-693-2320 | General Man: |
| 10134 | Capt'n John's Seafood | John | Fairbrother | 508-255-8721 | Manager |
| 10135 | The Adele Bannister House | Cheryl | Coppolino | 401-849-3093 | General Man: |
| 10138 | Blue Hill Inn & Country Club | Hwan | Tang | 508-893-0808 | Personnel Di |
| 10145 | The Clipper Ship Inn | Oren | Ben-Joseph | 978-546-0193 | Personnel M: |
| 10146 | Newport Mansion Guided Tours | Katherine | Foley | 401-849-6544 | Personnel Di |
| 10149 | Falling Leaves Tours | Jessica | Ropiak | 508-347-5331 | Director |
| 10150 | Colonial Caravan Tours | John | Logan | 978-371-8086 | Manager |
| 10151 | Granite State Resort | Christine | Faraci | 603-468-8866 | HR Manager |

Record: 1 of 45

fields appear in a different order

Notice that the query displays the fields from the Employer table, but in a different order. For example, the first and last names of each contact, as well as the contact's phone number, appear next to the employer name. This arrangement lets Elsa view pertinent contact information without having to scroll through the table. Rearranging the display of table data is one task you can perform with queries, so that table information appears in an order more suited to how you want to work with the information.

▶ **4.** Click the **Close** button  on the Query window title bar to close the Contacts query.

Even though a query can display table information in a different way, the information still exists in the table as it was originally entered. If you opened the Employer table, it would still show the fields in their original order.

Zack Ward, the director of marketing at NSJI, wants a list of all employers so that his staff can call them to check on their satisfaction with NSJI's services and recruits. He doesn't want the list to include all the fields in the Employer table (such as PostalCode and NAICSCode)—only the employer's contact information. To produce this list for Zack, you need to create a query using the Employer table.

## Creating, Sorting, and Navigating a Query

You can design your own queries or use an Access **Query Wizard**, which guides you through the steps to create a query. The Simple Query Wizard allows you to select records and fields quickly, and it is an appropriate choice for producing the employer list Zack wants. You can choose this wizard either by clicking the New button to open a dialog box listing several wizards for creating a query, or by double-clicking the "Create query by using wizard" option, which automatically starts the Simple Query Wizard.

### To start the Simple Query Wizard:

▶ **1.** Double-click **Create query by using wizard**. The first Simple Query Wizard dialog box opens. See Figure 1-10.

**First Simple Query Wizard dialog box** ◀ **Figure 1-10**

Because Contacts is the only query object in the Seasonal database, it is listed in the Tables/Queries box by default. You need to base the query you're creating on the Employer table.

▶ **2.** Click the **Tables/Queries** list arrow, and then click **Table: Employer** to select the Employer table as the source for the new query. The Available Fields list box now lists the fields in the Employer table.

You need to select fields from the Available Fields list box to include them in the query. To select fields one at a time, click a field and then click the ⌐ > ⌐ button. The selected field moves from the Available Fields list box on the left to the Selected Fields list box on the right. To select all the fields, click the ⌐ >> ⌐ button. If you change your mind or make a mistake, you can remove a field by clicking it in the Selected Fields list box and then clicking the ⌐ < ⌐ button. To remove all selected fields, click the ⌐ << ⌐ button.

Each Simple Query Wizard dialog box contains buttons on the bottom that allow you to move to the previous dialog box (Back button), move to the next dialog box (Next button), or cancel the creation process (Cancel button) and return to the Database window. You can also finish creating the object (Finish button) and accept the wizard's defaults for the remaining options.

Zack wants his list to include data from only the following fields: EmployerName, City, StateProv, ContactFirstName, ContactLastName, and Phone. You need to select these fields to include them in the query.

### To create the query using the Simple Query Wizard:

▶ **1.** Click **EmployerName** in the Available Fields list box, and then click the ⌐ > ⌐ button. The EmployerName field moves to the Selected Fields list box.

▶ **2.** Repeat Step 1 for the fields **City**, **StateProv**, **ContactFirstName**, **ContactLastName**, and **Phone**, and then click the **Next** button. The second, and final, Simple Query Wizard dialog box opens and asks you to choose a name for your query. This name will appear in the Queries list in the Database window. You'll change the suggested name (Employer Query) to "EmployerList."

▶ **3.** Click at the end of the highlighted name, use the **Backspace** key to delete the word "Query" and the space after "Employer," and then type **List**. Now you can view the query results.

▶ **4.** Click the **Finish** button to complete the query. Access displays the query results in Datasheet view.

▶ **5.** Click the **Maximize** button 🔲 on the Query window title bar to maximize the window. See Figure 1-11.

The datasheet displays the six selected fields for each record in the Employer table. The fields are shown in the order you selected them, from left to right.

The records are currently listed in order by the primary key field (EmployerID from the Employer table). This is true even though the EmployerID field is not included in the display of the query results. Zack prefers the records listed in order by state or province, so that his staff members can focus on all records for the employers in a particular state or province. To display the records in the order Zack wants, you need to sort the query results by the StateProv field.

## To sort the query results:

1. Click to position the insertion point anywhere in the State/Prov column. This establishes the State/Prov column as the current field.

2. Click the **Sort Ascending** button 🔼 on the Query Datasheet toolbar. Now the records are sorted in ascending alphabetical order by the values in the State/Prov column. All the records for Connecticut (CT) are listed first, followed by the records for Massachusetts (MA), Maine (ME), and so on.

   Notice that the navigation buttons are located at the bottom of the window. You navigate a query datasheet in the same way that you navigate a table datasheet.

3. Click the **Last Record** navigation button ▶❙. The last record in the query datasheet, for the Darby Inn & Restaurant, is now the current record.

4. Click the **Previous Record** navigation button ◀. Record 44 in the query datasheet is now the current record.

▶ **5.** Click the **First Record** navigation button ⏮. The first record is now the current record.

▶ **6.** Click the **Close Window** button ✕ on the menu bar to close the query.

A dialog box opens and asks if you want to save changes to the design of the query. This dialog box opens because you changed the sort order of the query results.

▶ **7.** Click the **Yes** button to save the query design changes and return to the Database window. Notice that the EmployerList query now appears in the Queries list box. In addition, because you maximized the Query window, now the Database window is also maximized. You need to restore the window.

▶ **8.** Click the **Restore Window** button 🗗 on the menu bar to restore the Database window.

The query results are not stored in the database; however, the query design is stored as part of the database with the name you specified. You can re-create the query results at any time by running the query again. You can also print the query datasheet using the Print button, just as you can to print a table datasheet. You'll learn more about creating and running queries in Tutorial 3.

After Zack views the query results, Elsa asks you to create a form for the Employer table so that her staff members can use the form to enter and work with data in the table easily.

## Creating and Navigating a Form

A **form** is an object you use to maintain, view, and print records in a database. Although you can perform these same functions with tables and queries, forms can present data in many customized and useful ways.

In Access, you can design your own forms or use a Form Wizard to create your forms automatically. A **Form Wizard** is an Access tool that asks you a series of questions, and then creates a form based on your answers. However, an **AutoForm Wizard** does not ask you questions. Instead, it places all the fields from a selected table (or query) on a form automatically, and then displays the form on the screen, making it the quickest way to create a form.

Elsa wants a form for the Employer table that will show all the fields for one record at a time, with fields listed one below another in a column. This type of form will make it easier for her staff to focus on all the data for a particular employer. You'll use the AutoForm: Columnar Wizard to create the form.

**To create the form using an AutoForm Wizard:**

▶ **1.** Click **Forms** in the Objects bar of the Database window to display the Forms list. The Forms list box does not contain any forms yet.

▶ **2.** Click the **New** button in the Database window to open the New Form dialog box. See Figure 1-12.

The top list box provides options for designing your own form or creating a form using one of the Form Wizards. In the bottom list box, you choose the table or query that will supply the data for the form.

▶ **3.** Click **AutoForm: Columnar** to select this AutoForm Wizard.

▶ **4.** Click the list arrow for choosing the table or query on which to base the form, and then click **Employer**.

▶ **5.** Click the **OK** button. The AutoForm Wizard creates the form and displays it in Form view. See Figure 1-13.

Form created by the AutoForm: Columnar Wizard ◄ Figure 1-13

**Trouble?** The placement of the Form View and Formatting toolbars might be different on your screen. If you want your screen to match the figures, you can use the mouse to drag a toolbar to a new location, using the dotted line at the left edge of a toolbar. However, the position of any toolbar does not affect your ability to complete the steps.

**Trouble?** The background of your form might look different from the one shown in Figure 1-13, depending on your computer's settings. If so, don't worry. You will learn how to change the form's style later in this text. For now, continue with the tutorial.

The form displays one record at a time in the Employer table. Access displays the field values for the first record in the table and selects the first field value (EmployerID). Each field name appears on a separate line (spread over two columns) and on the same line as its field value, which appears in a box. The widths of the boxes are different to accommodate the different sizes of the displayed field values; for example, compare the small box for the StateProv field value with the larger box for the EmployerName field value. The AutoForm: Columnar Wizard automatically placed the field names and values on the form and supplied the background style. Note as well that field names are displayed with spaces between them, such as "Contact First Name" instead of "ContactFirstName." (You'll learn how to control the display of field names in database objects, such as tables and forms, later in this text.)

To view and maintain data using a form, you must know how to move from field to field and from record to record. Notice that the Form window contains navigation buttons, similar to those available in Datasheet view, which you can use to display different records in the form. You'll use these now to navigate the form; then you'll save and close the form.

### To navigate, save, and close the form:

▶ 1. Click the **Next Record** navigation button ▶. The form now displays the values for the second record in the Employer table.

▶ 2. Click the **Last Record** navigation button ▶| to move to the last record in the table. The form displays the information for record 45, Lighthouse Tours.

▶ 3. Click the **Previous Record** navigation button ◀ to move to record 44.

▶ 4. Click the **First Record** navigation button |◀ to return to the first record in the Employer table.

Next, you'll save the form with the name "EmployerData" in the Seasonal database. Then the form will be available for later use.

▶ 5. Click the **Save** button 🖫 on the Form View toolbar. The Save As dialog box opens.

▶ 6. In the Form Name text box, click at the end of the highlighted word "Employer," type **Data**, and then press the **Enter** key. Access saves the form as EmployerData in the Seasonal database and closes the dialog box. Note, however, that the Form window title bar still displays the name "Employer"; you'll see how to control object names in the next tutorial.

▶ 7. Click the **Close** button ☒ on the Form window title bar to close the form and return to the Database window. Note that the EmployerData form is now listed in the Forms list box.

After attending a staff meeting, Zack returns with another request. He wants the same employer list you produced earlier when you created the EmployerList query, but he'd like the information presented in a more readable format. You'll help Zack by creating a report.

## Creating, Previewing, and Navigating a Report

A **report** is a formatted printout (or screen display) of the contents of one or more tables in a database. Although you can print data appearing in tables, queries, and forms, reports provide you with the greatest flexibility for formatting printed output. As with forms, you can design your own reports or use a Report Wizard to create reports automatically. Like other wizards, a **Report Wizard** guides you through the steps of creating a report.

Zack wants a report showing the same information contained in the EmployerList query that you created earlier. However, he wants the data for each employer to be grouped together, with one employer record below another, as shown in the report sketch in Figure 1-14.

Sketch of Zack's report | **Figure 1-14**

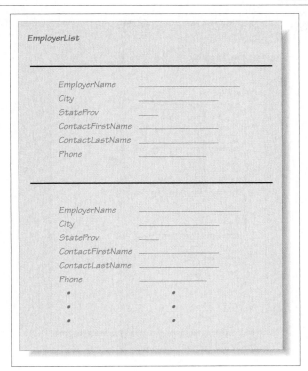

To produce the report for Zack, you'll use the AutoReport: Columnar Wizard, which is similar to the AutoForm: Columnar Wizard you used earlier when creating the EmployerData form. An **AutoReport Wizard**, like an AutoForm Wizard, places all the fields from a selected table (or query) on a report, making it the quickest way to create a report.

### To create the report using the AutoReport: Columnar Wizard:

1. Click **Reports** in the Objects bar of the Database window, and then click the **New** button in the Database window to open the New Report dialog box, which is similar to the New Form dialog box you saw earlier.

2. Click **AutoReport: Columnar** to select this wizard for creating the report.

    Because Zack wants the same data as in the EmployerList query, you need to choose that query as the basis for the report.

3. Click the list arrow for choosing the table or query on which to base the report, and then click **EmployerList**.

4. Click the **OK** button. The AutoReport Wizard creates the report and displays it in Print Preview, which shows exactly how the report will look when printed.

    To view the report better, you'll maximize the window and change the Zoom setting so that you can see the entire page.

5. Click the **Maximize** button 🔲 on the Report window title bar, click the **Zoom** list arrow (to the right of the value 100%) on the Print Preview toolbar, and then click **Fit**. The entire first page of the report is displayed in the window. See Figure 1-15.

**Figure 1-15** ▸ **First page of the report in Print Preview**

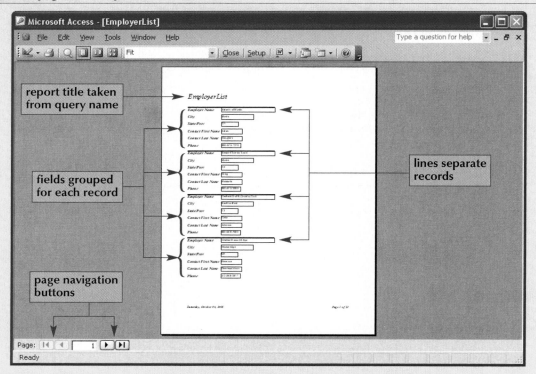

**Trouble?** The fonts used in your report might look different from the ones shown in Figure 1-15, depending on your computer's settings. If so, don't worry. You will learn how to change the report's style later in this text.

Each field from the EmployerList query appears on its own line, with the corresponding field value to the right and in a box. Horizontal lines separate one record from the next, visually grouping all the fields for each record. The name of the query—EmployerList—appears as the report's title.

Notice that the Print Preview window provides page navigation buttons at the bottom of the window, similar to the navigation buttons you've used to move through records in a table, query, and form. You use these buttons to move through the pages of a report.

▸ **6.** Click the **Next Page** navigation button ▶. The second page of the report is displayed in Print Preview.

▸ **7.** Click the **Last Page** navigation button ▶❙ to move to the last page of the report. Note that this page contains the fields for only one record. Also note that the box in the middle of the navigation buttons displays the number "12"; there are 12 pages in this report.

**Trouble?** Depending on the printer you are using, your report might have more or fewer pages, or might have more than one record on the last page. If so, don't worry. Different printers format reports in different ways, sometimes affecting the total number of pages and the number of records per page.

▸ **8.** Click the **First Page** navigation button ❙◀ to return to the first page of the report.

Zack likes how the report looks, and he wants to show it to his staff members to see if they approve of the format. He would like a printout of the report, but he doesn't need the entire report printed—only the first page.

## Printing Specific Pages of a Report

After creating a report, you typically print it to distribute it to others who need to view the report's contents. You can choose to print the entire report, using the Print toolbar button or the Print menu option, or you can select specific pages of a report to print. To specify certain pages to print, you must use the Print option on the File menu. In this case, you will print only the first page of the EmployerList report.

   **Note**: To complete the following steps, your computer must be connected to a printer.

### To print only the first page of the report:

▶ **1.** Click **File** on the menu bar, and then click **Print**. The Print dialog box opens. See Figure 1-16.

**Print dialog box** ◄ **Figure 1-16**

your settings
will vary

option for
specifying
a range of pages
to print

   **Trouble?** The settings shown for the Name, Type, and Where options in your Print dialog box will vary from those shown in the figure, depending on the printer you are using.

   The Print dialog box provides options for printing all the pages in the report or a specified range of pages. In this case, you will print just the first page of the report, so you need to specify a range of "From" page 1 "To" page 1.

▶ **2.** In the Print Range section, click the **Pages** option button. Notice that the insertion point now appears in the From box so that you can specify the first page to be printed.

▶ **3.** Type **1**, press the **Tab** key to move to the To box, and then type **1**. These settings will cause only the first page of the report to be printed.

▶ **4.** Click the **OK** button. The first page of the EmployerList report prints on your selected printer.

   **Trouble?** If your report did not print, make sure that your computer is connected to a printer, and that the printer is turned on and ready to print. Then repeat Steps 1 through 4.

   At this point, you could close the report without saving it because you can easily re-create it at any time. In general, it's best to save an object—report, form, or query—only if you anticipate using the object frequently or if it is time-consuming to create, because these objects use considerable storage space on your disk. However, Zack wants to keep the report until he receives feedback from his staff members about its layout, so he asks you to save it.

**To close and save the report:**

▶ **1.** Click the **Close Window** button ☒ on the menu bar. *Do not* click the Close button on the Print Preview toolbar.

**Trouble?** If you clicked the Close button on the Print Preview toolbar, you switched to Design view. Simply click the Close Window button ☒ on the menu bar, and then continue with the steps.

A dialog box opens and asks if you want to save the changes to the report design.

▶ **2.** Click the **Yes** button. The Save As dialog box opens.

▶ **3.** Click to the right of the highlighted text in the Report Name text box, type **Report**, and then click the **OK** button. Access saves the report as "EmployerListReport" and returns to the Database window.

Now that you've become familiar with the objects in the Seasonal database, Elsa suggests that you learn about some ways to manage your database.

# Managing a Database

One of the main tasks involved in working with database software is managing your databases and the data they contain. By managing your databases, you can ensure that they operate in the most efficient way, that the data they contain is secure, and that you can work with the data effectively. Some of the activities involved in database management include backing up and restoring a database, compacting and repairing a database, and converting a database for use in other versions of Access.

## Backing up and Restoring a Database

**Backing up** a database is the process of making a copy of the database file to protect your database against loss or damage. Experienced database users make it a habit to back up a database before they work with it for the first time, keeping the original data intact, and to make frequent backups while continuing to work with a database. Because a floppy disk can hold only the smallest of databases, it is not practical to store backup copies on a floppy disk. Most users back up their databases on tapes, recordable CDs, or hard disks.

With previous versions of Access, you could only make a backup copy using one of the following methods: Windows Explorer, My Computer, Microsoft Backup, or other backup software. With Access 2003, however, a new Back Up Database option enables you to back up your database file from within the Access program, while you are working on your database. Figure 1-17 shows the Save Backup As dialog box, which opens when you choose the Back Up Database option from the File menu.

**Save Backup As dialog box** | **Figure 1-17**

default filename for
backup copy of database

The Save Backup As dialog box is similar to the standard Save As dialog box found in Windows programs. Notice that the default filename for the backup copy consists of the same filename as the database you are backing up (in this example, "Seasonal") plus the current date. This file naming system makes it easy for you to keep track of your database backups and when they were created. (You will not actually back up the Seasonal database here; if you are working off a floppy disk, you will not have enough room on the disk to hold both the original database and its backup copy.)

To restore a backup database file, choose the same method you used to make the backup copy. For example, if you used the Microsoft Backup tool (which is one of the System Tools available from the All Programs menu and Accessories submenu in Windows), you must choose the Restore option for this tool to copy the database file to your database folder. If the existing database file and the backup copy have the same name, restoring the backup copy might replace the existing file. If you want to save the existing file, rename it before you restore the backup copy.

## Compacting and Repairing a Database

Whenever you open an Access database and work in it, the size of the database increases. Further, when you delete records and when you delete or replace database objects—such as queries, forms, and reports—the space that had been occupied on the disk by the deleted or replaced records or objects does not automatically become available for other records or objects. To make the space available, you must compact the database. **Compacting** a database rearranges the data and objects in a database to decrease its file size. Unlike making a backup copy of a database file, which you do to protect your database against loss or damage, you compact a database to make it smaller, thereby making more space available on your disk and letting you open and close the database more quickly. Figure 1-18 illustrates the compacting process; the red-orange elements in the figure represent database records and objects.

**Figure 1-18** **Compacting a database**

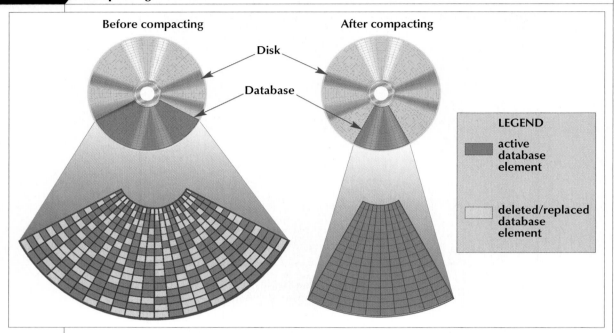

When you compact a database, Access repairs the database at the same time. In many cases, Access detects that a database is damaged when you try to open it and gives you the option to compact and repair it at that time. For example, the data in your database might become damaged, or corrupted, if you exit the Access program suddenly by turning off your computer. If you think your database might be damaged because it is behaving unpredictably, you can use the "Compact and Repair Database" option to fix it. With your database file open, point to the Database Utilities option on the Tools menu, and then choose the Compact and Repair Database option.

## Compacting a Database Automatically

Access also allows you to set an option for your database file so that every time you close the database, it will be compacted automatically.

Reference Window

### Compacting a Database Automatically

- Make sure the database file you want to compact automatically is open.
- Click Tools on the menu bar, and then click Options.
- Click the General tab in the Options dialog box.
- Click the Compact on Close check box to select it.
- Click the OK button.

You'll set the Compact on Close option now for the Seasonal database. Then, every time you subsequently close the Seasonal database, Access will compact the database file for you. After setting this option, you'll close the database.

**Important:** Because Access copies the database file and then compacts it on the same disk, you might run out of storage space if you compact a database stored on a floppy disk. Therefore, it is strongly recommended that you set the Compact on Close option *only* if your database is stored somewhere other than a floppy disk. However, if you must work with the Seasonal database on a floppy disk, per your instructor's requirements, you must also compact the database so that it will fit on the disk as you progress through the tutorials. Consult with your instructor or technical support staff to see if they recommend your using the Compact on Close option while working from a floppy disk.

### To set the option for compacting the Seasonal database:

▶ **1.** Make sure the Seasonal Database window is open.

▶ **2.** Click **Tools** on the menu bar, and then click **Options**. The Options dialog box opens.

▶ **3.** Click the **General** tab in the dialog box, and then click the **Compact on Close** check box to select it. See Figure 1-19.

**General tab of the Options dialog box** ◀ **Figure 1-19**

▶ **4.** Click the **OK** button to set the option.

**Trouble?** If you are working from a floppy disk, you might receive message or warning dialog boxes when setting this option. Click OK and continue with the tutorial. See your instructor or technical support staff if you have problems with this option.

▶ **5.** Click the **Close Window** button ☒ on the menu bar. Access closes the Seasonal database file and compacts it automatically.

**Note:** If the database you are compacting is located on a floppy disk, it is very important that you *wait until the compacting procedure is complete before removing the floppy disk.* Wait until the light on the floppy disk drive goes off and the whirring noise made by the floppy disk drive stops. If you remove the disk before compacting has finished, you could damage your database.

## Converting an Access 2000 Database

Another important database management task is **converting** a database so that you can work with it in a different version of Access. As noted earlier in this tutorial, the default file format for databases you create in Access 2003 is Access 2000. This enables you to work with the database in either the Access 2000, 2002, or 2003 versions of the software without having to convert it. This compatibility makes it easy for multiple users working with different versions of the software to share the same database and work more efficiently.

Sometimes, however, you might need to convert an Access 2000 database to another version. For example, if you need to share an Access 2000 database with a colleague who works on a laptop computer with Access 97 installed on it, you could convert the Access 2000 database to the Access 97 format. Likewise, you might want to convert an Access 2000 database to the Access 2002 file format if the database becomes very large. The Access 2002 file format is enhanced so that large databases run faster than in earlier versions of Access, making it more efficient for you to work with the information contained in them.

To convert a database, you would follow these steps (note that you will not actually convert a database now):

1. Make sure that Access is running (the database you want to convert can be open or closed).
2. Click Tools on the menu bar, point to Database Utilities, point to Convert Database, and then choose the format you want to convert to.
3. In the Database to Convert From dialog box (which appears only if the database you want to convert is closed), select the name of the database you want to convert, and then click the Convert button.
4. In the Convert Database Into dialog box, enter a new name for the converted database in the File name text box, and then click the Save button. If a message box opens with a caution about not being able to share files with a specific version of Access, click the OK button.

After converting a database, you can use it in the version of Access to which you converted the file. Note, however, that when you convert to a previous file format, such as converting from the Access 2000 file format to the Access 97 file format, you might lose some of the advanced features of the newer version and you might need to make some adjustments to the converted database. Simple databases, such as the Seasonal database, generally retain their data and formatting when converted. However, you could lose data and other information from more complex databases when you convert them to an earlier file format.

With the Employer and NAICS tables in place, Elsa can continue to build the Seasonal database and use it to store, manipulate, and retrieve important data for NSJI. In the following tutorials, you'll help Elsa complete and maintain the database, and you'll use it to meet the specific information needs of other NSJI employees.

**Review** | # Session 1.2 Quick Check

1. A(n) _____ is a question you ask about the data stored in a database.
2. Unless you specify otherwise, the records resulting from a query are listed in order by the _____.
3. The quickest way to create a form is to use a(n) _____.
4. Describe the form created by the AutoForm: Columnar Wizard.
5. After creating a report, the AutoReport Wizard displays the report in _____.
6. _____ a database rearranges the data and objects in a database to decrease its file size.

# Tutorial Summary

In this tutorial, you learned the basic concepts associated with databases, including how data is organized in a database and the functions of a relational database management system. You also learned how the Database window is the main control center for your work in Access, giving you options for viewing and manipulating all the objects in a database—tables, queries, forms, reports, and so on. By opening and navigating a table datasheet, you saw how the fields and records in a table are displayed and organized. Using various wizards, you also learned how to create queries, forms, and reports quickly in order to view and work with the data stored in a table in different ways. Finally, you were introduced to some of the important tasks involved in managing a database, including backing up, compacting, and converting a database.

# Key Terms

| | | |
|---|---|---|
| Access | Database window | query |
| Access window | datasheet | Query Wizard |
| AutoForm Wizard | Datasheet view | record |
| AutoReport Wizard | field | record number box |
| backing up | field selector | record selector |
| column selector | field value | relational database |
| common field | foreign key | relational database |
| compacting | form |    management system |
| converting | Form Wizard |    (RDBMS) |
| current record symbol | Groups bar | report |
| database | navigation buttons | Report Wizard |
| database management | Objects bar | row selector |
|    system (DBMS) | primary key | table |

# Review Assignments

**Data File needed for the Review Assignments: Seasons.mdb**

In the Review Assignments, you'll work with the Seasons database, which is similar to Elsa's database that you worked with in the tutorial. Complete the following steps:

1. Open the **Seasons** database, which is located in the Brief\Review folder provided with your Data Files.
2. Open the **Employers** table.
3. Use the appropriate navigation buttons to move to the last record in the table, and then up three records from the last record. Write down the field values for all the fields in this record.
4. Move back to the first record in the table, print the table datasheet, and then close the table.
5. Use the Simple Query Wizard to create a query that includes the City, EmployerName, ContactFirstName, ContactLastName, and Phone fields (in that order) from the **Employers** table. Name the query **EmployerPhoneList**. Sort the query results in ascending order by City. Print the query results, and then close and save the query.
6. Use the AutoForm: Columnar Wizard to create a form for the **Employers** table. Save the form as **EmployerInfo**, and then close the form.
7. Use the AutoReport: Columnar Wizard to create a report based on the **Employers** table. Print the first page of the report, and then close the report and save it as **Employers**.

8. Set the option for compacting the **Seasons** database on close. (*Note*: If you are working from a floppy disk, check with your instructor or technical support staff to confirm that you should set this option.)
9. Close the Seasons database.

**Apply**

*Use the skills you learned in the tutorial to work with the data contained in a video photography database.*

# Case Problem 1

**Data File needed for this Case Problem: Videos.mdb**

*Lim's Video Photography*   Several years ago, Youngho Lim left his position at a commercial photographer's studio and started his own business, Lim's Video Photography, located in San Francisco, California. Youngho quickly established a reputation as one of the area's best videographers, specializing in digital video photography. Youngho offers customers the option of storing edited videos on CD or DVD. His video shoots include weddings and other special events, as well as recording personal and commercial inventories for insurance purposes.

As his business continues to grow, Youngho relies on Access to keep track of information about clients, contracts, and so on. Youngho recently created an Access database named Videos to store data about his clients. You'll help Youngho complete and maintain the Videos database. Complete the following:

1. Open the **Videos** database, which is located in the Brief\Case1 folder provided with your Data Files.
2. Open the **Client** table, print the table datasheet, and then close the table.
3. Use the Simple Query Wizard to create a query that includes the ClientName, Phone, and City fields (in that order) from the **Client** table. Name the query **ClientList**. Print the query results, and then close the query.
4. Use the AutoForm: Columnar Wizard to create a form for the **Contract** table. Save the form as **ContractInfo**, and then close it.
5. Use the AutoReport: Columnar Wizard to create a report based on the **Contract** table. Print the first page of the report, and then close the report and save it as **Contracts**.
6. Set the option for compacting the **Videos** database on close. (*Note*: If you are working from a floppy disk, check with your instructor or technical support staff to confirm that you should set this option.)
7. Close the Videos database.

**Apply**

*Apply what you learned in the tutorial to work with the data for an e-commerce business in the food services industry.*

# Case Problem 2

**Data File needed for this Case Problem: Meals.mdb**

*DineAtHome.course.com*   After working as both a concierge in a local hotel and a manager of several restaurants, Claire Picard founded DineAtHome.course.com in Naples, Florida. Her idea for this e-commerce company was a simple one: to provide people with an easy-to-use, online service that would allow them to order meals from one or more area restaurants and have the meals delivered to their homes. DineAtHome acts as a sort of broker between restaurants and customers. The participating restaurants offer everything from simple fare to gourmet feasts. Claire's staff performs a variety of services, from simply picking up and delivering the meals to providing linens and table service for more formal occasions.

Claire created the Meals database in Access to maintain information about participating restaurants and their menu offerings. She needs your help in working with this database. Complete the following:

1. Open the **Meals** database, which is located in the Brief\Case2 folder provided with your Data Files.
2. Open the **Restaurant** table, print the table datasheet, and then close the table.
3. Use the Simple Query Wizard to create a query that includes the RestaurantName, OwnerFirstName, OwnerLastName, and City fields (in that order) from the **Restaurant** table. Name the query **OwnerList**.

**Explore**

4. Sort the query results in descending order by the City field. (*Hint:* Use a toolbar button.)
5. Print the query results, and then close and save the query.
6. Use the AutoForm: Columnar Wizard to create a form for the **Restaurant** table. Save the form as **RestaurantInfo**, and then close it.
7. Use the AutoReport: Columnar Wizard to create a report based on the **Restaurant** table. Maximize the Report window and change the Zoom setting to Fit.
8. Print just the first page of the report, and then close the report and save it as **Restaurants**.
9. Set the option for compacting the **Meals** database on close. (*Note:* If you are working from a floppy disk, check with your instructor or technical support staff to confirm that you should set this option.)
10. Close the Meals database.

**Challenge**

*Use what you've learned, and go a bit beyond, to work with a database that contains information about a zoo.*

# Case Problem 3

**Data File needed for this Case Problem: Redwood.mdb**

***Redwood Zoo***   The Redwood Zoo is a small zoo located in the picturesque city of Gig Harbor, Washington, on the shores of Puget Sound. The zoo is ideally situated, with the natural beauty of the site providing the perfect backdrop for the zoo's varied exhibits. Although there are larger zoos in the greater Seattle area, the Redwood Zoo is considered to have some of the best exhibits of marine animals. The newly constructed polar bear habitat is a particular favorite among patrons.

Michael Rosenfeld is the director of fundraising activities for the Redwood Zoo. The zoo relies heavily on donations to fund both ongoing exhibits and temporary displays, especially those involving exotic animals. Michael created an Access database named Redwood to keep track of information about donors, their pledges, and the status of funds. You'll help Michael maintain the Redwood database. Complete the following:

1. Open the **Redwood** database, which is located in the Brief\Case3 folder provided with your Data Files.

**Explore**

2. Use the "Type a question for help" box to ask the following question: "How do I rename an object?" Click the topic "Rename a database object" and read the displayed information. Close the Microsoft Office Access Help window and the task pane. Then, in the Redwood database, rename the **Table1** table as **Donor**.
3. Open the **Donor** table, print the table datasheet, and then close the table.

**Explore**

4. Use the Simple Query Wizard to create a query that includes all the fields in the **Donor** table *except* the MI field. (*Hint:* Use the [>>] and [<] buttons to select the necessary fields.) Name the query **Donors**.

**Explore**

5. Sort the query results in descending order by the Class field. (*Hint:* Use a toolbar button.) Print the query results, and then close and save the query.

**Explore**

6. Use the AutoForm: Columnar Wizard to create a form for the **Fund** table. Open the Microsoft Access Help task pane. (*Hint:* Click Help on the menu bar, and then click Microsoft Office Access Help.) Type the keywords "find a specific record in a form" in the Search for text box, and then click the Start searching button. Select the topic "Find a record in a datasheet or form," then choose the topic related to finding a record by record number. Read the displayed information. Close the Microsoft Office Access Help window and the task pane. Use the record number box to move to record 7 (Polar Bear Park), and then print the form for the current record only. (*Hint:* Use the Selected Record(s) option in the Print dialog box to print the current record.) Save the form as **FundInfo**, and then close it.

7. Use the AutoReport: Columnar Wizard to create a report based on the **Donor** table. Maximize the Report window and change the Zoom setting to Fit.

**Explore**

8. Use the View menu to view all seven pages of the report at the same time in Print Preview.

9. Print just the first page of the report, and then close and save it as **Donors**.

10. Set the option for compacting the **Redwood** database on close. (*Note:* If you are working from a floppy disk, check with your instructor or technical support staff to confirm that you should set this option.)

**Explore**

11. Convert the **Redwood** database to Access 2002–2003 file format, saving the converted file as **Redwood2002** in the Brief\Case3 folder. Then convert the **Redwood** database to Access 97 file format, saving the converted file as **Redwood97** in the Brief\Case3 folder. Using Windows Explorer or My Computer, view the contents of your Brief\Case3 folder, and note the file sizes of the three versions of the Redwood database. Describe the results.

12. Close the Redwood database.

# Case Problem 4

**Challenge**

*Work with the skills you've learned, and explore some new skills, to manage the data for an outdoor adventure company.*

**Data File needed for this Case Problem: Trips.mdb**

***Mountain River Adventures***   Several years ago, Connor and Siobhan Dempsey moved to Boulder, Colorado, drawn by their love of the mountains and their interest in outdoor activities of all kinds. This interest led them to form the Mountain River Adventures center. The center began as a whitewater rafting tour provider, but quickly grew to encompass other activities, such as canoeing, hiking, camping, fishing, and rock climbing.

From the beginning, Connor and Siobhan have used computers to help them manage all aspects of their business. They recently installed Access and created a database named Trips to store information about clients, equipment, and the types of guided tours they provide. You'll work with the Trips database to manage this information. Complete the following:

1. Open the **Trips** database, which is located in the Brief\Case4 folder provided with your Data Files.

2. Open the **Client** table.

**Explore**

3. Open the Microsoft Access Help task pane. (*Hint:* Click Help on the menu bar, and then click Microsoft Office Access Help.) Type the keyword "print" in the Search for text box, and then click the Start searching button. Scroll down the list, click the topic "Set page setup options for printing," and then click "For a table, query, form, or report." Read the displayed information. Close the Microsoft Office Access Help window and the task pane. Set the option for printing in landscape orientation, and then print the **Client** table datasheet. Close the table.

**Explore**

4. Use the Simple Query Wizard to create a query that includes the ClientName, City, StateProv, and Phone fields (in that order) from the **Client** table. Name the query **ClientInfo**.

5. Sort the query results in descending order by StateProv. (*Hint:* Use a toolbar button.)

6. Print the query results, and then close and save the query.

**Explore**

7. Use the AutoForm: Columnar Wizard to create a form for the **Client** table. Use the Microsoft Access Help task pane to search for information on how to find a specific record in a form. Select the topic "Find a record in a datasheet or form," then choose the topic related to finding a record by record number. Read the displayed information. Close the Microsoft Office Access Help window and the task pane. Use the record number box to move to record 18, and then print the form for the current record only. (*Hint:* Use the Selected Record(s) option in the Print dialog box to print the current record.) Save the form as **ClientInfo**, and then close it.

**Explore**

8. Use the AutoReport: Tabular Wizard to create a report based on the **Client** table. Maximize the Report window and change the Zoom setting to Fit. Use the Two Pages button on the Print Preview toolbar to view both pages of the report in Print Preview. Print the first page of the report in landscape orientation, and then close and save the report as **Clients**.

9. Set the option for compacting the **Trips** database on close. (*Note*: If you are working from a floppy disk, check with your instructor or technical support staff to confirm that you should set this option.)

**Explore**

10. Convert the **Trips** database to Access 2002–2003 file format, saving the converted file as **Trips2002** in the Brief\Case4 folder. Then convert the **Trips** database to Access 97 file format, saving the converted file as **Trips97** in the Brief\Case4 folder. Using Windows Explorer or My Computer, view the contents of your Brief\Case4 folder, and note the file sizes of the three versions of the Trips database. Describe the results.

11. Close the Trips database.

# Internet Assignments

**Research**

*Use the Internet to find and work with data related to the topics presented in this tutorial.*

The purpose of the Internet Assignments is to challenge you to find information on the Internet that you can use to work effectively with this software. The actual assignments are updated and maintained on the Course Technology Web site. Log on to the Internet and use your Web browser to go to the Student Online Companion for New Perspectives Office 2003 at **www.course.com/np/office2003**. Click the Internet Assignments link, and then navigate to the assignments for this tutorial.

## SAM Assessment and Training

**Assess**

If you have a SAM user profile, you may have access to hands-on instruction, practice, and assessment of the skills covered in this tutorial. Log in to your SAM account and go to your assignments page to see what your instructor has assigned.

**Reinforce**

Databases

# Lab Assignments

The New Perspectives Labs are designed to help you master some of the key concepts and skills presented in this text. The steps for completing this Lab are located on the Course Technology Web site. Log on to the Internet and use your Web browser to go to the Student Online Companion for New Perspectives Office 2003 at **www.course.com/np/office2003**. Click the Lab Assignments link, and then navigate to the assignments for this tutorial.

**Review**

# Quick Check Answers

### Session 1.1

1. field
2. common field
3. primary key; foreign key
4. records; fields
5. current record symbol
6. Use the horizontal and vertical scroll bars to view fields or records not currently visible in the datasheet; use the navigation buttons to move vertically through the records.
7. Access saves changes to the active database to disk automatically, when a record is changed or added and when you close the database. You use the Save button in Access only to save changes to the design of an object, such as a table, or to the format of a datasheet—not to save the database file.

### Session 1.2

1. query
2. primary key
3. AutoForm Wizard
4. The form displays each field name to the left of its field value, which appears in a box; the widths of the boxes represent the size of the fields.
5. Print Preview
6. Compacting

## Objectives

**Session 2.1**
- Learn the guidelines for designing databases and setting field properties
- Create a new database
- Create and save a table
- Define fields and specify a table's primary key

**Session 2.2**
- Add records to a table
- Modify the structure of a table
- Delete, move, and add fields
- Change field properties
- Update field property changes
- Copy records and import tables from another Access database
- Delete and change records

# Creating and Maintaining a Database

*Creating the Northeast Database, and Creating, Modifying, and Updating the Position Table*

## Case

## Northeast Seasonal Jobs International (NSJI)

The Seasonal database contains two tables—the Employer table and the NAICS table. These tables store data about NSJI's employer customers and the NAICS codes for pertinent job positions, respectively. Elsa Jensen also wants to track information about each position that is available at each employer's place of business. This information includes the position title and wage. Elsa asks you to create a third table, named Position, in which to store the position data.

Because this is your first time creating a new table, Elsa suggests that you first create a new database, named "Northeast," and then create the new Position table in this database. This will keep the Seasonal database intact. Once the Position table is completed, you then can import the Employer and NAICS tables from the Seasonal database into your new Northeast database.

Some of the position data Elsa needs is already stored in another NSJI database. After creating the Position table and adding some records to it, you'll copy the records from the other database into the Position table. Then you'll maintain the Position table by modifying it and updating it to meet Elsa's specific data requirements.

## Student Data Files

**▼ Brief**

▽ **Tutorial folder**
NEJobs.mdb

▽ **Review folder**
Elsa.mdb

▽ **Case1 folder**
Events.mdb
Videos.mdb *(cont.)*

▽ **Case2 folder**
Customer.mdb
Meals.mdb *(cont.)*

▽ **Case3 folder**
Pledge.mdb
Redwood.mdb *(cont.)*

▽ **Case4 folder**
Groups.mdb
Rafting.xls
Trips.mdb *(cont.)*

# Guidelines for Designing Databases

A database management system can be a useful tool, but only if you first carefully design the database so that it meets the needs of its users. In database design, you determine the fields, tables, and relationships needed to satisfy the data and processing requirements. When you design a database, you should follow these guidelines:

- **Identify all the fields needed to produce the required information.** For example, Elsa needs information about employers, NAICS codes, and positions. Figure 2-1 shows the fields that satisfy these information requirements.

| Figure 2-1 | Elsa's data requirements |
| --- | --- |

| | |
| --- | --- |
| EmployerID | ContactFirstName |
| PositionID | ContactLastName |
| PositionTitle | Position |
| EmployerName | Wage |
| Address | HoursPerWeek |
| City | NAICSCode |
| StateProv | NAICSDesc |
| PostalCode | StartDate |
| Country | EndDate |
| Phone | ReferredBy |
| Openings | Website |

- **Group related fields into tables.** For example, Elsa grouped the fields relating to employers into the Employer table and the fields related to NAICS codes into the NAICS table. The other fields are grouped logically into the Position table, which you will create, as shown in Figure 2-2.

| Figure 2-2 | Elsa's fields grouped into tables |
| --- | --- |

| Employer table | NAICS table | Position table |
| --- | --- | --- |
| EmployerID | NAICSCode | PositionID |
| EmployerName | NAICSDesc | PositionTitle |
| Address | | Wage |
| City | | HoursPerWeek |
| StateProv | | Openings |
| PostalCode | | ReferredBy |
| Country | | StartDate |
| ContactFirstName | | EndDate |
| ContactLastName | | |
| Position | | |
| Phone | | |
| Website | | |

- **Determine each table's primary key.** Recall that a primary key uniquely identifies each record in a table. Although a primary key is not mandatory in Access, it's usually a good idea to include one in each table. Without a primary key, selecting the exact record that you want can be a problem. For some tables, one of the fields, such as a Social Security or credit card number, naturally serves the function of a primary key. For other tables, two or more fields might be needed to function as the primary key. In these cases, the primary key is referred to as a **composite key**. For example, a school grade table would use a combination of student number and course code to serve as the primary key. For a third category of tables, no single field or combination of fields can uniquely identify a record in a table. In these cases, you need to add a field whose sole purpose is to serve as the table's primary key. For Elsa's tables, EmployerID is the primary key for the Employer table, NAICSCode is the primary key for the NAICS table, and PositionID will be the primary key for the Position table.

- **Include a common field in related tables.** You use the common field to connect one table logically with another. For example, Elsa's Employer and Position tables will include the EmployerID field as a common field. Recall that when you include the primary key from one table as a field in a second table to form a relationship, the field is called a foreign key in the second table; therefore, the EmployerID field will be a foreign key in the Position table. With this common field, Elsa can find all positions available at a particular employer; she can use the EmployerID value for an employer and search the Position table for all records with that EmployerID value. Likewise, she can determine which employer has a particular position available by searching the Employer table to find the one record with the same EmployerID value as the corresponding value in the Position table.

- **Avoid data redundancy.** When you store the same data in more than one place, **data redundancy** occurs. With the exception of common fields to connect tables, you should avoid redundancy because it wastes storage space and can cause inconsistencies, if, for instance, you type a field value one way in one table and a different way in the same table or in a second table. Figure 2-3, which contains portions of potential data to be stored in the Employer and Position tables, shows an example of incorrect database design that has data redundancy in the Position table; the EmployerName field is redundant, and one value was entered incorrectly, in three different ways.

**Incorrect database design with data redundancy**    **Figure 2-3**

**Employer table**

| Employer ID | Employer Name | Address | Phone |
|---|---|---|---|
| 10122 | BeanTown Tours | 105 State Street, Boston, MA 02109 | 617-451-1970 |
| 10125 | Boston Harbor Excursions | 75 Atlantic Avenue, Boston, MA 02110 | 617-235-1800 |
| 10126 | BaySide Inn & Country Club | 354 Oceanside Drive, Brewster, MA 02631 | 508-283-5775 |
| 10190 | The Briar Rose Inn | 105 Queen Street, Charlottetown PE C1A 8R4 | 902-626-1595 |
| 10191 | Windsor Alpine Tours | 14 Longmeadow Road, Laconia, NH 03246 | 603-266-9233 |
| 10198 | Trudel Spa & Resort | 40 Rue Rivard, North Hatley QC J0B 2C0 | 819-842-7783 |

data redundancy

**Position table**

| Position ID | Employer ID | Employer Name | Position Title | Hours/Week |
|---|---|---|---|---|
| 2040 | 10126 | DaySide Inn & Country Club | Waiter/Waitress | 32 |
| 2045 | 10122 | BeanTown Tours | Tour Guide | 24 |
| 2053 | 10190 | The Briar Rose Inn | Host/Hostess | 24 |
| 2066 | 10198 | Trudel Spa & Resort | Lifeguard | 32 |
| 2073 | 10126 | Baside Inn & Country Club | Pro Shop Clerk | 24 |
| 2078 | 10191 | Windsor Alpine Tours | Ski Patrol | 30 |
| 2079 | 10191 | Windsor Alpine Tours | Day Care | 35 |
| 2082 | 10125 | Boston Harbor Excursions | Reservationist | 40 |
| 2111 | 10126 | BaySide Inn Club | Kitchen Help | 32 |

inconsistent data

- **Determine the properties of each field.** You need to identify the **properties**, or characteristics, of each field so that the DBMS knows how to store, display, and process the field values. These properties include the field's name, maximum number of characters or digits, description, valid values, and other field characteristics. You will learn more about field properties later in this tutorial.

The Position table you need to create will contain the fields shown in Figure 2-2, plus the EmployerID field as a foreign key. Before you create the new Northeast database and the Position table, you first need to learn some guidelines for setting field properties.

# Guidelines for Setting Field Properties

As just noted, the last step of database design is to determine which values to assign to the properties, such as the name and data type, of each field. When you select or enter a value for a property, you **set** the property. Access has rules for naming fields, choosing data types, and setting other properties for fields.

## Naming Fields and Objects

You must name each field, table, and other object in an Access database. Access then stores these items in the database, using the names you supply. It's best to choose a field or object name that describes the purpose or contents of the field or object, so that later you can easily remember what the name represents. For example, the three tables in the Northeast database will be named Employer, NAICS, and Position, because these names suggest their contents.

The following rules apply to naming fields and objects in Access:

- A name can be up to 64 characters long.
- A name can contain letters, numbers, spaces, and special characters, except for a period (.), exclamation mark (!), accent grave (`), and square brackets ([ ]).
- A name cannot start with a space.
- A table or query name must be unique within a database. A field name must be unique within a table, but it can be used again in another table.

In addition, experienced users of databases follow these conventions for naming fields and objects:

- Capitalize the first letter of each word in the name.
- Avoid extremely long names because they are difficult to remember and reference.
- Use standard abbreviations, such as Num for Number, Amt for Amount, and Qty for Quantity.
- Avoid using spaces or special characters in names. According to standard database naming conventions, spaces and special characters should not be included in names. However, you can change how a field name is displayed in database objects—tables, forms, reports, and so on—by setting the field's Caption property. (You'll learn about setting the Caption property later in this tutorial.)

## Assigning Field Data Types

You must assign a data type for each field. The **data type** determines what field values you can enter for the field and what other properties the field will have. For example, the Position table will include a StartDate field, which will store date values, so you will assign the date/time data type to this field. Then Access will allow you to enter and manipulate only dates or times as values in the StartDate field.

Figure 2-4 lists the 10 data types available in Access, describes the field values allowed for each data type, explains when you should use each data type, and indicates the field size of each data type.

**Data types for fields** ◄ **Figure 2-4**

| Data Type | Description | Field Size |
|---|---|---|
| Text | Allows field values containing letters, digits, spaces, and special characters. Use for names, addresses, descriptions, and fields containing digits that are not used in calculations. | 0 to 255 characters; 50 characters default |
| Memo | Allows field values containing letters, digits, spaces, and special characters Use for long comments and explanations. | 1 to 65,535 characters; exact size is determined by entry |
| Number | Allows positive and negative numbers as field values. Numbers can contain digits, a decimal point, commas, a plus sign, and a minus sign. Use for fields that you will use in calculations, except calculations involving money. | 1 to 15 digits |
| Date/Time | Allows field values containing valid dates and times from January 1, 100 to December 31, 9999. Dates can be entered in mm/dd/yy (month, day, year) format, several other date formats, or a variety of time formats, such as 10:35 PM. You can perform calculations on dates and times, and you can sort them. For example, you can determine the number of days between two dates. | 8 bytes |
| Currency | Allows field values similar to those for the number data type. Unlike calculations with number data type decimal values, calculations performed using the currency data type are not subject to round-off error. | Accurate to 15 digits on the left side of the decimal separator and to 4 digits on the right side |
| AutoNumber | Consists of integers with values controlled by Access. Access automatically inserts a value in the field as each new record is created. You can specify sequential numbering or random numbering, which guarantees a unique field value, so that such a field can serve as a table's primary key. | 9 digits |
| Yes/No | Limits field values to yes and no, on and off, or true and false. Use for fields that indicate the presence or absence of a condition, such as whether an order has been filled or whether an employee is eligible for the company dental plan. | 1 character |
| OLE Object | Allows field values that are created in other programs as objects, such as photographs, video images, graphics, drawings, sound recordings, voice-mail messages, spreadsheets, and word-processing documents. These objects can be linked or embedded. | 1 gigabyte maximum; exact size depends on object size |
| Hyperlink | Consists of text used as a hyperlink address. A hyperlink address can have up to three parts: the text that appears in a field or control; the path to a file or page; and a location within the file or page. Hyperlinks help you to connect your application easily to the Internet or an intranet. | Up to 64,000 characters total for the three parts of a hyperlink data type |
| Lookup Wizard | Creates a field that lets you look up a value in another table or in a predefined list of values. | Same size as the primary key field used to perform the lookup |

## Setting Field Sizes

The **Field Size property** defines a field value's maximum storage size for text, number, and AutoNumber fields only. The other data types have no Field Size property because their storage size is either a fixed, predetermined amount or is determined automatically by the field value itself, as shown in Figure 2-4. A text field has a default field size of 50 characters; you can also set its field size by entering a number from 0 to 255. For example, the PositionTitle and ReferredBy fields in the Position table will be text fields with a size of 30 characters each. This field size will accommodate the values that will be entered in each of these fields (titles and names, respectively).

When you use the number data type to define a field, you should set the field's Field Size property based on the largest value that you expect to store in that field. Access processes smaller data sizes faster, using less memory, so you can optimize your database's performance and its storage space by selecting the correct field size for each field. For example, it would be wasteful to use the Long Integer setting when defining a field that will store only whole numbers ranging from 0 to 255, because the Long Integer setting will use four bytes of storage space. A better choice would be the Byte setting, which uses one byte of storage space to store the same values. Field Size property settings for number fields are as follows:

- **Byte:** Stores whole numbers (numbers with no fractions) from 0 to 255 in one byte
- **Integer:** Stores whole numbers from −32,768 to 32,767 in two bytes
- **Long Integer** (default)**:** Stores whole numbers from −2,147,483,648 to 2,147,483,647 in four bytes
- **Single:** Stores positive and negative numbers to precisely seven decimal places and uses four bytes
- **Double:** Stores positive and negative numbers to precisely 15 decimal places and uses eight bytes
- **Replication ID:** Establishes a unique identifier for replication of tables, records, and other objects and uses 16 bytes
- **Decimal:** Stores positive and negative numbers to precisely 28 decimal places and uses 12 bytes

## Setting Field Captions

The **Caption property** specifies how a field name will appear in datasheets and in other database objects, such as forms and reports. If you don't specify a caption, Access uses the field name as the default column heading in datasheets and as the default label in forms and reports. Because field names should not include spaces, some names might be difficult to read. For example, the Position table will include a field named "HoursPerWeek." This name looks awkward and might be confusing to users of the database. By setting the Caption property for this field to "Hours/Week," you can improve the readability of the field name displayed.

Elsa documented the design for the new Position table by listing each field's name, data type, size (if applicable), caption (if applicable), and description, as shown in Figure 2-5. Note that Elsa assigned the text data type to the PositionID, PositionTitle, EmployerID, and ReferredBy fields; the currency data type to the Wage field; the number data type to the HoursPerWeek and Openings fields; and the date/time data type to the StartDate and EndDate fields.

| Figure 2-5 | Design for the Position table |
| --- | --- |

| Field Name | Data Type | Field Size | Caption | Description |
| --- | --- | --- | --- | --- |
| PositionID | Text | 4 | Position ID | Primary key |
| PositionTitle | Text | 30 | Position Title | |
| EmployerID | Text | 5 | Employer ID | Foreign key |
| Wage | Currency | | | Rate per hour |
| HoursPerWeek | Number | Integer | Hours/Week | Work hours per week |
| Openings | Number | Integer | | Number of openings |
| ReferredBy | Text | 30 | Referred By | |
| StartDate | Date/Time | | Start Date | Month/day/year |
| EndDate | Date/Time | | End Date | Month/day/year |

With Elsa's design in place, you're ready to create the new Northeast database and the Position table.

# Creating a New Database

Access provides different ways for you to create a new database: you can use a Database Wizard, create a blank database, copy an existing database file, or use one of the database templates available on the Microsoft Web site. When you use a **Database Wizard**, the wizard guides you through the database creation process and provides the necessary tables, forms, and reports for the type of database you choose—all in one operation. Using a Database Wizard is an easy way to start creating a database, but only if your data requirements closely match one of the supplied templates. When you choose to create a blank database, you need to add all the tables, forms, reports, and other objects after you create the database file. Creating a blank database provides the most flexibility, allowing you to define objects in the way that you want, but it does require that you define each object separately. Whichever method you choose, you can always modify or add to your database after you create it.

The following steps outline the process for creating a new database using a Database Wizard:

1. If necessary, click the New button on the Database toolbar to display the New File task pane.
2. In the Templates section of the task pane, click the "On my computer" option. The Templates dialog box opens.
3. Click the Databases tab, and then choose the Database Wizard that most closely matches the type of database you want to create. Click the OK button.
4. In the File New Database dialog box, choose the location in which to save the new database, specify its name, and then click the Create button.
5. Complete each of the wizard dialog boxes, clicking the Next button to move through them after making your selections.
6. Click the Finish button when you have completed all the wizard dialog boxes.

None of the Database Wizards matches the requirements of the new Northeast database, so you'll use the Blank Database option to create it.

**To create the Northeast database:**

1. Start Access, and make sure your Data Files are in the proper location.
2. In the Open section of the Getting Started task pane, click **Create a new file**. The New File task pane is displayed.
3. Click **Blank database**. The File New Database dialog box opens. This dialog box is similar to the Open dialog box.
4. Click the **Save in** list arrow, and then click the drive that contains your Data Files.
5. Navigate to the **Brief\Tutorial** folder, and then click the **Open** button.
6. In the File name text box, double-click the text **db1** to select it, and then type **Northeast**.

    **Trouble?** If your File name text box contains an entry other than "db1," select whatever text is in this text box, and continue with the steps.
7. Click the **Create** button. Access creates the Northeast database in the Brief\Tutorial folder included with your Data Files, and then displays the Database window for the new database with the Tables object selected.

Now you can create the Position table in the Northeast database.

# Creating a Table

Creating a table involves naming the fields and defining the properties for the fields, specifying a primary key (and a foreign key, if applicable) for the table, and then saving the table structure. You will use Elsa's design (Figure 2-5) as a guide for creating the Position table in the Northeast database.

**To begin creating the Position table:**

► **1.** Click the **New** button in the Database window. The New Table dialog box opens. See Figure 2-6.

| **Figure 2-6** | **New Table dialog box** |
| --- | --- |

**click to design your own table**

**other ways to define a table**

**Trouble?** If the New File task pane opens, you clicked the New button 🔲 on the Database toolbar instead of the New button in the Database window. Click the Close button to close the task pane, and then repeat Step 1.

In Access, you can create a table from entered data (Datasheet View), define your own table (Design View), use a wizard to automate the table creation process (Table Wizard), or use a wizard to import or link data from another database or other data source (Import Table or Link Table). For the Position table, you will define your own table.

► **2.** Click **Design View** in the list box, and then click the **OK** button. The Table window opens in Design view. (Note that you can also double-click the "Create table in Design view" option in the Database window to open the Table window in Design view.) See Figure 2-7.

**Table window in Design view** ◀ **Figure 2-7**

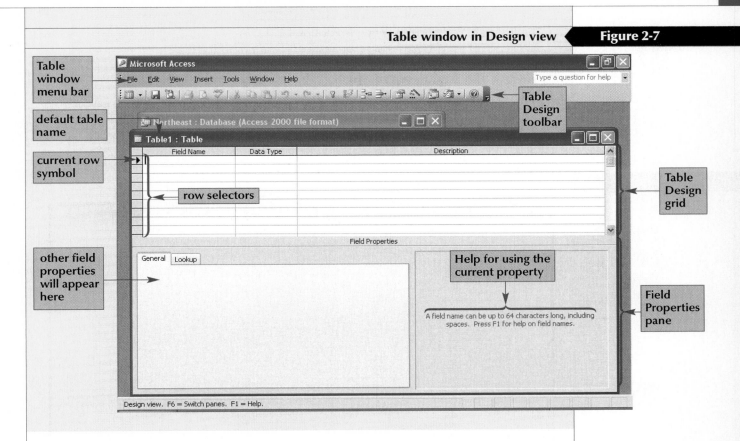

You use **Design view** to define or modify a table structure or the properties of the fields in a table. If you create a table without using a wizard, you enter the fields and their properties for your table directly in the Table window in Design view.

## Defining Fields

Initially, the default table name, Table1, appears on the Table window title bar, the current row symbol is positioned in the first row selector of the Table Design grid, and the insertion point is located in the first row's Field Name box. The purpose or characteristics of the current property (Field Name, in this case) appear in the right side of the Field Properties pane. You can display more complete Help information about the current property by pressing the **F1 key**.

You enter values for the Field Name, Data Type, and Description field properties in the Table Design grid. You select values for all other field properties, most of which are optional, in the Field Properties pane. These other properties will appear when you move to the first row's Data Type text box.

### Defining a Field in a Table

Reference Window

- In the Database window, select the table, and then click the Design button to open the Table window in Design view.
- Type the field name.
- Select the data type.
- Type or select other field properties, as appropriate.

The first field you need to define is PositionID.

### To define the PositionID field:

1. Type **PositionID** in the first row's Field Name text box, and then press the **Tab** key (or press the **Enter** key) to advance to the Data Type text box. The default data type, Text, appears highlighted in the Data Type text box, which now also contains a list arrow, and field properties for a text field appear in the Field Properties pane. See Figure 2-8.

| Figure 2-8 | Table window after entering the first field name |
| --- | --- |

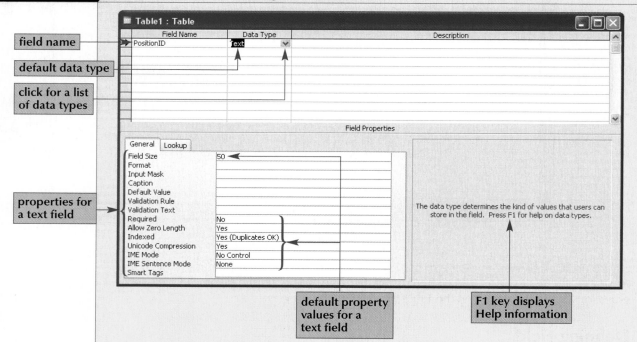

field name

default data type

click for a list of data types

properties for a text field

default property values for a text field

F1 key displays Help information

Notice that the right side of the Field Properties pane now provides an explanation for the current property, Data Type. You can display Help information about the current property by pressing the F1 key.

**Trouble?** If you make a typing error, you can correct it by clicking to position the insertion point, and then using either the Backspace key to delete characters to the left of the insertion point or the Delete key to delete characters to the right of the insertion point. Then type the correct text.

Because the PositionID numbers will not be used in calculations, you will assign the text data type (as opposed to the number data type) to the PositionID field.

2. Press the **Tab** key to accept Text as the data type and to advance to the Description text box.

Next you'll enter the Description property value as "Primary key." You can use the **Description property** to enter an optional description for a field to explain its purpose or usage. A field's Description property can be up to 255 characters long, and its value appears on the status bar when you view the table datasheet. Note that specifying "Primary key" for the Description property does *not* establish the current field as the primary key; you use a toolbar button to specify the primary key, which you will do later in this session.

3. Type **Primary key** in the Description text box.

Notice the Field Size property for the text field. The default setting of "50" is displayed. You need to change this number to "4" because all PositionID values at NSJI contain only 4 digits.

4. Double-click the number **50** in the Field Size property box to select it, and then type **4**.

By default, the Caption property for a field is blank. You need to set this property for the PositionID field to display "Position ID" as the column or label name in tables, forms, reports, and so on. (Refer to the Access Help system for a complete description of all the properties available for the different data types.)

5. Click to position the insertion point in the Caption property box, and then type **Position ID**. The definition of the first field is completed. See Figure 2-9.

PositionID field defined | **Figure 2-9**

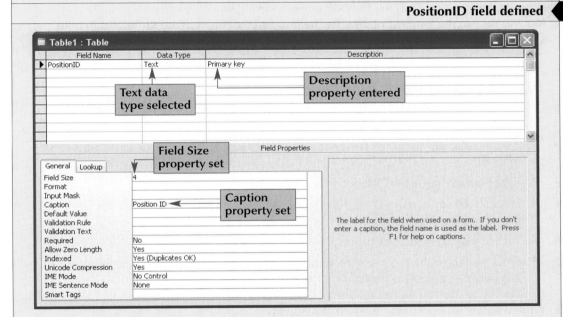

Elsa's Position table design shows PositionTitle as the second field. You will define PositionTitle as a text field with a Field Size of 30, which is a sufficient length for any title values that will be entered. You'll also set the Caption property for this field.

## To define the PositionTitle field:

1. In the Table Design grid, place the insertion point in the second row's Field Name text box, type **PositionTitle** in the text box, and then press the **Tab** key to advance to the Data Type text box.

2. Press the **Tab** key to accept Text as the field's data type.

According to Elsa's design (Figure 2-5), you do not need to enter a description for this field. If you've assigned a descriptive field name and the field does not fulfill a special function (such as primary key), you usually do not enter a value for the optional Description property. PositionTitle is a field that does not require a value for its Description property.

Next, you'll change the Field Size property to 30. Note that when defining the fields in a table, you can move between the Table Design grid and the Field Properties pane of the Table window by pressing the **F6 key**.

3. Press the **F6** key to move to the Field Properties pane. The current entry for the Field Size property, 50, is highlighted.

4. Type **30** to set the Field Size property.

Finally, you need to set the Caption property for the field. In addition to clicking to position the insertion point in a property's box, you can press the Tab key to move from one property to the next.

5. Press the **Tab** key three times to move to the Caption property, and then type **Position Title**. You have completed the definition of the second field.

The third field in the Position table is the EmployerID field. Recall that this field will serve as the foreign key in the Position table, allowing you to relate data from the Position table to data in the Employer table. The field must be defined in the same way in both tables—that is, a text field with a field size of 5.

## To define the EmployerID field:

1. Place the insertion point in the third row's Field Name text box, type **EmployerID** in the text box, and then press the **Tab** key to advance to the Data Type text box.

2. Press the **Tab** key to accept Text as the field's data type and to advance to the Description text box.

3. Type **Foreign key** in the Description text box.

4. Press the **F6** key to move to the Field Properties pane. The current entry for the Field Size property, 50, is highlighted.

5. Type **5** to set the Field Size property.

6. Press the **Tab** key three times to move to the Caption property, and then type **Employer ID**. You have completed the definition of the third field. See Figure 2-10.

| Figure 2-10 | Table window after defining the first three fields |
| --- | --- |

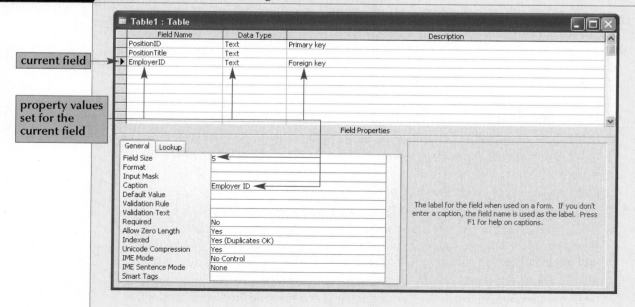

The fourth field is the Wage field, which will display values in the currency format.

## To define the Wage field:

1. Place the insertion point in the fourth row's Field Name text box, type **Wage** in the text box, and then press the **Tab** key to advance to the Data Type text box.

2. Click the **Data Type** list arrow, click **Currency** in the list box, and then press the **Tab** key to advance to the Description text box.

3. Type **Rate per hour** in the Description text box.

   Elsa wants the Wage field values to be displayed with two decimal places, and she does not want any value to be displayed by default for new records. So, you need to set the Decimal Places and Default Value properties accordingly. The **Decimal Places property** specifies the number of decimal places that will be displayed to the right of the decimal point.

4. Click the **Decimal Places** text box to position the insertion point there. A list arrow appears on the right side of the Decimal Places text box.

   When you position the insertion point or select text in many Access text boxes, Access displays a list arrow, which you can click to display a list box with options. You can display the list arrow and the list box simultaneously if you click the text box near its right side.

5. Click the **Decimal Places** list arrow, and then click **2** in the list box to specify two decimal places for the Wage field values.

   Next, notice the **Default Value property**, which specifies the value that will be automatically entered into the field when you add a new record. Currently this property has a setting of 0. Elsa wants the Wage field to be empty (that is, to contain *no* default value) when a new record is added. Therefore, you need to delete the 0 so that Access, by default, will display no value in the Wage field for a new record.

6. Select **0** in the Default Value text box either by dragging the pointer or double-clicking the mouse, and then press the **Delete** key.

The next two fields in the Position table—HoursPerWeek and Openings—are number fields with a field size of Integer. Also, for each of these fields, Elsa wants the values displayed with no decimal places, and she does not want a default value displayed for the fields when new records are added. You'll define these two fields next.

## To define the HoursPerWeek and Openings fields:

1. Position the insertion point in the fifth row's Field Name text box, type **HoursPerWeek** in the text box, and then press the **Tab** key to advance to the Data Type text box.

2. Click the **Data Type** list arrow, click **Number** in the list box, and then press the **Tab** key to advance to the Description text box.

3. Type **Work hours per week** in the Description text box.

4. Click the right side of the **Field Size** text box, and then click **Integer** to choose this setting. Recall that the Integer field size stores whole numbers in two bytes.

5. Click the right side of the **Decimal Places** text box, and then click **0** to specify no decimal places.

6. Move to the Caption property, and then type **Hours/Week**.

7. Select the value **0** in the Default Value text box, and then press the **Delete** key.

8. Repeat the preceding steps to define the **Openings** field as the sixth field in the Position table. For the Description, enter the text **Number of openings**. You do not have to set the Caption property for the Openings field.

According to Elsa's design (Figure 2-5), the final three fields to be defined in the Position table are ReferredBy, a text field, and StartDate and EndDate, both date/time fields. You'll define these three fields next.

### To define the ReferredBy, StartDate, and EndDate fields:

1. Position the insertion point in the seventh row's Field Name text box, type **ReferredBy** in the text box, press the **Tab** key to advance to the Data Type text box, and then press the **Tab** key again to accept the default Text data type.

2. Change the default Field Size of 50 to **30** for the ReferredBy field.

3. Set the Caption property for the field to **Referred By**.

4. Position the insertion point in the eighth row's Field Name text box, type **StartDate**, and then press the **Tab** key to advance to the Data Type text box.

5. Click the **Data Type** list arrow, click **Date/Time** to select this type, press the **Tab** key, and then type **Month/day/year** in the Description text box.

   Elsa wants the values in the StartDate field to be displayed in a format showing the month, the day, and a four-digit year, as in the following example: 03/11/2006. You use the Format property to control the display of a field value.

6. In the Field Properties pane, click the right side of the **Format** text box to display the list of predefined formats. As noted in the right side of the Field Properties pane, you can either choose a predefined format or enter a custom format.

   **Trouble?** If you see a list arrow instead of a list of predefined formats, click the list arrow to display the list.

   None of the predefined formats matches the exact layout Elsa wants for the StartDate values. Therefore, you need to create a custom date format. Figure 2-11 shows some of the symbols available for custom date and time formats. (A complete description of all the custom formats is available in Help.)

**Figure 2-11**  **Symbols for some custom date formats**

| Symbol | Description |
|--------|-------------|
| / | date separator |
| d | day of the month in one or two numeric digits, as needed (1 to 31) |
| dd | day of the month in two numeric digits (01 to 31) |
| ddd | first three letters of the weekday (Sun to Sat) |
| dddd | full name of the weekday (Sunday to Saturday) |
| w | day of the week (1 to 7) |
| ww | week of the year (1 to 53) |
| m | month of the year in one or two numeric digits, as needed (1 to 12) |
| mm | month of the year in two numeric digits (01 to 12) |
| mmm | first three letters of the month (Jan to Dec) |
| mmmm | full name of the month (January to December) |
| yy | last two digits of the year (01 to 99) |
| yyyy | full year (0100 to 9999) |

Elsa wants the dates to be displayed with a two-digit month (mm), a two-digit day (dd), and a four-digit year (yyyy). You'll enter this custom format now.

7. Click the **Format** list arrow to close the list of predefined formats, and then type **mm/dd/yyyy**. See Figure 2-12.

**Specifying the custom date format**     **Figure 2-12**

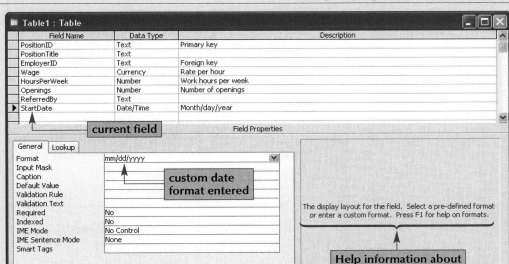

8. Set the Caption property for the field to **Start Date**.

Next, you'll define the ninth and final field, EndDate. This field will have the same definition and properties as the StartDate field.

9. Place the insertion point in the ninth row's Field Name text box, type **EndDate**, and then press the **Tab** key to advance to the Data Type text box.

You can select a value from the Data Type list box as you did for the StartDate field. Alternately, you can type the property value in the text box or type just the first character of the property value.

10. Type **d**. The value in the ninth row's Data Type text box changes to "date/Time," with the letters "ate/Time" highlighted. See Figure 2-13.

**Figure 2-13**    Selecting a value for the Data Type property

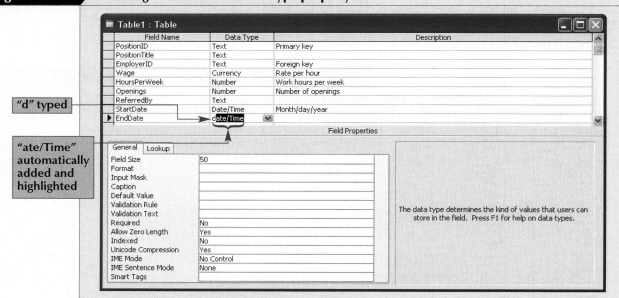

11. Press the **Tab** key to advance to the Description text box, and then type **Month/day/year**. Note that Access changes the value for the Data Type property to Date/Time.

12. In the Format text box, type **mm/dd/yyyy** to specify the custom date format for the EndDate field.

13. Set the Caption property for the field to **End Date**.

You've finished defining the fields for the Position table. Next, you need to specify the primary key for the table.

## Specifying the Primary Key

Although Access does not require a table to have a primary key, including a primary key offers several advantages:

- A primary key uniquely identifies each record in a table.
- Access does not allow duplicate values in the primary key field. If a record already exists with a PositionID value of 1320, for example, Access prevents you from adding another record with this same value in the PositionID field. Preventing duplicate values ensures the uniqueness of the primary key field.
- When a primary key has been specified, Access forces you to enter a value for the primary key field in every record in the table. This is known as **entity integrity**. If you do not enter a value for a field, you have actually given the field what is known as a **null value**. You cannot give a null value to the primary key field because entity integrity prevents Access from accepting and processing that record.
- Access stores records on disk in the same order as you enter them but displays them in order by the field values of the primary key. If you enter records in no specific order, you are ensured that you will later be able to work with them in a more meaningful, primary key sequence.
- Access responds faster to your requests for specific records based on the primary key.

## Specifying a Primary Key for a Table

- In the Table window in Design view, click the row selector for the field you've chosen to be the primary key.
- If the primary key will consist of two or more fields, press and hold down the Ctrl key, and then click the row selector for each additional primary key field.
- Click the Primary Key button on the Table Design toolbar.

According to Elsa's design, you need to specify PositionID as the primary key for the Position table.

### To specify PositionID as the primary key:

▶ **1.** Position the pointer on the row selector for the PositionID field until the pointer changes to a ➜ shape. See Figure 2-14.

Specifying PositionID as the primary key | **Figure 2-14**

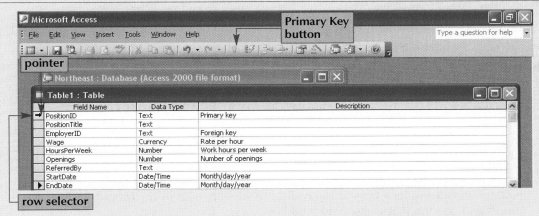

▶ **2.** Click the mouse button. The entire first row of the Table Design grid is highlighted.
▶ **3.** Click the **Primary Key** button 🔑 on the Table Design toolbar, and then click a row other than the first to deselect the first row. A key symbol appears in the row selector for the first row, indicating that the PositionID field is the table's primary key. See Figure 2-15.

PositionID selected as the primary key | **Figure 2-15**

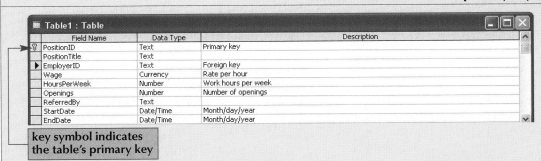

If you specify the wrong field as the primary key, or if you later change your mind and do not want the designated primary key field to be the table's primary key, you can select the field and then click the Primary Key button on the Table Design toolbar again, which will remove the key symbol and the primary key designation from the field. Then you can choose another field to be the primary key, if necessary.

You've defined the fields for the Position table and specified its primary key, so you can now save the table structure.

## Saving the Table Structure

The last step in creating a table is to name the table and save the table's structure on disk. Once the table is saved, you can use it to enter data in the table.

| Reference Window | Saving a Table Structure |
|---|---|

- Click the Save button on the Table Design toolbar.
- Type the name of the table in the Table Name text box of the Save As dialog box.
- Click the OK button (or press the Enter key).

According to Elsa's plan, you need to save the table you've defined as "Position."

### To name and save the Position table:

▶ 1. Click the **Save** button 🖫 on the Table Design toolbar. The Save As dialog box opens.

▶ 2. Type **Position** in the Table Name text box, and then press the **Enter** key. Access saves the table with the name Position in the Northeast database. Notice that Position now appears instead of Table1 in the Table window title bar.

Recall that in Tutorial 1 you set the Compact on Close option for the Seasonal database so that it would be compacted automatically each time you closed it. Now you'll set this option for your new Northeast database, so that it will be compacted automatically. (*Note*: If you are working from a floppy disk, check with your instructor or technical support staff to confirm that you should set this option.)

### To set the option for compacting the Northeast database automatically:

▶ 1. Click **Tools** on the menu bar, and then click **Options**. The Options dialog box opens.

▶ 2. Click the **General** tab in the dialog box, and then click the **Compact on Close** check box to select it.

▶ 3. Click the **OK** button to set the option.

The Position table is now complete. In Session 2.2, you'll continue to work with the Position table by entering records in it, modifying its structure, and maintaining data in the table. You will also import two tables, Employer and NAICS, from the Seasonal database into the Northeast database.

## Session 2.1 Quick Check

1. What guidelines should you follow when designing a database?
2. What is the purpose of the Data Type property for a field?
3. For which three types of fields can you assign a field size?
4. You use the _____ property to specify how a field name appears in datasheets, forms, and reports.
5. In Design view, which key do you press to move between the Table Design grid and the Field Properties pane?
6. A(n) _____ value, which results when you do not enter a value for a field, is not permitted for a primary key.

# Session 2.2

## Adding Records to a Table

You can add records to an Access table in several ways. A table datasheet provides a simple way for you to add records. As you learned in Tutorial 1, a datasheet shows a table's contents in rows and columns. Each row is a separate record in the table, and each column contains the field values for one field in the table. If you are currently working in Design view, you first must change from Design view to Datasheet view in order to view the table's datasheet.

Elsa asks you to add the two records shown in Figure 2-16 to the Position table. These two records contain data for positions that have recently become available at two employers.

**Records to be added to the Position table** ◄ **Figure 2-16**

| PositionID | PositionTitle | EmployerID | Wage | HoursPerWeek | Openings | ReferredBy | StartDate | EndDate |
|---|---|---|---|---|---|---|---|---|
| 2021 | Waiter/Waitress | 10155 | 9.50 | 30 | 1 | Sue Brown | 6/30/2006 | 9/15/2006 |
| 2017 | Tour Guide | 10149 | 15.00 | 20 | 1 | Ed Curran | 9/21/2006 | 11/1/2006 |

### To add the records in the Position table datasheet:

1. If you took a break after the previous session, make sure that Access is running and that the Position table of the Northeast database is open in Design view. To open the table in Design view from the Database window, right-click the **Position** table, and then click **Design View** on the shortcut menu.

   Access displays the fields you defined for the Position table in Design view. Now you need to switch to Datasheet view so that you can enter the two records for Elsa.

2. Click the **View** button for Datasheet view ▦ on the Table Design toolbar. The Table window opens in Datasheet view. See Figure 2-17.

**Figure 2-17** Table window in Datasheet view

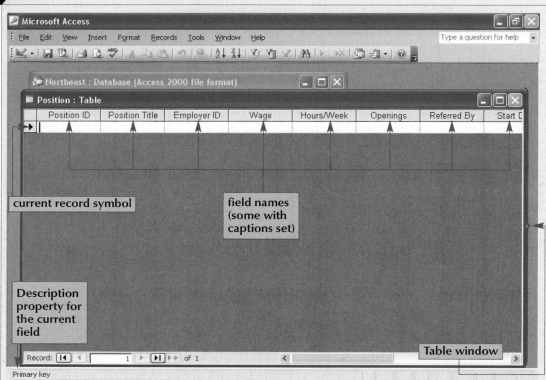

The table's nine fields appear at the top of the datasheet, with captions displayed for those fields whose Caption property you set. Some of the field names might not be visible, depending on the size of your monitor. The current record symbol in the first row's record selector identifies the currently selected record, which contains no data until you enter the first record. The insertion point is located in the first row's PositionID field, whose Description property appears on the status bar.

3. Type **2021**, which is the first record's PositionID field value, and then press the **Tab** key. Each time you press the Tab key, the insertion point moves to the right to the next field in the record. See Figure 2-18.

**Datasheet for Position table after entering the first field value**    **Figure 2-18**

symbol for the record being edited

next new record symbol

field value entered

insertion point

current record

**Position : Table**

| Position ID | Position Title | Employer ID | Wage | Hours/Week | Openings | Referred By | Start D |
|---|---|---|---|---|---|---|---|
| 2021 | | | | | | | |

Record: |◄| ◄ | 1 | ► |►I|►*| of 1

> **Trouble?** If you make a mistake when typing a value, use the Backspace key to delete characters to the left of the insertion point or the Delete key to delete characters to the right of the insertion point. Then type the correct value. If you want to correct a value by replacing it entirely, drag to select the value, and then type the correct value.

The **pencil symbol** in the first row's record selector indicates that the record is being edited. The **star symbol** in the second row's record selector identifies the second row as the next one available for a new record. Notice that all the fields are initially empty; this occurs because you set the Default Value property for the fields (as appropriate) to remove any values and leave them blank.

▶ 4. Type **Waiter/Waitress** in the PositionTitle field, and then press the **Tab** key. The insertion point moves to the EmployerID field.

▶ 5. Type **10155** and then press the **Tab** key. The insertion point moves to the right side of the Wage field.

Recall that the PositionID, PositionTitle, and EmployerID fields are all text fields and that the Wage field is a currency field. Field values for text fields are left-aligned in their boxes, and field values for number, date/time, and currency fields are right-aligned in their boxes.

▶ 6. Type **9.5** and then press the **Tab** key. Access displays the field value with a dollar sign and two decimal places ($9.50), as specified by the currency format. You do not need to type the dollar sign, commas, or decimal point (for whole dollar amounts) because Access adds these symbols automatically for you.

▶ 7. In the HoursPerWeek field, type **30**, press the **Tab** key, type **1** in the Openings field, and then press the **Tab** key.

▶ 8. Type **Sue Brown** in the ReferredBy field, and then press the **Tab** key. Depending on your monitor's resolution and size, the display of the datasheet might shift so that the next field, StartDate, is completely visible.

▶ 9. Type **6/30/2006** in the StartDate field, and then press the **Tab** key. Access displays the value as 06/30/2006, as specified by the custom date format (mm/dd/yyyy) you set for this field. The insertion point moves to the final field in the table, EndDate.

**10.** Type **9/15/2006** in the EndDate field, and then press the **Tab** key. Access displays the value as 09/15/2006, shifts the display of the datasheet back to the left, stores the first completed record in the Position table, removes the pencil symbol from the first row's record selector, advances the insertion point to the second row's PositionID text box, and places the current record symbol in the second row's record selector.

Now you can enter the values for the second record.

**11.** Refer back to Figure 2-16, and repeat Steps 3 through 10 to add the second record to the table. Access saves the record in the Position table, and moves the insertion point to the beginning of the third row. See Figure 2-19.

| Figure 2-19 | **Position table datasheet after entering the second record** |

Notice that "Record 3 of 3" appears around the navigation buttons, even though the table contains only two records. Access is anticipating that you will enter a new record, which would be the third of three records in the table. If you moved the insertion point to the second record, the display would change to "Record 2 of 2."

Notice that the two records are currently listed in the order in which you entered them. However, once you close the table or change to another view, and then redisplay the table datasheet, the records will be listed in primary key order by the values in the PositionID field.

# Modifying the Structure of an Access Table

Even a well-designed table might need to be modified. For example, the government at all levels and competitors place demands on a company to track more data and to modify the data it already tracks. Access allows you to modify a table's structure in Design view: you can add and delete fields, change the order of fields, and change the properties of the fields.

After holding a meeting with her staff members and reviewing the structure of the Position table and the format of the field values in the datasheet, Elsa has several changes she wants you to make to the table. First, she has decided that it's not necessary to keep track of the name of the person who originally requested a particular position, so she wants you to delete the ReferredBy field. Next, she wants the Openings field moved to the end of the table. She also wants you to add a new yes/no field, named Experience, to the table to indicate whether the available position requires that potential recruits have prior experience in that type of work. The Experience field will be inserted between the HoursPerWeek and StartDate fields. Finally, she thinks that the Wage field should remain a currency field, but she wants the dollar signs removed from the displayed field values in the datasheet so the values are easier to read. Figure 2-20 shows Elsa's modified design for the Position table.

**Modified design for the Position table** ◀ **Figure 2-20**

| Field Name | Data Type | Field Size | Caption | Description |
|---|---|---|---|---|
| PositionID | Text | 4 | Position ID | Primary key |
| PositionTitle | Text | 30 | Position Title | |
| EmployerID | Text | 5 | Employer ID | Foreign key |
| Wage | Currency | | | Rate per hour |
| HoursPerWeek | Number | Integer | Hours/Week | Work hours per week |
| Experience | Yes/No | | | Experience required |
| StartDate | Date/Time | | Start Date | Month/day/year |
| EndDate | Date/Time | | End Date | Month/day/year |
| Openings | Number | Integer | | Number of openings |

You'll begin modifying the table by deleting the ReferredBy field.

## Deleting a Field

After you've defined a table structure and added records to the table, you can delete a field from the table structure. When you delete a field, you also delete all the values for the field from the table. Therefore, before you delete a field you should make sure that you want to do so—and that you choose the correct field to delete.

**Deleting a Field from a Table Structure**                          Reference Window

- In the Table window in Design view, right-click the row selector for the field you want to delete, both to select the field and to display the shortcut menu.
- Click Delete Rows on the shortcut menu.

You need to delete the ReferredBy field from the Position table structure.

### To delete the ReferredBy field:

▶ **1.** Click the **View** button for Design view ▨ on the Table Datasheet toolbar. The Table window for the Position table opens in Design view.

▶ **2.** Position the pointer on the row selector for the ReferredBy field until the pointer changes to a ➡ shape.

▶ **3.** Right-click to select the entire row for the ReferredBy field and display the shortcut menu, and then click **Delete Rows**.

A dialog box opens asking you to confirm the deletion.

▶ **4.** Click the **Yes** button to close the dialog box and to delete the field and its values from the table. See Figure 2-21.

| Figure 2-21 | Table structure after deleting ReferredBy field |

You have deleted the ReferredBy field in the Table window, but the change doesn't take place in the table on disk until you save the table structure. Because you have other modifications to make to the table, you'll wait until you finish them all before saving the modified table structure to disk.

## Moving a Field

To move a field, you use the mouse to drag it to a new location in the Table window in Design view. Your next modification to the Position table structure is to move the Openings field to the end of the table, as Elsa requested.

### To move the Openings field:

▶ **1.** Click the **row selector** for the Openings field to select the entire row.

▶ **2.** If necessary, scroll the Table Design grid so that you can see both the selected Openings field and the empty row below the EndDate field at the same time.

▶ **3.** Place the pointer in the row selector for the Openings field, click the ⬉ pointer, and then drag the ⬉ pointer to the row selector below the EndDate row selector. See Figure 2-22.

| Figure 2-22 | Moving a field in the table structure |

▶ **4.** Release the mouse button. Access moves the Openings field below the EndDate field in the table structure.

**Trouble?** If the Openings field did not move, repeat Steps 1 through 3, making sure you firmly hold down the mouse button during the drag operation.

## Adding a Field

Next, you need to add the Experience field to the table structure between the HoursPerWeek and StartDate fields. To add a new field between existing fields, you must insert a row. You begin by selecting the field that will be below the new field you want to insert.

Reference Window

### Adding a Field Between Two Existing Fields

- In the Table window in Design view, right-click the row selector for the row above which you want to add a new field, to select the field and display the shortcut menu.
- Click Insert Rows on the shortcut menu.
- Define the new field by entering the field name, data type, description (optional), and any property specifications.

### To add the Experience field to the Position table:

▶ **1.** Right-click the **row selector** for the StartDate field to select this field and display the short-cut menu, and then click **Insert Rows**. Access adds a new, blank row between the HoursPerWeek and StartDate fields. See Figure 2-23.

**After inserting a row in the table structure** ◀ **Figure 2-23**

You'll define the Experience field in the new row of the Position table. Access will add this new field to the Position table structure between the HoursPerWeek and StartDate fields.

▶ **2.** Click the **Field Name** text box for the new row, type **Experience**, and then press the **Tab** key.

The Experience field will be a yes/no field that will specify whether prior work experience is required for the position.

▶ **3.** Type **y**. Access completes the data type as "yes/No."

▶ **4.** Press the **Tab** key to select the yes/no data type and to move to the Description text box.

Notice that Access changes the value in the Data Type text box from "yes/No" to "Yes/No."

▶ **5.** Type **Experience required** in the Description text box.

Elsa wants the Experience field to have a Default Value property value of "No," so you need to set this property.

▶ **6.** In the Field Properties pane, click the **Default Value** text box, type **no**, and then press the **Tab** key. Notice that Access changes the Default Value property value from "no" to "No." See Figure 2-24.

**Figure 2-24** **Experience field added to the Position table**

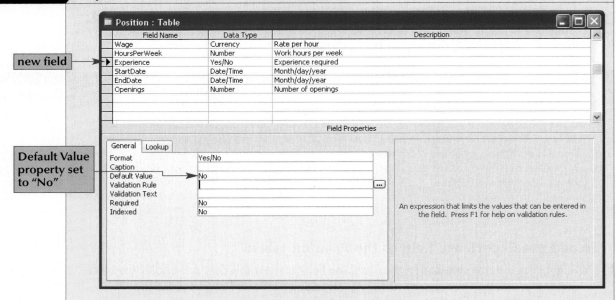

You've completed adding the Experience field to the Position table in Design view. As with the other changes you've made in Design view, however, the Experience field is not added to the Position table in the Northeast database until you save the changes to the table structure.

## Changing Field Properties

Elsa's last modification to the table structure is to remove the dollar signs from the Wage field values displayed in the datasheet—repeated dollar signs are unnecessary and they clutter the datasheet. As you learned earlier when defining the StartDate and EndDate fields, you use the Format property to control the display of a field value.

### To change the Format property of the Wage field:

1. Click the **Description** text box for the Wage field. The Wage field is now the current field.

2. Click the right side of the **Format** text box to display the Format list box. See Figure 2-25.

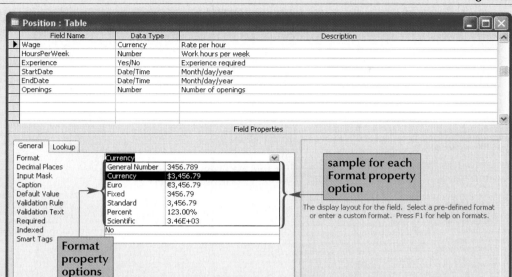

To the right of each Format property option is a field value whose appearance represents a sample of the option. The Standard option specifies the format Elsa wants for the Wage field.

▶ **3.** Click **Standard** in the Format list box to accept this option for the Format property.

Notice the Property Update Options button 🖉, which appears next to the Format property text box. This button allows you to have changes to properties take effect in other database objects.

## Updating Field Property Changes

When you change a field's property in Design view, you can update the corresponding property on forms and reports that include the field you've modified. For example, in the preceding steps, you changed the Format property of the Wage field to Standard. If the Northeast database included forms or reports that contained the Wage field, you could choose to **propagate**, or update, the modified property in those forms and reports so that their Wage field values would be displayed in the Standard format.

### To see the options for updating field property changes:

▶ **1.** Position the pointer on the **Property Update Options** button 🖉, and then click the list arrow that appears. A menu of related options is displayed. See Figure 2-26.

**Figure 2-26** **Updating changes to field properties**

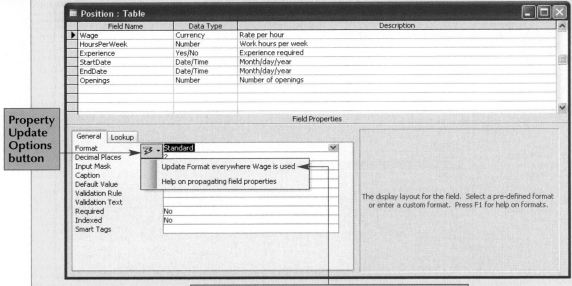

The "Help on propagating field properties" option takes you to a Help window for more information. The Update option allows you to select the objects you want to update with the property change.

2. Click **Update Format everywhere Wage is used**. A message box opens, indicating that no objects needed to be updated. This is because the Northeast database does not currently contain any forms or reports that might include the Wage field. If the database did contain such objects, the Update Properties dialog box would open, and you could then select the forms and reports containing the field that needs to be updated.

3. Click the **OK** button to close the message box. The Property Update Options button is no longer displayed in the Field Properties pane.

Elsa wants you to add a third record to the Position table datasheet. Before you can add the record, you must save the modified table structure, and then switch to the Position table datasheet.

**To save the modified table structure, and then switch to the datasheet:**

1. Click the **Save** button 🖫 on the Table Design toolbar. The modified table structure for the Position table is stored in the Northeast database. Note that if you forget to save the modified structure and try to close the table or switch to another view, Access will prompt you to save the table before you can continue.

2. Click the **View** button for Datasheet view 🖽 on the Table Design toolbar. The Position table datasheet opens. See Figure 2-27.

**Datasheet for the modified Position table** | **Figure 2-27**

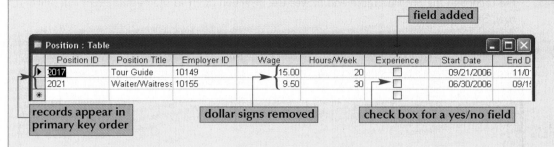

field added

records appear in primary key order

dollar signs removed

check box for a yes/no field

Notice that the ReferredBy field no longer appears in the datasheet, the Openings field is now the rightmost column (you might need to scroll the datasheet to see it), the Wage field values do not contain dollar signs, and the Experience field appears between the HoursPerWeek and StartDate fields. The Experience column contains check boxes to represent the yes/no field values. Empty check boxes signify "No," which is the default value you assigned to the Experience field. A check mark in the check box indicates a "Yes" value. Also notice that the records appear in ascending order based on the value in the PositionID field, the Position table's primary key, even though you did not enter the records in this order.

Elsa asks you to add a third record to the table. This record is for a position that requires prior work experience.

## To add the record to the modified Position table:

1. Click the **New Record** button on the Table Datasheet toolbar. The insertion point moves to the PositionID field for the third row, which is the next row available for a new record.

2. Type **2020**. The pencil symbol appears in the row selector for the third row, and the star appears in the row selector for the fourth row. Recall that these symbols represent a record being edited and the next available record, respectively.

3. Press the **Tab** key. The insertion point moves to the PositionTitle field. Recall that "PositionTitle" is the name of the field as it is stored in the database, and "Position Title" is the value specified for this field's Caption property. (This text generally refers to fields by their field names, not by their captions.)

4. Type **Host/Hostess**, press the **Tab** key to move to the EmployerID field, type **10163**, and then press the **Tab** key again. The Wage field is now the current field.

5. Type **18.5** and then press the **Tab** key. Access displays the value as "18.50" (with no dollar sign).

6. Type **32** in the HoursPerWeek field, and then press the **Tab** key. The Experience field is now the current field.

   Recall that the default value for this field is "No," which means the check box is initially empty. For yes/no fields with check boxes, you press the Tab key to leave the check box unchecked; you press the spacebar or click the check box to add or remove a check mark in the check box. Because this position requires experience, you need to insert a check mark in the check box.

7. Press the **spacebar**. A check mark appears in the check box.

8. Press the **Tab** key, type **6/15/2006** in the StartDate field, press the **Tab** key, and then type **10/1/2006** in the EndDate field.

▶ **9.** Press the **Tab** key, type **1** in the Openings field, and then press the **Tab** key. Access saves the record in the Position table and moves the insertion point to the beginning of the fourth row. See Figure 2-28.

**Figure 2-28** | **Position table datasheet with third record added**

record added

"No" values    "Yes" value

As you add records, Access places them at the end of the datasheet. If you switch to Design view and then return to the datasheet, or if you close the table and then open the datasheet, Access will display the records in primary key sequence.

For many of the fields, the columns are wider than necessary for the field values. You can resize the datasheet columns so that they are only as wide as needed to display the longest value in the column, including the field name or caption (if set). Resizing datasheet columns to their best fit improves the display of the datasheet and allows you to view more fields at the same time.

### To resize the Position datasheet columns to their best fit:

▶ **1.** Place the pointer on the line between the PositionID and PositionTitle field names until the pointer changes to a ✛ shape.

▶ **2.** Double-click the pointer. The PositionID column is resized so that it is only as wide as the longest value in the column (the caption for the field name, in this case).

▶ **3.** Double-click the ✛ pointer on the line to the right of each remaining field name to resize all the columns in the datasheet to their best fit. See Figure 2-29.

**Figure 2-29** | **Datasheet after resizing all columns to their best fit**

| Position ID | Position Title | Employer ID | Wage | Hours/Week | Experience | Start Date | End Date | Openings |
|---|---|---|---|---|---|---|---|---|
| 2017 | Tour Guide | 10149 | 15.00 | 20 | ☐ | 09/21/2006 | 11/01/2006 | 1 |
| 2021 | Waiter/Waitress | 10155 | 9.50 | 30 | ☐ | 06/30/2006 | 09/15/2006 | 1 |
| 2020 | Host/Hostess | 10163 | 18.50 | 32 | ☑ | 06/15/2006 | 10/01/2006 | 1 |
| | | | | | ☐ | | | |

Notice that all nine fields in the Position table are now visible in the datasheet if they were not visible before.

You have modified the Position table structure and added one record. Next, you need to obtain the rest of the records for this table from another database, and then import the two tables from the Seasonal database (Employer and NAICS) into your Northeast database.

# Obtaining Data from Another Access Database

Sometimes the data you need for your database might already exist in another Access database. You can save time in obtaining this data by copying and pasting records from one database table into another or by importing an entire table from one database into another.

## Copying Records from Another Access Database

You can copy and paste records from a table in the same database or in a different database only if the tables have the same structure—that is, the tables contain the same fields in the same order. Elsa's NEJobs database in the Brief\Tutorial folder included with your Data Files has a table named AvailablePositions that has the same table structure as the Position table. The records in the AvailablePositions table are the records Elsa wants you to copy into the Position table.

Other programs, such as Microsoft Word and Microsoft Excel, allow you to have two or more documents open at a time. However, you can have only one database open at a time for your current Access session. Therefore, you need to close the Northeast database, open the AvailablePositions table in the NEJobs database, select and copy the table records, close the NEJobs database, reopen the Position table in the Northeast database, and then paste the copied records. (*Note:* If you have a database open and then open a second database, Access will automatically close the first database for you.)

### To copy the records from the AvailablePositions table:

1. Click the **Close** button ☒ on the Table window title bar to close the Position table. A message box opens asking if you want to save the changes to the layout of the Position table. This box appears because you resized the datasheet columns to their best fit.

2. Click the **Yes** button in the message box.

3. Click the **Close** button ☒ on the Database window title bar to close the Northeast database.

4. Click the **Open** button 🖝 on the Database toolbar to display the Open dialog box.

5. If necessary, display the list of your Data Files in the **Brief\Tutorial** folder.

6. Open the database file named **NEJobs**. The Database window opens. Notice that the NEJobs database contains only one table, the AvailablePositions table. This table contains the records you need to copy.

7. Click **AvailablePositions** in the Tables list box (if necessary), and then click the **Open** button in the Database window. The datasheet for the AvailablePositions table opens. See Figure 2-30. Note that this table contains a total of 62 records.

**Figure 2-30** **Datasheet for the NEJobs database's AvailablePositions table**

click here to select all records →

total number of records in the table →

| Position ID | Position Title | Employer ID | Wage | Hours/Week | Experience | Start Date | End Date | Openings |
|---|---|---|---|---|---|---|---|---|
| 2004 | Host/Hostess | 10197 | 17.00 | 24 | ☐ | 07/01/2006 | 09/30/2006 | 1 |
| 2007 | Tour Guide | 10146 | 18.75 | 20 | ☑ | 05/15/2006 | 10/31/2006 | 2 |
| 2010 | Kitchen Help | 10135 | 13.00 | 40 | ☐ | 06/01/2006 | 10/01/2006 | 1 |
| 2015 | Concierge | 10159 | 22.00 | 40 | ☑ | 09/01/2006 | 03/01/2007 | 1 |
| 2025 | Kitchen Help | 10145 | 12.50 | 32 | ☐ | 07/01/2006 | 10/01/2006 | 2 |
| 2027 | Waiter/Waitress | 10130 | 10.00 | 32 | ☐ | 06/30/2006 | 10/01/2006 | 2 |
| 2028 | Cook | 10194 | 25.00 | 40 | ☑ | 08/01/2006 | 12/15/2006 | 1 |
| 2033 | Lifeguard | 10138 | 20.50 | 24 | ☑ | 06/15/2006 | 09/15/2006 | 1 |
| 2034 | Waiter/Waitress | 10162 | 10.25 | 30 | ☐ | 05/31/2006 | 11/01/2006 | 3 |
| 2036 | Reservationist | 10151 | 14.75 | 32 | ☐ | 10/01/2006 | 03/31/2007 | 1 |
| 2037 | Gift Shop Clerk | 10159 | 13.50 | 35 | ☐ | 09/01/2006 | 03/01/2007 | 1 |
| 2040 | Waiter/Waitress | 10126 | 10.50 | 32 | ☑ | 05/01/2006 | 10/01/2006 | 2 |
| 2041 | Housekeeping | 10133 | 12.00 | 40 | ☐ | 05/15/2006 | 10/15/2006 | 3 |
| 2045 | Tour Guide | 10122 | 17.00 | 24 | ☐ | 05/31/2006 | 10/01/2006 | 1 |
| 2048 | Front Desk Clerk | 10170 | 16.50 | 32 | ☐ | 07/01/2006 | 11/01/2006 | 1 |
| 2049 | Pro Shop Clerk | 10218 | 17.00 | 40 | ☑ | 05/01/2006 | 10/15/2006 | 1 |
| 2053 | Host/Hostess | 10190 | 15.75 | 24 | ☐ | 07/01/2006 | 09/01/2006 | 2 |
| 2055 | Greenskeeper | 10195 | 18.00 | 30 | ☑ | 06/01/2006 | 10/01/2006 | 1 |
| 2056 | Reservationist | 10156 | 15.00 | 24 | ☐ | 05/31/2006 | 10/15/2006 | 1 |
| 2058 | Main Office Clerk | 10152 | 14.25 | 32 | ☐ | 12/01/2006 | 04/01/2007 | 1 |

Record: I◄ ◄ 1 ► ►I ►✱ of 62

Elsa wants you to copy all the records in the AvailablePositions table. You can select all records by clicking the row selector for the field name row.

▶ **8.** Click the **row selector** for the field name row (see Figure 2-30). All the records in the table are now highlighted, which means that Access has selected all of them.

▶ **9.** Click the **Copy** button 📋 on the Table Datasheet toolbar. All the records are copied to the Clipboard.

**Trouble?** If a Clipboard panel opens in the task pane, click its Close button to close it, and then continue with Step 10.

▶ **10.** Click the **Close** button ✕ on the Table window title bar. A message box opens asking if you want to save the data you copied to the Clipboard.

▶ **11.** Click the **Yes** button in the message box. The message box closes, and then the table closes.

▶ **12.** Click the **Close** button ✕ on the Database window title bar to close the NEJobs database.

To finish copying and pasting the records, you must open the Position table and paste the copied records into the table.

## To paste the copied records into the Position table:

▶ **1.** Click **File** on the menu bar, and then click **Northeast** in the list of recently opened databases. The Database window opens, showing the tables for the Northeast database.

▶ **2.** In the Tables list box, click **Position** (if necessary), and then click the **Open** button in the Database window. The datasheet for the Position table opens.

You must paste the records at the end of the table.

▶ **3.** Click the **row selector** for row four, which is the next row available for a new record. Make sure the entire row is selected (highlighted).

▶ **4.** Click the **Paste** button 📋 on the Table Datasheet toolbar. A message box opens asking if you are sure you want to paste the records (62 in all).

**Trouble?** If the Paste button 🖺 is not available, click the row selector for row four, make sure that the entire row is selected, and then repeat Step 4.

5. Click the **Yes** button. All the records are pasted from the Clipboard, and the pasted records remain highlighted. See Figure 2-31. Notice that the table now contains a total of 65 records—the three original records plus the 62 copied records.

Table after copying and pasting records ◀ **Figure 2-31**

original records (3)

pasted records (62)   table now contains 65 records

6. Click the **Close** button ☒ on the Table window title bar to close the Position table.

## Importing a Table from Another Access Database

When you **import** a table from one Access database to another, you place a copy of the table—including its structure, field definitions, and field values—in the database into which you import it. There are two ways to import a table from another Access database into your current database: using the Get External Data option on the File menu, or using the Import Table Wizard, which is available in the New Table dialog box. You'll use both methods to import the two tables from the Seasonal database into your Northeast database.

### To import the Employer and NAICS tables:

1. Make sure the Northeast Database window is open on your screen.

2. Click **File** on the menu bar, point to **Get External Data**, and then click **Import**. The Import dialog box opens. This dialog box is similar to the Open dialog box.

3. Display the list of files in your Brief\Tutorial folder, click **Seasonal**, and then click the **Import** button. The Import Objects dialog box opens. See Figure 2-32.

**Figure 2-32** ▶ **Import Objects dialog box**

table objects in the Seasonal database

The Tables tab of the dialog box lists both tables in the Seasonal database—Employer and NAICS. Note that you can import other objects as well (queries, forms, reports, and so on).

▶ 4. Click **Employer** in the list of tables, and then click the **OK** button. The Import Objects dialog box closes, and the Employer table is now listed in the Northeast Database window.

Now you'll use the Import Table Wizard to import the NAICS table. (Note that you could also use the Select All button in the Import Objects dialog box to import all the objects listed on the current tab at the same time.)

▶ 5. Click the **New** button in the Database window, click **Import Table** in the New Table dialog box, and then click the **OK** button. The Import dialog box opens.

▶ 6. If necessary, display the list of files in your Brief\Tutorial folder, click **Seasonal**, and then click the **Import** button. The Import Objects dialog box opens, again displaying the tables in the Seasonal database.

▶ 7. Click **NAICS** in the list of tables, and then click the **OK** button to import the NAICS table into the Northeast database.

Now that you have all the records in the Position table and all three tables in the Northeast database, Elsa examines the records to make sure they are correct. She finds one record in the Position table that she wants you to delete and another record that needs changes to its field values.

# Updating a Database

**Updating**, or **maintaining**, a database is the process of adding, changing, and deleting records in database tables to keep them current and accurate. You've already added records to the Position table. Now Elsa wants you to delete and change records.

## Deleting Records

To delete a record, you need to select the record in Datasheet view, and then delete it using the Delete Record button on the Table Datasheet toolbar or the Delete Record option on the shortcut menu.

## Deleting a Record

- In the Table window in Datasheet view, click the row selector for the record you want to delete, and then click the Delete Record button on the Table Datasheet toolbar (or right-click the row selector for the record, and then click Delete Record on the shortcut menu).
- In the dialog box asking you to confirm the deletion, click the Yes button.

Elsa asks you to delete the record whose PositionID value is 2015 because this record was entered in error; the position for this record does not exist. The fourth record in the table has a PositionID value of 2015. This record is the one you need to delete.

### To delete the record:

▶ **1.** Open the Position table in Datasheet view.

▶ **2.** Right-click the **row selector** for row four. Access selects the fourth record and displays the shortcut menu. See Figure 2-33.

Deleting a record ◀ **Figure 2-33**

**selected record**

**click here to delete the selected record**

▶ **3.** Click **Delete Record** on the shortcut menu. Access deletes the record and opens a dialog box asking you to confirm the deletion. Because the deletion of a record is permanent and cannot be undone, Access prompts you to make sure that you want to delete the record.

**Trouble?** If you selected the wrong record for deletion, click the No button. Access ends the deletion process and continues to display the selected record. Repeat Steps 2 and 3 to delete the correct record.

▶ **4.** Click the **Yes** button to confirm the deletion and close the dialog box.

Elsa's final update to the Position table involves changes to field values in one of the records.

## Changing Records

To change the field values in a record, you must first make the record the current record. Then you position the insertion point in the field value to make minor changes or select the field value to replace it entirely. In Tutorial 1, you used the mouse with the scroll bars and the navigation buttons to navigate the records in a datasheet. You can also use keystroke combinations and the F2 key to navigate a datasheet and to select field values.

The **F2 key** is a toggle that you use to switch between navigation mode and editing mode:

- In **navigation mode**, Access selects an entire field value. If you type while you are in navigation mode, your typed entry replaces the highlighted field value.
- In **editing mode**, you can insert or delete characters in a field value based on the location of the insertion point.

Figure 2-34 shows some of the navigation mode and editing mode keystroke techniques.

**Figure 2-34** ▶ **Navigation mode and editing mode keystroke techniques**

| Press | To Move the Selection in Navigation Mode | To Move the Insertion Point in Editing Mode |
|---|---|---|
| ← | Left one field value at a time | Left one character at a time |
| → | Right one field value at a time | Right one character at a time |
| Home | Left to the first field value in the record | To the left of the first character in the field value |
| End | Right to the last field value in the record | To the right of the last character in the field value |
| ↑ or ↓ | Up or down one record at a time | Up or down one record at a time and switch to navigation mode |
| Tab or Enter | Right one field value at a time | Right one field value at a time and switch to navigation mode |
| Ctrl+Home | To the first field value in the first record | To the left of the first character in the field value |
| Ctrl+End | To the last field value in the last record | To the right of the last character in the field value |

The record Elsa wants you to change has a PositionID field value of 2125. Some of the values were entered incorrectly for this record, and you need to enter the correct values.

## To modify the record:

▶ 1. Make sure the PositionID field value for the fourth record is still highlighted, indicating that the table is in navigation mode.

▶ 2. Press the **Ctrl+End** keys. Access displays records from the end of the table and selects the last field value in the last record. This field value is for the Openings field.

▶ 3. Press the **Home** key. The first field value in the last record is now selected. This field value is for the PositionID field.

▶ 4. Press the ↑ key. The PositionID field value for the previous record (PositionID 2125) is selected. This record is the one you need to change.

Elsa wants you to change these field values in the record: PositionID to 2124, EmployerID to 10163, Wage to 14.50, Experience to "Yes" (checked), and EndDate to 10/15/2006.

▶ 5. Type **2124**, press the **Tab** key twice, type **10163**, press the **Tab** key, type **14.5**, press the **Tab** key twice, press the **spacebar** to insert a check mark in the Experience check box, press the **Tab** key twice, and then type **10/15/2006**. The changes to the record are complete. See Figure 2-35.

**Table after changing field values in a record** ◀ **Figure 2-35**

| | | | | | | | | | |
|---|---|---|---|---|---|---|---|---|---|
| | 2115 | Gift Shop Clerk | 10154 | 13.00 | 25 | ☐ | 05/01/2006 | 09/30/2006 | 1 |
| | 2117 | Housekeeping | 10220 | 13.50 | 30 | ☐ | 06/30/2006 | 09/30/2006 | 3 |
| | 2118 | Greenskeeper | 10218 | 17.00 | 32 | ☐ | 05/01/2006 | 11/01/2006 | 1 |
| | 2120 | Lifeguard | 10154 | 19.00 | 32 | ☑ | 06/15/2006 | 09/30/2006 | 2 |
| | 2122 | Kitchen Help | 10151 | 13.00 | 35 | ☐ | 09/01/2006 | 03/31/2007 | 3 |
| | 2123 | Main Office Clerk | 10170 | 14.50 | 32 | ☐ | 07/01/2006 | 11/15/2006 | 1 |
| 🖉 | 2124◀ | Kitchen Help | 10163◀ ▶14.50 | | 40 | ▶☑ | 06/01/2006 | 10/15/2006◀ | 2 |
| | 2127 | Waiter/Waitress | 10185 | 10.50 | 40 | ☐ | 12/01/2006 | 05/01/2007 | 1 |
| ✳ | | | | | | ☐ | | | |

**field values changed**

Record: I◀ ◀ 63 ▶ ▶I ▶✳ of 64

You've completed all of Elsa's updates to the Position table. Now you can close the Northeast database.

▶ 6. Close the Position table, and then close the Northeast database.

Elsa and her staff members approve of the revised table structure for the Position table. They are confident that the table will allow them to easily track position data for NSJI's employer customers.

## Session 2.2 Quick Check

Review

1. What does a pencil symbol in a datasheet's row selector represent? A star symbol?
2. What is the effect of deleting a field from a table structure?
3. How do you insert a field between existing fields in a table structure?
4. A field with the _____ data type can appear in the table datasheet as a check box.
5. Describe the two ways in which you can display the Import dialog box, so that you can import a table from one Access database to another.
6. In Datasheet view, what is the difference between navigation mode and editing mode?

## Tutorial Summary

Review

In this tutorial, you learned how to create and save a new database and how to create and save a new table in that database. With this process, you also learned some important guidelines for designing databases and tables, and for setting field properties. You worked in Design view to define fields, set properties, specify a table's primary key, and modify a table's structure. Then you worked in Datasheet view to add records to the new table, both by entering them directly in the datasheet and by copying records from another Access database. To complete the database design, you imported tables from another Access database into the new database you created. Finally, you updated the database by deleting records and changing values in records.

# Key Terms

| | | |
|---|---|---|
| Caption property | editing mode | navigation mode |
| composite key | entity integrity | null value |
| data redundancy | F1 key | pencil symbol |
| data type | F2 key | propagate |
| Database Wizard | F6 key | properties |
| Decimal Places property | Field Size property | set (a property) |
| Default Value property | import | star symbol |
| Description property | maintain (a database) | update (a database) |
| Design view | | |

**Practice**

*Take time to practice the skills you learned in the tutorial using the same case scenario.*

# Review Assignments

**Data File needed for the Review Assignments: Elsa.mdb**

Elsa needs a database to track data about the students recruited by NSJI and about the recruiters who find jobs for the students. She asks you to create the database by completing the following:

1. Start Access, and make sure your Data Files are in the proper location.
2. Create a new, blank database named **Recruits** and save it in the Brief\Review folder included with your Data Files.
3. Use Design view to create a new table using the table design shown in Figure 2-36.

**Figure 2-36**

| Field Name | Data Type | Description | Field Size | Caption | Other Properties |
|---|---|---|---|---|---|
| SSN | Text | Primary key | 30 | | |
| Salary | Currency | | | | Format: Currency<br>Default Value: (blank) |
| FirstName | Text | | 50 | First Name | |
| MiddleName | Text | | 30 | Middle Name | |
| LastName | Text | | 50 | Last Name | |

4. Specify SSN as the primary key field, and then save the table as **Recruiter**.
5. Add the recruiter records shown in Figure 2-37 to the **Recruiter** table.

**Figure 2-37**

| SSN | Salary | FirstName | MiddleName | LastName |
|---|---|---|---|---|
| 892-77-1201 | 40,000 | Kate | Teresa | Foster |
| 901-63-1554 | 38,500 | Paul | Michael | Kirnicki |
| 893-91-0178 | 40,000 | Ryan | James | DuBrava |

6. Make the following changes to the structure of the **Recruiter** table:
   a. Move the Salary field so that it appears after the LastName field.
   b. Add a new field between the LastName and Salary fields, using the following properties:

   | | |
   |---|---|
   | Field Name: | BonusQuota |
   | Data Type: | Number |
   | Description: | Number of recruited students needed to receive bonus |
   | Field Size: | Byte |
   | Decimal Places: | 0 |
   | Caption: | Bonus Quota |
   | Default Value: | (blank) |

   c. Change the format of the Salary field so that commas are displayed, dollar signs are not displayed, and no decimal places are displayed in the field values.
   d. Save the revised table structure.
7. Use the **Recruiter** datasheet to update the database as follows:
   a. Enter these BonusQuota values for the three records: 60 for Kate Foster; 60 for Ryan DuBrava; and 50 for Paul Kirnicki.
   b. Add a record to the Recruiter datasheet with the following field values:

   | | |
   |---|---|
   | SSN: | 899-40-2937 |
   | FirstName: | Sonia |
   | MiddleName: | Lee |
   | LastName: | Xu |
   | BonusQuota: | 50 |
   | Salary: | 39,250 |

8. Close the Recruiter table, and then set the option for compacting the **Recruits** database on close. (*Note*: If you are working off a floppy disk, check with your instructor or technical support staff to confirm that you should set this option.)
9. Elsa created a database with her name as the database name. In that database, the RecruiterEmployees table has the same format as the Recruiter table you created. Copy all the records from the **RecruiterEmployees** table in the **Elsa** database (located in the Brief\Review folder provided with your Data Files) to the end of the **Recruiter** table in the **Recruits** database.
10. Delete the MiddleName field from the Recruiter table structure, and then save the table structure.
11. Resize all columns in the datasheet for the Recruiter table to their best fit.
12. Print the Recruiter table datasheet, and then save and close the table.
13. Create a table named **Student** using the Import Table Wizard. The table you need to import is named **Student**, which is one of the tables in the **Elsa** database located in the Brief\Review folder provided with your Data Files.
14. Make the following modifications to the structure of the **Student** table in the **Recruits** database:
    a. Enter the following Description property values:
       StudentID: Primary key
       SSN:       Foreign key value of the recruiter for this student
    b. Change the Field Size property for both the FirstName field and the LastName field to 15.
    c. Move the BirthDate field so that it appears between the Nation and Gender fields.
    d. Change the format of the BirthDate field so that it displays only two digits for the year instead of four.
    e. Save the table structure changes. (Answer "Yes" to any warning messages about property changes and lost data.)

15. Switch to Datasheet view, and then resize all columns in the datasheet to fit the data.
16. Delete the record with the StudentID value DRI9901 from the **Student** table.
17. Save, print, and then close the Student datasheet.
18. Close the Recruits database.

# Case Problem 1

**Data Files needed for this Case Problem: Videos.mdb (*cont. from Tutorial 1*) and Events.mdb**

***Lim's Video Photography***   Youngho Lim uses the Videos database to maintain information about the clients, contracts, and events for his video photography business. Youngho asks you to help him maintain the database by completing the following:

1. Open the **Videos** database located in the Brief\Case1 folder provided with your Data Files.
2. Use Design view to create a table using the table design shown in Figure 2-38.

**Figure 2-38**

| Field Name | Data Type | Description | Field Size | Caption | Other Properties |
|---|---|---|---|---|---|
| ShootID | Number | Primary key | Long Integer | Shoot ID | Decimal Places: 0 Default Value: (blank) |
| ShootType | Text | | 2 | Shoot Type | |
| ShootTime | Date/Time | | | Shoot Time | Format: Medium Time |
| Duration | Number | # of hours | Single | | Default Value: (blank) |
| Contact | Text | person who booked shoot | 30 | | |
| Location | Text | | 30 | | |
| ShootDate | Date/Time | | | Shoot Date | Format: mm/dd/yyyy |
| ContractID | Number | Foreign key | Integer | Contract ID | Decimal Places: 0 Default Value: (blank) |

3. Specify ShootID as the primary key, and then save the table as **Shoot**.
4. Add the records shown in Figure 2-39 to the Shoot table.

**Figure 2-39**

| ShootID | ShootType | ShootTime | Duration | Contact | Location | ShootDate | ContractID |
|---|---|---|---|---|---|---|---|
| 927032 | AP | 4:00 PM | 3.5 | Ellen Quirk | Elm Lodge | 9/27/2006 | 2412 |
| 103031 | HP | 9:00 AM | 3.5 | Tom Bradbury | Client's home | 10/30/2006 | 2611 |

5. Youngho created a database named Events that contains a table with shoot data named ShootEvents. The Shoot table you created has the same format as the ShootEvents table. Copy all the records from the **ShootEvents** table in the **Events** database (located in the Brief\Case1 folder provided with your Data Files) to the end of the **Shoot** table in the **Videos** database.
6. Modify the structure of the Shoot table by completing the following:
   a. Delete the Contact field.
   b. Move the ShootDate field so that it appears between the ShootType and ShootTime fields.

7. Save the revised table structure, switch to Datasheet view, and then resize all columns in the datasheet for the Shoot table to their best fit.
8. Use the **Shoot** datasheet to update the database as follows:
   a. For ShootID 421032, change the ShootTime value to 7:00 PM, and change the Location value to Le Bistro.
   b. Add a record to the Shoot datasheet with the following field values:
      ShootID:      913032
      ShootType:    SE
      ShootDate:    9/13/2006
      ShootTime:    1:00 PM
      Duration:     2.5
      Location:     High School football field
      ContractID:   2501
9. Switch to Design view, and then switch back to Datasheet view so that the records appear in primary key sequence by ShootID. Resize any datasheet columns to their best fit, as necessary.
10. Print the Shoot table datasheet, and then save and close the table.
11. Create a table named **ShootDesc** using the Import Table Wizard. The table you need to import is named **ShootDesc**, which is one of the tables in the **Events** database located in the Brief\Case1 folder provided with your Data Files.
12. Make the following modifications to the structure of the **ShootDesc** table in the **Videos** database:
    a. Enter the following Description property values:
       ShootType:   Primary key
       ShootDesc:   Description of shoot
    b. Change the Field Size property for ShootType to 2.
    c. Change the Field Size property for ShootDesc to 30.
    d. Enter the following Caption property values:
       ShootType:   Shoot Type
       ShootDesc:   Shoot Desc
13. Save the revised table structure (answer "Yes" to any warning messages about property changes and lost data), switch to Datasheet view, and then resize both datasheet columns to their best fit.
14. Print the ShootDesc table datasheet, and then save and close the table.
15. Close the Videos database.

## Case Problem 2

**Challenge**

*Challenge yourself by using the Table Wizard to create a new table to store order data for this e-commerce business.*

**Explore**

**Data Files needed for this Case Problem: Meals.mdb (*cont. from Tutorial 1*) and Customer.mdb**

***DineAtHome.course.com***   Claire Picard uses the Meals database to track information about local restaurants and orders placed at the restaurants by the customers of her e-commerce business. You'll help her maintain this database by completing the following:

1. Open the **Meals** database located in the Brief\Case2 folder provided with your Data Files.
2. Use the Table Wizard to create a new table named **Order** in the **Meals** database, as follows:
   a. Base the new table on the Orders sample table, which is one of the sample tables in the Business category.
   b. Add the following fields to your table (in the order shown): OrderID, CustomerID, and OrderDate.

   c. Click CustomerID in the "Fields in my new table" list, and then use the Rename Field button to change the name of this field to RestaurantID. Click the Next button.
   d. Specify the name **Order** (not the default "Orders") for the new table, and choose the option for setting the primary key yourself. Click the Next button.
   e. Specify OrderID as the primary key field, and select the option "Numbers and/or letters I enter when I add new records." Click the Next button.
   f. In the next dialog box, click the Relationships button, click the option "The tables aren't related," click the OK button, and then click the Next button.
   g. In the final Table Wizard dialog box, choose the option for modifying the table design. Click the Finish button.

**Explore**

3. Modify the structure of the Order table as follows:
   a. For the OrderID field, make the following changes:
      Data Type:       Number
      Description:     Primary key
      Decimal Places:  0
      Default Value:   blank (no value specified)
   b. For the RestaurantID field, make the following changes:
      Description:     Foreign key
      Decimal Places:  0
      Caption:         Restaurant ID
   c. For the OrderDate field, make the following changes:
      Format:          Long Date
      Input Mask:      blank (delete the entry from this property's text box)
4. Add a new field as the fourth field in the table, below OrderDate, with the following properties:
   Field Name:     OrderAmt
   Data Type:      Currency
   Description:    Total amount of order
   Format:         Fixed
   Caption:        Order Amt
   Default Value:  blank (no value specified)
5. Save the modified table structure.
6. Add the records shown in Figure 2-40 to the Order table.

**Figure 2-40**

| OrderID | RestaurantID | OrderDate | OrderAmt |
|---------|--------------|-----------|----------|
| 3117 | 131 | 4/2/06 | 155.35 |
| 3123 | 115 | 5/1/06 | 45.42 |
| 3020 | 120 | 1/15/06 | 85.50 |
| 3045 | 108 | 3/16/06 | 50.25 |

7. Claire created a database named Customer that contains a table with order data named OrderRecords. The Order table you created has the same format as the OrderRecords table. Copy all the records from the **OrderRecords** table in the **Customer** database (located in the Brief\Case2 folder provided with your Data Files) to the end of the **Order** table in the **Meals** database.
8. Resize all columns in the datasheet for the Order table to their best fit.
9. For OrderID 3039, change the OrderAmt value to 87.30.

10. Delete the record for OrderID 3068.
11. Print the Order table datasheet, and then save and close the table.
12. Close the Meals database.

# Case Problem 3

**Data Files needed for this Case Problem: Redwood.mdb (*cont. from Tutorial 1*) and Pledge.mdb**

*Redwood Zoo*   Michael Rosenfeld continues to track information about donors, their pledges, and the status of funds to benefit the Redwood Zoo. Help him maintain the Redwood database by completing the following:

1. Open the **Redwood** database located in the Brief\Case3 folder provided with your Data Files.
2. Create a table named **Pledge** using the Import Table Wizard. The table you need to import is named **PledgeRecords**, which is located in the **Pledge** database in the Brief\Case3 folder provided with your Data Files.
3. After importing the PledgeRecords table, use the shortcut menu to rename the table to **Pledge** in the Database window.
4. Modify the structure of the **Pledge** table by completing the following:
   a. Enter the following Description property values:
      PledgeID:   Primary key
      DonorID:    Foreign key
      FundCode:   Foreign key
   b. Change the format of the PledgeDate field to mm/dd/yyyy.
   c. Change the Data Type of the TotalPledged field to Currency with the Standard format.
   d. Specify a Default Value of B for the PaymentMethod field.
   e. Specify a Default Value of F for the PaymentSchedule field.
   f. Save the modified table structure.
5. Switch to Datasheet view, and then resize all columns in the datasheet to their best fit.
6. Use the **Pledge** datasheet to update the database as follows:
   a. Add a new record to the Pledge table with the following field values:
      PledgeID:            2695
      DonorID:             59045
      FundCode:            P15
      PledgeDate:          7/11/2006
      TotalPledged:        1000
      PaymentMethod:       B
      PaymentSchedule:     M
   b. Change the TotalPledged value for PledgeID 2499 to 150.
   c. Change the FundCode value for PledgeID 2332 to B03.
7. Print the Pledge table datasheet, and then save and close the table.
8. Close the Redwood database.

**Challenge**

*Explore two new ways to create tables containing trip information — by importing an Excel worksheet and by entering records first in Datasheet view.*

**Explore**

# Case Problem 4

**Data Files needed for this Case Problem: Trips.mdb (*cont. from Tutorial 1*), Rafting.xls, and Groups.mdb**

***Mountain River Adventures*** Connor and Siobhan Dempsey use the Trips database to track the data about the guided tours they provide. You'll help them maintain this database by completing the following:

1. Open the **Trips** database located in the Brief\Case4 folder provided with your Data Files.

2. Use the Import Spreadsheet Wizard to create a new table named **RaftingTrip**. The data you need to import is contained in the **Rafting** workbook, which is a Microsoft Excel file located in the Brief\Case4 folder provided with your Data Files.
    a. Select the Import Table option in the New Table dialog box.
    b. Change the entry in the Files of type list box to display the list of Excel workbook files in the Brief\Case4 folder.
    c. Select the **Rafting** file and then click the Import button.
    d. In the Import Spreadsheet Wizard dialog boxes, choose the Sheet1 worksheet; choose the option for using column headings as field names; select the option for choosing your own primary key; specify TripID as the primary key; and enter the table name (**RaftingTrip**). Otherwise, accept the wizard's choices for all other options for the imported data.

3. Open the **RaftingTrip** table and resize all datasheet columns to their best fit.

4. Modify the structure of the RaftingTrip table by completing the following:
    a. For the TripID field, enter a Description property of "Primary key", change the Field Size property to Long Integer, set the Decimal Places property to 0, and set the Caption property to Trip ID.
    b. For the River field, change the Field Size property to 45.
    c. For the TripDistance field, enter a Description property of "Distance in miles", change the Field Size property to Integer, set the Decimal Places property to 0, and set the Caption property to Trip Distance.
    d. For the TripDays field, enter a Description property of "Number of days for the trip", change the Field Size property to Single, and set the Caption property to Trip Days.
    e. For the FeePerPerson field, change the Data Type to Currency, set the Format property to Fixed, and set the Caption property to Fee Per Person.
    f. Save the table structure. If you receive any warning messages about lost data or integrity rules, click the Yes button.

5. Switch to Datasheet view, and then resize all datasheet columns to their best fit.

6. Use the **RaftingTrip** datasheet to update the database as follows:
    a. For TripID 3142, change the TripDistance value to 20.
    b. Add a new record to the RaftingTrip table with the following field values:
       TripID:        3675
       River:         Colorado River (Grand Canyon)
       TripDistance:  110
       TripDays:      2.5
       FeePerPerson:  215
    c. Delete the record for TripID 3423.

7. Print the RaftingTrip table datasheet, and then save and close the table.

**Explore**

8. Create a new table named **Booking**, based on the data shown in Figure 2-41 and according to the following steps:

**Figure 2-41**

| BookingID | ClientID | TripDate | TripID | People |
|-----------|----------|----------|--------|--------|
| 410 | 330 | 6/5/06 | 3529 | 4 |
| 403 | 315 | 7/1/06 | 3107 | 7 |
| 411 | 311 | 7/5/06 | 3222 | 5 |

  a. Select the Datasheet View option in the New Table dialog box.
  b. Enter the three records shown in Figure 2-41. (Do *not* enter the field names at this point.)
  c. Switch to Design view, supply the table name, and then answer "No" if asked if you want to create a primary key.
  d. Enter the field names and properties for the five fields, as shown in Figure 2-42.

**Figure 2-42**

| Field Name | Data Type | Description | Field Size | Caption | Other Properties |
|------------|-----------|-------------|------------|---------|------------------|
| BookingID | Number | Primary key | Long Integer | Booking ID | Decimal Places: 0 |
| ClientID | Number | Foreign key | Integer | Client ID | Decimal Places: 0 |
| TripDate | Date/Time | | | Trip Date | Format: Short Date |
| TripID | Number | Foreign key | Long Integer | Trip ID | Decimal Places: 0 |
| People | Number | Number of people in the group | Byte | | Decimal Places: 0 |

9. Specify BookingID as the primary key, and then save the changes to the table structure.
10. Switch to Datasheet view, and then resize all datasheet columns to their best fit.
11. Connor created a database named Groups that contains a table with booking data named GroupInfo. The Booking table you created has the same format as the GroupInfo table. Copy all the records from the **GroupInfo** table in the **Groups** database (located in the Brief\Case4 folder provided with your Data Files) to the end of the **Booking** table in the **Trips** database.
12. Resize all columns in the Booking datasheet to their best fit (if necessary).
13. Print the Booking datasheet, and then save and close the table.
14. Close the Trips database.

**Research**

*Use the Internet to find and work with data related to the topics presented in this tutorial.*

# Internet Assignments

The purpose of the Internet Assignments is to challenge you to find information on the Internet that you can use to work effectively with this software. The actual assignments are updated and maintained on the Course Technology Web site. Log on to the Internet and use your Web browser to go to the Student Online Companion for New Perspectives Office 2003 at **www.course.com/np/office2003**. Click the Internet Assignments link, and then navigate to the assignments for this tutorial.

## SAM Assessment and Training

If you have a SAM user profile, you may have access to hands-on instruction, practice, and assessment of the skills covered in this tutorial. Log in to your SAM account and go to your assignments page to see what your instructor has assigned.

**Review**

# Quick Check Answers

### Session 2.1

1. Identify all the fields needed to produce the required information, group related fields into tables, determine each table's primary key, include a common field in related tables, avoid data redundancy, and determine the properties of each field.
2. The Data Type property determines what field values you can enter for the field and what other properties the field will have.
3. text, number, and AutoNumber fields
4. Caption
5. F6
6. null

### Session 2.2

1. the record being edited; the next row available for a new record
2. The field and all its values are removed from the table.
3. In Design view, right-click the row selector for the row above which you want to insert the field, click Insert Rows on the shortcut menu, and then define the new field.
4. yes/no
5. Make sure the database into which you want to import a table is open, click the File menu, point to Get External Data, and then click Import; or, click the New button in the Database window, click Import Table in the New Table dialog box, and then click the OK button.
6. In navigation mode, the entire field value is selected, and anything you type replaces the field value; in editing mode, you can insert or delete characters in a field value based on the location of the insertion point.

# Querying a Database

*Retrieving Information About Employers and Their Positions*

## Case

## Northeast Seasonal Jobs International (NSJI)

At a recent company meeting, Elsa Jensen and other NSJI employees discussed the importance of regularly monitoring the business activity of the company's employer clients. For example, Zack Ward and his marketing staff track employer activity to develop new strategies for promoting NSJI's services. Matt Griffin, the manager of recruitment, needs to track information about available positions, so that he can find student recruits to fill those positions. In addition, Elsa is interested in analyzing other aspects of the business, such as the wage amounts paid for different positions at different employers. You can satisfy all these informational needs for NSJI by creating and using queries that retrieve information from the Northeast database.

## Student Data Files

▼ **Brief**

▽ **Tutorial folder**
   Northeast.mdb *(cont.)*

▽ **Review folder**
   Recruits.mdb *(cont.)*

▽ **Case1 folder**
   Videos.mdb *(cont.)*

▽ **Case2 folder**
   Meals.mdb *(cont.)*

▽ **Case3 folder**
   Redwood.mdb *(cont.)*

▽ **Case4 folder**
   Trips.mdb *(cont.)*

# Introduction to Queries

As you learned in Tutorial 1, a query is a question you ask about data stored in a database. For example, Zack might create a query to find records in the Employer table for only those employers located in a specific state or province. When you create a query, you tell Access which fields you need and what criteria Access should use to select the records.

Access provides powerful query capabilities that allow you to:

- display selected fields and records from a table
- sort records
- perform calculations
- generate data for forms, reports, and other queries
- update data in the tables in a database
- find and display data from two or more tables

Most questions about data are generalized queries in which you specify the fields and records you want Access to select. These common requests for information, such as "Which employers are located in Quebec?" or "How many waiter/waitress positions are available?" are called **select queries**. The answer to a select query is returned in the form of a datasheet. The result of a query is also referred to as a **recordset**, because the query produces a set of records that answers your question.

More specialized, technical queries, such as finding duplicate records in a table, are best formulated using a Query Wizard. A Query Wizard prompts you for information by asking a series of questions and then creates the appropriate query based on your answers. In Tutorial 1, you used the Simple Query Wizard to display only some of the fields in the Employer table; Access provides other Query Wizards for more complex queries. For common, informational queries, it is easier for you to design your own query than to use a Query Wizard.

Zack wants you to create a query to display the employer ID, employer name, city, contact first name, contact last name, and Web site information for each record in the Employer table. He needs this information for a market analysis his staff is completing on NSJI's employer clients. You'll open the Query window to create the query for Zack.

# Query Window

You use the Query window in Design view to create a query. In Design view, you specify the data you want to view by constructing a query by example. When you use **query by example** (**QBE**), you give Access an example of the information you are requesting. Access then retrieves the information that precisely matches your example.

For Zack's query, you need to display data from the Employer table. You'll begin by starting Access, opening the Northeast database, and displaying the Query window in Design view.

**To start Access, open the Northeast database, and open the Query window in Design view:**

▶ 1. Start Access and open the **Northeast** database located in the Brief\Tutorial folder provided with your Data Files. The Northeast database is displayed in the Database window.

▶ 2. Click **Queries** in the Objects bar of the Database window, and then click the **New** button. The New Query dialog box opens. See Figure 3-1.

New Query dialog box    **Figure 3-1**

You'll design your own query instead of using a Query Wizard.

▶ **3.** If necessary, click **Design View** in the list box.

▶ **4.** Click the **OK** button. Access opens the Show Table dialog box on top of the Query window. (Note that you could also have double-clicked the "Create query in Design view" option in the Database window.) Notice that the title bar of the Query window shows that you are creating a select query.

The query you are creating will retrieve data from the Employer table, so you need to add this table to the Select Query window.

▶ **5.** Click **Employer** in the Tables list box (if necessary), click the **Add** button, and then click the **Close** button. Access places the Employer table's field list in the Select Query window and closes the Show Table dialog box.

To display more of the fields you'll be using for creating queries, you'll maximize the Select Query window.

▶ **6.** Click the **Maximize** button 🔲 on the Select Query window title bar. See Figure 3-2.

Select query in Design view    **Figure 3-2**

In Design view, the Select Query window contains the standard title bar, the menu bar, the status bar, and the Query Design toolbar. On the toolbar, the Query Type button shows a select query; the icon on this button changes according to the type of query you are creating. The title bar on the Select Query window displays the query type (Select Query) and the default query name (Query1). You'll change the default query name to a more meaningful one later when you save the query.

The Select Query window in Design view contains a field list and the design grid. The **field list** contains the fields for the table you are querying. The table name appears at the top of the list box, and the fields are listed in the order in which they appear in the table. You can scroll the field list to see more fields, or you can expand the field list box by dragging its borders to display all the fields and the complete field names.

In the **design grid**, you include the fields and record selection criteria for the information you want to see. Each column in the design grid contains specifications about a field you will use in the query. You can choose a single field for your query by dragging its name from the field list to the design grid. Alternatively, you can double-click a field name to place it in the next available design grid column.

When you are constructing a query, you can see the query results at any time by clicking the View button or the Run button on the Query Design toolbar. In response, Access displays the query datasheet (or recordset), which contains the set of fields and records that results from answering, or **running**, the query. The order of the fields in the query datasheet is the same as the order of the fields in the design grid. Although the query datasheet looks just like a table datasheet and appears in Datasheet view, a query datasheet is temporary, and its contents are based on the criteria you establish in the design grid. In contrast, a table datasheet shows the permanent data in a table. However, you can update data while viewing a query datasheet, just as you can when working in a table datasheet or form.

If the query you are creating includes every field from the specified table, you can use one of the following three methods to transfer all the fields from the field list to the design grid:

- Click and drag each field individually from the field list to the design grid. Use this method if you want the fields in your query to appear in an order that is different from the order in the field list.
- Double-click the asterisk in the field list. Access places the table name followed by a period and an asterisk (as in "Employer.*") in the design grid, which signifies that the order of the fields is the same in the query as it is in the field list. Use this method if you don't need to sort the query or specify conditions for the records you want to select. The advantage of using this method is that you do not need to change the query if you add or delete fields from the underlying table structure. Such changes are reflected automatically in the query.
- Double-click the field list title bar to highlight all the fields, and then click and drag one of the highlighted fields to the design grid. Access places each field in a separate column and arranges the fields in the order in which they appear in the field list. Use this method when you need to sort your query or include record selection criteria.

Now you'll create and run Zack's query to display selected fields from the Employer table.

# Creating and Running a Query

The default table datasheet displays all the fields in the table, in the same order as they appear in the table. In contrast, a query datasheet can display selected fields from a table, and the order of the fields can be different from that of the table, enabling those viewing the query results to see only the information they need and in the order they want.

Zack wants the Employer table's EmployerID, EmployerName, City, ContactFirstName, ContactLastName, and Website fields to appear in the query results. You'll add each of these fields to the design grid.

### To select the fields for the query, and then run the query:

▸ **1.** Drag **EmployerID** from the Employer field list to the design grid's first column Field text box, and then release the mouse button. See Figure 3-3.

**Field added to the design grid** ◂ **Figure 3-3**

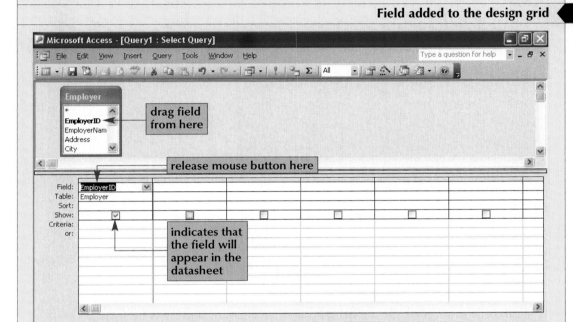

In the design grid's first column, the field name EmployerID appears in the Field text box, the table name Employer appears in the Table text box, and the check mark in the Show check box indicates that the field will be displayed in the datasheet when you run the query. Sometimes you might not want to display a field and its values in the query results. For example, if you are creating a query to show all employers located in Massachusetts, and you assign the name "EmployersInMassachusetts" to the query, you do not need to include the StateProv field value for each record in the query results—every StateProv field value would be "MA" for Massachusetts. Even if you choose not to include a field in the display of the query results, you can still use the field as part of the query to select specific records or to specify a particular sequence for the records in the datasheet.

▸ **2.** Double-click **EmployerName** in the Employer field list. Access adds this field to the second column of the design grid.

▸ **3.** Scrolling the Employer field list as necessary, repeat Step 2 for the **City**, **ContactFirstName**, **ContactLastName**, and **Website** fields to add these fields to the design grid in that order.

**Trouble?** If you double-click the wrong field and accidentally add it to the design grid, you can remove the field from the grid. Select the field's column by clicking the pointer ↓ on the bar above the Field text box for the field you want to delete, and then press the Delete key (or click Edit on the menu bar, and then click Delete Columns).

Having selected the fields for Zack's query, you can now run the query.

4. Click the **Run** button ⏷ on the Query Design toolbar. Access runs the query and displays the results in Datasheet view. See Figure 3-4.

Figure 3-4 **Datasheet displayed after running the query**

The six fields you added to the design grid—EmployerID, EmployerName, City, ContactFirstName, ContactLastName, and Website—appear in the datasheet, and the records are displayed in primary key sequence by EmployerID. Access selected a total of 45 records for display in the datasheet.

Zack asks you to save the query as "EmployerAnalysis" so that he can easily retrieve the same data again.

5. Click the **Save** button 🖫 on the Query Datasheet toolbar. The Save As dialog box opens.

6. Type **EmployerAnalysis** in the Query Name text box, and then press the **Enter** key. Access saves the query with the specified name in the Northeast database and displays the name in the title bar.

When viewing the results of the query, Zack noticed a couple of changes that need to be made to the data in the Employer table. The Adele Bannister House recently developed a Web site, so the Website field for this record needs to be updated. In addition, the contact information has changed for the Alpine Touring Center.

# Updating Data Using a Query

Although a query datasheet is temporary and its contents are based on the criteria in the query design grid, you can update the data in a table using a query datasheet. In this case, Zack has changes he wants you to make to records in the Employer table. Instead of making the changes in the table datasheet, you can make them in the EmployerAnalysis query datasheet. The underlying Employer table will be updated with the changes you make.

### To update data using the EmployerAnalysis query datasheet:

▶ **1.** For the record with EmployerID 10135 (The Adele Bannister House), click the check box in the Website field to place a check mark in it.

▶ **2.** For the record with EmployerID 10152 (Alpine Touring Center), change the ContactFirstName field value to **Mary** and change the ContactLastName field value to **Grant**.

▶ **3.** Click the **Close Window** button ⊠ on the menu bar to close the query. Note that the EmployerAnalysis query appears in the list of queries.

▶ **4.** Click the **Restore Window** button 🗗 on the menu bar to return the Database window to its original size.

Now you will check the Employer table to verify that the changes you made in the query datasheet were also made to the Employer table records.

▶ **5.** Click **Tables** in the Objects bar of the Database window, click **Employer** in the list of tables, and then click the **Open** button. The Employer table datasheet opens.

▶ **6.** For the record with EmployerID 10135, scroll the datasheet to the right to verify that the Website field contains a check mark. For the record with EmployerID 10152, scroll to the right to see the new contact information (Mary Grant).

▶ **7.** Click the **Close** button ⊠ on the Employer table window to close it.

Matt also wants to view specific information in the Northeast database. However, he needs to see data from both the Employer table and the Position table at the same time. To view data from two tables at the same time, you need to define a relationship between the tables.

# Defining Table Relationships

One of the most powerful features of a relational database management system is its ability to define relationships between tables. You use a common field to relate one table to another. The process of relating tables is often called performing a **join**. When you join tables that have a common field, you can extract data from them as if they were one larger table. For example, you can join the Employer and Position tables by using the EmployerID field in both tables as the common field. Then you can use a query, a form, or a report to extract selected data from each table, even though the data is contained in two separate tables, as shown in Figure 3-5. In the Positions query shown in Figure 3-5, the PositionID, PositionTitle, and Wage columns are fields from the Position table, and the EmployerName and StateProv columns are fields from the Employer table. The joining of records is based on the common field of EmployerID. The Employer and Position tables have a type of relationship called a one-to-many relationship.

**Figure 3-5** ▸ **One-to-many relationship and sample query**

## One-to-Many Relationships

A **one-to-many relationship** exists between two tables when one record in the first table matches zero, one, or many records in the second table, and when one record in the second table matches exactly one record in the first table. For example, as shown in Figure 3-5, employers 10126 and 10191 each have two available positions, and employers 10122, 10125, 10190, and 10198 each have one available position. Every position has a single matching employer.

Access refers to the two tables that form a relationship as the primary table and the related table. The **primary table** is the "one" table in a one-to-many relationship; in Figure 3-5, the Employer table is the primary table because there is only one employer for each available position. The **related table** is the "many" table; in Figure 3-5, the Position table is the related table because there can be many positions offered by each employer.

Because related data is stored in two tables, inconsistencies between the tables can occur. Consider the following scenarios:

- Matt adds a position record to the Position table for a new employer, Glen Cove Inn, using EmployerID 10132. Matt did not first add the new employer's information to the Employer table, so this position does not have a matching record in the Employer table. The data is inconsistent, and the position record is considered to be an **orphaned record**.
- Matt changes the EmployerID in the Employer table for BaySide Inn & Country Club from 10126 to 10128. Two orphaned records for employer 10126 now exist in the Position table, and the database is inconsistent.

• Matt deletes the record for Boston Harbor Excursions, employer 10125, in the Employer table because this employer is no longer an NSJI client. The database is again inconsistent; one record for employer 10125 in the Position table has no matching record in the Employer table.

You can avoid these problems by specifying referential integrity between tables when you define their relationships.

## Referential Integrity

**Referential integrity** is a set of rules that Access enforces to maintain consistency between related tables when you update data in a database. Specifically, the referential integrity rules are as follows:

• When you add a record to a related table, a matching record must already exist in the primary table, thereby preventing the possibility of orphaned records.
• If you attempt to change the value of the primary key in the primary table, Access prevents this change if matching records exist in a related table. However, if you choose the **cascade updates option**, Access permits the change in value to the primary key and changes the appropriate foreign key values in the related table, thereby eliminating the possibility of inconsistent data.
• When you attempt to delete a record in the primary table, Access prevents the deletion if matching records exist in a related table. However, if you choose the **cascade deletes option**, Access deletes the record in the primary table and also deletes all records in related tables that have matching foreign key values. Note, however, that you should *rarely* select the cascade deletes option, because setting this option might cause you to inadvertently delete records you did not intend to delete.

Now you'll define a one-to-many relationship between the Employer and Position tables so that you can use fields from both tables to create a query that will retrieve the information Matt needs. You will also define a one-to-many relationship between the NAICS (primary) table and the Employer (related) table.

## Defining a Relationship Between Two Tables

When two tables have a common field, you can define a relationship between them in the Relationships window. The **Relationships window** illustrates the relationships among a database's tables. In this window, you can view or change existing relationships, define new relationships between tables, and rearrange the layout of the tables in the window.

You need to open the Relationships window and define the relationship between the Employer and Position tables. You'll define a one-to-many relationship between the two tables, with Employer as the primary table and Position as the related table, and with EmployerID as the common field (the primary key in the Employer table and a foreign key in the Position table). You'll also define a one-to-many relationship between the NAICS and Employer tables, with NAICS as the primary table and Employer as the related table, and with NAICSCode as the common field (the primary key in the NAICS table and a foreign key in the Employer table).

### To define the one-to-many relationship between the Employer and Position tables:

▶ **1.** Click the **Relationships** button [icon] on the Database toolbar. The Show Table dialog box opens on top of the Relationships window. See Figure 3-6.

| Figure 3-6 | Show Table dialog box |

You must add each table participating in a relationship to the Relationships window.

▶ **2.** Click **Employer** (if necessary), and then click the **Add** button. The Employer field list is added to the Relationships window.

▶ **3.** Click **Position**, and then click the **Add** button. The Position field list is added to the Relationships window.

▶ **4.** Click the **Close** button in the Show Table dialog box to close it and reveal the entire Relationships window.

So that you can view all the fields and complete field names, you'll first move the Position field list box further to the right, and then resize both field list boxes.

▶ **5.** Click the Position field list title bar and drag the list to the right (see Figure 3-7), and then release the mouse button.

▶ **6.** Use the ↔ pointer to drag the right side of each list box to widen it until the complete field names are displayed, and then use the ↕ pointer to drag the bottom of each list box to lengthen it until all the fields are visible. Make sure that both field list boxes no longer contain scroll bars, and that they are sized and positioned similar to those shown in Figure 3-7.

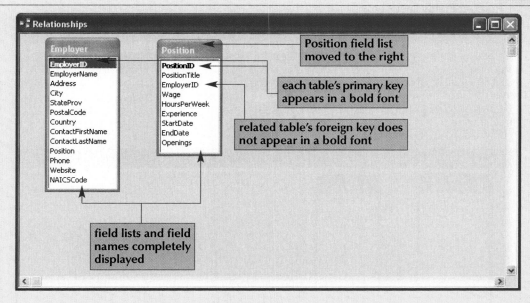

Notice that EmployerID in the Employer table appears in a bold font; this indicates that the field is the table's primary key (the same is true of PositionID in the Position table). On the other hand, the EmployerID field in the Position table is not bold, which is a reminder that this field is the foreign key in this table.

To form the relationship between the two tables, you drag the common field of EmployerID from the primary table to the related table. Then Access opens the Edit Relationships dialog box, in which you select the relationship options for the two tables.

► 7. Click **EmployerID** in the Employer field list, and then drag it to **EmployerID** in the Position field list. When you release the mouse button, the Edit Relationships dialog box opens. See Figure 3-8.

The primary table, related table, and common field appear at the top of the dialog box. The type of relationship, One-To-Many, appears at the bottom of the dialog box. When you click the Enforce Referential Integrity check box, the two cascade options become available. If you select the Cascade Update Related Fields option, Access changes the appropriate foreign key values in the related table when you change a primary key value in the primary table. You will not select the Cascade Delete Related Records option, because doing so could cause you to delete records that you did not want to delete; this option is rarely selected.

▶ **8.** Click the **Enforce Referential Integrity** check box, and then click the **Cascade Update Related Fields** check box.

▶ **9.** Click the **Create** button to define the one-to-many relationship between the two tables and to close the dialog box. The completed relationship appears in the Relationships window. See Figure 3-9.

| Figure 3-9 | Defined relationship in the Relationships window |

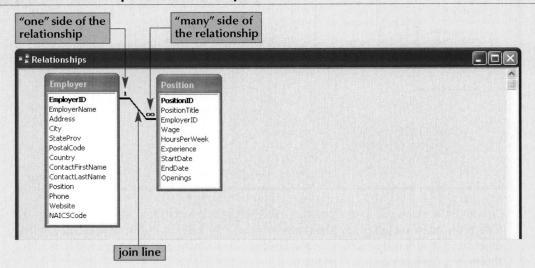

The **join line** connects the EmployerID fields, which are common to the two tables. The common field joins the two tables, which have a one-to-many relationship. The "one" side of the relationship has the digit 1 at its end, and the "many" side of the relationship has the infinity symbol ∞ at its end. The two tables are still separate tables, but you can use the data in them as if they were one table.

Now you need to define the one-to-many relationship between the NAICS and Employer tables. In this relationship, NAICS is the primary ("one") table because there is only one code for each employer. Employer is the related ("many") table because there are multiple employers with the same NAICS code.

### To define the one-to-many relationship between the NAICS and Employer tables:

▶ **1.** Click the **Show Table** button 🔲 on the Relationship toolbar. The Show Table dialog box opens on top of the Relationships window.

▶ **2.** Click **NAICS** in the list of tables, click the **Add** button, and then click the **Close** button to close the Show Table dialog box. The NAICS field list appears in the Relationships window to the right of the Position field list. To make it easier to define the relationship, you'll move the NAICS field list below the Employer and Position field lists.

▶ **3.** Click the NAICS field list title bar and drag the list until it is below the Position table (see Figure 3-10), and then release the mouse button.

Because the NAICS table is the primary table in this relationship, you need to drag the NAICSCode field from the NAICS field list to the Employer field list.

▶ **4.** Click and drag the **NAICSCode** field in the NAICS field list to the **NAICSCode** field in the Employer field list. When you release the mouse button, the Edit Relationships dialog box opens.

▶ **5.** Click the **Enforce Referential Integrity** check box, and then click the **Cascade Update Related Fields** check box.

▶ **6.** Click the **Create** button to define the one-to-many relationship between the two tables and close the dialog box. The completed relationship appears in the Relationships window. See Figure 3-10.

Both relationships defined ◀ **Figure 3-10**

With both relationships defined, you have connected the data among the three tables in the Northeast database.

▶ **7.** Click the **Save** button 🖫 on the Relationship toolbar to save the layout in the Relationships window.

▶ **8.** Click the **Close** button ⊠ on the Relationships window title bar. The Relationships window closes, and you return to the Database window.

You've established relationships among the three tables in the Northeast database, so you can now create queries that let Matt view data from the Employer table and the Position table at the same time.

# Creating a Multi-table Query

Now that you have joined the Employer and Position tables, you can create a query to produce the information Matt wants. To help him determine his recruiting needs, Matt wants a query that displays the EmployerName, City, and StateProv fields from the Employer table and the Openings, PositionTitle, StartDate, and EndDate fields from the Position table.

### To create, run, and save the query using the Employer and Position tables:

▶ 1. Click **Queries** in the Objects bar of the Database window, and then double-click **Create query in Design view**. The Show Table dialog box opens on top of the Query window in Design view.

You need to add the Employer and Position tables to the Query window.

▶ 2. Click **Employer** in the Tables list box (if necessary), click the **Add** button, click **Position**, click the **Add** button, and then click the **Close** button. The Employer and Position field lists appear in the Query window, and the Show Table dialog box closes. Note that the one-to-many relationship between the two tables is shown in the Query window. Also, notice that the join line is thick at both ends; this signifies that you selected the option to enforce referential integrity. If you had not selected this option, the join line would be thin at both ends and neither the "1" nor the infinity symbol would appear, even though there is a one-to-many relationship between the two tables.

You need to place the EmployerName, City, and StateProv fields from the Employer field list into the design grid, and then place the Openings, PositionTitle, StartDate, and EndDate fields from the Position field list into the design grid. This is the order in which Matt wants to view the fields in the query results.

▶ 3. Double-click **EmployerName** in the Employer field list to place EmployerName in the design grid's first column Field text box.

▶ 4. Repeat Step 3 to add the **City** and **StateProv** fields from the Employer table, so that these fields are placed in the second and third columns of the design grid.

▶ 5. Repeat Step 3 to add the **Openings**, **PositionTitle**, **StartDate**, and **EndDate** fields (in that order) from the Position table, so that these fields are placed in the fourth through seventh columns of the design grid.

The query specifications are completed, so you can now run the query.

▶ 6. Click the **Run** button 📭 on the Query Design toolbar. Access runs the query and displays the results in the datasheet.

▶ 7. Click the **Maximize** button 🔲 on the Query window title bar. See Figure 3-11.

**Figure 3-11** ▶ **Datasheet for the query based on the Employer and Position tables**

| Employer Name | City | State/Prov | Openings | Position Title | Start Date | End Date |
|---|---|---|---|---|---|---|
| BeanTown Tours | Boston | MA | 1 | Tour Guide | 05/31/2006 | 10/01/2006 |
| Boston Harbor Excursions | Boston | MA | 1 | Reservationist | 06/01/2006 | 10/01/2006 |
| BaySide Inn & Country Club | Brewster | MA | 2 | Waiter/Waitress | 05/01/2006 | 10/01/2006 |
| BaySide Inn & Country Club | Brewster | MA | 1 | Pro Shop Clerk | 05/01/2006 | 11/01/2006 |
| Seaview Restaurant | Falmouth | MA | 2 | Waiter/Waitress | 06/30/2006 | 10/01/2006 |
| Claire's Cottages | Orleans | MA | 3 | Housekeeping | 05/01/2006 | 10/15/2006 |
| The Inn at Plum Hill | Vineyard Haven | MA | 3 | Housekeeping | 05/15/2006 | 10/15/2006 |
| Capt'n John's Seafood | Orleans | MA | 2 | Kitchen Help | 07/01/2006 | 09/01/2006 |
| The Adele Bannister House | Newport | RI | 1 | Kitchen Help | 06/01/2006 | 10/01/2006 |
| The Adele Bannister House | Newport | RI | 1 | Host/Hostess | 05/01/2006 | 09/01/2006 |
| Blue Hill Inn & Country Club | Chatham | MA | 1 | Lifeguard | 06/15/2006 | 09/15/2006 |
| The Clipper Ship Inn | Rockport | MA | 2 | Kitchen Help | 07/01/2006 | 10/01/2006 |
| The Clipper Ship Inn | Rockport | MA | 2 | Housekeeping | 06/15/2006 | 10/01/2006 |
| The Clipper Ship Inn | Rockport | MA | 3 | Waiter/Waitress | 06/01/2006 | 10/15/2006 |

Only the seven selected fields from the Employer and Position tables appear in the datasheet. The records are displayed in order according to the values in the primary key field, EmployerID, even though this field is not included in the query datasheet.

Matt plans on frequently tracking the data retrieved by the query, so he asks you to save the query as "EmployerPositions."

▶ **8.** Click the **Save** button 🖫 on the Query Datasheet toolbar. The Save As dialog box opens.

▶ **9.** Type **EmployerPositions** in the Query Name text box, and then press the **Enter** key. Access saves the query with the specified name and displays the name in the title bar.

Matt decides he wants the records displayed in alphabetical order by employer name. Because the query displays data in order by the field value of EmployerID, which is the primary key for the Employer table, you need to sort the records by EmployerName to display the data in the order Matt wants.

# Sorting Data in a Query

**Sorting** is the process of rearranging records in a specified order or sequence. Sometimes you might need to sort data before displaying or printing it to meet a specific request. For example, Matt might want to review position information arranged by the StartDate field because he needs to know which positions are available earliest in the year. On the other hand, Elsa might want to view position information arranged by the Openings field for each employer, because she monitors employer activity for NSJI.

When you sort data in a query, you do not change the sequence of the records in the underlying tables. Only the records in the query datasheet are rearranged according to your specifications.

To sort records, you must select the **sort field**, which is the field used to determine the order of records in the datasheet. In this case, Matt wants the data sorted by the employer name, so you need to specify EmployerName as the sort field. Sort fields can be text, number, date/time, currency, AutoNumber, yes/no, or Lookup Wizard fields, but not memo, OLE object, or hyperlink fields. You sort records in either ascending (increasing) or descending (decreasing) order. Figure 3-12 shows the results of each type of sort for different data types.

**Sorting results for different data types** ◀ **Figure 3-12**

| Data Type | Ascending Sort Results | Descending Sort Results |
|---|---|---|
| Text | A to Z | Z to A |
| Number | lowest to highest numeric value | highest to lowest numeric value |
| Date/Time | oldest to most recent date | most recent to oldest date |
| Currency | lowest to highest numeric value | highest to lowest numeric value |
| AutoNumber | lowest to highest numeric value | highest to lowest numeric value |
| Yes/No | yes (check mark in check box) then no values | no then yes values |

Access provides several methods for sorting data in a table or query datasheet and in a form. One method, clicking a toolbar sort button, lets you sort the displayed records quickly.

## Using a Toolbar Button to Sort Data

The **Sort Ascending** and **Sort Descending buttons** on the toolbar allow you to sort records immediately, based on the values in the selected field. First you select the column on which you want to base the sort, and then you click the appropriate sort button on the toolbar to rearrange the records in either ascending or descending order. Unless you save the datasheet or form after you've sorted the records, the rearrangement of records is temporary.

Recall that in Tutorial 1 you used the Sort Ascending button to sort query results by the StateProv field. You'll use this same button to sort the EmployerPositions query results by the EmployerName field.

### To sort the records using a toolbar sort button:

▸ 1. Click any visible EmployerName field value to establish the field as the current field (if necessary).

▸ 2. Click the **Sort Ascending** button ↑↓ on the Query Datasheet toolbar. The records are rearranged in ascending order by employer name. See Figure 3-13.

| Figure 3-13 | **Sorting records on a single field in a datasheet** |

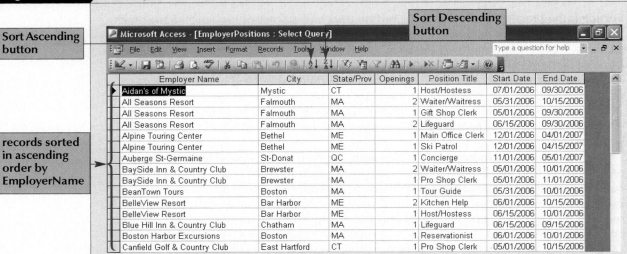

After viewing the query results, Matt decides that he'd prefer to see the records arranged by the value in the PositionTitle field, so that he can identify the types of positions he needs to fill. He also wants to display the records in descending order according to the value of the Openings field, so that he can easily see how many openings there are for each position. In addition, he wants the Openings field values to be displayed in the rightmost column of the query results so that they stand out in the query datasheet. To produce the results Matt wants, you need to sort using two fields.

## Sorting Multiple Fields in Design View

Sort fields can be unique or nonunique. A sort field is **unique** if the value of the sort field for each record is different. The EmployerID field in the Employer table is an example of a unique sort field because each employer record has a different value in this field. A sort field is **nonunique** if more than one record can have the same value for the sort field. For example, the PositionTitle field in the Position table is a nonunique sort field because more than one record can have the same PositionTitle value.

When the sort field is nonunique, records with the same sort field value are grouped together, but they are not in a specific order within the group. To arrange these grouped records in a specific order, you can specify a **secondary sort field**, which is a second field that determines the order of records that are already sorted by the **primary sort field** (the first sort field specified). Note that the primary sort field is *not* the same as a table's primary key field. A table has at most one primary key, which must be unique, whereas any field in a table can serve as a primary sort field.

Access lets you select up to 10 different sort fields. When you use the toolbar sort buttons, the sort fields must be in adjacent columns in the datasheet. You highlight the adjacent columns, and Access sorts first by the first column and then by each remaining highlighted column in order from left to right.

Matt wants the records sorted first by the PositionTitle field and then by the Openings field. The two fields are adjacent, but not in the correct left-to-right order, so you cannot use the toolbar buttons to sort them. You could move the Openings field to the right of the PositionTitle field in the query datasheet. However, you can specify only one type of sort—either ascending or descending—for selected columns in the query datasheet. This is not what Matt wants; he wants the PositionTitle field values to be sorted in ascending alphabetical order and the Openings field values to be sorted in descending order. To accomplish the differing sort orders for the PositionTitle and Openings fields, you must specify the sort fields in Design view.

In the Query window in Design view, Access first uses the sort field that is leftmost in the design grid. Therefore, you must arrange the fields you want to sort from left to right in the design grid, with the primary sort field being the leftmost. In Design view, multiple sort fields do not have to be adjacent to each other, as they do in Datasheet view; however, they must be in the correct left-to-right order.

## Sorting a Query Datasheet

- In the query datasheet, select the column or adjacent columns on which you want to sort.
- Click the Sort Ascending button or the Sort Descending button on the Query Datasheet toolbar.

*or*

- In Design view, position the fields serving as sort fields from left (primary sort field) to right, and then select the sort order for each sort field.

To achieve the results Matt wants, you need to switch to Design view, move the Openings field to the right of the EndDate field, and then specify the sort order for the two fields.

### To select the two sort fields in Design view:

▶ 1. Click the **View** button for Design view ![] on the Query Datasheet toolbar to open the query in Design view.

First, you'll move the Openings field to the right of the EndDate field, because Matt wants the Openings field to be the rightmost column in the query results. Remember, in Design view, the sort fields do not have to be adjacent, and non-sort fields can appear between sort fields. So, you will move the Openings field to the end of the query design, following the EndDate field.

▶ 2. If necessary, click the right arrow in the design grid's horizontal scroll bar a few times to scroll to the right so that both the Openings and EndDate fields are completely visible.

▶ 3. Position the pointer in the Openings field selector until the pointer changes to a ↓ shape, and then click to select the field. See Figure 3-14.

**Figure 3-14** ▶ **Selected Openings field**

**4.** Position the pointer in the Openings field selector, and then click and drag the pointer 🔓 to the right until the vertical line on the right of the EndDate field is highlighted. See Figure 3-15.

**Figure 3-15** ▶ **Dragging the field in the design grid**

**5.** Release the mouse button. The Openings field moves to the right of the EndDate field.

The fields are now in the correct order for the sort. Next, you need to specify an ascending sort order for the PositionTitle field and a descending sort order for the Openings field.

**6.** Click the right side of the **PositionTitle Sort** text box to display the list arrow and the sort options, and then click **Ascending**. You've selected an ascending sort order for the PositionTitle field, which will be the primary sort field. The PositionTitle field is a text field, and an ascending sort order will display the field values in alphabetical order.

**7.** Click the right side of the **Openings Sort** text box, click **Descending**, and then click in one of the empty text boxes to the right of the Openings field to deselect the setting. You've selected a descending sort order for the Openings field, which will be the secondary sort field, because it appears to the right of the primary sort field (PositionTitle) in the design grid. See Figure 3-16.

**Selecting two sort fields in Design view** ◀ **Figure 3-16**

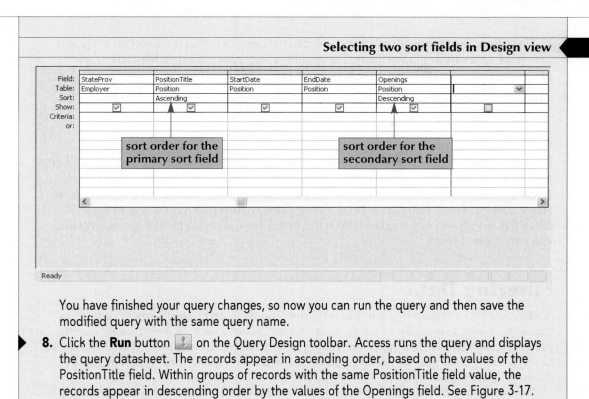

Ready

You have finished your query changes, so now you can run the query and then save the modified query with the same query name.

▶ **8.** Click the **Run** button 🔲 on the Query Design toolbar. Access runs the query and displays the query datasheet. The records appear in ascending order, based on the values of the PositionTitle field. Within groups of records with the same PositionTitle field value, the records appear in descending order by the values of the Openings field. See Figure 3-17.

**Datasheet sorted on two fields** ◀ **Figure 3-17**

When you save the query, all of your design changes—including the selection of the sort fields—are saved with the query. The next time Matt runs the query, the records will appear sorted by the primary and secondary sort fields.

▶ **9.** Click the **Save** button 🖫 on the Query Datasheet toolbar to save the revised EmployerPositions query.

Matt recently spoke with a recruit who is interested in clerk positions that are available in New Hampshire. So, Matt wants to concentrate on records that match those criteria. Selecting only the records with a PositionTitle field value that contains the word "Clerk" and a StateProv field value of "NH" is a temporary change that Matt wants in the datasheet, so you do not need to switch to Design view and change the query. Instead, you can apply a filter.

# Filtering Data

A **filter** is a set of restrictions you place on the records in an open datasheet or form to *temporarily* isolate a subset of the records. A filter lets you view different subsets of displayed records so that you can focus on only the data you need. Unless you save a query or form with a filter applied, an applied filter is not available the next time you run the query or open the form.

The simplest technique for filtering records is Filter By Selection. **Filter By Selection** lets you select all or part of a field value in a datasheet or form, and then display only those records that contain the selected value in the field. Another technique for filtering records is to use **Filter By Form**, which changes your datasheet to display empty fields. Then you can select a value from the list arrow that appears when you click any blank field to apply a filter that selects only those records containing that value.

| Reference Window | **Using Filter By Selection** |
|---|---|

- In the datasheet or form, select all or part of the field value that will be the basis for the filter.
- Click the Filter By Selection button on the toolbar.

For Matt's request, you first need to select just the word "Clerk" in the PositionTitle field, and then use Filter By Selection to display only those query records with this same partial value. Then you will filter the records further by selecting only those records with a value of "NH" in the StateProv field.

### To display the records using Filter By Selection:

▶ **1.** In the query datasheet, locate the first occurrence of a PositionTitle field containing the word "Clerk," and then select **Clerk** in that field value.

▶ **2.** Click the **Filter By Selection** button 🏏 on the Query Datasheet toolbar. Access displays the filtered results. Only the 10 query records that have a PositionTitle field value containing the word "Clerk" appear in the datasheet. The status bar's display (FLTR), the area next to the navigation buttons, and the selected Remove Filter button on the toolbar all indicate that the records have been filtered. See Figure 3-18.

**Using Filter By Selection** | Figure 3-18

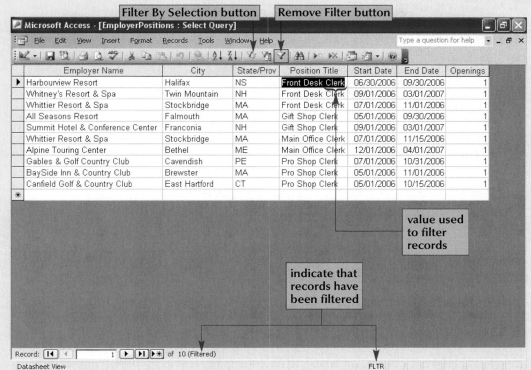

Next, Matt wants to view only those records with a StateProv value of NH, because the recruit is interested in positions in NH only.

▶ **3.** Click in any StateProv field value of **NH**, and then click the **Filter By Selection** button 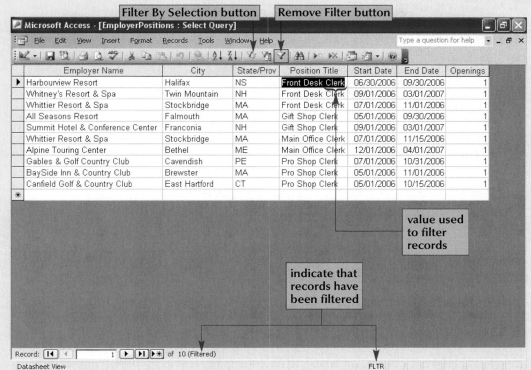 on the Query Datasheet toolbar. The filtered display now shows only the 2 records for clerk positions available in New Hampshire.

Now you can redisplay all the query records by clicking the Remove Filter button; this button works as a toggle to switch between the filtered and nonfiltered displays.

▶ **4.** Click the **Remove Filter** button on the Query Datasheet toolbar. Access redisplays all the records in the query datasheet.

▶ **5.** Click the **Save** button on the Query Datasheet toolbar, and then click the **Close Window** button on the menu bar to save and close the query and return to the Database window.

▶ **6.** Click the **Restore Window** button on the menu bar to return the Database window to its original size.

The queries you've created will help NSJI employees retrieve just the information they want to view. In the next session, you'll continue to create queries to meet their information needs.

# Session 3.1 Quick Check

1. What is a select query?
2. Describe the field list and the design grid in the Query window in Design view.
3. How are a table datasheet and a query datasheet similar? How are they different?
4. The _____ is the "one" table in a one-to-many relationship, and the _____ is the "many" table in the relationship.
5. _____ is a set of rules that Access enforces to maintain consistency between related tables when you update data in a database.
6. For a date/time field, how do the records appear when sorted in ascending order?
7. True or False: When you define multiple sort fields in Design view, the sort fields must be adjacent to each other.
8. A(n) _____ is a set of restrictions you place on the records in an open datasheet or form to isolate a subset of records temporarily.

# Session 3.2

# Defining Record Selection Criteria for Queries

Matt wants to display employer and position information for all positions with a start date of 07/01/2006, so that he can plan his recruitment efforts accordingly. For this request, you could create a query to select the correct fields and all records in the Employer and Position tables, select a StartDate field value of 07/01/2006 in the query datasheet, and then click the Filter By Selection button to filter the query results to display only those positions starting on July 1, 2006. However, a faster way of displaying the data Matt needs is to create a query that displays the selected fields and only those records in the Employer and Position tables that satisfy a condition.

Just as you can display selected fields from a database in a query datasheet, you can display selected records. To tell Access which records you want to select, you must specify a condition as part of the query. A **condition** is a criterion, or rule, that determines which records are selected. To define a condition for a field, you place the condition in the field's Criteria text box in the design grid.

A condition usually consists of an operator, often a comparison operator, and a value. A **comparison operator** asks Access to compare the value in a database field to the condition value and to select all the records for which the relationship is true. For example, the condition >15.00 for the Wage field selects all records in the Position table having Wage field values greater than 15.00. Figure 3-19 shows the Access comparison operators.

**Figure 3-19** ▶ **Access comparison operators**

| Operator | Meaning | Example |
|---|---|---|
| = | equal to (optional; default operator) | ="Hall" |
| < | less than | <#1/1/99# |
| <= | less than or equal to | <=100 |
| > | greater than | >"C400" |
| >= | greater than or equal to | >=18.75 |
| <> | not equal to | <>"Hall" |
| Between ... And... | between two values (inclusive) | Between 50 And 325 |
| In () | in a list of values | In ("Hall", "Seeger") |
| Like | matches a pattern that includes wildcards | Like "706*" |

## Specifying an Exact Match

For Matt's request, you need to create a query that will display only those records in the Position table with the value 07/01/2006 in the StartDate field. This type of condition is called an **exact match** because the value in the specified field must match the condition exactly in order for the record to be included in the query results. You'll use the Simple Query Wizard to create the query, and then you'll specify the exact match condition.

### To create the query using the Simple Query Wizard:

▶ 1. If you took a break after the previous session, make sure that Access is running, the Northeast database is open, and the Queries object is selected in the Database window.

▶ 2. Double-click **Create query by using wizard**. Access opens the first Simple Query Wizard dialog box, in which you select the tables (or queries) and fields for the query.

▶ 3. Click the **Tables/Queries** list arrow, and then click **Table: Position**. The fields in the Position table appear in the Available Fields list box. Except for the PositionID and EmployerID fields, you will include all fields from the Position table in the query.

▶ 4. Click the >> button. All the fields from the Available Fields list box move to the Selected Fields list box.

▶ 5. Scroll up and click **PositionID** in the Selected Fields list box, click the < button to move the PositionID field back to the Available Fields list box, click **EmployerID** in the Selected Fields list box, and then click the < button to move the EmployerID field back to the Available Fields list box.

Matt also wants certain information from the Employer table included in the query results. Because he wants the fields from the Employer table to appear in the query datasheet to the right of the fields from the Position table fields, you need to click the last field in the Selected Fields list box so that the new Employer fields will be inserted below it in the list.

▶ 6. Click **Openings** in the Selected Fields list box.

▶ 7. Click the **Tables/Queries** list arrow, and then click **Table: Employer**. The fields in the Employer table now appear in the Available Fields list box. Notice that the fields you selected from the Position table remain in the Selected Fields list box.

▶ 8. Click **EmployerName** in the Available Fields list box, and then click the > button to move EmployerName to the Selected Fields list box, below the Openings field.

▶ 9. Repeat Step 8 to move the **StateProv**, **ContactFirstName**, **ContactLastName**, and **Phone** fields into the Selected Fields list box. (Note that you can also double-click a field to move it from the Available Fields list box to the Selected Fields list box.)

▶ 10. Click the **Next** button to open the second Simple Query Wizard dialog box, in which you choose whether the query will display records from the selected tables or a summary of those records. Summary options show calculations such as average, minimum, maximum, and so on. Matt wants to view the details for the records, not a summary.

▶ 11. Make sure the **Detail (shows every field of every record)** option button is selected, and then click the **Next** button to open the last Simple Query Wizard dialog box, in which you choose a name for the query and complete the wizard. You need to enter a condition for the query, so you'll want to modify the query's design.

▶ 12. Type **July1Positions**, click the **Modify the query design** option button, and then click the **Finish** button. Access saves the query as July1Positions and opens the query in Design view. See Figure 3-20.

| Figure 3-20 | Query in Design view |
|---|---|

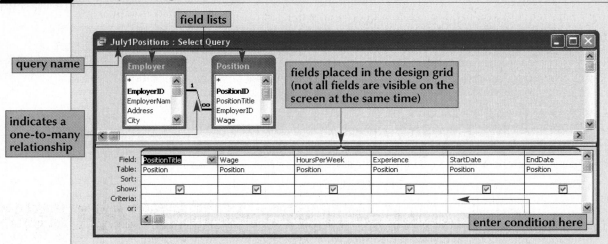

The field lists for the Employer and Position tables appear in the top portion of the window, and the join line indicating a one-to-many relationship connects the two tables. The selected fields appear in the design grid. Not all of the fields are visible in the grid; to see the other selected fields, you need to scroll to the right using the horizontal scroll bar.

To display the information Matt wants, you need to enter the condition for the StartDate field in its Criteria text box. Matt wants to display only those records with a start date of 07/01/2006.

### To enter the exact match condition, and then run the query:

▶ 1. Click the **StartDate Criteria** text box, type **07/01/2006**, and then press the **Enter** key. The condition changes to #7/1/2006#.

Access automatically placed number signs (#) before and after the condition. You must place date and time values inside number signs when using these values as selection criteria. If you omit the number signs, however, Access will include them automatically.

▶ 2. Click the **Run** button on the Query Design toolbar. Access runs the query and displays the selected field values for only those records with a StartDate field value of 07/01/2006. A total of 9 records are selected and displayed in the datasheet. See Figure 3-21.

| Figure 3-21 | Datasheet displaying selected fields and records |
|---|---|

▶ 3. Click the **Save** button on the Query Datasheet toolbar to save the query.

Matt would like to see more fields and records on the screen at one time. He asks you to maximize the datasheet, change the datasheet's font size, and resize all the columns to their best fit.

## Changing a Datasheet's Appearance

You can change the characteristics of a datasheet, including the font type and size of text in the datasheet, to improve its appearance or readability. As you learned in Tutorial 2, you can also resize the datasheet columns to view more columns on the screen at the same time.

You'll maximize the datasheet, change the font size from the default 10 points to 8, and then resize the datasheet columns.

### To change the font size and resize columns in the datasheet:

1. Click the **Maximize** button 🔲 on the Query window title bar.

2. Click **Format** on the menu bar, and then click **Font** to open the Font dialog box.

3. Scroll the Size list box, click **8**, and then click the **OK** button. The font size for the entire datasheet changes to 8.

   Next, you need to resize the columns to their best fit, so that each column is just wide enough to fit the longest value in the column. Instead of resizing each column individually, as you did in Tutorial 2, you'll select all the columns and resize them at the same time.

4. Position the pointer in the PositionTitle field selector. When the pointer changes to a ⬇ shape, click to select the entire column.

5. Click the right arrow on the horizontal scroll bar until the Phone field is fully visible, and then position the pointer in the Phone field selector until the pointer changes to a ⬇ shape.

6. Press and hold the **Shift** key, and then click the mouse button. All the columns are selected. Now you can resize all of them at once.

7. Position the pointer at the right edge of the Phone field selector until the pointer changes to a ⬌ shape. See Figure 3-22.

**Preparing to resize all columns to their best fit** ◄ **Figure 3-22**

8. Double-click the mouse button. All columns are resized to their best fit, which makes each column just large enough to fit the longest *visible* value in the column, including the field name at the top of the column.

9. Scroll to the left, if necessary, so that the PositionTitle field is visible, and then click any field value box (except an Experience field value) to deselect all columns. See Figure 3-23.

| Figure 3-23 | Datasheet after changing font size and column widths |

> **Trouble?** Your screen might show more or fewer columns, depending on the monitor you are using.

▶ **10.** Save and close the query. You return to the Database window.

After viewing the query results, Matt decides that he would like to see the same fields, but only for those records whose Wage field value is equal to or greater than 17.00. He needs this information when he recruits students who require a higher wage per hour for the available positions. To create the query needed to produce these results, you need to use a comparison operator to match a range of values—in this case, any Wage value greater than or equal to 17.00.

## Using a Comparison Operator to Match a Range of Values

Once you create and save a query, you can click the Open button to run it again, or you can click the Design button to change its design. Because the design of the query you need to create next is similar to the July1Positions query, you will change its design, run the query to test it, and then save the query with a new name, which keeps the July1Positions query intact.

### To change the July1Positions query design to create a new query:

▶ **1.** Click the **July1Positions** query in the Database window (if necessary), and then click the **Design** button to open the July1Positions query in Design view.

▶ **2.** Click the **Wage Criteria** text box, type **>=17**, and then press the **Tab** key three times. See Figure 3-24.

| Figure 3-24 | Changing a query's design to create a new query |

Matt's new condition specifies that a record will be selected only if its Wage field value is 17.00 or higher. Before you run the query, you need to delete the condition for the StartDate field.

3. With the StartDate field condition highlighted, press the **Delete** key. Now there is no condition for the StartDate field.

4. Click the **Run** button ![run] on the Query Design toolbar. Access runs the query and displays the selected fields for only those records with a Wage field value greater than or equal to 17.00. A total of 19 records are selected. See Figure 3-25.

| | Running the modified query | Figure 3-25 |

only records with a Wage value greater than or equal to 17.00 are selected

So that Matt can display this information again, as necessary, you'll save the query as HighWageAmounts.

5. Click **File** on the menu bar, and then click **Save As** to open the Save As dialog box.

6. In the text box for the new query name, type **HighWageAmounts**. Notice that the As text box specifies that you are saving the data as a query.

7. Click the **OK** button to save the query using the new name. The new query name appears in the title bar.

8. Close the Query window and return to the Database window.

Elsa asks Matt for a list of the positions with a start date of 07/01/2006 for only the employers in Prince Edward Island. She wants to increase NSJI's business activity throughout eastern Canada (Prince Edward Island in particular), especially in the latter half of the year. To produce this data, you need to create a query containing two conditions—one for the position's start date and another to specify only the employers in Prince Edward Island (PE).

# Defining Multiple Selection Criteria for Queries

Multiple conditions require you to use **logical operators** to combine two or more conditions. When you want a record selected only if two or more conditions are met, you need to use the **And logical operator**. In this case, Elsa wants to see only those records with a StartDate field value of 07/01/2006 *and* a StateProv field value of PE. If you place conditions in separate fields in the *same* Criteria row of the design grid, all conditions in that row must be met in order for a record to be included in the query results. However, if you place conditions in *different* Criteria rows, a record will be selected if at least one of the conditions is met. If none of the conditions is met, Access does not select the record. When you place conditions in different Criteria rows, you are using the **Or logical operator**. Figure 3-26 illustrates the difference between the And and Or logical operators.

**Figure 3-26** **Logical operators And and Or for multiple selection criteria**

## The And Logical Operator

To create Elsa's query, you need to modify the existing July1Positions query to show only the records for employers located in Prince Edward Island and offering positions starting on 07/01/2006. For the modified query, you must add a second condition in the same Criteria row. The existing condition for the StartDate field finds records for positions that start on July 1, 2006; the new condition "PE" in the StateProv field will find records for employers in Prince Edward Island. Because the conditions appear in the same Criteria row, the query will select records only if both conditions are met.

After modifying the query, you'll save it and then rename it as "PEJuly1Positions," overwriting the July1Positions query, which Matt no longer needs.

### To modify the July1Positions query and use the And logical operator:

1. With the Queries object selected in the Database window, click **July1Positions** (if necessary), and then click the **Design** button to open the query in Design view.

2. Scroll the design grid to the right, click the **StateProv Criteria** text box, type **PE**, and then press the ↓ key. See Figure 3-27.

**Query to find positions in PE that start on 07/01/2006**  Figure 3-27

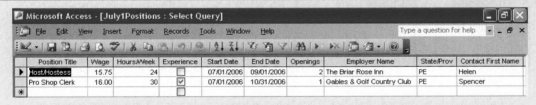

| Field: | StartDate | EndDate | Openings | EmployerName | StateProv | ContactFirstName | Conta |
|---|---|---|---|---|---|---|---|
| Table: | Position | Position | Position | Employer | Employer | Employer | Emplo |
| Sort: | | | | | | | |
| Show: | ☑ | ☑ | ☑ | ☑ | ☑ | ☑ | |
| Criteria: | #7/1/2006# | | | | "PE" | | |
| or: | | | | | | | |

**And logical operator; conditions entered in the same row**

Notice that Access added quotation marks around the entry "PE"; you can type the quotation marks when you enter the condition, but if you forget to do so, Access will add them for you automatically.

The condition for the StartDate field is already entered, so you can run the query.

**3.** Run the query. Access displays in the datasheet only those records that meet both conditions: a StartDate field value of 07/01/2006 and a StateProv field value of PE. Two records are selected. See Figure 3-28.

**Results of query using the And logical operator** ◀ Figure 3-28

Microsoft Access - [July1Positions : Select Query]

File   Edit   View   Insert   Format   Records   Tools   Window   Help          Type a question for help

| Position Title | Wage | Hours/Week | Experience | Start Date | End Date | Openings | Employer Name | State/Prov | Contact First Name |
|---|---|---|---|---|---|---|---|---|---|
| Host/Hostess | 15.75 | 24 | ☐ | 07/01/2006 | 09/01/2006 | 2 | The Briar Rose Inn | PE | Helen |
| Pro Shop Clerk | 16.00 | 30 | ☑ | 07/01/2006 | 10/31/2006 | 1 | Gables & Golf Country Club | PE | Spencer |
| * | | | ☐ | | | | | | |

Now you can save the changes to the query and rename it.

**4.** Save and close the query. You return to the Database window.

**5.** Right-click **July1Positions** in the Queries list box, and then click **Rename** on the shortcut menu.

**6.** Press the **Home** key to position the insertion point to the left of the text "July," type **PE**, and then press the **Enter** key. The query name is now PEJuly1Positions.

Now Elsa can run the PEJuly1Positions query whenever she needs to know which employers in Prince Edward Island are offering positions starting on 07/01/2006.

## Using Multiple Undo and Redo

Access allows you to undo and redo multiple actions when you are working in Design view for tables, queries, forms, reports, and so on. For example, when working in the Query window in Design view, if you specify multiple selection criteria for a query, you can use the multiple undo feature to remove the criteria—even after you run and save the query.

To see how this feature works, you will reopen the PEJuly1Positions query in Design view, delete the two criteria, and then reinsert them using multiple undo.

### To modify the PEJuly1Positions query and use the multiple undo feature:

► **1.** Open the **PEJuly1Positions** query in Design view.

► **2.** Select the StartDate Criteria value, **#7/1/2006#**, and then press the **Delete** key. The StartDate Criteria text box is now empty.

► **3.** Press the **Tab** key four times to move to and select **"PE"**, the StateProv Criteria value, and then press the **Delete** key.

► **4.** Run the query. Notice that the results display all records for the fields specified in the query design grid.

► **5.** Click the **View** button for Design view  on the Query Datasheet toolbar to switch back to Design view.

Now you will use multiple undo to reverse the edits you made and reinsert the two conditions.

► **6.** Click the **list arrow** for the Undo button on the Query Design toolbar. A menu appears listing the actions you can undo. See Figure 3-29.

| Figure 3-29 | Using multiple undo |
| --- | --- |

Two items, both named "Cell Edit," are listed in the Undo list box. These items represent the two changes you made to the query design—first deleting the StartDate condition and then deleting the StateProv condition. If you select an action that is below other items in the list, you will undo all the actions above the one you select, in addition to the one you select. Currently no actions are selected, so the list box indicates "Undo 0 actions."

► **7.** Position the pointer over the second occurrence of **Cell Edit** in the list. Notice that both undo actions are highlighted, and the list box indicates that you can undo two actions.

► **8.** Click the second occurrence of **Cell Edit**. Both actions are "undone," and the two conditions are redisplayed in the query design grid. The multiple undo feature makes it easy for you to test different criteria for a query and, when necessary, to undo your actions based on the query results.

Notice that the Redo button and list arrow are now available. You can redo the actions you've just undone.

► **9.** Click the **list arrow** for the Redo button on the Query Design toolbar. The Redo list box indicates that you can redo the two cell edits.

► **10.** Click the **list arrow** for the Redo button again to close the Redo list box without selecting any option.

► **11.** Close the query. Click the **No** button in the message box that opens, asking if you want to save your changes. You return to the Database window.

Matt has another request for information. He knows that it can be difficult to find student recruits for positions that offer fewer than 30 hours of work per week or that require prior work experience. So that his staff can focus on such positions, Matt wants to see a list of those positions that provide less than 30 hours of work or that require experience. To create this query, you need to use the Or logical operator.

## The Or Logical Operator

For Matt's request, you need a query that selects a record when either one of two conditions is satisfied or when both conditions are satisfied. That is, a record is selected if the HoursPerWeek field value is less than 30 *or* if the Experience field value is "Yes" (checked). You will enter the condition for the HoursPerWeek field in the Criteria row and the condition for the Experience field in the "or" criteria row, thereby using the Or logical operator.

To display the information Matt wants to view, you'll create a new query containing the EmployerName and City fields from the Employer table and the PositionTitle, HoursPerWeek, and Experience fields from the Position table. Then you'll specify the conditions using the Or logical operator.

### To create the query and use the Or logical operator:

▶ **1.** In the Database window, double-click **Create query in Design view**. The Show Table dialog box opens on top of the Query window in Design view.

▶ **2.** Click **Employer** in the Tables list box (if necessary), click the **Add** button, click **Position**, click the **Add** button, and then click the **Close** button. The Employer and Position field lists appear in the Query window, and the Show Table dialog box closes.

▶ **3.** Double-click **EmployerName** in the Employer field list to add the EmployerName field to the design grid's first column Field text box.

▶ **4.** Repeat Step 3 to add the **City** field from the Employer table, and then add the **PositionTitle**, **HoursPerWeek**, and **Experience** fields from the Position table.

Now you need to specify the first condition, <30, in the HoursPerWeek field.

▶ **5.** Click the **HoursPerWeek Criteria** text box, type **<30** and then press the **Tab** key.

Because you want records selected if either of the conditions for the HoursPerWeek or Experience fields is satisfied, you must enter the condition for the Experience field in the "or" row of the design grid.

▶ **6.** Press the ↓ key, and then type **Yes** in the "or" text box for Experience. See Figure 3-30.

**Query window with the Or logical operator** ◀ **Figure 3-30**

| Field: | EmployerName | City | PositionTitle | HoursPerWeek | Experience | | |
|---|---|---|---|---|---|---|---|
| Table: | Employer | Employer | Position | Position | Position | | |
| Sort: | | | | | | | |
| Show: | ☑ | ☑ | ☑ | ☑ | ☑ | ☐ | |
| Criteria: | | | | <30 | | | |
| or: | | | | | Yes | | |

Or logical operator; conditions entered in different rows

▶ **7.** Run the query. Access displays only those records that meet either condition: an HoursPerWeek field value less than 30 or an Experience field value of "Yes" (checked). A total of 35 records are selected.

Matt wants the list displayed in alphabetical order by EmployerName. The first record's EmployerName field is highlighted, indicating the current field.

▶ **8.** Click the **Sort Ascending** button 🔼 on the Query Datasheet toolbar.

▶ **9.** Resize all datasheet columns to their best fit. Scroll through the entire datasheet to make sure that all values are completely displayed. Deselect all columns when you are finished resizing them, and then return to the top of the datasheet. See Figure 3-31.

**Figure 3-31** ▶ **Results of query using the Or logical operator**

▶ **10.** Save the query with the name **HoursOrExperience**, and then close the query.

Next, Elsa wants to use the Northeast database to perform calculations. She is considering offering a 2% bonus per week to the student recruits in higher paid positions, based on employer recommendation, and she wants to know exactly what these bonuses would be.

# Performing Calculations

In addition to using queries to retrieve, sort, and filter data in a database, you can use a query to perform calculations. To perform a calculation, you define an **expression** containing a combination of database fields, constants, and operators. For numeric expressions, the data types of the database fields must be number, currency, or date/time; the constants are numbers such as .02 (for the 2% bonus); and the operators can be arithmetic operators (+ − * /) or other specialized operators. In complex expressions, you can enclose calculations in parentheses to indicate which one should be performed first. In expressions without parentheses, Access calculates in the following order of precedence: multiplication and division before addition and subtraction. When operators have equal precedence, Access calculates them in order from left to right.

To perform a calculation in a query, you add a calculated field to the query. A **calculated field** is a field that displays the results of an expression. A calculated field appears in a query datasheet or in a form or report; however, it does not exist in a database. When you run a query that contains a calculated field, Access evaluates the expression defined by the calculated field and displays the resulting value in the query datasheet, form, or report.

## Creating a Calculated Field

To produce the information Elsa wants, you need to open the HighWageAmounts query and create a calculated field that will multiply each Wage field value by each HoursPerWeek value, and then multiply that amount by .02 to determine the 2% weekly bonus Elsa is considering.

To enter an expression for a calculated field, you can type it directly in a Field text box in the design grid. Alternately, you can open the Zoom box or Expression Builder and use either one to enter the expression. The **Zoom box** is a large text box for entering text, expressions, or other values. To use the Zoom box, however, you must know all the parts of the expression you want to create. **Expression Builder** is an Access tool that makes it easy for you to create an expression; it contains a box for entering the expression, buttons for common operators, and one or more lists of expression elements, such as table and field names. Unlike a Field text box, which is too small to show an entire expression at one time, the Zoom box and Expression Builder are large enough to display lengthy expressions. In most cases, Expression Builder provides the easiest way to enter expressions, because you don't have to know all the parts of the expression; you can choose the necessary elements from the Expression Builder dialog box.

---

### Using Expression Builder

Reference Window

- Open the query in Design view.
- In the design grid, position the insertion point in the Field text box of the field for which you want to create an expression.
- Click the Build button on the Query Design toolbar.
- Use the expression elements and common operators to build the expression, or type the expression directly.
- Click the OK button.

---

You'll begin by copying, pasting, and renaming the HighWageAmounts query, keeping the original query intact. You'll name the new query "HighWagesWithBonus." Then you'll modify this query in Design view to show only the information Elsa wants to view.

### To copy the HighWageAmounts query and paste the copy with a new name:

1. Right-click the **HighWageAmounts** query in the list of queries, and then click **Copy** on the shortcut menu.

2. Right-click an empty area of the Database window, and then click **Paste** on the shortcut menu. The Paste As dialog box opens.

3. Type **HighWagesWithBonus** in the Query Name text box, and then press the **Enter** key. The new query appears in the query list, along with the original HighWageAmounts query.

Now you're ready to modify the HighWagesWithBonus query to create the calculated field for Elsa.

## To modify the HighWagesWithBonus query:

▶ **1.** Open the **HighWagesWithBonus** query in Design view.

Elsa wants to see only the EmployerName, PositionTitle, and Wage fields in the query results. First, you'll delete the unnecessary fields, and then you'll move the EmployerName field so that it appears first in the query results.

▶ **2.** Scroll the design grid to the right until the HoursPerWeek and EmployerName fields are visible at the same time.

▶ **3.** Position the pointer on the HoursPerWeek field selector until the pointer changes to a ⬇ shape, click and hold down the mouse button, drag the mouse to the right to highlight the HoursPerWeek, Experience, StartDate, EndDate, and Openings fields, and then release the mouse button.

▶ **4.** Press the **Delete** key to delete the five selected fields.

▶ **5.** Use this same method to delete the StateProv, ContactFirstName, ContactLastName, and Phone fields from the query design grid.

Next, you'll move the EmployerName field to the left of the PositionTitle field so that the Wage values will appear next to the calculated field values in the query results.

▶ **6.** Scroll the design grid back to the left (if necessary), select the **EmployerName** field, and then use the pointer ▷ to drag the field to the left of the PositionTitle field. See Figure 3-32.

**Figure 3-32** ▶ **Modified query before adding the calculated field**

Now you're ready to use Expression Builder to enter the calculated field in the HighWagesWithBonus query.

## To add the calculated field to the HighWagesWithBonus query:

▶ **1.** Position the insertion point in the blank Field text box to the right of the Wage field, and then click the **Build** button ⚒ on the Query Design toolbar. The Expression Builder dialog box opens. See Figure 3-33.

Initial Expression Builder dialog box ▶ **Figure 3-33**

You use the common operators and expression elements to help you build an expression. Note that the HighWagesWithBonus query is already selected in the list box on the lower left; the fields included in the original version of the query are listed in the center box.

The expression for the calculated field will multiply the Wage field values by the HoursPerWeek field values, and then multiply that amount by the numeric constant .02 (which represents a 2% bonus). To include a field in the expression, you select the field and then click the Paste button. To include a numeric constant, you simply type the constant in the expression.

▶ **2.** Click **Wage** in the field list, and then click the **Paste** button. [Wage] appears in the expression box.

To include the multiplication operator in the expression, you click the asterisk (**\***) button. Note that you do not include spaces between the elements in an expression.

▶ **3.** Click the **\*** button in the row of common operators, click **HoursPerWeek** in the field list, and then click the **Paste** button. The expression multiplies the Wage values by the HoursPerWeek values.

▶ **4.** Click the **\*** button in the row of common operators, and then type **.02**. You have finished entering the expression. See Figure 3-34.

Completed expression for the calculated field ▶ **Figure 3-34**

Note that you also could have typed the expression directly into the expression box, instead of clicking the field names and the operator.

> **5.** Click the **OK** button. Access closes the Expression Builder dialog box and adds the expression to the design grid in the Field text box for the calculated field.
>
> Next, you need to specify a name for the calculated field as it will appear in the query results.
>
> **6.** Press the **Home** key to position the insertion point to the left of the expression.
>
> You'll enter the name WeeklyBonus, which is descriptive of the field's contents; then you'll run the query.
>
> **7.** Type **WeeklyBonus:**. *Make sure you include the colon following the field name.* The colon is needed to separate the field name from its expression.
>
> **8.** Run the query. Access displays the query datasheet, which contains the three specified fields and the calculated field with the name "WeeklyBonus." Resize all datasheet columns to their best fit. See Figure 3-35.

**Figure 3-35** | **Datasheet displaying the calculated field**

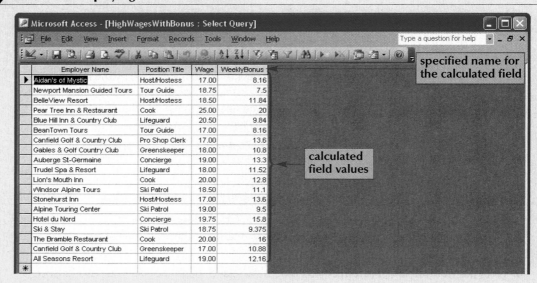

> **Trouble?** If the calculated field name does not appear correctly, as shown in Figure 3-35, you might not have included the required colon. Switch to Design view, then repeat Steps 7 and 8, making sure that you type the colon following the field name, to separate it from the calculated field's expression.

Notice the WeeklyBonus value for Ski & Stay; the value appears with three decimal places (9.375). Currency values should have only two decimal places, so you need to format the WeeklyBonus calculated field so that all values appear in the Fixed format with two decimal places. You'll also set the Caption property for the calculated field so that it is displayed in the same way as other field names, with a space between words.

## To format the calculated field:

> **1.** Switch to Design view.
>
> **2.** Right-click the **WeeklyBonus** calculated field in the design grid to open the shortcut menu, and then click **Properties**. The property sheet for the selected field opens. The property sheet for a field provides options for changing the display of field values in the datasheet.

3. Click the right side of the **Format** text box to display the list of formats, and then click **Fixed**. This format specifies no commas or dollar signs, which are unnecessary for the calculated field and would only clutter the worksheet.

4. Click the right side of the **Decimal Places** text box, and then click **2**.

5. Press the **Tab** key twice to move to the Caption property, and then type **Weekly Bonus**. See Figure 3-36.

**Property sheet settings to format the calculated field** ◄ **Figure 3-36**

Now that you have formatted the calculated field, you can run the query.

6. Close the Field Properties window, and then save and run the query. The calculated field now displays the name "Weekly Bonus," and the value for Ski & Stay now correctly appears as 9.38.

7. Close the query.

Elsa prepares a report on a regular basis that includes a summary of information about the wages paid to student recruits. She lists the minimum hourly wage paid, the average wage amount, and the maximum hourly wage paid. She asks you to create a query to determine these statistics from data in the Position table.

## Using Aggregate Functions

You can calculate statistical information, such as totals and averages, on the records selected by a query. To do this, you use the Access aggregate functions. **Aggregate functions** perform arithmetic operations on selected records in a database. Figure 3-37 lists the most frequently used aggregate functions. Aggregate functions operate on the records that meet a query's selection criteria. You specify an aggregate function for a specific field, and the appropriate operation applies to that field's values for the selected records.

| Figure 3-37 | Frequently used aggregate functions |
| --- | --- |

| Aggregate Function | Determines | Data Types Supported |
| --- | --- | --- |
| Avg | Average of the field values for the selected records | AutoNumber, Currency, Date/Time, Number |
| Count | Number of records selected | AutoNumber, Currency, Date/Time, Memo, Number, OLE Object, Text, Yes/No |
| Max | Highest field value for the selected records | AutoNumber, Currency, Date/Time, Number, Text |
| Min | Lowest field value for the selected records | AutoNumber, Currency, Date/Time, Number, Text |
| Sum | Total of the field values for the selected records | AutoNumber, Currency, Date/TIme, Number |

To display the minimum, average, and maximum of all the wage amounts in the Position table, you will use the Min, Avg, and Max aggregate functions for the Wage field.

### To calculate the minimum, average, and maximum of all wage amounts:

1. Double-click **Create query in Design view**, click **Position**, click the **Add** button, and then click the **Close** button. The Position field list is added to the Query window, and the Show Table dialog box closes.

   To perform the three calculations on the Wage field, you need to add the field to the design grid three times.

2. Double-click **Wage** in the Position field list three times to add three copies of the field to the design grid.

   You need to select an aggregate function for each Wage field. When you click the Totals button on the Query Design toolbar, a row labeled "Total" is added to the design grid. The Total row provides a list of the aggregate functions that you can select.

3. Click the **Totals** button Σ on the Query Design toolbar. A new row labeled "Total" appears between the Table and Sort rows in the design grid. See Figure 3-38.

| Figure 3-38 | Total row inserted in the design grid |
| --- | --- |

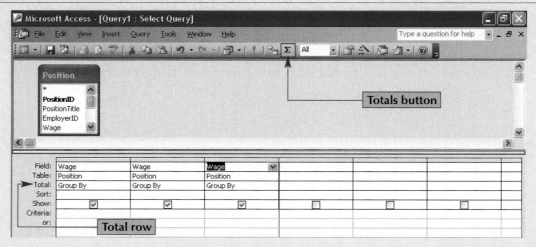

In the Total row, you specify the aggregate function you want to use for a field.

▶ **4.** Click the right side of the first column's **Total** text box, and then click **Min**. This field will calculate the minimum amount of all the Wage field values.

When you run the query, Access automatically will assign a datasheet column name of "MinOfWage" for this field. You can change the datasheet column name to a more descriptive or readable name by entering the name you want in the Field text box. However, you must also keep the field name Wage in the Field text box, because it identifies the field whose values will be calculated. The Field text box will contain the datasheet column name you specify followed by the field name (Wage) with a colon separating the two names.

▶ **5.** Position the insertion point to the left of Wage in the first column's Field text box, and then type **Minimum Wage:**. *Be sure that you type the colon following the name.*

▶ **6.** Click the right side of the second column's **Total** text box, and then click **Avg**. This field will calculate the average of all the Wage field values.

▶ **7.** Position the insertion point to the left of Wage in the second column's Field text box, and then type **Average Wage:**.

▶ **8.** Click the right side of the third column's **Total** text box, and then click **Max**. This field will calculate the maximum amount of all the Wage field values.

▶ **9.** Position the insertion point to the left of Wage in the third column's Field text box, and then type **Maximum Wage:**.

The query design is completed, so you can run the query.

▶ **10.** Run the query. Access displays one record containing the three aggregate function values. The single row of summary statistics represents calculations based on the 64 records selected by the query.

You need to resize the three columns to their best fit to see the column names.

▶ **11.** Resize all columns to their best fit, and then position the insertion point in the field value in the first column. See Figure 3-39.

**Results of the query using aggregate functions** ◀  **Figure 3-39**

▶ **12.** Save the query as **WageStatistics**, and then close the query.

Elsa also wants her report to include the same wage statistics (minimum, average, and maximum) for each type of position. She asks you to display the wage statistics for each different PositionTitle value in the Position table.

## Using Record Group Calculations

In addition to calculating statistical information on all or selected records in selected tables, you can calculate statistics for groups of records. For example, you can determine the number of employers in each state or province, or the average wage amount by position.

To create a query for Elsa's latest request, you can modify the current query by adding the PositionTitle field and assigning the Group By operator to it. The **Group By operator** divides the selected records into groups based on the values in the specified field. Those records with the same value for the field are grouped together, and the datasheet displays one record for each group. Aggregate functions, which appear in the other columns of the design grid, provide statistical information for each group.

You need to modify the current query to add the Group By operator for the PositionTitle field. This will display the statistical information grouped by position for the 64 selected records in the query. As you did earlier, you will copy the WageStatistics query and paste it with a new name, keeping the original query intact, to create the new query.

### To copy and paste the query, and then add the PositionTitle field with the Group By operator:

▶ 1. Right-click the **WageStatistics** query in the list of queries, and then click **Copy** on the shortcut menu.

▶ 2. Right-click an empty area of the Database window, and then click **Paste** on the shortcut menu.

▶ 3. Type **WageStatisticsByPosition** in the Query Name text box, and then press the **Enter** key.

   Now you're ready to modify the query design.

▶ 4. Open the **WageStatisticsByPosition** query in Design view.

▶ 5. Double-click **PositionTitle** in the Position field list to add the field to the design grid. Group By, which is the default option in the Total row, appears for the PositionTitle field.

   You've completed the query changes, so you can run the query.

▶ 6. Run the query. Access displays 16 records—one for each PositionTitle group. Each record contains the three aggregate function values and the PositionTitle field value for the group. Again, the summary statistics represent calculations based on the 64 records selected by the query. See Figure 3-40.

| Figure 3-40 | **Aggregate functions grouped by PositionTitle** |

▶ 7. Save and close the query, and then close the Northeast database.

   **Trouble?** If a dialog box opens and asks if you want to empty the Clipboard, click the Yes button.

The queries you've created and saved will help Elsa, Zack, Matt, and other employees to monitor and analyze the business activity of NSJI's employer customers. Now any NSJI staff member can run the queries at any time, modify them as needed, or use them as the basis for designing new queries to meet additional information requirements.

## Session 3.2 Quick Check

Review

1. A(n) _____ is a criterion, or rule, that determines which records are selected for a query datasheet.
2. In the design grid, where do you place the conditions for two different fields when you use the And logical operator? The Or logical operator?
3. To perform a calculation in a query, you define a(n) _____ containing a combination of database fields, constants, and operators.
4. How does a calculated field differ from a table field?
5. What is an aggregate function?
6. The _____ operator divides selected records into groups based on the values in a field.

## Tutorial Summary

Review

In this tutorial, you learned how to create queries in Design view, and how to run and save queries. You also learned how you can use the query datasheet to update the data contained in the underlying database table. This tutorial presented one of the most important database concepts—defining table relationships. You learned how to define a one-to-many relationship between two tables in a database, and how to enforce referential integrity as part of the relationship. After defining this relationship, you created a query based on data in the two tables. You learned how to sort and filter query results to view records in a particular order and to view different subsets of the displayed records. Using record selection criteria, you specified an exact match in a query, used a comparison operator to match a range of values, and used the And and Or logical operators to meet various requests for data retrieval. Finally, you created a calculated field in the Expression Builder dialog box to display the results of an expression in a query, and you used aggregate functions and the Group By operator to calculate and display statistical information in a query.

## Key Terms

| | | |
|---|---|---|
| aggregate function | Filter By Form | recordset |
| And logical operator | Filter By Selection | referential integrity |
| calculated field | Group By operator | related table |
| cascade deletes option | join | Relationships window |
| cascade updates option | join line | run (query) |
| comparison operator | logical operator | secondary sort field |
| condition | nonunique sort field | select query |
| design grid | one-to-many relationship | sort |
| exact match | Or logical operator | Sort Ascending button |
| expression | orphaned record | Sort Descending button |
| Expression Builder | primary sort field | sort field |
| field list | primary table | unique sort field |
| filter | query by example (QBE) | Zoom box |

**Practice**

*Build on what you learned in the tutorial by practicing those skills using the same case scenario.*

# Review Assignments

**Data File needed for the Review Assignments: Recruits.mdb (*cont. from Tutorial 2*)**

Elsa needs information from the Recruits database, and she asks you to query the database by completing the following:

1. Open the **Recruits** database located in the Brief\Review folder provided with your Data Files.

2. Create a select query based on the **Student** table. Display the StudentID, FirstName, and LastName fields in the query results; sort in ascending order based on the LastName field values; and select only those records whose Nation value equals Ireland. (*Hint*: Do not display the Nation field values in the query results.) Save the query as **StudentsFromIreland**, run the query, and then print the query datasheet.

3. Use the **StudentsFromIreland** datasheet to update the **Student** table by changing the FirstName field value for StudentID OMA9956 to Richard. Print the query datasheet, and then close the query.

4. Define a one-to-many relationship between the primary **Recruiter** table and the related **Student** table. Resize the field lists, as necessary, to display all the field names. Select the referential integrity option and the cascade updates option for the relationship.

5. Use Design view to create a select query based on the **Recruiter** and **Student** tables. Select the fields FirstName, LastName, City, and Nation from the **Student** table, and the fields BonusQuota, Salary, and SSN from the **Recruiter** table, in that order. Sort in ascending order based on the Nation field values. Select only those records whose SSN equals "977-07-1798." (*Hint*: Do not display the SSN field values in the query results.) Save the query as **WolfeRecruits**, and then run the query. Resize all columns in the datasheet to fit the data. Print the datasheet, and then save and close the query.

6. Use Design view to create a query based on the **Recruiter** table that shows all recruiters with a BonusQuota field value between 40 and 50, and whose Salary field value is greater than 35000. (*Hint*: Refer to Figure 3-19 to determine the correct comparison operator to use.) Display all fields except SSN from the **Recruiter** table. Save the query as **BonusInfo**, and then run the query.

7. Switch to Design view for the **BonusInfo** query. Create a calculated field named RaiseAmt that displays the net amount of a 3% raise to the Salary values. The expression for the calculated field will begin with the Salary field, and add to it the result of multiplying the Salary field by .03. Display the results in descending order by RaiseAmt. Save the query as a new query named **SalariesWithRaises**, and then run the query.

8. Switch to Design view for the **SalariesWithRaises** query, and then change the format of the calculated field to the Standard format, with no decimal places. Also change the caption property of the calculated field to "Raise Amt." Run the query. Resize all columns in the datasheet to fit the data, print the query datasheet, and then save and close the query.

9. In the Database window, copy the **StudentsFromIreland** query, and then paste it with the new name **StudentsFromHollandPlusYoungerStudents**. Open the new query in Design view. Modify the query to display only those records with a Nation field value of Holland or with a BirthDate field value greater than 1/1/85. Also, modify the query to include the Nation field values in the query results. Save and run the query. Resize all columns in the datasheet to fit the data, print the query datasheet, and then save and close the query.

10. Create a new query based on the **Recruiter** table. Use the Min, Max, and Avg aggregate functions to find the lowest, highest, and average values in the Salary field. Name the three aggregate fields Lowest Salary, Highest Salary, and Average Salary, respectively. Save the query as **SalaryStatistics**, and then run the query. Resize all columns in the datasheet to fit the data, print the query datasheet, and then save and close the query.

11. Open the **SalaryStatistics** query in Design view. Modify the query so that the records are grouped by the BonusQuota field. Save the query as **SalaryStatisticsByBonusQuota**, run the query, print the query datasheet, and then close the query.

12. Close the Recruits database.

# Case Problem 1

**Data File needed for this Case Problem: Videos.mdb (*cont. from Tutorial 2*)**

***Lim's Video Photography*** Youngho Lim wants to view specific information about his clients and video shoot events. He asks you to query the Videos database by completing the following:

1. Open the **Videos** database located in the Brief\Case1 folder provided with your Data Files.

2. Define the necessary one-to-many relationships between the database tables, as follows: between the primary **Client** table and the related **Contract** table, between the primary **Contract** table and the related **Shoot** table, and between the primary **ShootDesc** table and the related **Shoot** table. (*Hint*: Add all four tables to the Relationships window, and then define the three relationships.) Resize the field lists, as necessary, to display all the field names. Select the referential integrity option and the cascade updates option for each relationship.

3. Create a select query based on the **Client** and **Contract** tables. Display the ClientName, City, ContractDate, and ContractAmt fields, in that order. Sort in ascending order based on the ClientName field values. Run the query, save the query as **ClientContracts**, and then print the datasheet.

4. Use Filter By Selection to display only those records with a City field value of Oakland in the **ClientContracts** datasheet. Print the datasheet and then remove the filter. Save and close the query.

5. Open the **ClientContracts** query in Design view. Modify the query to display only those records with a ContractAmt value greater than or equal to 600. Run the query, save the query as **ContractAmounts**, and then print the datasheet.

6. Switch to Design view for the **ContractAmounts** query. Modify the query to display only those records with a ContractAmt value greater than or equal to 600 and with a City value of San Francisco. Also modify the query so that the City field values are not displayed in the query results. Run the query, save it as **SFContractAmounts**, print the datasheet, and then close the query.

7. Close the Videos database.

**Create**

*Follow the steps provided and use the figures as guides to create queries for an e-commerce company in the food services industry.*

# Case Problem 2

**Data File needed for this Case Problem: Meals.mdb (*cont. from Tutorial 2*)**

***DineAtHome.course.com*** Claire Picard is completing an analysis of the orders placed at restaurants that use her company's services. To help her find the information she needs, you'll query the Meals database by completing the following:

1. Open the **Meals** database located in the Brief\Case2 folder provided with your Data Files.
2. Define a one-to-many relationship between the primary **Restaurant** table and the related **Order** table. Resize the field lists, as necessary, to display all the field names. Select the referential integrity option and the cascade updates option for the relationship.
3. Use Design view to create a select query based on the **Restaurant** and **Order** tables. Display the fields RestaurantName, City, OrderAmt, and OrderDate, in that order. Sort in descending order based on the OrderAmt field values. Select only those records whose OrderAmt value is greater than 150. Save the query as **LargeOrders**, and then run the query.
4. Use the **LargeOrders** datasheet to update the **Order** table by changing the OrderAmt value for the first record in the datasheet to 240.25. Print the datasheet, and then close the query.
5. Use Design view to create a select query based on the **Restaurant** and **Order** tables. For all orders placed on 03/21/2006, display the OrderID, OrderAmt, OrderDate, and RestaurantName fields. Save the query as **March21Orders**, and then run the query. Switch to Design view, modify the query so that the OrderDate values do not appear in the query results, and then save the modified query. Run the query, print the query results, and then close the query.
6. Create and save the query whose results are shown in Figure 3-41. Print the query datasheet, and then close the query.

**Figure 3-41**

show only records that are located in Naples and have a Web site

7. Create and save the query whose results are shown in Figure 3-42. Print the query datasheet, and then close the query.

**Figure 3-42**

primary sort field

secondary sort field

show only orders placed on 3/14/2006 or 3/15/2006

8. Create and save the query whose results are shown in Figure 3-43 to display statistics for the OrderAmt field. Print the query datasheet.

**Figure 3-43**

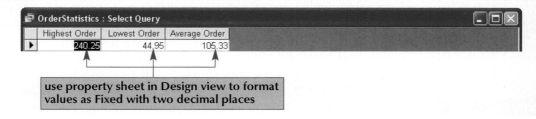

use property sheet in Design view to format values as Fixed with two decimal places

9. Change the query to display the same statistics grouped by RestaurantName. (*Hint*: Use the Show Table button on the Query Design toolbar to add the **Restaurant** table to the query.) Save the query as **OrderStatisticsByRestaurant**. Run the query, print the query results, and then close the query.
10. Close the Meals database.

**Challenge**

*Use the skills you learned in the tutorial, plus some new ones, to create queries that display information about a zoo and its patrons.*

**Explore**

# Case Problem 3

**Data File needed for this Case Problem: Redwood.mdb (*cont. from Tutorial 2*)**

***Redwood Zoo*** Michael Rosenfeld wants to find specific information about the donors and their pledge amounts for the Redwood Zoo. You'll help him find the information in the Redwood database by completing the following:

1. Open the **Redwood** database located in the Brief\Case3 folder provided with your Data Files.
2. Define the necessary one-to-many relationships between the database tables, as follows: between the primary **Donor** table and the related **Pledge** table, and between the primary **Fund** table and the related **Pledge** table. (*Hint*: Add all three tables to the Relationships window, and then define the two relationships.) Resize the field lists, as necessary, to display all the field names. Select the referential integrity option and the cascade updates option for each relationship.
3. Use Design view to create a select query that, for all pledges with a TotalPledged field value of greater than 200, displays the DonorID (from the **Donor** table), FirstName, LastName, PledgeID, TotalPledged, and FundName fields. Sort the query in ascending order by TotalPledged. Save the query as **LargePledges**, and then run the query.
4. Use the **LargePledges** datasheet to update the **Pledge** table by changing the TotalPledged field value for PledgeID 2976 to 750. Print the query datasheet, and then close the query.
5. Use Design view to create a select query that, for all donors who pledged less than $150 or who donated to the Whale Watchers fund, displays the PledgeID, PledgeDate, TotalPledged, FirstName, and LastName fields. Save the query as **PledgedOrWhaleWatchers**, run the query, and then print the query datasheet. Change the query to select all donors who pledged less than $150 and who donated to the Whale Watchers fund. Save the revised query as **PledgedAndWhaleWatchers**, and then run the query. Close the query.

**Explore**

6. Use Design view to create a select query that displays the DonorID (from the **Donor** table), TotalPledged, PaymentMethod, PledgeDate, and FundName fields. Save the query as **PledgesAfterCosts**. Create a calculated field named Overhead that displays the results of multiplying the TotalPledged field values by 15% (to account for overhead costs). Save the query, and then create a second calculated field named NetPledge that displays the results of subtracting the Overhead field values from the TotalPledged field values. Format the calculated fields as Fixed and set an appropriate caption for the NetPledge field. Display the results in ascending order by TotalPledged. Save the modified query, and then run the query. Resize all datasheet columns to their best fit, print the query results, and then save and close the query.

**Explore**

7. Use the **Pledge** table to display the sum, average, and count of the TotalPledged field for all pledges. Then do the following:
   a. Specify column names of Total Pledge, Average Pledge, and Number of Pledges.
   b. Change properties so that the values in the Total Pledge and Average Pledge columns display two decimal places and the Fixed format.
   c. Save the query as **PledgeStatistics**, run the query, resize all datasheet columns to their best fit, and then print the query datasheet. Save the query.
   d. Change the query to display the sum, average, and count of the TotalPledged field for all pledges by FundName. (*Hint:* Use the Show Table button on the Query Design toolbar to add the **Fund** table to the query.) Save the query as **PledgeStatisticsByFund**, run the query, print the query datasheet, and then close the query.

8. Close the Redwood database.

**Challenge**

*Challenge yourself by creating queries, including a new type of query, for an outdoor adventure company.*

# Case Problem 4

**Data File needed for this Case Problem: Trips.mdb** (*cont. from Tutorial 2*)

***Mountain River Adventures*** Connor and Siobhan Dempsey want to analyze data about their clients and the rafting trips they take. Help them query the Trips database by completing the following:

1. Open the **Trips** database located in the Brief\Case4 folder provided with your Data Files.

**Explore**

2. Define the necessary one-to-many relationships between the database tables, as follows: between the primary **Client** table and the related **Booking** table, and between the primary **RaftingTrip** table and the related **Booking** table. (*Hint:* Add all three tables to the Relationships window, and then define the two relationships.) Resize the field lists, as necessary, to display all the field names. Select the referential integrity option and the cascade updates option for each relationship.

3. For all clients, display the ClientName, City, StateProv, BookingID, and TripDate fields. Save the query as **ClientTripDates**, and then run the query. Resize all datasheet columns to their best fit. In Datasheet view, sort the query results in ascending order by the TripDate field. Print the query datasheet, and then save and close the query.

4. For all clients from Colorado (CO), display the ClientName, City, StateProv, TripID, People, and TripDate fields. Sort the query in ascending order by City. Save the query as **ColoradoClients**, and then run the query. Modify the query to remove the display of the StateProv field values from the query results. Save the modified query, run the query, print the query datasheet, and then close the query.

**Explore**

5. For all clients who are not from Colorado or who are taking a rafting trip in the month of July 2006, display the ClientName, City, StateProv, BookingID, TripDate, and TripID fields. (*Hint*: Refer to Figure 3-19 to determine the correct comparison operators to use.) Sort the query in descending order by TripDate. Save the query as **OutOfStateOrJuly**, run the query, and then print the query datasheet. Change the query to select all clients who are not from Colorado and who are taking a rafting trip in the month of July 2006. Sort the query in ascending order by StateProv. Save the query as **OutOfStateAndJuly**, run the query, print the query datasheet, and then close the query.

6. For all bookings, display the BookingID, TripDate, TripID (from the **Booking** table), River, People, and FeePerPerson fields. Save the query as **TripCost**. Then create a calculated field named TripCost that displays the results of multiplying the People field values by the FeePerPerson field values. Display the results in descending order by TripCost. Set the Caption property of the calculated field to "Trip Cost". Run the query, resize all datasheet columns to their best fit, print the query datasheet, and then save and close the query.

7. Use the **RaftingTrip** table to determine the minimum, average, and maximum FeePerPerson values for all trips. Then do the following:
   a. Specify column names of Lowest Fee, Average Fee, and Highest Fee.
   b. Use the property sheet for each column to format the results as Fixed with two decimal places.
   c. Save the query as **FeeStatistics**, run the query, resize all datasheet columns to their best fit, print the query datasheet, and then save the query again.

**Explore**

   d. Revise the query to show the fee statistics grouped by People. (*Hint*: Use the Show Table button on the Query Design toolbar to add the **Booking** table to the query.) Save the revised query as **FeeStatisticsByPeople**, run the query, print the query datasheet, and then close the query.

**Explore**

8. Use the "Type a question for help" box to ask the following question: "How do I create a Top Values query?" Click the topic "Show only the high or low values in a query (MDB)." Read the displayed information, and then close the Microsoft Office Access Help window and the task pane. Open the **TripCost** query in Design view, and then modify the query to display only the top five values for the TripCost field. Save the query as **TopTripCost**, run the query, print the query datasheet, and then close the query.

9. Close the Trips database.

**Research**

*Use the Internet to find and work with data related to the topics presented in this tutorial.*

## Internet Assignments

The purpose of the Internet Assignments is to challenge you to find information on the Internet that you can use to work effectively with this software. The actual assignments are updated and maintained on the Course Technology Web site. Log on to the Internet and use your Web browser to go to the Student Online Companion for New Perspectives Office 2003 at **www.course.com/np/office2003**. Click the Internet Assignments link, and then navigate to the assignments for this tutorial.

**Review**

# Quick Check Answers

## Session 3.1

1. a general query in which you specify the fields and records you want Access to select
2. The field list contains the table name at the top of the list box and the table's fields listed in the order in which they appear in the table; the design grid displays columns that contain specifications about a field you will use in the query.
3. A table datasheet and a query datasheet look the same, appearing in Datasheet view, and can be used to update data in a database. A table datasheet shows the permanent data in a table, whereas a query datasheet is temporary and its contents are based on the criteria you establish in the design grid.
4. primary table; related table
5. Referential integrity
6. oldest to most recent date
7. False
8. filter

## Session 3.2

1. condition
2. in the same Criteria row; in different Criteria rows
3. expression
4. A calculated field appears in a query datasheet, form, or report but does not exist in a database, as does a table field.
5. a function that performs an arithmetic operation on selected records in a database
6. Group By

## Objectives

**Session 4.1**
- Create a form using the Form Wizard
- Change a form's AutoFormat
- Find data using a form
- Preview and print selected form records
- Maintain table data using a form

**Session 4.2**
- Create a form with a main form and a subform
- Create a report using the Report Wizard
- Check errors in a report
- Insert a picture in a report
- Preview and print a report

# Creating Forms and Reports

*Creating a Position Data Form, an Employer Positions Form, and an Employers and Positions Report*

## Case

### Northeast Seasonal Jobs International (NSJI)

Elsa Jensen wants to continue enhancing the Northeast database to make it easier for NSJI employees to find and maintain data. In particular, she wants the database to include a form based on the Position table to make it easier for employees to enter and change data about available positions. She also wants the database to include a form that shows data from both the Employer and Position tables at the same time. This form will show the position information for each employer along with the corresponding employer data, providing a complete picture of NSJI's employer clients and their available positions.

In addition, Zack Ward would like the database to include a formatted report of employer and position data so that his marketing staff members will have printed output when completing market analyses and planning strategies for selling NSJI's services to employer clients. He wants the information to be formatted attractively, perhaps by including a picture or graphic image on the report for visual interest.

## Student Data Files

**▼ Brief**

▽ **Tutorial folder**
  Globe.bmp
  Northeast.mdb *(cont.)*

▽ **Review folder**
  Recruits.mdb *(cont.)*
  Travel.bmp

▽ **Case1 folder**
  Camcord.bmp
  Videos.mdb *(cont.)*

▽ **Case2 folder**
  Meals.mdb *(cont.)*
  Server.bmp

▽ **Case3 folder**
  Animals.bmp
  Redwood.mdb *(cont.)*

▽ **Case4 folder**
  Raft.gif
  Trips.mdb *(cont.)*

# Creating a Form Using the Form Wizard

As you learned in Tutorial 1, a form is an object you use to maintain, view, and print records in a database. In Access, you can design your own forms or use a Form Wizard to create them for you automatically.

Elsa asks you to create a new form that her staff can use to view and maintain data in the Position table. In Tutorial 1, you used the AutoForm Wizard to create the EmployerData form in the Seasonal database. The **AutoForm Wizard** creates a form automatically, using all the fields in the selected table or query. To create the form for the Position table, you'll use the Form Wizard. The **Form Wizard** allows you to choose some or all of the fields in the selected table or query, choose fields from other tables and queries, and display the selected fields in any order on the form. You can also apply an existing style to the form to format its appearance quickly.

### To open the Northeast database and activate the Form Wizard:

1. If you are working with a floppy disk, you need to delete a file from the disk to make sure you have enough space to complete this tutorial. Using My Computer or Windows Explorer, delete **NEJobs** from the Brief\Tutorial folder. (You only need to delete this file if you are working with a floppy disk.)

2. Start Access and open the **Northeast** database located in the Brief\Tutorial folder provided with your Data Files.

3. Click **Forms** in the Objects bar of the Database window.

4. Click the **New** button in the Database window. The New Form dialog box opens.

5. Click **Form Wizard**, click the list arrow for choosing a table or query, click **Position** to select this table as the source for the form, and then click the **OK** button. The first Form Wizard dialog box opens. See Figure 4-1.

**Figure 4-1** ▶ **First Form Wizard dialog box**

Elsa wants the form to display all the fields in the Position table, but in a different order. She would like the Experience field to appear at the bottom of the form so that it stands out, making it easier to determine if a position requires prior work experience.

## To finish creating the form using the Form Wizard:

1. Click **PositionID** in the Available Fields list box (if necessary), and then click the ☐ > ☐ button to move the field to the Selected Fields list box.

2. Repeat Step 1 to select the **PositionTitle**, **EmployerID**, **Wage**, **HoursPerWeek**, **StartDate**, **EndDate**, **Openings**, and **Experience** fields, in that order. Remember, you can also double-click a field to move it from the Available Fields list box to the Selected Fields list box.

3. Click the **Next** button to display the second Form Wizard dialog box, in which you select a layout for the form. See Figure 4-2.

Choosing a layout for the form ◄ **Figure 4-2**

The layout choices are Columnar, Tabular, Datasheet, Justified, PivotTable, and PivotChart. A sample of the selected layout appears on the left side of the dialog box.

4. Click each of the option buttons and review the corresponding sample layout.

The Tabular and Datasheet layouts display the fields from multiple records at one time, whereas the Columnar and Justified layouts display the fields from one record at a time. The PivotTable and PivotChart layouts display summary and analytical information. Elsa thinks the Columnar layout is the appropriate arrangement for displaying and updating data in the table, so you'll choose this layout.

5. Click the **Columnar** option button (if necessary), and then click the **Next** button. Access displays the third Form Wizard dialog box, in which you choose a style for the form. A sample of the selected style appears in the box on the left. If you choose a style, which is called an **AutoFormat**, and decide you'd prefer a different one after the form is created, you can change it. See Figure 4-3.

**Trouble?** Don't be concerned if a different form style is selected in your dialog box instead of the one shown in Figure 4-3. The dialog box displays the most recently used style, which might be different on your computer.

**Figure 4-3** ▶ **Choosing a style for the form**

sample of the
selected style

Form
Wizard
styles

▶ **6.** Click each style and review the corresponding sample.

Elsa likes the Expedition style and asks you to use it for the form.

▶ **7.** Click **Expedition**, and then click the **Next** button. Access displays the final Form Wizard dialog box and shows the Position table's name as the default form name. "Position" is also the default title that will appear in the form's title bar.

You'll use "Position Data" as the form name and, because you don't need to change the form's design at this point, you'll display the form.

▶ **8.** Click the insertion point to the right of Position in the text box, press the **spacebar**, type **Data**, and then click the **Finish** button. The completed form opens in Form view. See Figure 4-4.

**Figure 4-4** ▶ **Completed form for the Position table**

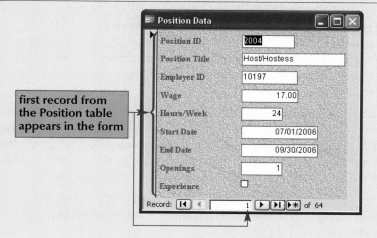

first record from
the Position table
appears in the form

After viewing the form, Elsa decides that she doesn't like the form's style; the background makes the field names a bit difficult to read. She asks you to change the form's style.

# Changing a Form's AutoFormat

You can change a form's appearance by choosing a different AutoFormat for the form. As you learned when you created the Position Data form, an AutoFormat is a predefined style for a form (or report). The AutoFormats available for a form are the ones you saw when you selected the form's style using the Form Wizard. To change an AutoFormat, you must switch to Design view.

**Reference Window**

## Changing a Form's AutoFormat

- Display the form in Design view.
- Click the AutoFormat button on the Form Design toolbar to open the AutoFormat dialog box.
- In the Form AutoFormats list box, click the AutoFormat you want to apply to the form, and then click the OK button.

## To change the AutoFormat for the Position Data form:

▶ **1.** Click the **View** button for Design view ![icon] on the Form View toolbar. The form is displayed in Design view. See Figure 4-5.

Form displayed in Design view | **Figure 4-5**

**Trouble?** If your screen displays any window other than those shown in Figure 4-5, click the Close button ![X] on the window's title bar to close it.

You use Design view to modify an existing form or to create a form from scratch. In this case, you need to change the AutoFormat for the Position Data form.

▶ **2.** Click the **AutoFormat** button ![icon] on the Form Design toolbar. The AutoFormat dialog box opens.

▶ **3.** Click the **Options** button to display the AutoFormat options. See Figure 4-6.

**Figure 4-6** ▶ **AutoFormat dialog box**

A sample of the selected AutoFormat appears to the right of the Form AutoFormats list box. The options at the bottom of the dialog box let you apply the selected AutoFormat or just its font, color, or border.

Elsa decides that she prefers the Standard AutoFormat, because its field names and field values are easy to read.

▶ **4.** Click **Standard** in the Form AutoFormats list box, and then click the **OK** button. The AutoFormat dialog box closes, the Standard AutoFormat is applied to the form, and the Form window in Design view becomes the active window.

▶ **5.** Click the **View** button for Form view 📧 on the Form Design toolbar. The form is displayed in Form view with the new AutoFormat. See Figure 4-7.

**Figure 4-7** ▶ **Form displayed with the new AutoFormat**

You have finished modifying the format of the form and can now save it.

▶ **6.** Click the **Save** button 🖫 on the Form View toolbar to save the modified form.

Elsa wants to use the Position Data form to view some data in the Position table. To view data, you need to navigate the form. As you learned in Tutorial 1, you navigate a form in the same way that you navigate a table datasheet. Also, the navigation mode and editing mode keystroke techniques you used with datasheets in Tutorial 2 are the same when navigating a form.

### To navigate the Position Data form:

▶ 1. Press the **Tab** key to move to the PositionTitle field value, and then press the **End** key to move to the Experience field. Because the Experience field is a yes/no field, its value is not highlighted; instead, a dotted outline appears around the field name to indicate that it is the current field.

▶ 2. Press the **Home** key to move back to the PositionID field value. The first record in the Position table still appears in the form.

▶ 3. Press the **Ctrl+End** keys to move to the Experience field for record 64, which is the last record in the table. The record number for the current record appears in the record number box between the navigation buttons at the bottom of the form.

▶ 4. Click the **Previous Record** navigation button ◀ to move to the Experience field in record 63.

▶ 5. Press the ↑ key twice to move to the EndDate field in record 63.

▶ 6. Click the insertion point between the numbers "0" and "6" in the EndDate field value to switch to editing mode, press the **Home** key to move the insertion point to the beginning of the field value, and then press the **End** key to move the insertion point to the end of the field value.

▶ 7. Click the **First Record** navigation button ◀◀ to move to the EndDate field value in the first record. The entire field value is highlighted because you have switched from editing mode to navigation mode.

▶ 8. Click the **Next Record** navigation button ▶ to move to the EndDate field value in record 2, the next record.

Elsa asks you to display the records for The Clipper Ship Inn, whose EmployerID value is 10145, because she wants to review the available positions for this employer.

# Finding Data Using a Form

The **Find command** lets you search for data in a form or datasheet so you can display only those records you want to view. You choose a field to serve as the basis for the search by making that field the current field; then you enter the value you want Access to match in the Find and Replace dialog box. You can use the Find command by clicking the toolbar Find button or by using the Edit menu.

| Finding Data in a Form or Datasheet | Reference Window |
|---|---|

- Make the field you want to search the current field.
- Click the Find button on the toolbar to open the Find and Replace dialog box.
- In the Find What text box, type the field value you want to find.
- Complete the remaining options, as necessary, to specify the type of search to conduct.
- Click the Find Next button to begin the search.
- Click the Find Next button to continue searching for the next match.
- Click the Cancel button to stop the search operation.

You need to find all records in the Position table for The Clipper Ship Inn, whose EmployerID is 10145.

## To find the records using the Position Data form:

1. Click in the **EmployerID** field value box. This is the field that you will search for matching values.

2. Click the **Find** button 🏔 on the Form View toolbar. The Find and Replace dialog box opens. Note that the Look In list box shows the name of the field that Access will search (in this case, the current EmployerID field), and the Match list box indicates that Access will find values that match the entire entry in the field. You could choose to match only part of a field value or only the beginning of each field value.

3. If the Find and Replace dialog box covers the form, move the dialog box by dragging its title bar. If necessary, move the Position Data form window so that you can see both the dialog box and the form at the same time. See Figure 4-8.

**Figure 4-8** | **Find and Replace dialog box**

4. In the Find What text box, type **10145** and then click the **Find Next** button. The Position Data form now displays record 7, which is the first record for EmployerID 10145.

5. Click the **Find Next** button. Access displays record 47, which is the second record for EmployerID 10145.

6. Click the **Find Next** button. Access displays record 48, which is the third record for EmployerID 10145.

7. Click the **Find Next** button. Access displays a dialog box informing you that the search is finished.

8. Click the **OK** button to close the dialog box.

The search value you enter can be an exact value, such as the EmployerID 10145 you just entered, or it can include wildcard characters. A **wildcard character** is a placeholder you use when you know only part of a value or when you want to start or end with a specific character or match a certain pattern. Figure 4-9 shows the wildcard characters you can use when finding data.

Wildcard characters | Figure 4-9

| Wildcard Character | Purpose | Example |
| --- | --- | --- |
| * | Match any number of characters. It can be used as the first and/or last character in the character string. | th* finds the, that, this, therefore, and so on |
| ? | Match any single alphabetic character. | a?t finds act, aft, ant, apt, and art |
| [] | Match any single character within the brackets. | a[fr]t finds aft and art but not act, ant, and apt |
| ! | Match any character not within brackets. | a[!fr]t finds act, ant, and apt but not aft and art |
| - | Match any one of a range of characters. The range must be in ascending order (a to z, not z to a). | a[d-p]t finds aft, ant, and apt but not act and art |
| # | Match any single numeric character. | #72 finds 072, 172, 272, 372, and so on |

Elsa wants to view the position records for two employers: George's Restaurant & Galley (EmployerID 10180) and Moondance Inn & Ski Resort (EmployerID 10185). Matt Griffin, the manager of recruitment, knows of some student recruits with prior work experience who are interested in working for these employers. Elsa wants to see which positions, if any, require experience. You'll use the * wildcard character to search for these employers' positions.

### To find the records using the * wildcard character:

1. Click **10145** in the Find What text box to select the entire value, and then type **1018***.

   Access will match any field value in the EmployerID field that starts with the digits 1018.

2. Click the **Find Next** button. Access displays record 64, which is the first record found for EmployerID 10185. Note that the Experience field value is unchecked, indicating that this position does not require experience.

3. Click the **Find Next** button. Access displays record 25, which is the first record found for EmployerID 10180. Again, the Experience field value is unchecked.

4. Click the **Find Next** button. Access displays record 42, which is the second record found for EmployerID 10185. In this case, the Experience field value is checked, indicating that this position requires prior work experience.

5. Click the **Find Next** button. Access displays a dialog box informing you that the search is finished.

6. Click the **OK** button to close the dialog box.

7. Click the **Cancel** button to close the Find and Replace dialog box.

Of the three positions, only one requires experience—PositionID 2089. Elsa asks you to use the form to print the data for record 42, which is for PositionID 2089, so that she can give the printout to Matt.

# Previewing and Printing Selected Form Records

Access prints as many form records as can fit on a printed page. If only part of a form record fits on the bottom of a page, the remainder of the record prints on the next page. Access allows you to print all pages or a range of pages. In addition, you can print the currently selected form record.

Before printing record 42, you'll preview the form record to see how it will look when printed. Notice that the current record number (in this case, 42) appears in the record number box at the bottom of the form.

### To preview the form and print the data for record 42:

▶ 1. Click the **Print Preview** button ☐ on the Form View toolbar. The Print Preview window opens, showing the form records for the Position table in miniature. If you clicked the Print button now, all the records for the table would be printed, beginning with the first record.

▶ 2. Click the **Maximize** button ☐ on the form's title bar.

▶ 3. Click the **Zoom** button ☐ on the Print Preview toolbar, and then use the vertical scroll bar to view the entire page. Each record from the Position table appears in a separate form. See Figure 4-10.

| Figure 4-10 | **Print Preview window displaying form records** |

▶ 4. Click the **Restore Window** button ☐ on the Print Preview menu bar, and then click the **Close** button on the Print Preview toolbar to return to the table in Form view.

The record that you need to print, PositionID 2089, appears in the form. To print selected records you need to use the Print dialog box.

▶ **5.** Click **File** on the menu bar, and then click **Print**. The Print dialog box opens.

▶ **6.** Click the **Selected Record(s)** option button to print the current form record (record 42).

▶ **7.** Click the **OK** button to close the dialog box and to print the selected record.

Elsa has identified several updates, as shown in Figure 4-11, that she wants you to make to the Position table. You'll use the Position Data form to update the data in the Position table.

**Updates to the Position table** ◀ **Figure 4-11**

| PositionID | Update Action |
| --- | --- |
| 2033 | Change HoursPerWeek to 35 <br> Change StartDate to 6/30/2006 |
| 2072 | Delete record |
| 2130 | Add new record for PositionID 2130: <br> PositionTitle = Housekeeping <br> EmployerID = 10151 <br> Wage = 12.50 <br> HoursPerWeek = 30 <br> StartDate = 6/1/2006 <br> EndDate = 10/15/2006 <br> Openings = 2 <br> Experience = No |

# Maintaining Table Data Using a Form

Maintaining data using a form is often easier than using a datasheet, because you can concentrate on all the changes required to a single record at one time. You already know how to navigate a form and find specific records. Now you'll make the changes Elsa requested to the Position table, using the Position Data form.

First, you'll update the record for PositionID 2033.

## To change the record using the Position Data form:

▶ **1.** Make sure the Position Data form is displayed in Form view.

When she reviewed the position data to identify possible corrections, Elsa noted that 10 is the record number for PositionID 2033. If you know the number of the record you want to display, you can type the number in the record number box and press the Enter key to go directly to that record.

▶ **2.** Select **42** in the record number box, type **10**, and then press the **Enter** key. Record 10 (PositionID 2033) is now the current record.

You need to change the HoursPerWeek field value to 35 and the StartDate field value to 06/30/2006 for this record.

3. Click the insertion point to the left of the number 2 in the HoursPerWeek field value, press the **Delete** key twice, and then type **35**. Note that the pencil symbol appears in the upper-left corner of the form, indicating that the form is in editing mode.

4. Press the **Tab** key to move to and select the StartDate field value, type **6/30/2006**, and then press the **Enter** key. See Figure 4-12.

| Figure 4-12 | Position record after changing field values |
| --- | --- |

You have completed the changes for PositionID 2033. Elsa's next update is to delete the record for PositionID 2072. The employer client recently informed Elsa that a full-time, permanent employee has been hired for this position, so it is no longer available for student recruits.

## To delete the record using the Position Data form:

1. Click anywhere in the PositionID field value to make it the current field.

2. Click the **Find** button 🔍 on the Form View toolbar. The Find and Replace dialog box opens.

3. Type **2072** in the Find What text box, click the **Find Next** button, and then click the **Cancel** button. The record for PositionID 2072 is now the current record.

4. Click the **Delete Record** button on the Form View toolbar. A dialog box opens, asking you to confirm the record deletion.

5. Click the **Yes** button. The dialog box closes, and the record for PositionID 2072 is deleted from the table.

Elsa's final maintenance change is to add a record for a new position available at the Granite State Resort.

## To add the new record using the Position Data form:

1. Click the **New Record** button on the Form View toolbar. Record 64, the next record available for a new record, becomes the current record. All field value boxes are empty, and the insertion point is positioned at the beginning of the field value box for PositionID.

▶ **2.** Refer to Figure 4-13 and enter the value shown for each field. Press the **Tab** key to move from field to field.

**Completed form for the new record** ◀ Figure 4-13

**Trouble?** Compare your screen with Figure 4-13. If any field value is wrong, correct it now, using the methods described earlier for editing field values.

▶ **3.** After entering the value for Openings, press the **Tab** key twice (if necessary). Record 65, the next record available for a new record, becomes the current record, and the record for PositionID 2130 is saved in the Position table.

You've completed Elsa's changes to the Position table, so you can close the Position Data form.

▶ **4.** Click the **Close** button ⊠ on the form's title bar. The form closes, and you return to the Database window. Notice that the Position Data form is listed in the Forms list box.

So that all your database objects will be named consistently, you'll rename the form object to "PositionData" (one word). This will not affect how the form title (caption) is displayed when you work with the form in Form view; it will still appear as "Position Data" (two words).

▶ **5.** Right-click **Position Data** in the Forms list box, and then click **Rename** on the shortcut menu.

▶ **6.** Delete the space between the words "Position" and "Data," and then press the **Enter** key. The form object name is now "PositionData."

   The PositionData form will enable Elsa and her staff to enter and maintain data easily in the Position table. In the next session, you'll create another form for working with data in both the Position and Employer tables at the same time. You'll also create a report showing data from both tables.

# Session 4.1 Quick Check

Review

**1.** Describe the difference between creating a form using the AutoForm Wizard and creating a form using the Form Wizard.

**2.** What is an AutoFormat, and how do you change one for an existing form?

**3.** Which table record is displayed in a form when you press the Ctrl+End keys while you are in navigation mode?

**4.** You can use the Find command to search for data in a form or _____.

**5.** Which wildcard character matches any single alphabetic character?

**6.** How many form records does Access print by default on a page?

# Session 4.2

Elsa would like you to create a form so that she can view the data for each employer and its available positions at the same time. The type of form you need to create will include a main form and a subform.

## Creating a Form with a Main Form and a Subform

To create a form based on two tables, you must first define a relationship between the two tables. In Tutorial 3, you defined a one-to-many relationship between the Employer (primary) and Position (related) tables, so you are ready to create the form based on both tables.

When you create a form containing data from two tables that have a one-to-many relationship, you actually create a **main form** for data from the primary table and a **subform** for data from the related table. Access uses the defined relationship between the tables to join them automatically through the common field that exists in both tables.

Elsa and her staff will use the form when contacting employers about their available positions. The main form will contain the employer ID and name, contact first and last names, and phone number for each employer. The subform will contain the position ID and title, wage, hours per week, experience, start and end dates, and number of openings for each position.

You'll use the Form Wizard to create the form.

### To create the form using the Form Wizard:

▶ 1. If you took a break after the previous session, make sure that Access is running and the **Northeast** database is open.

▶ 2. Make sure the Forms object is selected in the Database window, and then click the **New** button. The New Form dialog box opens.

   When creating a form based on two tables, you first choose the primary table and select the fields you want to include in the main form; then you choose the related table and select fields from it for the subform.

▶ 3. Click **Form Wizard**, click the list arrow for choosing a table or query, click **Employer** to select this table as the source for the main form, and then click the **OK** button. The first Form Wizard dialog box opens, in which you select fields in the order you want them to appear on the main form.

   Elsa wants the form to include only the EmployerID, EmployerName, ContactFirstName, ContactLastName, and Phone fields from the Employer table.

▶ 4. Click **EmployerID** in the Available Fields list box (if necessary), and then click the ⟩ button to move the field to the Selected Fields list box.

▶ 5. Repeat Step 4 for the **EmployerName**, **ContactFirstName**, **ContactLastName**, and **Phone** fields.

   The EmployerID field will appear in the main form, so you do not have to include it in the subform. Otherwise, Elsa wants the subform to include all the fields from the Position table.

▶ 6. Click the **Tables/Queries** list arrow, and then click **Table: Position**. The fields from the Position table appear in the Available Fields list box. The quickest way to add the fields you want to include is to move all the fields to the Selected Fields list box, and then to remove the only field you don't want to include (EmployerID).

7. Click the $\boxed{>>}$ button to move all the fields from the Position table to the Selected Fields list box.

8. Click **Position.EmployerID** in the Selected Fields list box, and then click the $\boxed{<}$ button to move the field back to the Available Fields list box. Note that the table name (Position) is included in the field name to distinguish it from the same field (EmployerID) in the Employer table.

9. Click the **Next** button. The next Form Wizard dialog box opens. See Figure 4-14.

**Choosing a main/subform format** ◄ **Figure 4-14**

In this dialog box, the list box on the left shows the order in which you will view the selected data: first by data from the primary Employer table, and then by data from the related Position table. The form will be displayed as shown in the right side of the dialog box, with the fields from the Employer table at the top in the main form, and the fields from the Position table at the bottom in the subform. The selected option button specifies a main form with a subform. The Linked forms option creates a form structure in which only the main form fields are displayed. A button with the subform's name on it appears on the main form; you can click this button to display the associated subform records.

The default options shown in Figure 4-14 are correct for creating a form with Employer data in the main form and Position data in the subform.

## To finish creating the form:

1. Click the **Next** button. The next Form Wizard dialog box opens, in which you choose the subform layout.

   The Tabular layout displays subform fields as a table, whereas the Datasheet layout displays subform fields as a table datasheet. The PivotTable and PivotChart layouts display summary and analytical information. The layout choice is a matter of personal preference. You'll use the Datasheet layout.

2. Click the **Datasheet** option button (if necessary), and then click the **Next** button. The next Form Wizard dialog box opens, in which you choose the form's style.

   Elsa wants all forms in the Northeast database to have the same style, so you will choose Standard, which is the same style you applied to the PositionData form.

▶ **3.** Click **Standard** (if necessary), and then click the **Next** button. The next Form Wizard dialog box opens, in which you choose names for the main form and the subform.

You will use the name "Employer Positions" for the main form and the name "Position Subform" for the subform. (Later, you'll rename the form objects so that their names do not include spaces.)

▶ **4.** Click the insertion point to the right of the last letter in the Form text box, press the **spacebar**, and then type **Positions**. The main form name is now Employer Positions. The Position Subform name is already set.

You have answered all the Form Wizard's questions.

▶ **5.** Click the **Finish** button. After a few moments, the completed form opens in Form view.

Some of the columns in the subform are not wide enough to display the field names entirely. You need to resize the columns to their best fit.

▶ **6.** Double-click the pointer ╋ at the right edge of each column in the subform, scrolling the subform to the right, as necessary, to display additional columns. Scroll the subform all the way back to the left. The columns are resized to their best fit. See Figure 4-15.

| Figure 4-15 | Main form with subform in Form view |

In the main form, Access displays the fields from the first record in the Employer table in columnar format. The records in the main form appear in primary key sequence by EmployerID. EmployerID 10122 has one related record in the Position table; this record is shown in the subform datasheet. The form shows that BeanTown Tours has one available position for a Tour Guide.

Notice that the subform is not wide enough to display all the fields from the Position table. Although the subform includes a horizontal scroll bar, which allows you to view the other fields, Elsa wants all the fields from the Position table to be visible in the subform at the same time. Even if you maximized the Form window, the subform would still not display all of the fields. You need to widen the main form and the subform in Design view.

## Modifying a Form in Design View

Just as you use Design view to modify the format and content of tables and queries, you also use Design view to modify a form. You can change the fields that are displayed on a form, and modify their size, location, format, and so on. You need to open the Employer Positions form in Design view and resize the Position subform to display all the fields at the same time.

### To widen the Position subform:

▶ **1.** Click the **View** button for Design view  on the Form View toolbar to display the form in Design view.

▶ **2.** Click the **Maximize** button  to enlarge the window. See Figure 4-16.

**Form with subform displayed in Design view** ◀ **Figure 4-16**

**Trouble?** If the subform appears as a white box instead of a datasheet as in Figure 4-16, click the View button for Form view 🖾 on the Form Design toolbar, and then click the View button for Design view 🗹 on the Form View toolbar.

▶ **3.** Click the **Form Header** bar for the subform (refer to Figure 4-16) to select the subform. Notice that small boxes appear around the subform's border. These boxes, which are called **handles**, indicate that the subform is selected and can be manipulated.

▶ **4.** Position the pointer on the right-center sizing handle so it changes to a ↔ shape, and then click and drag the handle to the right, to the mark just before the 6.5-inch mark on the horizontal ruler. See Figure 4-17.

**Figure 4-17** **Resizing the Position subform**

**5.** Release the mouse button. The subform section is resized. Notice that the main form section is also resized.

**6.** Switch back to Form view. Notice that all the field names in the Position subform are now visible.

**7.** Click the **Restore Window** button 🗗 on the menu bar to restore the form to its original size. Now you need to resize the Form window in Form view so that all the fields will be displayed when the Form window is not maximized.

**8.** Position the pointer on the right edge of the form so it changes to a ↔ shape, and then click and drag the right edge of the form to resize it so that it matches the form shown in Figure 4-18. Make sure the bottom of the form does not include a horizontal scroll bar; the absence of a scroll bar indicates that all fields are fully visible.

**Figure 4-18** **Form with all subform fields visible**

**9.** Save the modified form.

Two sets of navigation buttons appear at the bottom of the Form view window. You use the top set of navigation buttons to select records from the related table in the subform, and the bottom set to select records from the primary table in the main form.

You'll use the navigation buttons to view different records.

### To navigate to different main form and subform records:

▶ 1. Click the **Last Record** navigation button ▶I in the main form. Record 45 in the Employer table for Lighthouse Tours becomes the current record in the main form. The subform shows that this employer has one available Tour Guide position.

▶ 2. Click the **Previous Record** navigation button ◀ in the main form. Record 44 in the Employer table for Harbor Whale Watch Tours becomes the current record in the main form.

▶ 3. Select **44** in the record number box for the main form, type **32**, and then press the **Enter** key. Record 32 in the Employer table for Windsor Alpine Tours becomes the current record in the main form. This employer has two available positions.

▶ 4. Click the **Last Record** navigation button ▶I in the subform. Record 2 in the Position table becomes the current record in the subform.

You have finished your work with the form, so you can close it.

▶ 5. Close the form. Both the main form, Employer Positions, and the subform, Position Subform, appear in the Forms list box. Note that you can open each form separately in Design view and make changes to it. For example, if you open and modify the Position Subform, the changes you make will appear the next time you use the Employer Positions form, since it also contains the subform.

Now you'll rename the two form objects so that their names do not include spaces, and all the database objects are named consistently.

▶ 6. Right-click **Employer Positions**, click **Rename**, delete the space between the words "Employer" and "Positions," and then press the **Enter** key. Repeat this procedure for the Position Subform object so that the names of both objects do not contain spaces.

You've finished your work for Elsa on the forms in the Northeast database.

# Creating a Report Using the Report Wizard

As you learned in Tutorial 1, a report is a formatted printout of the contents of one or more tables in a database. In Access, you can create your own reports or use the Report Wizard to create them for you. Like the Form Wizard, the **Report Wizard** asks you a series of questions and then creates a report based on your answers. Whether you use the Report Wizard or design your own report, you can change the report's design after you create it.

Zack wants you to create a report that includes selected employer data from the Employer table and all the available positions from the Position table for each employer. Zack has sketched a design of the report he wants (Figure 4-19). Like the EmployerPositions form you just created, which includes a main form and a subform, the report will be based on both tables, which are joined in a one-to-many relationship through the common EmployerID field. As shown in the sketch in Figure 4-19, the selected employer data from the primary Employer table includes the employer ID and name, city, state or province, contact first and last names, and phone number. Below the data for each employer, the report will include the position ID and title, wage, hours per week, experience, start and end dates, and openings data from the related Position table. The set of field values for each position is called a **detail record**.

**Figure 4-19** **Report sketch for the Employers and Positions report**

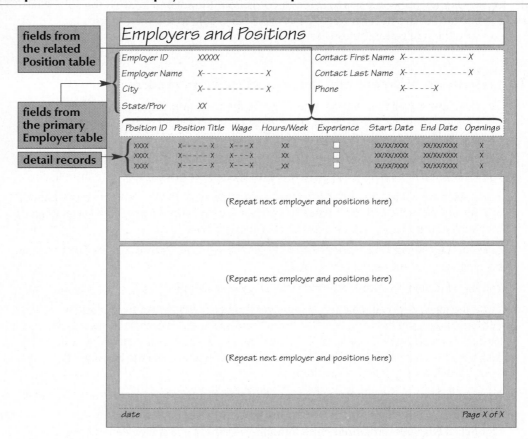

You'll use the Report Wizard to create the report according to the design in Zack's sketch.

## To start the Report Wizard and select the fields to include in the report:

▶ **1.** Click **Reports** in the Objects bar of the Database window to display the Reports list box. You have not yet created any reports.

▶ **2.** Click the **New** button in the Database window. The New Report dialog box opens.

As was the case when you created the form with a subform, initially you can choose only one table or query to be the data source for the report. Then you can include data from other tables. You will select the primary Employer table in the New Report dialog box.

▶ **3.** Click **Report Wizard**, click the list arrow for choosing a table or query, and then click **Employer**.

▶ **4.** Click the **OK** button. The first Report Wizard dialog box opens.

In the first Report Wizard dialog box, you select fields in the order you want them to appear on the report. Zack wants the EmployerID, EmployerName, City, StateProv, ContactFirstName, ContactLastName, and Phone fields from the Employer table to appear on the report.

▶ **5.** Click **EmployerID** in the Available Fields list box (if necessary), and then click the [ > ] button. The field moves to the Selected Fields list box.

▶ **6.** Repeat Step 5 to add the **EmployerName**, **City**, **StateProv**, **ContactFirstName**, **ContactLastName**, and **Phone** fields to the report.

▶ **7.** Click the **Tables/Queries** list arrow, and then click **Table: Position**. The fields from the Position table appear in the Available Fields list box.

The EmployerID field will appear on the report with the employer data, so you do not have to include it in the detail records for each position. Otherwise, Zack wants all the fields from the Position table to be included in the report.

▶ **8.** Click the [ >> ] button to move all the fields from the Available Fields list box to the Selected Fields list box.

▶ **9.** Click **Position.EmployerID** in the Selected Fields list box, click the [ < ] button to move the selected field back to the Available Fields list box, and then click the **Next** button. The second Report Wizard dialog box opens. See Figure 4-20.

Choosing a grouped or ungrouped report ◀ **Figure 4-20**

You can choose to arrange the selected data grouped by table, which is the default, or ungrouped. For a **grouped report**, the data from a record in the primary table appears as a group, followed on subsequent lines of the report by the joined records from the related table. For the report you are creating, data from a record in the Employer table appears in a group, followed by the related records for each employer from the Position table. An example of an ungrouped report would be a report of records from the Employer and Position tables in order by PositionID. Each position and its associated employer data would appear together on one or more lines of the report; the data would not be grouped by table.

You can display tips and examples for the choices in the Report Wizard dialog box by clicking the "Show me more information" button.

### To display tips about the options in the Report Wizard dialog box:

▶ **1.** Click the ⊠ button. The Report Wizard Tips dialog box opens. Read the information shown in the dialog box.

You can display examples of different grouping methods by clicking the ⊠ button ("Show me examples").

▶ **2.** Click the ⊠ button. The Report Wizard Examples dialog box opens.

You can display examples of different grouping methods by clicking the ⊠ buttons.

▶ **3.** Click each ⊠ button in turn, review the displayed example, and then click the **Close** button to return to the Report Wizard Examples dialog box.

▶ **4.** Click the **Close** button to return to the Report Wizard Tips dialog box, and then click the **Close** button to return to the second Report Wizard dialog box.

The default options shown on your screen are correct for the report Zack wants, so you can continue responding to the Report Wizard questions.

### To finish creating the report using the Report Wizard:

▶ **1.** Click the **Next** button. The next Report Wizard dialog box opens, in which you choose additional grouping levels.

Two grouping levels are shown: one for an employer's data, and the other for an employer's positions. Grouping levels are useful for reports with multiple levels, such as those containing monthly, quarterly, and annual totals, or for those containing city and country groups. Zack's report contains no further grouping levels, so you can accept the default options.

▶ **2.** Click the **Next** button. The next Report Wizard dialog box opens, in which you choose the sort order for the detail records. See Figure 4-21.

| Figure 4-21 ▶ | **Choosing the sort order for detail records** |

The records from the Position table for an employer represent the detail records for Zack's report. He wants these records to appear in increasing, or ascending, order by the value in the PositionID field. The Ascending option is already selected by default. To change to descending order, you simply click this button, which acts as a toggle between the two sort orders. Also, notice that you can sort on multiple fields, as you can with queries.

**3.** Click the **1** list arrow, click **PositionID**, and then click the **Next** button. The next Report Wizard dialog box opens, in which you choose a layout and page orientation for the report. See Figure 4-22.

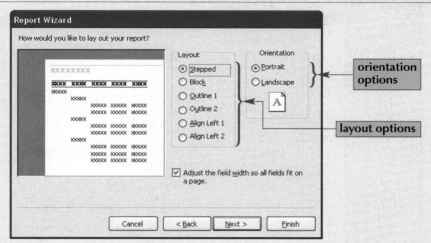

A sample of each layout appears in the box on the left.

**4.** Click each layout option and examine each sample that appears.

You'll use the Outline 2 layout option because it resembles the layout shown in Zack's sketch of the report. Also, because of the number of fields in the Position table, the information would fit better in a wide format; therefore, you'll choose the landscape orientation.

**5.** Click the **Outline 2** option button, click the **Landscape** option button, and then click the **Next** button. The next Report Wizard dialog box opens, in which you choose a style for the report.

A sample of the selected style, or AutoFormat, appears in the box on the left. You can always choose a different AutoFormat after you create the report, just as you can when creating a form. Zack likes the appearance of the Corporate AutoFormat, so you'll choose this one for your report.

**6.** Click **Corporate** (if necessary), and then click the **Next** button. The last Report Wizard dialog box opens, in which you choose a report name, which also serves as the printed title on the report.

According to Zack's sketch, the report title you need to specify is "Employers and Positions." (You'll rename the report object later so that its name does not contain spaces and conforms with other object names in the database.)

**7.** Type **Employers and Positions** and then click the **Finish** button. The Report Wizard creates the report based on your answers and saves it as an object in the Northeast database. Then Access opens the Employers and Positions report in Print Preview.

To view the report better, you need to maximize the Report window.

**8.** Click the **Maximize** button 🔲 on the Employers and Positions title bar.

To view the entire page, you need to change the Zoom setting.

**9.** Click the **Zoom** list arrow on the Print Preview toolbar, and then click **Fit**. The first page of the report is displayed in Print Preview. See Figure 4-23.

**Figure 4-23** | **Report displayed in Print Preview**

When a report is displayed in Print Preview, you can use the pointer to toggle between a full-page display and a close-up display of the report. Zack asks you to check the report to see if any adjustments need to be made. For example, some of the field titles or values might not be displayed completely, or you might need to move fields to enhance the report's appearance. To do so, you need to view a close-up display of the report.

### To view a close-up display of the report:

▶ **1.** Click the pointer 🔍 at the top center of the report. The display changes to show a close-up view of the report. See Figure 4-24.

Close-up view of the report  Figure 4-24

**Trouble?** Scroll your screen as necessary so that it matches the screen in Figure 4-24.

The letter "D" is missing from the end of the PositionID field name, the letter "H" is not fully displayed at the beginning of the HoursPerWeek field name, and the letter "e" is not visible at the end of the Experience field name. To fix these problems, you need to switch to Design view.

▶ **2.** Click the **View** button for Design view ![icon] on the Print Preview toolbar. Access displays the report in Design view. See Figure 4-25.

| Figure 4-25 | Report displayed in Design view |

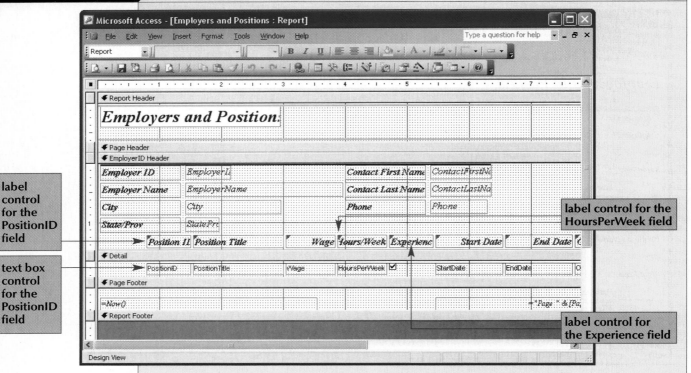

**Trouble?** If your screen displays any window other than the one shown in Figure 4-25, click the Close button ☒ on the window's title bar to close it.

You use the Report window in Design view to modify existing reports and to create custom reports. Each item on a report in Design view is called a **control**. For example, the PositionID field consists of two controls: the **label** "PositionID," which appears on the report to identify the field value, and the PositionID **text box**, in which the actual field value appears.

3.   Click the label control for the PositionID field to select it. Handles appear on the border around the control, indicating that the control is selected and can be manipulated. See Figure 4-26.

| Figure 4-26 | Selecting the PositionID label control |

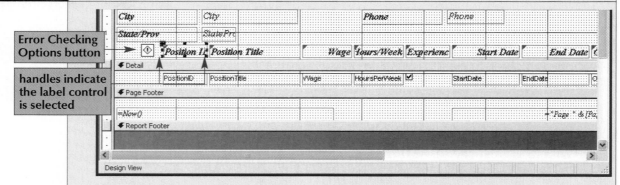

Notice also that a button appears to the left of the selected control. This button allows you to check for possible errors in your report.

# Checking Errors in a Report

When you work with a report (or a form) in Design view, Access provides automatic error checking to help you make sure that your report is designed correctly. The **Error Checking Options** button (see Figure 4-26) appears any time Access identifies a possible error. You can choose one of the options provided by this button to determine if there is, indeed, an error in your report.

## To check for errors in the report:

1. Position the pointer on the **Error Checking Options** button ⊕ and then click the list arrow that appears. A menu opens listing options associated with the possible error. See Figure 4-27.

**Menu displayed for possible error**     **Figure 4-27**

identified error for the selected control

click to view more options

In this case, the PositionID label is identified as a "new unassociated label," meaning that it does not have an associated text box in which to display the field values. Access identifies this as a potential error because the PositionID label appears in one section of the report, the EmployerID Header section, and its text box appears in another section of the report, the Detail section. Typically a label and its associated text box appear in the same section of the report. Because the selected report design places these controls in different sections, Access flags the error as an unassociated label.

2. Click **Error Checking Options** in the menu. The Options dialog box opens. See Figure 4-28.

**Options dialog box**     **Figure 4-28**

option for enabling or disabling error checking in forms and reports

potential errors are flagged with this color

The Enable error checking option allows you to turn this feature on or off (it is on by default). Note that the selected error indicator color is green. Each label in the EmployerID Header section whose associated text box is in the Detail section has a small green triangle in the upper-left corner of the label box, indicating a potential error for that label.

Because each of these labels does have an associated text box in the Detail section, there are no errors in the report design and you can safely ignore the error checking.

**3.** Click the **Cancel** button to close the Options dialog box.

**4.** Click the list arrow for the **Error Checking Options** button ⬦, and then click **Ignore Error**.

**5.** Click in the empty space next to the PositionID label to deselect it. Notice that the green triangle is no longer displayed in the upper-left corner of the label, because you chose to ignore the error. You could follow this same procedure for the other labels in this section, but there is no need to do so; each of the labels flagged with a green triangle does have an associated text box in the Detail section, so the report design is correct.

Now that you've determined there are no errors in the report design, you can proceed with fixing the labels that are not completely displayed.

### To fix the display of the PositionID label in the report:

**1.** Click the **PositionID** label to select it. You need to widen the label control for the PositionID field so that the entire field name is visible in the report.

**2.** Position the pointer on the center-left handle of the PositionID label control until the pointer changes to a ↔ shape.

**3.** Click and drag the pointer to the left until the left edge of the control is aligned with the mark just after the half-inch mark on the horizontal ruler. See Figure 4-29.

Figure 4-29 | Resizing the PositionID label control

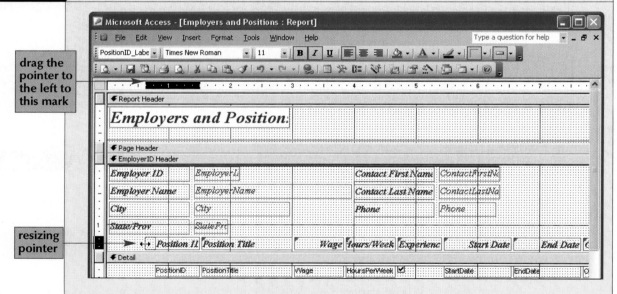

**4.** Release the mouse button. The label is wider, and the full name, Position ID, is visible.

To fix the problem with the HoursPerWeek and Experience labels, you first need to reduce the size of the Wage label, which currently takes up too much space in the report and crowds the other labels. However, you should also resize the Wage label's associated text box so that the displayed Wage values are aligned appropriately below the Wage label in the report. You can select multiple controls and resize them at the same time.

## To fix the display of the other labels in the report:

▶ 1. Click the **Wage** label, press and hold the **Shift** key, and then click the **Wage** text box in the Detail section. Both controls have handles around them, indicating that they are selected.

▶ 2. Position the pointer on the center-right handle of the Wage label control until the pointer changes to a ↔ shape. Click and drag the pointer to the left until the right edges of both selected controls are aligned with the **3.5**-inch mark on the horizontal ruler, and then release the mouse button. Both controls are reduced in size, and you can now widen the HoursPerWeek label. Note that you do not have to widen the HoursPerWeek text box, only the label.

▶ 3. Click the **HoursPerWeek** label (which contains the text Hours/Week), position the pointer on the center-left handle, click and drag the pointer to the left to the next mark on the horizontal ruler, and then release the mouse button. The complete label is now visible.

▶ 4. Click in an empty space of the EmployerID Header section to deselect the label. See Figure 4-30.

Controls after resizing ◀ Figure 4-30

Finally, you need to correct the problem with the Experience field name. To do so, you first need to reduce the width of the StartDate label and its associated text box; then you can widen just the Experience label control.

▶ 5. Click the **StartDate** label, press and hold the **Shift** key, and then click the **StartDate** text box in the Detail section. Both controls have handles around them, indicating that they are selected.

▶ 6. Position the pointer on the center-left handle of the StartDate label control, click and drag the pointer to the right to the **5.75**-inch mark on the horizontal ruler, and then release the mouse button. Both controls are reduced in size, and you can now widen the Experience label.

▶ 7. Click the **Experience** label, position the pointer on the center-right handle, click and drag the pointer to the right to the **5.5**-inch mark on the horizontal ruler, and then release the mouse button.

Now you need to switch back to Print Preview and make sure that the complete names for the PositionID, HoursPerWeek, and Experience fields are visible.

▶ 8. Click the **View** button for Print Preview 🔍 on the Report Design toolbar. The report appears in Print Preview. Notice that the PositionID, HoursPerWeek, and Experience labels are now completely displayed.

**Trouble?** If any of the labels in your report are not completely displayed, return to Design view and use the same resizing technique to correct the size of labels and/or associated text boxes, as necessary.

▶ 9. Click **File** on the menu bar, and then click **Save** to save the modified report.

Zack decides that he wants the report to include a graphic image to the right of the report title, for visual interest. You can add the graphic to the report by inserting a picture.

# Inserting a Picture in a Report

In Access, you can insert a picture or other graphic image to enhance the appearance of a report or form. Sources of graphic images include files created in Microsoft Paint and other drawing programs, and scanned files. The file containing the picture you need to insert is named Globe, and it is located in the Brief\Tutorial folder provided with your Data Files.

### To insert the picture in the report:

▶ 1. Click the **Close** button on the Print Preview toolbar to display the report in Design view. See Figure 4-31.

| Figure 4-31 | Inserting a picture in Design view |
| --- | --- |

Zack wants the picture to appear on the first page of the report only; therefore, you need to insert the picture in the **Report Header** section (see Figure 4-31). Any text or picture placed in this section appears once at the beginning of the report.

▶ 2. Click the **Report Header** bar to select this section of the report. The bar is highlighted to indicate that the section is selected.

▶ 3. Click **Insert** on the menu bar, and then click **Picture**. The Insert Picture dialog box opens. If necessary, open the **Brief\Tutorial** folder provided with your Data Files.

▶ 4. Click **Globe** to select the picture for the report, and then click the **OK** button. The picture is inserted in the left side of the Report Header section, covering some of the report title text. See Figure 4-32.

| Figure 4-32 | Picture inserted in the report |
| --- | --- |

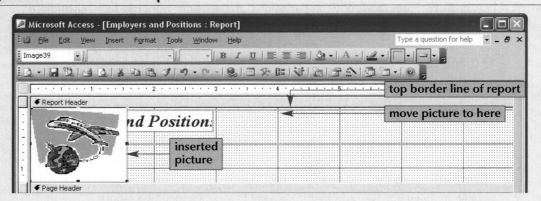

Notice that handles appear around the picture's border, indicating that the picture is selected and can be manipulated.

Zack wants the picture to appear to the right of the report title, so you need to move the picture using the mouse.

**5.** Position the pointer on the picture until the pointer changes to a  shape, and then click and drag the mouse to move the picture to the right so that its left edge aligns with the 4-inch mark on the horizontal ruler and its top edge is just below the top border line above the report title (see Figure 4-32).

**6.** Release the mouse button. The picture appears in the new position. Notice that the height of the Report Header section increased slightly to accommodate the picture. See Figure 4-33.

**Repositioned picture in the report** ◄ **Figure 4-33**

**Trouble?** If your picture appears in a different location from the one shown in Figure 4-33, use the pointer  to reposition the picture until it is in approximately the same position shown in the figure. Be sure that the top edge of the picture is below the top border line of the report.

**7.** Switch to Print Preview. The report now includes the inserted picture. If necessary, click the **Zoom** button 🔍 on the Print Preview toolbar to display the entire report page. See Figure 4-34.

**Print Preview of report with picture** ◄ **Figure 4-34**

**Trouble?** If the picture covers the gray line at the top of the report, switch to Design view and use the pointer to position the picture in the correct location. Then repeat Step 7.

▶ 8. Save the modified report.

The report is now completed. You'll print just the first page of the report so that Zack can review the report layout and the inserted picture.

**To print page 1 of the report:**

▶ 1. Click **File** on the menu bar, and then click **Print**. The Print dialog box opens.

▶ 2. In the Print Range section, click the **Pages** option button. The insertion point now appears in the From text box so that you can specify the range of pages to print.

▶ 3. Type **1** in the From text box, press the **Tab** key to move to the To text box, and then type **1**. These settings specify that only page 1 of the report will be printed.

▶ 4. Click the **OK** button. The Print dialog box closes, and the first page of the report is printed.

Zack approves of the report layout and contents, so you can close the report.

▶ 5. Click the **Close Window** button ✖ on the menu bar. You return to the Database window.

**Trouble?** If you click the Close button on the Print Preview toolbar by mistake, you switch to Design view. Click the Close Window button ✖ on the menu bar.

Recall that when you created the report, you specified the name "Employers and Positions" so that this title would appear on the report. Now you need to rename the report object so that its name is consistent with the names of other database objects (that is, with no spaces in the object name). Renaming the report object will not affect the specified title of the report.

▶ 6. Right-click **Employers and Positions** in the Database window, and then click **Rename**.

▶ 7. Change the name of the report to **EmployersAndPositions**, and then press the **Enter** key.

▶ 8. Close the Northeast database.

Elsa is satisfied that the forms you created—the PositionData form and the EmployerPositions form—will make it easier to enter, view, and update data in the Northeast database. The EmployersAndPositions report presents important information about NSJI's employer clients in an attractive and professional format, which will help Zack and his staff in their marketing efforts.

**Review**

# Session 4.2 Quick Check

1. In a form that contains a main form and a subform, what data is displayed in the main form and what data is displayed in the subform?
2. Describe how you use the navigation buttons to move through a form containing a main form and a subform.
3. Each item on a report in Design view is called a(n) _____.
4. The _____ button appears any time Access identifies a possible error in a report (or form) while you are working on the design of the report (or form).
5. To insert a picture in a report, the report must be displayed in _____.
6. Any text or pictures placed in the _____ section of a report will appear only on the first page of the report.

# Tutorial Summary

In this tutorial, you learned how to create a form using the Form Wizard and how to change the form's AutoFormat after you created it. Using the navigation buttons provided at the bottom of the form window and various keyboard techniques, you moved through the records in a form. You also used the Find command to locate specific form records, and included wildcard characters to search for records by specifying only a partial field value. In addition, you previewed and printed selected form records, and maintained table data using a form. With the one-to-many relationship already established between the necessary tables, you were able to create a form with a main form and a subform to display data from both tables at the same time. You also used the Report Wizard to create a report displaying data from two related tables. Working in Design view, you modified the report by resizing label and text box controls. You also learned about the new Error Checking Options button, which identifies potential design errors in a form or report and helps you to correct them, if necessary. Finally, you learned how to insert and reposition a picture in a report to add visual interest.

## Key Terms

| | | |
|---|---|---|
| AutoForm Wizard | Form Wizard | Report Header section |
| AutoFormat | grouped report | Report Wizard |
| control | handles | subform |
| detail record | label control | text box control |
| Error Checking Options | main form | wildcard character |
| Find command | | |

# Review Assignments

**Data Files needed for the Review Assignments: Recruits.mdb (*cont. from Tutorial 3*) and Travel.bmp**

Elsa wants to enhance the Recruits database with forms and reports, and she asks you to complete the following:

1. Open the **Recruits** database located in the Brief\Review folder provided with your Data Files.
2. Use the Form Wizard to create a form based on the **Student** table. Select all fields for the form, the Columnar layout, the SandStone style, and the title **Student Data** for the form.
3. Use the form you created in the previous step to print the fifth form record. Change the AutoFormat to Sumi Painting, save the changed form, and then print the fifth form record again.
4. Use the **Student Data** form to update the Student table as follows:
   a. Use the Find command to move to the record with StudentID STO1323. Change the field values for FirstName to Nathaniel, City to Perth, and BirthDate to 4/2/85 for this record.
   b. Use the Find command to move to the record with StudentID KIE2760, and then delete the record.
   c. Add a new record with the following field values:
      StudentID:  SAN2540
      FirstName:  Pedro
      LastName:  Sandes
      City:      Barcelona

Nation:      Spain
BirthDate:   5/1/85
Gender:      M
SSN:         977-07-1798

   d. Print only this form record, and then close the form.
5. Rename the form object to **StudentData**.
6. Use the Form Wizard to create a form containing a main form and a subform. Select the FirstName, LastName, and SSN fields from the **Recruiter** table for the main form, and select all fields except SSN from the **Student** table for the subform. Use the Datasheet layout and the Sumi Painting style. Specify the title **Recruiter Students** for the main form and the title **Student Subform** for the subform. Resize all columns in the subform to their best fit. Use Design view to resize the main form and the subform so that all fields are visible in the subform at the same time. Resize the Form window in Form view, as necessary, so that all fields are visible at the same time. Print the fourth main form record and its subform records. Save and close the form. Rename the main form object to **RecruiterStudents** and the subform object to **StudentSubform**.
7. Use the Report Wizard to create a report based on the primary Recruiter table and the related Student table. Select all fields from the **Recruiter** table, and then select all fields from the **Student** table except SSN, in the following order: FirstName, LastName, City, Nation, BirthDate, Gender, StudentID. Sort the detail records in ascending order by Nation. Choose the Align Left 2 layout and the Formal style for the report. Specify the title **Recruiters and Students** for the report.
8. Display the **Recruiters and Students** report in Design view and maximize the Report window. Then do the following:
   a. Choose the error checking option to ignore the error identified for the Nation label control.
   b. Reduce the size of the Nation label control by one mark on the horizontal ruler (from the right); then widen the FirstName label control to the left so that it is fully displayed in the report.
   c. Reduce the size of both the City label control and its associated text box in the Detail section so that their left edges begin at the mark immediately before the 3-inch mark on the horizontal ruler. Then widen the LastName label control to the right so that it is fully displayed in the report.
   d. Widen the Gender label control to the right to the mark immediately after the 5-inch mark on the horizontal ruler; the Gender label control should touch the adjacent StudentID label control.
9. Switch to Print Preview and make sure that all the labels are completely displayed.
10. Insert the **Travel** picture, which is located in the Brief\Review folder provided with your Data Files, in the Report Header section of the **Recruiters and Students** report. Position the picture so that its left edge aligns with the 4-inch mark on the horizontal ruler and its top edge is just below the top border line of the report.
11. Print only the first page of the report, and then close and save the modified report.
12. Rename the report object to **RecruitersAndStudents**.
13. If your database is stored on a floppy disk, you will need to turn off the Compact on Close feature before closing the **Recruits** database because there isn't enough room on the disk to compact the database. If your database is stored on a hard drive or a network drive, no action is necessary.
14. Close the Recruits database.

**Apply**

*Using what you learned in the tutorial, create forms and a report to work with and display data about video photography events.*

# Case Problem 1

**Data Files needed for this Case Problem: Videos.mdb (*cont. from Tutorial 3*) and Camcord.bmp**

*Lim's Video Photography*   Youngho Lim wants the Videos database to include forms and reports that will help him track and view information about his clients and their video shoot events. You'll create the necessary forms and reports by completing the following:

1. Open the **Videos** database located in the Brief\Case1 folder provided with your Data Files.
2. Use the Form Wizard to create a form based on the **Client** table. Select all fields for the form, the Columnar layout, and the Ricepaper style. Specify the title **Client Data** for the form.
3. Change the AutoFormat for the Client Data form to Standard.
4. Use the Find command to move to the record with ClientID 338, and then change the Address field value for this record to 2150 Brucewood Avenue.
5. Use the **Client Data** form to add a new record with the following field values:
   ClientID:       351
   ClientName:   Peters, Amanda
   Address:       175 Washington Street
   City:             Berkeley
   State:           CA
   Zip:             94704
   Phone:         510-256-1007
   Print only this form record, and then save and close the form.
6. Rename the form object to **ClientData**.
7. Use the Form Wizard to create a form containing a main form and a subform. Select all the fields from the **Client** table for the main form, and select all fields except ClientID from the **Contract** table for the subform. Use the Tabular layout and the Standard style. Specify the title **Contracts by Client** for the main form and the title **Contract Subform** for the subform.
8. Print the seventh main form record and its subform records, and then close the **Contracts by Client** form.
9. Rename the main form object to **ContractsByClient** and the subform object to **ContractSubform**.
10. Use the Report Wizard to create a report based on the primary Client table and the related Contract table. Select all the fields from the **Client** table, and select all the fields from the **Contract** table except ClientID. Sort the detail records in ascending order by ContractID. Choose the Align Left 2 layout and the Casual style. Specify the title **Client Contracts** for the report.
11. Switch to Design view, and then widen the Phone text box control so that the Phone field values are completely displayed in the report, if necessary.
12. Insert the **Camcord** picture, which is located in the Brief\Case1 folder provided with your Data Files, in the Report Header section of the **Client Contracts** report. Position the picture so that its left edge aligns with the 4-inch mark on the horizontal ruler and its top edge is just below the top border line of the report.
13. Print only the first page of the report, and then close and save the modified report.
14. Rename the report object to **ClientContracts**.
15. Close the Videos database.

**Challenge**

*Challenge yourself by creating and working with a form and a report for this e-commerce business.*

# Case Problem 2

**Data Files needed for this Case Problem: Meals.mdb** (*cont. from Tutorial 3*) **and Server.bmp**

*DineAtHome.course.com* Claire Picard continues her work with the Meals database to track and analyze the business activity of the restaurants she works with and their customers. To help her, you'll enhance the Meals database by completing the following:

1. Open the **Meals** database located in the Brief\Case2 folder provided with your Data Files.

2. Use the Form Wizard to create a form containing a main form and a subform. Select the RestaurantID, RestaurantName, City, Phone, and Website fields from the **Restaurant** table for the main form, and select all fields except RestaurantID from the **Order** table for the subform. Use the Datasheet layout and the Industrial style. Specify the title **Restaurant Orders** for the main form and the title **Order Subform** for the subform. Resize all columns in the subform to their best fit. Print the first main form record and its displayed subform records.

3. For the form you just created, change the AutoFormat to SandStone, and resize the Phone text box control so that the complete field value is displayed in the form. Save the changed form, and then print the first main form record and its subform records.

4. Navigate to the third record in the subform for the first main record, and then change the OrderAmt field value to 107.80.

5. Use the Find command to move to the record with RestaurantID 118, and then change the Phone field value to 941-272-1772.

**Explore** ▶ 6. Use the appropriate wildcard character to find all records with the word "House" anywhere in the restaurant name. (*Hint*: You must enter the wildcard character before and after the text you are searching for.) How many records did you find? Close the **Restaurant Orders** form.

7. Rename the main form object to **RestaurantOrders** and the subform object to **OrderSubform**.

**Explore** ▶ 8. Use the Report Wizard to create a report based on the primary Restaurant table and the related Order table. Select the RestaurantID, RestaurantName, Street, City, OwnerFirstName, and OwnerLastName fields from the **Restaurant** table, and select all fields from the **Order** table except RestaurantID. In the third Report Wizard dialog box, specify the OrderDate field as an additional grouping level. Sort the detail records by OrderAmt in *descending* order. Choose the Align Left 1 layout and the Bold style for the report. Specify the title **Orders by Restaurants** for the report.

9. Insert the **Server** picture, which is located in the Brief\Case2 folder provided with your Data Files, in the Report Header section of the **Orders by Restaurants** report. Leave the picture in its original position at the left edge of the Report Header section.

**Explore** ▶ 10. Use the "Type a question for help" box to ask the following question: "How do I move a control in front of or behind other controls?" Click the topic "Move one or more controls," and then click the subtopic "Move a control in front of or behind other controls." Read the information and then close the Help window and the Search Results task pane. Make sure the **Server** picture is still selected, and then move it behind the Orders by Restaurants title.

**Explore** ▶ 11. Use the "Type a question for help" box to ask the following question: "How do I change the background color of a control?" Click the topic "Change the background color of a control or section." Read the information and then close the Help window and the Search Results task pane. Select the Orders by Restaurant title object, and then change its background color to Transparent.

12. Display the report in Print Preview. Print just the first page of the report, and then close and save the report.

13. Rename the report object to **OrdersByRestaurants**.
14. Close the Meals database.

**Challenge**

*Use what you learned, plus some new skills, to create forms and a report to work with and display data about a zoo's patrons.*

# Case Problem 3

**Data Files needed for this Case Problem: Redwood.mdb (*cont. from Tutorial 3*) and Animals.bmp**

***Redwood Zoo*** Michael Rosenfeld wants to create forms and reports for the Redwood database. You'll help him create these database objects by completing the following:

1. Open the **Redwood** database located in the Brief\Case3 folder provided with your Data Files.
2. If your Redwood database is stored on a floppy disk, you will need to delete the files **Redwood97.mdb** and **Redwood2002.mdb** from your disk so you will have enough room to complete the steps. If your database is stored on a hard drive or a network drive, no action is necessary.
3. Use the Form Wizard to create a form based on the **Pledge** table. Select all fields for the form, the Columnar layout, and the Blueprint style. Specify the title **Pledge Info** for the form.
4. Use the **Pledge Info** form to update the **Pledge** table as follows:
   a. Use the Find command to move to the record with PledgeID 2490, and then change the FundCode to B11 and the TotalPledged amount to 75.
   b. Add a new record with the following values:
      PledgeID:           2977
      DonorID:            59021
      FundCode:           M23
      PledgeDate:         12/15/2006
      TotalPledged:       150
      PaymentMethod:   C
      PaymentSchedule:  S
   c. Print just this form record.
   d. Delete the record with PledgeID 2900.
5. Change the AutoFormat of the **Pledge Info** form to Expedition, save the changed form, and then use the form to print the last record in the **Pledge** table. Close the form.
6. Rename the form object to **PledgeInfo**.
7. Use the Form Wizard to create a form containing a main form and a subform. Select all the fields from the **Donor** table for the main form, and select the PledgeID, FundCode, PledgeDate, and TotalPledged fields from the **Pledge** table for the subform. Use the Datasheet layout and the Expedition style. Specify the title **Donors and Pledges** for the main form and the title **Pledge Subform** for the subform.
8. Display record 11 in the main form. Print the current main form record and its subform records, and then close the **Donors and Pledges** form.
9. Rename the main form object to **DonorsAndPledges** and the subform object to **PledgeSubform**.

**Explore**
10. Use the Report Wizard to create a report based on the primary Donor table and the related Pledge table. Select the DonorID, FirstName, LastName, and Class fields from the **Donor** table, and select all fields from the **Pledge** table except DonorID. In the third Report Wizard dialog box, specify the FundCode field as an additional grouping level. Sort the detail records in *descending* order by TotalPledged. Choose the Align Left 2 layout, Landscape orientation, and the Soft Gray style. Specify the title **Donors and Pledges** for the report.

11. Insert the **Animals** picture, which is located in the Brief\Case3 folder provided with your Data Files, in the Report Header section of the **Donors and Pledges** report. Position the picture so that its left edge aligns with the 4-inch mark on the horizontal ruler and its top edge is just below the top border line of the report.

**Explore** ▶ 12. Use the "Type a question for help" box to ask the following question: "How do I add a special effect to an object?" Click the topic "Make a control appear raised, sunken, shadowed, chiseled, or etched." Read the information, and then close the Help window and the Search Results task pane. Add the Shadowed special effect to the **Animals** picture, and then save the report.

**Explore** ▶ 13. Print only pages 1 and 7 of the report, and then close it.

14. Rename the report object to **DonorsAndPledges**.

15. If your database is stored on a floppy disk, you will need to turn off the Compact on Close feature before closing the **Redwood** database because there isn't enough room on the disk to compact the database. If your database is stored on a hard drive or a network drive, no action is necessary.

16. Close the **Redwood** database.

**Create**

*With the figures provided as guides, create a form and a report to display and manage data for this outdoor adventure company.*

# Case Problem 4

**Data Files needed for this Case Problem: Trips.mdb** (*cont. from Tutorial 3*) **and Raft.gif**

***Mountain River Adventures*** Connor and Siobhan Dempsey want to create forms and reports that will help them track and analyze data about their customers and the rafting trips they take. Help them enhance the Trips database by completing the following:

1. Open the **Trips** database located in the Brief\Case4 folder provided with your Data Files.

2. Create the form shown in Figure 4-35. Be sure to resize all columns in the subform to their best fit.

**Figure 4-35** ▶

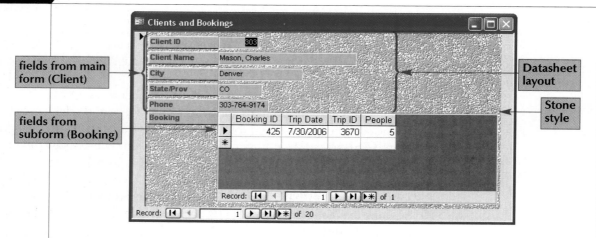

3. Using the form you just created, print the ninth main form record and its subform records.

4. Navigate to the second record in the subform for the ninth main record, and then change the People field value to 7.

5. Use the Find command to move to the record with ClientID 330, and then change the ClientName field value to Shaffer, Devon.

6. Use the appropriate wildcard character to find all records with a City value that begins with the letter "D." How many records did you find? Close the form.

7. Rename the form object to **ClientsAndBookings**.
8. Use the Report Wizard to create the report shown in Figure 4-36.

**Figure 4-36**

Callout labels on the figure:

- Raft picture inserted
- fields from primary table (Client)
- fields from related table (Booking)
- Align Left 1 layout and Formal style
- detail records sorted by TripDate in ascending order

*Hints*: Resize the Phone text box control in order to fully display the Phone field values in the report. When inserting the Raft picture (located in the Brief\Case4 folder provided with your Data Files), position the picture so that its left edge aligns with the 3-inch mark on the horizontal ruler and its top edge is just below the top border line of the report. Also, use the bottom center handle to resize the Raft picture so that it fits within the lines of the report header.

**Explore**

9. Insert the same **Raft** picture in the Report Footer section of the **Client Bookings** report. (Items placed in the Report Footer section appear only once, at the end of the report.) Position the picture so that its right edge aligns with the right edge of the report, at approximately the 6.5-inch mark on the horizontal ruler. Save the report.

**Explore**

10. View the first two pages of the report in Print Preview at the same time. (*Hint*: Use a toolbar button.) Use the Page navigation buttons to move through the report, displaying two pages at a time. Print only the first and last pages of the report, and then close the report.
11. Rename the report object to **ClientBookings**.
12. Close the Trips database.

**Research**

*Use the Internet to find and work with data related to the topics presented in this tutorial.*

# Internet Assignments

The purpose of the Internet Assignments is to challenge you to find information on the Internet that you can use to work effectively with this software. The actual assignments are updated and maintained on the Course Technology Web site. Log on to the Internet and use your Web browser to go to the Student Online Companion for New Perspectives Office 2003 at **www.course.com/np/office2003**. Click the Internet Assignments link, and then navigate to the assignments for this tutorial.

**Assess**

## SAM Assessment and Training

If you have a SAM user profile, you may have access to hands-on instruction, practice, and assessment of the skills covered in this tutorial. Log in to your SAM account and go to your assignments page to see what your instructor has assigned.

**Review**

# Quick Check Answers

### Session 4.1

1. The AutoForm Wizard creates a form automatically using all the fields in the selected table or query; the Form Wizard allows you to choose some or all of the fields in the selected table or query, choose fields from other tables and queries, and display fields in any order on the form.
2. An AutoFormat is a predefined style for a form (or report). To change a form's AutoFormat, display the form in Design view, click the AutoFormat button on the Form Design toolbar, click the new AutoFormat in the Form AutoFormats list box, and then click the OK button.
3. the last record in the table
4. datasheet
5. the question mark (?)
6. as many form records as can fit on a printed page

### Session 4.2

1. The main form displays the data from the primary table, and the subform displays the data from the related table.
2. You use the top set of navigation buttons to select and move through records from the related table in the subform, and the bottom set to select and move through records from the primary table in the main form.
3. control
4. Error Checking Options
5. Design view
6. Report Header

New Perspectives on

# Microsoft® Office Access 2003

# Read This Before You Begin: Tutorials 5–8

## To the Student

### Data Files

To complete the Level II Access Tutorials (Tutorials 5 through 8), you need the starting student Data Files. Your instructor will either provide you with these Data Files or ask you to obtain them yourself.

The Level II Access tutorials require the following folders to complete the Tutorials, Review Assignments, and Case Problems.

Intro\Tutorial folder
Intro\Review folder
Intro\Case1 folder
Intro\Case2 folder
Intro\Case3 folder
Intro\Case4 folder

You will need to copy these folders from a file server, a standalone computer, or the Web to the drive and folder where you will be storing your Data Files. (These Data Files can not be stored on floppy disks.) Your instructor will tell you which computer, drive letter, and folder(s) contain the files you need. You can also download the files by going to www.course.com; see the inside back or front cover for more information on downloading the files, or ask your instructor or technical support person for assistance.

The Data Files you work with in each tutorial in Level II build on the work you did in the previous tutorial. Thus when you begin Tutorial 6, you will use the Data Files that resulted after you completed the steps in Tutorial 5, the Tutorial 5 Review Assignments, and the Tutorial 5 Case Problems.

### Course Labs

There are no Course Labs for the Level II Access tutorials.

## To the Instructor

The Data Files and Course Labs are available on the Instructor Resources CD for this title. Follow the instructions in the Help file on the CD to install the programs to your network or standalone computer. See the "To the Student" section above for information on how to set up the Data Files that accompany this text.

You are granted a license to copy the Data Files and Course Labs to any computer or computer network used by students who have purchased this book.

## System Requirements

**If you are going to work through this book using your own computer, you need:**

- **Computer System** PC with Pentium 133-MHz or higher processor; Pentium III recommended. Microsoft Windows 2000 operating system with Service Pack 3 or later, Windows XP recommended.

These tutorials assume a typical installation of Microsoft Access 2003.

- **Data Files** You will not be able to complete the tutorials or exercises in this book using your own computer until you have the necessary starting Data Files.

## Objectives

**Session 5.1**
- Modify table designs using lookup fields, input masks, and data validation rules
- Use a subdatasheet and identify object dependencies

**Session 5.2**
- Use the Like, In, And, Not, and Or operators in queries
- Create a parameter query

**Session 5.3**
- Use query wizards to create a crosstab query, a find duplicates query, and a find unmatched query
- Create a top values query

# Enhancing a Table's Design and Creating Advanced Queries

*Making the Jobs Database Easier to Use*

## Case

### Northeast Seasonal Jobs International (NSJI)

Several years ago, Elsa Jensen founded Northeast Seasonal Jobs International (NSJI), a small Boston firm that serves as a job broker between foreign students seeking part-time, seasonal work and resort businesses located in New England and the eastern provinces of Canada. At first the company focused mainly on summer employment, but as the business continued to grow, Elsa increased the scope of operations to include all types of seasonal opportunities, including foliage tour companies in the fall and ski resorts in the winter.

Elsa incorporated the use of computers in all aspects of the business, including financial management, payroll, accounts payable, and student recruitment. Her company developed the Jobs database of employer and position data and uses **Microsoft Office Access 2003** (or simply **Access**) to manage it.

The Jobs database contains tables, queries, forms, and reports that Zack Ward, director of marketing, and Matt Griffin, manager of recruitment, use to track employers and their positions.

Elsa, Zack, and Matt are pleased with the information they get from the Jobs database. They are interested in taking better advantage of the power of Access to make the database easier to use and to create more sophisticated queries. For example, Zack wants to obtain lists of employers with certain area codes, and Matt needs a list of positions in a specified state or province. Elsa wants

## Student Data Files

▼ **Intro**

▽ **Tutorial folder**
    Jobs.mdb

▽ **Review folder**
    Students.mdb

▽ **Case1 folder**
    Clients.mdb

▽ **Case2 folder**
    Delivery.mdb

▽ **Case3 folder**
    Donors.mdb

▽ **Case4 folder**
    Outdoors.mdb

▽ **Case5 folder**
    (No starting Data Files)

to change the design of the Employer and Position tables. She wants to make entering the NAICS code value for an Employer record easier, improve the appearance of Phone field values, verify the correct entry of country and date values, and learn more about subdatasheets. (NAICS codes are the North American Industry Classification System codes used to classify businesses by their activities.) In this tutorial, you'll modify and customize the Jobs database to meet NSJI's goals.

# Session 5.1

## Creating a Lookup Wizard Field

The Employer table in the Jobs database contains information about the seasonal businesses with available jobs that NSJI fills with qualified foreign students. Elsa wants to make entering data in the table easier for her staff. In particular, data entry is easier if they do not need to remember the correct NAICS code for each employer. Because the Employer and NAICS tables have a one-to-many relationship, Elsa asks you to change the Employer table's NAICSCode field, which is a foreign key to the NAICS table, to a lookup field. A **lookup field** lets the user select a value from a list of possible values. For the NAICSCode field, the user will be able to select from the list of NAICS descriptions in the NAICS table rather than having to remember the correct NAICS code. Access will store the NAICS code in the NAICSCode field in the Employer table, but both the NAICS code and the NAICS description will appear in Datasheet view when entering or changing a code value. This arrangement makes entering and changing NAICS values easier for the user and guarantees that the NAICS code is valid. You use a **Lookup Wizard field** in Access to create a lookup field in a table.

Elsa asks you to change the NAICSCode field in the Employer table to a lookup field. You begin by opening the Jobs database and then opening the Employer table in Design view.

### To change the NAICSCode field to a lookup field:

▶ 1. Make sure you have created your copy of the Access Data Files, and that your computer can access them.

**Trouble?** If you don't have the Access Data Files, you need to get them before you can proceed. Your instructor will either give you the Data Files or ask you to obtain them from a specified location (such as a network drive). In either case, be sure that you make a backup copy of your Data Files before you start using them, so that the original files will be available on your copied disk in case you need to start over because of an error or problem. If you have any questions about the Data Files, see your instructor or technical support person for assistance.

**Trouble?** If you are not sure where to store your Data Files, read the "Read This Before You Begin" page or ask your instructor for help.

▶ 2. Start Access, open the **Jobs** database in the Intro\Tutorial folder provided with your Data Files, and then open the **Employer** table in Design view.

**Trouble?** If a dialog box opens with a message about installing the Microsoft Jet Service Pack, see your instructor or technical support person for assistance. You must have the appropriate Service Pack installed in order to open and work with Access databases safely.

**Trouble?** If a dialog box opens, warning you that the Jobs database may not be safe, click the Open button. Your security level is set to Medium, which is the security setting that lets you choose whether or not to open a database that contains macros, VBA, or certain types of queries. The Jobs database does not contain objects that will harm your computer, so you can safely open the database.

**Trouble?** If a dialog box opens, warning you that Access can't open the Jobs database due to security restrictions, click the OK button, click Tools on the menu bar, point to Macro, click Security, click the Medium option button, click the OK button, restart your computer if you're requested to do so, and then repeat Step 2. Your security level was set to High, which is the security setting that lets you open a database that contains macros, VBA, or certain types of queries only from trusted sources. Because the Jobs database does not contain objects that will harm your computer, you need to change the security setting to Medium and then safely open the Jobs database.

3. Scroll down (if necessary) to the NAICSCode field, click the right side of the **Data Type** text box for the NAICSCode field, and then click **Lookup Wizard**. The first Lookup Wizard dialog box opens. See Figure 5-1.

First Lookup Wizard dialog box  Figure 5-1

**Trouble?** If a list arrow appeared when you clicked the Data Type text box instead of a list box of data types, click the Data Type list arrow and then click Lookup Wizard. When you position the insertion point or select text in many Access text boxes, Access displays a list arrow, which you can click to display a list box with options. You can display the list arrow and the list box simultaneously if you click the text box near its right side.

This dialog box lets you specify a list of allowed values for the NAICSCode field in a record in the Employer table. You can specify a table or query from which users select the value, or you can enter a new list of values. You want the NAICSCode values to come from the NAICS table.

4. Make sure the option for looking up the values in a table or query is selected, and then click the **Next** button to display the next Lookup Wizard dialog box.

5. Click **Table: NAICS**, and then click the **Next** button to display the next Lookup Wizard dialog box. See Figure 5-2.

**Figure 5-2**   **Selecting the NAICS table fields**

This dialog box lets you select the lookup fields from the NAICS table. You need to select the NAICSCode field because it's the common field that links the NAICS and Employer tables. You also must select the NAICSDesc field because Elsa wants the user to be able to select from a list of NAICS descriptions when entering a new employer record or changing an existing NAICS code value.

▶ 6. Click the >> button to select both fields from the NAICS table, and then click the **Next** button to display the next Lookup Wizard dialog box. This dialog box lets you choose a sort order for the list box entries. Elsa wants the entries to appear in ascending NAICSDesc order. Note that ascending is the default sort order.

▶ 7. Click the **1** list arrow, click **NAICSDesc**, and then click the **Next** button. See Figure 5-3.

**Figure 5-3**   **Adjusting the widths of lookup columns**

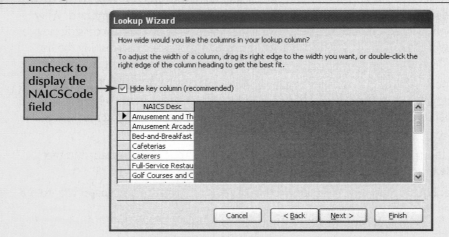

In this dialog box, the selected "Hide key column (recommended)" option means that the list of NAICSCode values will not appear in the Employer table datasheet; only the list of NAICSDesc values will appear. If you uncheck this option, the NAICSCode values will appear in the Employer table datasheet, but both field values will appear in a lookup list when you enter or change a value. The user can then select the correct NAICS code from the displayed codes and descriptions. Access will automatically store only the selected NAICSCode value in the Employer table. Elsa decides that she wants to display the NAICSCode field, so you'll remove the check mark for this option. In this dialog box, you can also adjust the widths of the displayed columns. Note that when you resize a column to its best fit, Access resizes the column so that the widest column heading and the visible field values fit the column width. However, some field values that aren't visible in this dialog box might be wider than the column width, so you must scroll down the column to make sure you don't have to repeat the column resizing.

8. Click the **Hide key column (recommended)** check box to deselect it, click the **NAICSCode** column selector, press and hold down the **Shift** key, click the **NAICSDesc** column selector to select both columns, release the **Shift** key, and then place the pointer on the right edge of the NAICSDesc field column heading. When the pointer changes to a ✛ shape, double-click to resize the columns to their best fits, scroll down the columns to make sure you don't have to repeat the resizing, and then click the **Next** button.

In the dialog box that appears next, you select the field(s) you want to store in the table. You'll store the NAICSCode field in the Employer table, but you won't store the NAICSDesc field in the table.

9. Make sure **NAICSCode** is selected in the Available Fields list box, and then click the **Next** button.

In the dialog box that appears next, you specify the field name for the lookup field. Because you'll be storing the NAICSCode field in the table, you'll accept the default field name, NAICSCode.

10. Click the **Finish** button.

To create the lookup field, Access must save the table design and join the NAICS and Employer tables in a one-to-many relationship. Access can then store the correct NAICSCode value in the Employer table. A dialog box opens asking you to confirm saving the table.

11. Click the **Yes** button. Access creates the lookup field, and you return to the Employer table in Design view. See Figure 5-4.

**Lookup Wizard field defined** ◀ **Figure 5-4**

The Data Type value for the NAICSCode field is still Text because this field contains text data. However, when you update the field, Access uses the NAICSCode field value to look up and display in the Employer table datasheet both NAICS codes and descriptions from the NAICS table.

After viewing a query that displays NAICSDesc field values, Elsa noticed that the NAICSCode field value stored in the Employer table for Boston Harbor Excursions is incorrect. She asks you to test the new lookup field to select the correct code. To do so, you need to switch to Datasheet view.

## To change the NAICSCode lookup field value:

▶ 1. Switch to Datasheet view.

The NAICSCode field values are in column 13. After you scroll to the right to view the NAICSCode column, you'll no longer be able to verify that you're changing the correct field value because the EmployerID and EmployerName fields will be hidden. You'll freeze those two columns so they remain visible in the datasheet as you scroll to the right.

▶ 2. Click the **Employer ID** column selector, press and hold down the **Shift** key, click the **Employer Name** column selector to select both columns, and then release the **Shift** key.

▶ 3. Click **Format** on the menu bar, click **Freeze Columns**, and then click anywhere in the datasheet to deselect the first two columns. A dark vertical line now separates the two left-most columns from the other columns. The dark line indicates that these two columns will remain visible no matter where you scroll in the datasheet. See Figure 5-5.

| Figure 5-5 | Freezing the first two datasheet columns |
| --- | --- |

You'll scroll to the right to view the rightmost columns in the datasheet.

▶ 4. Scroll to the right until you see the NAICS Code and Comments columns. Notice that the Employer ID and Employer Name columns, the two leftmost columns, remain visible.

▶ 5. Click **72232** in the NAICS Code column for record 2, and then click the list arrow to display the list of NAICSCode and NAICSDesc field values from the NAICS table. See Figure 5-6.

**List of NAICSCode and NAICSDesc field values** ◀ **Figure 5-6**

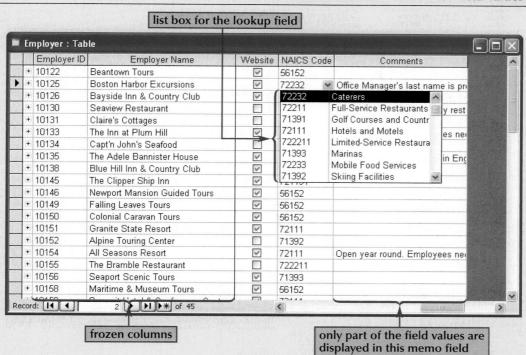

list box for the lookup field

frozen columns

only part of the field values are displayed in this memo field

6. Click **Marinas** to select the NAICSCode field value of 71393. The list box closes and 71393 appears in the NAICS Code text box; this new value will be stored in the Employer table for this column.

The Comments column is a memo field that NSJI staff members use to store explanations about the employer, its contact person, and its positions. The Comments field values are partially hidden because the datasheet column is not wide enough. You'll increase the datasheet row height so more of the Comments field values will be visible.

7. Place the pointer between the row selectors for rows 2 and 3, and, when the pointer changes to a ✛ shape, drag the edge down to the approximate position shown in Figure 5-7. Note that you could have increased the row height by placing the pointer between any two row selectors.

| Figure 5-7 | Datasheet rows resized |

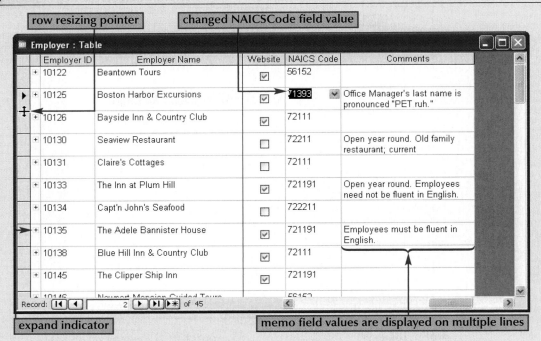

All datasheet rows are resized to the same height.

Elsa notices that a plus symbol appears to the left of the EmployerID field in the Employer table datasheet and asks what function it serves. You investigate and find that when you defined the one-to-many relationship between the Employer and Position tables in Tutorial 3, Access automatically added plus symbols to the Employer datasheet. These plus symbols let you view an employer's related Position table records in a subdatasheet.

# Displaying Related Records in a Subdatasheet

For tables such as the Employer and Position tables, which have a one-to-many relationship, you can display records from the related table—the Position table in this case—as a **subdatasheet** in the datasheet of the primary table—the Employer table in this case. When you first open a datasheet, its subdatasheets are not expanded. To display the Position subdatasheet for a specific employer, you click the **expand indicator** ⊞ in the row for that employer. Next, you'll display the Position subdatasheet for Beantown Tours.

### To display Position table records in a subdatasheet:

▶ **1.** Click the **expand indicator** ⊞ for Beantown Tours, which is EmployerID 10122. The subdatasheet for Beantown Tours opens. See Figure 5-8.

**Trouble?** If your Employer table datasheet does not contain expand indicators, you won't be able to perform this set of steps. Review the steps, and continue with the next section.

Position subdatasheet expanded ◄ **Figure 5-8**

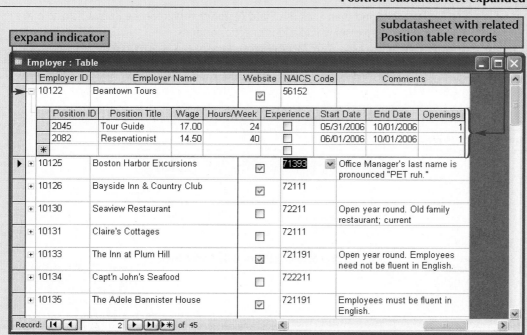

With the subdatasheet open, you can navigate and update it, just as you can a normal datasheet. Elsa now understands the subdatasheet feature and has no updates, so you'll collapse the subdatasheet.

► **2.** Click the **expand indicator** ⊟ for Beantown Tours. The subdatasheet for employer 10122 closes.

► **3.** Save your datasheet changes, and then scroll to the left until you see the Phone field in the Employer datasheet.

Elsa asks you to change the appearance of the Phone field in the Employer table to a standard telephone number format.

# Using the Input Mask Wizard

The Phone field in the Employer table is a 10-digit number that's difficult to read because it appears with none of the special formatting characters usually associated with a telephone number. For example, the Phone field value for Beantown Tours, which appears as 6174511970, would be more readable in any of the following formats: 617-451-1970, 617.451.1970, 617/451-1970, or (617) 451-1970. Elsa asks you to use the 617-451-1970 style for the Phone field.

Elsa wants hyphens to appear as literal display characters whenever users enter Phone field values. A **literal display character** is a special character that automatically appears in specific positions of a field value; users don't need to type literal display characters. To include these characters, you need to create an **input mask**, a predefined format used to enter and display data in a field. An easy way to create an input mask is to use the **Input Mask Wizard**, an Access tool that guides you in creating a predefined format for a field. You must use the Input Mask Wizard in Design view.

## To use the Input Mask Wizard for the Phone field:

1. Switch to Design view, and then click the **Field Name** text box for the Phone field to make it the current field and to display its Field Properties options.

2. Click the **Input Mask** text box in the Field Properties pane. A Build button […] appears to the right of the Input Mask text box.

3. Click the **Build** button […] next to the Input Mask text box. The first Input Mask Wizard dialog box opens. See Figure 5-9.

| Figure 5-9 | Input Mask Wizard dialog box |
| --- | --- |

scrollable list of predefined input masks

sample values for the corresponding input masks

practice area

**Trouble?** If a dialog box opens and tells you that this feature is not installed, insert your Office 2003 CD into the correct drive, and then click the Yes button. If you do not have an Office 2003 CD, ask your instructor or technical support person for help.

You can scroll the Input Mask list box, select the input mask you want, and then enter representative values to practice using the input mask.

4. If necessary, click **Phone Number** in the Input Mask list box to select it.

5. Click the far left side of the **Try It** text box. (___) ___-____ appears in the Try It text box. As you type a phone number, Access replaces the underscores, which are placeholder characters.

   **Trouble?** If your insertion point is not immediately to the right of the left parenthesis, press the ← key until it is.

6. Type **9876543210** to practice entering a sample phone number. The input mask formats the typed value as (987) 654-3210.

7. Click the **Next** button. The next Input Mask Wizard dialog box opens. In it, you can change the input mask and placeholder character. Because you can change an input mask easily after the Input Mask Wizard finishes, you'll accept all wizard defaults.

8. Click the **Finish** button. The Input Mask Wizard creates the phone number input mask, placing it in the Input Mask text box for the Phone field. See Figure 5-10.

**Phone number input mask created by the Input Mask Wizard** ◄ **Figure 5-10**

The characters preceding the first semicolon represent the input mask. The symbols in the default phone number input mask of !(999) 000-0000;;_ have the meanings shown in Figure 5-11.

**Input mask characters** ◄ **Figure 5-11**

| Input Mask Character | Description |
| --- | --- |
| ! | Input mask is displayed from right to left, rather than the default of left to right. Characters typed into the mask always fill in from left to right. |
| 9 | Digit or space can be entered. Entry is not required. |
| 0 | Digit only can be entered. Entry is required. |
| ;; | The character between the first and second semicolon determines whether to store in the database the literal display characters such as the hyphen and parentheses. If left blank or a value of 1, do not store the literal characters. If a value of 0, store the literal characters. |
| _ | Placeholder character because it follows the second semicolon |
| ( ) - | Literal display characters |

Elsa wants to view the Phone field with the default input mask before you change it for her.

## To view and change the input mask for the Phone field:

▶ **1.** Save your table design change. Because you've modified a field property, the Property Update Options button appears to the left of the Input Mask property.

▶ **2.** Click the **Property Update Options** button, and then click **Update Input Mask everywhere Phone is used**. The Update Properties dialog box opens. See Figure 5-12.

| Figure 5-12 | Update Properties dialog box |

objects dependent on the Phone field

Because the EmployerPositions form and the PositionsByEmployer report display Phone field values from the Employer table, Access will automatically change the Phone field's Input Mask property in these objects to your new input mask. This capability to update field properties in objects automatically when you modify a table field property is called **property propagation**. Although the Update Properties dialog box displays no queries, property propagation does occur with queries automatically. Property propagation is limited to field properties such as the Decimal Places, Description, Format, and Input Mask properties.

3. Click the **Yes** button. The Update Properties dialog box closes, Access updates the Input Mask property for the Phone field in these two objects, and the Property Update Options button closes.

4. Switch to Datasheet view.

5. Scroll the table to the right until the Phone field is visible. The Phone field values now have the format specified by the input mask.

6. Switch to Design view.

   The input mask changed from !(999) 000-0000;;_ to !\(999") "000\-0000;;_. The backslash character (\) causes the character that follows it to appear as a literal display character. Characters enclosed in quotation marks also appear as literal display characters.

7. Change the input mask to **!999\-000\-0000;;_** in the Input Mask text box for the Phone field.

8. Repeat Steps 1 through 5 to save your table design change, update the changed property on the two dependent objects, and switch to Datasheet view to review the input mask. The Phone field values now have the format Elsa requested. See Figure 5-13.

| Figure 5-13 | After changing the Phone field input mask |

**Employer : Table**

| Employer ID | Employer Name | Position | Phone | Website | NAICS Code | |
|---|---|---|---|---|---|---|
| 10122 | Beantown Tours | Office Manager | 617-451-1970 | ☑ | 56152 | |
| 10125 | Boston Harbor Excursions | Office Manager | 617-235-1800 | ☑ | 71393 | Office N pronoul |
| 10126 | Bayside Inn & Country Club | General Manager | 508-283-5775 | ☑ | 72111 | |
| 10130 | Seaview Restaurant | Manager | 508-776-8593 | ☐ | 72211 | Open y restaur |
| 10131 | Claire's Cottages | Manager | 508-822-1328 | ☐ | 72111 | |

Phone field with input mask

9. Close the Employer table.

Because Elsa wants her staff to store only standard 10-digit U.S. and Canadian phone numbers for NSJI employers, the input mask you've created will enforce the standard entry and display format that Elsa desires. However, this input mask does not allow values such as 617-USE-NSJI, 617.451.1970, 617/451-1970, (617) 451-1970, and most phone numbers from other countries. If you need to store phone numbers in a variety of formats, it's best to define the Phone field as a text field without an input mask and let users enter the literal display characters.

After each change to the Phone field's input mask, Access gave you the option to update, selectively and automatically, the Phone field's Input Mask property in other objects in the database. Elsa asks if there's an easy way to determine which objects are affected by changes made to other objects. To show Elsa how to determine the dependencies among objects in an Access database, you'll open the Object Dependencies task pane.

## Identifying Object Dependencies

An **object dependency** exists between two objects when a change to the properties of data in one object affects the properties of data in the other object. Dependencies between Access objects (tables, queries, forms, and so on) can occur in various ways. For example, the Employer and Position tables are dependent on each other because they have a one-to-many relationship. As another example, because the Employer table uses the NAICS table to obtain the NAICSDesc field to display along with the NAICSCode field, these two tables have a dependency. Any query, form, or other object that uses fields from the Employer table is dependent on the Employer table. Any form or report that uses fields from a query is directly dependent on the query and is indirectly dependent on the tables that provide the data to the query. Large databases contain hundreds of objects, so it would be useful to have a way to view the dependencies among objects easily before you attempt to delete or modify an object. The **Object Dependencies task pane** displays a collapsible list of the dependencies among the objects in an Access database; you click the list's expand indicators to show or hide different levels of dependencies. Next, you'll open the Object Dependencies task pane to show Elsa the object dependencies in the Jobs database.

### To open and use the Object Dependencies task pane:

1. Right-click **Employer** in the Tables list box, and then click **Object Dependencies** on the shortcut menu to open the Object Dependencies task pane. See Figure 5-14.

**Figure 5-14**    **After opening the Object Dependencies task pane**

**Trouble?** If a dialog box opens asking you if you want to update the information about object dependencies, click the OK button.

The Object Dependencies list box displays the objects that depend on the Employer table, the object name that appears at the top of the task pane. If you change the design of the Employer table, the objects in the list box might be affected by the change. Changing a property for a field in the Employer table that's also used by another listed object affects that other object. If the other object does not use the field you are changing, that other object is not affected.

2. Click the **Position** link in the Object Dependencies task pane. The Position table opens in Design view, so you can review the fields and determine that the EmployerID field in the Position table is a foreign key to the Employer table. This foreign key is the basis for the relationship between the Employer and Position tables and is the reason that the two tables have an object dependency.

3. Close the Position table, and then click the **expand indicator** ⊞ for the Position table in the Object Dependencies task pane. The list expands to display all the tables, queries, and forms that depend on the Position table.

4. Scroll down the Object Dependencies task pane to view the objects that depend on the Position table, and then click the **Objects that I depend on** option button to view the objects that affect the Employer table.

5. Click the **Things that cause dependencies** link to display Help about object dependencies, read the displayed information, and then close the Microsoft Access Help window.

**Trouble?** If a Help page about object dependencies does not appear, close the Microsoft Access Help window and continue with the next step.

6. Close the Object Dependencies task pane.

Elsa now better understands object dependencies and how to identify them by using the Object Dependencies task pane.

# Defining Data Validation Rules

Elsa wants to limit the entry of Country field values in the Employer table to Canada and USA because NSJI employer clients are located in only these two countries. In addition, Elsa wants to make sure that a StartDate field value entered in a Position table record is chronologically earlier than the EndDate field value in the same record. She's concerned that typing errors might produce incorrect query results and cause other problems. To provide these data-entry capabilities, you'll set field validation properties for the Country field in the Employer table and set table validation properties in the Position table.

## Defining Field Validation Rules

To prevent a user from entering a value other than Canada or USA in the Country field, you can create a **field validation rule** that verifies a field value by comparing it to a constant or a set of constants. You create a field validation rule by setting the Validation Rule and the Validation Text field properties. The **Validation Rule property** value specifies the valid values that users can enter in a field. The **Validation Text property** value will be displayed in a dialog box if the user enters an invalid value (in this case, a value other than Canada or USA). After you set these two Country field properties in the Employer table, Access will prevent users from entering an invalid Country field value in the Employer table and in all current and future queries and forms.

You'll now set the Validation Rule and Validation Text properties for the Country field in the Employer table.

### To create and test a field validation rule for the Country field:

▶ **1.** Open the **Employer** table in Design view, and then click the **Country Field Name** text box to make that row the current row.

To make sure that the only values entered in the Country field are Canada or USA, you'll specify a list of valid values in the Validation Rule text box.

▶ **2.** Click the **Validation Rule** text box, type **Canada or USA**, and then press the **Tab** key.

When you pressed the Tab key, the Validation Rule changed to "Canada" Or "USA". You can set the Validation Text property to a value that appears in a dialog box that opens if a user enters a value not listed in the Validation Rule text box.

▶ **3.** Type **Must be Canada or USA** in the Validation Text text box. See Figure 5-15.

| Figure 5-15 | Validation properties for the Country field |

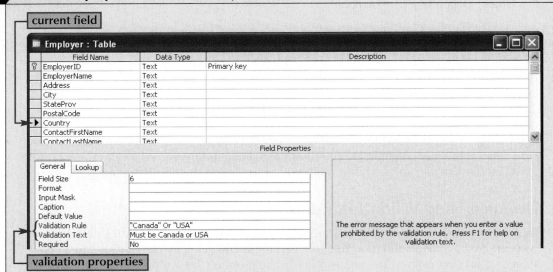

You can now save the table design changes and then test the validation properties.

4. Save your table design changes, and click the **Yes** button when asked if you want to test the existing Country field values in the Employer table against the new validation rule.

   Access tests the existing records in the Employer table against the validation rule. If any record violates the rule, you are prompted to continue testing or to revert to the previous Validation Rule property setting. Next, you'll test the validation rule.

5. Switch to Datasheet view, and then scroll the table to the right until the Country field is visible.

6. Double-click **USA** in the first row's Country field text box, type **Spain**, and then press the **Tab** key. A dialog box opens containing the message "Must be Canada or USA," which is the Validation Text property setting you created in Step 3.

7. Click the **OK** button, and then click the **Undo typing** button 🔄 on the Table Datasheet toolbar. The first row's Country field value again has its original value, USA.

8. Close the Employer table, and then click the **Yes** button if asked to save the table design changes.

Now that you've finished entering the field validation rule for the Country field in the Employer table, you'll next enter the table validation rule for the date fields in the Position table.

## Defining Table Validation Rules

To make sure that a user enters a StartDate field value in the Position table that is chronologically earlier than the record's EndDate field value, you can create a **table validation rule** that compares one field value in a table record to another field value in the same record to verify their relative accuracy. Once again you'll use the Validation Rule and Validation Text properties, but this time you'll set these properties for the table instead of for an individual field.

You'll now set the Validation Rule and Validation Text properties to compare the StartDate and EndDate field values in the Position table.

### To create and test a table validation rule in the Position table:

1. Open the **Position** table in Design view, and then click the **Properties** button 🗗 on the Table Design toolbar to open the Table Properties dialog box.

    To make sure that each StartDate field value is chronologically earlier than, or less than, each EndDate field value, you'll compare the two field values in the Validation Rule text box.

2. Click the **Validation Rule** text box, type **[StartDate]<[EndDate]**, and then press the **Tab** key. Make sure you type the brackets to enclose the field names. If you omit the brackets, Access automatically inserts quotation marks around the field names, in effect treating the field names as field values, and the table validation rule will not work correctly.

3. Type **The start date must be earlier than the end date** in the Validation Text text box. See Figure 5-16.

**Setting table validation properties** ◄ **Figure 5-16**

You can now test the validation properties.

4. Close the Table Properties dialog box, save your table design changes, and then click the **Yes** button when asked if you want to test the existing dates in the Position table against the new validation rule.

5. Switch to Datasheet view, select the EndDate field value in the first record, type **9/30/2005**, press the **Tab** key to advance to the Openings column, and then press the **Tab** key to complete your changes to the record. A dialog box opens containing the message "The start date must be earlier than the end date," which is the Validation Text property setting you entered in Step 3.

    Unlike field validation rule violations, which Access detects immediately after you finish your field entry and advance to another field, Access detects table validation rule violations when you finish all changes to the current record and advance to another record.

6. Click the **OK** button, and then press the **Esc** key to undo your change to the EndDate field value.

7. Close the Position table.

8. If you are not continuing on to the next session, close the Jobs database, and then exit Access.

You've completed Elsa's design changes to the Employer and Position tables. In the next session, you'll create queries that Elsa and her staff need.

**Review**

# Session 5.1 Quick Check

**1.** What is a lookup field?

**2.** What is a subdatasheet?

**3.** A(n) _____ is a predefined format you use to enter and display data in a field.

**4.** What is property propagation?

**5.** Define the Validation Rule property, and give an example of when you would use it.

**6.** Define the Validation Text property, and give an example of when you would use it.

# Session 5.2

# Using a Pattern Match in a Query

You are now ready to create the queries that Elsa, Matt, and Zack requested. You are already familiar with queries that use an exact match or a range of values (for example, queries that use the >= and < comparison operators) to select records. Access provides many other operators for creating select queries. These operators let you create more complicated queries that are difficult or impossible to create with exact match or range of values selection criteria.

Elsa, Matt, and Zack created a list of questions they want to answer using the Jobs database:

- Which employers have the 508 area code?
- What is the employer information for employers located in Maine (ME), New Hampshire (NH), or Vermont (VT)?
- What is the position information for all positions *except* those with the titles Lifeguard or Ski Patrol?
- What is the position information for those Waiter/Waitress or Kitchen Help positions located in Massachusetts (MA) or New Hampshire (NH)?
- What is the position information for positions in a particular state or province? For this query, the user needs to be able to specify the state or province.

Next, you will create the queries necessary to answer these questions. Zack wants to view the records for all employers within the 508 area code. He plans to travel in their area next week and wants to contact them. To answer Zack's question, you can create a query that uses a pattern match. A **pattern match** selects records with a value for the designated field that matches the pattern of the simple condition value, in this case, employers with the 508 area code. You do this using the Like comparison operator.

The **Like comparison operator** selects records by matching field values to a specific pattern that includes one or more of these wildcard characters: asterisk (*), question mark (?), and number symbol (#). The asterisk represents any string of characters, the question mark represents any single character, and the number symbol represents any single digit. Using a pattern match is similar to using an exact match, except that a pattern match includes wildcard characters.

To create the query, you must first place the Employer table field list in the Query window in Design view.

## To create the new query in Design view:

1. If you took a break after the previous session, make sure that Access is running, and that the **Jobs** database is open.

2. Click **Queries** in the Objects bar of the Database window, and then click the **New** button. The New Query dialog box opens.

3. Click **Design View** in the list box (if necessary), and then click the **OK** button. The Show Table dialog box opens on top of the Query window.

4. Click **Employer** in the Tables list box (if necessary), click the **Add** button, and then click the **Close** button. Access places the Employer table field list in the Query window.

5. Double-click the **title bar** of the Employer field list to highlight all the fields, and then drag the highlighted fields to the first column's Field text box in the design grid. Access places each field in a separate column in the design grid, in the same order that the fields appear in the table. See Figure 5-17.

**Adding the fields for the pattern match query**  Figure 5-17

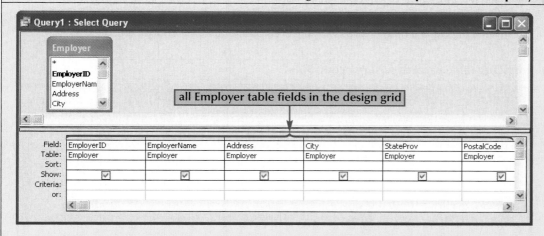

**Trouble?** If Employer.* appears in the first column's Field text box, you dragged the * from the field list instead of the highlighted fields. Press the Delete key, and then repeat Step 5.

Now you will enter the pattern match condition Like "508*" for the Phone field. Access will select records with a Phone field value of 508 in positions one through three. The asterisk (*) wildcard character specifies that any characters can appear in the remaining positions of the field value.

## To specify records that match the specified pattern:

1. Scroll the design grid until the Phone field is visible.

2. Click the **Phone Criteria** text box, and then type **Like "508*"**. See Figure 5-18.

   Note that if you omit the Like operator, Access automatically adds it when you run the query.

| Figure 5-18 | **Record selection based on matching a specific pattern** |

3. Click the **Run** button  on the Query Design toolbar, scroll the Query window until the Phone field is visible, and then reduce the row height, as shown in Figure 5-19. The query results display the nine records with the area code 508 in the Phone field.

| Figure 5-19 | **Employer table records for area code 508** |

Now you can save the query.

4. Click the **Save** button on the Query Datasheet toolbar. The Save As dialog box opens.

5. Type **508AreaCode** in the Query Name text box, and then press the **Enter** key. Access saves the query in the Jobs database.

Next, Zack asks you to create a query that displays information about employers in Maine (ME), New Hampshire (NH), or Vermont (VT). He wants a printout of the employer data for his administrative aide, who will contact these employers. To produce the results Zack wants, you'll create a query using a list-of-values match.

# Using a List-of-Values Match in a Query

A **list-of-values match** selects records whose value for the designated field matches one of two or more simple condition values. You could accomplish this by including several Or conditions in the design grid, but the In comparison operator provides an easier and clearer way to do this. The **In comparison operator** lets you define a condition with a list of two or more values for a field. If a record's field value matches one value from the list of defined values, then Access selects and includes that record in the query results.

   To display the information Zack requested, you want to select records if their StateProv field value equals ME, NH, or VT. These are the values you will use with the In comparison operator.

## To create the query using a list-of-values match:

▶ **1.** Switch to Design view.

   First, you need to delete the condition for the previous query you created.

▶ **2.** Click the **Phone Criteria** text box, press the **F2** key to highlight the entire condition, and then press the **Delete** key to remove the condition.

   Now you can enter the criteria for the new query using the In comparison operator. When you use this operator, you must enclose the list of values you want to match within parentheses and separate the values with commas. In addition, for Text data types you must enclose each value in quotation marks, but you don't use the quotation marks for Number data type fields.

▶ **3.** Scroll the design grid to the left to display the StateProv column, click the **StateProv Criteria** text box, and then type **In ("ME","NH","VT")**. See Figure 5-20.

**Record selection based on matching field values to a list of values** ◀ **Figure 5-20**

| Field: | StateProv | PostalCode | Country | ContactFirstName | ContactLastName | Position |
|---|---|---|---|---|---|---|
| Table: | Employer | Employer | Employer | Employer | Employer | Employer |
| Sort: | | | | | | |
| Show: | ☑ | ☑ | ☑ | ☑ | ☑ | ☑ |
| Criteria: | In ("ME","NH","VT") | | | | | |
| or: | | | | | | |

**list-of-values selection criterion**

▶ **4.** Run the query. Access displays the recordset, which shows the 14 records with ME, NH, or VT in the StateProv field.

   Now you can print the query results in landscape for Zack. Although Zack doesn't need this information again, you'll save this query so that the printed results contain an appropriate heading, and then you'll delete the query.

▶ **5.** Click **File** on the menu bar, click **Save As**, type **EmployersInSelectedStates** in the Save Query text box, and then press the **Enter** key.

▶ **6.** Click **File** on the menu bar, click **Page Setup** to open the Page Setup dialog box, click the **Page** tab, click the **Landscape** option button, and then click the **OK** button.

▶ **7.** Click the **Print** button 🖨 on the Query Datasheet toolbar, and then close the query.

▶ **8.** Right-click **EmployersInSelectedStates** in the Queries list box, click **Delete** on the shortcut menu, and then click the **Yes** button to confirm the query deletion.

Matt recruited several students who qualify for any position except Lifeguard and Ski Patrol. He'd now like to see which positions are available for those students. You can provide Matt with this information by creating a query with the Not logical operator.

# Using the Not Operator in a Query

The **Not logical operator** negates a criterion or selects records for which the designated field does not match the criterion. For example, if you enter Not = "CT" in the Criteria text box for the StateProv field in the Employer table, the query results show records that do not have the StateProv field value CT, that is, records of all employers not located in Connecticut.

To create Matt's query, you will combine the Not logical operator with the In comparison operator to select positions whose PositionTitle field value is not in the list ("Lifeguard","Ski Patrol"). The WeeklyWages query has the fields that Matt needs to see in the query results.

## To create the query using the Not logical operator:

1. Open the **WeeklyWages** query in Design view.

2. Click the **PositionTitle Criteria** text box, and then type **Not In ("Lifeguard","Ski Patrol")** for the condition. See Figure 5-21.

| Figure 5-21 | Record selection based on not matching a list of values |

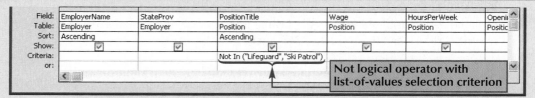

**Trouble?** Your screen might show only part of the criterion in the PositionTitle Criteria text box.

3. Run the query. The recordset displays only those records with a PositionTitle field value that is not Lifeguard and is not Ski Patrol. The recordset includes a total of 58 of the 64 position records.

4. Scroll down the datasheet to make sure that no Lifeguard or Ski Patrol positions appear in your results.

Matt wants a printed copy of the query results.

5. Switch to Print Preview, and use the navigation buttons to preview the report. Notice that you can't print all seven columns on one page, so you'll change to landscape orientation.

6. Click the **Setup** button on the Print Preview toolbar to open the Page Setup dialog box, click the **Page** tab, click the **Landscape** option button, and then click the **OK** button.

7. Print the query results.

Now you can close the query without saving it, because Matt does not need to run this query again.

8. Close the query without saving your design changes.

You now are ready to create the query to answer Matt's question about Waiter/Waitress or Kitchen Help positions located in Massachusetts (MA) or New Hampshire (NH).

# Using Both the And and Or Operators in the Same Query

Matt wants to see the employer names, states/provinces, position titles, wages, hours per week, number of openings, and weekly wages for employers in Massachusetts or New Hampshire that have openings for Waiter/Waitress or Kitchen Help positions. To create this query, you must use the And logical operator and the Or logical operator to create two compound conditions. That is, you will create conditions that select records for employers located in Massachusetts *or* in New Hampshire *and* have Waiter/Waitress positions *or* Kitchen Help positions. Figure 5-22 shows which records you need to select.

| **Records selected based on the conditions in Matt's query** | | | | **Figure 5-22** |
|---|---|---|---|---|

|  | **MA** | **NH** | **Other StateProv Value** |
|---|---|---|---|
| Waiter/Waitress | Yes | Yes | No |
| Kitchen Help | Yes | Yes | No |
| Other Position Value | No | No | No |

Because Matt wants to see the same fields used in the WeeklyWages query, you will use this query as the basis for your new query.

### To create the query using the And logical operator with the Or logical operator:

▶ 1. Open the **WeeklyWages** query in Design view.

  Matt wants to view data for employers in Massachusetts (MA) or New Hampshire (NH). You have several choices for specifying the required Or logical operator. One choice is to type "MA" in the StateProv Criteria text box and then type "NH" in the StateProv or text box. A second choice is to type "MA" Or "NH" in the StateProv Criteria text box. A third choice, and the one you'll use, is the In comparison operator.

▶ 2. Click the **StateProv Criteria** text box, type **In (MA,NH)** and then press the **Enter** key. The StateProv condition changes to In ("MA","NH") because Access adds quotation marks automatically to fields defined with the Text data type.

  To use the And logical operator, you need to enter the condition for the PositionTitle field in the same row as the StateProv condition. This time you'll use the Or logical operator for the condition in the PositionTitle column.

▶ 3. Type **"Waiter/Waitress" Or "Kitchen Help"** in the PositionTitle Criteria text box, and then press the **Enter** key. See Figure 5-23.

| **And with Or conditions in the design grid** | **Figure 5-23** |
|---|---|

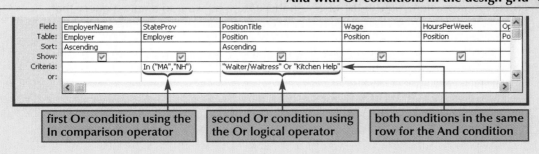

| Field: | EmployerName | StateProv | PositionTitle | Wage | HoursPerWeek | Op |
|---|---|---|---|---|---|---|
| Table: | Employer | Employer | Position | Position | Position | Po |
| Sort: | Ascending |  | Ascending |  |  |  |
| Show: | ☑ | ☑ | ☑ | ☑ | ☑ |  |
| Criteria: |  | In ("MA","NH") | "Waiter/Waitress" Or "Kitchen Help" |  |  |  |
| or: |  |  |  |  |  |  |

| first Or condition using the In comparison operator | second Or condition using the Or logical operator | both conditions in the same row for the And condition |
|---|---|---|

**Trouble?** Your screen might show only part of the criterion in the PositionTitle Criteria text box.

▶ **4.** Run the query. Access displays the query results. See Figure 5-24.

**Figure 5-24** ▶ **Results of query using And with Or**

New Hampshire employers selected

| Employer Name | State/Prov | Position Title | Wage | Hours/Week | Openings | Weekly Wages |
|---|---|---|---|---|---|---|
| All Seasons Resort | MA | Waiter/Waitress | 10.00 | 30 | 2 | 300.00 |
| Bayside Inn & Country Club | MA | Waiter/Waitress | 10.50 | 32 | 2 | 336.00 |
| Capt'n John's Seafood | MA | Kitchen Help | 12.00 | 40 | 2 | 480.00 |
| Granite State Resort | NH | Kitchen Help | 13.00 | 35 | 3 | 455.00 |
| Moondance Inn & Ski Resort | NH | Waiter/Waitress | 10.50 | 40 | 1 | 420.00 |
| The Berkshire House | MA | Kitchen Help | 13.00 | 32 | 1 | 416.00 |
| The Berkshire House | MA | Waiter/Waitress | 9.50 | 30 | 2 | 285.00 |
| The Bramble Restaurant | MA | Waiter/Waitress | 9.50 | 30 | 1 | 285.00 |
| The Clipper Ship Inn | MA | Kitchen Help | 12.50 | 32 | 2 | 400.00 |
| The Clipper Ship Inn | MA | Waiter/Waitress | 12.00 | 32 | 3 | 384.00 |
| The Clipper Ship Inn | MA | Waiter/Waitress | 10.00 | 32 | 2 | 320.00 |

Massachusetts employers selected

Waiter/Waitress or Kitchen Help positions

Record: |◄ ◄| | 1 | ► ►| ►* | of 11

The query results show records for employers in Massachusetts or New Hampshire that have either Waiter/Waitress or Kitchen Help positions. Next, you'll save the query with a new name (to keep the original query intact), and then you'll close the query.

▶ **5.** Click **File** on the menu bar, click **Save As**, type **SpecialStateProvPositions** in the Save Query text box, and then press the **Enter** key.

▶ **6.** Close the query.

**Trouble?** If necessary, scroll the Queries list box to the left to display all the queries.

You are now ready to create the query to satisfy Matt's request for information about positions in a particular state or province.

# Creating a Parameter Query

Matt's final query asks for records in the WeeklyWages query for employers in a particular state or province. For this query, he wants to specify the state or province, such as RI (Rhode Island), QC (Quebec), or NS (Nova Scotia).

To create this query, you will modify the existing WeeklyWages query. You could create a simple condition using an exact match for the StateProv field, but you would need to change it in Design view every time you run the query. Instead, you will create a parameter query. A **parameter query** displays a dialog box to prompt you to enter one or more criteria values when you run the query. In this case, you want to create a query that prompts you for the state or province of the employers to select from the table. You enter the prompt in the Criteria text box for the StateProv field.

When Access runs the query, it will open a dialog box and prompt you to enter the state or province. Access then creates the query results, just as if you had changed the criteria in Design view.

## Creating a Parameter Query

- Create a select query that includes all fields to appear in the query results. Also choose the sort fields and set the criteria that do not change when you run the query.
- Decide which fields will use prompts when the query runs. In the Criteria text box for each of these fields, type the prompt you want to appear in a message box when you run the query, and enclose the prompt in brackets.

Now you can open the WeeklyWages query in Design view and change its design to create the parameter query.

### To create the parameter query based on an existing query:

1. Open the **WeeklyWages** query in Design view.

   Next, you must enter the criteria for the parameter query. In this case, Matt wants the query to prompt users to enter the state or province for the position information they want to view. So, you need to enter the prompt in the Criteria text box for the StateProv field. Brackets must enclose the text of the prompt.

2. Click the **StateProv Criteria** text box, type **[Enter the state or province:]** and then press the **Enter** key. See Figure 5-25.

**Specifying the prompt for the parameter query** | Figure 5-25

prompt text

   **Trouble?** Your screen might show only part of the criterion in the StateProv Criteria text box.

3. Run the query. Access displays a dialog box prompting you for the name of the state or province. See Figure 5-26.

**Enter Parameter Value dialog box** | Figure 5-26

enter value here

prompt

The bracketed text you specified in the Criteria text box of the StateProv field appears above a text box, in which you must type a StateProv field value. You must enter the value so that it matches the spelling of a StateProv field value in the table, but you can enter the value in either lowercase or uppercase letters. Matt wants to see all positions in Nova Scotia (NS).

4. Type **NS**, and then press the **Enter** key. The recordset displays the data for the three positions in Nova Scotia. See Figure 5-27.

| Figure 5-27 | **Results of the parameter query** |

Matt plans to run this query frequently to monitor available positions by state or province, so he asks you to save it with a new name. You'll save the query as WeeklyWagesParameter.

▶ **5.** Click **File** on the menu bar, and then click **Save As**. The Save As dialog box opens.

▶ **6.** Press the **End** key, type **Parameter**, press the **Enter** key, and then close the query.

Matt asks what happens if he doesn't enter a value in the dialog box when he runs the WeeklyWagesParameter query. You run the query to show Matt the answer to his question.

▶ **7.** Right-click **WeeklyWagesParameter** in the Queries list box to select it and to display the shortcut menu, and then click **Open** on the shortcut menu. The Enter Parameter Value dialog box opens.

If you click the OK button or press the Enter key, you'll run the parameter query without entering a value for the StateProv field criterion.

▶ **8.** Click the **OK** button. Access displays no records in the query results.

When you run the WeeklyWagesParameter query and enter NS in the dialog box, Access runs the query the same way as if you had entered *"NS"* in the StateProv Criteria text box in the design grid; Access displays all Nova Scotia employer records. When you do not enter a value in the dialog box, Access runs the query the same way as if you had entered *null* in the StateProv Criteria text box. Because none of the records has a null StateProv field value, Access displays no records. Recall that a null field value is the absence of a value for the field.

Matt asks if there's a way to display records for a selected StateProv field value when he enters its value in the dialog box and to display all records when he doesn't enter a value. To provide this feature, you need to change the Criteria text box in the design grid for the StateProv column. You'll change the entry from *[Enter the state or province:]* to *Like [Enter the state or province:] & "*"*. The **& (ampersand)** symbol is a concatenation operator that joins expressions. When you run the parameter query with this new entry, you get one of the following recordsets:

- If you enter NS in the dialog box, the entry is the same as *Like "NS" & "*"*, which becomes *Like "NS*"* after the concatenation operation. That is, Access selects all records whose StateProv field values have NS in the first two positions and any characters in the remaining positions. Because the StateProv field values are all two-character values, the recordset displays only Nova Scotia employers.
- If you enter N in the dialog box, the entry is the same as *Like "N*"*, and the recordset displays employers in Nova Scotia (NS) and New Hampshire (NH), the only StateProv field values that begin with the letter N.
- If you enter no value in the dialog box, the entry is the same as *Like Null & "*"*, which becomes *Like "*"* after the concatenation operation, and the recordset displays employers in all states and provinces.

Now you'll modify the parameter query to satisfy Matt's request and test the new version of the query.

## To modify and test the parameter query:

▶ 1. Switch to Design view.

▶ 2. Right-click the **StateProv Criteria** text box, and then click **Zoom** on the shortcut menu to open the Zoom dialog box.

The Zoom dialog box has a large text box for entering text, expressions, and other values. You'll use the Zoom dialog box to modify the value in the StateProv Criteria text box.

▶ 3. Position the insertion point to the left of the expression in the Zoom dialog box, type **Like**, press the **spacebar**, press the **End** key, press the **spacebar**, and then type **& "*"**. See Figure 5-28.

**Modified value in the StateProv Criteria text box** ◀ **Figure 5-28**

Now you can test the modified parameter query.

▶ 4. Click the **OK** button to close the Zoom dialog box, save your query design changes, and then run the query.

First, you'll test the query to display positions in Nova Scotia.

▶ 5. Type **NS**, and then press the **Enter** key. The recordset displays the data for the three positions in Nova Scotia.

Now you'll test the query without entering a value when prompted.

▶ 6. Switch to Design view, run the query, and then click the **OK** button. The recordset displays all 64 original records in the query results.

Finally, you'll test the query and enter N in the dialog box.

▶ 7. Switch to Design view, run the query, type **N**, and then press the **Enter** key. The recordset displays the 14 records for employers in New Hampshire and Nova Scotia.

▶ 8. Close the query.

▶ 9. If you are not continuing on to the next session, close the Jobs database, and then exit Access.

The Employer and Position table design changes you made and the queries you created will make the Jobs database easier to use. In the next session, you will create a top values query and use query wizards to create three additional queries.

# Session 5.2 Quick Check

1. Which comparison operator selects records based on a specific pattern?
2. What is the purpose of the asterisk (*) in a pattern match query?
3. When do you use the In comparison operator?
4. How do you negate a selection criterion?
5. When do you use a parameter query?

# Session 5.3

## Creating a Crosstab Query

Elsa is considering expanding the business to include more states and provinces in which NSJI operates. Many factors will affect her decision, but her first area of interest is determining how much business NSJI conducts in Canada versus the United States and how the number of openings affects each country's business. She asks you to create a crosstab query using the Crosstab Query Wizard to provide the information she needs.

A **crosstab query** performs aggregate function calculations on the values of one database field and displays the results in a spreadsheet format. An **aggregate function** performs an arithmetic operation on selected records in a database. Figure 5-29 lists the aggregate functions you can use in a crosstab query. A crosstab query can also display one additional aggregate function value that summarizes the set of values in each row. The crosstab query uses one or more fields for the row headings on the left and one field for the column headings at the top.

**Figure 5-29** ▷ **Aggregate functions used in crosstab queries**

| Aggregate Function | Definition |
| --- | --- |
| Avg | Average of the field values |
| Count | Number of the nonnull field values |
| First | First field value |
| Last | Last field value |
| Max | Highest field value |
| Min | Lowest field value |
| StDev | Standard deviation of the field values |
| Sum | Total of the field values |
| Var | Variance of the field values |

Figure 5-30 shows two query recordsets—the first from a select query and the second from a related crosstab query. The title bar indicates the type of query.

Both queries are based on the PotentialIncome query, which joins the Employer and Position tables, but the crosstab query provides more valuable information. For each record in the Employer table that has one or more records in the Position table, the select query uses the Group By operator to display the StateProv and Country fields from the Employer table and the EmployerID field from the Position table. The select query also includes calculated fields that display the sum of the number of openings and the sum of the placement fees for each group. Notice that there are many rows for TotalOpenings values of 1, 2, 3, and so on, and many records for Canada and the USA. (Not all records are currently visible on the screen.) Note that the PlacementFee field is a calculated field; for each position filled, NSJI calculates the placement fee it charges employers by multiplying the weekly wages (multiply the HoursPerWeek and Wage fields in the Position table) for a position by two.

On the other hand, the crosstab query displays just one row for each different TotalOpenings value. The Total Openings column in the crosstab query identifies each row, and the field values for the Country field in the select query become the rightmost column headings in the crosstab query. The crosstab query uses the Sum aggregate function on the PlacementFee field to produce the displayed values in the Total Of PlacementFee, Canada, and USA columns. The Total Of PlacementFee column represents the total of the PlacementFee values for each row in the select query. For example, you can use the crosstab query to see that all employers with two total openings in Canada have total placement fees of $3,552.00, and that all employers with two total openings in the USA have total placement fees of $18,650.00. You could extract the same data from a select query, but the crosstab query does it for you automatically. Using the crosstab query recordset, Elsa can quickly see the total placement fees in each country for each number of total openings.

The quickest way to create a crosstab query is to use the **Crosstab Query Wizard**, which guides you through the steps for creating one. You could also change a select query to a crosstab query using the Query Type button on the Query Design toolbar. (Refer to the Help system for more information on creating a crosstab query without using a wizard.)

| Reference Window | **Using the Crosstab Query Wizard** |
|---|---|

- In the Database window, click Queries in the Objects bar to display the Queries list, and then click the New button.
- Click Crosstab Query Wizard, and then click the OK button.
- Complete the Wizard dialog boxes to select the table or query on which to base the crosstab query, select the row heading field or fields, select the column heading field, select the calculation field and its aggregate function, and enter a name for the crosstab query.

The crosstab query you will create, which is similar to the one shown in Figure 5-30, has the following characteristics:

- The PotentialIncome query in the Jobs database is the basis for the new crosstab query; it includes the EmployerID, StateProv, Country, TotalOpenings, and PlacementFee fields.
- The TotalOpenings calculated field from the Potential Income query is the leftmost column in the crosstab query and identifies each crosstab query row.
- The field values that appear in the Employer table for the Country field identify the rightmost columns of the crosstab query.
- The crosstab query applies the Sum aggregate function to the PlacementFee calculated field from the PotentialIncome query and displays the resulting total values in the Canada and USA columns of the query results. If one country has two or more employers with the same number of total openings, then the sum of the total openings appears in the intersecting cell of the crosstab query results.
- The total of the PlacementFee values appears for each row in a column with the heading Total Of PlacementFee.

You are now ready to create the crosstab query based on the PotentialIncome query. The crosstab query will show NSJI's placement fees in each country based on the number of total openings.

### To start the Crosstab Query Wizard:

1. If you took a break after the previous session, make sure that Access is running, and that the **Jobs** database is open.

2. Click **Queries** in the Objects bar of the Database window, and then click the **New** button. The New Query dialog box opens.

3. Click **Crosstab Query Wizard**, and then click the **OK** button. The first Crosstab Query Wizard dialog box opens.

You'll now use the Crosstab Query Wizard to create the crosstab query for Elsa.

## To finish the Crosstab Query Wizard:

▸ **1.** Click the **Queries** option button in the View section to display the list of queries in the Jobs database, and then click **Query: PotentialIncome**. See Figure 5-31.

Choosing the table or query for the crosstab query ◂ Figure 5-31

PotentialIncome query selected

Crosstab Query Wizard

Which table or query contains the fields you want for the crosstab query results?

Query: NAICSAndEmployers
Query: PotentialIncome
Query: PotentialIncomeByEmployer
Query: PotentialPlacementFees
Query: ReportedWeeklyWages
Query: SelectedEmployerInfo
Query: SpecialStateProvPositions
Query: WageStatistics

To include fields from more than one table, create a query containing all the fields you need and then use this query to make the crosstab query.

View
○ Tables  ● Queries  ○ Both

click to display Queries list

Sample:

| | Header1 | Header2 | Header3 |
|---|---|---|---|
| | TOTAL | | |

Cancel   < Back   Next >   Finish

▸ **2.** Click the **Next** button to open the next Crosstab Query Wizard dialog box, in which you choose the field (or fields) for the row headings. Because Elsa wants the crosstab query to display one row for each TotalOpenings value, you will select that field for the row headings.

▸ **3.** In the Available Fields list box, click **TotalOpenings**, and then click the [ > ] button to move TotalOpenings to the Selected Fields list box. When you select a field, Access changes the sample crosstab query in the bottom of the dialog box to illustrate your choice.

▸ **4.** Click the **Next** button to open the next Crosstab Query Wizard dialog box, in which you select the field values that will serve as column headings. Elsa wants to see the potential income by country, so you need to select the Country field for the column headings.

▸ **5.** Click **Country** in the list box, and then click the **Next** button.

In the Crosstab Query Wizard dialog box that appears next, you choose the field that will be calculated for each row and column intersection and the function to use for the calculation. The results of the calculation will appear in the row and column intersections of the query results. Elsa needs to calculate the sum of the PlacementFee field value for each row and column intersection.

▸ **6.** Click **PlacementFee** in the Fields list box, click **Sum** in the Functions list box, and then make sure that the **Yes, include row sums** check box is checked. The Yes, include row sums option creates a column showing the overall totals for the values in each row of the query recordset. See Figure 5-32.

**Figure 5-32** Completed crosstab query design

7. Click the **Next** button to open the final Crosstab Query Wizard dialog box, in which you choose the query name.

8. Type **PlacementFeeCrosstab** in the text box, be sure the option button for viewing the query is selected, and then click the **Finish** button. Access saves the crosstab query, and then displays the query recordset.

9. Resize all the columns in the query recordset to their best fit, and then click **TotalOpenings 1** to deselect any selected value or columns. See Figure 5-33.

**Figure 5-33** Crosstab query recordset

The query recordset contains one row for each TotalOpenings field value. The Total Of PlacementFee column shows the total placement fees for employers with that total number of openings. The columns labeled Canada and USA show the total placement fees for employers with that total number of openings in each country.

You can now close the completed query.

10. Close the query, and then click the **Yes** button when asked to save the query layout changes.

Access uses unique icons to represent different types of queries. The crosstab query icon appears in the Queries list box to the left of the PlacementFeeCrosstab query. This icon looks different from the icon that appears to the left of the other queries, which are all select queries.

Next, Elsa wants her staff to concentrate on filling those positions for employers with two or more different available positions. Filling these positions will give NSJI the best chance for repeat business with these employers in future years. To find the information Elsa needs, you'll create a find duplicates query.

## Creating a Find Duplicates Query

A **find duplicates query** is a select query that finds duplicate records in a table or query. You can create this type of query using the **Find Duplicates Query Wizard**. A find duplicates query searches for duplicate values based on the fields you select as you answer the Wizard's questions. For example, you might want to display all employers that have the same name, all students who have the same phone number, or all products that have the same description. Using this type of query, you can locate duplicates to avert potential problems (for example, you might have inadvertently assigned two different numbers to the same product), or you can eliminate duplicates that cost money (for example, you could send just one advertising brochure to all customers having the same address).

You can meet Elsa's request by using the Find Duplicates Query Wizard to display records for employers that appear more than once in the EmployerPositions query, which lists 64 available positions and their related employers.

### Using the Find Duplicates Query Wizard

Reference Window

- In the Database window, click Queries in the Objects bar to display the Queries list, and then click the New button.
- Click Find Duplicates Query Wizard, and then click the OK button.
- Complete the Wizard dialog boxes to select the table or query on which to base the query, select the field or fields to check for duplicate values, select the additional fields to include in the query results, enter a name for the query, and then click the Finish button.

You'll use the Find Duplicates Query Wizard to create and run a new query to display duplicate employer names in the EmployerPositions query results.

### To create the query using the Find Duplicates Query Wizard:

1. Click **Queries** in the Objects bar of the Database window (if necessary), and then click the **New** button to open the New Query dialog box.

2. Click **Find Duplicates Query Wizard**, and then click the **OK** button. The first Find Duplicates Query Wizard dialog box opens. In this dialog box, you select the table or query on which to base the new query. You'll use the EmployerPositions query.

3. Click the **Queries** option button in the View section to display the list of queries, click **Query: EmployerPositions**, and then click the **Next** button. Access opens the next Find Duplicates Query Wizard dialog box, in which you choose the fields you want to check for duplicate values.

▸ **4.** In the Available fields list box, click **EmployerName** (if necessary), click the ⊃ button to select the EmployerName field as the field to check for duplicate values, and then click the **Next** button. In the next Find Duplicates Query Wizard dialog box, you select the additional fields you want displayed in the query results.

Elsa also wants all remaining fields to be included in the query results.

▸ **5.** Click the ⊃⊃ button to move all fields from the Available Fields list box to the Additional query fields list box, and then click the **Next** button. Access opens the final Find Duplicates Query Wizard dialog box, in which you enter a name for the query. You'll use EmployersWithMultiplePositions as the query name.

▸ **6.** Type **EmployersWithMultiplePositions** in the text box, be sure the option button for viewing the results is selected, and then click the **Finish** button. Access saves the query, and then displays the 47 records for employers with two or more different available positions. See Figure 5-34.

| Figure 5-34 | Query recordset for employers with multiple positions |

| Employer Name | City | State/Prov | Position Title | Openings | Start Date | End Da |
|---|---|---|---|---|---|---|
| All Seasons Resort | Falmouth | MA | Gift Shop Clerk | 1 | 05/01/2006 | 09/30/2 |
| All Seasons Resort | Falmouth | MA | Lifeguard | 2 | 06/15/2006 | 09/30/2 |
| All Seasons Resort | Falmouth | MA | Waiter/Waitress | 2 | 05/31/2006 | 10/15/2 |
| Alpine Touring Center | Bethel | ME | Ski Patrol | 1 | 12/01/2006 | 04/15/2 |
| Alpine Touring Center | Bethel | ME | Main Office Clerk | 1 | 12/01/2006 | 04/01/2 |
| Bayside Inn & Country Club | Brewster | MA | Waiter/Waitress | 2 | 05/01/2006 | 10/01/2 |
| Bayside Inn & Country Club | Brewster | MA | Pro Shop Clerk | 1 | 05/01/2006 | 11/01/2 |
| Beantown Tours | Boston | MA | Tour Guide | 1 | 05/31/2006 | 10/01/2 |
| Beantown Tours | Boston | MA | Reservationist | 1 | 06/01/2006 | 10/01/2 |
| Belleview Resort | Bar Harbor | ME | Kitchen Help | 2 | 06/01/2006 | 10/15/2 |
| Belleview Resort | Bar Harbor | ME | Host/Hostess | 1 | 06/15/2006 | 10/01/2 |
| Canfield Golf & Country Club | East Hartford | CT | Pro Shop Clerk | 1 | 05/01/2006 | 10/15/2 |
| Canfield Golf & Country Club | East Hartford | CT | Greenskeeper | 1 | 05/01/2006 | 11/01/2 |
| Gables & Golf Country Club | Cavendish | PE | Pro Shop Clerk | 1 | 07/01/2006 | 10/31/2 |

Record: ◀◀ ◀ 1 ▶ ▶▶ ▶✳ of 47

Elsa asks you to print the query recordset before you close it.

▸ **7.** Change the page orientation to landscape, print the query recordset, and then click the **Close** button ☒ on the Query window to close it and return to the Database window.

After giving Elsa the printed query results, she asks you to find the records for employers with no available positions. These are employers who have placed their positions with NSJI in the past, but who have chosen not to place their current positions. Elsa wants to contact these employers and persuade them to continue doing business with NSJI. To provide Elsa with a list of these employers, you need to create a find unmatched query.

# Creating a Find Unmatched Query

A **find unmatched query** is a select query that finds all records in a table or query that have no related records in a second table or query. For example, you could display all customers who have not placed orders or all non-degree students who are not currently enrolled in classes. Such a query provides information for Elsa to solicit business from the inactive customers and for a school administrator to contact the students to find out their future educational plans. You can use the **Find Unmatched Query Wizard** to create this type of query.

## Using the Find Unmatched Query Wizard

- If necessary, click Queries in the Objects bar of the Database window.
- Click the New button, click Find Unmatched Query Wizard, and then click the OK button.
- Complete the Wizard dialog boxes to select the table or query on which to base the new query, select the table or query that contains the related records, specify the common field in each table or query, select the additional fields to include in the query results, enter a name for the query, and then click the Finish button.

Elsa wants to know which employers have no available positions. These employers are inactive, and she will contact them to determine their interest in filling future positions through NSJI. To create a list of inactive employers, you will use the Find Unmatched Query Wizard to display only those records from the Employer table with no matching EmployerID field value in the Position table.

### To create the query using the Find Unmatched Query Wizard:

▶ 1. Click **Queries** in the Objects bar of the Database window (if necessary), and then click the **New** button to open the New Query dialog box.

▶ 2. Click **Find Unmatched Query Wizard**, and then click the **OK** button. The first Find Unmatched Query Wizard dialog box opens. In this dialog box, you select the table or query on which to base the new query. You'll use the Employer table.

▶ 3. Click **Table: Employer** (if necessary) in the list box to select this table, and then click the **Next** button to open the next Find Unmatched Query Wizard dialog box, in which you choose the table that contains the related records. You'll select the Position table.

▶ 4. Click **Table: Position** in the list box, and then click the **Next** button to open the next dialog box, in which you choose the common field for both tables. See Figure 5-35.

**Selecting the common field**   **Figure 5-35**

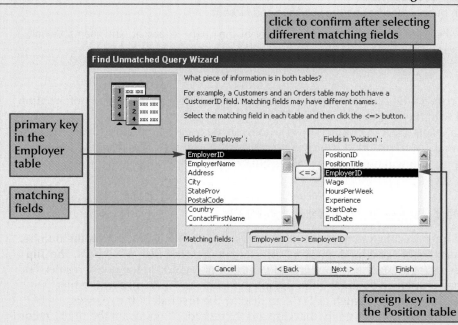

click to confirm after selecting different matching fields

primary key in the Employer table

matching fields

foreign key in the Position table

Notice that EmployerID is highlighted in each list box because it is the common field: EmployerID is the primary key in the primary Employer table, and EmployerID is the foreign key in the related Position table. The Matching fields box shows EmployerID <=> EmployerID to indicate the common field.

5. Click the **Next** button to open the next Find Unmatched Query Wizard dialog box, in which you choose the fields you want to see in the query recordset. Elsa wants the query recordset to display the EmployerName, City, StateProv, ContactFirstName, ContactLastName, and Phone fields.

6. Click **EmployerName** in the Available fields list box, and then click the > button to select this field. Use the same procedure to select the **City**, **StateProv**, **ContactFirstName**, **ContactLastName**, and **Phone** fields, and then click the **Next** button to open the final dialog box, in which you enter the query name.

7. Type **InactiveEmployers**, be sure the option button for viewing the results is selected, and then click the **Finish** button. Access saves the query and then displays the query recordset.

8. Resize all the columns in the query recordset to their best fit, and then click **Boston** in the City column to deselect any selected value or columns. See Figure 5-36.

| Figure 5-36 | InactiveEmployers query recordset |

**InactiveEmployers : Select Query**

| Employer Name | City | State/Prov | Contact First Name | Contact Last Name | Phone |
|---|---|---|---|---|---|
| Boston Harbor Excursions | Boston | MA | Beth | Petr | 617-235-1800 |
| Seaview Restaurant | Falmouth | MA | Donald | Bouwman | 508-776-8593 |
| Claire's Cottages | Orleans | MA | Claire | Markovicz | 508-822-1328 |
| Falling Leaves Tours | Sturbridge | MA | Jessica | Ropiak | 508-347-5331 |
| Colonial Caravan Tours | Concord | MA | John | Logan | 978-371-8086 |
| Maritime & Museum Tours | Salem | MA | Olivia | Alexander | 978-745-0202 |
| Seaside Excursions | Camden | ME | Scott | Moreau | 207-812-9954 |

The query recordset includes information for the seven inactive employers. Elsa asks you to print the query recordset before you save and close it.

9. Change the page orientation to landscape, print the query recordset, and then save and close the query.

Elsa will contact these seven inactive employers using the printed contact information you created with the find unmatched query.

Next, Elsa wants Zack to contact those employers who have the highest placement fee amounts to make sure that NSJI is providing satisfactory service. To display the information Elsa wants, you will create a top values query.

# Creating a Top Values Query

Whenever a query displays a large group of records, you might want to limit the number to a more manageable size by displaying, for example, just the first 10 records. The **Top Values property** for a query lets you limit the number of records in the query results. For the Top Values property, you enter either an integer (such as 10, to display the first 10 records) or a percentage (such as 50%, to display the first half of the records).

Suppose you have a select query that displays 45 records. If you want the query recordset to show only the first five records, you can change the query by entering a Top Values property value of either 5 or 10%. If the query contains a sort and the last record that Access can display is one of two or more records with the same value for the primary sort field, Access displays all records with that matching key value.

Reference Window

## Creating a Top Values Query

- In Design view, create a select query with the necessary fields and sorting and selection criteria.
- Enter the number of records (or percentage of records) you want selected in the Top Values text box on the Query Design toolbar.
- Click the Run button on the Query Design toolbar.

Elsa wants to see the EmployerName, ContactFirstName, ContactLastName, and Phone fields from the Employer table, and the TotalOpenings and PlacementFee fields from the PotentialIncome query, for employers with the highest 25% placement fee amounts. You will create a new query and then use the Top Values property to produce this information for Elsa.

## To create the query:

▶ **1.** Click **Queries** in the Objects bar of the Database window (if necessary), click the **New** button to open the New Query dialog box, make sure that **Design View** is selected, and then click the **OK** button. The Show Table dialog box opens on top of the Query window in Design view.

You need to add field lists for the Employer table and the PotentialIncome query to the Query window.

▶ **2.** Double-click **Employer**, click the **Queries** tab in the Show Table dialog box, double-click **PotentialIncome**, click the **Close** button to close the Show Table dialog box, and then drag the right edge of the PotentialIncome field list to widen it. Field lists for the Employer table and the PotentialIncome query appear in the Query window. See Figure 5-37.

**Joining a table and a query in the Query window** ◀ **Figure 5-37**

Employer table field list

PotentialIncome query field list

join line

**Trouble?** If a join line does not connect the two field lists, close the query without saving your design changes, click Tools on the menu bar, click Options, click the Tables/Queries tab, click the Enable AutoJoin check box, click the OK button, and then repeat Steps 1 and 2.

The join line connects the EmployerID fields, which are common to the table and query, even though you haven't created a relationship between the two objects. Access created the join because the automatic join option is enabled and the two objects each have a field (EmployerID) with the same name and a compatible data type, and the EmployerID field is a primary key in the Employer table. If you disable automatic joins, you can create a join in the Query window by dragging the primary key field from its field list to the common field in the other field list.

Now you can add the fields requested by Elsa to the design grid.

3. In the Employer field list, double-click **EmployerName**, double-click **ContactFirstName**, double-click **ContactLastName**, and then double-click **Phone**, scrolling as necessary, to add these four fields to the design grid.

4. In the PotentialIncome field list, double-click **TotalOpenings**, and then double-click **PlacementFee**, scrolling as necessary, to add these two fields to the design grid.

5. Click the right side of the **PlacementFee Sort** text box to display the sort order options, and then click **Descending**. The query will display the highest placement fee amounts first.

6. Click the **Run** button ![] on the Query Design toolbar. The query recordset shows the 38 records for employers with placement fee amounts. The records appear in descending order sorted by the PlacementFee field.

You can now set the Top Values property to limit the query recordset to the highest 25% placement fee amounts, so Zack can contact employers in this category.

### To set the Top Values property of the query:

1. Switch to Design view.

2. Click the **Top Values** list arrow on the Query Design toolbar, and then click **25%**. See Figure 5-38.

**Figure 5-38** **Creating the top values query**

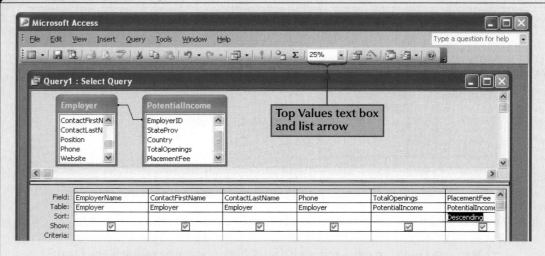

3. Run the query, resize all columns in the query recordset to their best fit, and then click **Total Openings 9** to deselect any selected value or columns. Access displays 10 records in the query recordset; these records represent the employers with the highest 25% placement fee amounts (25% of the original 38 records). See Figure 5-39.

**Top values query recordset** ◄ **Figure 5-39**

top 25% of the records selected

| Employer Name | Contact First Name | Contact Last Name | Phone | Total Openings | Placement Fee |
|---|---|---|---|---|---|
| The Clipper Ship Inn | Oren | Ben-Joseph | 978-546-0193 | 9 | $6,804.00 |
| Granite State Resort | Christine | Faraci | 603-468-8866 | 7 | $6,074.00 |
| The Inn at Plum Hill | Michele | Yasenak | 508-693-2320 | 6 | $5,175.00 |
| All Seasons Resort | Chelsea | Petraitis | 508-389-0777 | 5 | $4,282.00 |
| Hotel du Nord | Martine | Normand | 514-842-4623 | 4 | $4,010.00 |
| Belleview Resort | Akash | Shah | 207-288-1961 | 3 | $3,504.00 |
| Stonehurst Inn | Gavin | McDonough | 902-484-8354 | 3 | $3,400.00 |
| Windsor Alpine Tours | Michael | Engber | 603-266-9233 | 3 | $3,322.50 |
| Ski & Stay | Nathan | Weiss | 802-253-0809 | 4 | $3,123.00 |
| Canfield Golf & Country Club | Celia | Johnson | 860-569-7580 | 2 | $2,448.00 |

records listed in descending order by the PlacementFee field

Elsa asks you to print a copy of the query recordset so Zack can contact the employers. Because Zack will work from the printed results, you won't save the query.

4. Change the page orientation to landscape, and then print the query recordset.

5. Close the query without saving it, close the Jobs database, and then exit Access.

Elsa and Zack will use the information provided by the queries you created to contact employers.

## Session 5.3 Quick Check

**Review**

1. What is the purpose of a crosstab query?
2. What are the four query wizards you can use to create a new query?
3. What is a find duplicates query?
4. What does a find unmatched query do?
5. What happens when you set a query's Top Values property?
6. What happens if you set a query's Top Values property to 2 and the first five records have the same value for the primary sort field?

## Tutorial Summary

**Review**

In this tutorial, you learned how to enhance a table's design by creating lookup fields and input masks and by defining field and table validation rules. You also learned how to display subdatasheet records and identify object dependencies. Building on your earlier work with simple queries, you learned how to use pattern and list-of-values matches, the Not operator, and the And operator with the Or operator. Finally, you learned how to create parameter, crosstab, find duplicates, find unmatched, and top values queries.

# Key Terms

& (ampersand)
Access
aggregate function
crosstab query
Crosstab Query Wizard
field validation rule
find duplicates query
Find Duplicates
    Query Wizard
find unmatched query
Find Unmatched
    Query Wizard

In comparison operator
input mask
Input Mask Wizard
Like comparison operator
list-of-values match
literal display character
lookup field
Lookup Wizard field
Microsoft Office Access 2003
Not logical operator
Object Dependencies
    task pane

object dependency
parameter query
pattern match
property propagation
subdatasheet
table validation rule
Top Values property
Validation Rule property
Validation Text property

---

**Practice**

*Take time to practice the skills you learned in the tutorial using the same case scenario.*

# Review Assignments

**Data File needed for the Review Assignments: Students.mdb**

The Students database contains information about NSJI's recruiters and overseas students. The Recruiter table in the database contains records of the recruiters employed by NSJI to find students for seasonal work and match them with NSJI's client employers. The Student table contains student information. The database contains several other objects, including queries, forms, and reports. Elsa wants you to make changes to the design of the Student table and to create some new queries. Complete the following:

1. Open the **Students** database, which is located in the Intro\Review folder provided with your Data Files.

2. Open the **Student** table in Design view. Change the SSN field data type to Lookup Wizard. Look up values in the **Recruiter** table; select the SSN, FirstName, and LastName fields from the **Recruiter** table; sort in ascending order by the LastName field; do not hide the key column; resize all fields to their best fit; and accept all other Lookup Wizard default choices. View the **Student** table datasheet, resize the SSN column to its best fit, and then save the table.

3. Define a field validation rule for the Gender field in the **Student** table. Acceptable field values for the Gender field are F and M. Use the message "Gender must be F or M" to notify a user who enters an invalid Gender field value. Save your table changes, test the field validation rule for the Gender field, and verify that the lookup feature of the SSN field works properly. Make sure the field values are the same as they were before you tested.

4. Modify the first record in the **Student** table datasheet by changing the FirstName, LastName, BirthDate, and Gender field values to your name, birth date, and gender. If necessary, resize the FirstName and LastName columns, and save your datasheet changes. Close the table.

5. Use the Input Mask Wizard to add an input mask to the SSN field in the **Recruiter** table. Select the Social Security Number input mask, and then click the Finish button. Change the default input mask to 000\-00\-0000;;_. Update the Input Mask property everywhere the SSN field is used. Test the input mask by typing over an existing SSN field value, being sure not to change the value by pressing the Esc key after you type the last digit in the SSN field.

6. In the **Recruiter** table recordset, display the subdatasheet for record 4 (Ryan DuBrava), note the number of records in the subdatasheet, and then close the subdatasheet. Repeat these steps for record 7 (Colleen Murphy), record 10 (Elijah Slomich), and record 13 (Vincent Tumbido). Close the table, and then open the Object Dependencies task pane for the **Student** table. Create a Word or text document in which you report your subdatasheet results and list the objects that depend on the **Student** table and the objects that the **Student** table depends on. Close the task pane.

7. Create a query to find all records in the **Student** table in which the Nation field value starts with either the letter A or the letter I. Display all fields in the query recordset. Save the query as **StudentsFromSelectedCountries**, run the query, and then print the query recordset. Keep the query open.

8. Modify the query you created in Step 7. Use the modified query to find all records in the **Student** table in which the Nation field value does not start with the letter S. Sort the query in ascending order by the Nation field. Save the query as **StudentsFromSelectedCountriesModified**, run the query, print the query recordset, and then close the query.

9. Create a query to find all records from the **Recruiter** table in which the BonusQuota field value is 40, 50, or 60. Use a list-of-values match for the selection criteria. (*Hint*: Recall that you do not include quotation marks around these values because the BonusQuota field uses a Number data type.) Display all fields in the query recordset. Save the query as **SelectedBonusQuotas**, run the query, print the query recordset, and then close the query.

10. Create a query to select all records in the **Student** table for females from Australia or Germany. Display the FirstName, LastName, City, Nation, and Gender fields in the query recordset. Sort the query in ascending order by the LastName field. Save the query as **FemalesFromAustraliaOrGermany**, run the query, print the query recordset, and then close the query.

11. Create a parameter query to select the **Student** table records for a Nation field value that the user specifies. If the user doesn't enter a Nation field value, select all records from the table. Display all fields in the query recordset. Save the query as **NationParameter**. Run the query and enter Ireland as the Nation field value. Print the query recordset and then close the query.

12. Create a crosstab query based on the **Student** table. Use the Nation field values for the row headings, the Gender field values for the column headings, and the count of the StudentID field as the summarized value. Save the query as **StudentCrosstab**, resize the columns in the query recordset to their best fit, print the query recordset, and then save and close the query.

13. Create a find duplicates query based on the **Student** table. Select City and Nation as the fields that might contain duplicates, and select the FirstName and LastName fields as additional fields in the query recordset. Save the query as **FindDuplicateStudentLocations**, view and print the query recordset, and then close the query.

14. Create a find unmatched query that finds all records in the **Recruiter** table for which there is no matching record in the **Student** table. Display all fields from the **Recruiter** table in the query recordset. Save the query as **RecruitersWithoutMatchingStudents**, run the query, print the query recordset, and then close the query.

15. Create a query to select all records and display all fields from the **Student** table. Sort the query in ascending order by the BirthDate field. Use the Top Values property to select the top 25% of records. Save the query as **OldestStudents**, run the query, print the query recordset, and then close the query.
16. Close the **Students** database, and then exit Access.

**Apply**

*Use the skills you learned in the tutorial to work with the data contained in a video photography database.*

# Case Problem 1

**Data File needed for this Case Problem: Clients.mdb**

*Lim's Video Photography*   Youngho Lim owns a videography business, Lim's Video Photography. Located in San Francisco, California, the company specializes in digital video photography and offers customers the option of storing edited videos on CD or DVD. His video shoots include weddings and other special events, as well as recording personal and commercial inventories for insurance purposes. Youngho created an Access database named Clients to store data about his clients. He asks you to make changes to the design of the Client, Contract, and Shoot tables in this database and to create several new queries. You'll do so by completing the following steps:

1. Open the **Clients** database in the Intro\Case1 folder.
2. Open the **Shoot** table in Design view. Change the ShootType field data type to Lookup Wizard. Look up values in the **ShootDesc** table, select the ShootType and ShootDesc fields from the **ShootDesc** table, sort in ascending order by the ShootDesc field, do not hide the key column, resize both fields to their best fit, and accept all other Lookup Wizard default choices. View the **Shoot** table datasheet, verify that the lookup feature works properly without changing any field value, and then close the table.
3. Use the Input Mask Wizard to add an input mask to the Phone field in the **Client** table. Select the Phone Number input mask, and then click the Finish button. Change the default input mask to 999\/000\-0000;;_. Update the Input Mask property everywhere the Phone field is used. Test the input mask by typing over an existing Phone field value, being sure not to change the value by pressing the Esc key after you type the last digit in the Phone field.
4. Change the first record in the **Client** table datasheet so the ClientName field value is your name in the format: last name, comma, space, first name. Close the table.
5. Define a field validation rule for the ContractDate field in the **Contract** table. Acceptable field values for the ContractDate field are dates more recent than 1/1/2006. Use the message "Contract dates must be later than 1/1/2006" to notify a user who enters an invalid ContractDate field value. Save your table changes, test the field validation rule for the ContractDate field, making sure any tested field values are the same as they were before you tested, and then close the table.
6. Create a query to find all records in the **Client** table in which the Phone field value begins with 415. Display all fields from the **Client** table in the query recordset. Save the query as **415AreaCodes**, run the query, print the query recordset, and then close the query.
7. Create a query to find all records in the **Shoot** table in which the ShootType field value is AP, BP, or WE. Use a list-of-values match for the selection criterion, and include all fields from the **Shoot** table in the query recordset. Sort the query in ascending order by the ShootDate field and then in ascending order by the ShootTime field. Save the query as **MilestoneCelebrations**, run the query, and then print the query recordset in landscape orientation. Keep the query open.

8. Modify the query you created in Step 7. Use the modified query to find all records in the **Shoot** table in which the ShootType value is not any of: AP, BP, or WE. Save the query as **NotMilestoneCelebrations**, run the query, print the query recordset in landscape orientation, and then close the query.

9. Create a parameter query to select the **Shoot** table records for a ShootType field value that the user specifies. If the user doesn't enter a ShootType field value, select all records from the table. Include all fields from the **Shoot** table and the ContractAmt field from the **Contract** table in the query recordset. Save the query as **ShootTypeParameter**. Run the query and enter SE as the ShootType field value. Print the query recordset in landscape orientation, and then close the query.

10. Create a find duplicates query based on the **Shoot** table. Select ContractID as the field that might contain duplicates, and select all other fields in the table as additional fields in the query recordset. Save the query as **FindMultipleShootsPerContract**, view and print the query recordset, and then close the query.

11. Create a find unmatched query that finds all records in the **Client** table for which there is no matching record in the **Contract** table. Display all fields from the **Client** table in the query recordset. Save the query as **ClientsWithoutMatchingContracts**, run the query, print the query recordset, and then close the query.

**Explore**

12. Open the **ClientsAndTheirContracts** query, change the query to sort in descending order by the ContractAmt field, and then use the Top Values property to select the top 60% of records. (*Hint*: Recall that you can type values in the Top Values text box.) Save the query as **TopContracts**, run the query, print the query recordset, and then close the query.

13. Close the **Clients** database, and then exit Access.

**Apply**

*Apply what you learned in the tutorial to work with the data for an e-commerce business in the food services industry.*

# Case Problem 2

**Data File needed for this Case Problem: Delivery.mdb**

***DineAtHome.course.com*** DineAtHome.course.com in Naples, Florida, is an online service that lets people order meals from one or more area restaurants and delivers the meals to their homes. Participating restaurants offer everything from simple fare to gourmet feasts. Claire Picard, founder and owner, and her staff perform a variety of services, from simply picking up and delivering the meals to providing linens and table service for more formal occasions. Claire created the Delivery database to maintain information about participating restaurants and orders placed by customers. To make the database easier to use, Claire wants you to make changes to its table design and to create several queries. To do so, you'll complete the following steps:

1. Open the **Delivery** database in the Intro\Case2 folder.

2. Use the Input Mask Wizard to add an input mask to the OrderDate field in the **Order** table. Select the Short Date input mask, and then click the Finish button. Modify the default Short Date input mask by changing the two slashes to dashes. Next, type "mm-dd-yyyy" in the Format property text box for the OrderDate field to specify the data format. Test the input mask by typing over an existing OrderDate field value, being sure not to change the value by pressing the Esc key after you type the last digit in the OrderDate field. Resize the OrderDate column to its best fit, and then save and close the table.

3. Define a field validation rule for the DeliveryCharge field in the **Restaurant** table. Acceptable field values for the DeliveryCharge field are 0, 8, 10, and 15. Enter the message "Value must be 0, 8, 10, or 15" so it appears if a user enters an invalid DeliveryCharge field value. Save your table changes and then test the field validation rule for the DeliveryCharge field; make sure the field values are the same as they were before you tested.

4. Modify the first record in the **Restaurant** table datasheet by changing the OwnerFirstName and OwnerLastName field values to your name. Close the table.

5. Create a query to find all records in the **Order** table in which the RestaurantID field value is 108, 115, or 133. Use a list-of-values match for the selection criterion, and include all fields from the **Order** table in the query recordset. Sort the query in descending order by the OrderAmt field. Save the query as **SelectedRestaurants**, run the query, and then print the query recordset. Keep the query open.

6. Modify the query you created in Step 5. Use the modified query to find all records in the **Order** table in which the RestaurantID field value is not any of: 108, 115, or 133. Save the query as **SelectedRestaurantsModified**, run the query, print the query recordset, and then close the query.

7. Modify the **MarcoIslandRestaurants** query to select all records in which the City field value is Marco Island or Naples and the TakeoutOnly field value is No. Save the query as **MarcoIslandAndNaplesRestaurants**, run the query, print the query recordset, and then close the query.

8. Create a parameter query to select the **Restaurant** table records for a City field value that the user specifies. If the user doesn't enter a City field value, select all records from the table. Display all fields from the **Restaurant** table in the query recordset, except for the State, Website, and TakeoutOnly fields. Save the query as **RestaurantCityParameter**. Run the query and enter Naples as the City field value. Print the first page of the query recordset in landscape orientation, and then close the query.

9. Create a crosstab query based on the **RestaurantsAndOrders** query. Use the OrderDate field values for the row headings, the City field values for the column headings, and the sum of the OrderAmt field values as the summarized value. Save the query as **OrdersCrosstab**, resize the columns in the query recordset to their best fit, print the query recordset, and then save and close the query.

10. Create a find duplicates query based on the **Order** table. Select OrderDate as the field that might contain duplicates, and select all other fields in the table as additional fields in the query recordset. Save the query as **FindMultipleOrdersPerDay**, view and print the query recordset, and then close the query.

11. Create a find unmatched query that finds all records in the **Restaurant** table for which there is no matching record in the **Order** table. Select the RestaurantID, RestaurantName, and City fields from the **Restaurant** table. Save the query as **RestaurantsWithoutMatchingOrders**, run the query, print the query recordset, and then close the query.

12. Create a new query based on the **Order** table. Display all fields from the **Order** table in the recordset, sort in descending order by the OrderAmt field, and then use the Top Values property to select the top 25% of records. Save the query as **TopOrders**, run the query, print the query recordset, and then close the query.

13. Close the **Delivery** database, and then exit Access.

**Apply**

*Apply what you learned in the tutorial to work with a database that contains data about fundraising at a zoo.*

# Case Problem 3

**Data File needed for this Case Problem: Donors.mdb**

**Redwood Zoo**   The Redwood Zoo is a small zoo located in the picturesque city of Gig Harbor, Washington, on the shores of Puget Sound. The Redwood Zoo has some of the best exhibits of marine animals in the United States. Its newly constructed polar bear habitat is a particular favorite among patrons. The zoo relies heavily on donations to fund both permanent exhibits and temporary displays, especially those involving exotic animals. Michael Rosenfeld, director of fundraising activities, created the Donors database to track information about donors, their pledges, and the status of funds. Michael wants you to make changes to the table design and to create several queries. To do so, you'll complete the following steps:

1. Open the **Donors** database in the Intro\Case3 folder.
2. Open the **Pledge** table in Design view. Change the FundCode field data type to Lookup Wizard. Look up values in the **Fund** table, select the FundCode and FundName fields from the **Fund** table, sort in ascending order by the FundName field, do not hide the key column, resize both fields to their best fit, and accept all other Lookup Wizard default choices. View the **Pledge** table datasheet, test the lookup field without changing a field value, and then close the table.
3. Define a field validation rule for the Class field in the **Donor** table. Acceptable field values for the Class field are B, D, and P. Enter the message "Value must be B, D, or P", which appears if a user enters an invalid Class field value. Save your table changes and then test the field validation rule for the Class field; make sure the field values are the same as they were before you tested.
4. Modify the first record in the **Donor** table datasheet by changing the Title, FirstName, MI, and LastName field values to your title and name. Close the table, saving your changes.
5. Create a query to find all records in the **Pledge** table in which the FundCode field value starts with either the letter B or the letter M. Display all fields in the query recordset. Save the query as **PledgesFromSelectedFunds**, run the query, print the query recordset, and then close the query.
6. Create a query to find all records in the **Pledge** table in which the PaymentSchedule field value is M, Q, or S. Use a list-of-values match for the selection criterion, and display all fields from the **Pledge** table in the query recordset. Save the query as **SelectedPaymentSchedules**, run the query, and then print the query recordset in landscape orientation. Keep the query open.
7. Modify the query you created in Step 6. Use the modified query to find all records in the **Pledge** table in which the PaymentSchedule field value is not any of M, Q, or S. Save the query as **SelectedPaymentSchedulesModified**, run the query, print the query recordset in landscape orientation, and then close the query.
8. Create a query to select all records from the **Pledge** table with fund codes of B11 or P15 in which the payment method is either C or E. Display all fields in the query recordset. Save the query as **PaidBearFundPledges**, run the query, print the query recordset in landscape orientation, and then close the query.
9. Create a parameter query to select the **Pledge** table records for a FundCode field value that the user specifies. If the user doesn't enter a FundCode field value, select all records from the table. Display all fields from the **Pledge** table in the query recordset. Save the query as **FundCodeParameter**. Run the query and enter W13 as the FundCode field value. Print the query recordset in landscape orientation, and then close the query.

10. Create a crosstab query based on the **Pledge** table. Use the FundCode field values for the row headings, the PaymentMethod field values for the column headings, and the sum of the TotalPledged field as the summarized value. Save the query as **PledgeCrosstab**, resize the columns in the query recordset to their best fit, print the query recordset, and then save and close the query.

11. Create a find duplicates query based on the **Donor** table. Select LastName as the field that might contain duplicates, and select the remaining fields in the table as additional fields in the query recordset. Save the query as **FindDuplicateDonors**, view and print the query recordset, and then close the query.

12. Create a find unmatched query that finds all records in the **Fund** table for which there is no matching record in the **Pledge** table. Select all fields from the **Fund** table in the query recordset. Save the query as **FundsWithoutMatchingPledges**, run the query, print the query recordset, and then close the query.

13. Open the **DonorsAndPledges** query in Design view and sort the query recordset in descending order by the TotalPledged field. Use the Top Values property to select the top 15 records. Save the query as **TopPledges**, run the query, print the query recordset in landscape orientation, and then close the query.

14. Close the **Donors** database, and then exit Access.

# Case Problem 4

**Data File needed for this Case Problem: Outdoors.mdb**

***Mountain River Adventures*** Connor and Siobhan Dempsey own the Mountain River Adventures center, which offers clients their choice of outdoor activities, including white-water rafting, canoeing, hiking, camping, fishing, and rock climbing. To track their clients and bookings, they created the Outdoors database. Connor and Siobhan want you to make changes to the table design and to create several queries. To do so, you'll complete the following steps:

1. Open the **Outdoors** database in the Intro\Case4 folder.

2. Open the **Booking** table in Design view. Change the TripID field data type to Lookup Wizard. Look up values in the **RaftingTrip** table; select the TripID, River, and FeePerPerson fields from the **RaftingTrip** table; sort in ascending order by the River field; do not hide the key column; resize all fields to their best fit; and accept all other Lookup Wizard default choices. View the **Booking** table datasheet, resize the TripID column to its best fit, test the lookup field without changing field values, and then save and close the table.

3. Open the **Client** table in Design view. Change the StateProv field data type to Lookup Wizard. In the Lookup Wizard dialog box, create two columns and type the following pairs of values: CO and Colorado, NE and Nebraska, UT and Utah, and WY and Wyoming. Resize both columns to their best fit, and accept all other Lookup Wizard default choices. View the **Client** table datasheet, test the lookup field without changing field values, and then save and close the table.

4. Use the Input Mask Wizard to add an input mask to the Phone field in the **Client** table. Select the Phone Number input mask, and then click the Finish button. Change the default input mask to 999\-000\-0000;;_. Test the input mask by typing over an existing Phone field value, being sure not to change the value by pressing the Esc key after you type the last digit in the Phone field.

5. Change the first record in the **Client** table datasheet, so the ClientName field value is your name in the format: last name, comma, space, first name. Close the table.

6. In the **Client** table recordset, display the subdatasheets for the first three records, one at a time, and record the number of records in each subdatasheet. Close the table, and then open the Object Dependencies task pane for the **Booking** table. Create a Word or text document in which you report your subdatasheet results and in which you provide a list of the objects that depend on the **Booking** table and that the **Booking** table depends on. Close the task pane.

**Explore**

7. Define a field validation rule for the TripDays field in the **RaftingTrip** table. Acceptable field values for the TripDays field are values between 0.5 and 5.0, including those two values. Enter the message "Value must be between 0.5 and 5.0", which appears if a user enters an invalid TripDays field value. Save your table changes and then test the field validation rule for the TripDays field; make sure the field values are the same as they were before you tested.

8. Create a query to find all records in the **RaftingTrip** table in which the River field value starts with the word Arkansas. Display all fields in the query recordset. Save the query as **ArkansasTrips**, run the query, and then print the query recordset. Keep the query open.

9. Modify the query you created in Step 8. Use the modified query to find all records in the **RaftingTrip** table in which the River field value starts with a word other than Arkansas. Save the query as **NonArkansasTrips**, run the query, print the query recordset, and then close the query.

10. Create a query to find all records in the **Client** table where the StateProv field value is NE, UT, or WY. Use a list-of-values match for the selection criterion, and display all fields from the **Client** table in the query recordset. Save the query as **SelectedClients**, run the query, print the query recordset in landscape orientation, and then close the query.

11. Create a query to select all records from the **Booking** table with trip dates of 8/1/2006 or 8/11/2006 in which the number of people is either 5 or 6. Display all fields in the query recordset. Save the query as **AugustSelectedBookings**, run the query, print the query recordset, and then close the query.

12. Create a parameter query to select the **Client** table records for a StateProv field value that the user specifies. If the user doesn't enter a StateProv field value, select all records from the table. Display all fields from the **Client** table in the query recordset. Save the query as **StateProvParameter**. Run the query and enter CO as the StateProv field value. Print the query recordset in landscape orientation, and then close the query.

13. Create a crosstab query based on the **ClientsAndBookings** query. Use the StateProv field values for the row headings, the People field values for the column headings, and the count of the ClientID field as the summarized value. Save the query as **TripsCrosstab**, resize the columns in the query recordset to their best fit, print the query recordset, and then save and close the query.

14. Create a find unmatched query that finds all records in the **Client** table for which there is no matching record in the **Booking** table. Display the ClientName, City, and StateProv fields from the **Client** table in the query recordset. Save the query as **ClientsWithoutMatchingBookings**, run the query, print the query recordset, and then close the query.

15. Open the **Costs** query in Design view, and use the Top Values property to select the top 40% of the records. Save the query as **TopBookings**, run the query, resize all columns to their best fit, print the query recordset, and then save and close the query.

16. Close the **Outdoors** database, and then exit Access.

**Create**

*Work with the skills you've learned, and explore some new skills, to create a database for an Internet auction site.*

# Case Problem 5

**No Data Files needed for this Case Problem**

***eACH Internet Auction Site***   Chris and Pat Aquino own a successful Internet service provider (ISP) and want to expand their business to host an Internet auction site. The auction site will let sellers offer items for sale, such as antiques, first-edition books, vintage dolls, coins, art, stamps, glass bottles, autographs, and sports memorabilia. After a seller posts an item for sale, the auction site sells it to the buyer who places the highest bid. Before people can sell and bid on items, they must register with the auction site. Each item will be listed by subcategory within a general category, so bidders can easily find items of interest. For example, the general category of antiques might consist of several subcategories, including ancient world, musical instruments, and general.

Chris and Pat registered their Web site name eACH, which stands for *electronic Auction Collectibles Host*. Now they need to create a database to track people registered, items for sale, and bids received for those items. The process of creating a complete database—including all fields, tables, relationships, queries, forms, and other database objects—for eACH is an enormous undertaking. So you start with just a few database components, and then you will create additional objects in subsequent tutorials.

Complete the following steps to create the database and its initial objects:

1. Read the appendix titled "Relational Databases and Database Design" at the end of this book.
2. Use your Web browser to gather information about other Internet auction sites, so that you become familiar with common rules and requirements, categories and subcategories, fields and their attributes, and entities. (*Hint*: Yahoo (*www.yahoo.com*) lists names of several auction sites, and eBay (*www.ebay.com*) is a popular Internet auction site.)
3. The initial database structure includes the following relations and fields:
   a. The **Category** relation includes a unique category number and a category (the category name or description).
   b. The **Subcategory** relation includes a unique subcategory number, a subcategory name or description, and a category number.
   c. The **Registrant** relation includes a unique registrant number, last name, first name, middle initial, phone number, e-mail address, optional user ID, and password. Each person registers once and then can sell and bid on items.
   d. The **Item** relation includes a unique item number, the registrant who's selling the item, the subcategory number, a title (a short item description), a description (a fuller item description), a quantity (the number of identical items being sold separately, if there are more than one), a minimum bid amount in whole dollars, a duration (the number of days the site will accept bids for the item), an optional reserve price amount in whole dollars (the lowest sale price acceptable to the seller; this is not made available to bidders), and the date and time bidding started on the item.
4. Use the information in Step 3 to draw an entity-relationship diagram showing the entities (relations) and the relationships between the entities.
5. Build on Steps 3 and 4, creating on paper the initial database design for the eACH system. For each relation, identify all primary and foreign keys. For each field, determine attributes, such as data type, field size, and validation rules.

6. Create the database structure using Access. Use the database name **eACH**, and save the database in the Intro\Case5 folder provided with your Data Files. Create the tables with their fields. Be sure to set each field's properties correctly, select a primary key for each table, and then define the relationships between appropriate tables.

7. For each table, create a form that you'll use to view, add, edit, and delete records in that table.

8. For tables with one-to-many relationships, create a form with a main form for the primary table and a subform for the related table.

9. Design test data for each table in the database. You can research Internet auction sites to collect realistic values for categories, subcategories, and other fields, if necessary. Make sure your test data covers common situations. For example, your test data should include at least two sellers with multiple items for sale, one seller selling items in the same subcategory, another seller selling items in different subcategories, and at least one seller who currently has no items for sale. Each table should have at least 10 records. Include your name as one of the registrants, and include at least two items that you're selling.

10. Add the test data to your tables using the forms you created in Steps 7 and 8.

11. Open each table datasheet, resize all datasheet columns to their best fit, and then print each datasheet.

12. Set the option so that Access compacts the **eACH** database when you close it.

13. Use the Input Mask Wizard to add an appropriate input mask to one field in any table. Print the table's datasheet after adding the input mask.

14. Define data validation criteria for any one field in any table. Make sure to set both the Validation Rule and the Validation Text properties for the field.

15. For one of the foreign key fields in one of the tables, change the field's data type to Lookup Wizard. (*Hint*: Before you change the data type to Lookup Wizard, you must delete the relationship for which the field serves as the foreign key.) If necessary, resize the table datasheet, and then print the datasheet.

16. Create, test, save, and print one parameter query.

17. Close the **eACH** database, and then exit Access.

# Internet Assignments

The purpose of the Internet Assignments is to challenge you to find information on the Internet that you can use to work effectively with this software. The actual assignments are updated and maintained on the Course Technology Web site. Log on to the Internet and use your Web browser to go to the Student Online Companion for New Perspectives Office 2003 at **www.course.com/np/office2003**. Click the Internet Assignments link, and then navigate to the assignments for this tutorial.

## SAM Assessment and Training

If you have a SAM user profile, you may have access to hands-on instruction, practice, and assessment of the skills covered in this tutorial. Log in to your SAM account and go to your assignments page to see what your instructor has assigned.

# Quick Check Answers

## Session 5.1

1. A lookup field lets you select a value from a list of possible values, making data entry easier.
2. If two tables have a one-to-many relationship, when you display the primary table in Datasheet view, you can use a subdatasheet to display and edit the records from the related table.
3. input mask
4. Property propagation is an Access feature that updates control properties in objects when you modify table field properties.
5. The Validation Rule property specifies the valid values that users can enter in a field. For example, you could use this property to specify that users can enter only positive numeric values in a numeric field.
6. The Validation Text property value appears in a message box if the user violates the validation rule. For example, you could display the message "Must be a positive integer" if the user enters a value less than or equal to zero.

## Session 5.2

1. Like
2. The asterisk is a wildcard that represents any string of characters in a pattern match query.
3. Use the In comparison operator to define a condition with two or more values.
4. Use the Not logical operator to negate a condition.
5. Use a parameter query when you want to prompt the user to enter the selection criterion when the query runs.

## Session 5.3

1. A crosstab query performs aggregate function calculations on the values of one database field and displays the results in a spreadsheet format.
2. Simple Query Wizard, Crosstab Query Wizard, Find Duplicates Query Wizard, Find Unmatched Query Wizard
3. A find duplicates query is a select query that finds duplicate records in a table or query based on the values in one or more fields.
4. A find unmatched query is a select query that finds all records in a table or query that have no related records in a second table or query.
5. Setting a query's Top Values property lets you limit the number of records displayed in the query results.
6. Access displays the first five records.

## Objectives

**Session 6.1**
- Design and create a custom form
- View and print database documentation
- Add, select, and move controls

**Session 6.2**
- Resize, delete, and rename controls
- Add form headers and footers
- Add a picture to a form
- Create a multi-page form with tab controls
- Change a control to another control type
- Add combo boxes to a form

**Session 6.3**
- Add a subform to a form
- Add calculated controls to a form and a subform
- Change the tab order in a form
- Filter data in a form

# Creating Custom Forms

*Creating a Multi-page Form*

## Case

## Northeast Seasonal Jobs International (NSJI)

When Elsa Jensen and her staff began their project to improve the Jobs database, they initially concentrated on designing the Jobs database correctly and creating several needed queries. Although the Jobs database already has a few forms, Elsa wants a new form that would provide complete information about an employer and its positions.

In this tutorial, you will create the form for Elsa. In creating the form, you will use many Access form customization features, such as displaying data from two tables in a multi-page format, using combo boxes and calculated controls, and adding color and a picture to a form. These features will make it easier for Elsa and her staff to interact with the Jobs database.

## Student Data Files

▼**Intro**

▽ **Tutorial folder**

Jobs.mdb (*cont.*)
Plane.bmp

▽ **Review folder**

Students.mdb (*cont.*)
WorldMap.gif

▽ **Case1 folder**

Clients.mdb (*cont.*)
TV-VCR-L.bmp
TV-VCR-R.bmp

▽ **Case2 folder**

Delivery.mdb (*cont.*)
PlaceSet.gif

▽ **Case3 folder**

Donors.mdb (*cont.*)

▽ **Case4 folder**

Outdoors.mdb (*cont.*)
Kayak.bmp

▽ **Case5 folder**

eACH.mdb (*cont.*)

# Planning a Custom Form

Elsa has been using the EmployerPositions form to enter and view information about NSJI's employers and their positions. She likes having the information on a single form, but she prefers to display all fields from the Employer table instead of only a few. Also, Elsa prefers to have the fields rearranged and a picture added to the form. To make the form easier to read, she wants the employer and position information on separate pages, like the tabs in a dialog box. She asks you to create a new form to display information this way. Because this form differs significantly from the EmployerPositions form, you will create a new custom form.

To create a **custom form**, you can modify an existing form or design and create a form from scratch. In either case, you create a custom form in the Form window in Design view. You can design a custom form to match a paper form, to display some fields side by side and others top to bottom, to highlight certain sections with color, or to add special buttons and list boxes. A multi-page form displays the form on more than one page on a single screen. Each page is labeled with a tab; by clicking a tab, you can display the information on that page.

## Designing a Custom Form

Whether you want to create a simple or complex custom form, planning the form's content and appearance is always your first step. When you plan a form, you should keep in mind the following form design guidelines:

- Use forms to perform all database updates, because forms provide better readability and control than do table and query recordsets.
- Determine the fields and record source needed for each form. A form's **Record Source property** specifies the table or query that provides the fields for the form.
- Group related fields and position them in a meaningful, logical order.
- If users will refer to a source document while working with the form, design the form to match the source document closely.
- Identify each field value with a label that names the field, and align field values and labels for readability.
- Display calculated fields in a distinctive way, and prevent users from changing and updating them.
- Use default values, list boxes, and other form controls whenever possible to reduce user errors by minimizing keystrokes and limiting entries. A **control** is an item, such as a text box or command button, that you place in a form, report, or data access page.
- Use few colors, fonts, and graphics to keep the form uncluttered and to keep the focus on the data.
- Use a consistent style for all forms in a database.

After working with employer and position data using the EmployerPositions form for several weeks, Elsa's ideas for a better form led her to sketch the design for a custom form. Figure 6-1 shows Elsa's design for the custom form she wants you to create.

Notice that the top of the form displays a title and picture. Below these items are field values from the Employer table—the first employer line displays the EmployerID and EmployerName field values; and the second employer line displays the ContactFirstName, ContactLastName, and Phone field values. Also, notice that Elsa's form contains two pages. The first page, labeled "Employer Information," displays the employer's address, comments, and miscellaneous information. The second page, labeled "Positions," displays position information for the employer. Each field value from the Employer table is to appear in a text box, with identifying labels placed to the left of most field values. Each label will be the value of the field's Caption property (if any) or the field name. In Elsa's form design, a series of Xs indicates the locations and approximate lengths of each field value. For example, the five Xs following the Employer field label indicate that the field value (for the EmployerID field) is approximately five characters. The Position table fields appear in a **subform**, a separate form contained within another form, on the second page. Unlike the Employer table data, which appears on the first page with identifying labels to the left of the field values in text boxes, the Position table data appears in datasheet format with identifying column headings above the field values. Finally, the Total Openings field near the top of the form displays the total number of openings for the positions in the subform for the current employer.

## Removing the Lookup Feature

Elsa had designed the custom form before learning about the form design guidelines. The guidelines recommend performing all database updates using forms. As a result, NSJI won't use table or query datasheets to update the database, and Elsa asks if she should reconsider any of the design changes you made in the previous tutorial to the Employer and Position tables. The input mask and validation rule changes are necessary, but changing the NAICSCode field to a lookup field is unnecessary. A form combo box provides the same capability in a clearer, more flexible way. A **combo box** is a control that provides the features of a text box and a list box; it lets you choose a value from the list or type an entry. Before creating the custom form, you'll remove the lookup feature from the NAICSCode field.

### To remove the lookup feature from the NAICSCode field:

1. Start Access, open the **Jobs** database located in the Intro\Tutorial folder provided with your Data Files, and then open the **Employer** table in Design view.

2. Scroll down (if necessary) to the NAICSCode field, click its Field Name text box, and then click the **Lookup** tab in the Field Properties pane. The Field Properties pane now displays the lookup properties for the NAICSCode field. See Figure 6-2.

| Figure 6-2 | Lookup properties for the NAICSCode field |
| --- | --- |

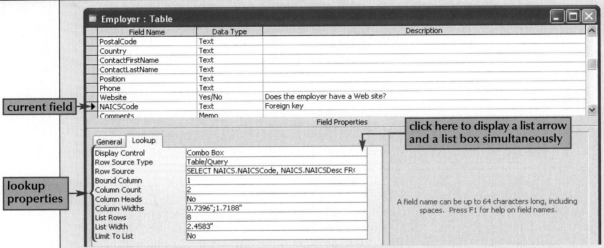

To remove the lookup feature for the NAICSCode field, you need to change the **Display Control property**, which specifies the default control used to display a field, from Combo Box to Text Box.

3. Click the right side of the **Display Control** text box, and then click **Text Box**. All the lookup properties in the Field Properties pane disappear, and the NAICSCode field changes back to a text field without lookup properties.

4. Click the **General** tab in the Field Properties pane and notice that the properties for a text field still apply to the NAICSCode field.

5. Save your table changes, switch to Datasheet view, scroll to the right until you can see the NAICSCode field, and then click one of the **NAICSCode** text boxes. A list arrow does not appear in the NAICSCode text box because the field is no longer a lookup field.

6. Close the Employer table.

Next, you'll view the table relationships to make sure that the tables in the Jobs database are related correctly.

**To view the table relationships in the Relationships window:**

1. Click the **Relationships** button ▣ on the Database toolbar to open the Relationships window. See Figure 6-3.

Jobs database tables in the Relationships window ◀ Figure 6-3

The primary Employer table and the related Position table have a one-to-many relationship with referential integrity enforced. The same is true for the primary Location table, which contains state/province abbreviations and names, and the related Employer table. The primary NAICS table and the related Employer table also have a one-to-many relationship, but the absence of symbols (the 1 and the infinity symbol) on the join line connecting these tables indicates that referential integrity is not enforced. You'll edit the relationship between the NAICS and Employer tables to enforce referential integrity.

2. Right-click the join line connecting the NAICS and Employer tables, and then click **Edit Relationship** to open the Edit Relationships dialog box.

3. Click the **Enforce Referential Integrity** check box, and then click the **OK** button. The join line connecting the NAICS and Employer tables is now similar to the join lines for the other two relationships.

4. Save your relationship changes.

Elsa asks you to print a copy of the database relationships to use as a reference, and she asks if other Access documentation is available.

# Printing Database Relationships and Using the Documenter

You can print the Relationships window to document the fields, tables, and relationships in a database. You can also use the **Documenter**, another Access tool, to create detailed documentation of all, or selected, objects in a database. For each selected object, the Documenter lets you print documentation such as the object's properties and relationships, and the fields used by the object and their properties. You can use the documentation to help you understand an object and to help you plan changes to that object.

| Reference Window | Using the Documenter |
|---|---|

- Start Access and open the database you want to document.
- Click Tools on the menu bar, point to Analyze, and then click Documenter.
- Select the object(s) you want to document.
- If necessary, click the Options button to select specific documentation options for the selected object(s), and then click the OK button.
- Click the OK button, print the documentation, and then close the Object Definition window.

Next, you'll print the Relationships window and use the Documenter to create documentation for the NAICS table. Elsa will show Matt and Zack the NAICS table documentation as a sample of the information that the Documenter provides.

### To print the Relationships window and use the Documenter:

▶ **1.** Click **File** on the menu bar, click **Print Relationships** to open the Relationships for Jobs report window, and then maximize the window.

▶ **2.** Click the **Setup** button on the Print Preview toolbar, click the **Page** tab, click the **Landscape** option button, click the **OK** button, and then scroll the window (if necessary) until you can see all the tables. See Figure 6-4.

| Figure 6-4 | Relationships for Jobs report |
|---|---|

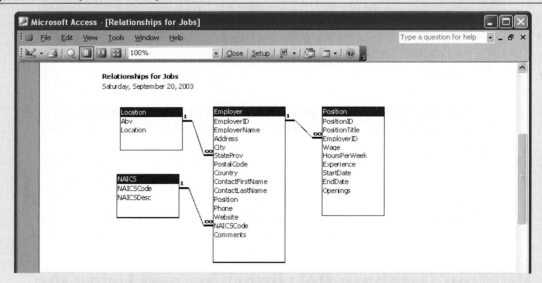

▶ **3.** Click the **Print** button 🖨 on the Print Preview toolbar. Access prints the Relationships for Jobs report.

▶ **4.** Click the **Close Window** button ✕ on the menu bar. A dialog box opens and asks if you want to save the report. Because you can easily create the report at any time, you won't save the report.

▶ **5.** Click the **No** button to close the report without saving changes, and then close the Relationships window.

Now you'll use the Documenter to create detailed documentation for the NAICS table as a sample to show Elsa.

6. Click **Tools** on the menu bar, point to **Analyze**, click **Documenter**, and then click the **Tables** tab (if necessary). The Documenter dialog box opens. See Figure 6-5.

**Documenter dialog box** ◀ **Figure 6-5**

click to display all database objects in the list box

option to select all objects in the list box

click to display more options for the selected object type

7. Click the **NAICS** check box, and then click the **Options** button. The Print Table Definition dialog box opens. See Figure 6-6.

**Print Table Definition dialog box** ◀ **Figure 6-6**

table documentation options

field documentation options

index documentation options

You select which documentation you want the Documenter to include for the selected table (Properties, Relationships, and Permissions by User and Group), its fields (Nothing; Names, Data Types, and Sizes; or Names, Data Types, Sizes, and Properties), and its indexes (Nothing; Names and Fields; or Names, Fields, and Properties). Elsa asks you to include all table documentation and the second options for fields and for indexes.

8. Make sure all check boxes are checked in the Include for Table section, click the **Names, Data Types, and Sizes** option button in the Include for Fields section (if necessary), click the **Names and Fields** option button in the Include for Indexes section (if necessary), click the **OK** button, and then click the **OK** button. The Object Definition window opens.

9. Click the **Zoom** list arrow on the Print Preview toolbar, click **100%**, and then scroll down the Object Definition window. See Figure 6-7.

| Figure 6-7 | Object Definition window for the NAICS table |

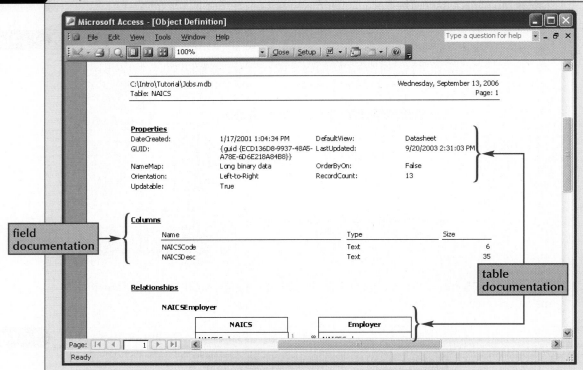

The Object Definition window displays table, field, and index documentation for the NAICS table.

▶ **10.** Scroll down the Object Definition window to view the remaining information in the documentation, print the documentation, and then close the Object Definition window to return to the Database window.

Elsa, Matt, and Zack will review the printout of the Relationships window and the documentation about the NAICS table and decide if they need further printed documentation. Next, you'll start working on Elsa's custom form.

# Creating a Custom Form

Using Elsa's design for the custom form, you are now ready to create it. You could use an AutoForm Wizard or the Form Wizard to create a basic form and then customize it in Design view. However, to create the form Elsa wants, you would need to make many modifications to a basic form, so you will design the entire form directly in Design view.

## The Form Window in Design View

You use the Form window in Design view to create and modify forms. To create Elsa's custom form, you'll create a blank form based on the Employer table and then add the Position table fields in a subform.

## Creating a Form in Design View

- In the Database window, click Forms in the Objects bar to display the Forms list.
- Click the New button to open the New Form dialog box, and then click Design View.
- Select the table or query on which to base the form, and then click the OK button.
- Place the necessary controls in the Form window in Design view. Modify the size, position, and other control properties as necessary.
- Click the Save button on the Form Design toolbar, and then enter a name for the form.

The form you'll create will be a bound form. A **bound form** is a form that has a table or query as its record source. You use bound forms for maintaining and displaying table data. **Unbound forms** are forms that do not have a record source and are usually used for forms that help users navigate among the objects in a database. Now you'll create a blank bound form based on the Employer table.

### To create a blank form in Design view:

▶ **1.** Click **Forms** in the Objects bar of the Database window, and then click the **New** button. The New Form dialog box opens.

▶ **2.** Click **Design View** (if necessary), click the list arrow for choosing a table or query, click **Employer**, and then click the **OK** button. Access opens the Form window in Design view.

▶ **3.** If necessary, click the **Maximize** button 🔲 on the Form window to maximize the window. See Figure 6-8.

Form window in Design view | **Figure 6-8**

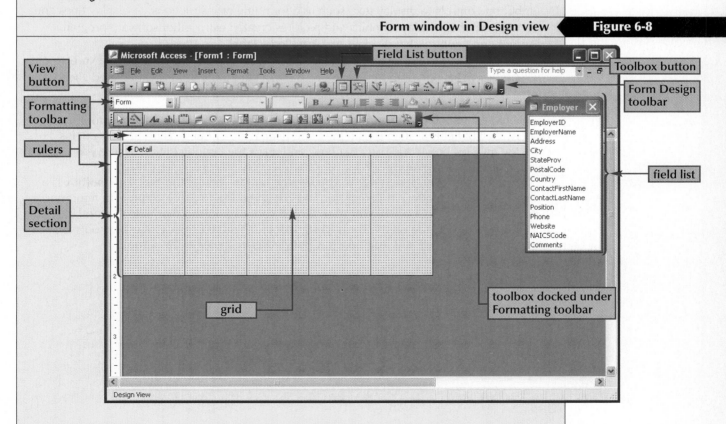

**Trouble?** If the rulers, grid, or toolbox do not appear, click View on the menu bar, and then click Ruler, Grid, or Toolbox to display the missing component. If the grid is still invisible, ask your instructor or technical support person for assistance. If the toolbox is not positioned as in Figure 6-8, click the Toolbox window's title bar and then drag it to the position shown.

**Trouble?** If the field list is not visible, click the Field List button [icon] on the Form Design toolbar to display it. If the field list is not positioned as in Figure 6-8, click the field list title bar and then drag it to the position shown. If necessary, resize the field list window so it matches the one shown Figure 6-8.

**Trouble?** If the Form Design toolbar or the Formatting toolbar does not appear, click View on the menu bar, point to Toolbars, and then click Form Design or Formatting (Form/Report) to display the missing toolbar.

**Trouble?** If the Form Design and Formatting toolbars appear on the same line or the Formatting toolbar is above the Form Design toolbar, drag the Formatting toolbar's move handle [icon] below the Form Design toolbar to the position shown in Figure 6-8.

The Form window in Design view contains the tools necessary to create a custom form. You create the form by placing controls on the blank form in the window. You can place three kinds of controls in a form:

- A **bound control** is connected, or bound, to a field in the underlying table or query. You use bound controls to display and maintain table field values.
- An **unbound control** is not connected to a field in an underlying table or query. You use unbound controls to display text, such as a form title or instructions; to display lines and rectangles; or to display graphics and pictures created using other software programs. An unbound control that displays text is called a **label**.
- A **calculated control** displays a value that is the result of an expression. The expression usually contains one or more fields, and the calculated control is recalculated each time any value in the expression changes.

To create a bound control, you use the Field List button on the Form Design toolbar to display a list of fields available from the underlying table or query. Then you drag fields from the field list box to the Form window, and place the bound controls where you want them to appear on the form.

To place other controls in a form, you use the buttons on the toolbox. The **toolbox** is a toolbar containing buttons that represent the tools you use to place controls in a form or report. ScreenTips are available for each tool. If you want to show or hide the toolbox, click the Toolbox button on the Form Design toolbar. Figure 6-9 describes the tools available on the toolbox. (You'll learn about Control Wizards later in this tutorial.)

**Summary of buttons available on the toolbox for a form or report** ◀ **Figure 6-9**

| Button | Button Name | Purpose in a Form or a Report | Control Wizard Available? |
|---|---|---|---|
| | Bound Object Frame | Display a frame for enclosing a bound OLE object stored in an Access database table | Yes |
| | Check Box | Display a check box control bound to a yes/no field | Yes |
| | Combo Box | Display a control that combines the features of a list box and a text box; you can type in the text box or select an entry in the list box to add a value to an underlying field | Yes |
| | Command Button | Display a control button you can use to link to an action, such as finding a record, printing a record, or applying a form filter | Yes |
| | Control Wizards | Activate Control Wizards for certain other toolbox tools | No |
| | Image | Display a graphic image | Yes |
| Aa | Label | Display text, such as titles or instructions; an unbound control | No |
| | Line | Display a line | No |
| | List Box | Display a control that contains a scrollable list of values | Yes |
| | More Controls | Display a list of all available controls | No |
| | Option Button | Display an option button control bound to a yes/no field | Yes |
| | Option Group | Display a group frame containing toggle buttons, option buttons, or check boxes | Yes |
| | Page Break | Begin a new screen in a form or a new page on a report | No |
| | Rectangle | Display a rectangle | No |
| | Select Objects | Select, move, size, and edit controls | No |
| | Subform/Subreport | Display data from a related table | Yes |
| | Tab Control | Display a tab control with multiple pages | No |
| ab | Text Box | Display a label attached to a text box that contains a bound control or a calculated control | No |
| | Toggle Button | Display a toggle button control bound to a yes/no field | Yes |
| | Unbound Object Frame | Display a frame for enclosing an unbound OLE object, such as a Microsoft Excel spreadsheet | Yes |

The Form window in Design view also contains a **Detail section**, which appears as a putty-colored rectangle. In this section, you place bound controls, unbound controls, and calculated controls for your form. You can change the size of the Detail section by dragging its edges. In the Detail section, the **grid** consists of the area with dotted and solid lines that help you position controls precisely in a form.

**Rulers** at the top and left edge of the Detail section define the horizontal and vertical dimensions of the form and serve as guides for placing controls in a form.

Your first task is to add bound controls to the Detail section for the EmployerID, EmployerName, ContactFirstName, ContactLastName, and Phone fields from the Employer table.

# Adding Fields to a Form

When you add a bound control to a form, Access adds a text box and, to its left, a label. The text box displays the field values from the underlying table or query on which the form is based, and the label identifies the values. To create a bound control, you display the field list by clicking the Field List button on the Form Design toolbar. Then you select one or more fields from the field list and drag the fields to place them on the form. You select a single field by clicking that field. You select two or more fields by holding down the Ctrl key and clicking each field; you select all fields by double-clicking the field list title bar.

Next, you'll add bound controls to the Detail section for five of the fields in the field list.

### To add bound controls from the Employer table to the grid:

1. Click **EmployerID** in the field list, press and hold the **Ctrl** key, click **EmployerName**, **ContactFirstName**, **ContactLastName**, and **Phone** in the field list, and then release the **Ctrl** key. You selected five fields.

2. Click one highlighted field and then drag it to the form's Detail section. Release the mouse button when the pointer 🖱 is positioned at the 1.5-inch mark on the horizontal ruler and at the top of the Detail section. Access adds five bound controls—one for the each of the five selected fields in the Employer field list—in the Detail section of the form. See Figure 6-10.

**Figure 6-10** | **Adding text boxes and attached labels as bound controls to a form**

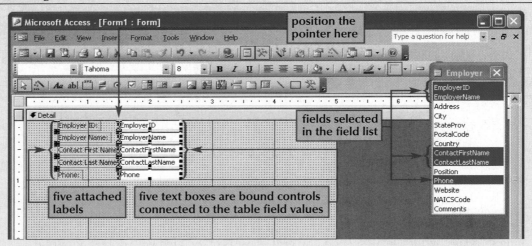

**Trouble?** You do not need to place your controls in exactly the same position as the controls in Figure 6-10. However, you should place them in approximately the same position. If you did not position the bound controls properly in the Detail section, click the Undo button 🔄 on the Form Design toolbar to delete the text boxes and labels from the Detail section. Then repeat Step 2 to add and position the bound controls.

**Trouble?** If the Control Wizards tool 🔧 on the toolbox is selected, click the Control Wizards tool 🔧 to deselect it.

3. Click the **Close** button ✕ on the field list to close it.

   Comparing the form's Detail section with Elsa's design, notice that you need only three of the five labels, so you'll delete two labels.

4. Click the gray area outside the Detail section to deselect all controls.

5. Right-click the **Employer Name label** to select it, and then click **Cut** on the shortcut menu.

6. Repeat Step 5 to delete the **Contact Last Name label**.

Working on a form in Design view might seem awkward at first. With practice you will become comfortable creating a custom form. To design a form productively, you should keep in mind the following suggestions:

- You can click the Undo button one or more times immediately after you make one or more errors or make undesired form adjustments.
- You should back up your database frequently, especially before you create new objects or before you make custom changes to existing objects. If you run into difficulty, you can revert to your most recent backup copy of the database.
- You should save your form after you've completed a portion of your work successfully and before you need to perform steps you've never done before. If you're not satisfied with subsequent steps, close the form without saving the changes you made since your last save, and then open the form and perform the steps again.
- You can always close the form, make a copy of the form in the Database window, and practice with the copy.

Compare your form's Detail section with Elsa's design, and notice that you need to arrange the labels and text boxes in two rows. To do so, you must select and move the controls.

## Selecting and Moving Controls

Five text boxes now appear in the form's Detail section, one below the other. Each text box is a bound control connected to a field in the underlying table. Three text boxes have labels attached to their left. Each text box and each label is a control on the form. When you select a control, eight squares, called handles, appear on its corners and edges. The larger handle in a control's upper-left corner is its **move handle**, which you use to move the control. You use the other seven handles, called **sizing handles**, to resize the control.

Reference Window

### Selecting and Moving Controls

- Click the control to select it. To select several controls at once, press and hold down the Shift key while clicking each control. Handles appear around all selected controls.
- To move a single selected control, drag the control's move handle to its new position.
- To move a group of selected controls, click any selected control (but do not click any of its handles), and then drag the group of selected controls to its new position.
- To move selected controls in small increments, hold down the Ctrl key and press the appropriate arrow key.

For Elsa's custom form, you must select the EmployerID and ContactFirstName controls and move them to the far left edge of the Detail section. Each control consists of a field-value text box and a corresponding label to its left.

### To select the EmployerID and ContactFirstName controls:

1. Hold down the **Shift** key, click the **EmployerID** text box, click the **ContactFirstName** text box, and then release the **Shift** key. Move handles, which are the larger handles, appear on the upper-left corners of the two selected text boxes and their attached labels. Sizing handles also appear, but only on the two text boxes. See Figure 6-11.

Figure 6-11 **Selecting two bound controls**

You can move a text box and its attached label together. To move them, place the pointer anywhere on the border of the text box, but not on a move handle or a sizing handle. When the pointer changes to a 🖐 shape, you can drag the text box and its attached label to the new location. As you move the controls, their outline moves and the rulers indicate their changing positions.

You can also move either a text box or its label individually. If you want to move the text box but not its label, for example, place the pointer on the text box's move handle. When the pointer changes to a 👆 shape, drag the text box to the new location. You use the label's move handle in a similar way to move just the label.

You'll now arrange the controls to match Elsa's design.

### To rearrange the controls in the Detail section:

1. Position the pointer on the EmployerID text box, but not on a move handle or a sizing handle. When the pointer changes to a 🖐 shape, drag the control as far left as you can, drag the control as far up as you can, and then release the mouse button. When the Employer ID and Contact First Name labels reach the left edge of the Detail section, you won't be able to move the labels and text boxes any further left. See Figure 6-12.

Figure 6-12 **After moving the EmployerID and ContactFirstName bound controls**

Next, you'll move the EmployerName text box to the right of the EmployerID text box.

2. Click the **EmployerName** text box, and then position the pointer on its move handle. When the pointer changes to a 👆 shape, drag the control to the top of the Detail section, so its left edge is on the 2.125-inch mark on the horizontal ruler, and then release the mouse button.

**Trouble?** If other form controls moved with the EmployerName text box, these other controls were also selected when you moved the EmployerName text box. To return the controls to their original positions, click the Undo button 🔄 on the Form Design toolbar, and then click the gray area outside the Detail section to deselect all selected controls. Repeat Step 2 to move the EmployerName text box.

According to Elsa's design, the three labels should be captioned "Employer:", "Contact:", and "Phone:". Before you finish arranging the controls in the Detail section, you'll modify the label text. To change the label text, you'll change each label's caption.

# Changing a Label's Caption

By default, the text in a label in a form for a bound control is defined by the associated text box's column name used in the underlying table or query. If the bound control is a table field, as is the case with this form, then the column name is the field name or, if you've set the field's Caption property, the Caption property value. If you want the label to display different text on the form, you need to change the label's **Caption property** value.

Reference Window

## Changing a Label's Caption

- Right-click the label to select it and to display the shortcut menu, and then click Properties to display the property sheet.
- If necessary, click the All tab to display the All page of the property sheet.
- Edit the existing label in the Caption text box; or click the Caption text box and press the F2 key to select the current value, and then type a new caption.
- Click the property sheet Close button to close it.

EmployerID, ContactFirstName, and Phone are the field names in the Employer table for the three bound controls in the report that still have attached labels. The "Phone:" label in the report matches Elsa's form design, but Elsa wants the other two labels to be "Employer:" and "Contact:", so you'll change the Caption property for these two labels.

## To change the Caption property value for the two labels:

1. Right-click the **Employer ID label**, which is the control to the left of the EmployerID text box, to select it and to display the shortcut menu, and then click **Properties** on the shortcut menu. The property sheet for the Employer ID label opens.

2. If necessary, click the property sheet title bar and drag the property sheet down to the lower-right corner of your screen, so that all controls in the Detail section are visible.

3. If necessary, click the **All** tab to display all properties for the selected Employer ID label.

   **Trouble?** If you do not see the word "Label" on your title bar or if Employer ID: is not the Caption property value, then you selected the wrong control in Step 1. Click the Employer ID label to change to the property sheet for this control.

4. Position the insertion point between the "D" and the colon in Employer ID: in the Caption text box, and then press the **Backspace** key three times. The Caption property value should now be Employer:. See Figure 6-13.

| Figure 6-13 | After changing the Caption property for the Employer ID label |

**Trouble?** The property sheet title bar, the Object list box, and the Name property on your screen might have a value other than the ones shown in Figure 6-13. Also, some property values in your property sheet, such as the Left and Top property values, might differ if your label's position slightly differs from the label position used as the basis for Figure 6-13. These differences cause no problems.

The property sheet title bar displays the object type (Label) and the Name property value (Label0—yours might differ). For most form controls, Access sets the Name property to the object type followed by a number; you can set the Name property to another value at any time.

▶ **5.** Click the **Contact First Name label** to select it. The property sheet now displays the properties for the Contact First Name label, and the Employer ID label in the Detail section now displays Employer:.

▶ **6.** Change the Caption property value for the label to **Contact:**

▶ **7.** Click the **Close** button ☒ on the property sheet to close it. The Contact First Name label in the Detail section now displays Contact:

As you create a form, you should periodically check your progress by displaying the form in Form view. You might find you want to make adjustments to your form in Design view. Next, you'll save the current form design and then view the form in Form view.

### To save the form and switch to Form view:

▶ **1.** Click the **Save** button 🖫 on the Form Design toolbar. The Save As dialog box opens.

▶ **2.** Type **EmployerInformation**, and then press the **Enter** key. Access saves the form in the Jobs database, and the form name appears in the title bar.

▶ **3.** Click the **View** button for Form view 🖾 on the Form Design toolbar. Access closes the Form window in Design view and displays the form in Form view. See Figure 6-14.

Access displays the EmployerID, EmployerName, ContactFirstName, ContactLastName, and Phone field values for the first record in the Employer table (Beantown Tours). You can use the navigation buttons to view other records from the table in the form.

4. Click the **Last Record** navigation button ▶I to view record 45 in the Employer table (Lighthouse Tours), and then click the **Previous Record** navigation button ◀ to view record 44 (Harbor Whale Watchers).

Form view reveals that you need to make some adjustments to the form design. The EmployerID, ContactFirstName, ContactLastName, and Phone text boxes are too large for the field values they contain; and the EmployerName text box is too small for the field value it contains. To correct these design problems, you will resize all five text boxes in Design view.

5. If you are not continuing on to the next session, close the Jobs database, and then exit Access.

So far, you have planned the custom form for Elsa, viewed and printed database documentation to verify table relationships, and started to add controls to the form. In the next session, you will continue your work with the main form by resizing and moving controls, adding a label and picture, changing the background color, and adding the two pages to the form to display employer address and miscellaneous information on one page and the employer's position information on the other page.

# Session 6.1 Quick Check

1. According to the form design guidelines, which object(s) should you use to perform all database updates?
2. What is a bound form, and when do you use bound forms?
3. What is the difference between a bound control and an unbound control?
4. The _____ consists of the dotted and solid lines that appear in the Detail section to help you position controls precisely in a form.
5. The _____ is a toolbar containing buttons that represent the tools you use to place controls in a form or a report.
6. The handle in a selected object's upper-left corner is the _____ handle.
7. How do you move a selected control and its label at the same time?
8. How do you change a label's caption?

# Session 6.2

## Resizing Controls

A selected control displays seven sizing handles: one on each side of the control and one at each corner except the upper-left corner. Recall that the upper-left corner displays the move handle. Positioning the pointer over a sizing handle changes the pointer to a two-headed arrow; the directions in which the arrows point indicate in which direction you can resize the selected control. When you drag a sizing handle, you resize the control. As you resize the control, a thin line appears inside the sizing handle to guide you in completing the task accurately.

| Reference Window | **Resizing a Control** |
| --- | --- |

- Click the control to select it and display the sizing handles.
- Place the pointer over the sizing handle you want, and then drag the edge of the control until it is the size you want.
- To resize selected controls in small increments, hold down the Shift key and press the appropriate arrow key.

You'll begin by resizing the EmployerID text box, which is much larger than necessary to display the five-digit EmployerID field value. Then you'll resize the other four controls appropriately.

### To resize the text boxes:

1. If you took a break after the previous session, make sure that Access is running, that the **Jobs** database in the Intro\Tutorial folder is open, and that the **EmployerInformation** form is open in Form view in a maximized window.

2. Switch to Design view, and then click the **EmployerID** text box to select it.

3. Place the pointer on the middle-right handle. When the pointer changes to a ↔ shape, drag the right border horizontally to the left until the text box is approximately the size shown in Figure 6-15.

   **Trouble?** If you accidentally change the vertical size of the text box, click the Undo button 🔄 on the Form Design toolbar, and then repeat Step 3.

   Now you will move the EmployerName control to its correct position and then resize the EmployerName text box.

4. Click the **EmployerName** text box to select it. Place the pointer on the EmployerName text box, but not on a move handle or a sizing handle. When the pointer changes to a 🖐 shape, drag the control to the left until its left edge is at the 1.75-inch mark on the horizontal ruler.

5. Place the pointer on the middle-right handle of the EmployerName text box control. When the pointer changes to a ↔ shape, drag the right border horizontally to the right until the right edge of the text box is at the 3.75-inch mark on the horizontal ruler. See Figure 6-15.

**EmployerID and EmployerName controls moved and resized** ◄ **Figure 6-15**

Next, you'll move and resize the remaining controls on the form.

▶ **6.** Select the **ContactFirstName** text box, move it and its attached label up until their top edges are at the 0.25-inch mark on the vertical ruler, and then drag the right edge of the ContactFirstName text box to the left until its right edge is at the 1.75-inch mark on the horizontal ruler. See Figure 6-16.

▶ **7.** Select the **ContactLastName** text box, move it until its top edge is at the 0.25-inch mark on the vertical ruler and its left edge is at the 1.875-inch mark on the horizontal ruler, and then drag the right edge of the ContactLastName text box to the left until its right edge is at the 2.75-inch mark on the horizontal ruler. See Figure 6-16.

▶ **8.** Select the **Phone** text box, and then move it and its attached label up until their top edges are at the 0.25-inch mark on the vertical ruler and the left edge of the label is at the 3-inch mark on the horizontal ruler. See Figure 6-16.

▶ **9.** Place the pointer on the **Phone** text box move handle and, when the pointer changes to a ⬆ shape, drag the control to the left to the 3.5-inch mark on the horizontal ruler. Make sure the top edge of the control remains at the 0.25-inch mark on the vertical ruler. See Figure 6-16.

▶ **10.** Resize the Phone text box by dragging its right edge to the left to the 4.25-inch mark on the horizontal ruler. See Figure 6-16.

**After moving and resizing all controls** ◄ **Figure 6-16**

▶ **11.** Save your design changes, and then switch to Form view to view the controls on the form. Navigate through the first several records, and notice that the text boxes are now the appropriate sizes for displaying the field values.

How do you know what size each control should be? When you design forms and other objects, it's a matter of trial and error. For forms, you make adjustments in Design view, switch to Form view and observe the placement and sizes of controls as you navigate the records, and then make further changes in Design view.

Now you will add the title and picture to the top of the form.

# Using Form Headers and Form Footers

The **Form Header** and **Form Footer sections** let you add titles, instructions, command buttons, and other controls to the top and bottom of your form, respectively. Controls placed in the Form Header or Form Footer sections remain on the screen whenever the form is displayed in Form view; they do not change when the contents of the Detail section change. To add either a header or footer to your form, you must first add both the Form Header and Form Footer sections as a pair to the Form window in Design view. If your form needs one of these sections but not the other, you can remove a section by setting its height to zero, which is the same method you would use to remove any form section. You can also prevent a section from appearing in Form view or in Print Preview by setting its Visible property to No. The **Visible property** determines if Access displays a control or section. Set the Visible property to Yes to display the control or section, and set the Visible property to No to hide it.

Reference Window

## Adding and Removing Form Header and Form Footer Sections

- Display the form in Design view.
- Click View on the menu bar, and then click Form Header/Footer to add a Form Header section and a Form Footer section to the form.
- To remove a Form Header or Form Footer section, drag its bottom edge up until the section area disappears or set the section's Visible property to No.

Elsa's design includes a title and a picture at the top of the form. Because these two controls will not change as you navigate through the form records, you will add them to a Form Header section in the form.

### To add Form Header and Form Footer sections to the form:

▶ **1.** Switch to Design view.

▶ **2.** Click **View** on the menu bar, and then click **Form Header/Footer**. Access inserts a Form Header section above the Detail section and a Form Footer section below the Detail section. See Figure 6-17.

**Adding the Form Header and Form Footer sections** | **Figure 6-17**

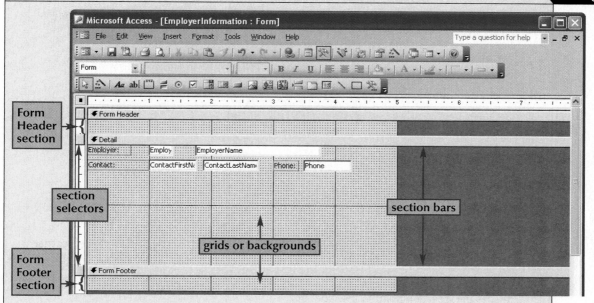

Each section consists of a **section selector** and a **section bar**, either of which you can click to select and set properties for the entire section, and the grid or background, which is where you place controls that you want to appear on the form.

Elsa's form design does not include any controls on the bottom of each form, so you don't need the Form Footer section. You'll remove it by changing its height to zero.

### To remove the Form Footer section:

1. Place the pointer at the bottom edge of the Form Footer section. When the pointer changes to a ✛ shape, drag the bottom edge of the section up until it disappears. Even though the words "Form Footer" remain, the area defining the section is set to zero, so the section will not appear in the form. If a future form design change makes adding controls to the Form Footer section necessary, you can restore the section by using the pointer to drag its bottom edge back down.

You can now add the title to the Form Header section using the Label tool on the toolbox.

## Adding a Label to a Form

Elsa's form design shows a title at the top of the form. You can add a title or other text to a form by using the **Label tool** on the toolbox.

**Reference Window** | **Adding a Label to a Form**

- If necessary, click the Toolbox button on the Form Design toolbar to display the toolbox.
- Click the Label tool on the toolbox.
- Place the pointer at the position for the upper-left corner of the label.
- Click the mouse button. Access places a box in the form where the label will appear.
- Type the text for the label in the label box.
- Click anywhere outside the label box to deselect it.

You'll begin by placing a label box for the title in the Form Header section.

### To place a label on the form:

1. Click the **Label** tool $Aa$ on the toolbox.

2. Move the pointer to the Form Header section. The pointer changes to a $^+A$ shape.

3. Position the center of the + portion of the pointer on the grid dot in the upper-left corner of the Form Header section. This is the location for the upper-left corner of the label.

4. Click the mouse button. Access inserts a small label box in the Form Header section and places the insertion point in the label box.

5. Type **NSJI Employer Information** in the label box, and then click the darker gray area outside the grids to deselect the label box. See Figure 6-18.

**Figure 6-18** ▶ **Label placed in the Form Header section**

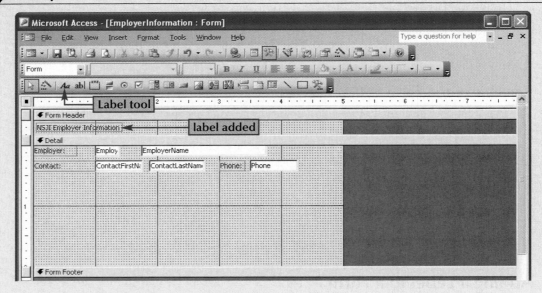

Elsa wants the title to be prominent on the form, so you will change the format of the label text to increase its font size and change its font weight to bold. You do this by using the buttons on the Formatting toolbar.

## To change the font size and weight for the title:

▶ **1.** Click the title label control to select it. Sizing handles appear on the control.

▶ **2.** Click the **Font Size** list arrow on the Formatting toolbar, and then click **14**.

▶ **3.** Click the **Bold** button **B** on the Formatting toolbar. See Figure 6-19.

Setting the properties for the title label control ◄ **Figure 6-19**

The label control now displays the title in 14-point, bold text. However, the label control is not large enough to display the entire title. You need to resize the label control so that it is large enough to display all the text. You could use the sizing handles to resize the label. However, using the Format menu is faster.

▶ **4.** Click **Format** on the menu bar, point to **Size**, and then click **To Fit**. The resized label control displays the entire title. In addition, the Form Header's size automatically increased to accommodate the new label size. See Figure 6-20.

Title label control resized to fit ◄ **Figure 6-20**

▶ **5.** Save your design changes.

Elsa also wants a picture at the top of the form. You will now add the picture to the Form Header section.

## Adding a Picture to a Form

Access lets you use files and data created by other software programs. To enhance the appearance of a form or report, for example, you can include a picture or another graphic image, such as a company logo or a photograph of a product. To do so, you use the **Image tool** on the toolbox.

Reference Window

## Adding a Picture to a Form

- Display the form in Design view.
- If necessary, click the Toolbox button on the Form Design toolbar to display the toolbox.
- Click the Image tool on the toolbox.
- Place the pointer at the position for the upper-left corner of the picture.
- Click the mouse button. Access places an outline in the form and opens the Insert Picture dialog box.
- If necessary, use the Look in list box to locate the picture file you want.
- Click the name of the picture file, and then click the OK button.

Elsa's picture was created in a graphics program and saved in a file named Plane. Now you'll add this picture to the upper-right area of the form.

### To place the picture on the form:

1. Click the **Image** tool on the toolbox.

2. Move the pointer to the Form Header section. The pointer changes to a shape.

3. Using the ruler as a guide, position the + portion of the pointer slightly below the top of the Form Header section, at the 3.25-inch mark on the horizontal ruler. (See Figure 6-20 for the correct position.) This is the location for the upper-left corner of the picture.

4. Click the mouse button. Access places an outline in the Form Header section and opens the Insert Picture dialog box.

5. Make sure **Tutorial** appears in the Look in list box, click **Plane** to select the picture file, and then click the **OK** button. The Insert Picture dialog box closes, and Access inserts the picture on the form. The Form Header section automatically enlarges to accommodate the image.

   Now, you'll reduce the height of the Form Header section, save your form changes, and then view the form.

6. Drag the bottom edge of the Form Header section up to the 0.875-inch mark on the vertical ruler.

7. Save your form changes, and then switch to Form view to view the form. See Figure 6-21.

Figure 6-21 **Viewing the form with the new header**

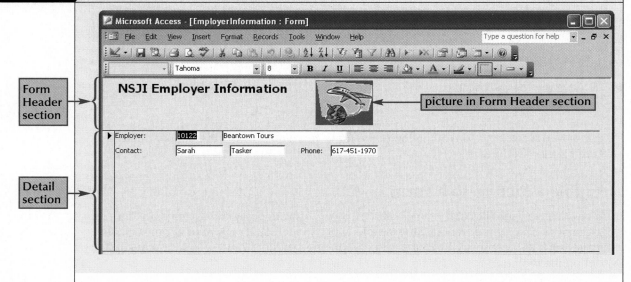

Elsa views the form and confirms that you correctly placed, formatted, and sized the title and picture. However, she wants you to change the background color of the form to dark teal to match the outline color of the picture, so that the picture will blend in better with the form.

# Changing the Background Color of a Form Control

You can change the background color of a form or of a specific section or control on the form by using the **Fill/Back Color button** available on the Formatting toolbar in Design view. Doing so can make a form more appealing and easy to use. For example, you can use a background color in a section that only certain users, such as customers, will complete.

Reference Window

### Changing the Background Color of a Control

- In Design view, click the control to select it.
- Click the Fill/Back Color list arrow on the Formatting toolbar to display the palette of available colors.
- Click the box of the color you want to apply to the control.

You need to change the background color of the Form Header and Detail sections of the form to match the outline color of the picture. This will cause the picture to blend in with the form.

### To change the background color of the Detail and Form Header sections:

1. Switch to Design view.

2. Click the **Detail selector** to make the Detail section the selected control. (See Figure 6-22.) Notice that the Detail section bar is highlighted as an indication that it is the current control.

3. Click the list arrow for the **Fill/Back Color** button  on the Formatting toolbar. Access displays the palette of available colors. See Figure 6-22.

**Changing the background color of the form sections** ◄ **Figure 6-22**

  4. Click the **teal** box in the color palette, the box in row 2, column 5. (See Figure 6-22.) The background color of the Detail section changes to teal.

   Now you need to apply the same color to the Form Header section. To do so, you do not have to redisplay the color palette; once you select a color from the palette, you can apply the color to other objects by simply clicking the Fill/Back Color button.

  5. Click the **Form Header selector** to make the Form Header section the selected control.

  6. Click the **Fill/Back Color** button 🖌 (not the list arrow) on the Formatting toolbar. The Form Header section now appears with the teal background.

   Now you can save the form and view your changes in Form view.

  7. Save your design changes, and then switch to Form view to view the form. See Figure 6-23.

**Figure 6-23**   **Form with new background color**

teal background color applied

   Next, you'll add a tab control to the form.

# Creating a Multi-page Form Using Tab Controls

You can create a multi-page form in two ways: use the **Page Break tool** to insert a page break control in the form, or use the **Tab Control tool** to insert a control that's called a tab control. If you insert a page break control in a form, users can move between the form pages by pressing the Page Up and Page Down keys. If you use a tab control, the control appears with tabs at the top, with one tab for each page. Users can switch between pages by clicking the tabs.

   Elsa wants to include a tab control with two pages on the EmployerInformation form. The first page of the tab control will contain employer information, such as the employer address, from the Employer table. The second page of the tab control will contain a sub-form with position information for the selected employer.

   First, you will resize the Detail section of the form to make room for the tab control.

### To resize the Detail section:

  1. Switch to Design view.

  2. Place the pointer on the right edge of the Detail section. When the pointer changes to a ⟷ shape, drag the section's edge to the right until it is at the 6.5-inch mark on the horizontal ruler.

   Now you can place the tab control on the form.

## To place the tab control on the form:

1. Click the **Tab Control** tool  on the toolbox.

2. Position the + portion of the pointer at the left edge of the Detail section, approximately 0.5 inches below the top of the Detail section, and then click the mouse button. (Refer to Figure 6-24 for the correct position of the tab control.) Access places a tab control in the Detail section.

   Now you will resize the tab control so that it is wide enough to display the remaining fields for the form.

3. Drag the middle-right sizing handle of the tab control to the right until it is three grid dots from the right edge of the form. See Figure 6-24.

Tab control placed in the Detail section and resized ◄ **Figure 6-24**

**Trouble?** The page tabs on your screen might show different page numbers in the labels, depending on how you completed the previous steps. This does not affect the form. Just continue with the tutorial.

The top of the tab control displays two tabs. Each tab indicates a separate page on the form. On the first page, you will place the controls for the fields from the Employer table. On the second page, you will place a subform displaying the fields from the Position table for that employer. The user can move between the two pages by clicking the tabs.

First, you'll add the fields from the Employer table to the first page of the tab control.

**To add the fields from the Employer table to the tab control:**

1. Click the **Field List** button 🔲 on the Form Design toolbar to display the field list.

2. Click the **Address** field in the field list, scroll to the end of the field list (if necessary), press and hold down the **Shift** key, click the **Comments** field, and then release the **Shift** key. You selected all fields in the list, except EmployerID and EmployerName.

   The ContactFirstName, ContactLastName, and Phone fields are already in the form, so you'll remove these three fields from your selection.

3. Press and hold down the **Ctrl** key, click the **ContactFirstName** field, click the **ContactLastName** field, click the **Phone** field, and then release the **Ctrl** key.

   Next, you'll drag the selected fields to the first page of the tab control. When you drag the fields over the central portion of the tab control, the central portion changes color; as you drag the fields near the tab control border, the entire tab control returns to its original color. The area that changes color shows you where you can release the mouse button to make sure the bound controls fit within the tab control.

4. Drag the selected fields to the tab control, and release the mouse button when the tab control changes color and when the pointer is approximately at the 1-inch mark on the horizontal ruler and at the 0.75-inch mark on the vertical ruler, making sure the pointer is still positioned in the area that changes color.

   Text boxes for the selected fields are added in a column to the tab control, with each text box's attached label to its left. To fit all the added bound controls to the tab control, Access automatically increases the height of the tab control at its bottom.

5. Close the field list, and then click a blank area of the tab control to deselect the bound controls.

Now you need to move and resize the controls to match Elsa's form design.

**To move and resize controls on the tab control:**

1. Click the **NAICSCode** text box to select it, and then position the pointer on one of its borders. When the pointer changes to a 🖐 shape, drag the bound control up and to the right until the left edge of the outline is at the 3-inch mark on the horizontal ruler and the top edge is at the 1.5-inch mark on the vertical ruler. Refer to Figure 6-25 for help in positioning the bound control.

   Next, you'll align the top of the NAICSCode bound control with the top of the PostalCode bound control.

2. Press and hold down the **Shift** key, click the **PostalCode** text box, click the **NAICS Code label** (the PostalCode text box and the NAICSCode text box and label should all have handles on their borders), click the **Postal Code** label, release the **Shift** key, click **Format** on the menu bar, point to **Align**, and then click **Top**. You aligned the top edges of the two bound controls.

   **Trouble?** If the NAICS Code label (or the NAICSCode text box) is not aligned with the other three controls, deselect all controls, select the NAICS Code label and the Postal Code label (or the NAICSCode text box and the PostalCode text box), click Format on the menu bar, point to Align, and then click Top.

   All the labels, except the Website label, have colons, so you'll add the colon to its caption, and then resize the label to fit.

3. Open the property sheet for the **Website label**, add a colon at the end of the control's Caption property, close the property sheet, and then size the control to fit.

   Unlike the other labels, the Website label is to the right of its associated check box, so you'll move the two Website controls independently.

4. Make sure the Website label is still selected, and then position the pointer on its move handle in the upper-left corner. When the pointer changes to a ✥ shape, drag the label above the NAICSCode label, align their left edges, and then align the bottom edges of the Website and State/Prov labels. (See Figure 6-25.)

5. Click the **Website** check box, move the control above the NAICSCode text box, align the two controls on their left edges, and then align the top edges of the Website label and the Website check box. (See Figure 6-25.)

6. Move, resize, and align the remaining controls. Use Figure 6-25 as a guide for positioning, sizing, and aligning the controls. Make sure to use the Align command on the Format menu to position pairs or larger groups of controls, aligning the controls on their top, left, or other edges.

**Employer fields placed in the tab control** ◀ **Figure 6-25**

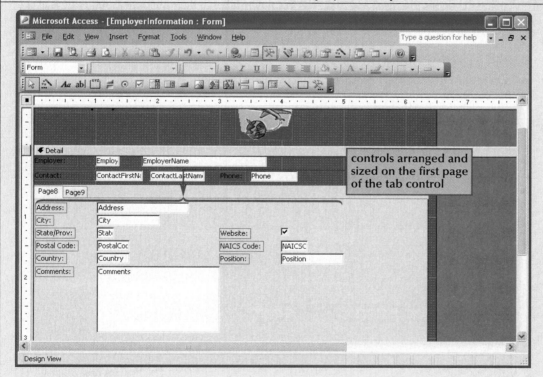

**Trouble?** You do not have to position your controls exactly where the controls appear in Figure 6-25. However, you should place them in approximately the same position. If you placed the controls incorrectly, move, resize, and align them now.

Elsa refers back to her form design and identifies two more changes. The Position label needs its Caption property changed to "Contact Position:". Also, you must size the Employer and Contact labels above the tab control to fit and then move them to the right so that they are closer to their associated text boxes. Finally, Elsa's design shows these labels as right-aligned. To align them, you will select all labels in a column and use the shortcut menu.

## Aligning Controls in a Form

- Select the objects you want to align.
- Right-click any one of the selected controls to display the shortcut menu.
- Point to Align, and then click the alignment you want.

Now you can change the Position label's Caption property and then resize, move, and align the two labels above the tab control.

### To change the Caption property and then resize, move, and right-align the labels:

1. Open the property sheet for the **Position label**, set the Caption property to **Contact Position:**, close the property sheet, and then size the control to fit.

2. Deselect all controls, press and hold down the **Shift** key, click the **Employer label**, click the **Contact label**, release the **Shift** key, and then size both controls to fit.

3. Place the pointer on the Employer label's move handle in the upper-left corner. When the pointer changes to a 👆 shape, drag the **Employer label** to the right until its left edge is at the 0.375-inch mark on the horizontal ruler. Refer to Figure 6-26 for help in positioning the label.

4. Make sure the Employer and Contact labels are still selected, and then right-click either of the selected label boxes to display the shortcut menu.

5. Point to **Align**, and then click **Right**. Access aligns the right edges of the label boxes. See Figure 6-26.

| Figure 6-26 | Sizing and aligning label boxes |

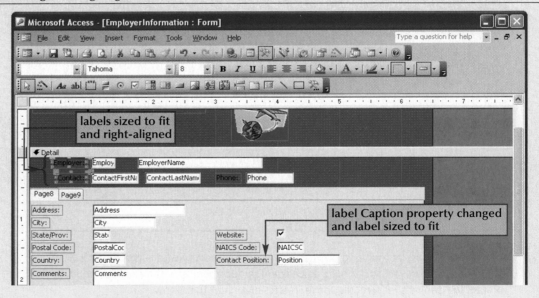

**Trouble?** If the text boxes also were aligned, click the Undo button on the Form Design toolbar, make sure that you select only the Employer and Contact labels (and that no other controls have sizing handles), and then repeat Steps 4 and 5.

6. Save your design changes, and then switch to Form view to view the form. See Figure 6-27.

**First record in Form view** ◄ **Figure 6-27**

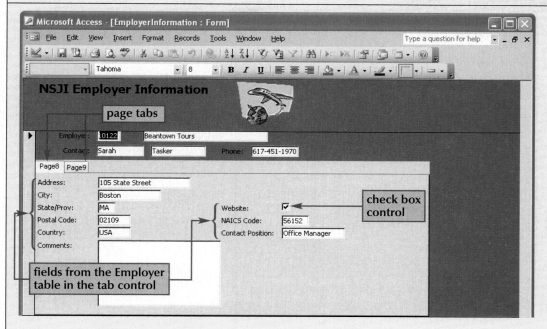

Elsa asks if you can change the Website field from a check box control to another control type.

# Changing a Control to Another Control Type

The Website field, which is a yes/no field, appears in a check box control in all objects by default. A check mark appears in the control when the field value is *yes*, and the control is unchecked when the field value is *no*. Clicking a check box control changes its value. You can also use toggle button and option button controls to display the value of a yes/no field; you click these controls to change the displayed value. A **toggle button** appears as a small button; a pressed or indented toggle button represents a *yes* value, and an unpressed or raised toggle button represents a *no* value. An **option button** appears as a white-filled circle; a dot inside the circle indicates a *yes* value, and an empty circle indicates a *no* value.

You can change from one of these three controls for a yes/no field to either of the other two controls in Design view. Elsa wants you to change the Website field to an option button because she prefers the look of that control in her custom form.

### To change the Website field to an option button:

► **1.** Switch to Design view.

► **2.** Click the **Website** check box, click **Format** on the menu bar, point to **Change To**, and then click **Option Button**. The Website control changes from a check box control to an option button control.

► **3.** Save your design changes, and then switch to Form view to view the form. See Figure 6-28.

**Figure 6-28** | **Website field changed to an option button control**

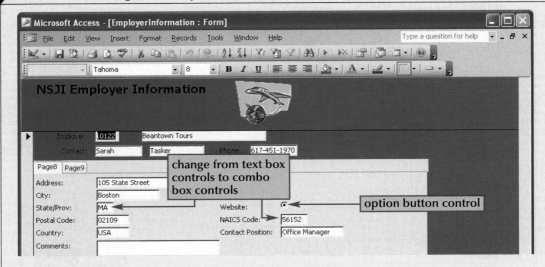

**4.** Use the navigation buttons to review the first few form records, noticing the appearance of the option button for Website field values of yes and no.

You can also change other types of controls; for example, you can change a text box to a label, list box, or combo box.

Elsa reminds you that you removed the lookup feature from the NAICSCode field because a combo box provides the same lookup capability in a form. Next, you'll add combo boxes to the custom form.

# Adding Combo Boxes to a Form

The Employer and Position tables in the Jobs database contain data necessary to manage NSJI's business. The NAICS table, which contains NAICS codes and descriptions, and the Location table, which contains state/province abbreviations and names, are lookup tables. A **lookup table** contains reference data that other tables in the database use. The StateProv and NAICSCode fields in the Employer table are foreign keys to these lookup tables, and you can use combo boxes on the custom form to maintain these fields more easily. Recall that a combo box is a control that provides the features of a text box and a list box; you can choose a value from the list or type an entry.

You use the **Combo Box tool** to add a combo box to a form. If you want help when defining the combo box, you can select one of the Access Control Wizards. A **Control Wizard** asks a series of questions and then uses your answers to create a control in a form or report. Access offers Control Wizards for the Combo Box, List Box, Option Group, Command Button, and Subform/Subreport tools, among others.

You will use the Combo Box Wizard to add combo boxes to the form for the NAICSCode and StateProv fields.

## To add a combo box to the form:

▶ **1.** Switch to Design view, and then deselect all controls.

First, you'll delete the NAICSCode and StateProv bound controls.

▶ **2.** Right-click the **NAICSCode** text box, click **Cut** on the shortcut menu to delete the NAICSCode text box and its attached label, right-click the **StateProv** text box, and then click **Cut** on the shortcut menu to delete the StateProv text box and its attached label.

▶ **3.** Make sure the **Control Wizards** tool 🔳 on the toolbox is selected.

▶ **4.** Click the **Combo Box** tool 🔳 on the toolbox.

First, you'll add a combo box in the tab control for the NAICSCode field.

▶ **5.** Position the + portion of the pointer above the Position text box and aligned with its left edge, and then click the mouse button. Access places a combo box control in the tab control and opens the first Combo Box Wizard dialog box.

You can use an existing table or query as the source for a new combo box, type the values for the combo box, or find a record based on the value you select in the combo box. In this case, you'll use the NAICS table as the basis for the new combo box.

## To use the Combo Box Wizard to add the combo box to the form:

▶ **1.** Make sure the **I want the combo box to look up the values in a table or query** option button is selected, click the **Next** button to open the next Combo Box Wizard dialog box, click **Table: NAICS**, and then click the **Next** button. Access opens the third Combo Box Wizard dialog box. This dialog box lets you select the fields from the NAICS table to appear as columns in the dialog box.

▶ **2.** Click the 🔲 >> button to move all available fields to the Selected Fields list box, and then click the **Next** button. This dialog box lets you choose a sort order for the combo box entries. Elsa wants the entries to appear in ascending NAICSDesc order.

▶ **3.** Click the **1** list arrow, click **NAICSDesc**, and then click the **Next** button to open the next Combo Box Wizard dialog box.

Similar to her earlier decision with the Lookup Wizard, Elsa wants both the NAICSCode and NAICSDesc fields to appear in the combo box.

▶ **4.** Click the **Hide key column (recommended)** check box to deselect it, resize both columns to their best fits, scrolling down the columns to make sure all values are visible and resizing again if they're not, and then click the **Next** button.

In this dialog box, you select the primary key from the lookup table.

▶ **5.** Make sure **NAICSCode** is selected in the Available Fields list box, and then click the **Next** button.

In this dialog box, you specify the field in the Employer table where you will store the selected NAICSCode value from the combo box. You'll store the value in the NAICSCode field in the Employer table.

▶ **6.** Click the **Store that value in this field** option button, click its list arrow, scroll the list box, click **NAICSCode**, and then click the **Next** button.

In this dialog box, you specify the control name for the combo box. You'll accept the default field name of NAICSCode.

7. Click the **Finish** button. The completed NAICSCode combo box displays in the form.

8. Set the Caption property for the label to **NAICS Code:** and resize the label to fit, move the combo box control to the position previously occupied by the NAICSCode bound control, aligning the combo box and its attached label as necessary, and then deselect all controls. See Figure 6-29.

| Figure 6-29 | NAICSCode combo box added to the form |

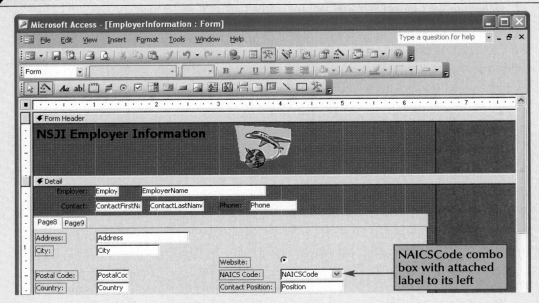

Next, you'll add a combo box to replace the StateProv bound control, using the Location table as the lookup table. The Location table contains the Abv and Location fields, and the Abv field is the table's primary key field.

9. Click the **Combo Box** tool on the toolbox, position the + portion of the pointer above the PostalCode text box and aligned with its left edge, and then click the mouse button.

10. Repeat Steps 1 through 8, using all fields in the Location table sorted by the Location field, hiding no fields, selecting Abv as the unique field, storing the Abv value in the StateProv field, setting **State/Prov:** as the ending combo box label, and aligning the combo box and its attached label as necessary into the positions previously occupied by the StateProv text box and its attached label.

Now you can save the form and view it in Form view.

## To view the combo boxes in Form view:

1. Save your design changes, switch to Form view to view the form, and then click the **NAICSCode** list arrow to open the control's list box. See Figure 6-30.

Two new combo boxes in Form view | **Figure 6-30**

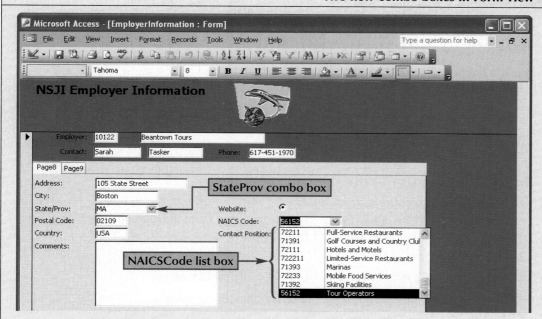

2. Click the **NAICSCode** list arrow to close the list box.

   **Trouble?** If you accidentally changed the NAICSCode field value, press the Esc key to undo the change, so that the NAICSCode field value is 56152.

3. Click the **StateProv** list arrow to open the control's list box, and then click the **StateProv** list arrow to close the list box.

   **Trouble?** If you accidentally changed the StateProv field value, press the Esc key to undo the change, so that the StateProv field value is MA.

4. Use the navigation buttons to review the first few form records, making sure that the combo box values change properly from record to record.

5. If you are not continuing on to the next session, close the Jobs database, and then exit Access.

You've made significant progress on Elsa's custom form. You added, resized, deleted, and renamed controls, and added a header, picture, combo boxes, and multi-page, tabbed form to the custom form. You also changed a check box to an option button. In the next session, you will continue your work with the main form by adding a subform on the second page of the tab control, adding calculated controls to the form, and changing the tab order in the form.

# Session 6.2 Quick Check

Review

1. How do you resize a control?
2. What is the Form Header section?
3. How do you add a picture created using another software program to a form?
4. Describe how you would use a Control Wizard to add a tab control to a form.
5. How do you align a group of labels?
6. To display a yes/no field you can use a check box control, a(n) _____ control, or a(n) _____ control.
7. A(n) _____ control provides the features of a text box and a list box.

## Session 6.3

# Adding a Subform to a Form

You use the **Subform/Subreport tool** on the toolbox to add a subform to a form. You can add the subform on your own, or you can get help adding the subform by using the SubForm Wizard.

You will use the SubForm Wizard to add the subform for the Position table records to the second page of the tab control.

### To add the subform to the tab control:

1. If you took a break after the previous session, make sure that Access is running, that the **Jobs** database in the Intro\Tutorial folder is open, and that the **EmployerInformation** form is open in Form view in a maximized window.

2. Switch to Design view.

3. Make sure the **Control Wizards** tool on the toolbox is selected.

4. Click the tab for the second page (the tab on the right) to select it.

5. Click the **Subform/Subreport** tool on the toolbox.

6. Position the + portion of the pointer near the upper-left corner of the tab control, just below the 0.875-inch mark on the vertical ruler and at the 0.5-inch mark on the horizontal ruler, and then click the mouse button. Access places a subform control in the tab control and opens the first SubForm Wizard dialog box.

You can use an existing table, query, or form as the record source for a new subform. In this case, you'll use the Position table as the basis for the new subform.

### To use the SubForm Wizard to add the subform to the form:

1. Make sure the **Use existing Tables and Queries** option button is selected, and then click the **Next** button. Access opens the next SubForm Wizard dialog box. This dialog box lets you select a table or query as the basis for the subform and then select the fields from that table or query.

2. Click the **Tables/Queries** list arrow to display the list of tables and queries in the Jobs database, and then click **Table: Position**. The Available Fields list box shows the fields in the Position table.

   Elsa's design includes all fields from the Position table in the subform, except the EmployerID field, which is already placed on the form from the Employer table.

3. Click the >> button to move all available fields to the Selected Fields list box, click **EmployerID** in the Selected Fields list box, click the < button, and then click the **Next** button to open the next SubForm Wizard dialog box. See Figure 6-31.

**Selecting the linking field** ◄ **Figure 6-31**

This dialog box lets you select the link between the Employer table and the Position table. EmployerID, as the common field between the two tables, links the two tables. Access uses the EmployerID field to display a record in the main form, which displays data from the Employer table, and to select and display the related records for that employer in the subform, which displays data from the Position table.

▶ **4.** Make sure the **Choose from a list** option button is selected and that the first link is highlighted, and then click the **Next** button. The next SubForm Wizard dialog box lets you specify a name for the subform.

▶ **5.** Type **EmployerInformationSubform** and then click the **Finish** button. Access inserts a subform object in the tab control. This is where the Position records will appear.

▶ **6.** Close the field list, and then maximize the Form window.

▶ **7.** Save your form changes, and then switch to Form view.

The tab control shows the employer information on the first page. You can view the position information for the employer by clicking the second page tab.

▶ **8.** Click the page tab on the right to display the position information. The subform displays the position data in a datasheet. See Figure 6-32.

**Viewing the subform on the tab control** ◄ **Figure 6-32**

**Trouble?** If the size of the columns in your datasheet differs, don't worry. You'll resize all columns to their best fit later.

**Trouble?** If the tab control isn't positioned below the contact and phone controls in the main form, switch to Design view, click the tab control to select it, drag it down until the control is positioned as shown in Figure 6-32, and then repeat Steps 7–8.

After viewing the form, Elsa identifies several modifications she wants you to make. The subform is not properly sized and the columns in the subform are not sized to their best fit. She wants you to resize the subform and its columns, so that the columns are entirely visible. Also, she asks you to delete the EmployerInformationSubform label and to edit the labels for the tabs in the tab control, so that they indicate the contents of each page.

You resize the subform and edit the labels in Design view. Then you can resize the subform columns in Form view.

### To resize the subform, delete its label, and edit the labels for the tabs:

1. Switch to Design view. Notice that in Design view, the subform data does not appear in a datasheet as it does in Form view. That difference causes no problem; you should ignore it.

2. If necessary, scroll down until you see the bottom of the subform. If necessary, click the right tab to select it.

    If you click a tab, you select the tab control, and sizing handles appear on its edges. If you want to select a subform positioned in a tab control, you should click one of the subform edges; sizing handles disappear from the tab control and appear on the edges of the subform, indicating that it's selected.

3. Select and then resize the subform on the right and left, so that the subform extends horizontally from the 0.25-inch mark to the 6.25-inch mark on the horizontal ruler. Then drag the bottom of the subform up to the 3-inch mark on the vertical ruler.

4. Deselect all controls, right-click the label for the subform control (make sure the subform no longer has sizing handles), and then click **Cut** on the shortcut menu to delete the label.

    Next, you'll change the labels on the tabs. To do so, you need to set the Caption property for each tab.

5. Right-click the subform page tab, and then click **Properties** on the shortcut menu to open the property sheet.

6. Click the **All** tab (if necessary), and then type **Positions** in the Caption text box. See Figure 6-33.

| Figure 6-33 | Setting the Caption property value for the page tab |
| --- | --- |

7. Click the page tab on the left, set the Caption property to **Employer Information**, close the property sheet, and then save your design changes.

Now you can view the form, and then resize the columns in the subform.

**To view the form and resize the columns in the subform:**

▶ **1.** Switch to Form view, and then click the **Positions** tab. The second page of the multi-page form displays the Position table records for Beantown Tours.

Before you resize the columns in the Positions subform, you'll change the font size in the subform datasheet.

▶ **2.** Make sure the PositionID field in the datasheet is the current field, and then change the font size to **8**. All text in the datasheet changes to Arial 8.

▶ **3.** Resize all datasheet columns to their best fit. See Figure 6-34.

Position table columns after resizing in the subform ◀ **Figure 6-34**

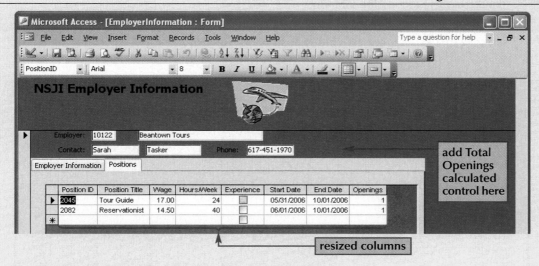

add Total Openings calculated control here

resized columns

▶ **4.** Practice navigating through the Employer and Position table records using the form. When you finish, click the **Employer Information** tab, and then click the main form's **First Record** navigation button to display the employer information for Beantown Tours.

▶ **5.** Save your form changes.

Elsa reviews her design for the custom form and reminds you that you need to add a calculated control to display an employer's total openings in the main form to the right of the phone number.

# Displaying a Subform's Calculated Control in the Main Form

Elsa wants the main form to display each employer's total number of openings in a calculated control. To calculate subtotals and overall totals in a form or report, you use the **Sum function**. The format for the Sum function you'll use is *=Sum([Openings])*. For the Sum function to calculate the total of an employer's Openings field values, which appear in the subform's Detail section, you'll place the calculated control in the subform's Form Footer section. However, Elsa wants the total openings displayed in the main form, not in the subform. Fortunately, the subform displays in Datasheet view by default, and Form Headers and Footers do not appear in Datasheet view, so the subform calculated control will not appear. Although the calculated control does not appear in the subform, the calculation occurs and you can add a calculated control to the main form that references the subform calculated control and displays the total openings in the main form.

## Adding a Calculated Control to a Subform's Form Footer Section

First, you'll open the subform in Design view in another window and add the calculated control to the subform's Form Footer section.

### To add a calculated control to the subform's Form Footer section:

1. Switch to Design view, click the **Positions** tab, and then click the subform border. Sizing handles appear around the subform.

2. Move the pointer to the subform border; when the pointer changes to a ✋ shape, right-click the border, and then click **Subform in New Window** on the shortcut menu. The subform opens in Design view. See Figure 6-35.

**Figure 6-35** **Subform in Design view**

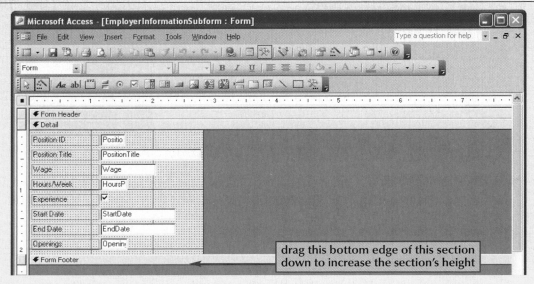

The subform's Detail section contains the Position table fields. As a subform in the main form, the fields appear as a datasheet even though the fields do not appear that way in Design view. The heights of the subform's Form Header and Form Footer sections are zero, meaning that these sections have been removed from the subform. You'll increase the height of the Form Footer section, so that you can add the calculated control to that section.

3. Place the pointer at the bottom edge of the Form Footer section. When the pointer changes to a ╪ shape, drag the bottom edge of the section down to the 0.5-inch mark on the vertical ruler.

Now you'll add a calculated control to the Form Footer section. To create the text box for the calculated control, you use the **Text Box tool** on the toolbox. Because the Form Footer section will not display, you do not need to position the control precisely.

4. Click the **Text Box** tool ab on the toolbox.

5. Position the + portion of the pointer near the top of the Form Footer section and at the 1-inch mark on the horizontal ruler, and then click the mouse button. Access places a text box control and an attached label control to its left in the Form Footer section.

   Next, you'll set the Name and Control Source properties for the text box. The **Name property** specifies the name of an object or control. The **Control Source property** specifies the source of the data that appears in the control; the Control Source property setting can be either a field name or an expression.

6. Open the property sheet for the text box in the Form Footer section, click the **All** tab (if necessary), select the entry in the Name text box (if necessary), type **txtOpeningsSum**, press the **Tab** key, and then type **=Sum([Openings])** in the Control Source text box. See Figure 6-36.

Setting properties for the subform calculated control  Figure 6-36

The calculated control's Name property setting (txtOpeningsSum) follows a common naming convention: *txt* is a prefix tag to identify the control type (a text box), *Openings* is the name for the related field, and *Sum* is a suffix tag to identify the control as a summary control. Read the Naming Conventions section in the appendix titled "Relational Databases and Database Design" for more information about naming conventions.

When you add the calculated control in the main form, you'll reference the subform's calculated control value by using its name. You've finished creating the subform calculated control, so you can return to the main form.

7. Close the property sheet, save your subform changes, and then click the **Close Window** button ⊠ on the menu bar. The subform closes, and you return to Design view for the main form.

Next, you'll add a calculated control in the main form to display an employer's total openings.

## Adding a Calculated Control to a Main Form

The subform's calculated control contains the employer's total openings, so you need to add a calculated control in the main form that references the value in the subform calculated control. To reference the subform calculated control, you'll set the main form's calculated control to =*EmployerInformationSubform.Form!txtOpeningsSum*. This expression asks Access to display the value of the txtOpeningsSum control that is located in the EmployerInformationSubform form, which is a form object. You'll add the calculated control to the right of the Phone field in the main form's Detail section.

## To add a calculated control to the main form's Detail section:

▶ **1.** Use the **Text Box** tool  on the toolbox to add a text box and attached label to the right of the Phone text box, clicking the + portion of the pointer at the 5.25-inch mark on the horizontal ruler. Don't be concerned about positioning the control precisely, because you'll resize and move the label and text box later.

▶ **2.** Open the property sheet for the label, set the Name property to **lblOpeningsTtl**, and set the Caption property to **Total Openings:**. See Figure 6-37.

| Figure 6-37 | Setting properties for the calculated control's label |
| --- | --- |

The label's Name property (lblOpeningsTtl) identifies the control as a label (lbl) control for the calculated field named txtOpeningsTtl, which is the name you'll give to the related text box; the *Ttl* suffix tag identifies the control as a total control. Next, you'll resize the label and text box controls and move them into position.

▶ **3.** Close the property sheet, right-click the label, point to **Size** on the shortcut menu, and then click **To Fit**.

▶ **4.** Resize the text box, and then move both controls to the positions shown in Figure 6-38.

| Figure 6-38 | Label and text box resized and moved in the main form |
| --- | --- |

Elsa asks you to change the appearance and properties of the calculated control so that users know it's a calculated control and so that it looks different from bound text boxes. In addition to the Name and Control Source properties, you'll set the following properties for the calculated control text box:

• Set the Tab Stop property to a value of No. The **Tab Stop property** specifies whether users can use the Tab key to move to a control on a form. If the Tab Stop property is set to No, users can't tab to the control.

- Set the ControlTip Text property to a value of *Calculated total number of openings for this employer*. The **ControlTip Text property** specifies the text that appears in a ScreenTip when users hold the mouse pointer over a control on a form.
- Set the Back Color property to teal. The **Back Color property** specifies the background color for a control on a form or report.
- Set the Special Effect property to a flat effect. The **Special Effect property** specifies the type of special effect applied to a control on a form or report. Choices for this property are Chiseled, Etched, Flat, Raised, Shadowed, and Sunken.

You can set many properties in the property sheet by typing a value in the property's text box, by selecting a value from the property's list box, or by double-clicking the property name. If you need to set a property by typing a long text entry, you can open the Zoom dialog box and type the entry in the dialog box. You can also use the Expression Builder to help you enter expressions.

Now you'll set the properties for the calculated control in the main form.

### To set properties for the calculated control in the main form:

▶ **1.** Open the property sheet for the text box, and then click the **All** tab (if necessary).

▶ **2.** Set the Name property to **txtOpeningsTtl**, right-click the **Control Source** text box, click **Zoom** on the shortcut menu, and then type **=EmployerInformationSubform.Form!txtOpeningsSum** in the Zoom dialog box. See Figure 6-39.

| Control Source property setting for the main form's calculated control ◀ | **Figure 6-39** |

▶ **3.** Click the **OK** button to close the Zoom dialog box.

▶ **4.** Scrolling the property sheet as necessary, set the Tab Stop property to **No**, and the ControlTip Text property to **Calculated total number of openings for this employer**.

You can set the Back Color property and the Special Effect property in the property sheet, but instead you'll use the Fill/Back Color and the Special Effect buttons on the Formatting toolbar to set these properties. Elsa wants the calculated control to have the same background color as its attached label; this background color is the color you set for the Detail section using the Fill/Back Color button earlier. Note that the default background color for form sections does not appear in the Fill/Back Color palette. If you want to set a control's background color to the default form section color, open the property sheet for a form section that has the default color, copy the section's Back Color property value, click the control, and then paste the copied value in the control's Back Color text box.

▶ **5.** Close the property sheet, and then click the **Fill/Back Color** button 🎨 on the Formatting toolbar. The calculated control now appears with the teal background.

**Trouble?** If your calculated control's background color is not teal, click the list arrow for the Fill/Back Color button on the Formatting toolbar, and then click the teal box in the color palette (row 2, column 5).

▶ **6.** Click the list arrow for the **Special Effect** button 🔲 on the Formatting toolbar, and then click the **Special Effect: Flat** button. The calculated control now appears with the flat special effect.

You've completed creating the calculated controls for the custom form, so you can save and view the form in Form view.

**7.** Save your form design changes, switch to Form view, click the **Restore Window** button 🗗 on the menu bar, drag the Form window title bar until the entire form is visible on the screen (if necessary), and then increase the form's width and height (see Figure 6-40). Notice that the Total Openings value of 2 appears even though the Positions tab isn't selected and the subform isn't visible.

**8.** Click the **Positions** tab, navigate to record 10 (The Clipper Ship Inn) in the main form, and then position the pointer on the **Total Openings** calculated control. See Figure 6-40.

| Figure 6-40 | Completed custom form in Form view |
| --- | --- |

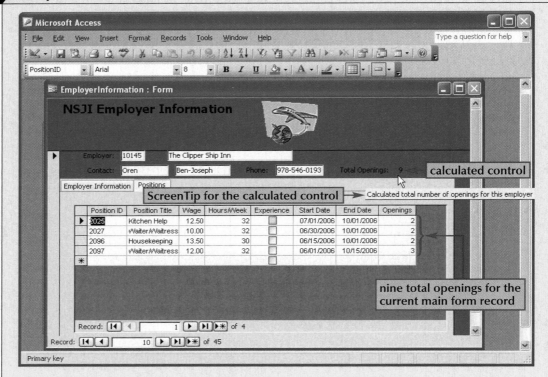

**Trouble?** If the subform moves up to cover the main form controls when you click the Positions tab, click the Employer Information tab, increase the height of the Form window, click the Positions tab, and then repeat these steps until the subform no longer moves up.

The ScreenTip appears when you hold the pointer on the main form's calculated control, which appears flat with a teal background. The four subform Position table records represent nine total openings, which matches the value displayed in the main form.

Elsa asks you to verify that users can't update the Total Openings calculated control in the main form and that users will tab in the correct order through the controls in the form.

# Changing the Tab Order in a Form

Pressing the Tab key in Form view moves the focus from one control to another control. **Focus** refers to the control that is currently active and awaiting user action; focus also refers to the object and record that is currently active. The order in which you move from control to control, or change the focus, in a form when you press the Tab key is called the

**tab order**. Elsa wants to verify that the tab order in the top portion of the main form is left-to-right, top-to-bottom, and that the tab order in the Employer Information tab is top-to-bottom, left-to-right. First, you'll verify that users can't update the Total Openings calculated control.

### To test the calculated control and modify the tab order:

▶ **1.** Select **9** in the Total Openings text box, and then press the **8** key. The Total Openings value remains at 9, and a message displays in the status bar. See Figure 6-41.

After attempting to update the calculated control  **Figure 6-41**

The status bar message warns you that you can't update, or edit, the calculated control because it's bound to an expression. The calculated control in the main form changes in value only when the value of the expression changes. Next, you'll determine the tab order of the fields at the top of the main form. Elsa wants the tab order to be across and then down.

▶ **2.** Select **10145** in the EmployerID text box, press the **Tab** key to advance to the EmployerName text box, and then press the **Tab** key three more times to advance to the ContactFirstName, ContactLastName, and Phone text boxes, in order. The tab order Elsa wants for the fields in the top portion of the main form (left-to-right, top-to-bottom) is correct. Now you'll determine the tab order of the fields in the Employer Information tab. Elsa wants the tab order to be top-to-bottom, left-to-right. (The tab order should be Address to City to StateProv to PostalCode to Country to Comments to Website to NAICSCode to Position.)

▶ **3.** Click the **Employer Information** tab, select **5 Cliffside Drive** in the Address text box (if necessary), press the **Tab** key to advance to the City text box, and then press the **Tab** key again. Instead of the focus advancing from the City text box to the StateProv text box, the focus advanced to the PostalCode text box.

▶ **4.** Press the **Tab** key six times, observing the tab order. The tab order doesn't match the order Elsa wants, so you'll change the tab order.

▶ **5.** Switch to Design view, click the **Employer Information** tab, click **View** on the menu bar, and then click **Tab Order**. The Tab Order dialog box opens. See Figure 6-42.

**Figure 6-42** | **Changing the tab order for the Employer Information tab**

Because you did not set the Name property for the two combo box controls, their names are Combo19 (your name might be different) for the NAICSCode text box and Combo21 (your name might be different) for the StateProv text box. The Auto Order button lets you create a left-to-right, top-to-bottom tab order automatically. First, you'll move the Combo21 entry above the PostalCode entry.

6. Click the box to the left of Combo21, and then drag the box above the PostalCode entry. The first five entries are now correct.

7. Repeat Step 6 to move the Comments entry above the Position entry and to move the Position entry below the Combo19 entry. From top to bottom the entries in the dialog box should be Address, City, Combo21, PostalCode, Country, Comments, Website, Combo19, and Position.

8. Click the **OK** button, save your table design changes, switch to Form view, and then tab through the controls in the Employer Information tab to make sure the tab order is correct.

   **Trouble?** If the tab order is incorrect, switch to Design view, click View on the menu bar, click Tab Order, move appropriate entries in the Tab Order dialog box, and then repeat Step 8.

   You've completed Elsa's custom form.

Elsa has a new request. She wants to see information for all employers in Massachusetts and Rhode Island that are tour operators. She wants to view this information using the EmployerInformation form. To display the results she wants, you will use a filter with a form.

# Using a Filter with a Form

Recall that a **filter** is a set of criteria you place on the records in an open form or datasheet to isolate a subset of the records temporarily. A filter is like a query, but it applies only to the open form or datasheet. If you want to use a filter at another time, you can save the filter as a query.

Five filter tools let you specify and apply filters in a form or datasheet: Filter By Selection, Filter Excluding Selection, Filter For Input, Filter By Form, and Advanced Filter/Sort. With the first four tools, you specify the filter directly in the form or datasheet. **Filter By Selection** filters records that contain a selected field value or a selected portion of a field value. **Filter Excluding Selection** filters records that do not contain the selected field value or the selected portion of a field value. For **Filter For Input** you enter a value or expression to filter only those records that contain the value or satisfy the expression. **Filter By Form** filters records that match multiple selection criteria using the same Access logical and comparison operators used in queries. After applying one of these filter tools, you can use the Sort Ascending or Sort Descending toolbar buttons to rearrange the records, if necessary.

**Advanced Filter/Sort** lets you specify multiple selection criteria and specify a sort order for selected records in the Filter window, in the same way you specify record selection criteria and sort orders for a query in Design view.

Before filtering the records to satisfy Elsa's request, you'll show her how to use the simpler filter tools.

## Using Simple Filters

Although Elsa has used simple filters with table and query datasheets, she's never used a filter with a form. You'll show Elsa some simple filters before you show her how to create the filter to answer her question.

### To select the records using simple filters:

1. Navigate to the first main form record (Beantown Tours), make sure the **Employer Information** tab is selected, select **MA** in the StateProv text box, and then click the **Filter By Selection** button on the Form View toolbar. Access displays the first of the 17 filtered records for employers in Massachusetts (MA). See Figure 6-43.

Using Filter By Selection in a form ◀ **Figure 6-43**

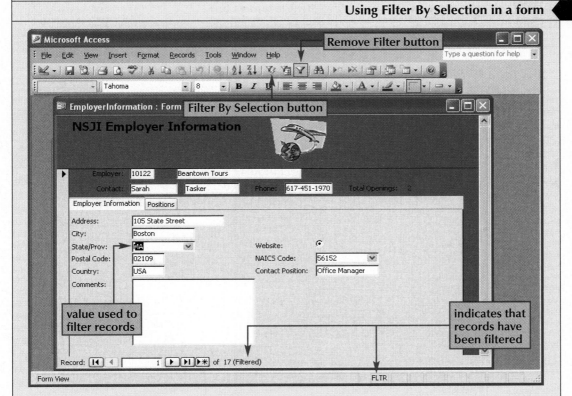

You can navigate through the main form records to verify that only employers from Massachusetts display. Next, after removing the filter, you'll use Filter Excluding Selection to exclude employers from Massachusetts.

▶ **2.** Click the **Remove Filter** button on the Form View toolbar, and then notice that the filter is removed and that 45 records are again available for viewing.

▶ **3.** Make sure **MA** is still selected in the StateProv text box, right-click the selected value to open the shortcut menu, and then click **Filter Excluding Selection**. Access displays the first of the 28 filtered records for employers not in Massachusetts.

Now you'll filter records for employers in New Hampshire (NH) and Nova Scotia (NS).

▶ **4.** Click the **Remove Filter** button on the Form View toolbar, right-click the **StateProv** text box, click **Filter For** on the shortcut menu, and then type **N\*** in the Filter For text box. See Figure 6-44.

| **Figure 6-44** | **Using Filter For Input in a form** |

The shortcut menu contains these filter options: Filter By Selection, Filter Excluding Selection, Filter For [Input], and Remove Filter/Sort. The typed expression of N\* will filter those records with StateProv field values that start with the letter N.

▶ **5.** Press the **Enter** key. Access displays the first of the eight filtered records for employers in New Hampshire and Nova Scotia.

▶ **6.** Navigate the main form records to verify that the filtered results are correct.

▶ **7.** Click the **Remove Filter** button on the Form View toolbar.

Next, you'll use Filter By Form to produce the results Elsa wants.

## Using Filter By Form

You can use Filter By Form to display Elsa's information for employers only in Massachusetts and Rhode Island that are tour operators.

## Selecting Records Using Filter By Form

- Open the form in Form view.
- Click the Filter By Form button on the Form View toolbar.
- Enter a simple selection criterion or an And condition in the first form, using the text boxes for the appropriate fields.
- If there is an Or condition, click the Or tab and enter the Or condition in the second form. Continue to enter Or conditions on separate forms by using the Or tab.
- Click the Apply Filter button on the Filter/Sort toolbar.

To answer Elsa's question, the multiple selection criteria you will enter are: Massachusetts *and* Tour Operators *or* Rhode Island *and* Tour Operators.

### To select the records using Filter By Form:

▶ 1. Click the **Filter By Form** button 🔳 on the Form View toolbar. Access displays a blank form. See Figure 6-45.

**Blank form for Filter By Form** ◀ **Figure 6-45**

On this blank form, you specify multiple selection criteria by entering conditions in the text boxes for the fields in a record. If you enter criteria in more than one field, you create the equivalent of an And condition—Access selects any record that matches all criteria. To create an Or condition, you enter the criteria for the first part of the condition in the field on the first (Look for) blank form, and then click the Or tab to display a new blank form. You enter the criteria for the second part of the condition on the "Or" blank form. Access selects any record that matches all criteria on the Look for form *or* all criteria on the Or form. Notice the expression (Like "N*") in the StateProv text box, which was how Access changed the expression (N*) that you entered in the Filter For text box. You need to clear the grid before you enter the new criteria.

▶ **2.** Click the **Clear Grid** button ☒ on the Filter/Sort toolbar, click the **StateProv** list arrow, and then click **MA** (the list box entries are alphabetical by name, not code). Access adds the criterion "MA" to the StateProv text box.

▶ **3.** Click the **NAICSCode** list arrow, and then click **Tour Operators**. Access adds the criterion "56152" to the NAICSCode text box.

You specified the logical operator (And) for the condition "MA" And "56152" (Massachusetts and Tour Operators). To add the rest of the criteria, you need to display the Or form.

▶ **4.** Click the **Or** tab to display a second blank form. The insertion point is in the text box for the NAICSCode field. Notice that a third tab, also labeled "Or," is now available in case you need to specify another Or condition.

▶ **5.** Click the **NAICSCode** list arrow, and then click **Tour Operators**.

▶ **6.** Click the **StateProv** list arrow, and then click **RI**. The form now contains the second And condition: "RI" And "56152" (Rhode Island and Tour Operators). See Figure 6-46.

| Figure 6-46 | **Completed Filter By Form** |
| --- | --- |

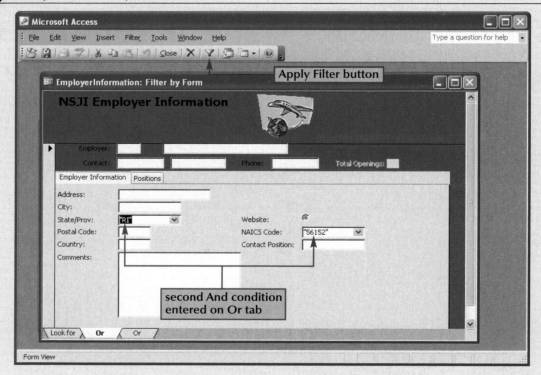

Combined with the Look for form, you now have the Or condition, and the complete Filter By Form conditions.

▶ **7.** Click the **Apply Filter** button ☑ on the Filter/Sort toolbar. Access applies the filter and displays the first record that matches the selection criteria (Beantown Tours, a tour operator in Massachusetts). The bottom of the screen shows that the filter selected six records. See Figure 6-47.

**First record that matches the filter criteria** | Figure 6-47

8. Click the main form's **Next Record** navigation button ▶ to display the second selected record (Newport Mansion Guided Tours, a tour operator in Rhode Island).

Now that you defined the filter, you can save it as a query, so that Elsa can easily view this information in the future.

## Saving a Filter as a Query

By saving a filter as a query, you can reuse the filter in the future by opening the saved query.

Reference Window

### Saving a Filter as a Query

- Create a filter using Filter By Selection, Filter Excluding Selection, Filter By Form, Filter For Input, or Advanced Filter/Sort.
- Click the Save As Query button on the Filter/Sort toolbar to open the Save As Query dialog box.
- Type the name for the query, and then press the Enter key (or click the OK button).

Next, you'll save the filter you just created as a query named TourOperatorsInMAandRI.

### To save the filter as a query:

▶ 1. Click the **Filter By Form** button 🖼 on the Form View toolbar. Access displays the form with the selection criteria.

▶ 2. Click the **Save As Query** button 💾 on the Filter/Sort toolbar. The Save As Query dialog box opens.

▶ 3. Type **TourOperatorsInMAandRI** in the Query Name text box, and then press the **Enter** key. Access saves the filter as a query in the Jobs database and closes the dialog box.

Now you can clear the selection criteria, close the Filter by Form window, and return to Form view.

▶ 4. Click the **Clear Grid** button ☒ on the Filter/Sort toolbar. Access removes the selection criteria from the forms.

▶ 5. Click the **Close** button on the Filter/Sort toolbar to close the Filter by Form window and return to Form view. The filter is still in effect in this window, so you need to remove it.

**Trouble?** If a dialog box opens and asks if you want to save your form changes, click the Yes button.

▶ 6. Click the **Remove Filter** button 🔽 on the Form View toolbar. The bottom of the screen shows that 45 records are available.

Next, to check that you saved the filter as a query, you'll switch to the Database window, leaving the form open, and you'll view the list of queries on the Queries tab.

### To switch to the Database window and view the query list:

▶ 1. Click the **Database Window** button 🖼 on the Form View toolbar.

▶ 2. Click **Queries** in the Objects bar of the Database window to display the Queries list box. The TourOperatorsInMAandRI query is now listed.

The next time Elsa wants to view the records selected by this query, she can apply the query to the form. If she simply runs the query, she will see the selected records, but they will not be shown in the EmployerInformation form. Instead, she can open the form and apply the saved query to select the records she wants to view in the form.

## Applying a Filter Saved as a Query

To see how to apply a query as a filter to a form, you will switch back to the open EmployerInformation form and apply the TourOperatorsInMAandRI query as a filter.

**Reference Window**

### Applying a Filter Saved as a Query

- Open the form to which you want to apply the filter.
- Click the Filter By Form button on the Form View toolbar.
- Click the Load from Query button on the Filter/Sort toolbar.
- Select the query you want to apply. Access loads the saved query into the Filter by Form window.
- Click the Apply Filter button on the Filter/Sort toolbar.

Now you'll activate the EmployerInformation form and apply the TourOperatorsInMAandRI query as a filter.

**To apply the filter saved as a query:**

▶ **1.** Click the **EmployerInformation** title bar to make the form the active object.

▶ **2.** Click the **Filter By Form** button 🔚 on the Form View toolbar.

**Trouble?** If your Filter by Form window already has the filter applied, click the Clear Grid button on the Filter/Sort toolbar to remove the filter.

▶ **3.** Click the **Load from Query** button 🖾 on the Filter/Sort toolbar. Access opens the Applicable Filter dialog box. See Figure 6-48.

Applicable Filter dialog box ◀ **Figure 6-48**

your list might show the filters in a different order

click to select filter saved as query

▶ **4.** Click **TourOperatorsInMAandRI** in the Filter list box, and then click the **OK** button. Access loads the saved query into the Filter by Form window.

▶ **5.** Click the **Apply Filter** button 🔽 on the Filter/Sort toolbar. Access applies the filter and displays the first filtered record in the form.

Now you'll remove the filter.

▶ **6.** Click the **Remove Filter** button 🔽 on the Form View toolbar.

If Elsa has more complex filter operations she needs to perform in the future, she'll need to use an advanced filter.

## Applying an Advanced Filter in a Form

Advanced Filter/Sort lets you specify multiple selection criteria and specify a sort order for the selected records in the Filter window, in the same way you specify record selection criteria and sort orders for a query in Design view.

| **Applying an Advanced Filter/Sort** | Reference Window |
|---|---|

- Open the table or query in Datasheet view, or open the form in Form view.
- Click Records on the menu bar, point to Filter, and then click Advanced Filter/Sort.
- Add to the design grid the fields you need to filter or sort.
- Specify the selection criteria, and select the sort fields and their sort orders.
- Click the Apply Filter button on the Filter/Sort toolbar to apply the filter.

Elsa wants to view employer data for USA employers that are not in the hotel and motel industry in ascending employer name sequence. To produce the results Elsa wants, you'll use an advanced filter/sort for the form.

### To create the advanced filter/sort for the form:

1. Click **Records** on the menu bar, point to **Filter**, and then click **Advanced Filter/Sort**. The Filter window opens on top of the EmployerInformation form. See Figure 6-49.

| Figure 6-49 | Filter window |
|---|---|

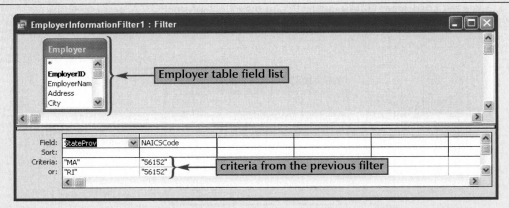

The Filter window looks the same as and functions similarly to the Query window in Design view. You add fields from the field list to the design grid just as you do with queries. However, you need to add only those fields for which you'll be specifying selection criteria and sorting specifications; all fields from the record source are included automatically in the filter results. The Employer table field list appears in the Filter window because it's the record source for the EmployerInformation form.

Notice that the criteria you used for the Filter By Form appear in the design grid, so you need to remove those criteria. Then you'll add the EmployerName, NAICSCode, and Country fields to the design grid, and you'll select the sort field.

2. Click the **Clear Grid** button ⊠ on the Filter/Sort toolbar, double-click **EmployerName** in the Employer field list, double-click **NAICSCode**, and then double-click **Country**, scrolling as necessary, to add these three fields to the design grid.

3. Click the right side of the **EmployerName Sort** text box to display the sort order options, and then click **Ascending**. The query will display the filtered records alphabetically by the EmployerName field values.

Next, you'll enter the selection criteria. Elsa wants to view USA employers that are not in the hotel and motel industry; the NAICS code 72111 identifies employers in that industry.

4. Click the **NAICSCode Criteria** text box, type **Not 72111**, and then press the **Tab** key. The condition changes to Not "72111".

5. In the Country Criteria text box type **USA**, and then press the **Tab** key. The condition changes to "USA". See Figure 6-50.

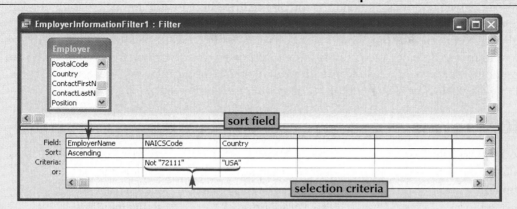

You've completed the filter, so you can now apply it.

▶ **6.** Click the **Apply Filter** button ▽ on the Filter/Sort toolbar. Access applies the filter and displays the first record that satisfies the selection criteria (USA employers not in the hotel and motel industry). The filter selected 29 records.

▶ **7.** Navigate the main form records to verify that only USA employers that are not in the hotel and motel industry have been selected.

As is the case with the other filter types, you can use the Remove Filter button to remove the filter. Now that Elsa knows how to create filters, you'll close the form and then exit Access.

▶ **8.** Close the form, close the Jobs database, and then exit Access.

You completed your work for Elsa by adding a subform and calculated controls to the custom form. You also changed the tab order, and filtered data. The custom form you created will make it easier for Elsa, Matt, Zack, and others at NSJI to enter, retrieve, and view information in the Jobs database.

## Session 6.3 Quick Check

Review

**1.** You use the _____ tool on the toolbox to add a subform to a form.

**2.** To calculate subtotals and overall totals in a form or report, you use the _____ function.

**3.** The Control Source property setting can be either a(n) _____ or a(n) _____ .

**4.** Explain the difference between the Tab Stop property and tab order.

**5.** What is focus?

**6.** What's the difference between Filter By Selection and Filter Excluding Selection?

**7.** How do you reuse a filter?

**8.** _____ lets you specify multiple selection criteria and specify a sort order for the selected records.

## Tutorial Summary

Review

In this tutorial, you examined general form design guidelines and learned how to use them in planning a custom form. You learned how to change a lookup field back to a text field, to print database relationships, and to use the Documenter. After creating a blank bound form, you learned how to add bound controls to a form, and to select, move, resize, delete, and rename controls. You also learned how to add and delete form headers and footers, to add a picture to a form, to create a multi-page form with tab controls, to change a control to another control type, to add combo boxes to a form, to add a subform to a form, to add calculated controls to a subform and a main form, and to change the tab order in a form. Finally, you learned how to filter data using Filter By Selection, Filter Excluding Selection, Filter For Input, Filter By Form, and Advanced Filter/Sort.

## Key Terms

| | | |
|---|---|---|
| Advanced Filter/Sort | Filter By Form | rulers |
| Back Color property | Filter By Selection | section bar |
| bound control | Filter Excluding Selection | section selector |
| bound form | Filter For Input | sizing handle |
| calculated control | focus | Special Effect property |
| Caption property | Form Footer section | subform |
| combo box | Form Header section | Subform/Subreport tool |
| Combo Box tool | grid | Sum function |
| control | Image tool | Tab Control tool |
| Control Source property | label | tab order |
| Control Wizard | Label tool | Tab Stop property |
| ControlTip Text property | lookup table | Text Box tool |
| custom form | move handle | toggle button |
| Detail section | Name property | toolbox |
| Display Control property | option button | unbound control |
| Documenter | Page Break tool | unbound form |
| Fill/Back Color button | Record Source property | Visible property |
| filter | | |

## Review Assignments

**Practice**

*Take time to practice the skills you learned in the tutorial using the same case scenario.*

**Data Files needed for the Review Assignments: Students.mdb (*cont. from Tutorial 5*) and WorldMap.gif**

Elsa wants you to create a custom form that displays and updates recruiters and the students they've recruited. She also wants you to filter data in a form and perform several other database tasks. You'll do so by completing the following:

1. Open the **Students** database in the Intro\Review folder provided with your Data Files.
2. Remove the lookup feature from the SSN field in the **Student** table.
3. Edit the relationship between the **Recruiter** and **Student** tables to enforce referential integrity.
4. Use the Documenter to document the **SalarieswithRaises** query. Select all query options; use the Names, Data Types, and Sizes option for fields; and use the Names and Fields option for indexes. Print the report produced by the Documenter.
5. Use Figure 6-51 and the following steps to create a multi-page form based on the **Recruiter** and **Student** tables.

**Figure 6-51**

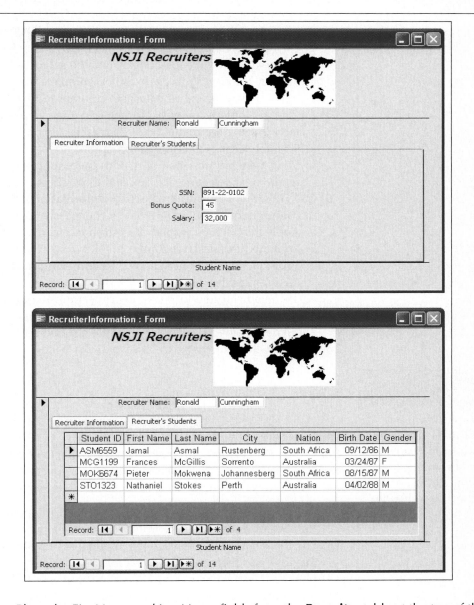

a. Place the FirstName and LastName fields from the **Recruiter** table at the top of the Detail section. Delete the LastName label and change the caption for the FirstName label to Recruiter Name:.

b. Insert a Form Header section and a Form Footer section in the form. Place a title label in the Form Header section. Enter the title NSJI Recruiters, and change its font to 14-point bold italic.

c. Place the **WorldMap** picture in the Form Header section to the right of the title. The file containing this picture is in the Intro\Review folder provided with your Data Files.

d. Place a label in the Form Footer section, and type your name in the label.

e. Place a tab control below the Recruiter Name label in the Detail section. On the first page of the tab control, place the remaining fields from the **Recruiter** table. Align the labels on the right, and move them closer to the text boxes. Resize the text boxes to appropriate widths.

f. On the second page of the tab control, place a subform based on the **Student** table, include all fields except for the SSN field from the table in the subform, and use SSN as the link field. Save the subform as **NSJIStudentSubform**.

g. Change the Caption property for each tab, and delete the subform label.

h. Resize the form, the tab control, and the subform. You might need to resize one or more of these controls again as you complete the remaining steps.

i. In Form view, resize all datasheet columns to their best fit.

j. If the tab order is incorrect for the Recruiter Name controls or for the controls on the Recruiter Information tab, correct the tab order.

k. Save the form as **RecruiterInformation**.

l. View the form, and then print both pages for record 10. (*Hint*: Print the selected record after selecting one tab, and then repeat the procedure for the other tab.)

6. Use Filter By Form with the **RecruiterInformation** form to select all records in which the bonus quota is 40 and the salary is either $28,500 or $29,000.

a. Apply the filter. How many records are selected?

b. Print the first filtered record.

c. Save the filter as a query named **RecruiterInformationFilter**. Close the filter, and then remove the filter.

7. Apply an advanced filter to the **RecruiterInformation** form, selecting records with a BonusQuota field value of 45 and a Salary field value greater than $32,000, and sorting in decreasing Salary order. Print the last filtered record. Close the form.

8. Close the **Students** database, and then exit Access.

### Create

*Use the skills you learned in the tutorial to work with the data contained in a video photography database and to create a custom form.*

## Case Problem 1

**Data Files needed for this Case Problem: Clients.mdb (*cont. from Tutorial 5*), TV-VCR-L.bmp, and TV-VCR-R.bmp**

***Lim's Video Photography*** Youngho Lim wants you to create a custom form that displays and updates clients and their contracts. He also wants you to filter data in a form and a datasheet and to perform several other database tasks. You'll do so by completing the following:

1. Open the **Clients** database in the Intro\Case1 folder provided with your Data Files.

2. Remove the lookup feature from the ShootType field in the **Shoot** table.

3. Edit the relationship between the **ShootDesc** and **Shoot** tables to enforce referential integrity, and then print the Relationships window.

4. Use the Documenter to document the **ShootDesc** table. Select all table options; use the Names, Data Types, and Sizes option for fields; and use the Names and Fields option for indexes. Print the report produced by the Documenter.

5. Use Figure 6-52 and the following steps to create a multi-page form based on the **Client** and **Contract** tables.

**Figure 6-52**

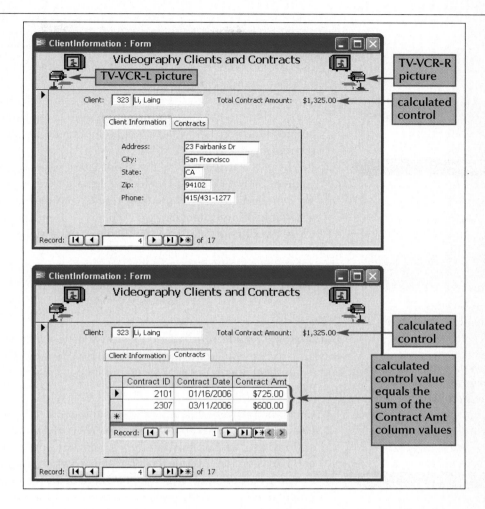

a. The main form is a bound form using the **Client** table. Fields from this table appear above the tab control and on the Client Information tab. Save the form as **ClientInformation**.

b. Fields from the **Contract** table appear in a subform named **ContractSubform** on the Contracts tab.

**Explore**

c. The calculated control, with its Format property set to Currency, displays the sum of the ContractAmt field values that appear in the subform. Set the calculated control's ControlTip Text property to "Calculated total contract amount for this client". Set the calculated control's Back Color property to the same value as the form's background color, and set the calculated control's Tab Stop property to No.

 d. The main form has a Form Header section that displays the title set in 12-point, bold font and two pictures: **TV-VCR-L** to the left of the title and **TV-VCR-R** to the right of the title. Both picture files are located in the Intro\Case1 folder provided with your Data Files.

 e. If the tab order is incorrect for the Client controls or for the controls on the Client Information tab, correct the tab order.

 f. View the form, and then print both pages for the first record.

6. Apply a filter to the **ClientInformation** form using Filter Excluding Selection, selecting records with City field values that are not equal to "San Francisco." How many records are filtered?

**Explore**

7. Apply an advanced filter to the **Shoot** table, selecting records with a ShootType field value of BP or WE and a Duration field value greater than 3.5, and sorting in increasing Duration order. Print the filter results, and then close the table without saving your table design changes.

8. Close the **Clients** database, and then exit Access.

**Create**

*Use the skills you learned in the tutorial to work with the data for an e-commerce business in the food services industry and to create two custom forms.*

# Case Problem 2

**Data Files needed for this Case Problem: Delivery.mdb** (*cont. from Tutorial 5*) **and PlaceSet.gif**

***DineAtHome.course.com***   Claire Picard wants you to create two custom forms that display and update data in the Delivery database. She also wants you to filter data in a form and a datasheet and to perform several other database tasks. You'll do so by completing the following:

1. Open the **Delivery** database in the Intro\Case2 folder provided with your Data Files.

2. Use the Documenter to document the **MarcoIslandRestaurants** query. Select all query options; use the Names, Data Types, and Sizes option for fields; and use the Names and Fields option for indexes. Print the report produced by the Documenter.

**Explore**

3. Create a custom form based on the **LargeOrders** query. Display all fields from the query in the form. Create your own design for the form. Add a label to the bottom of the Detail section, and enter your name in the label. Change the label's font so that your name appears in bold blue text. Change the OrderAmt text box format so that the field value appears in bold red text. Save the form as **LargeOrders**. In Form view, print the first record.

4. Use Filter By Form with the **LargeOrders** form to select all orders placed in Naples or East Naples for more than $110.

 a. Apply the filter. How many records are selected?

 b. Print the first filtered record.

 c. Save the filter as a query named **LargeOrdersFilter**. Close the form.

5. Use Figure 6-53 and the following steps to create a multi-page form based on the **Restaurant** and **Order** tables.

**Figure 6-53**

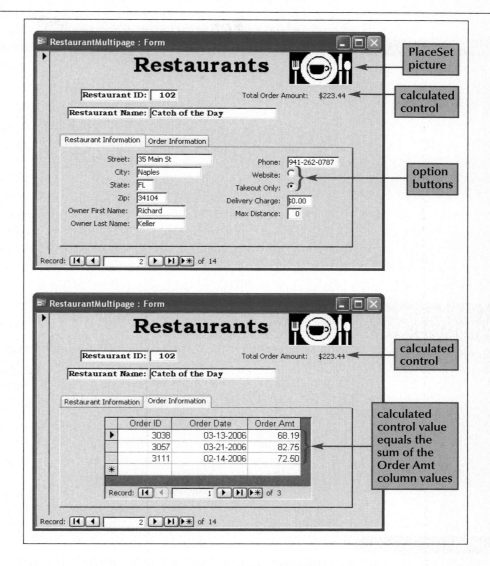

a. The main form is a bound form using the **Restaurant** table. Fields from this table appear above the tab control and on the Restaurant Information tab. Save the form as **RestaurantMultipage**.

b. Fields from the **Order** table appear in a subform named **RestaurantOrderSubform** on the Order Information tab.

**Explore**

c. The calculated control, formatted as Currency, displays the sum of the OrderAmt field values that appear in the subform. Set the calculated control's ControlTip Text property to "Calculated total order amount for this restaurant". Set the calculated control's Back Color property to the same value as the form's background color, and set the calculated control's Tab Stop property to No.

d. Change the two check box controls to option button controls.

e. Above the main form's tab control display the title set in 24-point, bold Bookman Old Style font, and one picture—**PlaceSet**—to the right of the title. The picture file is located in the Intro\Case2 folder provided with your Data Files.

f. If the tab order is incorrect for the Restaurant controls or for the controls on the Restaurant Information tab, correct the tab order.

g. View the form, and then print both pages for the first record.

6. Save the **RestaurantMultipage** form as **EnhancedRestaurantMultipage**. Make and save the following changes to the design of the new form:

a. Change the background color of the form's Detail section and the calculated control to light blue.

b. Use the Line/Border Width button to place a border (weight 2) around the title label.

c. Use the Font/Fore Color button to change the color of the title label to dark blue.

d. Draw one rectangle around the labels and text boxes for the RestaurantID, RestaurantName, and calculated controls.

e. Print both pages of the finished form for the first record, save your changes, and then close the form.

7. Apply an advanced filter to the **Order** table, selecting records with an OrderDate field value earlier than 3/16/2006 and an OrderAmt field value greater than $95, and sorting in decreasing OrderAmt order. Print the filter results, and then save and close the table.

8. Close the **Delivery** database, and then exit Access.

# Case Problem 3

**Data File needed for this Case Problem: Donors.mdb (*cont. from Tutorial 5*)**

***Redwood Zoo*** Michael Rosenfeld asks you to create a custom form for the Donors database so that he can better track pledges and costs for the zoo's funds. He also wants you to filter data and to perform other database tasks. You'll do so by completing the following:

1. Open the **Donors** database in the Intro\Case3 folder provided with your Data Files.

2. Remove the lookup feature from the FundCode field in the **Pledge** table.

3. Edit the relationship between the **Fund** and **Pledge** tables to enforce referential integrity, and then print the Relationships window.

4. Use the Documenter to document the **Fund** table. Select all table options; use the Names, Data Types, and Sizes option for fields; and use the Names and Fields option for indexes. Print the report produced by the Documenter.

5. Create a custom form based on the **Costs** query. Display all fields in the form. Use your own design for the form. Change the FundName label and text box format, so the label and field values appear in 10-point, bold, dark blue text on a light blue background. Add your name to the bottom of the form in the Form Footer section. Save the form as **Costs**, view the form, and then print the first record.

6. Apply the following filters to the **Costs** form:

a. Use Filter By Selection, selecting records with a PaymentMethod field value equal to B. How many records are selected?

b. Use Filter Excluding Selection, selecting records with PaymentMethod field values that are not equal to C. How many records are selected?

c. Use Filter For Input, selecting records with FundName field values that start with the letter B. How many records are selected?

d. Use Filter By Form, selecting records with PaymentMethod field values equal to C or E. How many records are selected?

7. Apply an advanced filter to the **Pledge** table, selecting records with a TotalPledged field value greater than or equal to 500 and a PaymentMethod field value equal to E, and sorting in increasing PledgeDate order. Print the filter results, and then save and close the table.

8. Close the **Donors** database, and then exit Access.

## Case Problem 4

**Data Files needed for this Case Problem: Outdoors.mdb (*cont. from Tutorial 5*) and Kayak.bmp**

***Mountain River Adventures*** Connor and Siobhan Dempsey want you to create two custom forms that display and update data in the Outdoors database. They also want you to filter data in a form and a datasheet and to perform other database tasks. You'll do so by completing the following:

1. Open the **Outdoors** database in the Intro\Case4 folder provided with your Data Files.

2. Remove the lookup feature from the TripID field in the **Booking** table.

3. Edit the relationship between the **RaftingTrip** and **Booking** tables to enforce referential integrity, and then print the Relationships window.

4. Use the Documenter to document the **COClients** query. Select all query options; use the Names, Data Types, and Sizes option for fields; and use the Names and Fields option for indexes. Print the report produced by the Documenter.

5. Create a custom form based on the **Costs** query. Display all fields in the form. Use your own design for the form, but place the title "Booked Trips," the **Kayak** picture (located in the Intro\Case4 folder), and your name in the Form Header section. Change the BookingID label and text box format so that the label and field value appear in 10-point, bold text on a light blue background. Save the form as **Costs**, view the form, and then print the first form record.

6. Use Filter By Form with the **Costs** form to select all records that have a FeePerPerson field value of over $100 or include trips on the Arkansas River.
   a. Apply the filter. How many records are selected?
   b. Print the first filtered record.
   c. Save the filter as a query named **CostsFilter**. Close the form.

7. Create a multi-page custom form named **ClientInformation** based on the **Client** and **Booking** tables by completing the following steps:
   a. Place the ClientName field in the Detail section of the form.
   b. On the first page of a tab control, display the other fields from the **Client** table. Make sure each field text box is an appropriate size. Change the Caption property for the first tab to Client Information.
   c. On the second page of the tab control, display all fields from the **Booking** table in a subform named **BookingSubform**. Resize the subform, change the Caption property for the second tab to Booking Information, delete the subform label, and resize the subform columns to their best fit.

**Apply**

*Apply what you learned in the tutorial to work with the data for an outdoor adventure company.*

**Explore**

**Explore**

    d. Add a calculated control in the main form to the right of the ClientName control. In this control display the sum of the People values that appear in the subform. Set the calculated control's ControlTip Text property to "Total people on trips for this client". Set the calculated control's Back Color property to the same value as the form's background color, and set the calculated control's Tab Stop property to No.

    e. View the form, print both pages for the first record, and then save and close the form.

8. Make a copy of the **ClientInformation** form, and save it as **ClientInformationEnhanced**. Make the following changes to the design of the new form:

    a. Change the background color of the form's Detail section (except the subform) and the calculated control to light blue.

    b. Use the Line/Border Width button to place a border (weight 2) around the ClientName label and field-value text box. Change the font size and weight for these controls, so that they stand out. Resize these controls, if necessary.

    c. Use the Font/Fore Color button to change the color of the Phone field value to red.

    d. Use the Special Effect button on the Form Design toolbar to change the display of the **BookingSubform** subform to raised.

    e. Print both pages of the finished form for the first record, and then save and close the form.

9. Apply an advanced filter to the **RaftingTrip** table, selecting records with a River field value that starts with the word "Colorado" and a TripDays field value less than 2, and sorting in decreasing FeePerPerson order. Print the filter results, and then save and close the table.

10. Close the **Outdoors** database, and then exit Access.

**Challenge**

*Work with the skills you've learned, and explore some new skills, to enhance a database for an Internet auction site.*

# Case Problem 5

**Data File needed for this Case Problem: eACH.mdb (*cont. from Tutorial 5*)**

*eACH Internet Auction Site*  Chris and Pat Aquino want you to create a custom form that displays and updates data in the eACH database. They also want you to filter data in a form and a datasheet and to perform other database tasks. You'll do so by completing the following:

1. Open the **eACH** database in the Intro\Case5 folder provided with your Data Files.

2. In Tutorial 5, you created a lookup field in one of your tables. Remove the lookup feature from this field.

3. Make sure that all table relationships enforce referential integrity, and then print the Relationships window.

4. Review all your database tables, queries, and forms to make sure that the removal of the lookup field did not affect them. If any object now has an incorrect reference to the lookup field, modify the object to correct the problem.

5. Use the Documenter to document one of your forms. Select all form options and use the Names option for sections and controls. Print the report produced by the Documenter.

6. On a piece of paper, sketch the design for a custom form. This form can be a new custom form or a customization of an existing form. The form must include at least the following features:
   a. at least one calculated field
   b. at least one combo box
7. Create two filters for the custom form you created in Step 6. One filter should use Filter By Form and the other filter should use Advanced Filter/Sort. Save both filters as queries.
8. Close the **eACH** database, and then exit Access.

# Internet Assignments

The purpose of the Internet Assignments is to challenge you to find information on the Internet that you can use to work effectively with this software. The actual assignments are updated and maintained on the Course Technology Web site. Log on to the Internet and use your Web browser to go to the Student Online Companion for New Perspectives Office 2003 at **www.course.com/np/office2003**. Click the Internet Assignments link, and then navigate to the assignments for this tutorial.

# SAM Assessment and Training

If you have a SAM user profile, you may have access to hands-on instruction, practice, and assessment of the skills covered in this tutorial. Log in to your SAM account and go to your assignments page to see what your instructor has assigned.

# Quick Check Answers

### Session 6.1

1. forms
2. A bound form is a form that has a table or query as its record source. You use bound forms for maintaining and displaying table data.
3. A bound control is connected to a field in the underlying table or query; an unbound control is not.
4. grid
5. toolbox
6. move
7. Click the control to select it, position the pointer anywhere on the border of the control (except not on a move or sizing handle), and then drag the control and its attached label.
8. Right-click the label, click Properties on the shortcut menu, click the All tab, and then change the entry in the Caption text box.

## Session 6.2

1. Select the control, position the pointer on a sizing handle, and then drag the pointer in the appropriate direction until it is the size you want.

2. The Form Header section lets you add titles, instructions, command buttons, and other controls to the top of a form. This section of the form does not change as you navigate through the records.

3. Open the form in Design view, click the Image tool on the toolbox, position the pointer at the location for the upper-left corner of the picture, click the mouse button, select the picture file, and then click the OK button.

4. Open the form in Design view, click the Tab Control tool on the toolbox, position the pointer in the form at the location for the upper-left corner of the tab control, and then click the mouse button.

5. Click a label, press and hold down the Shift key, click the other labels, release the Shift key, click Format on the menu bar, point to Align, and then click the appropriate alignment option.

6. toggle button, option button

7. combo box

## Session 6.3

1. Subform/Subreport

2. Sum

3. field name, expression

4. The Tab Stop property specifies whether users can use the Tab key to move to a control on a form. Tab order is the order in which you move from control to control, or change the focus, in a form when you press the Tab key.

5. Focus refers to the control that is currently active and awaiting user action; focus also refers to the object and record that is currently active.

6. Filter By Selection filters records that contain a selected field value or a selected portion of a field value. Filter Excluding Selection filters records that do not contain the selected field value or the selected portion of a field value.

7. Save the filter as a query, and then apply the query to an open form.

8. Advanced Filter/Sort

## Objectives

**Session 7.1**
- Customize an existing report
- Hide duplicate values in a report
- Add calculated controls to a report

**Session 7.2**
- Design and create a custom report
- Assign a conditional value to a calculated control
- Sort and group data in a report
- Add, move, resize, and align controls in a report

**Session 7.3**
- Add a subreport to a main report
- Add lines to a report
- Define conditional formatting rules
- Use domain aggregate functions

**Session 7.4**
- Add the date, page numbers, and title to a report
- Add a summary subreport to a main report
- Create and modify mailing labels

# Creating Custom Reports

*Creating a Potential Income Report*

## Case

## Northeast Seasonal Jobs International (NSJI)

At a recent staff meeting, Elsa Jensen indicated that she would like a new report created for the Jobs database. She wants a printed list of all positions for all NSJI employer clients. She also wants subtotals of the placement fee and potential income amounts from each employer and a grand total for all potential income amounts.

In this tutorial, you will create the report for Elsa. In building the report, you will use many Access report customization features—such as grouping data, adding a subreport, calculating totals, and adding lines to separate report sections. These features will enhance Elsa's report and make it easier to read.

## Student Data Files

▼**Intro**

▽ **Tutorial folder**
    Jobs.mdb (*cont.*)
    NSJILogo.gif

▽ **Review folder**
    Students.mdb (*cont.*)

▽ **Case1 folder**
    Clients.mdb (*cont.*)

▽ **Case2 folder**
    Delivery.mdb (*cont.*)
    DineLogo.gif

▽ **Case3 folder**
    Donors.mdb (*cont.*)

▽ **Case4 folder**
    Outdoors.mdb (*cont.*)

▽ **Case5 folder**
    eACH.mdb (*cont.*)

## Session 7.1

# Customizing an Existing Report

A **report** is the formatted, printed contents of one or more tables from a database. Although you can format and print data using datasheets, queries, and forms, reports offer you greater flexibility and provide a more professional, readable appearance. For example, NSJI can create reports from the database for billing statements and mailing labels.

Elsa needs a report using the EmployerPositions query as the record source. She used the Report Wizard to create an initial EmployerPositions report, but she is disappointed with the results. Wizards let you create reports easily, but you often need to fix formatting problems and add features to wizard-created reports. When you modify a report created by AutoReport or the Report Wizard, or when you design and create your own report, you produce a **custom report**. You need to produce a custom report whenever AutoReport or the Report Wizard cannot automatically create the specific report you need or when you need to fine-tune an existing report.

You'll review the EmployerPositions report so that Elsa can show you the changes she wants.

### To review the EmployerPositions report:

1. Start Access and open the **Jobs** database in the Intro\Tutorial folder provided with your Data Files.

2. Maximize the Database window, and then open the **EmployerPositions** report.

   You'll change the Zoom setting so that you can view the report contents more clearly.

3. Click the **Zoom** list arrow on the Print Preview toolbar, click **100%**, and then scroll down the report. See Figure 7-1.

**Figure 7-1** | **EmployerPositions report in Print Preview**

insert a space in the report title

widen column headings to display the entire column name

eliminate the display of these values

reduce the vertical space between lines

center values in the column

widen column to display the entire field value

Elsa wants you to make the following changes to the EmployerPositions report:

- Insert a space in the report title so that it becomes "Employer Positions."
- Increase the widths of the Openings and State/Prov column headings to display the entire column headings.
- Increase the width of the Employer Name column to display the full contents of each field value.
- Center the field values in the Openings column to avoid crowding the field values in the adjacent column.
- Reduce the vertical space between lines to single spacing.
- Eliminate the display of field values in the Position Title column when they repeat a previous field value.
- Print the grand total of the Openings field values at the end of the report.

You'll make the requested report changes in Design view.

## Report Window in Design View

The Report window in Design view is similar to the Form window in Design view, which you used in Tutorial 6 to create a custom form.

### To view the report in Design view:

▶ **1.** Click the **View** button for Design view 🖼 on the Print Preview toolbar. Access displays the report in Design view. See Figure 7-2.

Report window in Design view for the EmployerPositions report | Figure 7-2

**Trouble?** If the rulers, grid, or toolbox do not appear, click View on the menu bar, and then click Ruler, Grid, or Toolbox to display the missing component. If the grid still does not appear, see your instructor or technical support person for assistance. If the toolbox is not positioned as shown in Figure 7-2, click the Toolbox window's title bar, and then drag it into position.

**Trouble?** If the Report Design toolbar or the Formatting toolbar does not appear, click View, point to Toolbars, and then click Report Design or Formatting (Form/Report) to display the missing toolbar.

**Trouble?** If the Report Design and Formatting toolbars appear as one toolbar or if the Formatting toolbar is positioned above the Report Design toolbar, drag the Formatting toolbar move handle ⋮ below the Report Design toolbar to the position shown in Figure 7-2.

Notice that the Report window in Design view has many of the same components as the Form window in Design view. For example, the Report Design toolbar includes a Properties button and a Toolbox button. Both windows also have horizontal and vertical rulers, grids in each section, and a Formatting toolbar.

The Report window in Design view displays five sections for the EmployerPositions report: the Report Header section contains the report title, the Page Header section contains column heading labels and a horizontal line, the Detail section contains the bound controls to display the field values for each record in the record source query, the Page Footer section contains the current date and the page number, and the Report Footer section is blank.

Each Access report can have the seven different sections described in Figure 7-3.

| Figure 7-3 | Access report sections |

| Report Section | Description |
| --- | --- |
| Report Header | Appears once at the beginning of a report. Use it for report titles, company logos, report introductions, and cover pages. |
| Page Header | Appears at the top of each page of a report. Use it for column headings, report titles, page numbers, and report dates. If your report has a Report Header section, it precedes the first Page Header section. |
| Group Header | Appears before each group of records that has the same sort field value. Use it to print the group name and the field value that all records in the group have in common. A report can have up to 10 grouping levels. |
| Detail | Appears once for each record in the underlying table or query. Use it to print selected fields from the table or query and to print calculated values. |
| Group Footer | Appears after each group of records that has the same sort field value. It is usually used to print totals for the group. |
| Report Footer | Appears once at the end of the report. Use it for report totals and other summary information. |
| Page Footer | Appears at the bottom of each page of a report. Use it for page numbers and brief explanations of symbols or abbreviations. If your report has a Report Footer section, it precedes the Page Footer section on the last page of the report. |

You don't have to include all seven sections in a report. When you design a report, you determine which sections to include and what information to place in each section. Figure 7-4 shows a sample report produced from the Jobs database; it includes all seven sections.

**Sample report showing the seven sections of a report** ◣ **Figure 7-4**

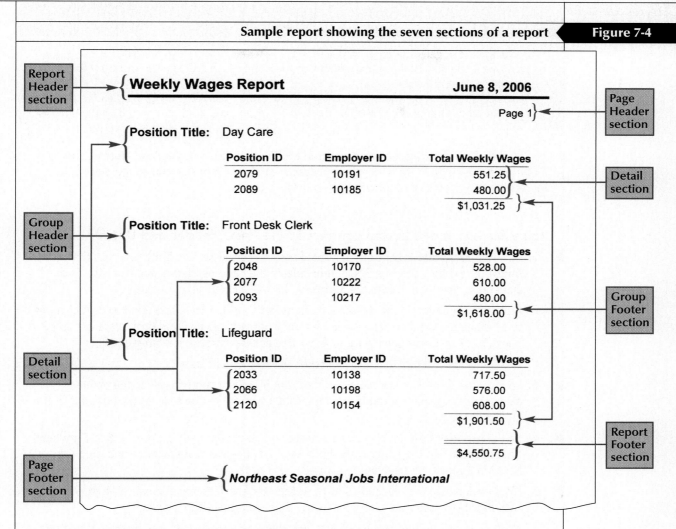

The Report Wizard used five of the seven report sections to create the EmployerPositions report for Elsa. To make Elsa's changes to the report, you'll make changes to four of the five sections.

## Resizing and Moving Controls

You need to resize and move controls in the report Page Header and Detail sections to correct the problems with the Openings, Employer Name, and State/Prov columns, which have truncated values. Just like with forms, you can move a text box and its attached label as a pair in the Report window. You can also move or resize any individual control or multiple selected controls. When you select a control, a move handle appears in its upper-left corner. This is the handle you use to reposition the selected control. Around its borders, a selected control also displays sizing handles, which you can use to resize a control in different directions.

## Moving and Resizing Controls

- In Design view, click the control to select it.
- To move a control, position the pointer on the control's move handle, and then drag the control to its new location.
- To resize a control, position the pointer on one of the control's sizing handles, and then drag the sizing handle until the control is the proper size.

You'll start by resizing the StartDate and EndDate controls in the Page Header and Detail sections, which are wider than necessary, to free up horizontal space before increasing the widths of other controls in these sections.

### To resize and move bound controls in the Page Header and Detail sections:

1. Click the **StartDate** text box in the Detail section, hold down the **Shift** key, click the **EndDate** text box, click the **Start Date** label in the Page Header section, click the **End Date** label, and then release the **Shift** key. You've selected all four controls.

2. Position the pointer on the middle-left sizing handle of the StartDate text box so it changes to a ↔ shape, and then drag the left border right until it's two grid dots to the left of the 5-inch mark on the horizontal ruler. All four selected controls are resized equally.

   Next, you'll reposition the StartDate text box and the Start Date label.

3. Position the pointer on the move handle of the StartDate text box. When the pointer changes to a ✋ shape, drag the control right, so its right edge touches the left edge of the EndDate text box.

4. Hold down the **Shift** key, click the **EndDate** text box to deselect it, click the **End Date** label to deselect it, and then release the **Shift** key. Only the StartDate text box and the Start Date label should be selected.

5. Right-click one of the selected controls to open the shortcut menu, point to **Align**, and then click **Right**. The selected controls are now aligned on their right edges.

   Next, you'll resize the State/Prov label, and then you'll move the label, its related text box, and the City controls to the right.

6. Right-click the **State/Prov** label, point to **Size**, and then click **To Fit**.

7. Hold down the **Shift** key, click the **StateProv** text box, click the **City** text box, click the **City** label, and then release the **Shift** key. All four controls are now selected.

8. Position the pointer on one of the selected controls. When the pointer changes to a ✋ shape, drag the controls to the right, so that the right edge of the State/Prov label is almost touching the left edge of the Start Date label.

   Now you'll increase the width of the EmployerName text box.

9. Click the **EmployerName** text box in the Detail section, and then drag its middle-right sizing handle ↔ to the right until its right edge touches the left edge of the City text box.

   Finally, you'll increase the width of the Openings label.

10. Right-click the **Openings** label, point to **Size**, and then click **To Fit**. See Figure 7-5.

**After resizing and moving controls in the Page Header and Detail sections** ◄ **Figure 7-5**

**Trouble?** If the controls on your screen are not resized and positioned as shown in Figure 7-5, adjust their widths and positions until they match.

Next, you'll insert a space in the report title and center the Openings field values.

## To correct the report title and center the Openings field values:

▶ **1.** Click the label in the Report Header section to select it, click between Employer and Positions in the label, press the **spacebar**, press the **Enter** key, right-click the label, point to **Size**, and then click **To Fit**.

▶ **2.** Click the **Openings** text box in the Detail section, and then click the **Center** button 🔳 on the Formatting toolbar.

Elsa wants you to reduce the vertical spacing between the lines that appear in the Detail section, so you'll move the controls in the section up to the top of the section and then reduce the height of the Detail section.

▶ **3.** Select all controls in the Detail section, and then drag the controls to the top of the Detail section.

**Trouble?** If you drag the controls too far up and they shift into the Page Header section, click the Undo button 🔳 on the Report Design toolbar and then repeat Step 3.

▶ **4.** Drag the bottom of the Detail section up until it touches the bottom of the controls in the Detail section.

▶ **5.** Save your report design changes.

For the EmployerPositions report the PositionTitle field is the primary sort field. Two or more consecutive detail report lines can have the same PositionTitle field value. In these cases, Elsa wants the PositionTitle field value printed for the first detail line but not for subsequent detail lines because she believes it makes the printed information easier to read.

# Hiding Duplicate Values in a Report

You use the **Hide Duplicates property** to hide a control in a report when the control's value is the same as that of the preceding record.

| Reference Window | **Hiding Duplicate Values in a Report** |
|---|---|

- Display the report in Design view.
- Open the property sheet for the field whose duplicate values you want to hide, set the Hide Duplicates property to Yes, and then close the property sheet.

Your next change is to hide duplicate PositionTitle field values in the Detail section.

### To hide the duplicate PositionTitle field values:

1. Click an unused portion of the Report window (see Figure 7-5) to deselect all controls.

2. Open the property sheet for the PositionTitle text box.

3. Click the **All** tab (if necessary), click the right side of the **Hide Duplicates** text box, and then click **Yes**. See Figure 7-6.

| Figure 7-6 | Hiding duplicate field values |
|---|---|

4. Close the property sheet.

You are now ready to calculate the total for the Openings field values.

# Calculating Grand Totals

Elsa wants the grand total of the Openings field values to print at the end of the report. To calculate subtotals and overall totals in a report, you use the Sum function. You place the Sum function in a Group Footer section to print each group's total. When placed in the Report Footer section, the Sum function prints the overall total. The function is the same one you used for forms, and its format is =Sum([*fieldname*]). When you use a function, you enclose the function's options in parentheses following the function name. For field names with spaces or special characters, you must enclose the field names in square brackets. For field names without spaces and special characters, the square brackets are optional; Access often adds the square brackets if you omit them in these latter cases. To create the appropriate text boxes in the footer sections for the Sum function, you use the Text Box tool on the toolbox.

## Calculating Totals in a Report

Reference Window

- Display the report in Design view.
- Click the Text Box tool on the toolbox.
- Position the pointer in the appropriate report section for the total—Group Footer for a group total or Report Footer for an overall report total.
- In the displayed text box, type =Sum([*fieldname*]) where *fieldname* is the name of the field to total.

To add the grand total to the report, you need to increase the height of the Report Footer section to make room for the text box that will contain the calculated control. Then you need to add a text box for the calculated control.

### To resize the Group Footer section and add the calculated control for the grand total:

1. Use the ✛ pointer to increase the height of the Report Footer section until six rows of grid dots are visible in the section.

   **Trouble?** If you increase the height of the section too much, reduce the section height by dragging the section back up.

   Next, you'll add the calculated control that will print the openings grand total.

2. Click the **Text Box** tool ab on the toolbox.

3. Position the pointer in the Report Footer section, and click when the pointer's plus symbol (+) is positioned three grid dots from the top of the section and at the 1-inch mark on the horizontal ruler. Access adds a text box with an attached label box to its left. Inside the text box is the description "Unbound." Recall that an unbound control is a control that is not linked to a database table field. See Figure 7-7.

**Figure 7-7** ▶ **Adding a text box in the Report Footer section**

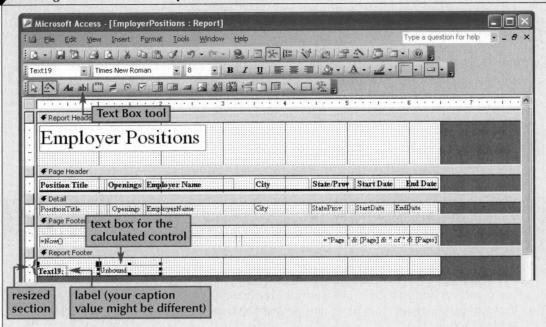

**Trouble?** The label on your screen might have a caption other than the one shown in Figure 7-7. That causes no problems.

You'll now add the Sum function to the text box, which contains the name Unbound.

▶ **4.** Right-click the **Unbound** text box, click **Properties** on the shortcut menu, click the **All** tab (if necessary), and then type **=Sum([Openings])** in the Control Source text box.

Now you'll set the label's Caption property and then resize and move the controls in the Report Footer section.

▶ **5.** Click the label, set the Caption property value to **Total Openings:** and then close the property sheet.

▶ **6.** Resize the label to fit, and then resize the calculated control, so that its right edge is at the 1.25-inch mark on the horizontal ruler.

▶ **7.** Move the label and calculated control together to the right, so that the right edge of the calculated control is at the 1.5-inch mark on the horizontal ruler.

Next, you'll verify the modified report in Print Preview.

## To view the modified EmployerPositions report in Print Preview:

▶ **1.** Save your design changes, and then switch to Print Preview. See Figure 7-8.

**Print Preview of the modified EmployerPositions report** ◄ Figure 7-8

Verify that you have completed Elsa's requested changes to the report. You need to navigate to the last report page to verify the grand total calculated control.

2. Use the navigation buttons to display page 2, and then scroll down the page until the calculated control is visible. See Figure 7-9.

**Grand total added to the EmployerPositions report** ◄ Figure 7-9

Elsa wants the report printed so she can bring it to a staff meeting.

▶ **3.** Click the **Print** button 🖨 on the Print Preview toolbar to print both pages of the report.

▶ **4.** Click the **Close Window** button ⊠ on the menu bar to close the report.

▶ **5.** If you are not continuing on to the next session, close the Jobs database, and then exit Access.

Now that you have completed the changes to the EmployerPositions report, you'll create Elsa's custom report in the next session. You'll review and modify the queries needed for the report, add a Group Header section to the report, and specify the sorting and grouping fields for the records. Finally, you will add, move, resize, and align controls in the report and change their captions and Can Grow properties.

| | |
|---|---|
| **Review** | **Session 7.1 Quick Check** |

**1.** What is a custom report?

**2.** Describe the seven sections of an Access report.

**3.** Why might you want to hide duplicate values in a report?

**4.** Which report section do you use to print overall totals?

# Session 7.2

## Designing a Custom Report

Before you create a custom report, you should first plan the report's contents and appearance. When you plan a report, keep in mind the following report design guidelines:

- Determine the purpose and record source for the report. Recall that the record source is a table or query that provides the fields for a form or report. If the report presents detailed information (a **detail report**), such as a list of all employers, then the report will display fields from the record source in the Detail section. If the report presents summary information (a **summary report**), such as total openings by state/province, then no detailed information appears; only grand totals and possibly subtotals appear based on calculations using fields from the record source.
- Determine the sort order for the information in the report.
- Identify any grouping fields in the report. A **grouping field** is a report sort field that includes a Group Header section before a group of records that has the same sort field value and that includes a Group Footer section after the group of records. A **Group Header section** usually displays the group name and the sort field value for the group. A **Group Footer section** usually displays subtotals or counts for the records in that group.
- Balance the report's attractiveness against its readability and economy. Keep in mind that an attractive, readable two-page report is more economical than a report of three pages or more. Unlike forms, which usually display one record at a time in the main form, reports display multiple records. Instead of arranging fields vertically as you do in a form, you usually should position fields horizontally across the page in a report. Typically, you single space the detail lines in a report. At the same time, make sure to include enough white space between columns.
- Group related fields and position them in a meaningful, logical order. For example, position identifying fields, such as names and codes, on the left. Group together all location fields, such as street and city, and position them in their usual order.
- Identify each column of field values with a column heading label that names the field.

- Include the report title, page number, and date on every page of the report.
- Identify the end of a report either by displaying grand totals or an end-of-report message.
- Use few colors, fonts, and graphics to keep the report uncluttered and to keep the focus on the information.
- Use a consistent style for all reports in a database.

After working with employer and position data using the EmployerPositions report for several weeks, Elsa's ideas for a better report led her to create a sketch of the design for a custom report. Figure 7-10 shows Elsa's design for the custom report she wants you to create.

**Design for the custom report** ◄ **Figure 7-10**

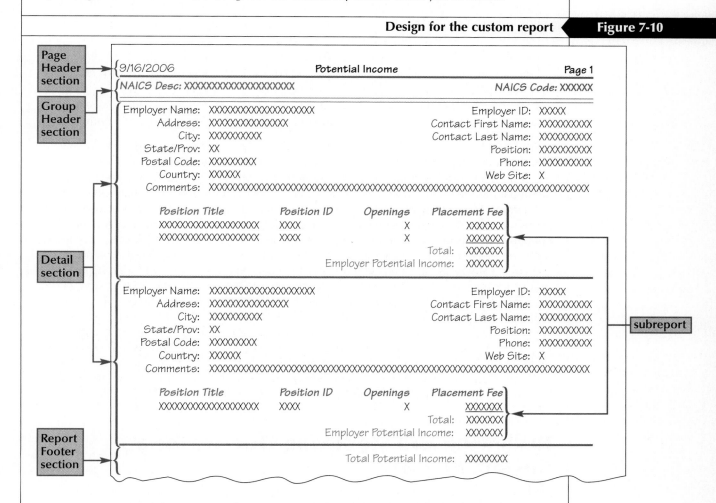

The report you need to create for Elsa will list the records for all employers and their positions. Elsa wants the report to group employers by values in the NAICSDesc field. The report will contain four sections:

- The Page Header section contains the report title ("Potential Income") centered between the current date on the left and the page number on the right. A thick blue horizontal line separates this section from the rest of the report page. From your work with AutoReport and the Report Wizard, you know that, by default, Access places the report title in the Report Header section and the date and page number in the Page Footer section. Elsa prefers the date, report title, and page number to appear at the top of each page, so you need to place this information in the custom report's Page Header section.

- The NAICS description and code will appear in the Group Header section. Two thin blue horizontal lines separate this section from the Detail section that follows.
- The Detail section will list all field values from the Employer table. Records within each NAICS group will appear in ascending order by employer name. Then for each employer's positions, the position title and ID, number of openings, and placement fee amount will print in ascending order by position title. In the Detail section shown in Figure 7-10, a series of Xs indicates the locations and relative lengths of the field values. The label for a field value will print to its left in the top portion of the Detail section and above the field value in the bottom portion of the Detail section. A thick blue horizontal line will print at the bottom of the Detail section to separate each employer and its positions from the next employer's data. The Placement Fee field in the Detail section is a calculated control based on the Openings, HoursPerWeek, and Wage field values in the Position table. The total for an employer's Placement Fee field values will appear in the Detail section after the employer's positions.
- Two potential income values—a subtotal in the Detail section for each employer's positions and an overall total in the Report Footer section—will be calculated controls.

The position data in the Detail section will appear in a **subreport**, a report contained within another report; the rest of Elsa's custom report constitutes the main report. You often use subreports to show summary information that can be either related or unrelated to the detail data in the main report. For example, Elsa might want to see a summary of the potential income amounts by country displayed at the end of the custom report; this would be a subreport related to the detail data. If the Jobs database included a Student table, which contained data about those students who've applied for the available positions, a summary of the counts of student applicants by country might appear in an unrelated subreport.

Why must you use a subreport to display the position information in Elsa's custom report? Elsa wants every employer to appear in the report, even those employers that do not have available positions. However, for those employers without available positions, Elsa doesn't want the position headings (Position Title, Position ID, Openings, and Placement Fee) and the position footings (the Total and Employer Potential Income lines) to appear in the report. You cannot suppress the printing of these headings and footings if they are in the main report. You can suppress them from printing only if they are in a subreport.

Before you start creating the custom report, you need to learn more details about NSJI's business and review the queries that you'll use for the report.

## Reviewing and Modifying Queries for a Custom Report

NSJI makes the money it needs to run its business by charging its employer clients a fee for each position filled. NSJI calculates this placement fee by multiplying the weekly wages for a position by two. Because the database does not contain a position's weekly wage amount, NSJI calculates the weekly wage value by multiplying the HoursPerWeek and Wage fields in the Position table. In addition to the placement fee, NSJI charges each employer a one-time search fee based on the total number of openings filled. For fewer than three openings filled, NSJI charges a $500 search fee; NSJI reduces the search fee to $200 if it fills three or more openings. Combining the search fee with the total placement fees for an employer produces the total income from the employer. The custom report you'll create for Elsa will show the placement fees and total income for each employer with the assumption that NSJI will fill all available openings for all positions. For this reason, the employer and overall income printed are considered potential income amounts.

The record source for a report (or form) can come from a single table, from a single query based on one or more tables, or from multiple tables and/or queries. Your report will contain data from the Employer, NAICS, and Position tables, but the report requirements are complicated enough that you'll need a total of three queries to supply the needed data. Elsa has already created the three queries: the NAICSAndEmployers query, the PotentialPlacementFees query, and the PotentialIncomeByEmployer query. You'll need to modify the third query before you start your work with the custom report.

The first existing query, the NAICSAndEmployers query, lists all fields from the NAICS and Employer tables. This query will supply the data for the report's Group Header section and for the employer data in the Detail section.

The second existing query, the PotentialPlacementFees query, lists the PositionID, PositionTitle, Openings, and EmployerID fields from the Position table. This query will provide the source data for the report's Detail section subreport, which is where the position data for an employer will print. The subreport also includes the Placement Fee column, which will print the calculated results of multiplying the Openings, HoursPerWeek, and Wage fields in the Position table by two. You can create a calculated control in a form or report, but then you wouldn't be able to calculate subtotals by employer and a grand total for the calculated control. However, you can calculate totals in a form or report for any field, including calculated fields, from a table or query used as the record source. Because Elsa wants subtotals by employer for the PlacementFee field values on her report, the existing PotentialPlacementFees query already includes the PlacementFee calculated field.

In most situations, these two queries would be the only data sources needed for Elsa's report. However, the report will list all employers, even those with no currently available positions. Elsa's report will not print the subreport for these employers for two reasons. First, printing a position-related column heading line and a subtotal in the subreport without any detail position data doesn't make sense and wouldn't look attractive. Second, for those employers without positions, Access will generate a data error for the subreport subtotals because Access doesn't let you calculate statistics when there are no records upon which to base the calculations. Because the subreport will not be printed for all employers, Access will generate a data error if you base your calculation for the grand total potential income on the individual employer potential incomes. Thus, the existing PotentialIncomeByEmployer query, which has the Position table as its record source, will serve as the source for the grand total of the new report's potential income value. This query is a statistical query that will list the total number of openings, total placement fees, and total potential income by employer for those clients with available positions.

Before modifying the PotentialIncomeByEmployer query, you'll review the other two queries that Elsa created for the report.

### To review the NAICSAndEmployers query:

1. If you took a break after the previous session, make sure that Access is running, that the **Jobs** database in the Tutorial folder is open, and that the Database window is open and maximized.

2. Open the **NAICSAndEmployers** query. Forty-five records—one for each record in the Employer table—appear in the recordset.

3. Scroll right to view the fields in the recordset, and then switch to Design view. See Figure 7-11.

**Figure 7-11** | **NAICSAndEmployers query in Design view**

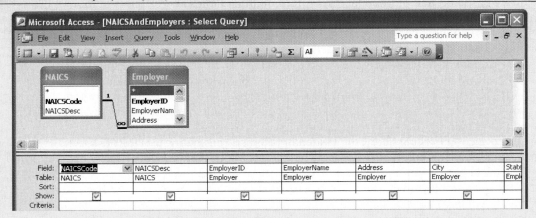

The NAICS and Employer tables are the source tables for the query. Both fields from the NAICS table—NAICSCode and NAICSDesc—appear in the design grid, as do all fields from the Employer table, except for the common NAICSCode field, which would be redundant if included in the query.

**4.** Close the query, and then restore the Database window.

Next, you'll review the design and recordset for the PotentialPlacementFees query, the second query Elsa developed for the new report.

## To review the PotentialPlacementFees query:

**1.** Open the **PotentialPlacementFees** query in Design view. The PositionID, PositionTitle, Openings, and EmployerID fields from the Position table appear in the design grid, along with the PlacementFee field, a calculated field.

**2.** Right-click the **PlacementFee Field** text box, click **Zoom** on the shortcut menu, and then position the insertion point to the right of the expression in the Zoom dialog box. See Figure 7-12.

**Figure 7-12** | **PlacementFee calculated field in the Zoom dialog box**

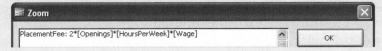

The PlacementFee calculated field entry in the Zoom dialog box determines an employer's placement fee for a position by multiplying the weekly wages (HoursPerWeek field times the Wage field) by two, and then multiplying by the number of openings (Openings field) for the position.

**3.** Click the **OK** button, and then run the query. The recordset displays the four fields from the Position table and the calculated field, PlacementFee. See Figure 7-13.

**Recordset displaying the PlacementFee calculated field** | Figure 7-13

PotentialPlacementFees : Select Query

| Position ID | Position Title | Openings | Placement Fee | Employer ID |
|---|---|---|---|---|
| 2004 | Host/Hostess | 1 | 816.00 | 10197 |
| 2007 | Tour Guide | 2 | 1,500.00 | 10146 |
| 2010 | Kitchen Help | 1 | 1,040.00 | 10135 |
| 2017 | Tour Guide | 1 | 600.00 | 10146 |
| 2020 | Host/Hostess | 1 | 1,184.00 | 10163 |
| 2021 | Waiter/Waitress | 1 | 570.00 | 10155 |
| 2025 | Kitchen Help | 2 | 1,600.00 | 10145 |
| 2027 | Waiter/Waitress | 2 | 1,280.00 | 10145 |
| 2028 | Cook | 1 | 2,000.00 | 10194 |
| 2033 | Lifeguard | 1 | 1,435.00 | 10138 |
| 2034 | Waiter/Waitress | 3 | 1,845.00 | 10162 |
| 2036 | Reservationist | 1 | 944.00 | 10151 |
| 2037 | Gift Shop Clerk | 1 | 945.00 | 10159 |
| 2040 | Waiter/Waitress | 2 | 1,344.00 | 10126 |

Record: |◄ ◄ 1 ► ►| ►* of 64

calculated field

**4.** Close the query, and then click the **No** button when asked if you want to save design changes to the query.

Next, you'll modify the third query needed for Elsa's custom report.

## Assigning a Conditional Value to a Calculated Field

The PotentialIncomeByEmployer query displays the total number of openings and total placement fees by employer. You'll modify the query by adding the calculation for the total potential income. For this calculation, you'll need to add either $200 (if the total number of openings is three or greater) or $500 (if the total number of openings is less than three) to an employer's total placement fees. To permit the calculated field to be one of two values based on a condition, you'll use the IIf (Immediate If) function. The **IIf function** lets you assign one value to a calculated field or control if a condition is true, and a second value if the condition is false. The format of the IIf function you'll use is: *IIf (TotalOpenings>=3, PlacementFee+200, PlacementFee+500)*. You interpret this function as: If the TotalOpenings field value is greater than or equal to 3, then set the calculated field value equal to the sum of the PlacementFee field value and 200; otherwise, set the calculated field value equal to the sum of the PlacementFee field value and 500.

Now you are ready to open and modify the statistical query.

## To open and modify the PotentialIncomeByEmployer query:

▶ **1.** Open the **PotentialIncomeByEmployer** query in Design view. See Figure 7-14.

**Figure 7-14** **PotentialIncomeByEmployer query in Design view**

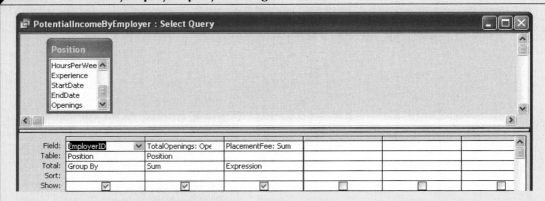

The PotentialIncomeByEmployer query calculates statistics for sets of records grouped by the EmployerID field, which uses the Group By operator. The TotalOpenings calculated field uses the Sum aggregate function to determine an employer's total number of openings.

▶ **2.** Right-click the **PlacementFee Field** text box, click **Zoom** on the shortcut menu, and then position the insertion point to the right of the expression in the Zoom dialog box. See Figure 7-15.

**Figure 7-15** **Expression for the PlacementFee calculated field**

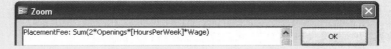

The PlacementFee calculated field determines an employer's total placement fee. When Elsa created the query, she used the same expression as she used for the PlacementFee calculated field in the PotentialPlacementFees query (see Figure 7-12), and she set the PlacementFee Total text box to Sum. However, after closing the PotentialIncomeByEmployer query, Access changed the expression to the one shown in Figure 7-15, adding the Sum aggregate function to the expression.

▶ **3.** Click the **OK** button. Notice that Access set the PlacementFee Total text box to Expression when it changed Elsa's expression for the calculated field. For calculated fields that include aggregate functions, such as Sum, or that include other calculated fields, you must set the field's Total value to Expression.

Next, you'll add to the design grid's fourth column the PotentialIncome calculated field that will determine an employer's total potential income using the IIf function.

▶ **4.** Right-click the **Field** text box in the fourth column, click **Zoom** on the shortcut menu, and then type **PotentialIncome: IIf (TotalOpenings>=3, PlacementFee+200, PlacementFee+500)**. See Figure 7-16.

**Figure 7-16** **Expression for the PotentialIncome calculated field**

**Trouble?** If your calculated field differs from that shown in Figure 7-16, correct it so it matches.

Because the expression includes the TotalOpenings calculated field, you'll set the PotentialIncome calculated field's Total value to Expression. You'll also set the field's Caption property to Potential Income.

▶ **5.** Click the **OK** button, click the right side of the **PotentialIncome Total** text box, scroll down the list, click **Expression**, click the **Properties** button 🔳 on the Query Design toolbar, set the Caption property to **Potential Income**, and then close the property sheet.

▶ **6.** Save the query, run the query, resize the Potential Income column in the recordset to its best fit, and then deselect the values or columns. The recordset displays the statistical query that includes the two calculated fields for each employer with available positions in the Position table. See Figure 7-17.

Recordset displaying the statistical query ◀ Figure 7-17

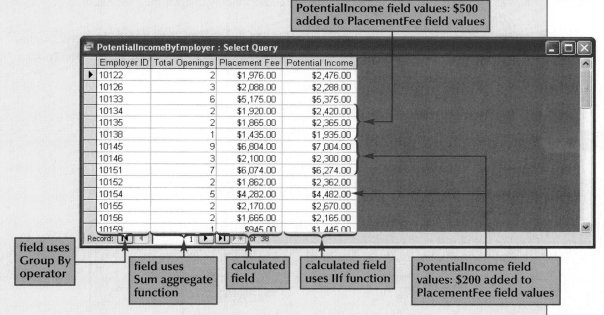

PotentialIncome field values: $500 added to PlacementFee field values

field uses Group By operator

field uses Sum aggregate function

calculated field

calculated field uses IIf function

PotentialIncome field values: $200 added to PlacementFee field values

Records 4, 5, and 6 have PotentialIncome field values of $500 more than their PlacementFee field values because their TotalOpenings field values are less than three. Records with TotalOpenings field values equal to three or greater, such as records 7, 8, 9, and 11, have PotentialIncome field values of $200 more than their PlacementFee field values.

▶ **7.** Save and then close the query.

You are now ready to create Elsa's report.

# Creating a Custom Report

You could use the Report Wizard to create the report and then modify it to match the report design. However, because you need to customize several components of the report, you will create a custom report in Design view. To do so, you need to display a blank report in Design view.

Reference Window

### Creating a Report in Design View

- In the Database window, click Reports in the Objects bar of the Database window to display the Reports list box.
- Click the New button in the Database window to open the New Report dialog box.
- Click Design View to select it (if necessary); for a bound form select the table or query on which you want to base the new report; and then click the OK button.

The main record source for the report you are creating is the NAICSAndEmployers query that you reviewed earlier in this tutorial. To begin, you need to create a blank report in Design view.

### To create a blank report in Design view:

▶ **1.** Click **Reports** in the Objects bar of the Database window to display the Reports list box, and then click the **New** button in the Database window to open the New Report dialog box.

▶ **2.** Click **Design View** (if necessary), click the list arrow to display the list of tables and queries in the Jobs database, scroll down and click **NAICSAndEmployers** to select this query as the main record source for the report, and then click the **OK** button. The Report window in Design view opens and displays a blank report.

▶ **3.** Click the **Maximize** button 🔲 on the Report window. See Figure 7-18.

| Figure 7-18 | Report window in Design view |
| --- | --- |

Field List button | Toolbox button | field list

Page Header section

Detail section

Page Footer section

Properties button

Sorting and Grouping button

**Trouble?** If the rulers, grid, or toolbox do not appear, click View on the menu bar, and then click Ruler, Grid, or Toolbox to display the missing component. If the grid still does not appear, see your instructor or technical support person for assistance. If the toolbox is not positioned as shown in Figure 7-18, click the Toolbox window's title bar, and then drag it into position.

**Trouble?** If the field list does not appear, click the Field List button 🔲 on the Report Design toolbar to display it. If the field list is not positioned and sized as shown in Figure 7-18, click the field list title bar, and then drag it to the position shown; use the mouse to resize the field list.

**Trouble?** If the Report Design toolbar or the Formatting toolbar does not appear, click View, point to Toolbars, and then click Report Design or Formatting (Form/Report) to display the missing toolbar.

**Trouble?** If the Report Design and Formatting toolbars appear as one toolbar or if the Formatting toolbar is positioned above the Report Design toolbar, drag the Formatting toolbar move handle 🔳 below the Report Design toolbar to the position shown in Figure 7-18.

Unlike the Form window in Design view, which initially displays only the Detail section in a blank form, the Report window also displays a Page Header section and a Page Footer section. Reports often contain these sections, so Access automatically includes them in a blank report.

According to Elsa's plan for the report (see Figure 7-10), the NAICSDesc and NAICSCode fields from the NAICSAndEmployers query will appear in a Group Header section, and the remaining 13 fields from the query will appear in the Detail section. Before you can add the NAICSDesc and NAICSCode fields to the report, you need to create the Group Header section by specifying the NAICSDesc field as a grouping field.

# Sorting and Grouping Data in a Report

Access lets you organize records in a report by sorting them using one or more sort fields. Each sort field can also be a grouping field. If you specify a sort field as a grouping field, you can include a Group Header section and a Group Footer section for the group. A Group Header section typically includes the name of the group, and a Group Footer section typically includes a count or subtotal for records in that group. Some reports have a Group Header section but not a Group Footer section, some reports have a Group Footer section but not a Group Header section, and some reports have both sections or have neither section.

You use the Sorting and Grouping button on the Report Design toolbar to select sort fields and grouping fields for a report. Each report can have up to 10 sort fields, and any of its sort fields can also be grouping fields.

**Sorting and Grouping Data in a Report**                                    Reference Window

- Display the report in Design view.
- Click the Sorting and Grouping button on the Report Design toolbar.
- Click the first Field/Expression list arrow in the Sorting and Grouping dialog box, and select the field to use as the primary sort field. In the Sort Order text box, select the sort order.
- Repeat the previous step to select secondary sort fields and their sort orders as necessary.
- To group data, click the field in the Field/Expression text box by which you want to group records. In the Group Properties section, set the grouping options for the field.
- Click the Close button on the Sorting and Grouping dialog box to close it.

Elsa wants records listed in ascending order based on the NAICSDesc field; the NAICSDesc and NAICSCode field values print at the beginning of each NAICSDesc group. For these reasons, you need to specify the NAICSDesc field as both the primary sort field and a grouping field. Elsa also wants the employer data listed in ascending order by employer name within each NAICSDesc group. So, you need to specify the EmployerName field as the secondary sort field.

### To select the sort fields and the group field:

▶ **1.** Click the **Sorting and Grouping** button on the Report Design toolbar. The Sorting and Grouping dialog box opens.

   The top section of the Sorting and Grouping dialog box lets you specify the sort fields for the records in the Detail section. For each sort field, the Group Properties section of the dialog box lets you designate the sort field as a grouping field and specify whether you want a Group Header section, a Group Footer section, and other options for the group.

▶ **2.** Click the list arrow in the first **Field/Expression** text box to display the list of available fields, and then click **NAICSDesc**. Ascending is the default sort order in the Sort Order text box, so you do not need to change this setting.

   You can now designate NAICSDesc as a grouping field and specify that you want a Group Header section for this group. This section will contain the NAICS description and code labels and field values.

▶ **3.** Click the right side of the **Group Header** text box to display a list arrow and a list of values, and then click **Yes**. Access adds a Group Header section named NAICSDesc Header to the Report window. See Figure 7-19.

| Figure 7-19 | Adding a group header section |
| --- | --- |

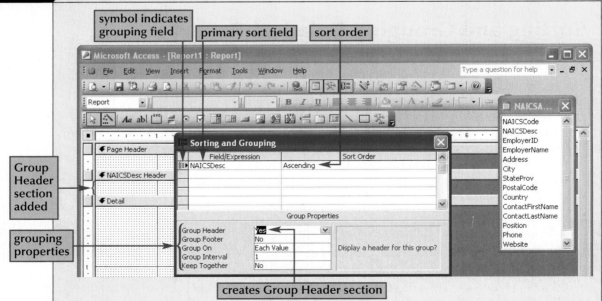

Notice the symbol placed to the left of the Field/Expression text box for NAICSDesc. That symbol indicates that you designated NAICSDesc as a grouping field.

You can now specify the secondary sort field and its sort order.

▶ **4.** Click the right side of the second **Field/Expression** text box to display the list of fields, and then click **EmployerName**. Once again, you do not need to change the default sort order, so you've finished setting the sorting and grouping options for the main report.

▶ **5.** Close the Sorting and Grouping dialog box.

Now that you've created the NAICSDesc Header section, you can add the fields from the field list to the correct sections of the report.

# Adding Fields to a Report

Your next task is to add bound controls to the Group Header and Detail sections for all the fields from the NAICSAndEmployers query. Recall that a bound control displays field values from the table or query that serves as the record source. You add bound controls to a report in the same way that you add them to a form.

| Adding Fields to a Form or Report | Reference Window |
|---|---|

- Display the report in Design view.
- If necessary, click the Field List button on the Report Design toolbar to display the field list.
- To place a single field on the report, position the pointer on the field name in the field list, drag the field name to the report, and then release the mouse button when the pointer is positioned correctly.
- To place all fields on the report, double-click the field list title bar to highlight them. Click anywhere in the highlighted area of the field list, and then drag the fields to the report. Release the mouse button when the pointer is positioned correctly.
- To select two or more consecutive fields in the field list, click the first field, hold down the Shift key, click the last field, and then release the Shift key. To select two or more non-consecutive fields, hold down the Ctrl key and click each field. To deselect a field, hold down the Ctrl key and click the field.

First, you need to add bound controls for the NAICSCode and NAICSDesc fields to the Group Header section. Then you'll add bound controls for the other fields to the Detail section.

### To add bound controls for all fields in the field list:

▶ **1.** Click **NAICSCode** in the field list, hold down the **Shift** key, click **NAICSDesc** in the field list, and then release the **Shift** key to highlight both fields.

▶ **2.** Click anywhere in the highlighted area of the field list (except the title bar), and then drag the fields to the NAICSDesc Header section. Release the mouse button when the pointer is positioned at the top of the NAICSDesc Header section and at the 3-inch mark on the horizontal ruler. You've added bound controls for the two selected fields. Each bound control consists of a text box and an attached label positioned to the left of the text box. See Figure 7-20. Notice that the text boxes are left aligned near the 3-inch mark; the labels are also left aligned.

**Trouble?** If you did not position the bound controls properly in the NAICSDesc Header section, click the Undo button on the Report Design toolbar, and then repeat Step 2. However, if the positioning of your controls differs just slightly from those shown in Figure 7-20, leave them where they are because you'll move all the controls later in this tutorial.

3. Double-click the field list title bar to highlight all the fields in the NAICSAndEmployers field list.

4. Hold down the **Ctrl** key, click **NAICSCode** in the field list, click **NAICSDesc** in the field list, and then release the **Ctrl** key. You've highlighted all fields in the field list, except the NAICSCode and NAICSDesc fields.

5. Drag the highlighted fields to the Detail section. Release the mouse button when the pointer ⊞ is positioned at the top of the Detail section and at the 3-inch mark on the horizontal ruler. You've added bound controls to the Detail section for the 13 selected fields. See Figure 7-20.

**Figure 7-20** ▶ **Adding bound controls to the report**

You've added all fields from the NAICSAndEmployers field list to the report, so you no longer need the field list open and can close it.

6. Close the field list.

You perform operations in the Report window in Design view the same as you perform operations in the Form window in Design view. These operations become easier with practice. Remember to use the Undo button, back up your database frequently, save your report changes frequently, and work from a copy of the report for complicated design changes. You can also click the Print Preview button at any time to view your progress on the report.

# Working with Controls

Two text boxes now appear in a column in the NAICSDesc Header section, and 12 text boxes and one check box now appear in a column in the Detail section. Each box is a bound control linked to a field in the underlying query and has an attached label box. The label boxes appear to the left of the text boxes and to the right of the check box. The labels identify the contents of the text boxes and the check box; the text boxes and check box will display the field values from the database.

According to Elsa's report design (see Figure 7-10), you need to reposition all labels and text boxes in the report. You'll also resize several text boxes.

### To move the controls in the NAICSDesc Header and Detail sections:

1. Deselect all controls.

2. Click the **NAICSDesc** label in the NAICSDesc Header section, position the pointer on the move handle in the upper-left corner of the label so the pointer changes to a ✋ shape, and then drag the label to the upper-left corner of the NAICSDesc Header section.

3. Refer to Figure 7-21 and use the procedures in Steps 1 and 2 to move the other labels and text boxes in the NAICSDesc Header and Detail sections to match the figure as closely as possible. The report's width will widen automatically from 5 inches to approximately 5.5 inches when you move the NAICSCode text box in the NAICSDesc Header section. See Figure 7-21.

**After moving the controls in the Report window**    **Figure 7-21**

You've made many modifications to the report design and should save the report before proceeding.

## To save the report design:

▶ **1.** Click the **Save** button 🔚 on the Report Design toolbar. The Save As dialog box opens.

▶ **2.** Type **PotentialIncome** in the Report Name text box, and then press the **Enter** key. The dialog box closes, and Access saves the PotentialIncome report in the Jobs database.

Next, you'll resize four text boxes—the NAICSDesc, EmployerName, Address, and Comments text boxes—so their field-value contents will be completely visible. Because the Comments field in the Employer table is a memo field, the Comments text box is a special case; comments about an employer can range from none to many lines of text. Thus, you'll need to resize the Comments text box for the minimal case of one line, but you want the text box to expand to display the entire field value when multiple lines are needed. Setting the Can Grow property of the Comments text box to Yes will do exactly this. The **Can Grow property**, when set to Yes, expands a text box vertically to fit the field value when the report is printed or previewed.

## To resize the text boxes and set the Can Grow property:

▶ **1.** Click the **Comments** text box in the Detail section, position the pointer on its middle-right sizing handle so it changes to a ↔ shape, and then drag the right border to the right to the 5.5-inch mark on the horizontal ruler.

▶ **2.** Position the pointer on the middle-bottom sizing handle of the Comments text box so it changes to a ↕ shape, and then drag the bottom border up until it's the same height as the bottom of the Comments label.

▶ **3.** Refer to Figure 7-22 and repeat Step 1 to resize the width of the **EmployerName** and **Address** text boxes in the Detail section and the width of the **NAICSDesc** text box in the NAICSDesc Header section.

| Figure 7-22 | After resizing four text boxes |

▶ **4.** Click the **Comments** text box, press the **F4** key to open the property sheet, set the Can Grow property to **Yes**, and then close the property sheet.

Now you need to align the two columns of labels in the Detail section on their right edges. You can align controls in a report or form using the **Align command**, which provides different options for aligning controls. For example, if you select controls in a column, you can use the Align Left option to align the left edges of the controls. Similarly, if you select controls in a row, you can use the Align Top option to align the top edges of the controls. The Align Right and Align Bottom options work the same way. A fifth option, Align To Grid, aligns selected controls with the grid dots in the Report window. To match Elsa's report design, you will use the Align Right option to align the labels in the Detail section. Then you'll save the modified report and preview it to see what it will look like when printed.

### To align the labels in the Detail section and then save and preview the report:

1. Deselect all controls.

2. Click the **EmployerName** label in the Detail section, hold down the **Shift** key, click each of the six labels below the EmployerName label, and then release the **Shift** key. This action selects the seven labels in the left column of the Detail section in preparation for aligning them on their right edges.

3. Right-click one selected label, point to **Align** on the shortcut menu, and then click **Right** to right-align the selected labels on the right.

   The Contact First Name and Contact Last Name labels are too close to their attached text boxes, so you need to move both controls to the left before you right-align the six labels in the right column of the Detail section.

4. Deselect all controls, move the **Contact First Name** label to the left until its right edge is at the 3.75-inch mark on the horizontal ruler, and then repeat the move for the **Contact Last Name** label.

5. Repeat Steps 1 through 3 for the six labels in the right column of the Detail section to right-align them, and then deselect all controls. See Figure 7-23.

After right-aligning the labels in the Detail section | **Figure 7-23**

As you create a report, you should periodically save your modifications to the report and preview your progress.

6. Save your report design changes, and then switch to Print Preview.

**7.** Scroll the Print Preview window so that you can see more of the report on the screen. The field values for the first two employers follow the first pair of NAICS field values. See Figure 7-24.

**Figure 7-24**    **Report displayed in Print Preview**

**8.** Navigate to Seaview Restaurant (page 7 or 8 of the Print Preview window). Notice that the Comments field value for Seaview Restaurant displays three lines of text, verifying that the Can Grow property is properly set for the field.

**9.** Click the **Close** button on the Print Preview toolbar to return to the Report window in Design view.

**10.** If you are not continuing on to the next session, close the Jobs database, and then exit Access.

You have completed your initial work on the report. In the next session, you will continue developing the report according to Elsa's design.

**Review**

# Session 7.2 Quick Check

1. What is a grouping field?
2. A(n) _____ is a report contained in another report.
3. The _____ function returns one of two values based on whether the condition being tested is true or false.
4. To select two or more consecutive fields in a field list, click the first field, hold down the _____ key, and then click the last field.
5. The _____ property, when set to Yes, expands a text box vertically to fit the field value when a report is printed or previewed.
6. How do you right-align controls in a column?

# Session 7.3

## Adding a Subreport Using Control Wizards

According to Elsa's design, the Potential Income report uses a subreport in the Detail section to include an employer's position information. Similar to a subform, a Control Wizard can help you create a subreport. You will use the SubReport Wizard to add the subreport based on the data from the PotentialPlacementFees query, which Elsa created and you reviewed at the beginning of Session 7.2.

### To add the subreport to the report's Detail section:

1. If you took a break after the previous session, make sure that Access is running, that the **Jobs** database in the Intro\Tutorial folder is open, and that the **PotentialIncome** report is open in Design view in a maximized window.

2. Make sure the **Control Wizards** tool 🖾 on the toolbox is selected, and then click the **Subform/Subreport** tool 🖼 on the toolbox.

3. Position the pointer's plus symbol (+) near the left edge of the Detail section, just below the 1.5-inch mark on the vertical ruler and in the third column of grid dots, and then click the mouse button. Access places a subreport control in the Detail section and opens the first SubReport Wizard dialog box.

   **Trouble?** If a dialog box opens and tells you that Microsoft can't start this Wizard, place your Office 2003 CD in the correct drive, and then click the Yes button. If you do not have this CD, ask your instructor or technical support person for help.

4. Make sure the **Use existing Tables and Queries** option button is selected, and then click the **Next** button. Access opens the next SubReport Wizard dialog box, in which you select the table or query on which the subreport is based and the fields from that table or query.

   You'll select all fields from the PotentialPlacementFees query.

5. Click the **Tables/Queries** list arrow to display the list of tables and queries in the Jobs database, click **Query: PotentialPlacementFees**, click the >> button to select all fields from the query, and then click the **Next** button to open the next SubReport Wizard dialog box.

   In this dialog box, you select the link between the main report and the subreport. You want to use the default option, which uses the EmployerID field as the common field between the two queries—the main report's NAICSAndEmployers source query includes the common field; so does the subreport's PotentialPlacementFees source query.

6. Make sure the **Choose from a list** option button is selected and the first link is highlighted, and then click the **Next** button. The next SubReport Wizard dialog box lets you specify a name for the subreport.

7. Type **PotentialIncomeSubreport**, and then click the **Finish** button. Access inserts a subreport control, which is where an employer's position records will appear, in the Detail section of the main report.

8. Save your report changes, close the field list, and then maximize the Report window. See Figure 7-25.

**Figure 7-25** After adding the subreport to the main report

**9.** Switch to Print Preview to review the report. See Figure 7-26.

**Figure 7-26** Print Preview of the subreport in the main report

**Trouble?** If the format of your labels differs, don't worry. You'll change the label format later in this tutorial.

Based on Elsa's report design, you'll need to make several changes to the subreport.

## Modifying a Subreport

In Elsa's report design (see Figure 7-10), the subreport includes columns for the Position Title, Position ID, Openings, and Placement Fee columns, but not for the Employer ID column. Also, the Position Title controls appear to the left of the Position ID controls. In addition, a line appears above the placement fee total. Before you open the subreport to modify it based on Elsa's report design, you'll delete the subreport label and change some subreport properties.

The subreport label does not appear in Elsa's report design, so you'll delete the label. In addition, you'll set the subreport's Can Shrink and Border Style properties. The **Can Shrink property**, when set to Yes, reduces the height of a control or section so that the data it contains is printed or previewed without leaving blank lines. You'll set the subreport's Can Shrink property to Yes. When an employer has no available positions, Elsa wants to avoid printing the blank space occupied by the empty subreport. Finally, the subreport includes a rectangular solid border by default; Elsa's report design does not include this border. You'll set the **Border Style property**, which specifies a control's border type, to Transparent, so that the rectangle is invisible.

### To delete the subreport label and set the Can Shrink and Border Style properties:

1. Switch to Design view, right-click the subreport label, and then click **Cut** on the shortcut menu to delete the label.

2. Right-click the subreport border to select it, and then click **Properties** to open the property sheet for the subreport.

3. If necessary, click the **Format** tab.

4. Set the Can Shrink property to **Yes**, set the Border Style property to **Transparent**, and then close the property sheet.

You could modify the subreport in the Report window of the Potential Income report. However, because the subreport is a separate report and making the subreport changes is easier in a separate window, you'll open the subreport in Design view in a new window. Then you'll modify the subreport design to match Elsa's design.

### To open the subreport in Design view:

1. If the subreport is not the currently selected control, click the subreport border. Sizing handles appear around the subreport.

2. Move the pointer to the subreport border; when the pointer changes to a 🖐 shape, right-click the mouse button, and then click **Subreport in New Window** on the shortcut menu. The PotentialIncomeSubreport report opens in Design view. See Figure 7-27.

**Subreport in Design view** | **Figure 7-27**

your label format might be different

exchange, resize, and reposition these controls

**Trouble?** If the labels in your Report Header section have different font properties from the labels shown in Figure 7-27, select the five labels, and then change their properties to match. Figure 7-27 shows labels set in 10-point, black, bold, Times New Roman font without italics; if you need to change these properties, use the buttons on the Formatting toolbar.

**Trouble?** If the text boxes and label boxes in your subreport have different widths from those shown in Figure 7-27, don't be concerned because you'll move and resize all the controls later in this tutorial.

Unlike the main report, which initially contained Detail, Page Header, and Page Footer sections when you created a blank report, the subreport contains a Report Header section and a Detail section. (Although the Page Header, Page Footer, and Report Footer sections appear in the subreport, their heights are set to zero. As a result, these three sections do not appear in Print Preview or in the printed subreport.) Labels appear as column headings in the Report Header section, and field-value text boxes appear in the Detail section.

To match Elsa's design, you'll move the three rightmost control pairs to the right, reduce the widths of the PositionID and PositionTitle controls so that you can exchange their positions, and then resize and reposition the four controls.

## To modify the subreport design:

1. Use the ↔ pointer to increase the width of the subreport so that its right edge is at the 5.25-inch mark on the horizontal ruler.

2. Deselect all controls (if necessary), select the three rightmost text boxes and the three rightmost labels, and then move the six controls to the right so that the right edge of the EmployerID text box is at the 5.25-inch mark on the horizontal ruler.

3. Deselect all controls, click the **Position Title** label, hold down the **Shift** key, click the **PositionTitle** text box, release the **Shift** key (both controls are now selected), and then use the middle-right sizing handle of either control to reduce the widths of the selected controls to approximately 0.5 inches.

4. Repeat Step 3 for the **Position ID** label and the **PositionID** text box.

5. Position the pointer on the PositionID text box; when the pointer changes to a ✋ shape, drag the two selected controls to the right of the PositionTitle controls.

6. Refer to Figure 7-28 to resize and reposition the PositionID label and text box and the PositionTitle label and text box, and to reposition (and resize, if necessary) the three rightmost labels and text boxes, and then use the ↔ pointer to decrease the width of the subreport so that its right edge is two grid dots beyond the 5-inch mark on the horizontal ruler.

| Figure 7-28 | After exchanging, resizing, and repositioning controls |
|---|---|

Because the EmployerID label and field value appear in the main report's Detail section, you need to prevent them from printing in the subreport by setting their Visible property. You use the **Visible property** to show or hide a control.

▶ **7.** Use the Shift key to select the **Employer ID label** and the **EmployerID** text box.

▶ **8.** Press the **F4** key to open the property sheet. The text "Multiple selection" in the property sheet title bar and the empty Object list box both indicate that you'll set properties for two or more controls. See Figure 7-29.

Property sheet for multiple controls ◀ **Figure 7-29**

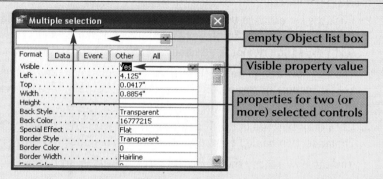

▶ **9.** Set the Visible property to **No**, and then close the property sheet.

Elsa wants all labels in the subreport formatted with blue, bold, italic Times New Roman font. The labels' font is already bold Times New Roman, so you need to set their font additionally to blue italics. You can use the **Font/Fore Color button** on the Formatting toolbar to change a control's font color.

## To modify the labels' font to blue italics:

▶ **1.** Deselect all controls, use the Shift key to select the **Position Title**, **Position ID**, **Openings**, and **Placement Fee** labels; click the **Italic** button *I* on the Formatting toolbar, and then click the list arrow for the **Font/Fore Color** button A on the Formatting toolbar to open the palette of available colors. See Figure 7-30.

Changing the font color for selected labels ◀ **Figure 7-30**

▶ **2.** Click the **blue** box in the color palette in row 2 and column 6 (see Figure 7-30), and then deselect all controls. The selected labels' text color changes to blue.

Elsa's report design includes subreport totals for the placement fee and employer potential income amounts, so you need to add a Group Footer section for the EmployerID field to the subreport. Thus, EmployerID will be the primary sort field using an ascending sort order. Because Elsa wants the positions to print in ascending order by the position titles for an employer, the PositionTitle field will be the secondary sort field.

**To select the sort keys and the group field for the subreport:**

1. Click the **Sorting and Grouping** button [image] on the Report Design toolbar to open the Sorting and Grouping dialog box.

2. Click the list arrow in the first **Field/Expression** text box to display the list of available fields, and then click **EmployerID**. Ascending is the default sort order in the Sort Order text box, so you do not need to change this setting.

   You can now designate EmployerID as a grouping field and specify that you want a Group Footer section for this group. This section will contain the employer totals for the placement fee and potential income amounts.

3. Click the right side of the **Group Footer** text box, and then click **Yes**. Access adds a Group Footer section named EmployerID Footer to the Report window.

   You can now specify the secondary sort field and its sort order.

4. Click the right side of the second **Field/Expression** text box to display the list of fields, and then click **PositionTitle**. You've finished setting the sorting and grouping options for the subreport.

5. Close the Sorting and Grouping dialog box.

Next, you'll add a line to the EmployerID Footer section to separate the detail placement fees from the employer placement fee total.

# Adding Lines to a Report

You can use lines in a report to improve the report's readability and to group related information. The **Line tool** on the toolbox lets you add a line to a report or form.

You will add a horizontal line to the top of the EmployerID Footer section under the PlacementFee text box to separate the total employer placement fee from the column of individual placement fees for the employer on the printed report.

## To add a line to the subreport:

▶ **1.** Click the **Line** tool ◥ on the toolbox.

▶ **2.** Position the pointer in the EmployerID Footer section. The pointer changes to a ⁺◥ shape.

▶ **3.** Position the pointer's plus symbol (+) near the top of the EmployerID Footer section at the 3.625-inch mark on the horizontal ruler.

▶ **4.** Drag a horizontal line from left to right, so the end of the line aligns with the right edge of the PlacementFee text box in the Detail section, and then release the mouse button. See Figure 7-31.

Adding a line to the report ◀ **Figure 7-31**

**Trouble?** If the line is not straight or not positioned correctly, click the Undo button ↺ on the Report Design toolbar, and then repeat Steps 1 through 4. If the line is not the correct length, hold down the Shift key, and press one or more of the arrow keys until the line's length is the same as that of the line shown in Figure 7-31.

Next, you'll move the line to the top of the EmployerID Footer section.

▶ **5.** Hold down the **Ctrl** key, and then press the ↑ key until the line reaches the top of the EmployerID Footer section.

**Trouble?** If·the line jumps up to the bottom of the Detail section, hold down the Ctrl key and press the ↓ key until the line moves back to the top of the EmployerID Footer section.

Elsa asks you to remove the excess space above and below the five controls in the Detail section and to reduce the height of the Detail section.

▶ **6.** Select all five controls in the Detail section and place the pointer on a selected control; when the pointer changes to a ✋ shape, drag the controls straight up to the top of the Detail section.

▶ **7.** Using the buttons on the Formatting toolbar, make sure the font for the five controls in the Detail section is **Arial 8**.

▶ **8.** Position the pointer on the bottom edge of the Detail section; when the pointer changes to a ✛ shape, drag the bottom edge up until it touches the bottom of the text boxes in the Detail section.

▶ **9.** Save your subreport design changes.

Recall that the subreport's primary sort field is the EmployerID field and the secondary sort field is the PositionTitle field. For employers with several positions, two or more positions could possibly have the same PositionTitle field value. In these cases, Elsa wants the PositionTitle field value printed for the first position but not for subsequent positions because she believes that would make the position data easier to read. Your next change is to hide duplicate PositionTitle field values in the Detail section.

**To hide the duplicate PositionTitle field values:**

▶ **1.** Deselect all controls, and then open the property sheet for the PositionTitle text box in the Detail section.

▶ **2.** Click the **Format** tab (if necessary), and then set the Hide Duplicates property to **Yes**.

▶ **3.** Close the property sheet.

You are now ready to calculate the group totals for the placement fee and employer potential income amounts.

# Calculating Group Totals

Elsa wants the report to print each employer's subtotals for the placement fee and potential income amounts. You calculate subtotals for a group in the same way you calculate overall totals—use the Text Box tool to add a calculated control to the Group Footer section instead of the Report Footer section, and then use the Sum function to set the calculated control's Control Source property.

To add the two group totals to your report, you need to increase the height of the EmployerID Footer section to make room for the two text boxes that will contain the calculated controls. Then you need to add text boxes for the two calculated controls.

**To resize the Group Footer section and add the two calculated controls for the group totals:**

▶ **1.** Use the ✚ pointer to increase the height of the EmployerID Footer section until the bottom of the section is at the 0.5-inch mark on the vertical ruler.

Next, you'll add the first calculated control that will print the employer placement fee total.

▶ **2.** Click the **Text Box** tool [ab] on the toolbox.

▶ **3.** Position the pointer in the EmployerID Footer section, and click when the pointer's plus symbol (+) is positioned at the top of the section and aligns vertically with the left edge of the PlacementFee text box. Access adds a text box with an attached label box to its left. Inside the text box is the description "Unbound." Recall that an unbound control is a control that is not linked to a database table field. See Figure 7-32.

Adding a text box in the EmployerID Footer section ◄ **Figure 7-32**

**Trouble?** The label on your screen might have a caption or format other than the one shown in Figure 7-32. That causes no problems.

You'll now add the Sum function to the text box, which contains the name Unbound, and then set its Format property to Standard, which will print the values with two decimal places.

▶ **4.** Right-click the **Unbound** text box, click **Properties** on the shortcut menu, click the **All** tab, type **=Sum([PlacementFee])** in the Control Source text box, set the Format property to **Standard**, and then close the property sheet.

Now add a text box for the second calculated control. You'll use the IIf function for this calculated control.

▶ **5.** Repeat Steps 2 and 3, clicking when the pointer's plus symbol (+) is positioned in the EmployerID Footer section two grid dots below the other text box and vertically aligned with its left edge.

▶ **6.** Open the property sheet for the **Unbound** text box, right-click the **Control Source** text box, click **Zoom** on the shortcut menu, and then type **=IIf (Sum (Openings) >= 3, Sum (PlacementFee) + 200, Sum (PlacementFee) + 500)** in the Zoom box. See Figure 7-33.

Calculation for the employer potential income ◄ **Figure 7-33**

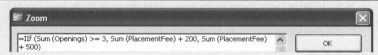

The calculation is the same one you used in the PotentialIncomeByEmployer query, except it includes the Sum function. Depending on whether the total number of openings for an employer is three or more, either $200 or $500 is added to the employer total placement fee.

Next, you'll set the calculated control's Format property to Standard.

▶ **7.** Click the **OK** button, set the Format property to **Standard**, and then close the property sheet.

▶ **8.** Using the buttons on the Formatting toolbar, make sure the font for the two text box controls in the EmployerID Footer section is **Arial 8**.

▶ **9.** Save your design changes, and then switch to Print Preview. See Figure 7-34.

**Figure 7-34** ▶ **Print Preview of the subreport**

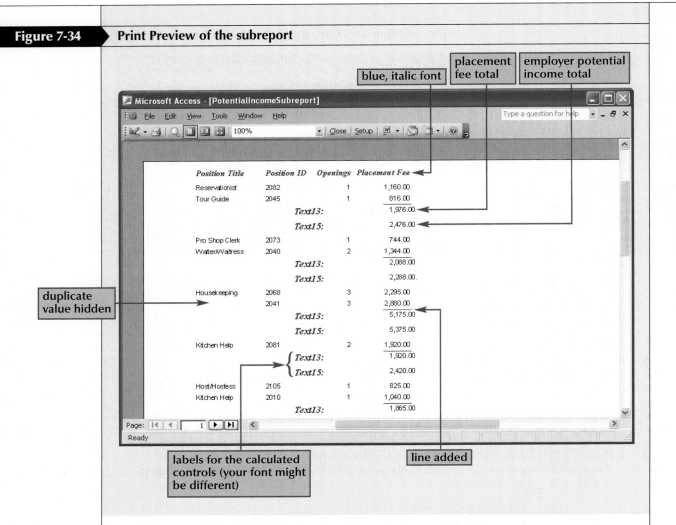

You still need to make several modifications to the subreport. The decimal points for the two calculated controls don't line up with the PlacementFee field values, so you'll need to resize the text boxes for the calculated controls. You'll set the Caption property for both labels, and then you'll resize and reposition them and change their font properties. Finally, Elsa wants to make it easier to use the report to find potential income amounts for employers with low- and high-income potential (under $2000 and over $5000, respectively).

First, you'll resize the text boxes and modify the properties for the two labels.

### To resize the text boxes and modify the label properties:

▶ **1.** Switch to Design view, and then deselect all controls.

▶ **2.** Select both text boxes in the EmployerID Footer section.

▶ **3.** Position the pointer on the middle-right sizing handle of either selected control, and then drag the right borders to the left so that they align with the right border of the PlacementFee text box in the Detail section.

▶ **4.** Using the middle-left sizing handle, repeat Step 3 to drag the left borders of the selected controls to the right until they are just to the left of the 3.5-inch mark on the horizontal ruler. (See Figure 7-35.)

**5.** Deselect the controls, open the property sheet for the top label in the EmployerID Footer section, set its Caption property to **Total:**, and then change its font size to **8** and make sure its font is blue **Times New Roman**, bold, and italic.

**6.** Click the bottom label in the EmployerID Footer section, set its Caption property to **Employer Potential Income:**, change its font size to **8** and make sure its font is blue **Times New Roman**, bold, and italic. Close the property sheet.

**7.** Resize and reposition both labels to match the labels shown in Figure 7-35, and then reduce the height of the EmployerID Footer section.

**After modifying the footer labels and text boxes** ◄ **Figure 7-35**

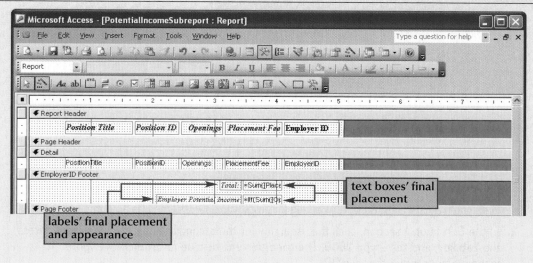

Your final subreport modification will allow Elsa to find employer potential income amounts under $2000 and over $5000 more easily.

# Defining Conditional Formatting Rules

One way to make employer potential income amounts easier to spot on the report is to use conditional formatting for the calculated control's text box in the EmployerID Footer section. **Conditional formatting** lets you change the format of a report or form control based on the control's value. For example, you can change the calculated control's font style or color when its value is more than $5000 and change its font to a different style or color when its value is less than $2000. All other values for the control print in the default font style or color. You can define up to a maximum of three conditional formats for each control.

**Defining Conditional Formatting for a Control**                                          Reference Window

- In Design view, right-click the control to select it, and then click Conditional Formatting on the shortcut menu.
- Select and enter the conditions, and then select the format options to be used.
- For a second or third conditional format, click the Add button.
- Click the OK button.

You will use bold text for employer potential income amounts over $5000 and bold, italic text for values under $2000.

### To define conditional formatting for the potential income amounts:

▶ **1.** Right-click the **Employer Potential Income** text box in the EmployerID Footer section, and then click **Conditional Formatting** on the shortcut menu. The Conditional Formatting dialog box opens. See Figure 7-36.

| Figure 7-36 | Conditional Formatting dialog box |
|---|---|

First, you'll define conditional formatting for employer potential income amounts under $2000.

▶ **2.** In the Condition 1 section, click the list arrow for the second list box, click **less than**, press the **Tab** key, and then type **2000**. The condition will be true for all employer potential income amounts less than $2000.

Now you need to select the format that will be used for the first condition.

▶ **3.** Click the **Bold** button **B** in the Condition 1 section, click the **Italic** button *I* in the Condition 1 section, and then click the **Add** button. You have defined the first condition and its format, and the Conditional Formatting dialog box expands so you can enter a second condition. See Figure 7-37.

| Figure 7-37 | After defining the first conditional format |
|---|---|

Next, you'll define the conditional formatting for employer potential income amounts over $5000.

▶ **4.** In the Condition 2 section, click the list arrow for the second list box, click **greater than**, press the **Tab** key, and then type **5000**. The condition will be true for all employer potential income amounts greater than $5000.

▶ **5.** In the Condition 2 section, click the **Bold** button $\boxed{\text{B}}$. You have defined the second condition and its format.

You've finished defining the conditional formats for the employer potential income amounts. Next, you'll accept the conditional formats, save your work, and then show Elsa how the subreport looks.

▶ **6.** Click the **OK** button, save your subreport design changes, switch to Print Preview, and then scroll down the page to verify that the default format and the two conditional formats produce the results you expected. See Figure 7-38.

**Print Preview showing conditional formats** ◀ **Figure 7-38**

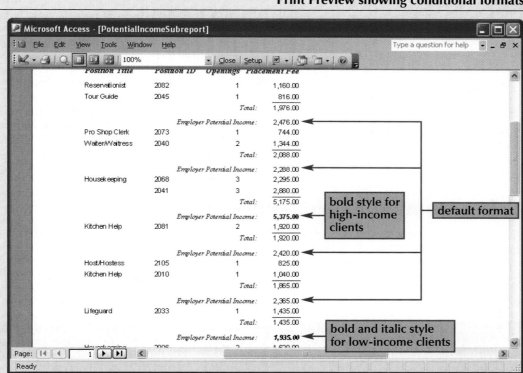

▶ **7.** Preview the remaining pages of the report to verify that the two conditional formats are correct.

You've completed the subreport design, so you'll return to Design view and close the subreport.

▶ **8.** Switch to Design view, and then click the **Close Window** button $\boxed{\times}$ on the menu bar. The subreport closes, and you return to Design view for the main report.

Now that you've completed the subreport, you'll check the progress of your report design in Print Preview.

**9.** Switch to Print Preview, and then scroll up the page (if necessary). The Group Header and Detail sections are displayed for the first employer. See Figure 7-39.

Figure 7-39 **Print Preview of the main report**

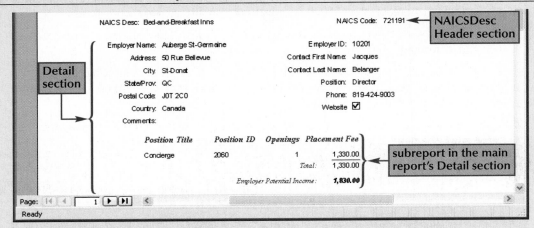

Comparing your report with Elsa's report design (see Figure 7-10), you can see that you've completed most of the work. Your remaining tasks include adding the current date, report title, and page number to the Page Header section; adding horizontal lines to all three sections of the main report; and adding a calculated control for the total potential income.

First, you'll add the calculated control to the Report Footer section.

# Using Domain Aggregate Functions

When you print a report, anything contained in the Report Footer section appears once at the end of the report. This section is often used to display overall totals. Elsa wants the report to print an overall total based on the employer potential income amounts. To include information in the Report Footer, you must first add both a Report Header section and a Report Footer section to the report.

Reference Window

## Adding and Removing Report Header and Report Footer Sections

- Display the report in Design view.
- To add the Report Header and Report Footer sections, click View on the menu bar, and then click Report Header/Footer.
- To remove a Report Header or Report Footer section, drag the bottom edge of that section up until the section area disappears.

Before adding the total potential income amount to the report, you need to add Report Header and Report Footer sections. Also, because you will not place any controls in the Report Header and Page Footer sections, you will remove these two sections.

**To add Report Header and Report Footer sections and remove report sections:**

▶ **1.** Switch to Design view.

▶ **2.** Click **View** on the menu bar, and then click **Report Header/Footer**. Access places a Report Header section at the top of the Report window and a Report Footer section at the bottom.

▶ **3.** Scrolling vertically as necessary, use the ╬ pointer to decrease the height of the Report Header and Page Footer sections to 0, and to decrease the height of the Detail section to 2.5 inches. The new height of the Detail section will allow sufficient room to add a horizontal line in this section below the subreport control. See Figure 7-40.

**Report sections added and removed** ◀ **Figure 7-40**

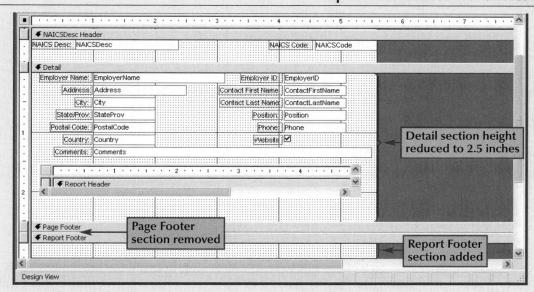

The subreport does not appear for those employers without available positions. Recall from Session 7.2 that this causes Access to generate a data error if you attempt to base your calculation for the total potential income amount on the individual employer potential incomes. For that reason, you modified the PotentialIncomeByEmployer query in Session 7.2. To calculate the total potential income amount for Elsa, you'll use the PotentialIncomeByEmployer query as the record source and a domain aggregate function to perform the calculation.

**Domain aggregate functions** calculate statistics for a set of records (recordset), or **domain**, from a table or a query. Figure 7-41 describes the available domain aggregate functions. You use aggregate functions, such as the Sum function you used in the subreport, when the fields you're using for the function are bound fields that appear in text boxes in the report. In contrast, you use domain aggregate functions when the record source is a table or query recordset that is not bound to the report.

**Figure 7-41** ▶ **Domain aggregate functions**

| Domain Aggregate Function | Description |
|---|---|
| DAvg | Calculates the average of the specified field values from the selected recordset |
| DCount | Calculates the number of records with nonnull values in the specified field from the selected recordset |
| DFirst | Provides the value in the specified field from the first physical record in the selected recordset |
| DLast | Provides the value in the specified field from the last physical record in the selected recordset |
| DLookup | Provides the value in the specified field from the selected recordset based on the specified criteria |
| DMax | Provides the maximum value of the specified field from the selected recordset |
| DMin | Provides the minimum value of the specified field from the selected recordset |
| DStDev | Estimates a population sample standard deviation of the specified field from the selected recordset |
| DStDevP | Estimates a population standard deviation of the specified field from the selected recordset |
| DSum | Calculates the sum of the specified field values from the selected recordset |
| DVar | Estimates a population sample variance of the specified field from the selected recordset |
| DVarP | Estimates a population variance of the specified field from the selected recordset |

To calculate the total potential income amount, you use the **DSum domain aggregate function**. You place the DSum function in a text box in the Report Footer section to print the overall total. The format for the DSum function is =DSum("expression", "domain", "criteria").

Reference Window | **Using a Domain Aggregate Function in a Report**

- Display the report in Design view.
- Add a text box to the Report Footer section.
- In the text box, set the Control Source property to =*DFunction*("*expression*", "*domain*", "*criteria*"), where *DFunction* is the domain aggregate function, *expression* is the field name in the domain or a calculation involving a field name in the domain, *domain* is the table or query name, and the optional *criteria* is a condition that restricts the records selected.

You need to add a text box for the DSum function in the Report Footer section.

### To add a text box in the Report Footer section and add the DSum function:

▶ **1.** Click the **Text Box** tool  on the toolbox, position the pointer in the Report Footer section, and click when the pointer's plus symbol (+) is at the top of the Report Footer section and approximately at the 3.5-inch mark on the horizontal ruler. Access adds a text box with an attached label box to its left.

You can now enter the DSum function for the text box.

▶ **2.** Open the property sheet for the **Unbound** text box, click the **All** tab (if necessary), right-click the **Control Source** text box, and then click **Zoom** on the shortcut menu.

▶ **3.** Type **=DSum("PotentialIncome", "[PotentialIncomeByEmployer]")** in the Zoom box. See Figure 7-42.

The DSum function will calculate the total of all the PotentialIncome field values in the PotentialIncomeByEmployer recordset.

Because Elsa wants the calculated value to print as a money field, you'll set the calculated control's Format and Decimal Places properties.

▶ **4.** Click the **OK** button to close the Zoom box, set the Format property to **Currency**, and then set the Decimal Places property to **2**.

Next, you'll set the label's Caption property, and then you'll format it similar to the labels for the calculated controls in the subreport—with blue, bold, italic Times New Roman 8-point font.

▶ **5.** Click the label in the Report Footer section, set the Caption property to **Total Potential Income:**, and then close the property sheet.

▶ **6.** Using the buttons on the Formatting toolbar, change the label's font size to **8** and make sure its font is blue **Times New Roman**, bold, and italic.

▶ **7.** If necessary, set the font for the calculated control in the Report Footer section to **Arial**.

Now you need to resize and reposition the label and text box in the Report Footer section.

▶ **8.** Refer to Figure 7-43 to resize and reposition the DSum text box in the Report Footer section, and to size to fit and reposition the label in the Report Footer section.

▶ **9.** Save your report design changes, switch to Print Preview, and then navigate to the last page of the report. The total potential income and its associated label appear below the information for the last employer and its one available position. See Figure 7-44.

**Figure 7-44** | **Print Preview of Report Footer section controls**

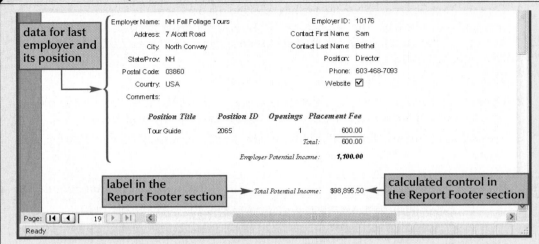

10. If you are not continuing on to the next session, close the Jobs database, and then exit Access.

You have completed the Report Footer section of the custom report. In the next session, you will complete the custom report according to Elsa's design.

## Review

## Session 7.3 Quick Check

1. The _____ property, when set to Yes, reduces the height of a control or section so that the data it contains is printed or previewed without leaving blank lines.
2. When you use Control Wizards to create a subreport, which non-empty sections does the Wizard create automatically?
3. You use the _____ property to show or hide a control.
4. To make small adjustments in the placement of a selected line, hold down the Ctrl key, and press a(n) _____ key.
5. To calculate and display subtotals, you place a calculated control in the _____ section.
6. What is the maximum number of conditional formats you can define for a control?
7. What is a domain?

# Session 7.4

## Adding the Date to a Report

According to Elsa's design, the Potential Income report includes the date in the Page Header section. To add the date to a report, you insert the Date function in a text box. The **Date function** returns the current date. The format of the Date function is =Date(). The equal sign (=) indicates that what follows it is an expression; Date is the name of the function; and the parentheses () indicate a function rather than simple text.

## Adding the Date to a Report

- Display the report in Design view.
- Click the Text Box tool on the toolbox, position the pointer where you want the date to appear, and then click to place the text box in the report.
- Click the text box, type =Date( ), and then press the Enter key; or set the text box's Control Source to =Date().

You need to insert the Date function in the Page Header section so that the current date will print on each page of the report.

### To add the Date function to the Page Header section:

1. If you took a break after the previous session, make sure that Access is running, that the **Jobs** database in the Intro\Tutorial folder is open, and that the **PotentialIncome** report is open in a maximized Print Preview window.

2. Switch to Design view, and make sure the Page Header section is visible on your screen.

3. Click the **Text Box** tool ab on the toolbox, position the pointer in the Page Header section, and then click when the pointer's plus symbol (+) is in the second row of grid dots at the 1-inch mark on the horizontal ruler (see Figure 7-45). Access adds a text box with an attached label box to its left.

4. Click the **Unbound** text box to position the insertion point and remove the word "Unbound," then type **=Date()** and press the **Enter** key. See Figure 7-45.

Adding the current date to the report      **Figure 7-45**

**Trouble?** The attached label on your screen might have a caption, such as "Text6," that differs from the one shown in Figure 7-45, depending on how you completed previous steps. That causes no problem.

5. Switch to Print Preview, and then scroll up to see the date in the Page Header section and to see the following sections of the report. See Figure 7-46.

**Figure 7-46** ▶ **Report with date in the Page Header section**

**Trouble?** Your year might appear with two digits instead of four digits as shown in Figure 7-46. Your date format might also differ, depending on your computer's date settings.

When you print or preview the report, the current date appears instead of the Date function you entered in the text box. The date label is unnecessary, so you can delete it. You'll also move the text box to the left edge of the Page Header section and then left-align the date in the text box.

### To delete the Date label and move and left-align the Date text box:

▶ **1.** Switch to Design view.

▶ **2.** Right-click the **Date label** located at the far left of the Page Header section, and then click **Cut** on the shortcut menu to delete the label.

▶ **3.** Click the **Date** text box, drag its move handle to the left edge of the Page Header section, and then click the **Align Left** button 📄 on the Formatting toolbar to left-align the date in the text box.

▶ **4.** Save your report design changes.

You are now ready to add page numbers to the Page Header section.

# Adding Page Numbers to a Report

You can print page numbers in a report by including an expression in the Page Header or Page Footer section. You can type the expression in an unbound control, just as you did for the Date function, or you can use the Page Numbers option on the Insert menu. The inserted page number expression automatically prints the correct page number on each page of a report.

**Reference Window** | **Adding Page Numbers to a Report**

- Display the report in Design view.
- Click the section in which you want to place page numbers.
- Click Insert on the menu bar, and then click Page Numbers.
- Select the formatting, position, and alignment options you want.
- Click the OK button to place the page number expression in the report.

Elsa wants the page number to be printed at the right side of the Page Header section, on the same line with the date. You'll use the Page Numbers option to insert the page number in the report.

### To add page numbers in the Page Header section:

1. Deselect all controls.

2. Click **Insert** on the menu bar, and then click **Page Numbers**. The Page Numbers dialog box opens.

   You use the Format options to specify the format of the page number. Elsa wants page numbers to appear as Page 1, Page 2, and so on. This is the Page N format option. You use the Position options to place the page numbers at the top of the page in the Page Header section or at the bottom of the page in the Page Footer section. Elsa's design shows page numbers at the top of the page.

3. Make sure that the **Page N** option button in the Format section and that the **Top of Page [Header]** option button in the Position section are both selected.

   The report design shows page numbers at the right side of the page. You can specify this placement in the Alignment list box.

4. Click the **Alignment** list arrow, and then click **Right**.

5. Make sure that the **Show Number on First Page** check box is checked, so the page number prints on the first page and all other pages as well. See Figure 7-47.

| Completed Page Numbers dialog box | Figure 7-47 |
| --- | --- |

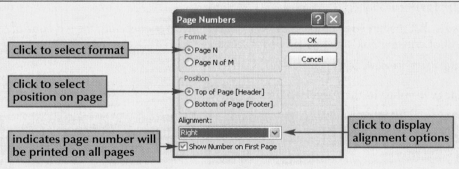

6. Click the **OK** button. The text box shown in Figure 7-48 appears in the upper-right corner of the Page Header section. The expression ="Page" & [Page] in the text box means that the printed report will show the word "Page" followed by a space and the page number.

| Page number expression added to the Report window | Figure 7-48 |
| --- | --- |

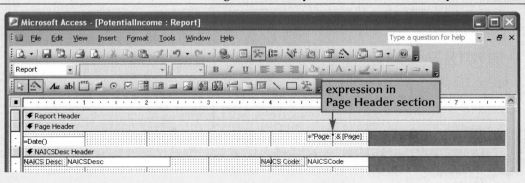

Elsa wants the word "Page," the page number, and the date to be bold. You could select both controls and then set both to bold at the same time. Or you could select one of the two controls, set it to bold, and then duplicate the formatting for the other control. To duplicate a control's formatting, you can use the Format Painter. The **Format Painter** lets you copy the format of a control to other controls in the report. With the Format Painter, creating several controls with the same font style, size, color, and special effect is easy.

Elsa's report design also shows the page number's bottom edge aligned with the date in the Page Header section.

### To use the Format Painter and to align controls:

▶ **1.** Click the **Date** text box to select it, and then click the **Bold** button [B] on the Formatting toolbar to change the date to bold.

▶ **2.** Click the **Format Painter** button [≪] on the Report Design toolbar.

▶ **3.** Click the **Page Number** text box. The Format Painter automatically formats the Page Number text box like the Date text box, changing its font to bold.

   You'll now align the bottom border of the Date and Page Number text boxes.

▶ **4.** Hold down the **Shift** key, click the **Page Number** text box, release the **Shift** key, click **Format** on the menu bar, point to **Align**, and then click **Bottom**. The bottom borders of the text boxes are now aligned.

▶ **5.** Make sure that the left edge of the Page Number text box is aligned with the left edge of the NAICSCode text box in the Page Header section.

▶ **6.** Switch to Print Preview. See Figure 7-49.

| Figure 7-49 | Date and page number in the Page Header section |

Now you are ready to add the title to the Page Header section.

## Adding a Title to a Report

Elsa's report design includes the title "Potential Income," which you'll add to the Page Header section. To emphasize the report title, Elsa asks you to change it to bold and increase its font size from 8 points, the default, to 14 points.

### To add the title to the Page Header section:

▶ **1.** Switch to Design view.

▶ **2.** Click the **Label** tool [Aa] on the toolbox, and then position the pointer in the Page Header section. The pointer changes to a ⁺A shape.

▶ **3.** Position the pointer's plus symbol (+) at the top of the Page Header section and at the 1.75-inch mark on the horizontal ruler, and then click the mouse button. Access places a very narrow text box in the Page Header section. When you start typing in this text box, it expands to accommodate the text.

4. Type **Potential Income**, and then press the **Enter** key. The Error Checking Options button appears to the left of the new label.

5. Position the pointer on the Error Checking Options button. A ScreenTip appears that describes the potential error. See Figure 7-50.

**Adding a label for the report title** ◀ **Figure 7-50**

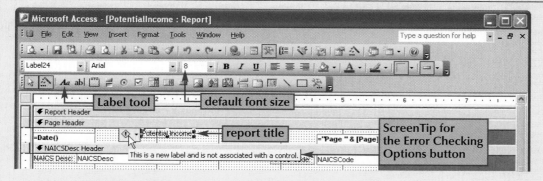

The ScreenTip indicates that the new label is not associated with a control, neither a bound control nor a calculated control. Because you don't want a label that contains a report title to be associated with another control, you want to ignore this potential error.

6. Click the **Error Checking Options** button, and then click **Ignore Error**.

The label is still selected, so you can increase the report title's font size and change the title to bold.

7. Click the **Font Size** list arrow on the Formatting toolbar, click **14**, and then click the **Bold** button **B** on the Formatting toolbar. The font size and style of the report title change from 8 points to 14 points and to bold. The label box is now too small to display the entire report title, so you need to resize the label box.

8. Click **Format** on the menu bar, point to **Size**, and then click **To Fit** to resize the report title text box.

Elsa wants to see how the report looks, so you'll switch to Print Preview to check the report against her design.

9. Save your report design changes, switch to Print Preview and, if necessary, scroll the Print Preview window to see more of the report. See Figure 7-51.

**Report title displayed in the Page Header section** ◀ **Figure 7-51**

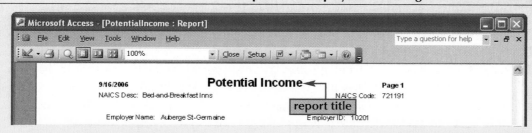

10. Review the first several pages of the report in Print Preview. Notice that the NAICSDesc Header section on page 5 appears near the bottom of the page, and the first employer name within this group appears at the top of the next page. See Figure 7-52.

| Figure 7-52 | Group Header section orphaned from group's first employer |
|---|---|

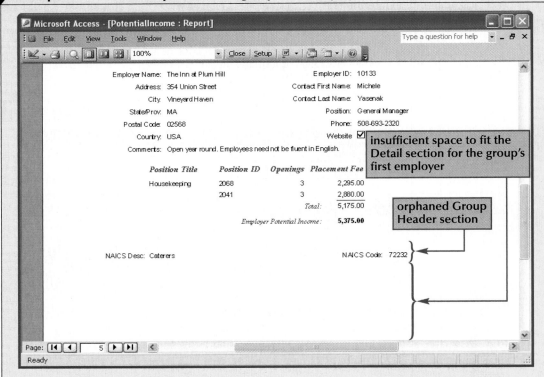

**Trouble?** If your Print Preview screen for page 5 doesn't match the one shown in Figure 7-52, navigate through the remaining Print Preview pages to find a similar Group Header section with the same problem. Depending on your printer driver, you might not find a similar Group Header section; in this case, simply continue with the tutorial.

The Group Header section shown in Figure 7-52 is an example of an orphaned header section. An **orphaned header section** appears by itself at the bottom of a page. Elsa prefers to see the NAICSDesc Header printed at the top of a page, just before the first employer name in the group. To do this, you'll set the Keep Together property for the NAICSDesc Header section. The **Keep Together property** prints a group header on a page only if there is enough room on the page to print the first detail record for the group; otherwise, the group header prints at the top of the next page.

Now you'll set the Keep Together property for the NAICSDesc Header section.

### To set the Keep Together property for the NAICSDesc Header section:

▶ **1.** Switch to Design view.

▶ **2.** Click the **Sorting and Grouping** button ⊞ on the Report Design toolbar to open the Sorting and Grouping dialog box. The NAICSDesc field is selected.

▶ **3.** Click the right side of the **Keep Together** text box, and then click **With First Detail**. The NAICSDesc Header section will now print on a page only if the first detail record for the group can also print on the page.

▶ **4.** Close the Sorting and Grouping dialog box.

**5.** Switch to Print Preview, and then navigate through the Print Preview pages to verify that the orphaned header section problem no longer exists.

**6.** Switch to Design view.

To make your report look like Elsa's report design, your final task is to add blue horizontal lines to the Page Header, NAICSDesc Header, and Detail sections. You'll first increase the height of the Page Header section so it will be easier to add the line below the three controls in the section.

## To add lines to the report:

**1.** Use the ✛ pointer to increase the height of the Page Header section to the 0.5-inch mark on the vertical ruler. The new height of the Page Header section will allow sufficient room to add a horizontal line in this section below the three controls.

You can now add a line under the controls in the Page Header section. If you want to make sure you draw a straight horizontal line, press the Shift key before you start drawing the line and release the Shift key after you've created the line.

**2.** Click the **Line** tool ◯ on the toolbox, position the pointer at the left edge of the Page Header section and on the bottom border of the Date text box, and then draw a horizontal line from left to right, ending at the 5-inch mark on the horizontal ruler.

Elsa's report design shows a thick blue line in the Page Header section, so you'll now change the line to match the design.

**3.** Click the list arrow for the **Line/Border Color** button ◢ on the Formatting toolbar, and then click the **blue** box in the color palette in row 2 and column 6. The line's color changes to blue.

**4.** Click the list arrow for the **Line/Border Width** button ▢ on the Formatting toolbar, and then click width **3**. The line changes to a thick blue line. See Figure 7-53.

**Adding a thick blue line in the Page Header section** ◀ **Figure 7-53**

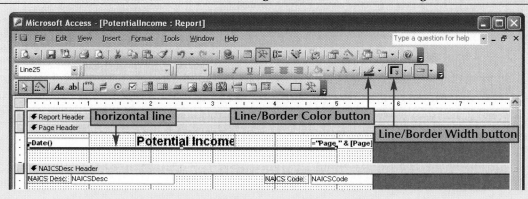

You need to place a copy of the thick blue line in the Detail section.

**5.** With the line selected, click the **Copy** button ▨ on the Report Design toolbar, click an empty area of the Detail section to make it the current section, and then click the **Paste** button ▨ on the Report Design toolbar. You've pasted a copy of the line at the top of the Detail section.

**6.** Position the pointer over the line in the Detail section; when it changes to a ✋ shape, drag the line straight down to the 2.25-inch mark on the vertical ruler.

You can now reduce the height of the Page Header and Detail sections.

**7.** Use the ✛ pointer to decrease the height of the Page Header section so that the bottom of the section touches the blue line, and then decrease the height of the Detail section to the 2.375-inch mark on the vertical ruler.

Elsa's report design shows two thin blue horizontal lines in the NAICSDesc Header section, so you'll now add these lines.

**8.** Click the **Line** tool ◻ on the toolbox, position the pointer on the left edge of the NAICSDesc Header section and in the row of grid dots just above the 0.25-inch mark on the vertical ruler, and then draw a horizontal line from left to right, ending at the 5-inch mark on the horizontal ruler.

**9.** Click the **Line/Border Color** button ◻ (not the list arrow) on the Formatting toolbar. The line changes to blue.

To draw the second line shown in Elsa's report design, you'll copy and paste the line you just drew.

**10.** Click the **Copy** button ◻ on the Report Design toolbar, and then click the **Paste** button ◻ on the Report Design toolbar. A copy of the line is positioned below it.

**11.** Drag the copied line straight up so that it's in the row of grid dots immediately below the original line. See Figure 7-54.

**Figure 7-54** ▶ **Adding lines to the report**

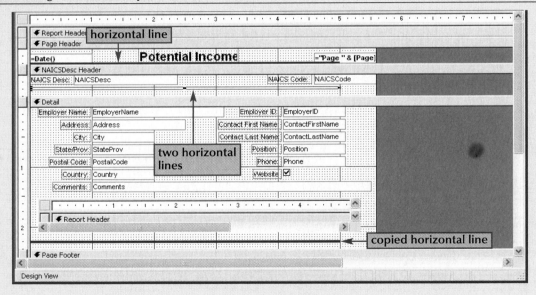

The Potential Income report is finished. You can now save the report and then preview its pages.

## To save and preview the report:

**1.** Save your report changes, and then switch to Print Preview to display the first page of the report. See Figure 7-55.

**Print Preview of page 1 of the final report** ◀ **Figure 7-55**

**2.** Use the navigation buttons to view the other pages of the report. In particular, note the information for Seaview Restaurant, which appears on approximately page 5. For this employer, the Comments field's Can Grow property has expanded its text box vertically to display its three lines of text. Also, because Seaview Restaurant has no available positions, the subreport's Can Shrink property removed the blank space for this control. See Figure 7-56.

**Can Grow and Can Shrink properties** ◀ **Figure 7-56**

**3.** Navigate to the last Print Preview page to view the overall total at the end of the report.

Elsa asks if it's possible to add another subreport to the PotentialIncome report.

# Adding a Summary Subreport

Elsa created the PlacementFeeByStateProv report, which is a summary report displaying total placement fees by state and province. She wants you to add this report as a subreport to the Report Footer section in the PotentialIncome main report. Although the main report already includes the PotentialIncomeSubreport report as a subreport in the Detail section, you can include additional subreports in the main report's Report Header and Report Footer sections.

You'll add Elsa's summary report to the PotentialIncome report's Report Footer section without using the Control Wizard; you'll set the subreport's Source Object property to use the PlacementFeeByStateProv report. The **Source Object property** identifies the report that is the source of a subreport in a main report.

### To add the summary report to the Report Footer section:

1. Switch to Design view, scroll down the window until the entire Report Footer section is visible, and then use the ⊹ pointer to increase the height of the Report Footer section to the 1.75-inch mark on the vertical ruler.

2. Click the **Control Wizards** tool ▨ on the toolbox to deselect it, and then click the **Subform/Subreport** tool ▦ on the toolbox.

3. Position the pointer's plus symbol (+) in the Report Footer section at the 1.5-inch mark on the horizontal ruler and at the 0.625-inch mark on the vertical ruler, and then click the mouse button. Access places a subreport control with attached label in the Report Footer section.

   Before you set the subreport's Source Object property, you'll delete the unneeded label and resize and reposition the subreport control.

4. Right-click the subreport label, and then click **Cut** on the shortcut menu to delete the label.

5. Make sure the subreport control's left edge is at the 1.5-inch mark on the horizontal ruler and its top edge is at the 0.5-inch mark on the vertical ruler.

6. Adjust the width of the subreport control so that its right edge is at the 3.75-inch mark on the horizontal ruler, and adjust its height so that its bottom edge is at the 1.5-inch mark on the vertical ruler.

7. Press the **F4** key to open the property sheet for the subreport, click the right side of the **Source Object** text box, click **Report.PlacementFeeByStateProv**, and then close the property sheet. See Figure 7-57.

**After adding the subreport control to the Report Footer section** Figure 7-57

Because you don't need the total potential income in the Report Footer section to print on the same page as the new subreport, you'll set the Keep Together property for the section to No.

▶ 8. Right-click the **Report Footer** selector bar, click **Properties** on the shortcut menu to open the property sheet for the section (make sure Section: ReportFooter appears in the property sheet title bar), set the Keep Together property to **No**, and then close the property sheet.

Now you'll save your report design changes and review the new subreport in Print Preview.

▶ 9. Save your report changes, switch to Print Preview, navigate to the last report page, and then scroll as necessary to display the entire subreport. See Figure 7-58.

**After adding a second subreport to the main report** Figure 7-58

**10.** Click the **Close Window** button ☒ on the menu bar to close the report and return to the Database window.

Now that you've finished the PotentialIncome report, Elsa wants to show you how she created the summary PlacementFeeByStateProv report.

### To review the summary report:

**1.** Open the **PlacementFeeByStateProv** report in Design view. See Figure 7-59.

| Figure 7-59 | Viewing the summary report in Design view |
|---|---|

The report design includes controls in the Report Header, StateProv Footer, and Report Footer sections; these sections are the ones you saw in the subreport when you viewed it after adding it to the PotentialIncome report. But the report design also includes controls in the Detail section. Why didn't you see those controls in the subreport? You'll open the property sheet for the Detail section to determine the answer.

**2.** Right-click the **Detail** selector bar, click **Properties** on the shortcut menu to open the property sheet for the section, and then click the **All** tab (if necessary). See Figure 7-60.

| Figure 7-60 | Viewing the property sheet for the Detail section |
|---|---|

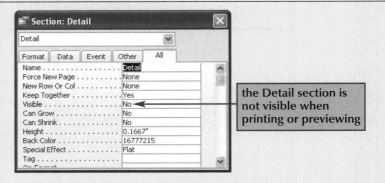

Notice that the Visible property for the Detail section is set to No. Recall that earlier in this tutorial you set the Visible property to No to hide the EmployerID text box and its attached label in the subreport's Detail section. In a similar way, you can set the Visible property to No to hide entire report sections. For a report that displays records in the Detail section and that has totals in Group Footer and Report Footer sections, you can change that report to a summary report by hiding its Detail section, as was done for this report.

Note that you can create the same summary report without setting the section's Visible property to No. You would need to delete the PlacementFee control in the Detail section and then delete the Detail section by reducing its height to zero. The PlacementFee field is a field in the report's record source, so you can calculate subtotals and totals in footer sections using that field.

▶ 3. Close the property sheet, switch to Print Preview, notice that the report is the same as the subreport you previously added to the main report, and then close the report.

Next, Elsa wants you to create mailing labels that can be used in mass mailings to NSJI's employer clients.

# Creating Mailing Labels

Elsa needs a set of mailing labels printed for all employers so she can mail a marketing brochure and other materials to them. The Employer table contains the name and address information that will serve as the record source for the labels. Each mailing label will have the same format: contact name on the first line; employer name on the second line; street address on the third line; city, state or province, and postal code on the fourth line; and country on the fifth line. In addition, Elsa wants the NSJI logo to appear on each mailing label.

You could create a custom report to produce the mailing labels, but using the Label Wizard is an easier and faster way to produce them. The **Label Wizard** provides templates for hundreds of standard label formats, each of which is uniquely identified by a label manufacturer's name and number; these templates specify the dimensions and arrangement of labels on each page. Standard label formats can have between one and five labels across a page; the number of labels printed on a single page also varies. Elsa's mailing labels are Avery number C2163; each sheet has 1.5-inch by 3.9-inch labels arranged in two columns and six rows on the page.

## Creating Mailing Labels and Other Labels

Reference Window

- In the Database window, click Reports in the Objects bar of the Database window to display the Reports list box.
- Click the New button in the Database window to open the New Report dialog box.
- Click Label Wizard to select it, select the table or query that contains the source data for the mailing labels, and then click the OK button.
- Select the label manufacturer and its product number, and then click the Next button.
- Select the label font, color, and style, and then click the Next button.
- Construct the label content by selecting the fields from the record source and specifying their placement and spacing on the label, and then click the Next button.
- Select the sort fields, click the Next button, specify the report name, and then click the Finish button.

You'll use the Label Wizard to create a report to produce mailing labels for all employer clients.

## To use the Label Wizard to create the mailing label report:

1. Make sure that **Reports** is selected in the Objects bar of the Database window, and then click the **New** button in the Database window to open the New Report dialog box.

2. Click **Label Wizard**, click the list arrow to display the list of tables and queries in the Jobs database, click **Employer** to select this table as the basis for your report, and then click the **OK** button. The first Label Wizard dialog box opens and asks you to select the standard or custom label you'll use.

3. Make sure that the **English** option button is selected in the Unit of Measure section, that the **Sheet feed** option button is selected in the Label Type section, and that **Avery** is selected in the Filter by manufacturer list box, and then click **C2163** in the Product number list box. See Figure 7-61.

**Figure 7-61** ▶ Selecting a standard label

select this Avery product number

make sure these options are selected

selected manufacturer

Because you've filtered the labels by Avery as the manufacturer, the top list box shows the Avery product number, dimensions, and number of labels across the page for each of its standard label formats. If your label manufacturer or its labels do not appear in the list box, you can create your own custom format for them. You can display the dimensions in the list in either inches or millimeters by choosing the appropriate option in the Unit of Measure section. You can also specify in the Label Type section whether the labels are on individual sheets or are continuous forms.

4. Click the **Next** button to open the second Label Wizard dialog box, in which you choose font specifications for the labels.

Elsa wants the labels to use 10-point Arial with a medium font weight and without italics or underlines. The font weight determines how light or dark the characters will print; you can choose from nine values ranging from thin to heavy.

5. If necessary, select **Arial** for the font name, **10** for the font size, and **Medium** for the font weight; make sure the Italic and the Underline check boxes are unchecked and that black is the text color; and then click the **Next** button to open the third Label Wizard dialog box, from which you select the data to appear on the labels.

As you select fields from the Available fields list box or type text for the label, the Prototype label box shows the format for the label. Elsa wants the mailing labels to print the ContactFirstName and ContactLastName fields on the first line; the EmployerName field on the second line; the Address field on the third line; the City, StateProv, and PostalCode fields on the fourth line; and the Country field on the fifth line. One space will separate the ContactFirstName and ContactLastName fields, the City and StateProv fields, and the StateProv and PostalCode fields.

6. Scroll down and click **ContactFirstName** in the Available fields list box, click the ⎡ > ⎤ button to move the field to the Prototype label box, press the **spacebar**, click **ContactLastName** in the Available fields list box (if necessary), and then click the ⎡ > ⎤ button (see Figure 7-62). The braces around the field names in the Prototype label box indicate that the name represents a field rather than text that you entered.

   **Trouble?** If you select the wrong field or type the wrong text, highlight the incorrect item in the Prototype label box, press the Delete key to remove the item, and then select the correct field or type the correct text.

7. Press the **Enter** key to move to the next line in the Prototype label box, and then use Figure 7-62 to complete the entries in the Prototype label box. Make sure you press the spacebar after selecting the City field and the StateProv field.

**Completed label prototype** ◄ **Figure 7-62**

8. Click the **Next** button to open the fourth Label Wizard dialog box, in which you choose the sort fields for the labels.

   Elsa wants PostalCode to be the primary sort field and EmployerName to be the secondary sort field.

9. Select the **PostalCode** field as the primary sort field, select the **EmployerName** field as the secondary sort field, and then click the **Next** button to open the last Label Wizard dialog box, in which you enter a name for the report.

10. Type **EmployerMailingLabels**, and then click the **Finish** button. Access saves the report as EmployerMailingLabels and then opens the Report window in Print Preview.

11. Click the **Zoom** list arrow on the Print Preview toolbar, and then click **Fit**. The first page of the report appears. Note that two columns of labels appear across the page. See Figure 7-63.

**Figure 7-63** | **Previewing the mailing labels**

Elsa wants the NSJI logo to appear on each mailing label, but first you'll review the mailing labels more closely to see if Elsa has other changes for you to make.

### To preview the mailing label report in greater detail:

1. Click the **Zoom** list arrow on the Print Preview toolbar, and then click **75%** to preview the report in greater detail. See Figure 7-64.

**Previewing the label content and sequence** | **Figure 7-64**

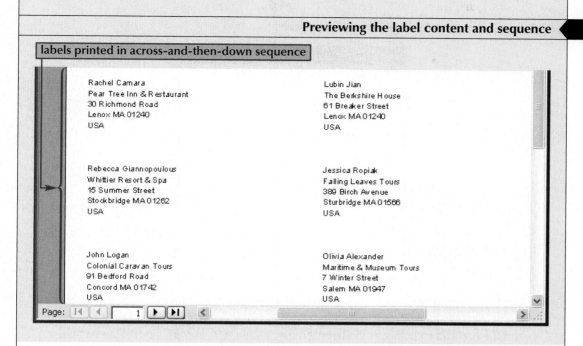

labels printed in across-and-then-down sequence

| | |
|---|---|
| Rachel Camara<br>Pear Tree Inn & Restaurant<br>30 Richmond Road<br>Lenox MA 01240<br>USA | Lubin Jian<br>The Berkshire House<br>61 Breaker Street<br>Lenox MA 01240<br>USA |
| Rebecca Giannopoulous<br>Whittier Resort & Spa<br>15 Summer Street<br>Stockbridge MA 01262<br>USA | Jessica Ropiak<br>Falling Leaves Tours<br>389 Birch Avenue<br>Sturbridge MA 01566<br>USA |
| John Logan<br>Colonial Caravan Tours<br>91 Bedford Road<br>Concord MA 01742<br>USA | Olivia Alexander<br>Maritime & Museum Tours<br>7 Winter Street<br>Salem MA 01947<br>USA |

Page: |◄ ◄ 1 ► ►|  <

The EmployerMailingLabels report is a **multiple-column report**, one that prints the same collection of field values in two or more sets across the page. The labels will print in ascending PostalCode order and then in ascending EmployerName order. The first label will print in the upper-left corner on the first page, the second label will print to its right, the third label will print under the first label, and so on. This style of multiple-column report is the across-and-then-down layout. Instead, Elsa wants the labels to print with the "down, then across" layout—the first label prints, the second label prints under the first, and so on. After the bottom label in the first column is printed, the next label is printed at the top of the second column. The "down, then across" layout is also called **newspaper-style columns**, or **snaking columns**.

Elsa also wants the NSJI logo to print above the employer name and address information, so you'll add the logo as a picture in the report.

## To change the layout and to add a picture to the mailing label report:

▶ 1. Switch to Design view. The Detail section, the only section in the report, is sized for a single label.

   First, you'll change the layout to snaking columns.

▶ 2. Click **File** on the menu bar, click **Page Setup**, and then click the **Columns** tab. The Page Setup dialog box displays the Columns options for the report. See Figure 7-65.

**Figure 7-65** | **Columns options in the Page Setup dialog box**

The Columns options in the Page Setup dialog box let you change the properties of a multiple-column report. In the Grid Settings section, you specify the number of column sets and the row and column spacing between the column sets. In the Column Size section, you specify the width and height of each column set. In the Column Layout section, you select between the "down, then across" and the "across, then down" layouts.

You can now change the layout for the labels.

3. Click the **Down, then Across** option button, and then click the **OK** button.

Because Elsa wants the NSJI logo printed above the employer data, you'll select all controls and move them down the Detail section.

4. Click **Edit** on the menu bar, and then click **Select All** to select all controls in the Detail section.

5. Position the pointer over one of the selected controls; when the pointer changes to a ♨ shape, drag the controls straight down in the Detail section until the top border of the top control is at the 0.375-inch mark on the vertical ruler.

Next, you'll add the NSJI logo above the employer information. You could add the logo to the report in the same way you added a picture to a form, by using the Image tool on the toolbox. Instead, you'll use the Picture option on the Insert menu.

6. Deselect all controls, click **Insert** on the menu bar, and then click **Picture**. The Insert Picture dialog box opens.

7. Make sure **Tutorial** appears in the Look in list box, click **NSJILogo** to select the picture file, and then click the **OK** button. The Insert Picture dialog box closes and the picture is inserted in the upper-left corner of the Detail section.

8. Move the picture straight to the right until its left edge is at the 2-inch mark on the horizontal ruler. See Figure 7-66.

**Final design for the mailing labels** ◄ **Figure 7-66**

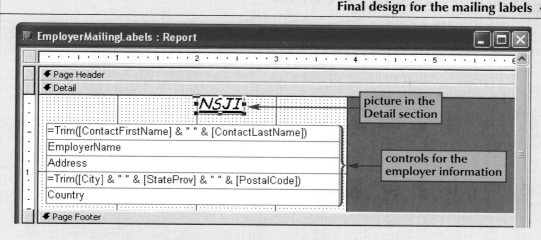

You've finished Elsa's changes, so you can now save and preview the report.

9. Save your report design changes, and then switch to Print Preview. The logo will print on each label, and the labels appear in the snaking-columns layout. See Figure 7-67.

**The completed labels in Print Preview** ◄ **Figure 7-67**

Because you've finished Elsa's reports, you can now close the Jobs database and exit Access.

10. Click the **Close** button ☒ on the Access window title bar to close the Jobs database and to exit Access.

Elsa is very pleased with the modified report and the two new reports, which will provide her with improved information and help expedite her written communications with NSJI's employer clients.

# Session 7.4 Quick Check

1. What do you type in a text box control to print the current date?
2. How do you insert a page number in the Page Header section?
3. You can use the _____ to copy the format of a control to other controls.
4. The Keep Together property prints a group header on a page only if there is enough room on the page to print the first _____ record for the group.
5. The Source Object property identifies the report that is the source of a _____ in a main report.
6. What is a multiple-column report?

# Tutorial Summary

In this tutorial, you customized a report created by the Report Wizard by modifying its controls, hiding duplicate values, and calculating grand totals. You then examined general report design guidelines, learned how to use the guidelines in planning a custom report, reviewed record source queries for the report, and learned how to assign a conditional value to a calculated field in a query. In creating the custom report, you sorted and grouped data; added fields and modified report controls; added two subreports; modified one subreport; added lines; calculated group totals; defined conditional formatting rules; used domain aggregate functions; and added the date, page numbers, and a title. Finally, you created mailing labels.

## Key Terms

| | | |
|---|---|---|
| Align command | DSum domain aggregate function | Line tool |
| Border Style property | | multiple-column report |
| Can Grow property | Font/Fore Color button | newspaper-style columns |
| Can Shrink property | Format Painter | orphaned header section |
| conditional formatting | Group Footer section | report |
| custom report | Group Header section | snaking columns |
| Date function | grouping field | Source Object property |
| detail report | Hide Duplicates property | subreport |
| domain | IIf function | summary report |
| domain aggregate function | Keep Together property | Visible property |
| | Label Wizard | |

# Review Assignments

**Data File needed for the Review Assignments: Students.mdb (*cont. from Tutorial 6*)**

Elsa wants you to create a custom report for the Students database that prints all recruiters and the students they've recruited. She also wants you to customize an existing report. You will perform the tasks for Elsa by completing the following steps:

1. Open the **Students** database in the Intro\Review folder provided with your Data Files.
2. Create a custom report based on the **Recruiter** table. Figure 7-68 shows a sample of the completed report. Refer to the figure as a guide as you complete Steps 3 through 7.

Figure 7-68

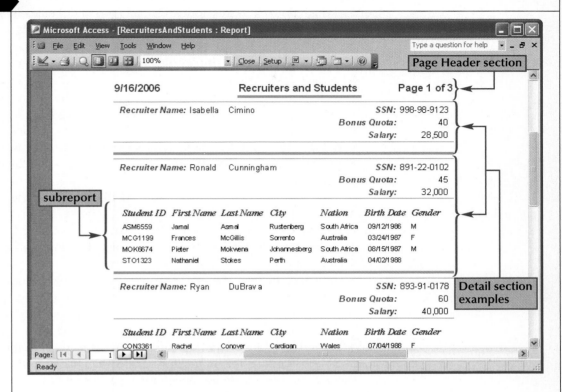

3. Use the **Recruiter** table as the record source for the main report.
4. Make the following modifications to the main report:
   a. Include the following sections in the main report: Page Header, Detail, and Page Footer.
   b. At the top center of the Page Header section, enter the report title and format it with dark blue, 12-point, bold, Arial font. Use the same format for the current date at the left edge of the section and for the page number at the right edge of the section. Use the "Page N of M" format for page numbers. Add a red line with a 3-point border width below the report title.
   c. Type your name in the top center of the Page Footer section with the same format that you used for the report title, and then save the report as **RecruitersAndStudents**.
   d. Add all fields from the **Recruiter** table to the Detail section, using Figure 7-68 as a guide.
   e. Delete the Last Name label. Change the caption for the First Name label to "Recruiter Name:", and resize the label to fit.
   f. Change all labels and text boxes in the Detail section to 10-point Arial font; format all the labels with dark blue, bold, italic font; and then size all labels to fit.
   g. Add a thin red line at the top of the Detail section, and add a thin red line below the Salary controls in the Detail section.
   h. Sort the recruiter records in ascending order by the LastName field, and then in ascending order by the FirstName field.
5. Use the following instructions to add a subreport using Control Wizards to the Detail section:
   a. Select all fields from the **Student** table, link the main report and subreport using the SSN field, and name the subreport **StudentSubreport**.
   b. Delete the subreport label.

  c. Open the subreport in a new window, and then delete the SSN label and text box.

  d. Make sure the text boxes' font is 8-point Arial and the labels' font is 11-point Times New Roman, dark blue, bold, italic. Resize all labels to their best fit.

  e. By switching between Design view and Print Preview, resize each text box so that it's just wide enough to display the entire field value, and move and resize the labels and text boxes as necessary.

  f. Left-align all text boxes and their corresponding labels.

  g. Move all text boxes straight up to the top of the Detail section to eliminate all extra blank space above the text boxes, and then reduce the height of the Detail section until the bottom of the section touches the bottom of the text boxes.

  h. Reduce the subreport's width until the right edge touches the right edge of the Gender controls.

  i. Sort the student records in ascending order by the LastName field, and then in ascending order by the FirstName field.

  j. Hide duplicate values for the Gender field.

  k. Save the subreport design changes, and then close the subreport.

6. Make the following modifications to the main report:

  a. By switching between Design view and Print Preview, reduce the width of the subreport control in the Detail section from the right as much as possible (approximately 6 inches or less).

  b. Set the subreport border style to Transparent, and set its Can Shrink property to Yes.

  c. Add a red line with a 3-point border width below the subreport control.

  d. Set the Can Shrink property of the Detail section to Yes. (*Hint*: Click the Detail section bar to make the entire section the current control.)

7. Save your report design changes, switch to Print Preview, print the report's first page, and then close the report.

8. Open the **Recruiters** report in Design view, and make the following modifications to the report:

  a. Reduce the vertical space between lines in the Detail section to single spacing.

  b. Center the BonusQuota field values.

  c. Change the sorting options to sort in increasing order on BonusQuota field values and then in increasing order on Salary field values.

  d. Add calculated controls to display salary subtotals for each BonusQuota field value and salary grand totals, formatting the controls as Standard with zero decimal points. Add a single line above the calculated control in the Group Footer section, and add two lines above the calculated control in the Report Footer section.

  e. Hide duplicate BonusQuota field values.

  f. Save your report design changes, print the report, and then close the report.

9. Close the **Students** database, and then exit Access.

<table>
<tr><td>

**Create**

*Use the skills you learned in the tutorial to work with the data contained in a video photography database.*

</td><td>

# Case Problem 1

Data File needed for this Case Problem: Clients.mdb (*cont. from Tutorial 6*)

***Lim's Video Photography*** Youngho Lim wants you to modify an existing report and to create a custom report and mailing labels for the Clients database. The custom report will be based on the results of two queries you will create. You will modify the report and create the queries, the custom report, and the mailing labels by completing the following steps:

1. Open the **Clients** database in the Intro\Case1 folder provided with your Data Files.

</td></tr>
</table>

2. Create two queries for the custom report following these instructions:
   a. For the first query, select the ShootDesc field from the **ShootDesc** table; and then select (in order) the ShootDate, Duration, Location, and ContractID fields from the **Shoot** table. Sort the query in ascending order by the ContractID field. Save the query as **ShootData**, run and print the query, and then close the query.
   b. For the second query, select all fields from the **Client** table; and then select all fields, except the ClientID field, from the **Contract** table. Sort the query in ascending order by the ContractID field. Save the query as **ClientsAndContracts**, run the query, print it in landscape orientation, and then close the query.
3. Create a custom report based on the **ClientsAndContracts** query. Figure 7-69 shows a sample of the completed report. Refer to the figure as a guide as you complete Steps 4 through 8.

**Figure 7-69**

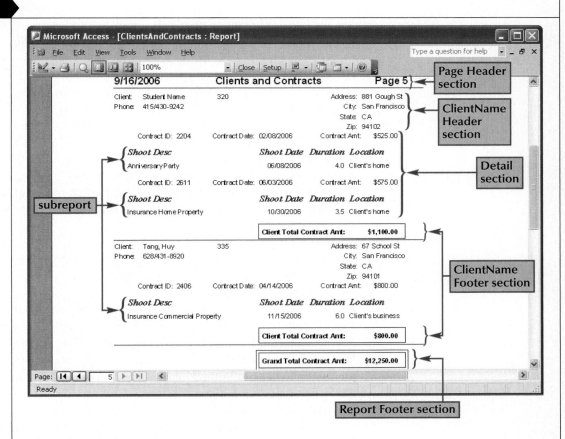

4. Use the **ClientsAndContracts** query as the record source for the main report.
5. Make the following modifications to the main report:
   a. You'll be directed to include the following sections in your report: Page Header, ClientName Header, Detail, ClientName Footer, Page Footer, and Report Footer.
   b. At the top center of the Page Header section, enter the report title and format it with Arial 12-point, bold font. Use the same format for the current date at the left edge of the section and for the page number at the right edge of the section. Below the controls in the Page Header section, add a blue line running from the left edge of the section to approximately the 5-inch mark on the horizontal ruler.
   c. Enter your name in the top center of the Page Footer section with the same format that you used for the report title, and then save the report as **ClientsAndContracts**.

d. Sort the main report records in ascending order by the ClientName field, and then in ascending order by the ContractID field. Add Group Header and Group Footer sections for the ClientName field, and set its Keep Together property to "Whole Group."

e. Add the ClientName, ClientID, Phone, Address, City, State, and Zip fields from the **ClientsAndContracts** query to the ClientName Header section. Delete the Client ID label, and change the caption for the Client Name label to "Client:". Resize and reposition the labels and text boxes in the ClientName Header section as shown in Figure 7-69, positioning the ClientID text box to the right of the ClientName text box.

f. Add the ContractID, ContractDate, and ContractAmt fields from the **ClientsAndContracts** query to the Detail section. Resize and reposition the labels and text boxes in the Detail section as shown in Figure 7-69.

6. Use the following instructions to add a subreport using Control Wizards to the Detail section:

a. Select all fields from the **ShootData** query, link the main report and subreport using the ContractID field, and name the subreport **ShootSubreport**.

b. Open the subreport in a new window, and then delete the ContractID text box and label.

c. By switching between Design view and Print Preview, resize each text box so that it's just wide enough to display the entire field value.

d. Resize and reposition the labels in the Report Header section and the text boxes in the Detail section until they're positioned as shown in Figure 7-69.

e. Move all text boxes straight up to the top of the Detail section to eliminate all extra blank space above the text boxes, and then reduce the height of the Detail section until the bottom of the section touches the bottom of the text boxes.

f. If necessary, reduce the subreport's width until its right edge touches the right edge of the Location controls.

g. Sort the subreport records in ascending order by the ShootDate field.

h. Save the subreport design changes, and then close the subreport.

7. Make the following modifications to the main report:

a. Delete the subreport label.

b. By switching between Design view and Print Preview, reduce the width of the subreport control in the Detail section from the right as much as possible.

c. Set the subreport border style to Transparent, and set its Can Shrink property to Yes.

d. Reduce the height of the Detail section to just below the subreport control, and then reduce the width of the main report as much as possible.

e. Add a text box to the ClientName Footer section, enter the function to calculate the total of the ContractAmt field values, format the calculated control as currency, change the label caption to "Client Total Contract Amt:", and then format both controls as bold. Resize and reposition the controls in the ClientName Footer section as shown in Figure 7-69.

**Explore**

f. Draw a rectangle around the controls in the ClientName Footer section, and then change the rectangle's border color to dark blue. Use the Send to Back option on the Format menu to position the rectangle.

g. Add the Report Footer section, but not the Report Header section, to the main report. Add a text box to the Report Footer section, enter the function to calculate the total of the ContractAmt field values, and format the calculated control as currency. Change the label caption to "Grand Total Contract Amt:", and then format both controls as bold. Resize and reposition the controls in the Report Footer section as shown in Figure 7-69.

**Explore**

    h. Draw a rectangle around the controls in the Report Footer section, and then change the rectangle's border color to dark blue. Use the Send to Back option on the Format menu to position the rectangle. Draw a second rectangle around the first rectangle, and then set its properties to match the properties for the inner rectangle.

    i. Add a dark blue line below the controls in the ClientName Footer section. Start the line at the left edge of the section and end it at approximately the 5-inch mark on the horizontal ruler.

    j. If necessary, reduce the height of the ClientName Footer and Report Footer sections to the bottom of the controls in the section.

8. Save your report design changes, switch to Print Preview, print the first and last pages of the report, and then close the report.

9. Open the **ClientsAndTheirContracts** report in Design view, and make the following modifications to the report:

    a. Insert spaces in the report title so that it becomes "Clients and Their Contracts" and then reduce the height of the Report Header section to the bottom of the report title label.

    b. Reduce the vertical space between lines in the Detail section to single spacing.

    c. Change the sorting options to sort in increasing order on City field values and then in decreasing order on ContractAmt field values.

    d. Add calculated controls to display ContractAmt subtotals for each City field value and City grand totals, formatting the controls as Currency. Add a single line above the calculated control in the Group Footer section, and add two lines above the calculated control in the Report Footer section.

    e. Hide duplicate City field values.

    f. Save your report design changes, print the report, and then close the report.

**Explore**

10. Create a copy of the **ClientsAndTheirContracts** report with the name **ClientsAndTheirContractsSummary**. Change the new report to a summary report, displaying the City and subtotal values in the Group Footer section and the grand total value in the Report Footer section. Modify the report title, column headings, and other controls until the report has a professional look.

11. Use the following instructions to create the mailing labels:

    a. Use the **Client** table as the record source for the mailing labels.

    b. Use Durable 1452 labels, and use the default font and color. (*Hint*: Make sure the Metric option button is selected in the Unit of Measure section.)

    c. For the prototype label, place ClientName on the first line; Address on the second line; and City, a space, State, a space, and Zip on the third line.

    d. Sort by Zip and then by ClientName, and then enter the report name **ClientLabels**.

    e. Print the first page of the report, and then close the report.

12. Close the **Clients** database, and then exit Access.

**Apply**

*Apply what you learned in the tutorial to work with the data for an e-commerce business in the food services industry.*

# Case Problem 2

**Data Files needed for this Case Problem: Delivery.mdb (*cont. from Tutorial 6*) and DineLogo.gif**

***DineAtHome.course.com*** Claire Picard wants you to create a custom report and mailing labels for the Delivery database. The custom report will be based on the results of a query you will create. You will create the query, the custom report, and the mailing labels by completing the following steps:

1. Open the **Delivery** database in the Intro\Case2 folder provided with your Data Files.

2. Create a new query based on the **Restaurant** and **Order** tables. Select all fields from the **Restaurant** table, and select all fields except RestaurantID from the **Order** table. Add a calculated field named BillTotal (Caption property value of Bill Total) that adds the OrderAmt and DeliveryCharge fields; use the IIf function to add an additional $2 to the BillTotal field if the City field value is Naples. Save the query as **RestaurantOrders**, and then close it.

3. Create a custom report based on the **RestaurantOrders** query. Figure 7-70 shows a sample of the completed report. Refer to the figure as a guide as you create the report.

**Figure 7-70**

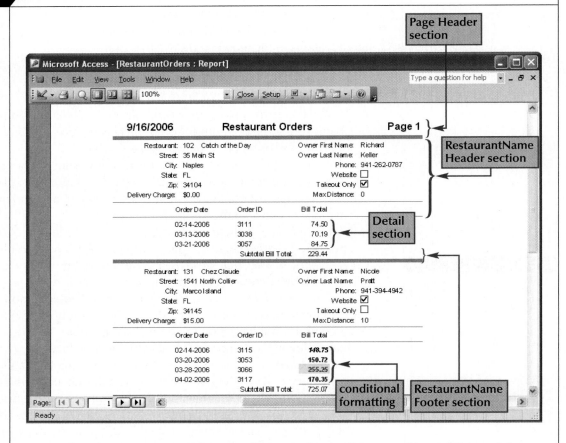

a. Sort the report records in ascending order by the RestaurantName field, and then in ascending order by the OrderDate field. Add Group Header and Group Footer sections for the RestaurantName field, and set its Keep Together property to "Whole Group."

b. In the RestaurantName Header section, add all fields from the **RestaurantOrders** query, except for the three **Order** table fields. Delete the RestaurantID label. Change the caption for the RestaurantName label to "Restaurant:", and then resize the label to fit. Resize and reposition the labels and text boxes as shown in Figure 7-70, placing the RestaurantID and RestaurantName text boxes to the right of the Restaurant label.

**Explore**

c. Add a red line to the RestaurantName Header section in the row of grid dots below the bottom controls. Start the line at the left edge of the section and end it at the 5-inch mark on the horizontal ruler. Save the report as **RestaurantOrders**.

d. From the **RestaurantOrders** query, add the OrderDate, OrderID, and BillTotal fields to the Detail section. Cut the three labels in the Detail section and paste them into the RestaurantName Header section. (*Hint*: Select the three labels, click the Cut button on the Report Design toolbar, click the RestaurantName Header bar, and then click the Paste button on the Report Design toolbar.) Delete the colons from the label captions.

e. Add a second red line to the RestaurantName Header section in the row of grid dots below the three labels, and then reduce the height of the section to the row of grid dots below the line.

**Explore**

f. Resize the three text boxes in the Detail section, move the text boxes to the top of the section, and then reduce the height of the section to the bottom of the text boxes. Define conditional formatting rules for the BillTotal field—use bold and italic font for values between 100 and 150, use bold for values between 150.01 and 200, and use a bold, dark blue font and a light yellow fill for values over 200. Set the BillTotal field's Format property to Fixed and its Decimal Places property to 2.

g. At the top center of the Page Header section, enter the report title and format it with 12-point, Arial, bold font. Use the same format for the current date at the left edge of the section and for the page number at the right edge of the section. Add a red line with a 4-point border width under the controls in the Page Header section. Start the line at the left edge of the section and end it at the 5-inch mark on the horizontal ruler. Reduce the height of the section to the row of grid dots below the line.

h. Add a text box to the RestaurantName Footer section, enter the function to calculate the total of the BillTotal field values, format the calculated control as Standard, and then change the label caption to "Subtotal Bill Total:". Add a short red line at the top of the section, above the calculated control. Next, add a red line with a 4-point border width below the controls in the section; extend the line from the left edge of the section to the 5-inch mark on the horizontal ruler. Reduce the height of the section to the row of grid dots below the line.

i. Add the Report Footer section, but not the Report Header section, to the report. Add a text box to the Report Footer section, enter the function to calculate the total of the BillTotal field values, format the calculated control as Standard, and then change the label caption to "Grand Total Bill Total:". Resize and reposition the controls in the Report Footer section. Add a red line with a 4-point border width below the controls in the section. Start the line at the left edge of the section and end it at the 5-inch mark on the horizontal ruler. See Figure 7-71.

**Figure 7-71**

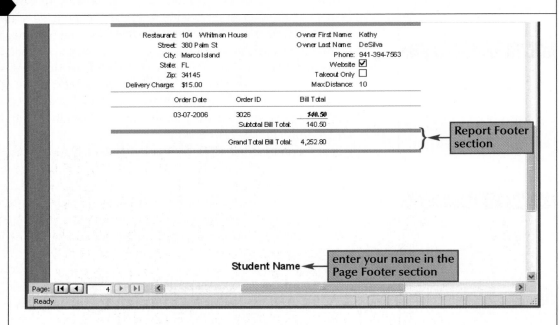

j. Enter your name in the top center of the Page Footer section with the same format you used for the report title.

4. Save your report design changes, switch to Print Preview, print the last page of the report, and then close the report.

5. Use the following instructions to create the mailing labels:

   a. Use the **Restaurant** table as the record source for the mailing labels.

   b. Use Avery C2160 labels, and use the default font and color. (*Hint*: Make sure the English option button is selected in the Unit of Measure section.)

   c. For the prototype label, place OwnerFirstName, a space, and OwnerLastName on the first line; RestaurantName on the second line; Street on the third line; and City, a space, State, a space, and Zip on the fourth line.

   d. Sort by Zip then by RestaurantName, and then type the report name **RestaurantLabels**.

   e. Select all controls in the Detail section, and then move them straight down until the top border of the top selected control is at the 0.75-inch mark on the vertical ruler.

   f. Add the **DineLogo** picture, located in the Intro\Case2 folder, to the upper-left corner of the Detail section.

   g. Save your report design changes, print the first page of the report, and then close the report.

6. Close the **Delivery** database, and then exit Access.

# Case Problem 3

**Data File needed for this Case Problem: Donors.mdb (*cont. from Tutorial 6*)**

***Redwood Zoo*** Michael Rosenfeld asks you to create a custom report for the Donors database so that he can better track pledges made by donors to the zoo's funds. You'll create the report by completing the following:

1. Open the **Donors** database in the Intro\Case3 folder provided with your Data Files.

2. Create a new query based on the **Donor** and **Pledge** tables. Select the FirstName and LastName fields from the **Donor** table; then select the FundCode, PledgeDate,

TotalPledged, and PaymentMethod fields from the **Pledge** table. Save the query as **DonorPledges**, and then close it.

3. Create a custom report based on the **Fund** table. Figure 7-72 shows the completed report. Refer to the figure as a guide as you complete Steps 4 through 8.

**Figure 7-72**

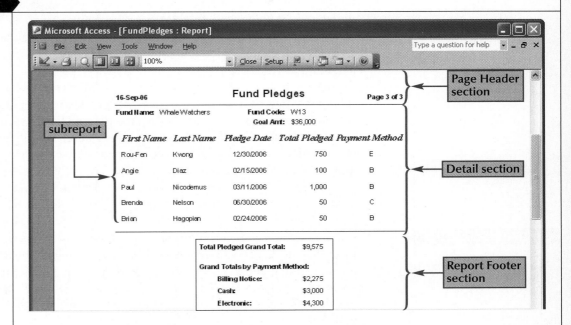

4. Use the **Fund** table as the record source for the main report.
5. Make the following modifications to the main report:
   a. Sort the report records in ascending order by the FundName field.
   b. At the top center of the Page Header section, enter the report title and format it with 13-point, Arial, bold font. Add the current date at the left edge of the section, change it to bold, and then set the Format property to Medium Date. Add the page number at the right edge of the section, using the "Page N of M" format for the page numbers, and then change it to bold. Add a line to the section below the controls. Extend the line from the left edge of the current date text box to the right edge of the page number text box. If necessary, reduce the height of the Page Header section to the bottom of the controls in the section.
   c. Type your name in the top center of the Page Footer section with the same format you used for the report title, and then save the report as **FundPledges**.
   d. Add the three fields from the **Fund** table to the Detail section. Make sure the labels are bold, and resize the labels to fit. Resize the text boxes, and reposition the labels and text boxes in the Detail section as shown in Figure 7-72.
6. Use the following instructions to add a subreport using Control Wizards to the Detail section:
   a. Select all fields from the **DonorPledges** query, link the main report and subreport using the FundCode field, and name the subreport **FundPledgesSubreport**.
   b. Open the subreport in a new window, and then delete the FundCode label and text box.
   c. Resize and reposition the labels and text boxes in the subreport as shown in Figure 7-72.

d. If necessary, reduce the subreport width until its right edge touches the right edge of the PaymentMethod controls.

e. Save the subreport design changes, and then close the subreport.

7. Make the following modifications to the main report:

a. Delete the subreport label.

b. By switching between Design view and Print Preview, reduce the width of the sub-report control in the Detail section from the right as much as possible.

c. Set the subreport border style to Transparent, and set its Can Shrink property to Yes.

d. To the Detail section below the subreport, add a line that's the same length as the line in the Page Header section.

e. Reduce the height of the Detail section to just below the line you drew below the subreport control, and then reduce the width of the main report as much as possible.

f. Add the Report Footer section, but not the Report Header section, to the main report. Add a text box to the Report Footer section, and then enter the DSum function to calculate the total of the TotalPledged field values from the **DonorPledges** query. Format the calculated control as Currency with zero decimal places, and then change the label caption's text to "Total Pledged Grand Total:" and its font to bold. Resize and reposition the two controls in the Report Footer section, as shown in Figure 7-72.

**Explore**

g. Add a label below the two controls in the Report Footer section, using the caption value "Grand Totals by Payment Method:" and changing the text to bold. Below the label in the Report Footer section, add three text boxes. For each text box, enter the DSum function to calculate the total of the TotalPledged field values from the **DonorPledges** query for each of the three PaymentMethod field values: B for a billing notice, C for cash, and E for electronic. (*Hint*: Use the same DSum function you used in Step 7f, but include the third optional *criteria* condition in the function. For example, use "PaymentMethod='B'" as the condition to calculate the total of the TotalPledged field values from billing notices as a payment method.) Set the captions for the three labels, format the text boxes as Currency with zero decimal places, and then resize and reposition the labels and text boxes.

**Explore**

h. Draw a rectangle around the controls in the Report Footer section, and then use the Send to Back option on the Format menu to position the rectangle.

i. If necessary, reduce the height of each section in the main report, and then reduce the width of the main report.

8. Save your report design changes, switch to Print Preview, print the first and last pages of the report, and then close the report.

9. Open the **Pledges** report in Design view, and make the following modifications to the report:

a. Reduce the height of the Report Header section to the bottom of the report title label.

b. Reduce the vertical space between lines in the Detail section to single spacing.

c. Center the DonorID field values.

d. Change the sorting options to sort in decreasing order on TotalPledged field values and then in decreasing order on NetPledge field values.

e. Add calculated controls to display NetPledge subtotals for each TotalPledged field value and NetPledge grand totals, formatting the controls as Currency. Add a single line above the calculated control in the Group Footer section, and add two lines above the calculated control in the Report Footer section.

f. Hide duplicate TotalPledged field values.

**Explore**

g. If the report doesn't fit on one page in Print Preview, modify the report design until it does.

h. Save your report design changes, print the report, and then close the report.

**Explore**

10. Create a copy of the Pledges report with the name **PledgesSummary**. Change the new report to a summary report, displaying the TotalPledged and subtotal values in the Group Footer section and the grand total value in the Report Footer section. Modify the report title, column headings, and other controls until the report has a professional look.
11. Close the **Donors** database, and then exit Access.

**Create**

*Use the skills you've learned in this tutorial to work with the data for an outdoor adventure company.*

# Case Problem 4

Data File needed for this Case Problem: Outdoors.mdb (*cont. from Tutorial 6*)

***Mountain River Adventures*** Connor and Siobhan Dempsey want you to create a custom report and mailing labels for the Outdoors database. You will create the custom report and the mailing labels by completing the following steps:

1. Start Access and then open the **Outdoors** database in the Intro\Case4 folder provided with your Data Files.
2. Create a new query based on the **RaftingTrip** and **Booking** tables. Select all fields from the **RaftingTrip** table, and select all fields except River from the **Booking** table. Add a calculated field named TripFee (Caption property value of Trip Fee) that multiplies the FeePerPerson and People fields; use the IIf function to reduce the TripFee by 10% if the People field value is greater than six. Set the calculated field's Format property to Standard. Save the query as **BookedRaftingTrips**, and then close it.
3. Complete Steps 4 through 8 to create a custom report based on the **Client** table, saving the report as **BookedTrips**.
4. Use the **Client** table as the record source for the main report.
5. Make the following modifications to the main report:
   a. Change the page orientation to landscape, and then change the width of the report to 7.5 inches.
   b. Sort the report records in ascending order by the ClientID field.
   c. At the top center of the Page Header section, enter the report title of Booked Trips, and format it with 12-point, Arial, bold font. Use the same format for the current date at the left edge of the section and for the page number at the right edge of the section. Add a black line with a 3-point border width to underline the controls in the Page Header section. Extend the line from the left edge of the section to approximately the 7.5-inch mark on the horizontal ruler. If necessary, reduce the height of the Page Header section to the bottom of the controls in the section.
   d. In the top center of the Page Footer section, type your name. Use the same format for your name that you used for the report title, and then save the report.
   e. Add the eight fields from the **Client** table to the Detail section. Move the ClientID, ClientName, Address, and City labels and text boxes in a column to the left. Move the StateProv, PostalCode, Country, and Phone labels and text boxes in a column to the right. Right-align the labels and left-align the text boxes.
6. Use the following instructions to add a subreport using Control Wizards to the Detail section:
   a. Select all fields from the **BookedRaftingTrips** query, link the main report and subreport using the ClientID field, and name the subreport **BookedTripsSubreport**.
   b. Open the subreport in a new window, and then delete the ClientID label and text box. Format the TripFee text box as Standard.

    c. Make sure the subreport page orientation is landscape, set its width to approximately 7.5 inches, and then resize and reposition its labels and text boxes. Switch between Print Preview and Design view to make sure that the labels and text boxes are aligned and that all field values are fully visible.

    d. Move all text boxes straight up to the top of the Detail section to eliminate all extra blank space above the text boxes, and then reduce the height of the Detail section until its bottom edge touches the bottom edges of the text boxes.

    e. Sort the subreport records in ascending order by the ClientID field, and then sort in ascending order by the TripDate field. Add a Group Footer section for the ClientID field, and set its Keep Together property to "Whole Group."

    f. Add a text box to the ClientID Footer section, enter the function to calculate the total of the TripFee field values, format the calculated control as Standard, and then change the label caption to "Subtotal Trip Fee:". At the top of the section, add a short black line above the calculated control; then below the controls in the section, add a black line with a 3-point border width that extends from the left edge of the section to the 7.5-inch mark on the horizontal ruler. Reduce the height of the section to the row of grid dots below the line.

    g. Save the subreport design changes, and then close the subreport.

7. Make the following modifications to the main report:

    a. Delete the subreport label.

    b. Change the width of the subreport control in the Detail section so that it extends from the left edge of the section to the 7.5-inch mark on the horizontal ruler.

    c. Set the subreport border style to Transparent, and set its Can Shrink property to Yes.

    d. Reduce the height of the Detail section to just below the subreport control.

    e. Add the Report Footer section, but not the Report Header section, to the main report. Add a text box to the Report Footer section, and then enter the DSum function to calculate the total of the TripFee field values from the **BookedRaftingTrips** query. Format the calculated control as Standard with two decimal places, and then change the label caption to "Grand Total Trip Fee:". Change the label font to 11-point Times New Roman, change its style to bold and italic, and change its color to blue. Resize and reposition the two controls in the Report Footer section so that the calculated control right-aligns with the subtotal amount.

**Explore**

    f. In the Report Footer section, add two text boxes below the text box you added in Step 7e. In the first text box that you have just added, use the DAvg function to calculate the average of the TripFee field values from the **BookedRaftingTrips** query. Format the DAvg text box as Standard with two decimal places. In the other text box, use the DCount function to calculate the total number of trips booked. (*Hints*: The DAvg and DCount functions use the same format as the DSum function. You can use the TripFee field for the DCount function.) Format the DCount text box as Standard with zero decimal places. Use the label captions "Average Trip Fee:" and "Total Trips:", and then change the labels to bold. Resize and reposition the labels and text boxes in the Report Footer section.

    g. If necessary, reduce the height of the Report Footer section in the main report.

8. Save your report design changes, switch to Print Preview, print the first and last pages of the report, and then close the report.

9. Open the **Costs** report in Design view, and make the following modifications to the report:

    a. Reduce the height of the Report Header section to the bottom of the report title label.

    b. Reduce the vertical space between lines in the Detail section to single spacing.

    c. Center the BookingID and People field values under their column headings.

d. Change the sorting options to sort in increasing order on River field values and then in decreasing order on TripCost field values.

e. Add calculated controls to display TripCost subtotals for each River field value and TripCost grand totals, formatting the controls as Currency. Add a single line above the calculated control in the Group Footer section, and add two lines above the calculated control in the Report Footer section.

f. Hide duplicate River field values.

**Explore**

g. If the report doesn't fit on one page in Print Preview, modify the report design until it does.

h. Save your report design changes, print the report, and then close the report.

10. Use the following instructions to create the mailing labels:

a. Use the **Client** table as the record source for the mailing labels.

b. Use Avery C2163 labels, with the default font and color settings. (*Hint*: Make sure the English option button is selected in the Unit of Measure section.)

c. For the prototype label, place ClientName on the first line; Address on the second line; City, a space, StateProv, a space, and PostalCode on the third line; and Country on the fourth line.

d. Sort by PostalCode and then by ClientName, and then enter the report name **ClientLabels**.

e. Change the column layout to "Down, then Across," print the first page of the report, and then save and close the report.

11. Close the **Outdoors** database, and then exit Access.

**Challenge**

*Work with the skills you've learned, and explore some new skills, to enhance a database for an Internet auction site.*

# Case Problem 5

**Data File needed for this Case Problem: eACH.mdb (*cont. from Tutorial 6*)**

*eACH Internet Auction Site* Chris and Pat Aquino want you to continue developing their Internet auction site for collectibles. Their auction site is now a proven success, with tens of thousands of bids placed daily. However, their costs have increased because they've had to install additional servers and high-speed communication lines to support the growing traffic at eACH. Income they earn from eACH offsets their costs—they charge a seller $2 to post an item plus an additional 3% of the item's final sale price. The number of items for sale varies dramatically each day, so Chris and Pat want you to design and then create a custom report to project income from the eACH database; the basis for the report will be a query you'll need to create. You will create the necessary query and report by completing the following steps:

1. Open the **eACH** database in the Intro\Case5 folder provided with your Data Files.

2. Create a select query based on all four tables in the database. Display the subcategory name from the **Subcategory** table; the category name from the **Category** table; the title from the **Item** table; the seller's last name and first name from the **Registrant** table; and the minimum bid from the **Item** table, in that order. Create a calculated field named ProjectedIncome that displays the results of adding $2 to 3% of the minimum bid. Format the calculated field as Standard with two decimal places. Sort the query in descending order by the ProjectedIncome field. Save the query as **ProjectedIncome**, run the query, resize all columns to their best fit, print the query in landscape orientation, and then save and close the query.

3. On a piece of paper, sketch the design for a custom report based on the **ProjectedIncome** query. The report must include at least the following features:
   a. A Page Header section that includes the report title, the current date, the page number, and column headings.
   b. A Group Header section that includes the subcategory name and category name, both sorted in ascending order.
   c. A Detail section that includes the title, seller's first name and last name, minimum bid, and ProjectedIncome field. (Hide duplicate values for the title.)
   d. A Group Footer section that includes an appropriate label and totals by subcategory for the minimum bid and ProjectedIncome field.
   e. A Report Footer section that includes an appropriate label and totals for the minimum bid and ProjectedIncome field.
4. Building on Step 3, create, test, and print the custom report. Save the report as **ProjectedIncomeBasedOnMinimumBid**. You might need to add records to your tables and modify existing records so that you have enough data and a sufficient level of variety to test your report features.
5. Close the **eACH** database, and then exit Access.

**Research**

*Use the Internet to find and work with data related to the topics presented in this tutorial.*

# Internet Assignments

The purpose of the Internet Assignments is to challenge you to find information on the Internet that you can use to work effectively with this software. The actual assignments are updated and maintained on the Course Technology Web site. Log on to the Internet and use your Web browser to go to the Student Online Companion for New Perspectives Office 2003 at **www.course.com/np/office2003**. Click the Internet Assignments link, and then navigate to the assignments for this tutorial.

**Assess**

## SAM Assessment and Training

If you have a SAM user profile, you may have access to hands-on instruction, practice, and assessment of the skills covered in this tutorial. Log in to your SAM account and go to your assignments page to see what your instructor has assigned.

**Review**

# Quick Check Answers

### Session 7.1

1. A custom report is a report you make by modifying a report created by AutoReport or the Report Wizard, or by creating a report from scratch in Design view.
2. The Report Header section appears once at the beginning of a report. The Page Header section appears at the top of each page of a report. The Group Header section appears once at the beginning of a new group of records. The Detail section appears once for each record in the underlying table or query. The Group Footer section appears once at the end of a group of records. The Report Footer section appears once at the end of a report. The Page Footer section appears at the bottom of each page of a report.
3. Hiding duplicate values makes a report easier to read; duplicate values clutter the report.
4. Report Footer section

## Session 7.2

1. A grouping field is a report sort field that includes a Group Header section before a group of records that has the same sort field value and that has a Group Footer section after the group of records.
2. subreport
3. IIf
4. Shift
5. Can Grow
6. Click a control, hold down the Shift key, click the other controls, release the Shift key, right-click a selected control, point to Align, and then click Right.

## Session 7.3

1. Can Shrink
2. Report Header and Detail sections; the heights of the Page Header, Page Footer, and Report Footer sections are set to zero
3. Visible
4. arrow
5. Group Footer
6. three
7. a recordset or set of records

## Session 7.4

1. =Date()
2. Click Insert on the menu bar; click Page Numbers; specify the format, position, and alignment of the page number; and then click the OK button.
3. Format Painter
4. detail
5. subreport
6. A multiple-column report prints the same collection of data in two or more sets across the page.

## Objectives

**Session 8.1**
- Export an Access table to an HTML document and view the document
- Use a wizard to create a data access page
- Update, sort, and filter a data access page using a Web browser
- Create a custom data access page

**Session 8.2**
- Create and use a PivotTable in a data access page
- Create and use a PivotChart in a data access page

**Session 8.3**
- Import and export XML files
- Export an Access query as an Excel worksheet
- Add a hyperlink field to an Access table
- Create hyperlinks to Office documents

# Integrating Access with the Web and with Other Programs

*Creating Web-Enabled and Integrated Information for the Jobs Database*

## Case

### Northeast Seasonal Jobs International (NSJI)

Elsa Jensen, Zack Ward, and Matt Griffin are pleased with the design and contents of the Jobs database. Their work has been made much easier because they are able to obtain the information they need from the database quickly. Matt feels that others in the company would benefit from gaining access to the Jobs database. Elsa asks Matt if he can make information in the database available to employees using the company network. That way, employees could obtain company information using their desktop and portable computers rather than using printouts and paper forms.

Zack mentions that most employees, such as the recruiters, do not need access to the entire database, nor should they be able to make changes to all the database objects. He proposes publishing the necessary Access data on the company's intranet, or internal network, as Web pages.

In this tutorial, you will use Access to make objects in the Jobs database available to employees on NSJI's internal network. You will also use Access to import and export XML files and integrate Access with other Office programs.

## Student Data Files

▼**Intro**

▽ **Tutorial folder**
Aidan.doc
Jobs.mdb *(cont.)*
Job.xml
NSJILogo.gif
NSJI-Tbl.htm
PearTree.doc

▽ **Case2 folder**
Choices.xml
Delivery.mdb *(cont.)*
Skillet.gif

▽ **Review folder**
NSJILogo.gif
NSJI-Tbl.htm
Students.mdb *(cont.)*

▽ **Case3 folder**
Donors.mdb *(cont.)*

▽ **Case5 folder**
eACH.mdb *(cont.)*
eACH-Rpt.htm
eACH-Tbl.htm

▽ **Case1 folder**
Clients.mdb *(cont.)*

▽ **Case4 folder**
Outdoors.mdb *(cont.)*

# Session 8.1

## Using the Web

The **Internet** is a worldwide collection of millions of interconnected computers and computer networks that share resources. The **World Wide Web** (or the **Web**) is a vast collection of digital documents available on the Internet. Each electronic document on the Web is called a **Web page**. A computer on which an individual or company stores Web pages for access on the Internet is called a **Web server**. Each Web page is assigned an Internet address called a **Uniform Resource Locator** (**URL**); the URL identifies where the Web page is stored—the location of both the Web server and the Web page on that server. For example, http://www.course.com/default.cfm is a URL that identifies the Web server (course.com) and the Web page (default.cfm) on that server. To view a Web page, you start a computer program called a **Web browser**, such as Microsoft Internet Explorer or Netscape Navigator. After you start the Web browser, you enter the Web page's URL. The Web browser uses the URL to find and retrieve the Web page, and then displays it on your computer screen.

Each Web page contains the necessary commands, called tags, for a Web browser to display the page's text and graphics. A **tag** describes how text is formatted, positions graphic images, or sets the document's background color or another visual characteristic of the Web page. A **hyperlink** is a tag that links one Web page to another or links to another location in the same Web page. When you click hyperlink text, the linked page opens. Hyperlinks connect Web pages throughout the Internet.

Most Web pages are created using a programming language called **HTML** (**HyperText Markup Language**). You can create a Web page by typing all the necessary HTML code into a text document, called an **HTML document**, and saving the document with the .htm or .html file extension. You can also use a program, such as Microsoft FrontPage, to create the HTML code for your Web pages without needing to learn HTML. Some programs, including Access, have built-in tools that convert objects to HTML documents for viewing on the Web.

When you use Access to create a Web page, the page can be either static or dynamic. A **static Web page** shows the state of a database object at the time the page was created. Any subsequent changes made to the database object, such as updates to field values in records, are not reflected in a static Web page. A **dynamic Web page** is updated automatically each time the page is viewed and therefore reflects the current state of the database object at that time. When you use a browser to open a Web page created from an Access database, you cannot make changes to the database using a static Web page, but you can change database data for certain types of dynamic Web pages. The type of Web page you create depends on how you want other users to be able to share and manipulate its information. In this tutorial, you'll work with both static and dynamic Web pages.

## Exporting an Access Query to an HTML Document

Matt asks you to create an HTML document for the EmployerPositions query. He wants this data to be available to the recruiters when they work outside the office to interview and screen students for available positions. The recruiters will access the company's intranet from laptop computers connected to telephone lines. The recruiters usually wait until they have completed all interviews for available positions before matching qualified applicants with appropriate jobs. For this reason, the recruiters only need to reference the available positions data, so Matt asks you to create a static Web page for the recruiters to use as a resource during the interview process.

Creating the necessary HTML document is not as difficult as it might appear at first. You will use the Export command on the shortcut menu, which automatically converts the selected database object to an HTML document.

Reference Window

## Exporting an Access Object to an HTML Document

- In the Database window, right-click the object (table, query, form, or report) you want to export, and then click Export on the shortcut menu.
- Enter the filename in the File name text box, and then select the location where you want to save the file.
- Click the Save as type list arrow, and then click HTML Documents.
- Click the Save formatted check box (if using a template), and then click the Export button.
- Select the template (if necessary), and then click the OK button.

To complete the following steps, you need to use Access and a Web browser. The steps in this tutorial are written for Internet Explorer, the Web browser used at NSJI. If you use Navigator or another browser, the steps you need to complete might be slightly different.

You'll export the EmployerPositions query as an HTML document.

### To export the EmployerPositions query as an HTML document:

1. Start Access, and then open the **Jobs** database located in the Intro\Tutorial folder provided with your Data Files.

2. Click **Queries** in the Objects bar of the Database window, right-click **EmployerPositions** to display the shortcut menu, and then click **Export**. The Export dialog box opens, displaying the type and name of the object you are exporting in its title bar—in this case, the EmployerPositions query.

   In this dialog box you specify the filename for the exported file and its type and location. You'll save the EmployerPositions query as an HTML document in the Intro\Tutorial folder.

3. Make sure the Save in list box displays the **Tutorial** folder.

4. Click the **Save as type** list arrow, and then scroll down the list and click **HTML Documents**. The query name is added to the File name text box automatically. See Figure 8-1.

**Figure 8-1** Export dialog box

folder to use to save the exported HTML document

option for saving the object as a datasheet

selected file type

default name for the HTML document

The Save formatted option lets you save the object formatted as a datasheet. If you do not choose this option, the object will appear without the field names as column headings. Matt wants the query saved in datasheet format.

▶ **5.** Click the **Save formatted** check box, and then click the **Export** button. The HTML Output Options dialog box opens.

This dialog box lets you specify an HTML template or use the default format when saving the object. An **HTML template** is a file that contains HTML instructions for creating a Web page with both text and graphics, together with special instructions that tell Access where to place the Access data on the Web page. Matt used a text-editing program to create an HTML template, named NSJI-Tbl, that you'll use. This template will automatically include the NSJI logo in all Web pages created with it. You need to locate Matt's template file in your Data Files.

▶ **6.** Make sure the **Select a HTML Template** check box is checked.

▶ **7.** If necessary, click the **Browse** button to open the HTML Template to Use dialog box, use the Look in list box to display the contents of the **Intro\Tutorial** folder, click **NSJI-Tbl**, and then click the **OK** button. Access closes the HTML Template to Use dialog box, returns to the HTML Output Options dialog box, and displays the location and filename for the HTML template. See Figure 8-2.

**Figure 8-2** HTML Output Options dialog box

your path to the NSJI-Tbl template might be different

data encoding options if you're not using a template

**Trouble?** If NSJI-Tbl does not appear in the Intro\Tutorial folder when you open the HTML Template to Use dialog box, click the Cancel button to return to the HTML Output Options dialog box so you can specify the template file manually. In the HTML Template text box, type the full path to the NSJI-Tbl.htm file in the Intro\Tutorial folder—for example, C:\Intro\Tutorial\NSJI-Tbl.htm.

▶ **8.** Click the **OK** button. The HTML Output Options dialog box closes, and the HTML document named EmployerPositions is saved in the Intro\Tutorial folder.

Now you can view the Web page.

# Viewing an HTML Document Using Internet Explorer

Matt asks to see the Web page you created. You can view the HTML document that you created using any Web browser. You'll view it using Internet Explorer.

---

### Viewing an HTML Document in a Web Browser

Reference Window

- If necessary, click View on the menu bar, point to Toolbars, and then click Web to display the Web toolbar.
- Click the Go button on the Web toolbar, and then click Open Hyperlink.
- Use the Browse button to select the file to open, and then click the Open button.
- Click the OK button.

---

You can now view the EmployerPositions query Web page.

### To view the EmployerPositions query Web page:

▶ **1.** If necessary, click **View** on the menu bar, point to **Toolbars**, and then click **Web**. Access displays the Web toolbar. See Figure 8-3.

**Displaying the Web toolbar** ◀ **Figure 8-3**

**Trouble?** If the Database and Web toolbars appear on the same line or the Web toolbar appears above the Database toolbar, drag the Web toolbar's move handle below the Database toolbar to the position shown in Figure 8-3.

▶ **2.** Click the **Go** button on the Web toolbar, and then click **Open Hyperlink**. Access opens the Open Internet Address dialog box, in which you can specify or browse for the URL of the Web page, or the path and filename of the HTML document, you want to view.

▶ **3.** Click the **Browse** button. Access opens the Browse dialog box.

▶ **4.** Make sure the Look in list box displays the **Tutorial** folder, click **EmployerPositions** in the list, and then click the **Open** button. The Browse dialog box closes, and the Address text box in the Open Internet Address dialog box now displays the path and filename for the EmployerPositions HTML document. See Figure 8-4.

| Figure 8-4 | Open Internet Address dialog box |
| --- | --- |

▶ **5.** Click the **OK** button. Internet Explorer starts and opens the EmployerPositions Web page. See Figure 8-5.

| Figure 8-5 | EmployerPositions query in the Internet Explorer window |
| --- | --- |

**Trouble?** If a dialog box opens and tells you that an unexpected error has occurred, click the OK button, click the Start button on the taskbar, point to Programs, click Internet Explorer, type the path to the EmployerPositions.html file in the Intro\Tutorial folder in the Address bar, and then press the Enter key.

**Trouble?** If another program opens, such as Microsoft Word, then Internet Explorer might not be installed on your computer. If the title bar on your screen displays "Microsoft Word," you can continue with the steps, but your screens will look different from those shown in the figures.

**Trouble?** If your computer has Navigator installed as its default browser, Navigator will start automatically and open the EmployerPositions Web page. If Navigator opens, your screens will look slightly different from those shown in the figures.

Changes that NSJI employees make to the Jobs database will not appear in the EmployerPositions Web page that you created because it is a static page—that is, it reflects the state of the EmployerPositions query in the Jobs database at the time you created it. If data in the EmployerPositions query changes, Matt will have to export the EmployerPositions Web page again.

Because this static Web page is not linked to the EmployerPositions query on which it is based, you cannot use your browser to make changes to its data. Before closing the EmployerPositions Web page, you'll try to change one of its field values.

### To attempt to change a field value, and then close the browser:

▶ **1.** Double-click **QC** in the State/Prov column for the first record (Auberge St-Germaine), and then type **NS**. The value of QC remains highlighted and unchanged, because the EmployerPositions Web page is a static page.

▶ **2.** Click the **Close** button ☒ on the Internet Explorer window title bar to close it and to return to the Database window.

▶ **3.** Click **View** on the menu bar, point to **Toolbars**, and then click **Web** to close the Web toolbar.

Matt asks if it's possible to create a dynamic Web page for the Position table that he and the recruiters can update using their browsers. To accomplish this task for Matt, you'll need to create a data access page.

# Creating a Data Access Page for an Access Table

A **data access page** (or simply a **page**) is a dynamic HTML document that you can open with a Web browser to view or update current data in an Access database. Unlike other database objects stored in an Access database, such as forms and reports, data access pages are stored outside the database as separate HTML documents. Like other database objects, however, a data access page also includes a page object in the Access database; this page object connects the HTML document with the bound fields in the database. This connection provides the dynamic element to the HTML document.

You can create a data access page either in Design view or by using a wizard. To create the data access page for the Position table, you'll use the Page Wizard.

### To create the data access page using the Page Wizard:

1. Click **Pages** in the Objects bar of the Database window to display the Pages list. The Pages list box does not contain any data access pages.

2. Click the **New** button in the Database window to open the New Data Access Page dialog box. This dialog box is similar to the ones you've used to create tables, queries, forms, and reports.

3. Click **Page Wizard** to select this wizard, click the list arrow for choosing the table or query on which to base the page, scroll down and click **Position**, and then click the **OK** button. The first Page Wizard dialog box opens, in which you select the fields you want to display in the data access page. You'll include all of the fields from the Position table.

   **Trouble?** If a message box opens to warn you that you won't be able to open the page in Design view in Access 2000, click the OK button. Although the Jobs database uses the Access 2000 file format, certain features, such as modifying a data access page's design, work in Access 2003 but not in Access 2000.

4. Click the >> button to select all of the fields from the Position table, and then click the **Next** button to open the next Page Wizard dialog box, in which you select the grouping levels for the data access page. See Figure 8-6.

| Figure 8-6 | Selecting grouping levels for a data access page |
| --- | --- |

The wizard selected the EmployerID field for a grouping level. Matt doesn't need any grouping levels for this data access page, so you'll delete the EmployerID field grouping level.

5. Click the **EmployerID** field on the right side of the dialog box, click the < button to delete the EmployerID grouping level and to place the field with the other Position table fields, and then click the **Next** button. In the Page Wizard dialog box, you select the sort fields for the data access page. Matt wants the records sorted in ascending order by the EmployerID field, and then in ascending order by the PositionTitle field.

6. Select the **EmployerID** field as the primary sort field and the **PositionTitle** field as the secondary sort field, and then click the **Next** button to open the last Page Wizard dialog box, in which you enter a name for the data access page. You'll use the default name, and then open the data access page in Access.

7. Click the **Open the page** option button, and then click the **Finish** button. Access opens the data access page in Page view. See Figure 8-7.

**Data access page created by the Page Wizard** | Figure 8-7

first record from
the Position table

record navigation
toolbar

This data access page, which has an appearance similar to a form, displays a record's field values one at a time from the Position table. The **record navigation toolbar**, which appears below the record, lets you move between records in the table, add and delete records, edit and undo entries, sort and filter data, and request Help. ScreenTips for each button on the record navigation toolbar appear if you position the pointer on a button, and 11 of the 13 buttons are familiar because you've seen them on other Access toolbars. The Save button 🔲 and the Undo button 🔄 are the two new buttons on the record navigation toolbar.

Matt wants to make sure that he can update the Position table using the data access page that you created. You can use a data access page to update data in Page view or with a Web browser, so you'll show Matt how to use both update methods. First, you'll save the data access page, and then you'll update a field value in Page view.

**To save the data access page, and then update a Position table field value in Page view:**

1. Click the **Save** button 🔲 on the Page View toolbar. The Save As Data Access Page dialog box opens. You'll save the data access page using the default name (Position) and type (Microsoft Data Access Pages).

2. Make sure the Save in list box displays the **Tutorial** folder, and then click the **Save** button. Unless it has been disabled, a message box opens to warn you that the page's connection string is an absolute path. See Figure 8-8.

**Connection string warning** | Figure 8-8

leave this
option
unchecked

**Trouble?** If the message box doesn't open, a previous user has disabled it. Continue with Step 4.

The **connection string** is a string, or text, expression that specifies the disk location and the database name used to connect a page to an Access database. When you specify a particular file on a specific disk drive, you provide what is called an **absolute path**. For example, if your Intro\Tutorial folder is located on drive C when you save the Position page, C:\Intro\Tutorial\Jobs.mdb would be the connection string expressed as an absolute path. If you want others to use the page, you must make sure the disk drive specified in the absolute path represents a Web server or network drive that others can access. After saving the page, if you want to change the connection string to a different disk drive, switch to Design view, right-click the data access page title bar, click Page Properties on the shortcut menu, click the Data tab, click the ConnectionString text box, click its Build button, click the Connection tab, modify the absolute path in the first text box, and then click the OK button.

You won't be changing the connection string because Matt won't be moving the Jobs database to NSJI's Web server until after you've completed all your work with it. Also, it's a good idea to view the message box every time you create a page as a reminder that you need to update the connection string if you move the database, so you'll leave the "Don't show this warning again" check box unchecked.

▶ 3. Make sure the **Don't show this warning again** check box is unchecked, and then click the **OK** button to save the page with the default name and type.

Next, you'll show Matt how to update position data on the page.

▶ 4. Double-click **40** in the Hours/Week text box, type **35**, and then press the **Tab** key. The value of the HoursPerWeek field is now 35. Note that several buttons on the record navigation toolbar changed from dimmed to active.

Next, you'll close the page.

▶ 5. Click the **Close** button ☒ on the Position window title bar. A message opens and warns you that your change to the HoursPerWeek field will be discarded because you didn't save it. You can save changes to a record automatically by navigating to another record or by clicking the Save button on the record navigation toolbar. You'll cancel the message, and then save your change.

▶ 6. Click the **Cancel** button, and then click the **Save** button 🖫 on the record navigation toolbar. Your change to the record is saved in the database, and the Save button and other buttons on the record navigation toolbar change from active to dimmed.

You've completed working in Page view, so you can close the page.

▶ 7. Click the **Close** button ☒ on the Position window title bar. The page closes, and you return to the Database window. Notice that the Position page is listed in the Pages list box.

Next, you'll view the page with your browser. Then you'll show Matt how to update data on a page using a browser; you'll change the HoursPerWeek field value for the first position for EmployerID 10122 back to 40.

# Updating Data in a Data Access Page Using Internet Explorer

You can view a data access page and update its data using Internet Explorer 5.0 or higher and Windows 2000 with Service Pack 3 or higher.

## Viewing and Updating Data in a Page Using Internet Explorer

- If necessary, click Pages in the Objects bar of the Database window.
- Right-click the data access page name, and then click Web Page Preview to start Internet Explorer and open the data access page.
- If changing an existing record, navigate to the desired record, make changes to the record, and then click the Save button on the record navigation toolbar.
- If deleting an existing record, navigate to the desired record, click the Delete button on the record navigation toolbar, and then click the Save button on the record navigation toolbar.
- If adding a record, click the New button on the record navigation toolbar, enter the field values for the record, and then click the Save button on the record navigation toolbar.

You can now view and update data in the page using Internet Explorer.

### To view and update data in the page using Internet Explorer:

1. Right-click **Position** in the Pages list box, and then click **Web Page Preview** to start Internet Explorer and open the Position page. See Figure 8-9.

    **Trouble?** If an Internet Explorer dialog box opens and indicates that the Position page is unavailable offline, click the OK button to close the dialog box. In Internet Explorer, click File on the menu bar, and then click Work Offline. You do not need an Internet connection to complete these steps.

**Page in the Internet Explorer window** ◀ **Figure 8-9**

You'll change the Hours/Week field value for position 2082 back to 40.

2. Double-click **35** in the Hours/Week text box, type **40**, press the **Tab** key, and then click the **Save** button 📑 on the record navigation toolbar. The value of the HoursPerWeek field is changed to 40 in the database.

Matt asks about the other buttons on the record navigation toolbar. Next, you'll show him how to sort and filter records using a data access page.

# Using a Data Access Page to Sort and Filter Records

The buttons on the record navigation toolbar for sorting and filtering data work the same for data access pages as they do for forms. You'll show Matt how to sort and filter records using a data access page based on a value in the StartDate field.

### To use a data access page to sort and filter records:

1. Click the **Start Date** text box, and then click the **Sort Descending** button [⤵] on the record navigation toolbar. Access rearranges the records in descending order by start date—records for 12/15/2006 appear first, followed by records for 12/01/2006, and so on.

   Next, you'll filter records, selecting just the records for those positions with a 12/15/2006 start date.

2. Click the **Start Date** text box, and then click the **Filter by Selection** button [▽] on the record navigation toolbar. Access filters the position records, displaying the first of four records having a start date field value of 12/15/2006. See Figure 8-10.

**Figure 8-10** | Using filter by selection in a data access page

Next you'll redisplay all the position records by clicking the Filter Toggle Button button.

3. Click the **Filter Toggle Button** button [▽] on the record navigation toolbar. Access makes all 64 records from the Position table available on the page.

4. Click the **Close** button [✕] on the Internet Explorer window title bar to close it and return to the Database window.

When visiting employers, the recruiters frequently require access to current information about employers and their positions at the same time. Elsa asks if it's possible to create a data access page that the recruiters can use to view and update current Jobs database information about employers and their positions. To do this, you'll create a custom data access page in Design view.

# Creating a Custom Data Access Page

Because of its connection to the database object on which it is based, every data access page is a dynamic HTML document. When you open a data access page, you are viewing current data from the source Access database. To create a data access page that recruiters can use to view and update data, you'll create a data access page that includes data selected from the Employer table and from the related Position table.

Just as with forms and reports, you could use a wizard to create a basic data access page and then customize it in Design view, or you could create a data access page from scratch in Design view. To create the data access page with the employer and position information for Elsa and the recruiters, you'll create the entire data access page in Design view.

## Creating a Blank Data Access Page in Design View

You use the Page window in Design view to create and modify data access pages. Similar to Design view for forms and reports, you select the fields for a data access page in Design view from the field list. Unlike previous field lists, which contain only the fields from the source table or query, the field list in the Page window contains all fields from the database. Thus, you don't need to select a source table or query for a data access page before opening the Page window in Design view. To create Elsa's data access page, you'll create a blank data access page and then add fields and controls to it.

---

**Creating a Data Access Page in Design View**                    Reference Window

- If necessary, click Pages in the Objects bar of the Database window to display the Pages list.
- Click the New button to open the New Data Access Page dialog box, click Design View (if necessary), click the OK button, and then if necessary click the OK button to close the warning message and to create a blank data access page.
- Place the necessary controls in the Page window in Design view. Modify the size, position, and other properties of the controls as necessary.
- Click the Save button on the Page Design toolbar, enter a name for the data access page, select a location for the data access page, and then click the Save button.

---

To create the data access page, you'll first create a blank data access page in the Page window in Design view.

### To create a blank data access page in Design view:

1. Maximize the Database window, and then click the **New** button in the Database window. The New Data Access Page dialog box opens.

2. Click **Design View** in the list box (if necessary), click the **OK** button, and then (if necessary) click the **OK** button if you're warned about the Access 2000 Design view issue. Access displays the Page window in Design view. See Figure 8-11.

| Figure 8-11 | Page window in Design view |
|---|---|

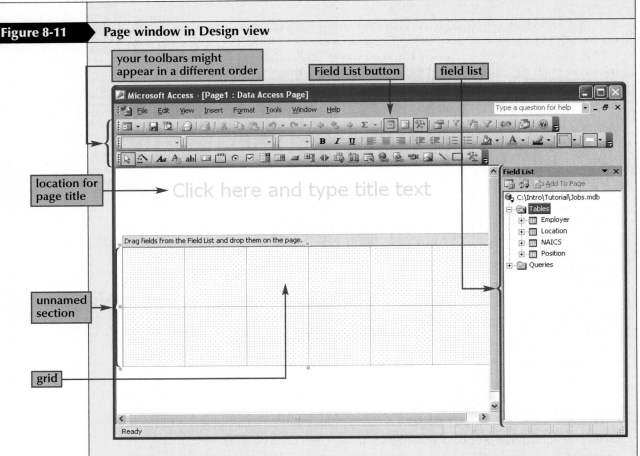

**Trouble?** If the grid or toolbox do not appear, click View on the menu bar, and then click Grid or Toolbox to display the missing component. If the grid is still invisible, ask your instructor or technical support person for assistance. If necessary, drag the toolbox to dock it below the Formatting toolbar.

**Trouble?** If the field list is not displayed, click the Field List button on the Page Design toolbar.

The Page window in Design view has many of the same components as the Form and Report windows in Design view. For example, these windows include a Formatting toolbar, a grid, a Properties button, a Field List button, and a Toolbox button.

Unlike the Form and Report windows in Design view, however, the Page window initially contains only one unnamed section, which is named after you place controls in it, and placeholder text for the title of your data access page. Also, the Field List window, which is also called the field list, contains all of the tables and queries in the database; you can select fields from one or more tables and queries to include in the data access page.

## Adding Fields to a Data Access Page

Because Elsa wants to see employers and their positions, your first task is to use the field list to add fields from the Employer table to the grid.

### To add fields to the grid from the field list for the Employer table:

▶ **1.** Click ⊞ next to Employer in the field list. The fields from the Employer table and a folder for related tables are now visible in the field list. See Figure 8-12.

**Fields and Related Tables folder for the Employer table** ◀ **Figure 8-12**

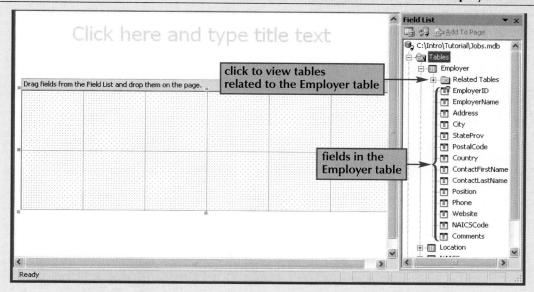

Elsa wants you to include only the EmployerName, City, and StateProv fields from the Employer table in the page.

▶ **2.** Double-click **EmployerName** in the field list. Access adds a bound control for the EmployerName field to the grid. The bound control consists of a text box and an attached label, similar to the bound controls you've used previously for forms and reports. Notice that the section name has changed to Header: Employer, which is referred to as the Employer Header section. Below the Employer Header section, Access adds the Employer Navigation section, which contains the record navigation toolbar.

▶ **3.** Repeat Step 2 to select the **City** and **StateProv** fields, in that order.

Elsa wants you to include the PositionTitle, Wage, HoursPerWeek, and Openings fields from the Position table on the page. To display the fields in the Position table, you'll expand the Employer table's Related Tables entry in the field list, which will display the Location, NAICS, and Position tables, and then expand the Position table. (If you had first selected fields from the Position table instead of from the Employer table, you would have expanded the Position table at the bottom of the field list.)

### To add fields to the grid from the field list for the Position table:

1. Click ⊞ next to Related Tables in the field list, and then click ⊞ next to Position in the field list. The Location, NAICS, and Position tables, which are related to the Employer table, are now visible in the field list, as are the fields from the Position table.

2. Click **PositionTitle** in the field list, press and hold the **Ctrl** key, click **Wage**, **HoursPerWeek**, and **Openings** in the field list, and then release the **Ctrl** key. All four fields are selected.

3. Drag the selected Position table fields from the field list to the bottom of the Employer Header section so that the text "Create new section below Employer" appears within a rectangle with a blue border. See Figure 8-13.

**Figure 8-13** | **Adding selected Position table fields to the grid**

4. Release the mouse button to open the Layout Wizard dialog box, in which you can choose a columnar or tabular layout for the new Position section, click the **Tabular** option button, click the **OK** button, and then scroll down the Page window. The four fields from the Position table are added to the grid in a new Position Header section, a new Position Navigation section is added above the Employer Navigation section, and a Position Caption section is added above the Position Header section. See Figure 8-14.

**Trouble?** If the Layout Wizard doesn't open and the four fields and their labels are added to the Position Header section, click the Position Header list arrow; click Caption; drag the four labels individually to the positions in the Position Caption section shown in Figure 8-14; decrease the height of the Position Caption section; drag the four text boxes individually to the positions in the Position Header section shown in Figure 8-14 (moving a text box also moves its label, so you'll need to select and move the labels back into position); decrease the height of the Position Header section; click the Position Title label, click it again, delete the colon; and then delete the colons at the end of the other three labels.

**Page after adding all required fields to the grid** | **Figure 8-14**

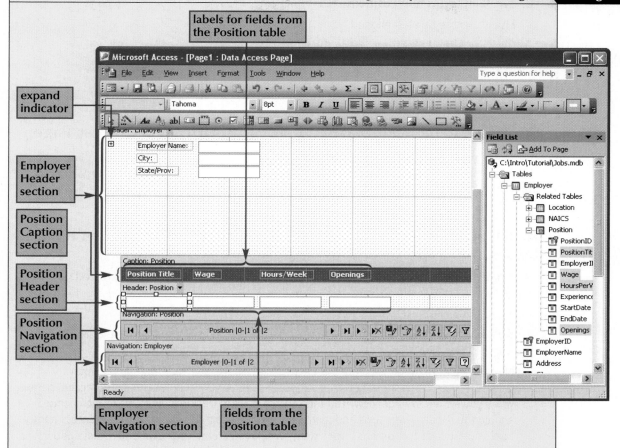

You're done with the field list, so you can close it.

▶ **5.** Click the **Close** button ✖ on the Field List window to close it, and then scroll to the top of the Page window.

Notice that an expand indicator ⊞ appears to the left of the Employer Name label in the Employer Header section. When you view the page in Page view or with a browser, the Employer Header and Employer Navigation sections will be displayed, but the Position Caption, Position Header, and Position Navigation sections will be hidden. Each employer record has an expand indicator, and clicking this control opens a section below the employer record that contains the position data for that employer. At the same time, the ⊞ changes to ⊟, which you can click to collapse (hide) the employer's positions. The expand indicators (⊞ and ⊟) provide the same features as the expand indicators you used with subdatasheets in Tutorial 5.

Next, you'll add a title to the page above the Employer Header section.

### To add a title to the page:

1. Click anywhere in the **Click here and type title text** placeholder at the top of the page. The text disappears and is replaced by a large insertion point.

2. Type **Employers and Positions**. Your typed entry becomes the title for the page.

   Elsa wants the title left aligned.

3. Click the **Align Left** button 🖺 on the Formatting toolbar.

Next, you'll modify the controls in the Employer Header section.

## Deleting, Moving, and Resizing Controls in a Data Access Page

Elsa wants you to delete the labels and to move and resize the text boxes in the Employer Header section. She feels that the field values without labels are self-explanatory, and she'd prefer to view the data for as many employers as possible at one time.

### To delete the labels, and then move and resize the text boxes in the Employer Header section:

1. Right-click the **Employer Name label** in the Employer Header section, and then click **Cut** on the shortcut menu to delete the label.

2. Repeat Step 1 to delete the **City label** and the **State/Prov label**.

   **Trouble?** If the Clipboard task pane opens, click the **Close** button ⊠ on the task pane to close it.

   Next, you'll move and resize the three text boxes. You usually identify some design changes, such as resizing text boxes to best fit the data they contain, in a data access page when you switch to Page view. You then switch back to Design view to make the changes, and continue changing views and identifying and making changes to the data access page until you are satisfied with its appearance. When you create your own data access pages, you will need to use Page view and Design view to identify changes you need to make to increase the effectiveness of the data access page.

3. Click the **EmployerName** text box (the top text box), and then use the 🖐 pointer to drag the text box into position, as shown in See Figure 8-15.

4. Use the ↔ pointer on the middle-right sizing handle to resize the **EmployerName** text box, as shown in Figure 8-15.

5. Repeat Step 3 for the two remaining text boxes, repeat Step 4 to reduce the width of the StateProv text box, and then click an empty area of the Employer Header section. See Figure 8-15.

After deleting labels and moving and resizing text boxes | **Figure 8-15**

Next, you'll finish your changes to the Employer Header section by reducing the section's height and applying a special effect to the text boxes.

## Resizing a Section and Applying a Special Effect

Elsa prefers a different special effect for the three text boxes in the Employer Header section. She also asks you to reduce the height of the section.

**To resize the Employer Header section, and then change the special effects for the text boxes:**

1. Position the pointer on the middle-bottom sizing handle of the Employer Header section; when the pointer changes to a ↕ shape, drag the bottom up until it's just below the text boxes. See Figure 8-16.

**Figure 8-16** After resizing the Employer Header section

Next, you'll change the special effect for each of the text boxes.

▶ **2.** Click the **EmployerName** text box (the leftmost text box in the Employer Header section), click the list arrow for the **Special Effect: None** button 🔲 on the Formatting toolbar, and then click the **Special Effect: Etched** button 🔲. The etched special effect is applied to the EmployerName text box.

▶ **3.** Click the **City** text box (the middle text box in the Employer Header section), and then click the **Special Effect: Etched** button 🔲 on the Formatting toolbar. The etched special effect is applied to the City text box.

▶ **4.** Repeat Step 3 for the **StateProv** text box.

You've made many changes to the page, so you'll save it.

▶ **5.** Click the **Save** button 🔲 on the Page Design toolbar. The Save As Data Access Page dialog box opens.

▶ **6.** Type **EmployersAndPositions** in the File name text box.

▶ **7.** If necessary, use the Save in list box to display the **Tutorial** folder, click the **Save** button, and then if necessary click the **OK** button in the message box that warns you about the connection string being an absolute path. Access saves the data access page as EmployersAndPositions in the Intro\Tutorial folder.

Elsa asks if you can change the number of employer records displayed on the page in Page view. The **DataPageSize property** specifies the number of records displayed in a data access page for a group. The default value is 10 for a grouped data access page and one for a non-grouped data access page. A **grouped data access page** uses two or more group levels to display information from general categories to specific details. For the EmployersAndPositions page, the first group level is data from the Employer table, and the second group level is data from the Position table. Data from the Employer table represents the general category, and data from the Position table represents the specific details.

Elsa asks you to increase the number of displayed employer records from 10 to 12.

## To set the DataPageSize property for the Employer Header section:

▶ **1.** Click the **Employer Header section** list arrow (see Figure 8-16), and then click **Group Level Properties** on the shortcut menu to open the property sheet for the Employer Header section group.

▶ **2.** Select the value in the DataPageSize text box, and then type **12**. Access will display 12 employers on each page. See Figure 8-17.

Property sheet for the Employer Header section  Figure 8-17

**3.** Close the property sheet.

Elsa is pleased with the data access page that you have created. She asks if there's a way to format the page to have a more interesting and professional appearance. Next, you'll select a theme for the page.

## Selecting a Theme

Before viewing the completed form, Elsa wants to know if you can easily change the overall style of the page. You can select a theme to add visual interest to the page. A **theme** is a collection of formats that determines the appearance of the controls, sections, body, and text in a data access page.

### To select a theme for a page:

**1.** Click **Format** on the menu bar, and then click **Theme**. The Theme dialog box opens. See Figure 8-18.

Theme dialog box  Figure 8-18

**Trouble?** If a dialog box opens and tells you that the Theme feature is not currently installed, insert your Microsoft Office 2003 CD in the correct drive, and then click the OK button. If you do not have an Office 2003 CD, ask your instructor or technical support person for help.

A sample of the default theme, the selected "(No Theme)" in the Choose a Theme list box, appears in the box on the right.

▶ 2. Click several of the styles in the Choose a Theme list box, and view the corresponding sample.

**Trouble?** If one of the themes you select displays an Install button instead of a sample, choose another theme from the list box.

▶ 3. Click **Axis** in the Choose a Theme list box, and then click the **OK** button. The selected theme is applied to the page.

**Trouble?** If an Install button appears in the sample box for the Axis theme, choose another theme that's already installed on your system.

The text in the four label controls in the Position Caption section is too large, so you'll change the font size and size the controls to fit.

▶ 4. Select the four controls in the Position Caption section, change their font size to **8**, click **Format** on the menu bar, point to **Size**, and then click **To Fit**.

Next, you'll change the font size for the three controls in the Employer Header section and the four controls in the Position Header section to match the font size in the Position Caption section.

▶ 5. Select the three controls in the Employer Header section, change their font size to **8**, select the four controls in the Position Header section, and then change their font size to **8**.

Next, you'll save your design changes and view the completed page.

## Saving and Viewing a Data Access Page

Elsa wants to view and update the completed data access page, but first you'll save the changes you made to it.

### To save, view, and update the completed page:

▶ 1. Save your design changes, and then click the **Close Window** button ⊠ on the Page Design window menu bar. The page closes, and you return to the Database window. Notice that the EmployersAndPositions page is listed in the Pages list box.

**Trouble?** If a dialog box opens warning you that one or more supporting files are missing, click the OK button, click Format on the menu bar, click Theme, click Axis (or the theme you previously chose, if the Axis theme wasn't available on your computer), click the OK button, save your design changes, and then click the Close Window button on the Page Design window menu bar.

▶ 2. Right-click **EmployersAndPositions** in the Pages list box, and then click **Web Page Preview**. Internet Explorer starts and opens the EmployersAndPositions page. See Figure 8-19.

Completed data access page | Figure 8-19

Next, you will show Elsa how to view an employer's position records.

3. Click the **expand indicator** ⊞ to the left of Beantown Tours (the first record). The two positions for Beantown Tours are displayed between Beantown Tours and the next employer record, the record navigation toolbar for positions appears, and the expand indicator changes to ⊟. See Figure 8-20.

Displaying the positions for Beantown Tours | Figure 8-20

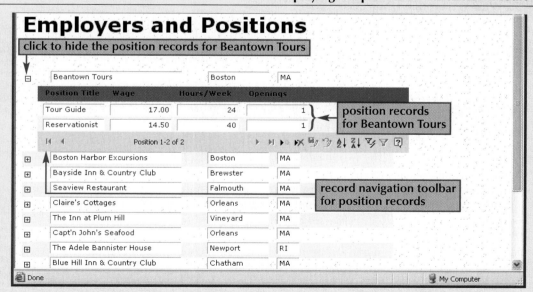

Elsa recently heard from Beantown Tours that they now have two Tour Guide openings, so you'll change the Openings field value for the first position record from 1 to 2.

▶ 4. Double-click **1** in the Openings column for the first position record (Tour Guide), type **2**, and then click the **Save** button 🖫 on the record navigation toolbar. The value of the Openings field is changed to 2 in the Jobs database.

▶ 5. Click the **expand indicator** ⊟ to the left of Beantown Tours. The two positions for Beantown Tours and the record navigation toolbar for positions are no longer displayed, and the expand indicator changes back to ⊞.

▶ 6. Use the navigation buttons (First, Previous, Next, and Last) to navigate through the pages.

You've completed your work with the EmployersAndPositions page, so you can close it.

▶ 7. Click the **Close** button ☒ on the Internet Explorer window title bar. Internet Explorer closes, and you return to the Database window.

▶ 8. If you are not continuing on to the next session, close the Jobs database, and then exit Access.

Elsa is pleased with the HTML documents and the data access pages that you created. Your work will make it easy to distribute important Jobs database information on the company's intranet. In the next session, you will continue working with data access pages to enhance the database further.

## Review

# Session 8.1 Quick Check

1. What is the World Wide Web, and what do you use to view the information it provides?
2. What is a hyperlink?
3. What is HTML?
4. What is an HTML template?
5. Explain the difference between a static Web page and a data access page.
6. A(n) _____ string is a string, or text, expression that specifies the disk location and database name used to connect a data access page to an Access database.
7. What is a grouped data access page?
8. What is a theme?

# Session 8.2

# Creating and Using a PivotTable in a Data Access Page

Elsa would like to extend the use of Web pages for the Jobs database. In particular, she wants to be able to use Web pages to analyze her business in a flexible way. You can use PivotTables in data access pages to provide the flexible analysis that Elsa needs. When used in a data access page, a **PivotTable**, also called a **PivotTable list**, is an interactive table that lets you analyze data dynamically using a Web browser. You can use a PivotTable in a data access page to view and organize data from a database, look for summary or detail information, and dynamically change the contents and organization of the table. Figure 8-21 shows a PivotTable in a data access page.

PivotTable in a data access page | **Figure 8-21**

A PivotTable contains the following basic components:

- The **PivotTable toolbar** lets you perform actions such as sorting and filtering when viewing and using a PivotTable.
- The **detail area**, consisting of a **detail field** and **detail values**, provides details or totals from a database. In Figure 8-21, the detail field is the Openings field from the Position table, and the detail values are the Openings field values.
- The **row area**, consisting of a **row field** and **row field items**, provides row groupings in the PivotTable. In Figure 8-21, the row field is the PositionTitle field from the Position table, and the row field items are the PositionTitle field values.
- The **column area**, consisting of a **column field** and **column field items**, provides column groupings in the PivotTable. In Figure 8-21, the column field is the StateProv field from the Employer table, and the column field items are the StateProv field values.
- The **filter area**, consisting of a **filter field** and **filter field items**, lets you restrict which data appears in the PivotTable. In Figure 8-21, the filter field is the Country field from the Employer table, and the filter field item is "Canada"—only Canadian provinces appear in the PivotTable.
- All the PivotTable areas—detail area, row area, column area, and filter area—can have multiple fields with associated field items.

When you use PivotTables in data access pages, you are not using Access 2003 features. Instead, the PivotTable uses the **Office PivotTable Component**, one of the **Office Web Components** that are part of Office 2003. Therefore, PivotTables can be used with other programs, such as Excel and FrontPage. You can also use PivotTables with Access forms and with Access table and query datasheets; the PivotTable view with these Access objects provides this capability.

## Adding a PivotTable to a Data Access Page

Matt and the recruiters have been very successful finding overseas students interested in the seasonal jobs NSJI brokers. To place all these students, Elsa and Zack need to find more employers with seasonal jobs. To help them determine which positions are popular and where they are popular, Elsa wants to analyze position openings by location (state/province) and by position title. You'll create a PivotTable in a data access page to let her perform this analysis.

Reference Window

### Adding a PivotTable to a Data Access Page

- If necessary, click Pages in the Objects bar of the Database window to display the Pages list.
- Click the New button to open the New Data Access Page dialog box, click Design View (if necessary), click the OK button, and then if necessary click the OK button to close the warning message and to create a blank data access page.
- Click the Office PivotTable tool on the toolbox, and then click the mouse button in the location on the page where you want to position the upper-left corner of the PivotTable.
- Use the fields from the field list to drag and drop the filter, row, column, and detail fields in the PivotTable. Add calculated and total fields to the PivotTable as needed.
- Modify the size of the PivotTable, and modify the size and other properties of the controls in the PivotTable.
- Click the Save button on the Page Design toolbar, enter a name for the data access page, select a location for the data access page, and then click the Save button.

You'll first create a blank data access page and add a PivotTable to the page.

### To create a PivotTable on a data access page:

1. If you took a break after the previous session, make sure that Access is running, that the **Jobs** database in the Intro\Tutorial folder is open, that **Pages** is selected in the Objects bar of the Database window, and that the Database window is maximized.

2. Click the **New** button in the Database window to open the New Data Access Page dialog box, click **Design View** in the list box (if necessary), click the **OK** button, and then if necessary click the **OK** button if you're warned about the Access 2000 Design view issue.

   You'll use the Office PivotTable tool on the toolbox to add a PivotTable control to the page.

3. Click the **Office PivotTable** tool 🔲 on the toolbox. The pointer changes to a ⁺🖳 shape when you move it over the data access page.

4. Move the pointer to the grid, and when the center of the pointer's plus symbol (+) is positioned on the grid dot in the upper-left corner, click the mouse button. Access adds a PivotTable control to the page and opens the field list. See Figure 8-22.

**After adding a PivotTable control to the page** | Figure 8-22

**Trouble?** If your PivotTable control doesn't contain drop areas (see Figure 8-22) or looks different from the PivotTable control in Figure 8-22, right-click the PivotTable control, click Commands and Options on the shortcut menu, click the Behavior tab, made sure the Expand indicator check box is checked, make sure the Drop areas check box is checked, make sure the Title bar check box is checked, make sure the Toolbar check box is checked, and then close the Commands and Options dialog box.

If you do not select a table or query as the basis for a page when you create a new page in Design view, the message "The query could not be processed: The "" object can not be found." appears inside the PivotTable control. After you add fields to the PivotTable, the message will disappear.

## Adding Fields to a PivotTable

For Elsa's analysis, she needs the Country and StateProv fields from the primary Employer table and the PositionTitle and Openings fields from the related Position table. Within the PivotTable, the Country field will be the filter field, the StateProv field will be the column field, the PositionTitle field will be the row field, and the Openings field will be the detail field.

First, you'll expand the Employer table in the field list to display its fields, and then you'll add the required fields from the field list to the PivotTable.

### To add fields to a PivotTable:

1. Click ⊞ next to Employer in the field list to display the fields from the Employer table and a folder for related tables.

2. Drag the **Country** field from the field list to the "Drop Filter Fields Here" section on the PivotTable so that the section's border color changes to blue. See Figure 8-23.

**Figure 8-23** | Adding the Country field as the filter field

**3.** Release the mouse button. A control for the Country field now appears in the filter section of the PivotTable. "All" below the Country field indicates that all country values will appear in the PivotTable—that is, no filter is currently applied. (See Figure 8-24.)

**Trouble?** If you move the wrong field to a PivotTable section or move a field to the wrong PivotTable section, right-click the field name in the PivotTable, click Remove Field on the shortcut menu, and then drag and drop the correct field to the correct section.

Next, you'll specify the StateProv field as the column field.

**4.** Drag the **StateProv** field from the field list to the "Drop Column Fields Here" section on the PivotTable so that the section's border color changes to blue, and then release the mouse button. A control for the StateProv field now appears in the column section of the PivotTable. The StateProv field is the column field, and its field values (CT, MA, and so on) are the column field items. See Figure 8-24.

**Figure 8-24** | After adding the Country and StateProv fields to the PivotTable

After adding the filter and column fields to the PivotTable, you no longer can see the drop areas for the row area and detail area, so you need to increase the PivotTable control's height and width. The border of the PivotTable has diagonal slashes, which indicates that the control's content is activated, so you can manipulate its inner controls, such as the filter and column fields. You use the PivotTable's sizing handles to change the control's size.

**5.** Use the ↔ pointer on the PivotTable's middle-right sizing handle to increase its width, and then use the ↕ pointer on the control's middle-bottom sizing handle to increase its height. See Figure 8-25.

**After resizing the PivotTable**  **Figure 8-25**

You need to drag and drop the PositionTitle and Openings fields from the related Position table into the PivotTable, so you'll expand the Related Tables entry in the field list and then expand the Position table.

**6.** Click ⊞ next to Related Tables in the field list, and then click ⊞ next to Position in the field list. The Location, NAICS, and Position tables, which are related to the Employer table, are now visible in the field list, as are the fields from the Position table.

**7.** Drag the **PositionTitle** field from the field list and drop it in the "Drop Row Fields Here" section on the PivotTable. A control for the PositionTitle field now appears in the row section of the PivotTable. The PositionTitle field is the row field, and its field values (Concierge, Cook, and so on) are the row field items. (See Figure 8-26.)

**8.** Drag the **Openings** field from the field list and drop it in the "Drop Totals or Detail Fields Here" section on the PivotTable. A control for the Openings field now appears in the detail section of the PivotTable. The Openings field is the detail field. The values in the body of the PivotTable are Openings field values from records in the Position table; for example, two Massachusetts (MA) employers each have one available position for a cook. See Figure 8-26.

**Figure 8-26**     **After adding the fields from the Jobs database to the PivotTable**

The PivotTable control is finished. Elsa wants you to add a title to the page and then open it in Page view.

## Using a PivotTable in Page View

Before viewing and using the PivotTable in Page view, you'll add a page title and then save the page. Also, because you've added all the required fields to the PivotTable, you'll close the field list.

### To add a page title, close the field list, and save the page:

▶ 1. Click anywhere on the **Click here and type title text** placeholder at the top of the page, and then type **Openings by State/Prov and Position**.

▶ 2. Close the field list, and then save the page as **OpeningsPivotTable** in the Intro\Tutorial folder. If necessary, click the **OK** button to close the dialog box containing the connection string warning message.

Next, you'll view the page in Page view.

### To view and use a PivotTable in Page view:

▶ 1. Click the **View** button for Page view 🖾 on the Page Design toolbar. The Page window opens in Page view. See Figure 8-27.

Initial view of the PivotTable in Page view

Figure 8-27

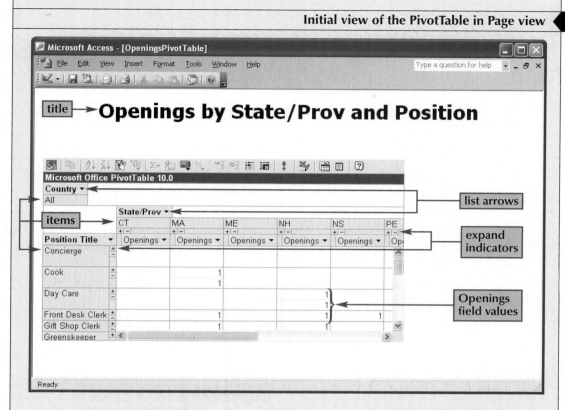

Elsa asks you to explain the purpose of the list arrows next to each field name. The list arrows let you filter the data displayed in the PivotTable. You can filter which countries, position titles, and states/provinces you want to view in the PivotTable. You'll filter to display openings in Canada.

2. Click the **Country** list arrow, click the **All** check box to clear all selections, click the **Canada** check box, and then click the **OK** button. Access applies the Country filter and displays openings in the provinces of Nova Scotia (NS), Prince Edward Island (PE), and Quebec (QC). See Figure 8-28.

Filtering data by country

Figure 8-28

In a similar way, you can filter selected position titles and selected states/provinces. To remove the Country filter, you could repeat Step 2 and click the All check box. You'll instead show Elsa a faster way to remove and then reapply the filter.

3. Click the **AutoFilter** button on the PivotTable toolbar. Access removes the Country filter and displays employers in all locations.

4. Click the **AutoFilter** button again to reapply the Country filter to display only employers in Canada.

   The PivotTable expand indicators ⊞ and ⊟ provide the same functionality as the expand indicators used with subdatasheets and data access pages. Unlike datasheets and data access pages, which display one expand indicator at a time, both PivotTable expand indicators appear for each row field item and column field item. However, clicking the expand indicator ⊞ has no effect if the item is already expanded, and clicking ⊟ has no effect if the item is already collapsed.

5. Click the **Concierge expand indicator** ⊞. Because the Concierge item is already expanded, clicking ⊞ did not change the PivotTable.

6. Click the **Concierge expand indicator** ⊟. The Concierge item collapses to a single line, and its two Openings field values are now hidden.

7. Click the **Concierge expand indicator** ⊞ again to show its details, and then click the rightmost column **Grand Total expand indicator** ⊞. See Figure 8-29.

| Figure 8-29 | Showing row grand totals |

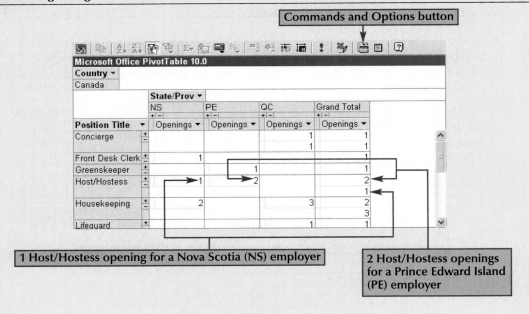

1 Host/Hostess opening for a Nova Scotia (NS) employer

2 Host/Hostess openings for a Prince Edward Island (PE) employer

A PivotTable automatically includes a grand total column and a grand total row. However, the grand total values do not function as you might expect when the PivotTable's detail area displays field values from a database. For example, instead of a grand total value of 3 openings appearing for the Canadian Host/Hostess position, each of the two individual Openings detail values appears in a separate row in the Grand Total column; the same happens in the grand total row. However, the grand total column and row values work as expected when the PivotTable's main body displays total field values.

## Adding a Total Field to a PivotTable

A **total field** summarizes values from a source field. For example, Elsa prefers to view the total number of openings for each position and location in the PivotTable instead of each individual Openings field value. For Elsa's request, you'll add a total field to the PivotTable's detail area that will calculate the sum of the Openings field values for each position in each state/province. Before adding the total field, you'll switch to Design view to increase the width and height of the PivotTable, and then you'll change the caption for the PivotTable title bar. Both of these design changes will make the PivotTable easier to use for identifying and viewing the data that Elsa needs.

### To change the PivotTable's dimensions and title bar caption:

1. Switch to Design view, click anywhere outside the PivotTable control to deselect it, and then click the PivotTable control to select the outer control. Sizing controls appear on the control's border, which does not have diagonal slashes.

2. Use the middle-right sizing handle to increase the width of the PivotTable until you can see the entire QC column field item, and then use the middle-bottom sizing handle to increase the height of the PivotTable until you can see the entire Housekeeping row field item.

   **Trouble?** If you increase the PivotTable's width or height too much, drag the sizing handle back to its correct position, click the grid that extends beyond the PivotTable, and then drag the grid's sizing handle so that its edge overlaps the PivotTable's edge.

   You can now change the PivotTable title bar caption.

3. Click the PivotTable title bar and, if the PivotTable border does not have diagonal slashes, click the PivotTable title bar until the control's border has diagonal slashes.

4. Click the **Commands and Options** button ⬚ on the PivotTable toolbar to open the Commands and Options dialog box, and then if necessary click the **Captions** tab. See Figure 8-30.

**Commands and Options dialog box** ◄ **Figure 8-30**

Serving a function similar to the property sheet, the Commands and Options dialog box lets you set property values, such as fonts and captions, for the internal controls on the PivotTable control.

5. Make sure the Select caption list box is set to **Report title bar**, select **Microsoft Office PivotTable 11.0** in the Caption text box (your version number might be different), type **Openings PivotTable** in the Caption text box, and then close the Commands and Options dialog box. The PivotTable title bar caption changes to Openings PivotTable.

Next, you'll add the total field to display the total number of openings in the PivotTable's detail area.

### To add the total field to the PivotTable's main body:

1. Click one of the Openings column headings (but not a list arrow for an Openings column heading) to select the detail column heading row, right-click the same Openings column heading, point to **AutoCalc** on the shortcut menu, and then click **Sum**. Access adds a new row for each position in the PivotTable that displays the total number of openings for the position in each state/province. See Figure 8-31.

| Figure 8-31 | After adding the total field |
| --- | --- |

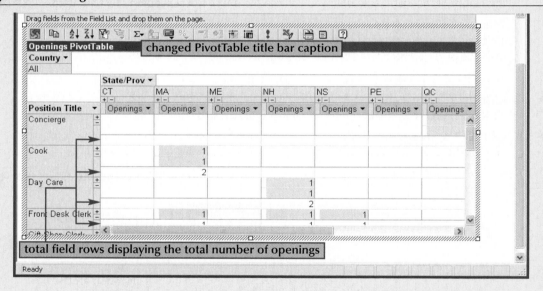

Elsa wants to view only the new total field, so you'll hide the detail number of openings values in the PivotTable.

2. Click the **Hide Details** button 📇 on the PivotTable toolbar. The detail values are now hidden, and only the total field values appear in the PivotTable's main body. See Figure 8-32.

**After adding the total field to the detail area**  Figure 8-32

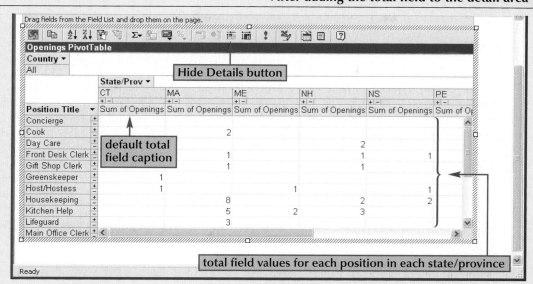

You can now change the default total field caption to a more meaningful description of the field's contents.

3. Right-click one of the Sum of Openings column headings, click **Commands and Options** on the shortcut menu to open the Commands and Options dialog box for the total field column heading, and then if necessary click the **Captions** tab.

4. Make sure that **Total** appears in the Select caption list box, change the Caption property to **Total Openings**, and then close the Commands and Options dialog box. The total field column headings change to the new Caption property value.

5. Save your design changes, switch to Page view, and then use the PivotTable's horizontal and vertical scroll bars to scroll down to the lower-right corner of the PivotTable. The Total Openings total field values appear in the PivotTable, along with a grand total row and a grand total column. See Figure 8-33.

**Completed PivotTable in Page view**  Figure 8-33

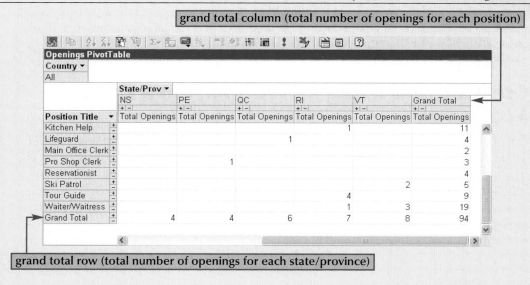

You've completed the PivotTable for Elsa, so you can close the data access page and open it using your browser.

6. Close the data access page, right-click **OpeningsPivotTable** in the Pages list box, and then click **Web Page Preview**.

Elsa wants to view a summary of the total openings in New Hampshire (NH) and Vermont (VT).

7. Click the **State/Prov** list arrow, click the **All** check box to clear all selections, click the **NH** check box, click the **VT** check box, click the **OK** button, and then scroll down if necessary until you see the Grand Total row. Access applies the State/Prov filter and displays total openings only in the states of New Hampshire and Vermont. See Figure 8-34.

| Figure 8-34 | Completed PivotTable in the Internet Explorer window |

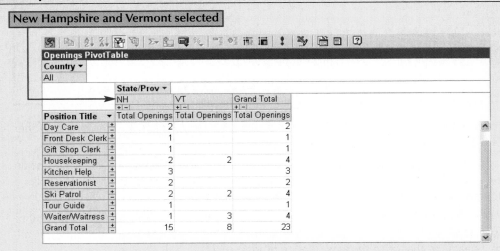

**Trouble?** If the Openings column headings appear instead of the Total Openings column headings, click the **Hide Details** button on the PivotTable toolbar.

8. Close the Internet Explorer window.

Elsa is so pleased with the PivotTable that you created for her that she immediately thinks of another data access page that would be helpful to her. She asks if you can create a data access page with a chart showing the total openings for each state/province. You'll create a PivotChart on a data access page to satisfy Elsa's request.

# Creating and Using a PivotChart in a Data Access Page

Office 2003 provides the **Office PivotChart Component** to assist you in adding a chart to a data access page, form, or datasheet. Using the Office PivotChart Component, you can create a **PivotChart**, an interactive chart that provides capabilities similar to a PivotTable. Figure 8-35 shows a PivotChart in a data access page.

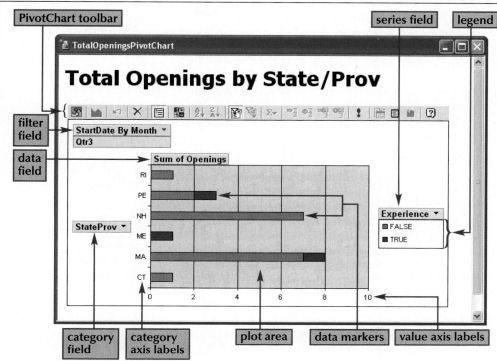

A PivotChart contains the following basic components:

- The **PivotChart toolbar** lets you perform actions such as sorting and filtering.
- The **plot area** provides a background for the data markers and gridlines. A **data marker** is a bar, dot, segment, or other symbol that represents a single data value. The **data field**, which is the Sum of Openings field in Figure 8-35, identifies which values the data markers represent and identifies each value displayed as a **value axis label**. Each **gridline**, which appears in Figure 8-35 as one of the vertical lines in the plot area, makes it easier to see the values represented by the data markers.
- The **category field** identifies each value that's displayed as a **category axis label**; each category axis label identifies an individual data marker. In Figure 8-35, the StateProv field is the category field; CT, MA, and the other states/provinces are the category axis labels. Therefore, the data markers show the total number of openings for each state/province.
- The **series field** identifies the data markers' subdivisions. In Figure 8-35, the Experience field is the series field, and the data markers show the portion of the total number of openings that require experienced workers. The **legend** provides a list of the series field values and how these values are indicated on the data markers.
- The **filter field** lets you restrict which data appears on the PivotChart. In Figure 8-35, the filter field is StartDate By Month, and a filter has been applied to include only those openings with start dates in the third quarter (Qtr3).

Using the Office PivotChart Component, you'll create a PivotChart in a data access page to let Elsa analyze total openings for each state/province. The data source for a PivotChart can be a single table, or a query based on one or more tables. Elsa wants the chart to include the StateProv field from the Employer table and the Openings, StartDate, and Experience fields from the Position table. The EmployerPositionsWithExperience query contains the fields needed for the PivotChart.

Reference Window

### Adding a PivotChart to a Data Access Page

- If necessary, click Pages in the Objects bar of the Database window to display the Pages list.
- Click the New button to open the New Data Access Page dialog box, click Design View (if necessary), click the OK button, and then if necessary click the OK button to close the warning message and to create a blank data access page.
- Click the Office Chart tool on the toolbox, and then click the mouse button in the location on the page where you want to position the upper-left corner of the PivotChart.
- Click the PivotChart control to open the Commands and Options dialog box. Select the data source, data link connection, table or query, and chart type for the PivotChart.
- Close the Commands and Options dialog box.
- From the field list add the category, data, filter, and series fields to the PivotChart.
- Modify the size of the PivotChart, and modify the size and other properties of the controls in the PivotChart.
- Click the Save button on the Page Design toolbar, enter a name for the data access page, select a location for the data access page, and then click the Save button.

You'll first create a blank data access page and add a PivotChart to the page.

### To create a PivotChart in a data access page:

▶ 1. Click **Pages** in the Objects bar of the Database window to display the Pages list (if necessary).

▶ 2. Click the **New** button in the Database window to open the New Data Access Page dialog box, click **Design View** in the list box (if necessary), click the **OK** button, and then if necessary click the **OK** button if you're warned about the Access 2000 Design view issue.

You'll use the Office Chart tool on the toolbox to add a PivotChart control to the page.

▶ 3. Click the **Office Chart** tool 🔳 on the toolbox. The pointer changes to a ⁺🔳 shape when you move it over the data access page.

▶ 4. Move the pointer to the grid, and when the center of the pointer's plus symbol (+) is positioned on the grid dot in the upper-left corner, click the mouse button. Access adds a PivotChart control to the page.

▶ 5. Click the PivotChart control. The Chart Wizard opens the Commands and Options dialog box. See Figure 8-36.

**Specifying the data source for the PivotChart** | **Figure 8-36**

Your first step is to choose the data source for the PivotChart. The data source for a PivotChart can be data you type into a datasheet, data from a table or query, or data from a Web page. Because the EmployerPositionsWithExperience query is the data source, you'll choose the second option.

▶ **6.** Click the **Data from a database table or query** option button, and then click the **Connection** button. The Commands and Options dialog box expands to include the Data Details and Type tabs, in addition to the original Data Source tab, and the Data Details tab is selected. You need to set the Connection text box to the Jobs database. Notice that as you make selections in the dialog boxes, the PivotChart control on the data access page changes to reflect your selections.

▶ **7.** Click the **Edit** button, use the Look in list box to open the **Intro\Tutorial** folder, click **Jobs** (if necessary), and then click the **Open** button. The Data Link Properties dialog box opens and displays the Jobs database as the selected database name. See Figure 8-37.

Figure 8-37 **Specifying the connection to the database**

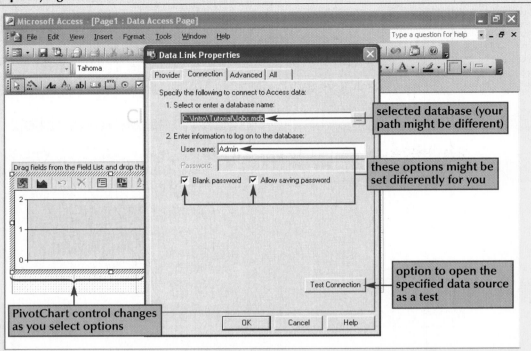

The second section of the dialog box contains a user name (yours might differ from the user name shown in Figure 8-37) and two check boxes. Because you don't want to type a password to establish a connection to the Jobs database and because the default user name is acceptable to Elsa, you won't change anything in the dialog box. If you click the Test Connection button, the Office PivotChart Component will test the accuracy of your data source settings by attempting to open the Jobs database. This test will fail because you already have the database open; the Office PivotChart Component can open the data source only if it's not currently in use. (You would use this option when you have started the Office PivotChart Component but have not opened the data source.)

8. Click the **OK** button to close the Data Link Properties dialog box and open the next dialog box. This dialog box displays the options you've previously selected, so you do not need to make any changes to it.

9. Click the **OK** button to close the dialog box and open the Select Table dialog box, click **EmployerPositionsWithExperience**, click the **OK** button, and then click the **Type** tab on the Commands and Options dialog box. See Figure 8-38.

**Selecting the chart type** | **Figure 8-38**

Next, you need to select the specific chart type you'll use for the PivotChart. Elsa suggests using a stacked column chart.

▶ **10.** Click **Column** in the left list box, click the stacked column chart type (row 1, column 2), and then close the Commands and Options dialog box. The PivotChart control now appears with the settings you selected in the dialog boxes, and the data access page field list might be open on your screen. See Figure 8-39.

**After adding the PivotChart control to the page** | **Figure 8-39**

The PivotChart control contains a toolbar and four areas: the filter area, the category area, the data area, and the series area. The filter area will contain any filter fields you need to filter data displayed in the PivotChart; Elsa initially doesn't need any filter fields. The category area will contain the category field whose values will appear as labels on the PivotChart's category axis where "Categories" currently appears; Elsa wants the StateProv field to be a category field. The series area will contain any series fields you need to represent groups of related data points or data markers on the PivotChart; Elsa wants the Experience field to be a series field. The data area will contain the data fields that will serve as data markers on the PivotChart; Elsa wants the Openings field to be the data field.

The four PivotChart areas are empty until you add fields from the field list to them. Before you add the fields to the PivotChart, you'll enlarge the PivotChart.

### To resize and add fields to a PivotChart:

▶ **1.** Use the ↔ pointer on the PivotChart's middle-right sizing handle to increase its width so that its right edge touches the right edge of the page grid.

▶ **2.** Use the ↕ pointer on the control's middle-bottom sizing handle to increase its height until you can see 1.25 at the top of the y-axis. (See Figure 8-40.)

▶ **3.** Click the PivotChart so that the border has diagonal slashes, and then click the **Field List** button ▤ on the PivotChart toolbar to open the field list. See Figure 8-40.

**Figure 8-40** ▶ **After enlarging the PivotChart and opening the field list**

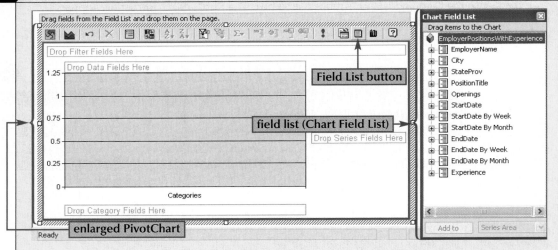

▶ **4.** Drag the **StateProv** field from in the field list to the category area on the PivotChart. The StateProv field is now a category field on the PivotChart.

**Trouble?** If the drop area for category fields is missing in your PivotChart, click the StateProv field in the field list, click the Add to list arrow at the bottom of the field list, click Category Area, and then click the Add to button.

**5.** Drag the **Experience** field from the field list to the series area on the PivotChart, and then drag the **Openings** field from the field list to the data area on the PivotChart. The Experience field is now a series field on the PivotChart, and the Openings field is now a data field on the PivotChart.

**Trouble?** If a drop area is missing in your PivotChart, click the field in the field list, click the Add to list arrow at the bottom of the field list, click the appropriate item in the list, and then click the Add to button.

Next, you'll add a left-aligned page title and save the page.

**6.** Click anywhere on the **Click here and type title text** placeholder at the top of the page, type **Total Openings by State/Prov**, press the **Delete** key to remove the blank line following the title line, and then click the **Align Left** button 📄 on the Formatting toolbar. Note that the field list no longer appears in the Page Design window.

**7.** Save the page as **TotalOpeningsPivotChart** in the Intro\Tutorial folder; if necessary, click the **OK** button if the connection string warning message appears. See Figure 8-41.

| Completed PivotChart in Design view | Figure 8-41 |
| --- | --- |

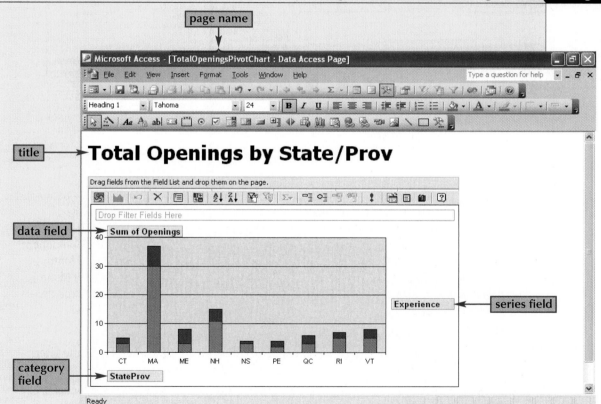

Elsa wants to view the PivotChart in Internet Explorer.

### To view the PivotChart in Internet Explorer:

**1.** Click the list arrow for the **View** button 📄 on the Page Design toolbar, and then click **Web Page Preview**. Internet Explorer starts and displays the TotalOpeningsPivotChart page.

> **2.** Click the **Show/Hide Legend** button 🗐 on the PivotChart toolbar to display the legend for the Experience series field, if necessary, click the **Field List** button 🗐 on the PivotChart toolbar, and then, if necessary, maximize the Internet Explorer window. See Figure 8-42.

| Figure 8-42 | Completed PivotChart in Web Page Preview |

The field list contains the eight fields from the EmployerPositionsWithExperience query and the Sum of Openings summary field, created automatically by the Office PivotChart Component when you added the Openings field as the data field to the PivotChart; the summary field appears as a Totals subentry. In addition, the Office PivotChart Component automatically added two field list entries (StartDate By Week and StartDate By Month) based on the StartDate field, and two entries (EndDate By Week and EndDate By Month) based on the EndDate field. These four date entries let you filter date fields by time divisions such as year, quarter, month, and day.

Elsa asks if she can view the total openings for a specific quarter of the year.

> **3.** Click ⊞ next to StartDate By Month in the field list, and then drag **Quarters** to the filter area on the PivotChart to add it as a filter field to the PivotChart.

> **4.** Click the **StartDate By Month** list arrow, click the **All** check box to clear all selections, click ⊞ next to 2006, click the **Qtr3** check box so that it's the only checked entry, and then click the **OK** button. Access applies the StartDate By Month filter and displays total openings in only those states/provinces that have openings with start dates in the third quarter. See Figure 8-43.

After viewing the filter, Elsa now wants to remove the filter field from the PivotChart.

5. Click the **StartDate By Month** filter field in the PivotChart control to make it the current selection, and then click the **Delete Selection** button ⊠ on the PivotChart toolbar to remove the filter field from the PivotChart.

Elsa now wants to replace the stacked column chart with a stacked bar chart. You need to change the chart type in Design view.

## To change the chart type of the PivotChart:

1. Close Internet Explorer, and then click the PivotChart control until the **Chart Type** button ⬛ on the PivotChart toolbar is activated.

2. Click the **Chart Type** button ⬛ on the PivotChart toolbar. The Commands and Options dialog box opens with the Type tab selected.

3. Click **Bar** in the left list box, and then click the stacked bar chart type (row 1, column 2). The chart changes to a stacked bar chart.

4. Close the Commands and Options dialog box.

   Elsa has no further changes to the PivotChart, so you'll save your design changes and close the page.

5. Save your changes, and then close the data access page.

6. If you are not continuing on to the next session, close the Jobs database, and then exit Access.

You have completed four data access pages for Elsa: a page created using the Page Wizard, a custom page using data from the Employer and Position tables, a custom page with a PivotTable, and a custom page with a PivotChart. In the next session, you will help Elsa use XML files and integrate Access data with other programs.

**Review**

# Session 8.2 Quick Check

1. What is a PivotTable?
2. Within a PivotTable you can choose fields from the field list to be the column field, the row field, the detail field, and the _____ field.
3. You can use the Office PivotTable Component to add a PivotTable to which three Access objects?
4. What's different about a PivotTable's expand indicators compared to the expand indicators that appear for datasheets and data access pages?
5. On a PivotTable, the _____ field summarizes field values from a source field.
6. On a PivotChart, the _____ field identifies which values are shown as value axis labels.
7. You can show/hide a legend for the _____ field on a PivotChart.

# Session 8.3

## Using XML

Matt has been tracking positions and the students hired for those positions. Elsa wants to add this data to the Jobs database; in response to her request, Matt has made the data available to Elsa in an XML document. **XML** (**Extensible Markup Language**) is a programming language that is similar in format to HTML, but is more customizable and suited to the exchange of data between different programs. Unlike HTML, which uses a fixed set of tags to describe how a Web page should look, developers can customize XML code to describe the data it contains and how that data should be structured.

## Importing an XML File as an Access Table

Access can import data from an XML file directly into a database table. Matt's XML file is named Job, and you'll import it as a table with the same name into the Jobs database.

**Reference Window** | **Importing an XML File as an Access Table**

- Click File on the menu bar, point to Get External Data, and then click Import.
- Click the Files of type list arrow, and then click XML.
- Use the Look in list box to select the XML document to import.
- Click the Import button to open the Import XML dialog box, click the Options button, select the desired import option, click the file to import, and then click the OK button.

Now you will import the Job.xml document as an Access database table.

### To import the XML document as an Access table:

1. If you took a break after the previous session, make sure that Access is running, that the **Jobs** database in the Intro\Tutorial folder is open, that the Database window is maximized, and that **Tables** is selected in the Objects bar of the Database window.

2. Click **File** on the menu bar, point to **Get External Data**, and then click **Import**. The Import dialog box opens.

3. If necessary, click the **Files of type** list arrow, scroll down, and then click **XML**.

4. Make sure the Look in list box displays the **Tutorial** folder provided with your Data Files, and then click **Job** to select it.

5. Click the **Import** button to open the Import XML dialog box, and then click the **Options** button. See Figure 8-44.

Import XML dialog box ◀ **Figure 8-44**

table name as defined in the XML document

option to import the table's structure and data

From the XML file, you can import just the table structure to a new table, import the table structure and data to a new table, or append the data in the XML file to an existing table. You'll import the table structure and data to a new table named Job.

6. Make sure the **Structure and Data** option button is selected, click **Job** in the list box, click the **OK** button, and then click the **OK** button when the import confirmation message box appears. The Job table has been imported to the Jobs database, and its data has been saved in a new table named Job. This table is now listed in the Tables list box of the Database window.

Elsa asks to view the data in the Job table.

7. Open the **Job** table in Datasheet view. Access displays the PositionID, StudentID, StartDate, and EndDate fields from the Job table, which contains 31 records. See Figure 8-45.

**Figure 8-45** | **Job table in Datasheet view**

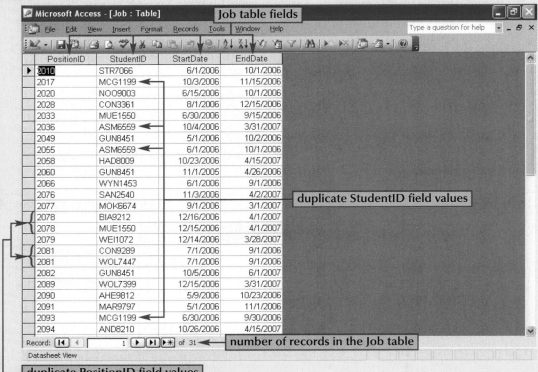

Notice the duplicate PositionID field values (2078 and 2081) and the duplicate StudentID field values (MCG1199 and ASM6559). Because of these duplicate field values, neither field can be the table's primary key. Neither the StartDate nor the EndDate field can serve as the table's primary key either, because they also contain duplicate field values. So what's the primary key for the Job table? It's the combination of the PositionID and StudentID fields; each pair of values for these two fields is unique. You'll verify the primary key by viewing the Job table in Design view.

8. Switch to Design view. Both the PositionID field and the StudentID field have the key symbol in their row selectors, so the combination of values in these two fields serves as the primary key for the Job table. See Figure 8-46.

**Figure 8-46** | **Job table in Design view**

9. Close the table.

Elsa just received a request that requires you to export the Position table as an XML file.

## Exporting an Access Table as an XML File

A regional nonprofit agency, which coordinates housing for international students, recently contacted Elsa and requested job-opening information for NSJI's client employers. The agency uses a specialized computer program, and the agency representative asked Elsa to provide the data as an XML file to make it easier for the agency to identify and process the data.

Just as you did when you exported the EmployerPositions query as an HTML document earlier in this tutorial, you'll use the Export command on the shortcut menu to export the Position table as an XML file.

Reference Window

### Exporting an Access Object as an XML File

- In the Database window, right-click the object (table, query, form, or report) you want to export, and then click Export on the shortcut menu.
- Enter the filename in the File name text box, and then select the location where you want to save the file.
- Click the Save as type list arrow, click XML, and then click the Export button.
- Click the Advanced button on the Export XML dialog box; set the data, schema, and presentation options; and then click the OK button.

You can now export the Position table as an XML file.

### To export the Position table as an XML file:

▶ **1.** Right-click **Position** in the Tables list to display the shortcut menu, and then click **Export**. The Export dialog box opens, displaying the type and name of the object you are exporting in its title bar—in this case, the Position table.

You'll save the Position table as an XML file in the Intro\Tutorial folder provided with your Data Files.

▶ **2.** Make sure the Save in list box displays the **Tutorial** folder for your Data Files.

▶ **3.** Type **NSJIEmployerPositions** in the File name text box, click the **Save as type** list arrow, scroll down the list and click **XML**, and then click the **Export** button. The Export XML dialog box opens.

Clicking the More Options button in the Export XML dialog box lets you view and change detailed options for exporting a database object to an XML file.

▶ **4.** Click the **More Options** button to reveal detailed export options in the Export XML dialog box. See Figure 8-47.

**Figure 8-47** ▶ **Data tab of the Export XML dialog box**

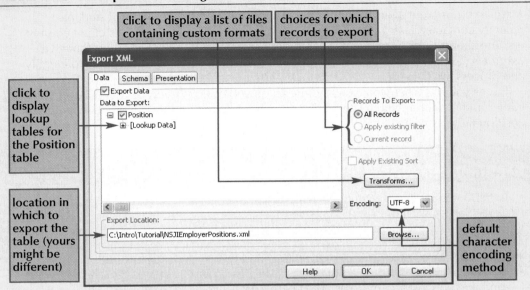

The Export Data check box, the Export Location text box, and the Records to Export option group display the selections you made in the previous step. You're exporting all records from the Position table, including the data in the records and the structure of the table, to the NSJIEmployerPositions.xml file in the Intro\Tutorial folder. The encoding option determines how characters will be represented in the exported XML file. The encoding choices are UTF-8, which uses 8 bits to represent each character, and UTF-16, which uses 16 bits to represent each character. You can also click the Transforms button if you have a special file that contains instructions for changing the exported data.

The agency didn't provide a transform file and requires the default encoding, but Elsa wants to review the tables that contain lookup data.

▶ **5.** Click ⊞ next to Lookup Data. The Employer table contains lookup data because it's the primary table in the one-to-many relationship with the related Position table. The agency's requirements don't include any lookup data, so make sure the Employer check box remains unchecked.

The Data tab settings are correct, so you'll verify the Schema tab settings.

▶ **6.** Click the **Schema** tab. See Figure 8-48.

**Schema tab of the Export XML dialog box** | **Figure 4-48**

option to export the table structure

option to include the table structure in the XML file

Along with the data from the Position table, you'll be exporting its table structure, including information about the table's primary key and indexes. You can include this information in a separate **XSD (XML Structure Definition)** file, or you can embed the information in the XML file. The agency wants a single XML file, so you'll embed the structure information in the XML file.

7. Click the **Embed schema in exported XML data document** option button to select that option and to dim the "Create separate schema document" list box, and then click the **Presentation** tab.

   The Presentation tab options let you export a separate **XSL (Extensible Stylesheet Language)** file containing the format specifications for the Position table data. Unlike HTML, XML provides no screen formatting information. An XSL file provides formatting instructions so that a browser or another program can display the data in the XML file in a readable way. The agency will import the Position table data directly into its computer program, which contains its own formatting instructions, so you will not export an XSL file.

8. Make sure that the **Export Presentation (HTML 4.0 Sample XSL)** check box is unchecked, and then click the **OK** button. Access closes the Export XML dialog box, creates the XML file in the Intro\Tutorial folder provided with your Data Files, and returns you to the Database window.

When contacted in the future, Elsa now knows how to create an XML file to give to the agency. If Elsa needs further information about XML, she can explore several Web sites. The XML section of the Student Online Companion page for Tutorial 8, located at *www.course.com/np/office2003/access*, contains links that you can follow to learn more about XML.

Elsa next wants to perform a detailed analysis on potential income data. To do so, she wants to work with the data in a Microsoft Excel worksheet.

# Exporting an Access Query as an Excel Worksheet

A spreadsheet (or worksheet) program, such as Microsoft Excel, is designed to assist you in analyzing data. Although a database management program provides some data analysis capabilities, it is primarily designed for storing and retrieving data. A worksheet program has many more powerful tools for analyzing data to create budgets, projections, and models.

You can export the contents of most Access objects, including tables, forms, and reports, to other Windows programs, including Excel.

| Reference Window | **Exporting an Access Object to an Excel Worksheet** |
|---|---|

- In the Database window, click the object you want to export to select it.
- Click the OfficeLinks list arrow, and then click Analyze It with Microsoft Excel.

Like many business owners, Elsa uses a worksheet program as a planning and budgeting tool for her business. She would like to use the potential income information to analyze the company's future income. She asks you to transfer the results of the PotentialIncomeByEmployer query to an Excel worksheet so that she can use Excel to perform the necessary analysis that she cannot perform using Access.

## To export the query results to an Excel worksheet:

1. Click **Queries** in the Objects bar of the Database window to display the queries list.

2. Click **PotentialIncomeByEmployer**, click the list arrow for the **OfficeLinks** button 🔛 on the Database toolbar, and then click **Analyze It with Microsoft Office Excel**. Access automatically starts Excel and places the query results in a new worksheet. See Figure 8-49.

| Figure 8-49 | **Query results in the Excel worksheet** |
|---|---|

**Trouble?** If Excel is not installed on your computer, another spreadsheet program might start. The specific program that starts and opens the query results is not important. Simply continue with the steps. If a spreadsheet program is not installed on your computer, ask your instructor or technical support person for help.

**Trouble?** If your screen displays any toolbars in addition to the Standard toolbar and the Formatting toolbar, click View on the menu bar, point to Toolbars, click the toolbar name to close the toolbar, and then repeat if necessary.

Notice that each field value is placed in a single cell in the worksheet. The field names are entered in the first row of cells in the worksheet. You can now use this data just as you would any other data in an Excel worksheet.

Elsa wants to see the total of the potential income amounts, so she asks you to create a grand total for the data in column D. You'll first add a line to separate the grand total amount from the other potential income amounts.

### To create the grand total amount:

▶ **1.** Scroll down the worksheet, and then click cell **D39** to select the rightmost cell in the last row of data in column D (see Figure 8-50).

▶ **2.** Click the list arrow for the **Borders** button 🔲 on the Formatting toolbar to display the list of border options, click the **Thick Bottom Border** button (the second choice in row two), and then click cell **E39**. Excel places a heavy border on the bottom of cell D39. See Figure 8-50.

**Adding a bottom border to the cell** ◀ **Figure 8-50**

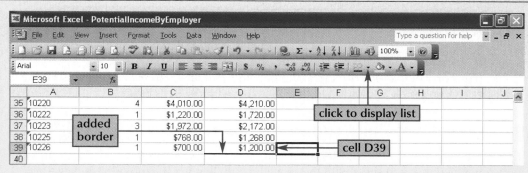

**Trouble?** If the Borders button is not visible on your Formatting toolbar, click the More Buttons button ▪ on the Formatting toolbar, and then click the Borders button 🔲.

**Trouble?** Your Borders button might look different from the one shown in Figure 8-50 and might be in a different position on the Formatting toolbar.

▶ **3.** Click cell **D40** to select it, and then click the **AutoSum** button Σ on the Standard toolbar. Excel automatically creates the formula to sum the contents of the cells above cell D40. See Figure 8-51.

| Figure 8-51 | **Formula to sum the contents of cells D2 through D39** |

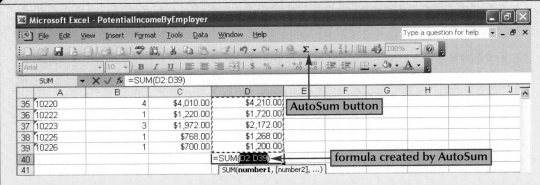

**4.** Press the **Enter** key to enter the formula. Excel displays the sum of the contents of cells D2 through D39 in cell D40. See Figure 8-52.

| Figure 8-52 | **Total added to cell D40** |

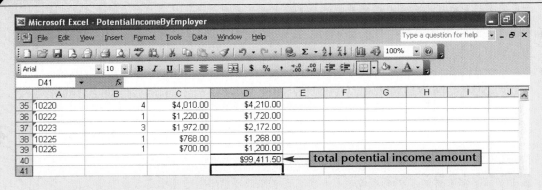

Elsa plans on doing more work with the data in Excel later. For now, you can save the worksheet, close Excel, and return to the Database window in Access.

## Saving the Worksheet and Exiting Excel

When you exported the PotentialIncomeByEmployer query results to Excel, Excel automatically saved the worksheet with the name PotentialIncomeByEmployer. Because you have made changes to the worksheet, you need to save them now before exiting Excel.

### To save and close the Excel worksheet:

**1.** Click the **Save** button on the Standard toolbar.

**2.** Click the **Close** button on the Excel window title bar to close the worksheet, exit Excel, and return to the Database window in Access.

When you exported the query results to Excel, Access placed a copy of the query results in the worksheet. The query results in the Excel worksheet are static, so any later changes made to the Access data will not be reflected in the Excel worksheet. Similarly, any changes made in the worksheet will not affect the Access data.

# Creating Hyperlinks to Other Office XP Documents

When Zack visits client employers, he keeps field notes about their positions in Word documents. Now he would like some way of connecting these notes with the corresponding records in the Position table. This connection would allow him to review his notes when he views the records in the table.

Each position's set of notes is a separate Word document. For example, Zack created a Word document named Aidan to enter his notes on the host/hostess position at Aidan's of Mystic. Similarly, his notes for the tour guide position at Newport Mansion Guided Tours are in a file named Newport, and the file for the cook position at Pear Tree Inn & Restaurant is named PearTree. To connect Zack's notes with the corresponding records in the Position table, you need to create a hyperlink field in the Position table.

## Creating a Hyperlink Field in a Table

Access lets you create a hyperlink field in a table. The field value in a hyperlink field is a hyperlink or pointer to another object. These objects can be database objects (such as tables or forms), a Word document, a named range in an Excel worksheet, or even a URL for a Web page. When you click a hyperlink field value, the associated program starts and opens the linked object.

---

| Creating a Hyperlink Field in a Table | Reference Window |
|---|---|

- Display the table in Design view.
- In a blank Field Name text box, type the name of the new field, and then press the Tab key.
- Click the Data Type list arrow, and then click Hyperlink.

---

You will create a hyperlink field in the Position table. The hyperlink field value will be a hyperlink to one of Zack's Word documents. When Zack clicks a hyperlink, Word will start and open the Word document that contains his notes.

### To add a hyperlink field to the Position table:

1. Open the **Position** table in Design view.
2. Click the **Field Name** text box in the first empty row, type **FieldNotes**, and then press the **Tab** key.
3. Click the **Data Type** list arrow, and then click **Hyperlink**. See Figure 8-53.

| Figure 8-53 | Adding a hyperlink field to a table |

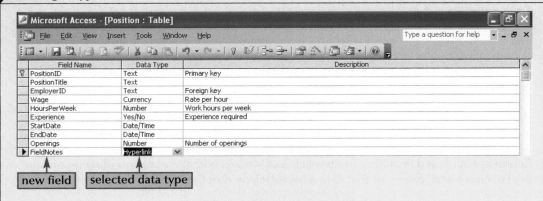

**4.** Save your table design change, and then switch to Datasheet view.

Now you can add the hyperlink field values to the new FieldNotes field in the Position table datasheet. These field values will be hyperlinks to the Word documents Zack created.

## Entering Hyperlink Field Values

When you add a field value in a hyperlink field, you can enter the name of an object, such as a table, form, worksheet, or document, or you can enter a URL to a Web page. You can type the field value directly into the field or you can use the Insert Hyperlink dialog box to enter it.

| Reference Window | **Entering a Hyperlink Field Value in a Table** |

- In Datasheet view, position the insertion point in the hyperlink field for the appropriate record.
- Click the Insert Hyperlink button on the Table Datasheet toolbar.
- Type the hyperlink's filename, URL, or object name in the Address text box, or select it by clicking the appropriate button.
- Change the Text to display the text box value, if necessary.
- Click the OK button.

You will use the Insert Hyperlink dialog box to enter the necessary hyperlink field values.

### To enter field values in the hyperlink field:

**1.** In Datasheet view, click the **FieldNotes** text box for the PositionID 2004 record (record 1).

**2.** Click the **Insert Hyperlink** button 🖳 on the Table Datasheet toolbar. The Insert Hyperlink dialog box opens.

**3.** If necessary, use the Look in list arrow to display the contents of the **Tutorial** folder in the Look in list box. See Figure 8-54.

Insert Hyperlink dialog box ◄ **Figure 8-54**

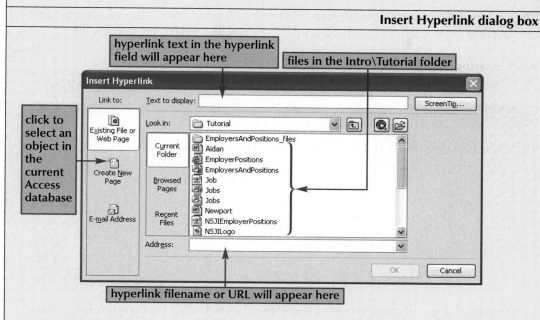

hyperlink text in the hyperlink field will appear here

files in the Intro\Tutorial folder

click to select an object in the current Access database

hyperlink filename or URL will appear here

In the Insert Hyperlink dialog box, you can type the hyperlink, select the link from the Look in list box, or select the link by using one of the buttons. You can click the Bookmark button or the Object in This Database button to select an object in the current Access database as the hyperlink.

The hyperlink for the first record is the file named Aidan.

4. Click **Aidan** in the Look in list box. The name of the Aidan file appears in the Address text box with a .doc extension, which is the extension for a Word document. This is the file that will open when you click the hyperlink field for record 1 in the Position table.

The Text to display text box shows what will be displayed as a field value in the database hyperlink field for record 1. You'll change the value of the Text to display text box to "Aidan's of Mystic" so that it is more descriptive.

5. Select **.doc** in the Text to display text box, and then type **'s of Mystic**. See Figure 8-55.

Entering a hyperlink field value and filename ◄ **Figure 8-55**

field value display text

hyperlink filename

6. Click the **OK** button to close the Insert Hyperlink dialog box. The display text for the hyperlink field value appears in the FieldNotes field for the first record. See Figure 8-56.

---

**Figure 8-56** ▶ **After entering a hyperlink field value**

**Trouble?** If you selected the wrong hyperlink value, right-click the hyperlink field value, point to Hyperlink on the shortcut menu, click Edit Hyperlink, and then repeat Steps 4 through 6.

7. Use the same procedure to enter hyperlink field values for the records for PositionID 2007 (record 2) and PositionID 2028 (record 9). For the PositionID 2007 record, select **Newport** as the filename and type **Newport Mansion Guided Tours** as the display text value; for the PositionID 2028 record, select **PearTree** as the filename and type **Pear Tree Inn & Restaurant** as the display text value.

8. Resize the FieldNotes column to its best fit and, if necessary, scroll to the right to view the entire column. Click in any empty FieldNotes text box to deselect the FieldNotes column. When you are finished, the Datasheet window should look like Figure 8-57.

---

**Figure 8-57** ▶ **Hyperlink field values entered for the three records**

**Trouble?** If you click a hyperlink in the datasheet instead of an empty FieldNotes text box, Access will start Word and open the hyperlinked file. Click the Close button ☒ on the Word title bar to close Word.

Notice that the hyperlink field values have a different appearance from the other field values. The hyperlink field values are shown in a different color and are underlined, indicating that they are hyperlinks.

Zack wants to test one of the new hyperlink fields in the Position table. You'll use a hyperlink to view his corresponding field notes for the Pear Tree Inn & Restaurant.

## Using a Hyperlink

When you click a hyperlink field value, its associated program starts and opens the linked object. When you click a value in the FieldNotes field, for example, Word will start and open the linked document.

### To use a hyperlink to open a Word document:

1. Click the **Pear Tree Inn & Restaurant** FieldNotes hyperlink. Word starts and opens the PearTree document, which contains Zack's field notes for Pear Tree Inn & Restaurant. See Figure 8-58.

Field notes for Pear Tree Inn & Restaurant in the PearTree document ◄ **Figure 8-58**

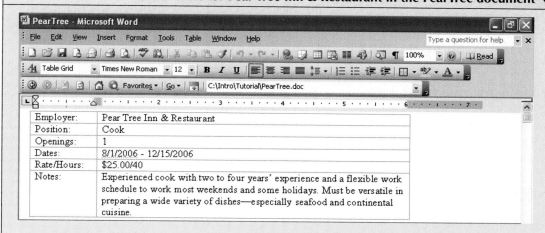

**Trouble?** If a message box opens warning you that hyperlinks can be harmful to your computer and data, click the Yes button to continue. The hyperlinks you added will not harm your computer.

**Trouble?** If Word is not installed on your computer, another program, such as WordPad, might start and open the field notes. The specific program that starts and opens the field notes is not important. Simply continue with the steps.

**Trouble?** If Word opens with a different Zoom setting, click the Zoom list arrow on the Standard toolbar, and then click 100%.

**Trouble?** If the Show/Hide button ¶ is selected, click the Show/Hide button ¶ to deselect it.

2. Click the **Close** button ⊠ on the Word window title bar to close the document, exit Word, and return to the Database window in Access.

Notice that the Pear Tree Inn & Restaurant hyperlink field value is a different color from the other hyperlink field values; this indicates that you've used the hyperlink. All hyperlinks will be the same color the next time you open the Jobs database.

You've finished your work for Zack and Elsa, so you can save your table layout changes and exit Access.

3. Save and close the Position table, and then exit Access.

Elsa, Zack, and Matt are very pleased with the data access pages and integration work you completed for them. They've learned enough to be able to do similar work on their own.

**Review**

## Session 8.3 Quick Check

1. _____ is a programming language that describes how a Web page should look; _____ is a programming language that describes the data it contains and how that data should be structured.
2. When you import or export an XML file using Access, is the data in the XML file static or dynamic?
3. When you use Access to export an XML file and an accompanying XSD file, what information is stored in the XSD file?
4. How do you export a table or query datasheet to Excel?
5. What does the field value of a hyperlink field represent?
6. How do you view a hyperlink that is named in a hyperlink field?

**Review**

## Tutorial Summary

In this tutorial, you learned how to integrate Access with the Web and with other programs. You exported an Access query to an HTML document and then used a Web browser to view the document. You also created a data access page using the Page Wizard and created three custom pages, one with a PivotTable and another with a PivotChart. Finally, you imported and exported XML files; exported a query as an Excel worksheet; and created a hyperlink field, entered hyperlink field values, and used a hyperlink.

## Key Terms

| | | |
|---|---|---|
| absolute path | HTML (HyperText Markup Language) | row field |
| category axis label | | row field items |
| category field | HTML document | series field |
| column area | HTML template | static Web page |
| column field | hyperlink | tag |
| column field items | Internet | theme |
| connection string | legend | total field |
| data access page | Office PivotChart Component | Uniform Resource Locator (URL) |
| data field | | value axis label |
| data marker | Office PivotTable Component | Web |
| DataPageSize property | Office Web Components | Web browser |
| detail area | page | Web page |
| detail field | PivotChart | Web server |
| detail values | PivotChart toolbar | World Wide Web |
| dynamic Web page | PivotTable | XML (Extensible Markup Language) |
| filter area | PivotTable list | |
| filter field | PivotTable toolbar | XSD (XML Structure Definition) |
| filter field items | plot area | |
| gridline | record navigation toolbar | XSL (Extensible Stylesheet Language) |
| grouped data access page | row area | |

**Practice**

*Take time to practice the skills you learned in the tutorial using the same case scenario.*

# Review Assignments

**Data Files needed for the Review Assignments: NSJILogo.gif, NSJI-Tbl.htm, and Students.mdb (*cont. from Tutorial 7*)**

Elsa wants you to export the data selected by the SelectedBonusQuotas query and the RecruitersAndStudents report as HTML documents so she can view these Access objects using her Web browser. In addition, she asks you to create additional Web pages based on objects in the Students database. Finally, she wants to use the data in the SelectedBonusQuotas query as an XML file and also work with the data in Excel, so she needs you to export the query into these data formats. To do so, you'll complete the following steps:

1. Open the **Students** database in the Intro\Review folder provided with your Data Files.
2. Export the **SelectedBonusQuotas** query as an HTML document to the Intro\Review folder, using the HTML template file named **NSJI-Tbl**, which is located in the Intro\Review folder. Use your Web browser to open the **SelectedBonusQuotas** HTML document, print the document, and then close your Web browser.
3. Use the AutoPage: Columnar Wizard to create a data access page based on the **SelectedBonusQuotas** query. Save the data access page in the Intro\Review folder as **SelectedQuotas**, sort the data access page in descending order based on the Salary field, move to the fourth record, print this record, and then close the data access page.
4. Create a custom data access page based on the **Recruiter** and **Student** tables. Use the design in Figure 8-59 as a guide.

**Figure 8-59**

a. Place the five fields from the **Recruiter** table in the Recruiter Header section.
b. Place the FirstName, LastName, Nation, and BirthDate fields from the **Student** table in the Student Header section.
c. Select the Axis theme. If this theme is not available on your computer, select another theme.
d. In the Recruiter Header section, if necessary, change the labels' font size to 8 and text boxes' font to Times New Roman 8; and then move and resize the labels and text boxes.

   e. Reduce the height of the Recruiter Header section, and set its DataPageSize property to 5.
   f. If necessary, change the labels' font size to 8 in the Student Caption section, and change the text boxes' font to Times New Roman 8.
   g. Use Recruiters with Students as the title for the data access page, left align the title, and then delete the blank line between the title and the Recruiter Header section.
   h. Save the data access page as **RecruitersWithStudents** in the Intro\Review folder.
   i. Close the data access page, use the Web Page Preview command to view the data access page, expand the third record (Kye Nguyen), print the Web page, and then close your Web browser.
5. Create a PivotChart on a new data access page as follows:
   a. Use the **Student** table as the data source for the PivotChart, and select the stacked column chart type.
   b. Increase the width of the PivotChart control so that you can see the control's Field List button. Select Nation as the category field, Gender as the series field, LastName as the data field, and SSN as the filter field.
   c. Increase the height and width of the PivotChart control so that you can see the nation values in the chart and all columns of data.
   d. Use Students by Nation as the title for the data access page.
   e. Save the data access page as **StudentsByNation** in the Intro\Review folder, and then close the data access page.
   f. Use the Web Page Preview command to view the data access page, display the legend, and then print the page.
   g. Use the SSN filter to select the first five recruiters, print the page, and then close your Web browser.
6. Export the **SelectedBonusQuotas** query as an XML file named **SelectedBonusQuotas** to the Intro\Review folder; do not create a separate XSD file.
7. Export the **SelectedBonusQuotas** query as an Excel worksheet. In the worksheet, add a calculation in cell E12 for the grand total salary, resize the Salary column (if necessary), print the worksheet, save the worksheet as SelectedBonusQuotas in the Intro\Review folder, and then close the worksheet.
8. Close the **Students** database, and then exit Access.

# Case Problem 1

**Apply**

*Use the skills you learned in the tutorial to work with the data contained in a video photography database.*

**Explore**

**Data File needed for this Case Problem: Clients.mdb (*cont. from Tutorial 7*)**

***Lim's Video Photography*** Youngho Lim wants to be able to use his Web browser to view data stored in the Clients database. He asks you to export table data and a report as Web pages, create data access pages, and export data to an XML file. To do so, you'll complete the following steps:

1. Open the **Clients** database in the Intro\Case1 folder provided with your Data Files.
2. Export the **ShootDesc** table as an HTML document to the Intro\Case1 folder; do not use a template. Use your Web browser to open the **ShootDesc** HTML document, print the page, and then close your Web browser.
3. Export the **ClientsAndContracts** report as an HTML document to the Intro\Case1 folder; do not use a template. Use your Web browser to open the **ClientsAndContracts** HTML document. Then scroll to the bottom of the document; use the First, Previous, Next, and Last links to navigate through the document; print page 4 of the report; and then close your Web browser. (*Note:* The report title will appear truncated on the right when you view the HTML document.)

4. Use the Page Wizard to create a data access page based on the **Client** table as follows:

   a. Select all fields from the **Client** table, do not select any grouping levels, sort in ascending order by the ClientName field, use Client Page as the title, and then open the page.

   b. Use the data access page to add a new record to the **Client** table with these values: ClientName of "Trent, Brenda", ClientID of 982, Address of 18 Sunset Rd, City of Hurley, State of CA, Zip of 94449, and Phone of 6286312041. Save the record.

   c. Close the page, saving it as **ClientPage** in the Intro\Case1 folder.

   d. Open the **Client** table datasheet, print the datasheet, and then close the table.

5. Create a custom data access page based on the **Client** and **Contract** tables. Use the design in Figure 8-60 as a guide.

**Figure 8-60**

a. Place the ClientID, ClientName, and Phone fields from the **Client** table in the Client Header section.

b. Place the ContractID, ContractDate, and ContractAmt fields from the **Contract** table in the Contract Header section.

c. Select the Expedition theme. If this theme is not available on your computer, select another theme.

d. In the Client Header section, delete the labels, and move and resize the text boxes to match Figure 8-60. Reduce the width of the text boxes in the Contract Header section.

**Explore**

e. Reduce the height of the Client Header section, set its DataPageSize property to 6, and then change its default sort to an ascending sort based on the ClientName field. (*Hint*: Set the DefaultSort property for the Client Header section in the Group Level Properties dialog box; use Help if you need more information about setting the DefaultSort property.)

f. Use Clients and Their Contracts as the title for the data access page, left align the title, and then delete the blank line between the title and the Client Header section.

g. Save the data access page as **ClientsAndTheirContracts** in the Intro\Case1 folder.

h. Close the data access page, use the Web Page Preview command to view the data access page, navigate to the page that contains the client record with your name, expand that record, print the Web page, and then close your Web browser.

6. Create a PivotTable on a new data access page as follows:

a. Select City from the **Client** table as the row field, ContractAmt from the **Contract** table as the detail field, ContractDate from the **Contract** table as the filter field, and ShootType from the **Shoot** table as the column field.

b. Increase the height and width of the PivotTable control so that you can see Grand Total row and the entire GR column. Set the PivotTable title bar caption to CityAndShootPivotTable.

c. Use City and Shoot PivotTable as the title for the data access page, and then delete the blank line between the title and the PivotTable.

d. Save the data access page as **CityAndShootPivotTable** in the Intro\Case1 folder.

e. Switch to Page view.

f. Use the ContractDate filter to select all April dates, print the page, and then close the page.

7. Export the **ClientContractAmounts** query as an XML file named **ClientContractAmounts** to the Intro\Case1 folder; do not create a separate XSD file.

8. Export the **ClientContractAmounts** query as an Excel worksheet. In the worksheet, add a calculation in cell D22 for the grand total contract amount, print the worksheet, and then save and close the worksheet.

9. Close the **Clients** database, and then exit Access.

# Case Problem 2

**Data Files needed for this Case Problem: Choices.xml, Delivery.mdb (*cont. from Tutorial 7*), and Skillet.htm**

***DineAtHome.course.com***  Claire Picard wants to be able to use her Web browser to view data stored in the Delivery database. She asks you to export data retrieved by a query and a report as HTML documents, create data access pages, and export data as XML documents and Excel worksheets. To do so, you'll complete the following steps:

1. Open the **Delivery** database in the Intro\Case2 folder provided with your Data Files.

2. Export the **LargeOrders** query as an HTML document to the Intro\Case2 folder; do not use a template. Use your Web browser to open the **LargeOrders** HTML document, print the page, and then close your Web browser.

3. Export the **RestaurantOrders** report as an HTML document to the Intro\Case2 folder; do not use a template. Use your Web browser to open the **RestaurantOrders** HTML document. Then scroll to the bottom of the document; use the First, Previous, Next, and Last links to navigate through the Web page; print the last page of the report; and then close your Web browser. (*Note:* The report title and some labels will appear truncated on the right when you view the HTML document.)

4. Use the AutoPage: Columnar Wizard to create a data access page based on the **Order** table, and then do the following:

a. Save the data access page in the Intro\Case2 folder as **OrderPage**.

b. Sort the data access page in descending order based on the OrderDate field.

c. Change the OrderAmt field value for OrderID 3123 from 45.42 to 55.77, and then print this record.

**Apply**

*Apply what you learned in the tutorial to work with the data for an e-commerce business in the food services industry.*

**Explore**

d. Filter the page, selecting all records with a RestaurantID field value of 131. (*Hint:* The second record should have that field value.) Print the last filtered record.

e. Close the data access page.

f. Open the **Order** table datasheet, print the datasheet, and then close the table.

5. Create a custom data access page based on the **Restaurant** and **Order** tables. Use the design in Figure 8-61 as a guide.

**Figure 8-61**

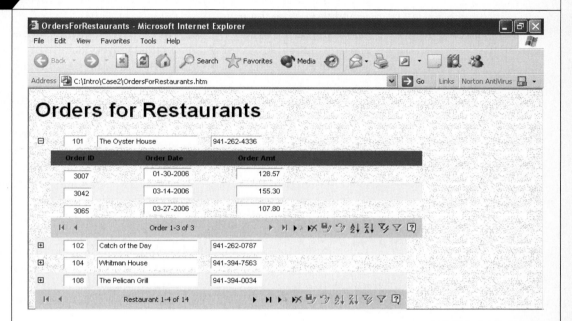

a. Place the RestaurantID, RestaurantName, and Phone fields from the **Restaurant** table in the Restaurant Header section.

b. Place the OrderID, OrderDate, and OrderAmt fields from the **Order** table in the Order Header section.

c. Select the Watermark theme. If this theme is not available on your computer, select another theme.

d. In the Restaurant Header section, delete the labels, and then move and resize the text boxes to match Figure 8-61. Reduce the width of the text boxes in the Order Header section.

e. Reduce the height of the Restaurant Header section, and then set its DataPageSize property to 4.

f. Use Orders for Restaurants as the title for the data access page, delete the blank line between the title and the Restaurant Header section, and then left align the title.

g. Save the data access page as **OrdersForRestaurants** in the Intro\Case2 folder.

h. Close the data access page, use the Web Page Preview command to view the data access page, expand the first record (The Oyster House), print the Web page, and then close your Web browser.

6. Create a PivotChart on a new data access page as follows:

a. Use the **RestaurantOrders** query as the data source for the PivotChart, and select the pie chart type.

b. Increase the width of the PivotChart control so that you can see the control's Field List button. Select City as the category field, Bill Total as the data field, and OrderDate By Month as the filter field.

   c. Increase the height and width of the PivotChart control so that you can see the entire PivotTable toolbar and the pie chart is a readable size.

   d. Use Restaurant Orders as the title for the data access page, delete the blank line between the title and the PivotChart, and then left align the title.

   e. Save the data access page as **RestaurantOrdersChart** in the Intro\Case2 folder.

   f. Use the Web Page Preview command to view the data access page, display the legend, and then print the page.

   g. Use the OrderDate By Month filter to select only the March orders, print the page, and then close the page.

7. Import the data and structure from the XML file named **Choices**, located in the Intro\Case2 folder, as a new table in the **Delivery** database. Open the imported **Selection** table, resize all columns to their best fit, print the first page, and then save and close the table.

8. Export the **Order** table as an XML file named **Order** in the Intro\Case2 folder; do not create a separate XSD file.

9. Export the **Order** table as an Excel worksheet. In the worksheet, add a calculation in cell D39 for the order grand total, print the worksheet, and then save and close the worksheet.

10. Claire has created a Web page in the Intro\Case2 folder containing a description about one of the meal selections. Add a hyperlink field named SelectionDetails to the **Selection** table. Add a hyperlink with the text "Sunshine Skillet" to the record for the Sunshine Skillet field value that opens the **Skillet** file located in the Intro\Case2 folder. Resize the SelectionDetails column to its best fit, and then click the hyperlink. View the short description in the Web page, print the description, and then close your browser.

11. Save and close the **Selection** table, close the **Delivery** database, and then exit Access.

**Apply**

*Apply what you learned in the tutorial to work with a database that contains data about fundraising at a zoo.*

# Case Problem 3

**Data File needed for this Case Problem: Donors.mdb** (*cont. from Tutorial 7*)

***Redwood Zoo*** Michael Rosenfeld wants you to create Web pages for the Donors database so he can use his Web browser to access and view data. To do so, you'll complete the following steps:

1. Open the **Donors** database in the Intro\Case3 folder provided with your Data Files.

2. Export the **Donor** table as an HTML document to the Intro\Case3 folder; do not use a template. Use your browser to open the **Donor** HTML document, print the page, and then close your browser.

**Explore**

3. Export the **FundPledges** report as an HTML document to the Intro\Case3 folder; do not use a template. Use your browser to open the **FundPledges** HTML document. Then scroll to the bottom of the document; use the First, Previous, Next, and Last links to navigate through the document; print the last page of the report; and then close your Web browser.

4. Use the AutoPage: Columnar Wizard to create a data access page based on the **Fund** table, and then do the following:

   a. Save the data access page in the Intro\Case3 folder as **FundPage**.

   b. Sort the data access page in descending order based on the GoalAmt field.

   c. Change the GoalAmt field value for record 2 (Kodiak Bear Exhibit) from $65,000 to $95,000.

d. Close the data access page.

e. Open the **Fund** table recordset, print the recordset, and then close the table.

5. Create a custom data access page based on the **Fund**, **Donor**, and **Pledge** tables. Use the design in Figure 8-62 as a guide.

**Figure 8-62**

a. Place the FundCode, FundName, and GoalAmt fields from the **Fund** table in the Fund Header section.

b. Place the PledgeDate and TotalPledged fields from the **Pledge** table, and the FirstName and LastName fields from the **Donor** table, in the Pledge Header section.

c. Select the Profile theme. If this theme is not available on your computer, select another theme.

d. In the Fund Header section, delete the labels, and then move and resize the text boxes.

e. Reduce the height of the Fund Header section, and then set its DataPageSize property to 3.

f. Use Pledges for Zoo Funds as the title for the data access page, change its font color to blue, delete the blank line between the title and the Fund Header section, and then left align the title.

g. Save the data access page as **PledgesForZooFunds** in the Intro\Case3 folder.

h. Close the data access page, use the Web Page Preview command to view the data access page, expand the third record (Bear Central), print the Web page, and then close your Web browser.

6. Create a PivotChart on a new data access page as follows:

a. Use the **DonorPledges** query as the data source for the PivotChart, and select the stacked bar chart type.

b. Increase the width of the PivotChart control so that you can see the control's Field List button. Select FundCode as the category field, TotalPledged as the data field, PaymentMethod as the series field, and PledgeDate By Month as the filter field.

    c. Increase the height and width of the PivotChart control so that you can see the entire PivotChart toolbar and all rows in the chart.

    d. Use Donor Pledges Chart as the title for the data access page, and then delete the blank line between the title and the PivotChart.

    e. Save the data access page as **DonorPledgesChart** in the Intro\Case3 folder.

    f. Close the data access page, use the Web Page Preview command to view the data access page, display the legend, and then print the page.

    g. Use the PledgeDate By Month filter to select pledges in the last two quarters, print the page, and then close the browser.

7. Export the **Pledge** table as an XML file named **Pledge** to the Intro\Case3 folder; do not create a separate XSD file.

8. Export the **Pledge** table as an Excel worksheet. In the worksheet, add a calculation in cell E30 for the total pledged grand total, print the worksheet in landscape orientation, and then save and close the worksheet.

9. Close the **Donors** database, and then exit Access.

# Case Problem 4

**Challenge**

*Use the skills you've learned, and explore some new skills, to work with the data for an outdoor adventure company.*

**Data File needed for this Case Problem: Outdoors.mdb (*cont. from Tutorial 7*)**

***Mountain River Adventures*** Connor and Siobhan Dempsey travel frequently and need to access data from the Outdoors database using their Web browsers. They ask you to export a query and a report as HTML documents, and to create data access pages based on database tables. Finally, they need to use the data in a query in Excel and also in another application that requires XML data. To make these changes, you'll complete the following steps:

1. Open the **Outdoors** database in the Intro\Case4 folder provided with your Data Files.

2. Export the **TripDates** query as an HTML document to the Intro\Case4 folder; do not use a template. Use your Web browser to open the **TripDates** HTML document, print the page, and then close your Web browser.

**Explore**

3. Export the **Bookings** report as an HTML document to the Intro\Case4 folder; do not use a template. Use your Web browser to open the **Bookings** HTML document. Then scroll to the bottom of the document; use the First, Previous, Next, and Last links to navigate through the Web page; print the last page of the report; and then close your Web browser.

4. Use the Page Wizard to create a data access page based on the **Costs** query as follows:

    a. Select all fields from the **Costs** query, select River as a grouping level, sort in ascending order by the TripDate field, use Costs Page as the title, and then open the page.

    b. Navigate to the last record (South Platte River), navigate to the second record for that group, and then print the page.

    c. Close the page, saving it as **CostsPage** in the Intro\Case4 folder.

**Explore**

5. Create a custom data access page based on the **Client** and **Booking** tables. Use the design in Figure 8-63 as a guide.

**Figure 8-63**

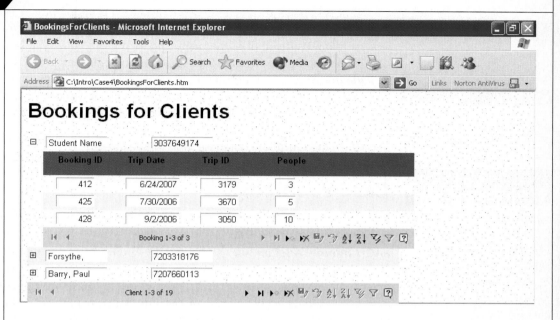

a. Place the ClientName and Phone fields from the **Client** table in the Client Header section.

b. Place the BookingID, TripDate, TripID, and People fields from the **Booking** table in the Booking Header section.

c. Select the Pixel theme. If this theme is not available on your computer, select another theme.

d. In the Client Header section, delete the labels, and then move and resize the text boxes.

e. In the Booking Header section, modify the width of the text boxes.

f. Reduce the height of the Client Header section, and then set its DataPageSize property to 3.

g. Use Bookings for Clients as the title for the data access page, delete the blank line between the title and the Client Header section, and then left align the title.

h. Save the data access page as **BookingsForClients** in the Intro\Case4 folder.

i. Close the data access page, use the Web Page Preview command to view the data access page, expand the record that contains your name, print the Web page, and then close your Web browser.

6. Create a PivotChart on a new data access page as follows:

a. Use the **BookedRaftingTrips** query as the data source for the PivotChart, and select the stacked bar chart type.

b. Increase the width of the PivotChart control so that you can see the control's Field List button. Select TripDays as the category field, TripFee as the data field, People as the series field, and River as the filter field.

c. Increase the height and width of the PivotChart control so that you can see the entire PivotChart toolbar and the individual bars are readable.

d. Use Booked Rafting Trips Chart as the title for the data access page, and then delete the blank line between the title and the PivotChart.

e. Save the data access page as **BookedRaftingTripsChart** in the Intro\Case4 folder.

f.  Close the data access page, use the Web Page Preview command to view the data access page, display the legend, and then print the page.

g.  Use the River filter to select trips for all rivers except those occurring on the Arkansas River, print the page, and then close your Web browser.

7.  Export the **BookedRaftingTrips** query as an XML file named **BookedRaftingTrips** to the Intro\Case4 folder; do not create a separate XSD file.

**Explore**

8.  Export the **BookedRaftingTrips** table as an Excel worksheet. In the worksheet, add a calculation in cell J24 for the grand total trip fee, print the worksheet to fit on one page, and then save and close the worksheet.

9.  Close the **Outdoors** database, and then exit Access.

# Case Problem 5

**Challenge**

*Work with the skills you've learned, and explore some new skills, to create additional objects for a database for an Internet auction site.*

**Data Files needed for this Case Problem: eACH.mdb (*cont. from Tutorial 7*), eACH-Rpt.htm, and eACH-Tbl.htm**

*eACH Internet Auction Site*   Chris and Pat Aquino want you to continue your development of their Internet auction site for collectibles. They want you to export some of the eACH database data as HTML documents for their registrants to view. They also want you to create two data access pages, an XML file, and a hyperlink field that's linked to Word documents. One of the data access pages will allow buyers to view categories with their subcategories when they're searching for items that might be of interest to them. They ask you to make the following changes to the eACH database:

1.  Open the **eACH** database in the Intro\Case5 folder provided with your Data Files.

2.  Export the **Item** table to an HTML document in the Intro\Case5 folder, using the HTML template named **eACH-Tbl**, which is located in the Intro\Case5 folder. Use your Web browser to open the **Item** HTML document, print the page, and then close your Web browser.

**Explore**

3.  Export the custom report you created in Tutorial 7 to an HTML document in the Intro\Case5 folder, using the HTML template named **eACH-Rpt**, which is located in the Intro\Case5 folder. Use your Web browser to open the HTML document that you created, print the report, and then close your Web browser.

4.  Use the AutoPage: Columnar Wizard to create a data access page based on the **Registrant** table, and then complete the following:

a.  Use the data access page to add a new record with your name to the **Registrant** table with additional data that you create.

b.  Sort the data access page in ascending order based on the field that contains the registrant's last name.

c.  Print the first record.

d.  Close the data access page, saving it as **RegistrantPage** in the Intro\Case5 folder.

**Explore**

5.  Design and then create a custom data access page that satisfies the following requirements:

a.  Place all the fields from the **Category** table in the Category Header section.

b.  Place all the fields, except for the common field, from the **Subcategory** table in the Subcategory Header section.

c.  Select the Edge theme. If this theme is not available on your computer, select another theme.

d.  In the Category Header section, move the labels and text boxes into a row, and then resize the text boxes. Resize the text boxes in the Subcategory Header section.

e. Reduce the height of the Category Header section, and then set its DataPageSize property to 4.

f. Use an appropriate title for the page.

g. Save the data access page as **CategoriesAndSubcategoriesPage** in the Intro\Case5 folder.

h. Close the page, use the Web Page Preview command to view the page, expand a record with related records, print the Web page, and then close your Web page.

6. Export the **Registrant** table as an XML file named **Registrant** to the Intro\Case5 folder; do not create a separate XSD file.

**Explore**

7. Given the test data you created in Tutorial 5, you should have at least two items you've posted for sale on eACH. To attract bidders to those items, you should include visuals and short descriptions of them by completing the following:

a. Create at least three Word documents and save them with appropriate filenames in the Intro\Case5 folder. In each document, write a short description for one of the items in your database. Also, include an appropriate graphic or picture (that you locate in the Microsoft Clip Art Gallery or download from the Internet) for the item. Save each document.

b. Add a hyperlink field named Visual to the **Item** table. Add hyperlink field values for each item that has a corresponding Word document.

c. Click the hyperlink for one of the items. View the Word document, print the document, and then close Word.

8. Close the **eACH** database, and then exit Access.

**Research**

# Internet Assignments

The purpose of the Internet Assignments is to challenge you to find information on the Internet that you can use to work effectively with this software. The actual assignments are updated and maintained on the Course Technology Web site. Log on to the Internet and use your Web browser to go to the Student Online Companion for New Perspectives Office 2003 at **www.course.com/np/office2003**. Click the Internet Assignments link, and then navigate to the assignments for this tutorial.

**Assess**

## SAM Assessment and Training

If you have a SAM user profile, you may have access to hands-on instruction, practice, and assessment of the skills covered in this tutorial. Log in to your SAM account and go to your assignments page to see what your instructor has assigned.

**Review**

# Quick Check Answers

### Session 8.1

1. The World Wide Web is a vast collection of digital documents stored on Web servers linked through the Internet, and you use a Web browser to view the information on the Web in the form of Web pages.

2. A hyperlink links one Web document to another.

3. HTML (HyperText Markup Language) is the language used to create most Web documents.

4. An HTML template is a file that contains HTML instructions for creating a Web page with both text and graphics, together with special instructions that tell Access where to place the Access data on the page.
5. A static Web page shows the state of the database object at the time the page was created. Any subsequent changes made to the database object, such as updates to field values in records, are not reflected in a static Web page. In contrast, a data access page is a dynamic HTML document that you can open with a Web browser to view or update current data in an Access database.
6. connection
7. A grouped data access page is a data access page that uses two or more group levels to display information from general categories to specific details.
8. A theme is a predefined style for a data access page.

## Session 8.2

1. A PivotTable is an interactive table that lets you analyze data dynamically using a Web browser.
2. filter
3. data access pages, forms, datasheets
4. For datasheets and data access pages, only one expand indicator appears at a time and is active; clicking the expand indicator causes the data to expand or collapse and to change to the other expand indicator. For PivotTables, both expand indicators appear, even though only one is active at any given time.
5. total
6. data
7. series

## Session 8.3

1. HTML; XML
2. static
3. The XSD (XML Structure Definition) file contains table structure information, including information about the table's primary key and indexes.
4. Select the table or query in the Database window, click the OfficeLinks list arrow, and then click Analyze It with Microsoft Excel.
5. a hyperlink or pointer to another object in the database, to a file, or to a Web page
6. Click the hyperlink field value to start the associated program and open the hyperlinked document or object.

New Perspectives on

# Microsoft® Office Access 2003

# Read This Before You Begin: Tutorials 9–12

## To the Student

### Data Files

To complete the Level III Access Tutorials (Tutorials 9 through 12), you need the starting student Data Files. Your instructor will either provide you with these Data Files or ask you to obtain them yourself.

The Level III Access tutorials require the following folders to complete the Tutorials, Review Assignments, and Case Problems.

Comp\Tutorial folder
Comp\Review folder
Comp\Case1 folder
Comp\Case2 folder
Comp\Case3 folder
Comp\Case4 folder
Comp\Case5 folder

You will need to copy these folders from a file server, a standalone computer, or the Web to the drive and folder where you will be storing your Data Files. (These Data Files can not be stored on floppy disks.) Your instructor will tell you which computer, drive letter, and folder(s) contain the files you need. You can also download the files by going to www.course.com; see the inside back or front cover for more information on downloading the files, or ask your instructor or technical support person for assistance.

The Data Files you work with in each tutorial in Level III build on the work you did in the previous tutorial. Thus in Tutorial 10, you will use the Data Files that resulted after you completed the steps in Tutorial 9, the Tutorial 9 Review Assignments, and the Case Problems.

### Course Labs

There are no Course Labs for the Level III Access tutorials.

## To the Instructor

The Data Files and Course Labs are available on the Instructor Resources CD for this title. Follow the instructions in the Help file on the CD to install the programs to your network or standalone computer. See the "To the Student" section above for information on how to set up the Data Files that accompany this text.

You are granted a license to copy the Data Files and Course Labs to any computer or computer network used by students who have purchased this book.

## System Requirements

**If you are going to work through this book using your own computer, you need:**

- **Computer System**  PC with Pentium 133-MHz or higher processor; Pentium III recommended. Microsoft Windows 2000 operating system with Service Pack 3 or later, Windows XP recommended.

These tutorials assume a typical installation of Microsoft Access 2003.

- **Data Files**  You will not be able to complete the tutorials or exercises in this book using your own computer until you have the necessary starting Data Files.

## Objectives

**Session 9.1**
- Create an action query to create a table
- Create action queries to append, delete, and update data

**Session 9.2**
- Define many-to-many and one-to-one relationships between tables
- View and create indexes for tables
- Learn about joining tables
- Join a table using a self-join

# Using Action Queries and Defining Table Relationships

*Enhancing User Interaction with the Overseas Database*

## Case

## Northeast Seasonal Jobs International (NSJI)

Several years ago, Elsa Jensen founded Northeast Seasonal Jobs International (NSJI), a small Boston firm that serves as a job broker between foreign students seeking part-time, seasonal work and resort businesses located in New England and the eastern provinces of Canada. At first the company focused mainly on summer employment, but as the business continued to grow, Elsa increased the scope of operations to include all types of seasonal opportunities, including foliage tour companies in the fall and ski resorts in the winter.

Elsa incorporated the use of computers in all aspects of the business, including financial management, payroll, accounts payable, and student recruitment. Her company developed the Overseas database of employer and position data and uses **Microsoft Office Access 2003** (or simply **Access**) to manage it.

The Overseas database contains tables, queries, forms, and reports that Elsa, Zack Ward, director of marketing, and Matt Griffin, manager of recruitment, use to track students, employers, and jobs.

Elsa, Zack, and Matt have found the Overseas database to be very useful in managing the company's data. They have asked you to continue enhancing the database by creating some advanced queries and integrating more tables into the database.

## Student Data Files

▼ **Comp**

▽ **Tutorial folder**
    Overseas.mdb

▽ **Review folder**
    Work.mdb

▽ **Case1 folder**
    Shoots.mdb

▽ **Case2 folder**
    AtHome.mdb

▽ **Case3 folder**
    ZooFunds.mdb

▽ **Case4 folder**
    Rivers.mdb

▽ **Case5 folder**
    BuySell.mdb

# Session 9.1

# Action Queries

Queries can do more than display answers to the questions you ask; they can also perform actions on the data in your database. An **action query** is a query that adds, changes, or deletes multiple table records at a time. For example, if the NAICS code changes for one business classification, Elsa can use an action query to update all employers in that business classification to the new NAICS code. (NAICS codes are the North American Industry Classification System codes used to classify businesses by their activities.) Because action queries modify many records in a table at a time, Access allows you to preview the query results before you actually run the action query. After you confirm that the query works correctly, you can save and run it as an action query.

Access provides four types of action queries: the make-table query, the append query, the delete query, and the update query.

A **make-table query** creates a new table by copying records from one or more existing tables. The new table can be an exact copy of the records in an existing table, a subset of the fields and records in an existing table, or a combination of the fields and records from two or more tables. Access does not delete the selected fields and records from the existing tables. You can use make-table queries, for example, to create backup copies of tables or to create customized tables for others to use. The new table reflects data at a point in time; future changes made to the underlying tables will not be reflected in the new table. You need to run the make-table query periodically if you want the newly created table to contain current data.

An **append query** adds records from existing tables or queries to the end of another table. For an append query, you choose the fields you want to append from one or more tables or queries; the selected data remains in the original tables. Usually you append records to history tables. A **history table** contains data that is no longer needed for current processing but that you might need to reference in the future. Tables containing data about cleared bank checks, former employees, inactive customers, and obsolete products are examples of history tables. Because the records you append to a history table are no longer needed for current processing, you can delete the records from the original table after you append the records to the history table.

A **delete query** deletes a group of records matching the criteria you specify from one or more tables. You choose which records you want to delete by entering selection criteria. Deleting records removes them permanently from the database. Quite often, delete queries are run after append queries have added those same records to history tables, allowing you to verify that you appended the correct records before you delete them.

An **update query** changes selected field values from selected records in one or more tables. You choose the fields and records you want to change by entering the selection criteria and the update rules. You can use update queries, for example, to increase the salaries of selected employee groups by a specified percentage or to change the billing dates of selected customers from one date to another. Update queries are particularly valuable in performing multiple updates to large tables.

## Creating a Make-Table Query

Elsa wants to call NSJI's employer clients in the bed-and-breakfast industry. The owners of these inns personally manage all aspects of their businesses and expect frequent contact by Elsa and her staff. She asks you to create a new table containing the EmployerName, ContactFirstName, ContactLastName, Phone, and NAICSCode fields from the Employer table records for all employers whose NAICS code is 721191, which is the code for businesses in the bed-and-breakfast industry. She wants to create a new table so she can modify it by adding notes that she will take when she calls the inn owners. By creating a new table, Elsa won't need to worry about disrupting or changing the data in any existing tables or in any objects on which those existing tables are based.

You can create the new table for Elsa by using a make-table query that uses fields from the Employer table in the Overseas database. When you run a make-table query, you create a new table. The records in the new table are based on the records in the query's underlying tables. The fields in the new table have the data type and field size of the fields in the query's underlying tables. The new table does not preserve the primary key designation or field properties such as the format or lookup properties.

## Creating a Make-Table Query

Reference Window

- Create a select query with the necessary fields and selection criteria.
- Click the Run button on the Query Design toolbar to preview the results.
- Switch to Design view to make any necessary changes. When the query is correct, click the list arrow for the Query Type button on the Query Design toolbar.
- Click Make-Table Query.
- In the Make Table dialog box, type the new table name in the Table Name list box. Make sure the Current Database option button is selected to include the new table in the current database; or, click the Another Database option button and enter the database name in the File Name text box. Then click the OK button.
- Click the Run button on the Query Design toolbar.
- Click the Yes button to confirm creating the new table.

Now you can create the new table using a make-table query. You'll base the make-table query on the Employer table to enter the fields and records that Elsa wants in the new table.

### To create and run the select query based on the Employer table:

1. Make sure you have created your copy of the Access Data Files, and that your computer can access them.

   **Trouble?** If you don't have the Access Data Files, you need to get them before you can proceed. Your instructor will either give you the Data Files or ask you to obtain them from a specified location (such as a network drive). In either case, be sure that you make a backup copy of your Data Files before you start using them, so that the original files will be available on your copied disk in case you need to start over, because of an error or problem. If you have any questions about the Data Files, see your instructor or technical support person for assistance.

   **Trouble?** If you are not sure where to store your Data Files, read the "Read This Before You Begin" page or ask your instructor for help.

2. Start Access, and then open the **Overseas** database located in the Comp\Tutorial folder provided with your Data Files.

   **Trouble?** If a dialog box opens with a message about installing the Microsoft Jet Service Pack, see your instructor or technical support person for assistance. You must have the appropriate Service Pack installed in order to open and work with Access databases safely.

   **Trouble?** If a dialog box opens, warning you that the Overseas database may not be safe, click the Open button. Your security level is set to Medium, which is the security setting that lets you choose whether or not to open a database that contains macros, VBA, or certain types of queries. The Overseas database does not contain objects that will harm your computer, so you can safely open the database.

**Trouble?** If a dialog box opens, warning you that Access can't open the Overseas database due to security restrictions, click the OK button, click Tools on the menu bar, point to Macro, click Security, click the Medium option button, click the OK button, restart your computer if you're requested to do so, and then repeat Step 2. Your security level was set to High, which is the security setting that lets you open a database that contains macros, VBA, or certain types of queries only from trusted sources. Because the Overseas database does not contain objects that will harm your computer, you need to change the security setting to Medium and then safely open the Overseas database.

3. Click **Queries** in the Objects bar of the Database window (if necessary), click the **New** button to open the New Query dialog box, make sure that **Design View** is selected, and then click the **OK** button.

4. Add the **Employer** table field list to the Query window, and then close the Show Table dialog box.

   Now you can add the fields that Elsa needs to the design grid.

5. In the Employer field list, double-click **EmployerName**, double-click **ContactFirstName**, double-click **ContactLastName**, double-click **Phone**, and then double-click **NAICSCode**, scrolling as necessary, to add these five fields to the design grid.

   Next, you'll enter the NAICSCode field's selection criterion of 721191 for bed-and-breakfast inns.

6. Click the **NAICSCode Criteria** text box, type **721191**, and then press the ↓ key. The condition changes to "721191". See Figure 9-1.

| Figure 9-1 | Select query on which to base the make-table query |

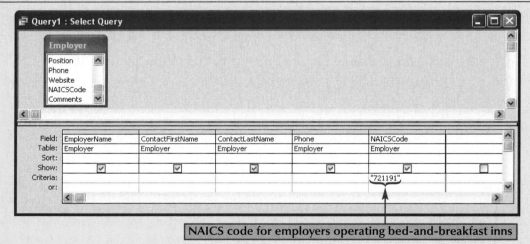

NAICS code for employers operating bed-and-breakfast inns

You've completed the select query, so now you can run it to make sure the recordset contains the data Elsa needs.

7. Run the query, and then resize all columns to their best fit. The query recordset shows the 11 records for employers operating bed-and-breakfast inns.

Now that you have the correct select query, you can change the query to a make-table query.

### To change the query type, and then run and save the make-table query:

1. Switch to Design view, click the list arrow for the **Query Type** button 🔲 on the Query Design toolbar, and then click **Make-Table Query**. Access opens the Make Table dialog box, in which you enter the name of the new table. See Figure 9-2.

Make Table dialog box ◀ **Figure 9-2**

option to create the new table in the Overseas database

option to create the new table in another database

enter the new table name here

2. In the Table Name list box, type **ContactEmployers**, make sure the **Current Database** option button is selected so that the new table will be included in the Overseas database, and then press the **Enter** key.

   Now that you have created and tested the query, you can run it to create the ContactEmployers table. After you run the query, you can save it, and then you can view the new table.

3. Run the query. Access opens a dialog box indicating that you are about to paste 11 rows into a new table. Because you are running an action query, which alters the contents of the database, Access gives you an opportunity to cancel the operation, if necessary, or to confirm it.

4. Click the **Yes** button. Access closes the dialog box, runs the make-table query to create the ContactEmployers table, and continues displaying the Query window in Design view.

5. Save the query as **ContactEmployersMakeTable**, and then close the query. The ContactEmployersMakeTable query appears in the Queries list with a special icon indicating that it is a make-table query.

   You can now open the ContactEmployers table to view the results of the make-table query.

6. Open the **ContactEmployers** table in Datasheet view, resize all datasheet columns to their best fit, and then deselect the columns (if necessary). See Figure 9-3.

ContactEmployers table datasheet ◀ **Figure 9-3**

**ContactEmployers : Table**

| EmployerName | ContactFirstName | ContactLastName | Phone | NAICSCode |
|---|---|---|---|---|
| The Inn at Plum Hill | Michele | Yasenak | 508-693-2320 | 721191 |
| The Adele Bannister House | Cheryl | Coppolino | 401-849-3093 | 721191 |
| The Clipper Ship Inn | Oren | Ben-Joseph | 978-546-0193 | 721191 |
| Darby Inn & Restaurant | Jahnavi | Sonthi | 802-987-4603 | 721191 |
| Lion's Mouth Inn | Bryce | Kervin | 802-253-9775 | 721191 |
| Moondance Inn & Ski Resort | Sonya | Krikorian | 603-635-9208 | 721191 |
| The Briar Rose Inn | Helen | MacDonald | 902-626-1595 | 721191 |
| Pear Tree Inn & Restaurant | Rachel | Camara | 413-637-4745 | 721191 |
| Auberge St-Germaine | Jacques | Belanger | 819-424-9003 | 721191 |
| Stonehurst Inn | Gavin | McDonough | 902-484-8354 | 721191 |
| The Berkshire House | Lubin | Jian | 413-637-9670 | 721191 |

The ContactEmployers table includes the EmployerName, ContactFirstName, ContactLastName, Phone, and NAICSCode fields for employers in the bed-and-breakfast industry. Notice that the make-table query did not include each field's Caption property setting from the Employer table in the ContactEmployers table. For example, Access uses the field name of EmployerName as a column heading in the ContactEmployer table, because the Caption property is null for the field, but Access uses the Caption property setting of Employer Name as a column heading in the Employer table.

▶ **7.** Save your datasheet changes, and then close the table.

Elsa can now make any necessary changes to the ContactEmployers table records when she contacts the employers without affecting the Employer table in the Overseas database.

## Creating an Append Query

Elsa has decided to expand the list of employers that she will call to ensure personalized service. She wants to add the EmployerName, ContactFirstName, ContactLastName, Phone, and NAICSCode fields for all employers with limited-service restaurants. She asks you to add these new records to the ContactEmployers table. You could make this change by modifying the selection criterion in the ContactEmployersMakeTable query to select employers with NAICS code field values of either 721191 (bed-and-breakfast inns) or 722211 (limited-service restaurants). If you ran this modified query, however, you would overwrite the existing ContactEmployers table with a new table. If Elsa had made any changes to the existing ContactEmployers records, creating a new table would overwrite these changes, as well.

Instead, you will modify the ContactEmployersMakeTable query to select only those employers with limited-service restaurants and change the query to an append query. When you run this new query, the selected records will be appended to the records in the existing ContactEmployers table.

| Reference Window | **Creating an Append Query** |
| --- | --- |

- Create a select query with the necessary fields and selection criteria.
- Click the Run button on the Query Design toolbar to preview the results.
- Switch to Design view to make any necessary changes. When the query is correct, click the list arrow for the Query Type button on the Query Design toolbar, and then click Append Query.
- In the Append dialog box, type the name of the table to which you want to append the selected records in the Table Name list box. Make sure the Current Database option button is selected to append the records in the current database; or, click the Another Database option button and enter the database name in the File Name text box. Then click the OK button. Access replaces the Show row in the design grid with the Append To row.
- Click the Run button on the Query Design toolbar.
- Click the Yes button to confirm appending the records to the table.

You can now modify the ContactEmployersMakeTable query to create the append query you'll use to include the additional employer data Elsa wants in the ContactEmployers table.

## To create the append query:

1. Open the **ContactEmployersMakeTable** query in Design view.

   You'll change the selection criterion to 722211, which is the NAICS code for limited-service restaurants.

2. Click the **NAICSCode Criteria** text box, press the **F2** key to highlight the entire condition, type **722211**, and then press the ↓ key. The condition changes to "722211". See Figure 9-4.

**Changing the selection criterion**  Figure 9-4

employers operating limited-service restaurants

Before you can run the query to append the records to the ContactEmployers table, you have to change it to an append query. It is always a good idea to test an action query before you run it, so you will first change the query to a select query and run it to make sure the correct records are selected. Then you will change it to an append query and run it to append the new records to the ContactEmployers table.

3. Click the list arrow for the **Query Type** button 🔲! on the Query Design toolbar, and then click **Select Query**.

4. Run the query, and then deselect the highlighted Employer Name column value. The query recordset shows the three records for employers with limited-service restaurant businesses. See Figure 9-5.

**Recordset displaying employers operating limited-service restaurants** Figure 9-5

These three records are the additional records you will append to the ContactEmployers table. Now that the results show that the query is correct, you can change the query to an append query.

5. Switch to Design view, click the list arrow for the **Query Type** button 🔲 on the Query Design toolbar, and then click **Append Query**. Access opens the Append dialog box, in which you enter the name of the table to which you want to append the data.

> **6.** Make sure **ContactEmployers** appears in the Table Name list box and that the **Current Database** option button is selected, and then click the **OK** button. Access replaces the Show row with the Append To row between the Sort and Criteria rows in the design grid. See Figure 9-6.

**Figure 9-6** | **Query window for the append query**

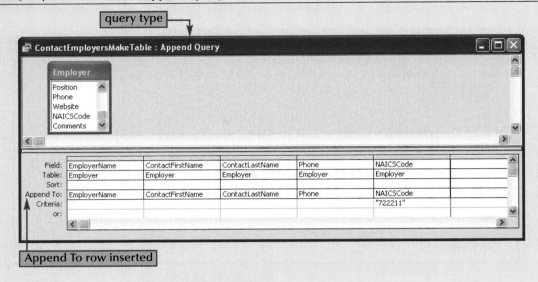

The Append To row in the design grid identifies the fields that the query will append to the designated table. The EmployerName, ContactFirstName, ContactLastName, Phone, and NAICSCode fields are selected and will be appended to the ContactEmployers table, which already contains these five fields for employers with bed-and-breakfast inns.

You can now run and then save the append query.

## To run and save the append query:

> **1.** Run the query. Access opens a dialog box warning that you are about to append three rows.

> **2.** Click the **Yes** button to acknowledge the warning. Access closes the dialog box, runs the append query, adds the three records to the ContactEmployers table, and continues displaying the Query window in Design view.

> **3.** Click **File** on the menu bar, and then click **Save As**. The Save As dialog box opens.

> **4.** Type **ContactEmployersAppend** in the Save Query To text box, and then press the **Enter** key. Access saves the query.

> **5.** Close the query. The ContactEmployersAppend query appears in the Queries list with a special icon indicating that it is an append query.

Next, you'll open the ContactEmployers table to make sure that the three records were appended to the table.

> **6.** Open the **ContactEmployers** table in Datasheet view.

The new records have been added to the ContactEmployers table. Because the ContactEmployers table does not have a primary key, the new records appear at the end of the table. You could arrange the records in a different order by sorting the records using the Sort Ascending or Sort Descending button on the Table Datasheet toolbar.

> **7.** Close the table.

## Creating a Delete Query

Elsa has contacted all the employers in the ContactEmployers table who have phone numbers in the 508 and 902 area codes. She asks you to delete these records from the ContactEmployers table so that the table contains only those records for employers she has not yet contacted. You can either delete the table records individually or create a delete query to remove them all at once.

Reference Window

### Creating a Delete Query

- Create a select query with the necessary fields and selection criteria.
- Click the Run button on the Query Design toolbar to preview the results.
- Switch to Design view to make any necessary changes. When the query is correct, click the list arrow for the Query Type button on the Query Design toolbar.
- Click Delete Query. Access replaces the Show and Sort rows in the design grid with the Delete row.
- Click the Run button on the Query Design toolbar.
- Click the Yes button to confirm deleting the records.

You'll create a delete query to delete the records of all the employers in the ContactEmployers table that have phone numbers in the 508 and 902 area codes. First, you'll create a select query to choose the correct records based on the area code criteria. Then you'll test the select query and change it to a delete query.

### To create the delete query:

1. Click **Queries** in the Objects bar of the Database window, click the **New** button to open the New Query dialog box, make sure that **Design View** is selected, and then click the **OK** button.

2. Add the **ContactEmployers** table field list to the Query window, and then close the Show Table dialog box.

3. Double-click the title bar of the ContactEmployers field list to select all the fields in the table, drag the pointer from the highlighted area of the field list to the design grid's first column Field text box, and then release the mouse button. Access adds all the fields to the design grid.

4. Click the **Phone Criteria** text box, type **Like "508*"**, press the ↓ key, and then type **Like "902*"**. Access will select a record only if the Phone field value starts with either 508 or 902.

5. Run the query. The query results display five records, each one with either a 508 or 902 area code. The select query is correct. See Figure 9-7.

**Five records to be deleted** ◀ | Figure 9-7

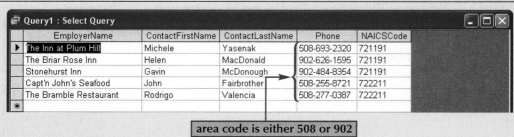

area code is either 508 or 902

**Trouble?** If your query did not select the correct five records, switch to Design view, correct the selection criteria as necessary, and then rerun the query.

Now that you have verified that the correct records are selected, you can change the query to a delete query.

6. Switch to Design view, click the list arrow for the **Query Type** button ▣ on the Query Design toolbar, and then click **Delete Query**. In the design grid, Access replaces the Sort and Show rows with the Delete row. See Figure 9-8.

| Figure 9-8 | Design view for the delete query |

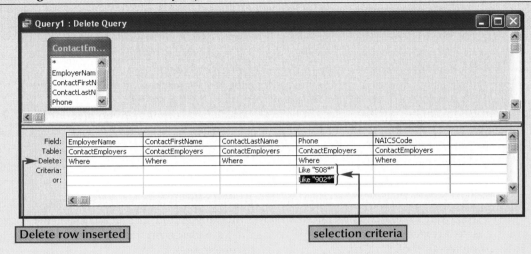

Delete row inserted          selection criteria

Now you can run the query and view the results in the ContactEmployers table.

### To run the delete query, and then view the results:

1. Run the query. Access opens a dialog box warning that you are about to delete five rows.

2. Click the **Yes** button to close the dialog box and run the delete query. Access deletes the five records in the ContactEmployers table and continues to display the Query window in Design view. Because you'll need to run this query only once, you won't save it.

3. Close the query, and then click the **No** button when Access asks if you want to save it.

   You can now open the ContactEmployers table to verify that the records have been deleted.

4. Open the **ContactEmployers** table in Datasheet view. The table now includes only nine records; five records were correctly deleted. See Figure 9-9.

| Figure 9-9 | ContactEmployers table after deleting five records |

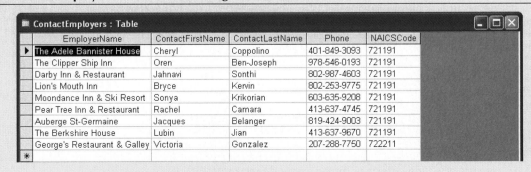

Elsa wants Zack and Matt to split the work of contacting the nine remaining employers in the ContactEmployers table. She asks you to add a new field to the table that will identify whether Zack or Matt will call the employer. To do so, you'll create an update query to add either Zack's or Matt's name to the ContactEmployers table.

## Creating an Update Query

Recall that an update query changes selected fields and records in one or more tables. In this case, you need to create a new field to contain Zack's or Matt's name, and then enter the appropriate values in this new field. You could enter the value for every record in the ContactEmployers table, but you can accomplish the same thing more quickly and with less chance of error by using an update query to enter the values at one time.

### Creating an Update Query

- Create a select query with the necessary fields and selection criteria.
- Click the Run button on the Query Design toolbar to preview the results.
- Switch to Design view to make any necessary changes. When the query is correct, click the list arrow for the Query Type button on the Query Design toolbar.
- Click Update Query. Access replaces the Show and Sort rows in the design grid with the Update To row.
- Type the updated values for the fields you need to update in their Update To text boxes.
- Click the Run button on the Query Design toolbar.
- Click the Yes button to confirm updating the records.

First, you will add a field named Caller to the ContactEmployers table. This new field will contain a field value of either "Zack" or "Matt" to indicate which NSJI employee will contact the employer.

### To add the new Caller field to the ContactEmployers table:

1. Switch to Design view.

2. Click the **Field Name** text box below the NAICSCode field, type **Caller**, and then press the **Tab** key twice to name the field and accept the default text data type.

   Because the new field will contain values of "Zack" or "Matt", which are 4 characters long, you'll change the field size for the new field to 4.

3. Press the **F6** key and then type **4** in the Field Size text box. This completes the addition of the Caller field to the ContactEmployers table. See Figure 9-10.

---

**Figure 9-10** ▷ **Caller field added to the ContactEmployers table**

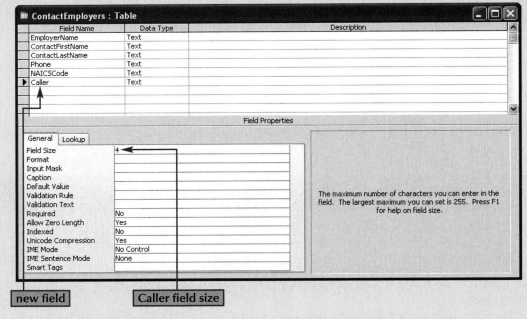

**new field** **Caller field size**

> **4.** Save your table structure changes, and then close the table.

Now you can create an update query to update the Caller field for the records in the ContactEmployers table. You'll change the Caller field value to "Zack" for each employer in the 413 and 802 telephone area codes and to "Matt" for all other employers.

### To create the update query to enter Caller field values:

> **1.** Click **Queries** in the Objects bar of the Database window, click the **New** button to open the New Query dialog box, make sure that **Design View** is selected, and then click the **OK** button.

> **2.** Add the **ContactEmployers** table field list to the Query window, and then close the Show Table dialog box.
>
> You will select the Phone and Caller fields for the query results. The Phone field lets you select records for customers in a particular telephone area code. The Caller field is the field you need to update.

> **3.** In the ContactEmployers field list, double-click the **Phone** and **Caller** fields to add these fields to the design grid, scrolling down the field list as necessary.
>
> You can now select the records for employers in the 413 and 802 telephone area codes and update the Caller field value for those records to "Zack."

> **4.** Click the **Phone Criteria** text box, and then type **Like "413*" Or Like "802*"**. Access will select a record only if the first three digits of the Phone field value are 413 or 802.

> **5.** Run the query. The query recordset displays four records, each one with either a 413 or 802 telephone area code. The select query is correct.
>
> Now that you have verified that the correct records are selected, you can change the query to an update query.

6.  Switch to Design view, click the list arrow for the **Query Type** button 🖻 on the Query Design toolbar, and then click **Update Query**. In the design grid, Access replaces the Sort and Show rows with the Update To row.

    You tell Access how you want to change a field value for the selected records by entering an expression in the field's Update To text box. An expression is a calculation resulting in a single value. You can type a simple expression directly into the Update To text box. If you need help creating a complicated expression, you can create it using Expression Builder, an Access tool that contains an expression box in which the expression is entered, buttons for common operators, and one or more lists of expression elements, such as table and field names. The expression in this case is simple, so you can type it directly in the Update To text box.

7.  Click the **Caller Update To** text box, type **Zack**, and then press the ↓ key. The condition changes to "Zack". See Figure 9-11.

Updating the Caller field   ◀   Figure 9-11

**Trouble?** Your screen might show only part of the criterion in the Phone Criteria text box.

8.  Run the query. Access opens a dialog box warning you that you are about to update four rows in the ContactEmployers table.

9.  Click the **Yes** button to close the dialog box and run the update query. Access updates the Caller field values for the employers with telephone area codes of 413 or 802 and leaves the Query window in Design view open.

Now you need to update the Caller field values for employers that Matt will contact. To do so, you'll modify the criteria and the "Update To" value for the existing update query.

## To update the remaining Caller field values:

1.  Double-click **Zack** in the Caller Update To text box to select it, and then type **Matt**. This is the Caller field value you'll use to update the remaining five records in the ContactEmployers table.

    Matt will call the remaining employers in the ContactEmployers table, so you'll use the Not logical operator to change the existing Phone criterion.

2.  Click the **Phone Criteria** text box, press the **Home** key to position the insertion point at the beginning of the criterion, and then type **Not (**

3. Press the **End** key to position the insertion point at the end of the criterion in the Phone text box, and then type **)** (a closing parenthesis). The entry in the Phone Criteria text box is now *Not (Like "413*" Or Like "802*")*, and Access will select a record only if the Phone field value starts with neither 413 nor 802. See Figure 9-12.

| Figure 9-12 | After changing the update query |
| --- | --- |

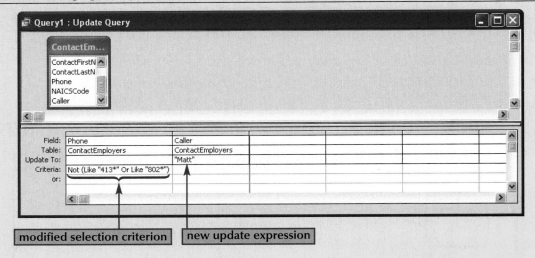

modified selection criterion | new update expression

4. Run the query, and then click the **Yes** button to confirm the update of five rows.
   You are finished updating the ContactEmployers table, so you can close the Query window. Because all the records have been updated, you do not need to save the query.
5. Close the query, and then click the **No** button when Access asks if you want to save it.

Now you can view the ContactEmployers table to see the results of the update operations.

## To view the updated ContactEmployers table:

1. Open the **ContactEmployers** table in Datasheet view. "Zack" is the Caller field value for records with telephone area codes of 413 and 802, and "Matt" is the Caller field value for the other records. See Figure 9-13.

| Figure 9-13 | ContactEmployers table with the updated Caller field values |
| --- | --- |

updated Contact field values

▶ **2.** Close the table.

You usually create an action query and run it for a special purpose. If you create and run an action query, save it, and accidentally run it again, you might update tables in unintended ways. Therefore, after you've run an action query, you usually shouldn't save it in your database. Because you saved the make-table and append queries after you ran them, you'll delete them now.

▶ **3.** Click **Queries** in the Objects bar of the Database window.

▶ **4.** Right-click **ContactEmployersAppend** in the Queries list, click **Delete** on the shortcut menu, and then click the **Yes** button to confirm the deletion.

▶ **5.** Repeat Step 4 to delete the **ContactEmployersMakeTable** query.

▶ **6.** If you are not continuing on to the next session, close the Overseas database, and then exit Access.

Elsa can now use action queries in her future work with the Overseas database. In the next session, you'll learn about the different types of relationships you can create between tables, and view and create indexes to increase a database's efficiency.

## Session 9.1 Quick Check

Review

**1.** What is an action query?

**2.** What precautions should you take before running an action query?

**3.** What is the difference between a make-table query and an append query?

**4.** What does a delete query do?

**5.** What does an update query do?

**6.** How does the design grid change when you create an update query?

# Session 9.2

# Relationships Between Database Tables

As you learned in Tutorial 3, a **one-to-many relationship** (abbreviated as **1:M**) exists between two tables when each record in the primary table matches zero, one, or many records in the related table, and when each record in the related table matches at most one record in the primary table. For example, Figure 9-14 shows a one-to-many relationship between portions of the Employer and Position tables and also shows a sample query based on the two tables. (Most examples in this session use portions of tables for illustrative purposes.) Employer 10151 has three positions, employer 10217 has one position, and employer 10125 has zero positions. The first four positions each have a single matching employer based on the Employer ID foreign key values. The fifth position with a Position ID value of 2199 has a null Employer ID foreign key value. Permitted foreign key values are governed by **referential integrity**, which is the rule that requires each *nonnull* foreign key value to match a primary key value in the primary table.

| **Figure 9-14** | **One-to-many relationship and sample query** |

You use the common field, the Employer ID column, to form the one-to-many relationship between the Employer and Position tables. When you join the two tables based on Employer ID column values, you can extract data from them as if they are one larger table. For example, you can join the Employer and Position tables to create the EmployerPositions query shown in Figure 9-14. In the EmployerPositions query, the Employer Name and State/Prov columns are from the Employer table, and the Position Title, Wage, and Hours/Week columns are from the Position table.

In addition to one-to-many relationships between tables, you can also relate tables through many-to-many and one-to-one relationships.

## Many-to-Many Relationships

A **many-to-many relationship** (abbreviated as **M:N**) exists between two tables when each record in the first table matches many records in the second table, and each record in the second table matches many records in the first table.

In the Overseas database, the Position table contains one record for each position offered by an employer, and the Student table contains one record for each student recruited by NSJI. Because a student can be employed in many positions (at different times), and each position can be filled by many students, the Position and Student tables have a many-to-many relationship, as shown in Figure 9-15.

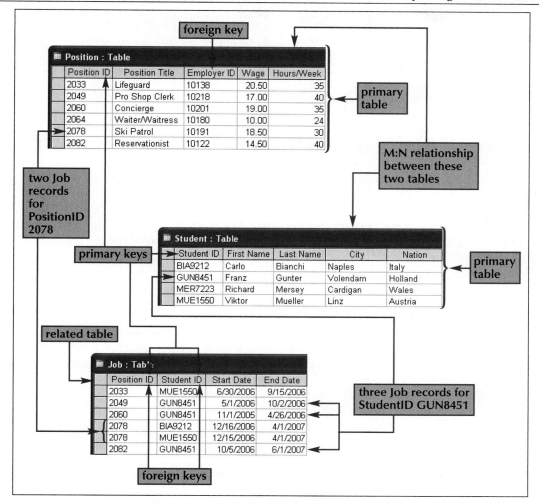

**Position and Student tables with a M:N relationship using the Job table**          Figure 9-15

When you have a many-to-many relationship between two tables, you must create a third table and form one-to-many relationships between the two original primary tables and the new related table. For instance, the Job table exists only because the Position and Student tables have a many-to-many relationship. Each record in the Job table contains two foreign keys: the Position ID column is a foreign key that allows you to join the Position table to the Job table; and the Student ID column is a foreign key that allows you to join the Student table to the Job table. For example, the first record in the Job table represents a Lifeguard position for Employer ID 10138 that was filled by Viktor Mueller with Student ID MUE1550. Franz Gunter, who has Student ID GUN8451, appears in three records in the Job table. These three Job table records appear in three different positions for Position ID column values of 2049, 2060, and 2082. Also, Position ID 2078 appears in two Job table records, each for a different student: Carlo Bianchi and Viktor Mueller. The primary key of the Job table is a composite key, consisting of the combination of the Position ID and Student ID columns. Each pair of values in this primary key is unique.

When you join tables that have a many-to-many relationship, you can extract data from them as if they were one larger table. For example, you can join the Student, Position, and Job tables to create the JobData query shown in Figure 9-16.

**Figure 9-16** ▶ **Query recordset produced by joining tables having a M:N relationship**

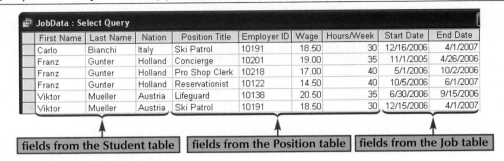

The Position ID column joins the Position and Job tables, and the Student ID column joins the Student and Job tables. In the JobData query, the First Name, Last Name, and Nation columns are from the Student table; the Position Title, Employer ID, Wage, and Hours/Week columns are from the Position table; and the Start Date and End Date columns are from the Job table. The first record in the query recordset shows data from the fourth record in the Job table, joined with data from the matching first record in the Student table and with data from the matching fifth record in the Position table.

## One-to-One Relationships

A **one-to-one relationship** (abbreviated as **1:1**) exists between two tables when each record in the first table matches at most one record in the second table, and each record in the second table matches at most one record in the first table. Most relationships between tables are either one-to-many or many-to-many; the primary use for one-to-one relationships is as entity subtypes. An **entity subtype** is a table whose primary key is a foreign key to a second table and whose fields are additional fields for the second table. For example, the Employer table and the BillingAddress table, which is an entity subtype, have a one-to-one relationship, as shown in Figure 9-17.

**Figure 9-17** ▶ **Employer and BillingAddress tables with a 1:1 relationship**

For most employer clients, the Address, City, State/Prov, PostalCode, and Country fields in the Employer table identify both the employer's location and billing address, which is where NSJI sends the employer's invoices. In a few cases, however, the billing address is different from the location address; additionally, the employer name used for billing purposes is different from the employer name in the Employer table. There are two ways to handle these two sets of names and addresses. The first way is to add BillingName, BillingStreet, BillingCity, BillingStateProv, BillingPostalCode, and BillingCountry fields to the Employer table. For those employers having a different billing name and address, store the appropriate values in these billing fields. For those employers having identical location and billing names and addresses, leave these billing fields null.

As shown in Figure 9-17, the second way to handle the two sets of addresses is to create the entity subtype named BillingAddress. In the BillingAddress table, EmployerID, which is the primary key, is also a foreign key to the Employer table. A record appears in the BillingAddress table only for those employers having a different billing name and address.

When you join tables that have a one-to-one relationship, you can extract data from them as if they were one larger table. For example, you can join the Employer and BillingAddress tables to create the BillingAddressData query shown in Figure 9-18.

**Query results produced by joining tables having a 1:1 relationship** ◄ **Figure 9-18**

| Employer ID | Employer Name | Billing Name | City | State/Prov |
|---|---|---|---|---|
| 10134 | Capt'n John's Seafood | RKJ Foods | Atlanta | GA |
| 10152 | Alpine Touring Center | Touring Centers USA | Denver | CO |
| 10156 | Seaport Scenic Tours | Scenic Tours Inc | New York | NY |
| 10159 | Summit Hotel & Conference Center | Bartley Hotels | Nashville | TN |
| 10195 | Gables & Golf Country Club | North Country Clubs | Montreal | QC |
| 10226 | Lighthouse Tours | Mr. Andrew Adgate | Block Island | RI |

**fields from the Employer table**     **fields from the BillingAddress table**

The Employer ID column joins the Employer and BillingAddress tables. In the query, the Employer ID and Employer Name columns are from the Employer table; and the Billing Name, City, and State/Prov columns are from the BillingAddress table. Only the six employers that have records in the BillingAddress table—because they have different billing addresses—appear in the BillingAddressData query recordset.

Next, you'll define a many-to-many relationship between the Position and Student tables, and a one-to-one relationship between the Employer and BillingAddress tables.

# Defining M:N and 1:1 Relationships Between Tables

Similar to how you defined one-to-many relationships in Tutorial 3, you define many-to-many and one-to-one relationships in the Relationships window. First, you'll open the Relationships window and define the many-to-many relationship between the Position and Student tables. You'll define a one-to-many relationship between the Position and Job tables, with Position as the primary table, Job as the related table, and PositionID as the common field (the primary key in the Position table and a foreign key in the Job table). Next, you'll define a one-to-many relationship between the Student and Job tables, with Student as the primary table, Job as the related table, and StudentID as the common field (the primary key in the Student table and a foreign key in the Job table).

### To define a many-to-many relationship between the Position and Student tables:

▶ 1. If you took a break after the previous session, make sure that Access is running, and that the **Overseas** database in the Comp\Tutorial folder is open.

▶ 2. Click the **Relationships** button on the Database toolbar to open the Relationships window.

   The NAICS, Location, Employer, Position, and Job field lists already appear in the Relationships window, so you need to add only the Student field list to the Relationships window.

▶ 3. Click the **Show Table** button on the Relationship toolbar to open the Show Table dialog box, double-click **Student** to add the Student field list to the Relationships window, and then click the **Close** button in the Show Table dialog box to close the dialog box and reveal the entire Relationships window.

▶ 4. Drag the Student field list title bar to the right until the Student field list is positioned as shown in Figure 9-19, and then use the pointer to drag the bottom border of the Student field list down until you can see all the fields in the list.

| **Figure 9-19** | **After adding the Student field list to the Relationships window** |

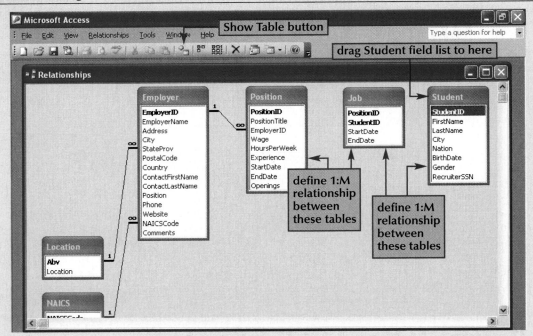

First, you'll define the one-to-many relationship between the Position and Job tables.

▶ 5. Click **PositionID** in the Position field list, and drag it to **PositionID** in the Job field list. When you release the mouse button, the Edit Relationships dialog box opens.

   The primary table, related table, and common field appear at the top of the dialog box. The type of relationship, One-To-Many, appears at the bottom of the dialog box. When you click the Enforce Referential Integrity check box, the two cascade options become available. If you select the Cascade Update Related Fields option, Access will change the appropriate foreign key values in the related table when you change a primary key value in the primary table. If you select the Cascade Delete Related Records option, when you delete a record in the primary table, Access will delete all records in the related table that have a matching foreign key value. As you did in Tutorial 3, you'll enforce referential integrity and cascade updates to related fields, but you won't cascade deletions to related records.

6. Click the **Enforce Referential Integrity** check box, and then click the **Cascade Update Related Fields** check box. You have now selected all the necessary relationship options.

7. Click the **Create** button to define the one-to-many relationship between the two tables and close the dialog box. The completed relationship appears in the Relationships window.

8. Repeat Steps 5 through 7 to define the one-to-many relationship between the primary Student table and the related Job table, using StudentID as the common field. See Figure 9-20.

| M:N relationship defined between the Position and Student tables | Figure 9-20 |

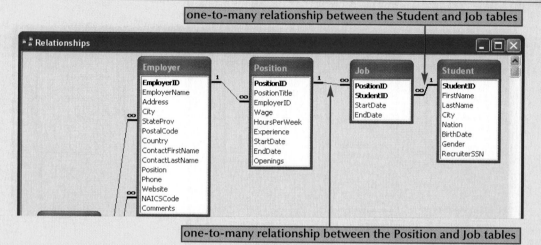

one-to-many relationship between the Student and Job tables

one-to-many relationship between the Position and Job tables

9. Click the **Save** button 🔲 on the Relationship toolbar to save the layout in the Relationships window.

Now you can add the BillingAddress table to the Relationships window and then define a one-to-one relationship between the Employer and BillingAddress tables.

## To define a one-to-one relationship between the Employer and BillingAddress tables:

1. Click the **Show Table** button 🔲 on the Relationship toolbar to open the Show Table dialog box, double-click **BillingAddress** to add the BillingAddress field list to the Relationships window, and then click the **Close** button in the Show Table dialog box to close the dialog box and reveal the entire Relationships window.

2. If necessary, drag the BillingAddress field list title bar up and to the left until the BillingAddress field list is positioned to the left of the Employer field list.

3. Use the ↕ pointer to drag the bottom border of the BillingAddress field list down until you can see all the fields in the list.

   Now you can define the one-to-one relationship between the primary Employer table and the related BillingAddress table.

4. Click **EmployerID** in the Employer field list, and drag it to **EmployerID** in the BillingAddress field list. When you release the mouse button, the Edit Relationships dialog box opens.

   The primary table, related table, and common field appear at the top of the dialog box. The type of relationship, One-To-One, appears at the bottom of the dialog box.

> ▶ **5.** Click the **Enforce Referential Integrity** check box, and then click the **Cascade Update Related Fields** check box. You have now selected all the necessary relationship options.
>
> ▶ **6.** Click the **Create** button to define the one-to-one relationship between the two tables and close the dialog box. The completed relationship appears in the Relationships window. Both sides of the relationship have the digit 1 at their ends to indicate a one-to-one relationship between the two tables. See Figure 9-21.

| Figure 9-21 | ▶ 1:1 relationship defined between the Employer and BillingAddress tables |

drag BillingAddress table list to here (if necessary)

one-to-one relationship

> ▶ **7.** Save your relationship changes, and then close the Relationships window.

Elsa asks you if her staff's work will take longer as the Overseas database grows in size with the addition of more table records. Specifically, she wants to know if queries will take longer to run. You tell her that using indexes will help make her queries run faster.

# Using Indexes for Table Fields

Suppose you need to find all the pages in a book that discuss a specific topic. The fastest, most accurate way to perform your search is to look up the topic in the book's index. In a similar fashion, you can create and use indexes to locate all the records in a table that contain specific values for one or more fields. An **index** is a list that relates field values to the records that contain those field values.

Access automatically creates and maintains an index for a table's primary key. For example, the Position table in the Overseas database includes an index for the PositionID field, which is the table's primary key. Conceptually, as shown in Figure 9-22, Access identifies each record in the Position table by its record number, and the PositionID index has two columns. The first column contains a PositionID value, and the second column contains the record number for that PositionID value. For instance, PositionID 2036 in the index has a record number value of 8; and record number 8 in the Position table contains the data for PositionID 2036.

Position table with index for PositionID field | **Figure 9-22**

Because PositionID values are unique, each row in the PositionID index has a single record number. When you or Access create indexes for non-primary-key fields, however, the indexes may contain multiple record numbers in a row. Figure 9-23 illustrates an EmployerID index for the Position table. Because EmployerID is a foreign key in the Position table (an employer can offer many positions), each EmployerID entry in the index can be associated with many record numbers. For instance, EmployerID 10151 in the index has record number values of 3, 7, and 8; and record numbers 3, 7, and 8 in the Position table contain the position data for EmployerID 10151.

Position table with index for EmployerID field | **Figure 9-23**

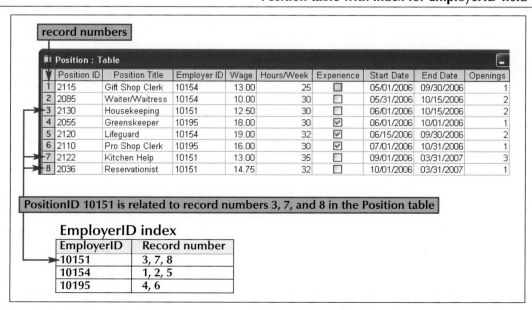

If an index exists for the EmployerID field in the Position table, queries that use EmployerID as a sort field or as a selection criterion will run faster. With small tables, the increased speed associated with indexes is not readily apparent. In practice, tables with hundreds of thousands or millions of records are common. In such cases, the increase in speed is dramatic. In fact, without indexes, many database operations in large tables would not be practical, because they would take too long to complete. Why the speed difference in these cases? To sort or select records from a large table without an index, Access must make numerous accesses to disk storage to retrieve table records, because the entire table can't fit in computer memory. In contrast, indexes are usually small enough to fit completely in computer memory, and Access sorts and selects records based on indexes with minimal need to access disk storage. Because accessing disk storage is very slow and performing operations in computer memory is very fast, using indexes in large tables is faster.

The speed advantage of using an index must be weighed against two disadvantages: the index adds disk storage requirements to the database, and it takes time to update the index as you add and delete records. Except for primary key indexes, you can add and delete indexes at any time. Thus, you can add an index if you think searching and query-ing would be faster as the number of records in the database increases. You can also delete an existing index if you later deem it to be unnecessary.

# Viewing Existing Indexes

You can view the existing indexes for a table by opening the table in Design view.

| Reference Window | **Viewing a Table's Existing Indexes** |
| --- | --- |

- Open the table in Design view.
- To view an index for a single field, click the field, and then view the Indexed property in the Field Properties pane.
- To view all indexes for a table or to view an index consisting of multiple fields, click the Indexes button on the Table Design toolbar.

Elsa wants to view the indexes for the Job table.

### To view the indexes for the Job table:

1. Open the **Job** table in Design view.
2. Click the **Indexes** button ⚡ on the Table Design toolbar. The Indexes window opens. See Figure 9-24.

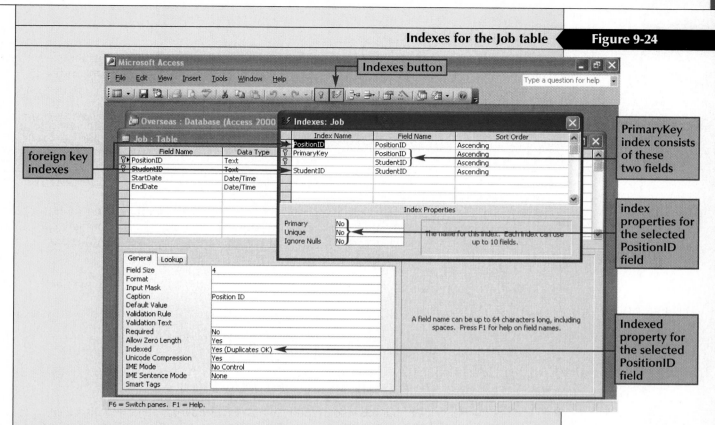

**Trouble?** If the Indexes window on your screen is positioned differently from the one shown in Figure 9-24, move it to the same position.

Because the PositionID field was selected when you opened the Indexes window, the properties in the Field Properties pane in the Table Design window pertain to this field. In particular, the Indexed property value of "Yes (Duplicates OK)" for the PositionID field specifies the use of an index that allows duplicate values. The properties in the Index Properties pane in the Indexes window apply to the highlighted PositionID index; these properties indicate that the PositionID index is not the primary key index, that values in this index do not need to be unique, and that all records (even those with null PositionID values) are included in the index.

Access automatically created the PositionID index when you specified the PositionID field as a foreign key in the Relationships window. Likewise, Access automatically created the StudentID index for the StudentID foreign key.

The second index, named PrimaryKey, consists of the table's composite key—the combination of the PositionID and StudentID fields. Because StudentID in the Indexes window's third row does not have an Index Name property value, both PositionID and StudentID comprise the PrimaryKey index. When Elsa created this table and specified the composite key, Access automatically created the PrimaryKey index.

Over the past few weeks, Elsa's staff has been monitoring the performance of the Overseas database by timing how long it takes to run queries. She wants her staff to let her know if the performance changes over the next few days after she creates an index for the StartDate field in the Job table.

# Creating an Index

You can create an index for a single field in the Indexes window or by setting its Indexed property in Design view. For a multiple-field index, however, you must create the index in the Indexes window.

**Reference Window** | **Creating an Index**

- Open the table in Design view.
- To create an index for a single field, click the field, and then set the Indexed property in the Field Properties pane.
- To create an index consisting of multiple fields, click the Indexes button on the Table Design toolbar, enter a name for the index in the Index Name text box, select the fields in the Field Name text boxes, and then set other properties as necessary for the index.

Next, you'll create an index for the StartDate field in the Job table by setting the field's Indexed property.

### To create an index for the StartDate field:

1. Click the Table window title bar to make it the active window.

2. Click the **StartDate Field Name** text box to make it the current field.

3. Click the right side of the **Indexed** property in the Field Properties pane, and then click **Yes (Duplicates OK)**. An index for the StartDate field is created with duplicate values allowed. Setting the Indexed property automatically created the StartDate index in the Indexes window. See Figure 9-25.

**Figure 9-25** | **After creating the StartDate index**

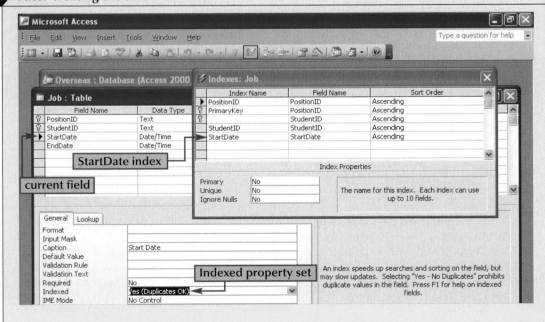

**4.** Click the **Close** button ⊠ on the Indexes window title bar to close the Indexes window. Now you'll save your changes to the table design and close the Table window.

**5.** Save your table design changes, and then close the table.

Elsa and her staff provide ongoing contact with all students placed in seasonal positions. However, Elsa has found that these students often feel more comfortable addressing some of their concerns and problems with one of their peers. Consequently, Elsa has chosen two students, Isadora Santiago and Carlo Bianchi, who are experienced and mature seasonal workers, to serve as contacts for the other students.

Elsa asks you to add a Contact field to the Student table, use an update query to place values into the Contact field, and then create a select query to provide the contact information as needed. The select query you'll create will require a special join using the Student table.

# Joining Tables

The design of the Overseas database includes a one-to-many relationship between the Employer and Position tables using EmployerID as the common field, which allows you to join the two tables to create a query based on data from both tables. The type of join you have used so far is an inner join. Two other types of joins are the outer join and the self-join.

## Inner and Outer Joins

An **inner join** is a join in which the DBMS selects records from two tables only when the records have the same value in the common field that links the tables. For example, in a database containing a table of student information and a table of class information, an inner join would show all student records that have a matching class record and all class records that have a matching student record. In the Overseas database, EmployerID is the common field for the Employer and Position tables. As shown in Figure 9-26, the results of a query based on an inner join of these two tables include only those records that have a matching EmployerID value. The record in the Employer table with an Employer ID column value of 10125 is not included in the query recordset, because it fails to match a record with the same Employer ID column value in the Position table. (That employer has no currently available positions.) Also, the record in the Position table with a Position ID column value 2199 is not included in the query recordset, because it has a null Employer ID column value. (The clerk entering the position in the Overseas database wasn't sure which employer offers that position and left the field value null.) Because primary key values can't be null, records with null foreign key values do not appear in a query recordset based on an inner join. You usually use an inner join whenever you perform a query based on more than one table; it is the default join you have used to this point.

| Figure 9-26 | Example of an inner join |

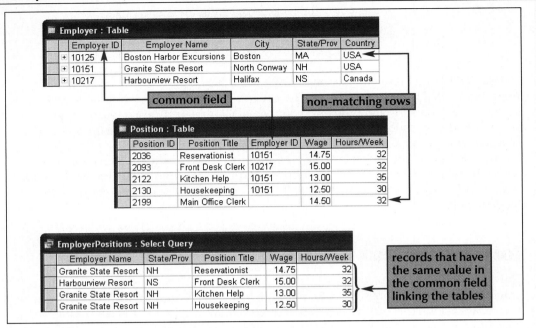

An **outer join** is a join in which the DBMS selects *all* records from one table and only those records from a second table that have matching common field values. For example, in a database containing a student table and a class table, an outer join would show all students whether or not the students are enrolled in a class, and another outer join would show all classes whether or not there are any students enrolled in them. In the Overseas database, you would use this kind of join if you wanted to see, for example, all records from the Employer table and also all matching records from the Position table. Figure 9-27 shows an outer join for the Employer and Position tables. All records from the Employer table appear in the query recordset, along with only matching records from the Position table. Notice that the Boston Harbor Excursions record from the Employer table appears even though it does not match a record in the Position table. The PositionID 2199 record in the Position table does not appear, however, because it does not match a record in the Employer table.

Example of an outer join ◀ **Figure 9-27**

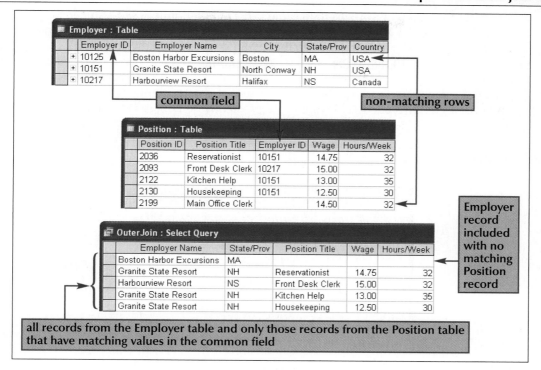

Another example of an outer join using the Employer and Position tables is shown in Figure 9-28. All records from the Position table appear in the query recordset, even the PositionID 2199 record that does not match a record in the Employer table. The Boston Harbor Excursions record from the Employer table does not appear, however, because it does not match a record in the Position table.

Another example of an outer join ◀ **Figure 9-28**

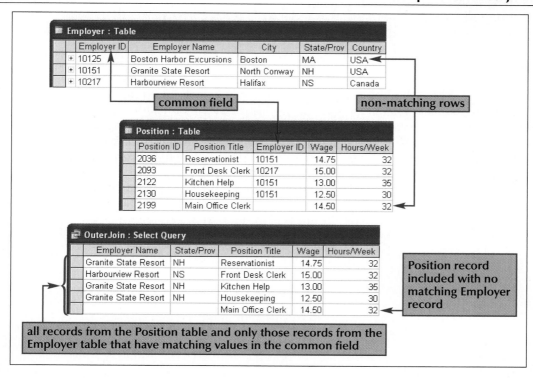

## Self-Joins

A table can also be joined with itself; this join is called a **self-join**. A self-join can be either an inner or outer join. For example, you would use this kind of join if you wanted to see records from the Student table together with information about each student's contact (either Isadora or Carlo). Figure 9-29 shows a self-join for the Student table. In this case, the self-join is an inner join because records appear in the query results only if the Contact field value matches a StudentID field value. To create this self-join, you would add two copies of the Student table to the Query window in Design view, and then join the Contact field of one Student table to the StudentID field of the other Student table.

**Figure 9-29**     **Example of a self-join**

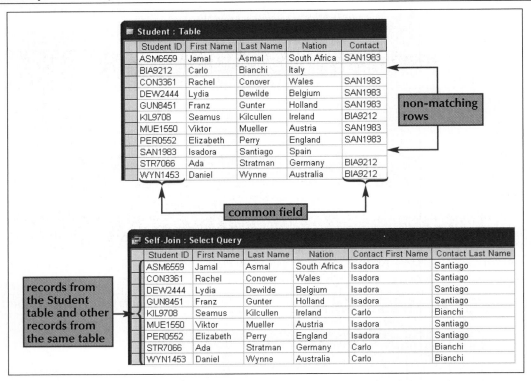

In Figure 9-29, the query results show the record for each student in the Student table and the contact information for that student. The contact information also comes from the Student table through the Contact field.

To produce the information Elsa requested, indicating whether Isadora or Carlo is the contact for a student, you'll need to create a self-join. First, you'll add the Contact field to the Student table, and then create and run an update query to place values into the Contact field. When you add the Contact field, you'll set its properties similar to the StudentID field.

## To add the Contact field and create and run an update query:

1. Open the **Student** table in Datasheet view, replace Student in the first record's FirstName field with your first name, and then replace Name in the first record's LastName field with your last name.

2. Switch to Design view, add to the end of the table a field named **Contact**, select the **Text** data type, set the Field Size to **7**, and then save and close the table.

3. Create a new query in Design view, adding the **Student** field list to the Query window.

   You'll need to add the StudentID, Nation, and Contact fields to the design grid. Elsa has assigned Carlo as the contact for all students from Australia, Germany, and Ireland, and Isadora as the contact for students from all other countries. To select the correct student records, you'll enter a selection criterion for the Nation field. You won't update Carlo and Isadora's Contact fields—neither is logically assigned to anyone—so you'll need to exclude their records from the update query by entering a selection criterion for the StudentID field. Finally, you'll be updating the Contact field.

4. Add the **StudentID**, **Nation**, and **Contact** fields to the design grid.

   To exclude Carlo and Isadora's records, you'll use the Not logical operator and the In comparison operator with Carlo's StudentID field value of BIA9212 and Isadora's StudentID field value of SAN1983. First, you'll update Carlo's contacts by using the In comparison operator to select students from Australia, Germany, and Ireland.

5. Click the **StudentID Criteria** text box, type **Not In ("BIA9212","SAN1983")**, press the **Tab** key to advance to the Nation text box, and then type **In ("Australia","Germany","Ireland")**. You've completed the selection criteria needed to choose the records you'll be updating for Carlo's contacts. See Figure 9-30.

**Query to select Carlo's contacts** ◀ **Figure 9-30**

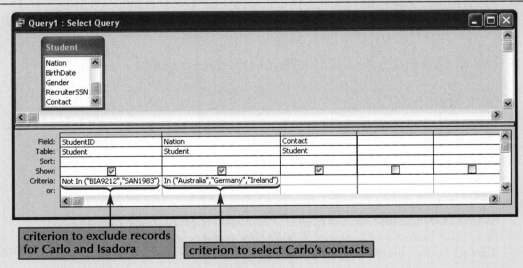

criterion to exclude records
for Carlo and Isadora

criterion to select Carlo's contacts

   **Trouble?** Your screen might show only part of the criteria in the StudentID and Nation Criteria text boxes.

6. Run the query to verify that the 15 records with Australia, Germany, and Ireland in the Nation field are selected, and then switch to Design view.

   Next, you'll change the query to an update query, add Carlo's StudentID field value as the Contact Update To value, and then run the update query.

7. Click the list arrow for the **Query Type** button 🗔 on the Query Design toolbar, and then click **Update Query**.

8. Type **"BIA9212"** in the Contact Update To text box, run the query, and then click the **Yes** button to confirm that you want to update 15 rows in the Student table.

   Now you need to update the Contact field values for Isadora's contacts. To do so, you'll add the Not logical operator to the beginning of the Nation Criteria text box, and change the Contact Update To value to Isadora's StudentID field value.

9. Click the **Nation Criteria** text box, press the **Home** key to position the insertion point at the beginning of the expression, type **Not (**, press the **End** key to position the insertion at the end of the expression, and then type **)** (a closing parenthesis).

10. Double-click **BIA9212** in the Contact Update To text box to select it, and then type **SAN1983**.

    You've completed the selection and update changes needed to update Isadora's contacts. See Figure 9-31.

| Figure 9-31 | **Query to update Isadora's contacts** |

criterion to select Isadora's contacts | Isadora's StudentID field value

Now you can run the query to update the remaining records in the Student table and to add Isadora's StudentID as the Contact field value.

### To run the update query and update the Contact field values:

1. Run the query, and then click the **Yes** button to confirm that you want to update 17 rows in the Student table.

   You are finished updating the Contact field in the Student table, so you can close the Query window. Because all the records have been updated, you do not need to save the query.

2. Close the query, and then click the **No** button when Access asks if you want to save it.

   Now you'll open the Student table to verify the updates.

3. Open the **Student** table in Datasheet view. The Contact field values are now equal to Carlo's StudentID field value of BIA9212 (for students from Australia, Germany, and Ireland) or Isadora's field value of SAN1983 (for students from all other countries). The Contact field values for Carlo's and Isadora's records are null. See Figure 9-32.

| | After updating the Contact field values in the Student table | Figure 9-32 |

Carlo's Contact field value is null

| | | Student ID | First Name | Last Name | City | Nation | Birth Date | Gender | Recruiter SSN | Contact |
|---|---|---|---|---|---|---|---|---|---|---|
| ► | + | AHE9812 | Student | Name | Clifden | Ireland | 02/02/1985 | F | 911-72-0005 | BIA9212 |
| | + | AND8210 | Daphne | Anderson | Edam | Holland | 09/28/1988 | F | 928-01-3456 | SAN1983 |
| | + | ASM6559 | Jamal | Asmal | Rustenberg | South Africa | 09/12/1986 | M | 891-22-0102 | SAN1983 |
| | + | BAN7807 | Karl | Bankemper | Dusseldorf | Germany | 10/01/1981 | M | 899-34-4506 | BIA9212 |
| | + | BIA9212 | Carlo | Bianchi | Naples | Italy | 12/24/1981 | M | 907-42-5625 | |
| | + | CAS1942 | Fernando | Castellena | Barcelona | Spain | 02/22/1985 | M | 977-07-1798 | SAN1983 |
| | + | CON3361 | Rachel | Conover | Cardigan | Wales | 07/04/1988 | F | 893-91-0178 | SAN1983 |
| | + | CON9289 | Emilio | Conti | Bologna | Italy | 09/30/1985 | M | 907-42-5625 | SAN1983 |
| | + | DEW2444 | Lydia | Dewilde | Brugge | Belgium | 12/05/1988 | F | 911-72-0005 | SAN1983 |
| | + | GUN8451 | Franz | Gunter | Volendam | Holland | 01/31/1984 | M | 928-01-3456 | SAN1983 |
| | + | HAD8009 | Maggie | Hadley | Amsterdam | Holland | 04/02/1989 | F | 928-01-3456 | SAN1983 |
| | + | HES7702 | Mallory | Hesse | Hamburg | Germany | 06/01/1982 | F | 911-72-0005 | BIA9212 |
| | + | JOH1414 | Eleanor | Johnson | Perth | Australia | 04/28/1987 | F | 899-40-2937 | BIA9212 |
| | + | KIL9708 | Seamus | Kilcullen | Galway | Ireland | 03/14/1983 | M | 977-07-1798 | BIA9212 |
| | + | MAR9797 | Chloe | Martin | Galway | Ireland | 06/24/1988 | F | 977-07-1798 | BIA9212 |
| | + | MCG1199 | Frances | McGillis | Sorrento | Australia | 03/24/1987 | F | 891-22-0102 | BIA9212 |
| | + | MER7223 | Richard | Mersey | Cardigan | Wales | 11/16/1988 | M | 893-91-0178 | SAN1983 |
| | + | MOK6674 | Pieter | Mokwena | Johannesberg | South Africa | 08/15/1987 | M | 891-22-0102 | SAN1983 |
| | + | MOR8340 | Jeffrey | Morris | London | England | 05/23/1987 | M | 893-91-0178 | SAN1983 |
| | + | MUE1550 | Viktor | Mueller | Linz | Austria | 08/06/1984 | M | 907-42-5625 | SAN1983 |

Record: [◄] [◄] 1 [►] [►I] [►*] of 34

updated Contact field values

**4.** Scroll down the table to verify all Contact field values and Isadora's null Contact field value, and then close the table.

The Contact field values in the Student table are the StudentID values for Carlo and Isadora. To produce the contact information in the format that Elsa requested—with the contact's first and last names—you need to create a self-join.

## Creating a Self-Join

You need to create a query to display the new contact information in the Student table. This query requires a self-join. To create the self-join, you need to add two copies of the Student field list to the Query window, and then add a join line from the StudentID field in one field list to the Contact field in the other. The Contact field is a foreign key that matches the primary key field StudentID. You can then create a query that can display Student information from one table and Contact information from the other table.

| Reference Window | **Creating a Self-Join** |
|---|---|

- In the Database window, click Queries in the Objects bar to display the Queries list, and then click the New button.
- Click Design View and then click the OK button.
- Double-click the table for the self-join, and then double-click the table a second time. Click the Close button.
- Click and drag a primary key field from one field list to the foreign key field in the other field list.
- Right-click the join line between the two tables, and then click Join Properties to open the Join Properties dialog box.
- Click the first option button to select an inner join, or click the second option button or the third option button to select an outer join, and then click the OK button.
- Select the fields, specify the selection criteria, select the sort options, and set other properties as appropriate for the query.

Now you'll create the self-join query to display the student contact information.

### To create the self-join query:

1. Click **Queries** in the Objects bar of the Database window, click the **New** button to open the New Query dialog box, make sure that **Design View** is selected, and then click the **OK** button.

2. Double-click **Student** to add the Student field list to the Query window.

3. Double-click **Student** again to add a second copy of the Student field list, and then click the **Close** button. Access identifies the left field list as Student and the right field list as Student_1 to distinguish the two copies of the table.

   You will now create a join between the two copies of the Student table by linking the StudentID field in the Student field list to the Contact field in the Student_1 field list. The Contact field is a foreign key that matches the primary key field StudentID.

4. Scroll the Student_1 field list until the Contact field is visible, and then click and drag the **StudentID** field from the Student field list to the **Contact** field in the Student_1 field list. Access adds a join line between the two fields. You can verify that this is an inner join query by opening the Join Properties dialog box.

5. Right-click the **join line** between the two tables, and then click **Join Properties** to open the Join Properties dialog box. See Figure 9-33.

| Figure 9-33 | Join Properties dialog box |
|---|---|

**Trouble?** If right-clicking the join line does not work, click View on the menu bar, and then click Join Properties to open the Join Properties dialog box.

The first option button is selected, indicating that this is an inner join. You would click the second or third option buttons for an outer join. Because the inner join is correct, you can cancel the dialog box and then add the necessary fields to the design grid.

6. Click the **Cancel** button and then, scrolling as necessary, double-click the following fields (in order) from the Student_1 field list: **StudentID**, **FirstName**, **LastName**, and **Nation**.

7. Double-click the following fields (in order) from the Student field list: **FirstName** and **LastName**.

8. Run the query, and then maximize the Query window. Access displays the recordset in increasing StudentID order with six fields and 32 records. See Figure 9-34.

**Initial self-join on the Student table** ◄ **Figure 9-34**

The query results display all students and their contacts. The query results do not display the Student records for Carlo and Isadora because their records contain null Contact field values. Remember that an inner join doesn't display records from the second table unless it contains a matching value in the common field. In the Student_1 table, the Contact field values for Carlo and Isadora are null, so the inner join doesn't select their records in the Student table.

**Trouble?** If your query results do not match Figure 9-34, click the View button for Design view to return to Design view, and review the preceding steps to make any necessary corrections to your query design. Then run the query again.

Access displays 32 of the 34 records from the Student table. The records for Carlo and Isadora have a null Contact field value and, therefore, are not displayed. Two field names in the query recordset are "First Name," and two field names are "Last Name." Elsa asks you to rename the two rightmost fields so that the query recordset will be easier to read. After you rename the necessary fields, the column names in the query recordset will be, from left to right, Student ID, First Name, Last Name, Nation, Contact First Name, and Contact Last Name.

### To rename the necessary fields:

▶ 1. Switch to Design view.

▶ 2. Right-click the fifth column's Field text box, click **Properties** on the shortcut menu to open the property sheet, click the **General** tab (if necessary), and then set the Caption property to **Contact First Name**.

▶ 3. Click the sixth column's Field text box, and then set the Caption property to **Contact Last Name**.

▶ 4. Close the property sheet, run the query, resize all columns to their best fit, and then click **StudentID AHE9812** to deselect any selected value or columns. The query recordset displays the new names for the fifth and sixth columns. See Figure 9-35.

| Figure 9-35 | ▶ | Final self-join on the Student table |
| --- | --- | --- |

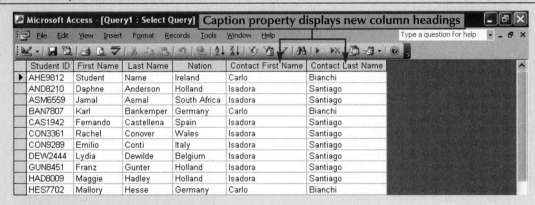

Elsa asks you to print a copy of the query recordset.

▶ 5. Save the query as **StudentContacts**, print the query recordset, close the query, and then exit Access.

The new queries that you created and the other work you completed will make it much easier for Elsa and her staff to enter, retrieve, and view information in the Overseas database.

| Review |
| --- |

# Session 9.2 Quick Check

1. What are the three types of relationships you can define between tables?
2. What is an entity subtype?
3. What is an index?
4. What is the difference between an inner join and an outer join?
5. What is a self-join?

**6.** Figure 9-36 lists the field names from two tables: Department and Employee.

Figure 9-36

| Department | Employee |
|---|---|
| DepartmentID | EmployeeSSN |
| DepartmentName | EmployeeName |
| PhoneNumber | DepartmentID |
| | Salary |
| | SupervisorSSN |

a. What is the primary key for each table?
b. What type of relationship exists between the two tables?
c. Is an inner join possible between the two tables? If so, give one example of an inner join.
d. Is an outer join possible between the two tables? If so, give one example of an outer join.
e. Is a self-join possible for one of the tables? If so, give one example of a self-join.

**Review**

# Tutorial Summary

In this tutorial, you created action queries, including make-table, append, delete, and update queries. You learned about one-to-many, many-to-many, and one-to-one relationships. You also learned about indexes and how to create them. Finally, you learned about inner joins, outer joins, and self-joins, and you created a self-join.

## Key Terms

| | | |
|---|---|---|
| action query | inner join | one-to-one relationship (1:1) |
| append query | make-table query | outer join |
| delete query | many-to-many | referential integrity |
| entity subtype | relationship (M:N) | self-join |
| history table | one-to-many | update query |
| index | relationship (1:M) | |

**Practice**

# Review Assignments

**Data File needed for the Review Assignments: Work.mdb**

*Take time to practice the skills you learned in the tutorial using the same case scenario.*

The Work database contains information about NSJI's recruiters and overseas students. The Recruiter table in the database contains records of the recruiters employed by NSJI to find students for seasonal work and to match them with the employers that are NSJI's clients. The Student table contains student information. The Country table contains records of the nations from which NSJI recruits students. Finally, the Territory table contains records indicating which recruiters cover which nations for NSJI. The database contains several other objects, including queries, forms, and reports. Elsa wants you to define a many-to-many relationship between the Recruiter and Country tables, and to create some new queries for her. To help with these requests, complete the following steps:

1. Open the **Work** database in the Comp\Review folder provided with your Data Files.
2. Open the **Student** table datasheet, and modify the first record by changing the FirstName, LastName, BirthDate, and Gender field values to your name, birth date, and gender. Close the table.
3. Define a many-to-many relationship between the **Recruiter** and **Country** tables, using the **Territory** table as the related table. Select the referential integrity option and the cascade updates option for the relationships. Print the Relationships window without saving the created report. Save your changes to the Relationships window and then close it.
4. Create a make-table query based on the **Recruiter** and **Territory** tables, selecting all fields from the **Recruiter** table and the Nation field from the **Territory** table. Use **RecruiterTerritory** as the new table name, and store the table in the current database. Run the query, and then close the query without saving it. Open the **RecruiterTerritory** table, print the table recordset, and then close the table.
5. Create an update query to select all records in the **RecruiterTerritory** table where the Nation field value is Ireland. Update the Nation field value to France, run the query, and then close the query without saving it. Open the **RecruiterTerritory** table, print the table recordset, and then close the table.
6. Create an append query based on the **Recruiter** and **Territory** tables, selecting all fields from the **Recruiter** table and the Nation field from the **Territory** table, selecting all records where the Nation field value is Ireland, and appending the selected records to the **RecruiterTerritory** table. Run the query, and then close the query without saving it. Open the **RecruiterTerritory** table, print the table recordset, and then close the table.
7. Create a delete query that deletes all records from the **RecruiterTerritory** table where the BonusQuota field value is 40 or 50. Run the query, and then close the query without saving it. Open the **RecruiterTerritory** table, print the table recordset, and then close the table.
8. Add an index named BonusQuota to the **Recruiter** table using the default property settings, and then save and close the table.
9. Create an outer join query between the **Country** and **Student** tables, selecting all records from the **Country** table and any matching records from the **Student** table. Display the Nation field from the **Country** table, and the FirstName, LastName, and City fields from the **Student** table in the query results. Save the query as **CountryAndStudentOuterJoin**, run the query, print the query recordset, and then close the query.
10. Close the **Work** database, and then exit Access.

**Apply**

*Use the skills you learned in the tutorial to work with the data contained in a video photography database.*

# Case Problem 1

**Data File needed for this Case Problem: Shoots.mdb**

*Lim's Video Photography*  Youngho Lim owns a videography business, Lim's Video Photography. Located in San Francisco, California, the company specializes in digital video photography and offers customers the option of storing edited videos on CD or DVD. His video shoots include weddings and other special events, as well as recording personal and commercial inventories for insurance purposes. Youngho has created an Access database named Shoots to store data about his clients and the work he does for them. The Client table contains client data, the ShootDesc table contains descriptions of the different categories of work Youngho does, the Contract table contains data about his client contracts, the Shoot table contains data about his contracted shooting assignments, the Billing table contains client invoice data, the Case table contains data about his CD/DVD storage units, and the CdStorage table contains data about each CD/DVD stored in his cases for his clients' shoots. The database contains several other objects including queries, forms, and reports. Youngho asks you to define a many-to-many relationship between the Case and Shoot tables and a one-to-one relationship between the Contract and Billing tables, and to create some new queries for him. To help Youngho with his requests, complete the following steps:

1. Open the **Shoots** database in the Comp\Case1 folder provided with your Data Files.
2. Modify the first record in the **Client** table datasheet by changing the ClientName field value to your name in the format: last name, comma, space, first name. Close the table.
3. Define a many-to-many relationship between the **Case** and **Shoot** tables, using the **CdStorage** table as the related table. Select the referential integrity option and the cascade updates option for the relationships.
4. Define a one-to-one relationship between the primary **Contract** table and the related **Billing** table. Select the referential integrity option and the cascade updates option for the relationship. Print the Relationships window without saving the created report. Save your changes to the Relationships window and then close it.
5. Create a make-table query based on the **Shoot** table, selecting all fields from the table and only those records where the ShootType field value is AP or BP. Use **SpecialShoot** as the new table name, and store the table in the current database. Run the query, and then close the query without saving it. Open the **SpecialShoot** table, print the table recordset, and then close the table.
6. Create an append query based on the **Shoot** table, selecting all fields from the table and only those records where the ShootType field value is DR or WE. Append the selected records to the **SpecialShoot** table. Run the query, and then close the query without saving it. Open the **SpecialShoot** table, print the table recordset, and then close the table.

7. Create a delete query that deletes all records from the **SpecialShoot** table where the Duration field value is less than 4.5. Run the query, and then close the query without saving it. Open the **SpecialShoot** table, print the table recordset, and then close the table.

8. Create an update query to select all records in the **CdStorage** table where the CaseID field value is 1. Update the CaseID field value to 5, run the query, and then close the query without saving it. Open the **CdStorage** table, print the table recordset, and then close the table.

9. Add an index named ShootID to the **CdStorage** table using the default property settings, and then save and close the table.

10. Create an outer join query between the **ShootDesc** and **Shoot** tables, selecting all records from the **ShootDesc** table and any matching records from the **Shoot** table. Display both fields from the **ShootDesc** table, and the ShootDate, Duration, and ContractID fields from the **Shoot** table in the query results. Save the query as **ShootDescAndShootOuterJoin**, run the query, print the query recordset, and then close the query.

11. Close the **Shoots** database, and then exit Access.

**Apply**

*Apply what you learned in the tutorial to work with the data for an e-commerce business in the food services industry.*

# Case Problem 2

**Data File needed for this Case Problem: AtHome.mdb**

***DineAtHome.course.com*** DineAtHome.course.com in Naples, Florida is an online service that lets people order meals from one or more area restaurants for home delivery. Participating restaurants offer everything from simple fare to gourmet feasts. Claire Picard, the founder and owner, and her staff perform a variety of services, from simply picking up and delivering meals to providing linens and table service for more formal occasions. Claire created the AtHome database to maintain information about participating restaurants and the orders placed by customers. The CreditCard table contains data about customers' credit cards, the Customer table contains customer name and phone data, the Order table contains data about the restaurant orders placed by customers, and the Restaurant table contains data about each restaurant. The database contains several other objects, including queries, forms, and reports. Claire wants you to define a many-to-many relationship between the Restaurant and Customer tables, create a one-to-one relationship between the Customer and CreditCard tables, and create several new queries. To do so, complete the following steps:

1. Open the **AtHome** database in the Comp\Case2 folder provided with your Data Files.

2. Modify the first record in the **Restaurant** table datasheet by changing the Owner First Name and Owner Last Name column values to your first and last names, respectively. Close the table.

3. Define a many-to-many relationship between the **Restaurant** and **Customer** tables, using the **Order** table as the related table. Select the referential integrity option and the cascade updates option for the relationship.

4. Define a one-to-one relationship between the primary **Customer** table and the related **CreditCard** table. Select the referential integrity option and the cascade updates option for the relationship. Print the Relationships window without saving the created report. Save your changes to the Relationships window and then close it.

5. Create a make-table query based on the **Order** table, selecting all fields from the table and only those records where the OrderDate field value is before 03/01/2006. Use **SpecialOrder** as the new table name, and store the table in the current database. Run the query, and then close the query without saving it. Open the **SpecialOrder** table, print the table recordset, and then close the table.

6. Create an append query based on the **Order** table, selecting all fields from the table and only those records where the OrderDate field value is after 3/31/2006. Append the selected records to the **SpecialOrder** table. Run the query, and then close the query without saving it. Open the **SpecialOrder** table, print the table recordset, and then close the table.

7. Create a delete query that deletes all records from the **SpecialOrder** table where the CustomerID field value equals 1. Run the query, and then close the query without saving it. Open the **SpecialOrder** table, print the table recordset, and then close the table.

8. Add an index named OrderDate to the **Order** table, using the default property settings, and then save and close the table.

9. Open the **Restaurant** table in Design view, delete the PostalCode index, and then save and close the table.

10. Create an outer join query between the **Customer** and **CreditCard** tables, selecting all records from the **Customer** table and any matching records from the **CreditCard** table. Display all fields from the **Customer** table, and the CardNum and ExpDate fields from the **CreditCard** table in the query results. Save the query as **CustomerAndCreditCardOuterJoin**, run the query, print the query recordset, and then close the query.

11. Close the **AtHome** database, and then exit Access.

# Case Problem 3

**Data File needed for this Case Problem: ZooFunds.mdb**

*Redwood Zoo*  The Redwood Zoo is a small zoo located in the picturesque city of Gig Harbor, Washington, on the shores of Puget Sound. The Redwood Zoo has some of the best exhibits of marine animals in the United States. Its newly constructed polar bear habitat is a particular favorite among patrons. The zoo relies heavily on donations to fund permanent exhibits and temporary displays, especially those involving exotic animals. Michael Rosenfeld, the director of fund-raising activities, created the ZooFunds database to manage information about donors, their pledges, and the status of funds. The Donor table contains data about people who donate money to the zoo, the Fund table contains data about the zoo's funding categories and their target donation amounts, the Invitation table contains data about the donors invited to the zoo's receptions, the Pledge table contains data about each donor's pledges, and the Reception table contains data about the zoo's scheduled fund-raising activities. The database contains several other objects, including queries, forms, and reports. Michael wants you to define a many-to-many relationship between the Reception and Donor tables, and to create several new queries. To do so, complete the following steps:

1. Open the **ZooFunds** database in the Comp\Case3 folder provided with your Data Files.
2. Modify the first record in the **Donor** table datasheet by changing the Title, FirstName, MI, and LastName field values to your title and name. Close the table.
3. Define a many-to-many relationship between the **Reception** and **Donor** tables, using the **Invitation** table as the related table. Select the referential integrity option and the cascade updates option for the relationships. Print the Relationships window without saving the created report. Save your changes to the Relationships window and then close it.

**Explore**

4. Create a make-table query based on the **Donor**, **Invitation**, and **Reception** tables, selecting all fields from the **Donor** table, the Accept field from the **Invitation** table, and the ReceptionID and DateHeld fields from the **Reception** table. Select those records with a ReceptionID field value of 51. Use **Reception51** as the new table name, and store the table in the current database. Run the query, and then close the query without saving it. Open the **Reception51** table in Design view, set the Accept field's Format property to Yes/No, save the table changes, switch to Datasheet view, resize all columns to their best fit, print the table recordset, and then save and close the table.
5. Create a delete query that deletes all records from the **Reception51** table where the Accept field value is No. Run the query, and then close the query without saving it. Open the **Reception51** table, print the table recordset, and then close the table.
6. Create an append query based on the **Donor**, **Invitation**, and **Reception** tables, selecting all fields from the **Donor** table, the Accept field from the **Invitation** table, and the ReceptionID and DateHeld fields from the **Reception** table. Select those records with a ReceptionID field value of 52 and an Accept field value of Yes, and append the selected records to the **Reception51** table. Run the query, and then close the query without saving it. Rename the **Reception51** table as **Reception51And52**, open it, print the table recordset, and then close the table.
7. Create an update query to select all records in the **Reception51And52** table where the ReceptionID field value is 52. Update the DateHeld field value to 5/5/2006, run the query, and then close the query without saving it. Open the **Reception51And52** table, print the table recordset, and then close the table.
8. Add an index named LastName to the **Reception51And52** table, using the default property settings, and then save and close the table. (*Hint*: Only the primary key field is unique.)
9. Create an outer join query between the **Fund** and **Pledge** tables, selecting all records from the **Fund** table and any matching records from the **Pledge** table. Display all fields from the **Fund** table, and the DonorID, PledgeDate, and TotalPledged fields from the **Pledge** table in the query results. Save the query as **FundAndPledgeOuterJoin**, run the query, print the query recordset, and then close the query.
10. Close the **ZooFunds** database, and then exit Access.

**Apply**

*Apply what you learned in the tutorial to work with the data for an outdoor adventure company.*

# Case Problem 4

**Data File needed for this Case Problem: Rivers.mdb**

*Mountain River Adventures*   Connor and Siobhan Dempsey own Mountain River Adventures center, which offers clients their choice of outdoor activities, including white-water rafting, canoeing, hiking, camping, fishing, and rock climbing. To keep track of their clients and bookings, they created the Rivers database. The Booking table contains data about client rafting trips, the Client table contains data about clients, the Guide table contains data about the raft guides employed by Mountain River Adventures, the RaftingTrip table contains data about the available river rafting excursions, and the Works table contains data about the guides assigned to each client trip. The database contains several other objects, including queries, forms, and reports. The Dempseys want you to define a many-to-many relationship between the Booking and Guide tables, and to create several new queries. To do so, complete the following steps:

1. Open the **Rivers** database in the Comp\Case4 folder provided with your Data Files.
2. Modify the first record in the **Client** table datasheet by changing the ClientName field value to your name in the format: last name, comma, space, first name. Close the table.
3. Define a many-to-many relationship between the **Booking** and **Guide** tables, using the **Works** table as the related table. Select the referential integrity option and the cascade updates option for the relationships. Print the Relationships window without saving the created report. Save your changes to the Relationships window and then close it.
4. Create a make-table query based on the **Client** and **Booking** tables, selecting the ClientName and StateProv fields from the **Client** table and the TripDate, TripID, and People fields from the **Booking** table. Select those records with a StateProv field value of NE. Save the table as **ClientTrips** in the current database. Run the query, and then close the query without saving it. Open the **ClientTrips** table, resize all columns to their best fit, print the table recordset, and then save and close the table.
5. Create an append query based on the **Client** and **Booking** tables, selecting the ClientName and StateProv fields from the **Client** table and the TripDate, TripID, and People fields from the **Booking** table. Select those records with a StateProv field value of UT or WY, and append the selected records to the **ClientTrips** table. Run the query, and then close the query without saving it. Open the **ClientTrips** table, print the table recordset, and then close the table.
6. Create a delete query that deletes all records from the **ClientTrips** table where the People field value is less than 5. Run the query, and then close the query without saving it. Open the **ClientTrips** table, and then print the table records.
7. Add an index named StateProv to the **ClientTrips** table, using the default property settings, and then save and close the table.
8. Create a self-join query based on the **Guide** table with GuideID as the primary key and LeadGuide as the foreign key. Select the GuideID, FirstName, and LastName fields from the related table (the table that has LeadGuide connected to the join line), and the GuideID, FirstName, and LastName fields from the primary table. Set each field's Caption property to Guide ID, First Name, Last Name, Lead Guide ID, Lead Guide First, and Lead Guide Last, respectively. Save the query as **GuideSelfJoin**, run the query, resize all columns to their best fit, print the query recordset, and then save and close the query.
9. Close the **Rivers** database, and then exit Access.

## Challenge

*Work with the skills you've learned, and explore some new skills, to create additional objects for a database for an Internet auction site.*

# Case Problem 5

**Data File needed for this Case Problem: BuySell.mdb**

***eACH Internet Auction Site*** Chris and Pat Aquino own a successful Internet service provider (ISP) and want to expand their business to host an Internet auction site named eACH. Before people can sell items and bid on items, they must register with eACH. After a seller posts an item for sale, it is sold at the auction site by accepting bids from buyers. Each item is listed by subcategory within category—for example, the general category of collectibles consists of several subcategories, including advertising, animation characters, comic books, and bears.

To keep track of these auctions, Chris and Pat have developed the BuySell database. The database has four tables: Category, Subcategory, Registrant, and Item. The Category table contains information about categories, and the Subcategory table contains information about subcategories. The Registrant table has one record for each person who sells and/or bids on items, and the Item table has one record for each item that is posted for sale. The database contains several other objects including queries, forms, and reports.

Chris and Pat want you to add a new table named Bid to the database to keep track of the bids placed by people on the items for sale. Also, they want you to define a many-to-many relationship between the Item and Registrant tables and to create several new queries. To help them with their requests, complete the following steps:

1. Open the **BuySell** database in the Comp\Case5 folder provided with your Data Files.
2. Create the new **Bid** table by defining the following fields:
   - BidID, an AutoNumber field, is the primary key field, with Bid ID as its Caption setting.
   - ItemID, a Number (Long Integer field size) field, is a foreign key to the **Item** table, with Item ID as its Caption setting. This field stores the item on which the bidder is placing a bid.
   - Bidder, a Number (Long Integer field size) field, is a foreign key to the **Registrant** table. This field stores the registrant who's making the bid.
   - BidTime, a Date/Time (General Date format) field with Bid Time as its Caption setting, stores the exact date and time the bid is made.
   - Bid, a Currency (Currency format with 2 decimal places) field, stores the amount of the bid.
3. Define a many-to-many relationship between the **Item** and **Registrant** tables, using the **Bid** table as the related table. Select the referential integrity option and the cascade updates option for the relationships. Print the Relationships window without saving the created report. Save your changes to the Relationships window and then close it.

## Explore

4. If the BidID field was deleted from the **Bid** table, what would be the primary key of the **Bid** table? (*Hint*: A registrant can bid on many items, and an item can have many registrants as bidders. However, it's possible for a registrant to place two or more bids on a single item.)

5. In Design view, add an index named LastName to the **Registrant** table, using the default property settings, and then save the table.

6. Delete the UserID index from the **Registrant** table, and then save and close the table.

**Explore**

7. Design test data for the **Bid** table, and then add the test data to the table. (*Hint*: Be sure you have at least one item without any bids, at least one item with a single bid, and at least three items with two or more bids. Also, be sure you have at least one registrant who's not placed a bid and not posted an item for sale, at least one registrant who's only a seller, at least one registrant who's only a bidder, at least one registrant who's placed bids on two or more items, and at least one registrant who's placed multiple bids on a single item.)

8. Create a make-table query based on the **Subcategory** table, saving the new table as **SpecialSubcategory** in the current database. Select all fields in the **Subcategory** table, and select those records with a CategoryID field value of 2. Run the query, save the make-table query as **Category2MakeTable**, and then close the query. Open the **SpecialSubcategory** table, resize the columns to their best fit, print the table recordset, and then save and close the table.

9. Create an append query to select all records from the **Subcategory** table where the CategoryID field value is either 4 or 6 and append them to the **SpecialSubcategory** table. Run the query, save the append query as **Category4Or6Append**, and then close the query. Open the **SpecialSubcategory** table, print the table records, and then close the table.

**Explore**

10. Create an outer join query between the **Category** and **Subcategory** tables, selecting all records from the **Category** table and any matching records from the **Subcategory** table. Display all fields from the **Category** table, and the SubcategoryID and Subcategory fields from the **Subcategory** table in the query results. Save the query as **CategoryAndSubcategoryOuterJoin**, run the query, print the query recordset, and then close the query.

11. Close the **BuySell** database, and then exit Access.

**Research**

# Internet Assignments

The purpose of the Internet Assignments is to challenge you to find information on the Internet that you can use to work effectively with this software. The actual assignments are updated and maintained on the Course Technology Web site. Log on to the Internet and use your Web browser to go to the Student Online Companion for New Perspectives Office 2003 at **www.course.com/np/office2003**. Click the Internet Assignments link, and then navigate to the assignments for this tutorial.

**Assess**

## SAM Assessment and Training

If you have a SAM user profile, you may have access to hands-on instruction, practice, and assessment of the skills covered in this tutorial. Log in to your SAM account and go to your assignments page to see what your instructor has assigned.

# Quick Check Answers

## Session 9.1

1. a query that adds, changes, or deletes multiple table records at a time
2. You should preview the results before running an action query to confirm that the correct records are selected.
3. A make-table query creates a new table from one or more existing tables. An append query adds records from existing tables or queries to the end of another table.
4. deletes a group of records from one or more tables
5. changes selected field values from selected records in one or more tables
6. Access replaces the Show and Sort rows in the design grid with the Update To row.

## Session 9.2

1. one-to-many (1:M), many-to-many (M:N), one-to-one (1:1)
2. a table whose primary key is a foreign key to a second table and whose fields are additional fields for the second table
3. a list that relates field values to the records that contain those field values
4. An inner join selects records from two tables when they have matching values in the common field(s). An outer join selects all records from one table and records from a second table whose common field value(s) match records in the first table.
5. a join between a table and itself
6. a. The primary key for the Department table is DepartmentID, and the primary key for the Employee table is EmployeeSSN.
   b. There is a one-to-many relationship between the primary Department table and the related Employee table.
   c. Yes, an inner join is possible based on the common field of DepartmentID. One example of an inner join is a list of all employees, including the EmployeeName, EmployeeSSN, and DepartmentName fields, in alphabetical order by EmployeeName.
   d. Yes, an outer join is possible. One example of an outer join is a list that shows all records from the Department table and their employees, even those departments without any employees currently assigned.
   e. Yes, a self-join is possible using the Employee table. The SupervisorSSN field is a foreign key that matches the primary key field EmployeeSSN, so you could list all employees and the supervisor name for each employee.

## Objectives

**Session 10.1**
- Design a switchboard and dialog box for a graphical user interface
- Run and add actions to macros
- Single step a macro
- Create a macro

**Session 10.2**
- Add a macro to a macro group
- Add a command button to a form
- Attach a macro to a command button
- Create a dialog box form
- Add a list box to a form
- Use an SQL statement to fill a list box with object names

**Session 10.3**
- Create a macro group
- Use the Switchboard Manager to create a switchboard

# Automating Tasks with Macros

*Creating a User Interface for the Overseas Database*

## Case

## Northeast Seasonal Jobs International (NSJI)

At a recent office automation conference, Elsa saw several database applications developed by database designers. The designers' applications used several advanced Access features to automate and control how a user interacts with Access. These features allowed the designers to create a custom user interface for a database. This interface made it much easier for inexperienced users to access the database, and it minimized the chance that an unauthorized user could change the design of any database objects.

Elsa would like to implement a similar user interface for the Overseas database. She would like the interface to display a list of available forms, reports, and queries in the database that the user can select by clicking a command button. This interface will make it much easier for NSJI employees to use the Overseas database, and it will reduce the chance that they will make undesirable changes to the design of the database objects.

## Student Data Files

▼**Comp**

▽ **Tutorial folder**
  Airplane.bmp
  Overseas.mdb (*cont.*)

▽ **Review folder**
  Globe.gif
  Work.mdb (*cont.*)

▽ **Case1 folder**
  Camera.bmp
  Shoots.mdb (*cont.*)

▽ **Case2 folder**
  AtHome.mdb (*cont.*)
  ServeHot.gif

▽ **Case3 folder**
  ZooFunds.mdb (*cont.*)

▽ **Case4 folder**
  Rivers.mdb (*cont.*)

▽ **Case5 folder**
  BuySell.mdb (*cont.*)

# Session 10.1

## Implementing a Graphical User Interface

A **user interface** is what you see and use when you communicate with a computer program. Not too long ago, most users communicated with a program by typing words that issued commands. You had to remember these commands, which were part of a command language. All the programs developed for today's popular operating environments, such as Microsoft Windows, provide graphical user interfaces. A **graphical user interface** (**GUI**) (pronounced "gooey") displays windows, menu bars, pull-down menus, dialog boxes, and graphical pictures, called icons, that you use to communicate with the program. All Microsoft Windows programs use a similar visual interface, so once you learn one program, you can easily learn another. Overall, a GUI benefits a user by simplifying work, improving productivity, and decreasing errors.

Elsa wants to provide an easier way to work with the Overseas database. The type of user interface you need for working with a database is called a switchboard.

## Switchboards

A **switchboard** is a form that appears when you open a database and that provides controlled access to the database's tables, forms, queries, and reports. When a user opens the database, Access opens a switchboard from which the user can choose an option. When you create a switchboard, you are essentially creating a new interface, and it's up to you to decide what options you want to give the user. Figure 10-1 shows the finished Overseas Database switchboard, which you will begin in this tutorial and finish in Tutorial 12.

| Figure 10-1 | Overseas Database switchboard |

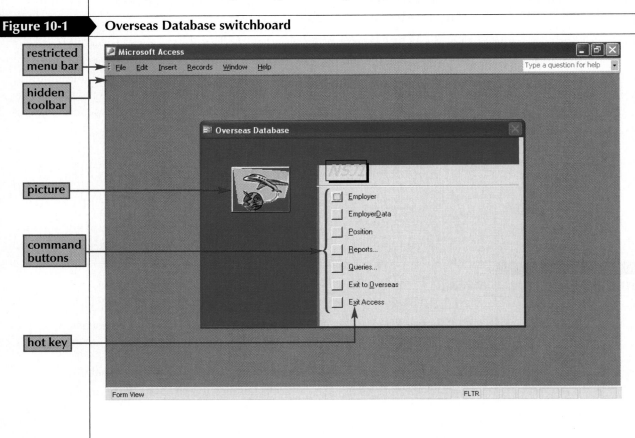

A typical switchboard provides the following items:

- Command buttons provide access to all the options and option groups available to the user. In the switchboard shown in Figure 10-1, for example, you can click a command button to open one of three forms (Employer, EmployerData, or Position), to open another switchboard with report options, to open a list of available queries, to close the switchboard and return to the Database window for the Overseas database, or to exit Access. When a selected form, query list, or report switchboard is closed, Access redisplays the Overseas Database switchboard, so the user can choose the next option. In other words, the user starts and ends with the switchboard and navigates between options from the switchboard.
- A restricted menu bar contains only those menu options that a user needs for manipulating data; there are no menu options for changing the database design.
- The toolbar is hidden to prevent users from accessing commands that they could potentially use to alter the database design.
- **Shortcut keys** (or **hot keys**), which are identified by the underlined letters in the words next to each command button option, let users select an option by pressing and holding down the Alt key while typing the underlined letter, instead of clicking a command button. You can also create shortcut keys for menu names, menu options, and toolbar buttons.
- Text boxes and pictures can be used to provide identification and visual appeal. The display of a small number of attractively designed pictures and text boxes can help users understand the switchboard's functions. Keep in mind, however, that too many graphics can be confusing or distracting.

A switchboard provides an attractive presentation for a user interface, but there are two more important reasons to use a switchboard instead of the Database window to work with a database. First, a switchboard lets you customize the organization of the user interface. Second, a switchboard prevents users from changing the design of tables, forms, queries, reports, and other objects. By hiding the Database window and toolbar and using a restricted menu bar, you limit users to just those database features that you want them to use. If you do not include any menu, toolbar, or command button options that let users open database objects in Design view, users cannot inadvertently or purposely change the design of the database.

The Reports and Queries command buttons on the Overseas Database switchboard include ellipses after the button names. As you know from your work in Windows, these ellipses signify that a dialog box containing additional options opens when you click these command buttons. To display the list of available reports, you will create the switchboard shown in Figure 10-2, which is similar in appearance to the Overseas Database switchboard.

**Reports switchboard** | **Figure 10-2**

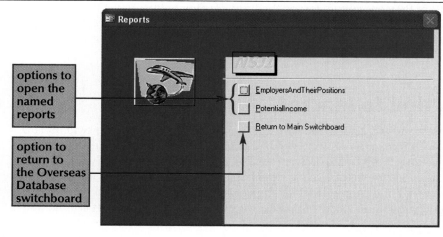

options to open the named reports

option to return to the Overseas Database switchboard

The Reports switchboard contains command buttons to open the EmployersAndTheirPositions report and the PotentialIncome report. It also has a command button to return to the Overseas Database switchboard, which is the main switchboard.

To display the list of available queries and their options, you will create a custom dialog box.

## Dialog Boxes

A **custom dialog box** is a form that resembles a dialog box, both in appearance and function. You use a custom dialog box to ask for user input, selection, or confirmation before an action is performed, such as opening the results of a query or printing a query. Figure 10-3 shows the finished Queries dialog box that you will create later in this tutorial for the Overseas database user interface.

| Figure 10-3 | Queries dialog box |
| --- | --- |

You will add a list box, which displays the queries available for selection, to the dialog box. You will also add three command buttons. A **command button** is a control on a form that starts an action, or a set of actions, when you click it. An **action** is an instruction to Access to perform an operation, such as opening a form or displaying a query in the Print Preview window. Command buttons can contain text, standard pictures available from Access, or pictures you supply, to indicate their functions. Clicking the Close command button on the dialog box returns you to the Overseas Database switchboard. The other command buttons contain pictures that identify their functions. The command button on the left has an icon of a magnifying glass over a piece of paper. This is the same icon shown on the Print Preview button. Just as the Print Preview button opens the Print Preview window, this command button opens the Print Preview window for the selected query. When you click the middle command button, the selected query opens in Datasheet view.

## Introduction to Macros

The command buttons and custom dialog boxes on the Overseas Database switchboard gain their power from macros—and from Visual Basic for Applications code. A **macro** is an action, or a set of actions, that you want Access to perform automatically for you. Macros automate repetitive tasks, such as opening forms, printing selected form records, and running queries. For example, clicking the Position command button on the Overseas Database switchboard causes Access to perform a macro containing the action that opens the Position form.

Access lets you automate most tasks using either macros or **Visual Basic for Applications (VBA)**, the programming language for Microsoft Office programs. As a beginner, you will find it easier to use macros than to create programs using VBA. With macros, you simply select a series of actions from a list to create a macro that does what you want it to do. To use VBA, you need to understand the VBA command language well enough to be able to write your own code. VBA does provide advantages over using macros, such as better error-handling capabilities and making your application easier to change. Macros, however, are useful for small applications and for simple tasks, such as opening and closing objects. Additionally, you cannot use VBA to assign actions to a specific key or key combination or to open an application in a special way, such as displaying a switchboard. For these types of actions, you must use macros. When you use Access, over 50 actions are available; Figure 10-4 shows several frequently used Access actions.

**Frequently used Access actions**     Figure 10-4

| Action | Description |
|---|---|
| Beep | Produces a beep tone through the computer's speakers |
| Close | Closes the specified window, or the active window if none is specified |
| FindRecord | Finds the first record, or the next record if the action is used again, that meets the specified criteria |
| Maximize | Maximizes the active window |
| MsgBox | Displays a message box containing a warning or informational message |
| OpenForm | Opens a form in Datasheet view, Design view, Form view, or Print Preview |
| PrintTo | Prints the active database object |
| Quit | Exits Microsoft Access |
| Restore | Restores a maximized or minimized window to its previous size |
| RunMacro | Runs a macro |
| SendKeys | Sends keystrokes to Microsoft Access or another active program |

Before you begin creating the Overseas Database switchboard and its supporting macros, you'll run an existing macro, named mcrEmployerData, that Elsa created after she returned from the conference. (*mcr* is a prefix tag to identify the macro object type. Read the Naming Conventions section in the appendix titled "Relational Databases and Database Design" for more information about naming conventions.)

# Running a Macro

You can directly run an existing macro in three different ways:

- In the Macro window, click the Run button on the Macro Design toolbar.
- Click Tools on the menu bar, point to Macro, click Run Macro, click the Macro Name list arrow, click the desired macro name, and then click the OK button.
- In the Database window, click Macros in the Objects bar, right-click the macro name, and then click Run.

You'll use the last method to run the mcrEmployerData macro.

### To run the mcrEmployerData macro:

1. Start Access, and then open the **Overseas** database located in the Comp\Tutorial folder provided with your Data Files.

   **Trouble?** If a dialog box opens with a message about installing the Microsoft Jet Service Pack, see your instructor or technical support person for assistance. You must have the appropriate Service Pack installed in order to open and work with Access databases safely.

   **Trouble?** If a dialog box opens, warning you that the Overseas database may not be safe, click the Open button. Your security level is set to Medium, which is the security setting that lets you choose whether or not to open a database that contains macros, VBA, or certain types of queries. The Overseas database does not contain objects that will harm your computer, so you can safely open the database.

   **Trouble?** If a dialog box opens, warning you that Access can't open the Overseas database due to security restrictions, click the OK button, click Tools on the menu bar, point to Macro, click Security, click the Medium option button, click the OK button, restart your computer if you're requested to do so, and then repeat Step 1. Your security level was set to High, which is the security setting that lets you open a database that contains macros, VBA, or certain types of queries only from trusted sources. Because the Overseas database does not contain objects that will harm your computer, you need to change the security setting to Medium and then safely open the Overseas database.

2. Click **Macros** in the Objects bar of the Database window, right-click **mcrEmployerData**, and then click **Run**. A message box opens. See Figure 10-5.

| Figure 10-5 | Using a macro action to open a message box |
|---|---|

Opening the message box is the first action Elsa added to the mcrEmployerData macro. A **message box** is a special type of dialog box that contains a message and a command button but no options. The message box remains on the screen until you click the OK button. This message box specifies that the next macro action will open the EmployerData form. When you click the OK button, the message box closes, and the macro resumes with the next action. Elsa added this message box and other message boxes to her practice macro so that she could more easily observe the other actions. In most situations, you don't include message boxes between steps as Elsa did in this macro.

3. Click the **OK** button. The next two actions in the mcrEmployerData macro are performed: the EmployerData form opens, and the second message box opens. See Figure 10-6.

**Second and third actions in the mcrEmployerData macro** ◄ **Figure 10-6**

**EmployerData : Form**

**NSJI Employer Information**

Overseas database

Sound a beep

OK

third action
opens the
message box

Employer: 10197    Aidan's of Myst

Contact: Aidan    Gaughan

Employer Information | Positions

Address:    390 West Main Road
City:    Mystic
State/Prov:    CT
Postal Code:    06355
Country:    USA
Comments:

Website:
NAICS Code:    72232
Contact Position:    Manager

Record: 1 of 45    second action opens the
EmployerData form

Calculating . . .

**4.** Click the **OK** button. A beep sounds, and the third message box opens. These are the fourth and fifth actions in the mcrEmployerData macro.

**Trouble?** If your computer doesn't have speakers, you won't hear a beep sound. If you do hear the beep, its sound varies depending on your computer and its settings.

**5.** Click the **OK** button. The EmployerData form is maximized, and the fourth message box opens. These are the sixth and seventh actions in the mcrEmployerData macro.

**6.** Click the **OK** button. The EmployerData form is restored, and the fifth message box opens. These are the eighth and ninth actions in the mcrEmployerData macro.

**7.** Click the **OK** button. The EmployerData form now displays record 17 for George's Restaurant & Galley, and the sixth message box opens. These are actions 10 and 11 in the mcrEmployerData macro.

**8.** Click the **OK** button. The EmployerData form closes (action 12—the last action in the mcrEmployerData macro), the mcrEmployerData macro ends, and the Database window becomes the active window.

Elsa suggests that you add some actions to the mcrEmployerData macro to learn about the Macro window and how to modify an existing macro.

# Adding Actions to a Macro

To modify the mcrEmployerData macro, you need to open the macro in the Macro window.

### To open the Macro window:

**1.** Right-click **mcrEmployerData** in the Macros list, and then click **Design View** on the short-cut menu. The mcrEmployerData macro opens in the Macro window. See Figure 10-7.

| Figure 10-7 | Macro window |
| --- | --- |

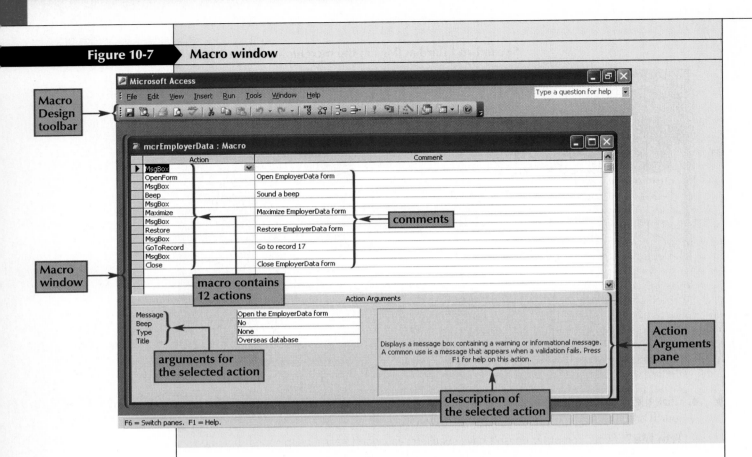

In the **Macro window**, you create and modify macros. Both the menu bar and toolbar for the Macro window have options that are specifically related to macros. The Macro window also includes an **Action column**, in which you enter the actions you want Access to perform, and a **Comment column**, in which you enter optional comments to document the specific actions. You usually don't enter comments for actions that are self-descriptive.

The first MsgBox action is the current action. Access documents the current action in the Action Arguments pane of the Macro window on the right; pressing the F1 key displays more detailed documentation about the action. On the left, Access lists the arguments associated with the current action. **Arguments** are additional facts Access needs to execute an action. The action for opening a message box, for example, needs the wording of the message to be displayed and the title bar's name as arguments.

You'll add two actions, the MsgBox and FindRecord actions, to the mcrEmployerData macro between the GoToRecord and the last MsgBox actions. For the FindRecord action, you'll find the record for EmployerID 10190. You use the **FindRecord action** to find the first record, or the next record if the action is used again, that meets the criteria specified by the FindRecord arguments.

The **MsgBox action** opens a message box and displays a warning or informational message. The macro containing a MsgBox action does not proceed to the next action until you click the OK button, so when you add this action to the mcrEmployerData macro, you'll have as much time as you need to read and react to the message box.

The MsgBox action requires four arguments: Message, Beep, Type, and Title, described as follows:

- Message contains the text that will appear in the message box when it is displayed.
- Beep is a Yes/No argument that specifies whether a beep will sound when the message box is opened.

- Type determines which icon, if any, appears in the message box to signify the critical level of the message. The icon choices are None (no icon), Critical (white X in a red ball), Warning? (blue question mark in a white balloon), Warning! (black exclamation point in a yellow triangle), and Information (blue letter I in a white balloon).
- Title contains the title that will appear in the message box title bar.

You'll now add the MsgBox and FindRecord actions to the mcrEmployerData macro.

## To add the actions to the mcrEmployerData macro:

1. Right-click the **row selector** for the last MsgBox action, which is action 11, and then click **Insert Rows**. Access adds a new, blank row between the GoToRecord and MsgBox actions.

   Because you'll be adding two actions, you need to insert a second blank row.

2. Repeat Step 1 to add a second blank row.

   You'll add the MsgBox action to the first blank row.

3. Click the right side of the first blank row's **Action** text box to display the list of actions, scroll down the list, and then click **MsgBox**. The list box closes, MsgBox becomes the new action, and four arguments for this action appear in the Action Arguments pane.

   You'll enter values for the Message and Title arguments, change the Beep argument value from Yes to No, and retain the default Type argument value of None. The description appearing on the right side of the Action Arguments pane changes as you select different action arguments on the left. The description is a brief explanation of the current action argument. If you need a more detailed explanation, press the F1 key to open the Microsoft Office Access Help window and a page related to the current action argument. You can also use Help to learn about specific actions and their arguments, and about macros in general.

4. Press the **F6** key to move the insertion point to the Message text box in the Action Arguments pane, type **Find EmployerID 10190**, press the **Tab** key, click the **Beep** list arrow, click **No**, press the **Tab** key twice, and then type **Overseas database** in the Title text box. See Figure 10-8.

**After adding the MsgBox action** ◄ **Figure 10-8**

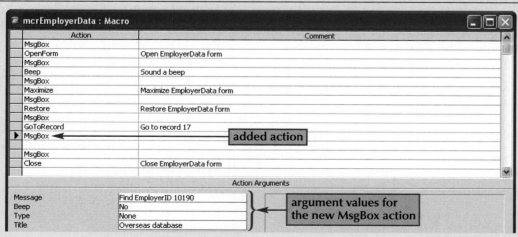

You'll now add the FindRecord action in the next row of the Action column.

5. Click the right side of the **Action** text box for the second row you added, scroll down the list, and then click **FindRecord**. The FindRecord action has seven arguments in the Action Arguments pane.

You need to type a comment and to set the Find What argument to a value of 10190. You'll accept the defaults for the other action arguments.

▶ **6.** Press the **Tab** key, type **Find EmployerID 10190** in the Comment text box, press the **F6** key to move the insertion point to the Find What text box, and then type **10190**.

When you create complicated macros with many actions, you'll find it useful to run through a macro one step at a time.

## Single Stepping a Macro

**Single stepping** executes a macro one action at a time, pausing between actions. You use single stepping to make sure you have placed actions in the right order and with the correct arguments. If you have problems with a macro, you can use single stepping to find the cause of the problems and to determine their proper corrections. The Single Step button on the Macro Design toolbar is a toggle you use to turn single stepping on and off. Once you turn on single stepping, it stays on for all macros until you turn it off.

---

**Reference Window** | **Single Stepping a Macro**

- In the Macro window, click the Single Step button on the Macro Design toolbar to enable single stepping.
- Click the Run button on the Macro Design toolbar. If necessary, click the Yes button to save the macro.
- In the Macro Single Step dialog box, click the Step button to execute the next action, click the Halt button to stop the macro, or click the Continue button to execute all remaining actions in the macro and turn off single stepping.

---

To get a clearer view of the effects of the actions in the mcrEmployerData macro, you can single step through it. First, you need to save your macro changes.

### To save the mcrEmployerData macro and then single step though it:

▶ **1.** Click the **Save** button 🔲 on the Macro Design toolbar to save your macro design changes.

▶ **2.** Click the **Single Step** button 🔄 on the Macro Design toolbar to turn on single stepping.

▶ **3.** Click the **Run** button ❗ on the Macro Design toolbar. The Macro Single Step dialog box opens. See Figure 10-9.

---

**Figure 10-9** ▶ **Macro Single Step dialog box**

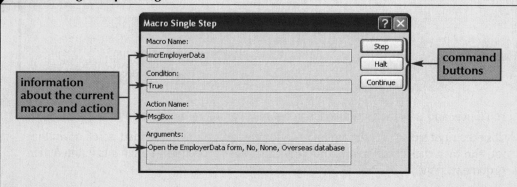

**Trouble?** If the first message box opens instead of the Macro Single Step dialog box, then you turned off single stepping in Step 2 when you clicked the button. Click the OK buttons to run the macro, and then repeat Steps 2 and 3.

When you single step through a macro, Access opens the Macro Single Step dialog box before performing each action. This dialog box shows the macro's name and the action's condition, name, and arguments. The action will be executed or not executed, depending on whether the condition is true or false. The three command buttons let you step through the macro one action at a time, halt the macro and return to the Macro window, or continue by executing all remaining actions without pausing. If you click the Continue button, you also turn off single stepping.

4. Click the **Step** button. Access runs the first action (MsgBox). Because the MsgBox action pauses the macro, the Macro Single Step dialog box remains hidden until you click the OK button in the message box.

5. Click the **OK** button to close the message box. The Macro Single Step dialog box shows the macro's second action (OpenForm).

6. Click the **Step** button. Access runs the second action by opening the EmployerData form and shows the macro's third action (MsgBox) in the Macro Single Step dialog box.

7. Click the **Step** button nine more times, and click the **OK** button four more times, making sure you read the Macro Single Step dialog box carefully and observe the actions that occur. At this point, the message box you added is open (Find EmployerID 10190), and record 17 is the current record in the Employer Data form.

8. Click the **OK** button, and then click the **Step** button. The FindRecord action runs, record 39 for EmployerID 10190 is now the current record in the EmployerData form, and the Macro Single Step dialog box shows the macro's last action (MsgBox).

9. Click the **Step** button two more times, and the **OK** button once. The Macro Single Step dialog box closes automatically after the last macro action is completed.

Elsa suggests you complete your practice with macros by creating a new macro and adding an action to a macro by dragging an object from the Database window.

# Creating a Macro

You use the Macro window to create and modify macros. To create the new macro, you'll create a blank macro and then add the actions to it.

Reference Window

**Creating a Macro**

- In the Database window, click Macros in the Objects bar to display the Macros list.
- Click the New button.
- Choose the actions and specify the arguments for the macro in the Macro window.
- Click the Save button on the Macro Design toolbar, and then enter a name for the macro in the Macro Name text box.
- Click the OK button.

Before you create the new macro, you need to turn off single stepping and close the mcrEmployerData macro.

**To turn off single stepping and close the mcrEmployerData macro:**

▶ 1. Click the **Single Step** button 🖅 on the Macro Design toolbar to turn off single stepping.

▶ 2. Click the **Close** button ☒ on the Macro window to close it and return to the Database window.

You'll create a practice macro named mcrPosition; this macro will contain actions to open and close the Position form.

**To create the mcrPosition macro:**

▶ 1. Click the **New** button in the Database window. The Macro window opens.

Because you can save a macro at any time, you'll save the blank macro immediately and name it mcrPosition.

▶ 2. Click the **Save** button 🖫 on the Macro Design toolbar. The Save As dialog box opens.

▶ 3. Type **mcrPosition** in the Macro Name text box, and then press the **Enter** key.

## Adding Actions by Dragging

Another way to add an action to a macro is by dragging an object from the Database window to a new row in the Macro window. When you do this, Access adds the appropriate action and specifies its default argument values. Figure 10-10 describes the effect of dragging each of the seven Access objects to a new row in the Macro window. For example, dragging a table creates an OpenTable action that opens the table in Datasheet view and permits editing or updating. To use this dragging technique, be sure that the Macro and Database windows are both visible. You can move the two windows until you see all the critical components of each window, or use the Tile Horizontally or Tile Vertically command on the Window menu.

**Figure 10-10** ▸ **Actions created by dragging objects from the Database window**

| Object Dragged | Action Created | Arguments and Their Default Values |
| --- | --- | --- |
| Table | OpenTable | View: Datasheet<br>Data Mode: Edit |
| Query | OpenQuery | View: Datasheet<br>Data Mode: Edit |
| Form | OpenForm | View: Form<br>Filter Name: none<br>Where Condition: none<br>Data Mode: none<br>Window Mode: Normal |
| Report | OpenReport | View: Print<br>Filter Name: none<br>Where Condition: none<br>Window Mode: Normal |
| Data Access Page | OpenDataAccessPage | View: Browse |
| Macro | RunMacro | Repeat Count: none<br>Repeat Expression: none |
| Module | OpenModule | Procedure Name: none |

## Creating an Action by Dragging

- Arrange the Macro and the Database windows so that both are visible.
- Drag a database object from the Database window to an Action text box in the Macro window. Access adds the appropriate macro action and sets its arguments to their default values.

Next, you'll use the dragging technique to add actions that open and close the Position form.

### To add actions using the dragging method:

1. Click **Window** on the menu bar, and then click **Tile Vertically** to tile the Macro and Database windows. See Figure 10-11.

**Macro and Database windows tiled vertically** | **Figure 10-11**

active Macro window

Database window

2. Click **Forms** in the Objects bar of the Database window to display the Forms list.

3. Drag **Position** from the Forms list box to the first row's Action text box in the Macro window. Access adds the OpenForm action for the Position form and sets the arguments to their default values.

4. Press the **Tab** key, and then type **Open Position form** in the Comment text box.

   Next, you'll add the MsgBox action so that you'll be able to see the opened Position form before you close it. You'll use the default values for the Beep and Type arguments.

5. Press the **Tab** key, click the **Action** list arrow, scroll down the list, and then click **MsgBox**.

6. Press the **F6** key, type **Close Position form** in the Message text box, press the **Tab** key three times, and then type **Overseas database** in the Title text box.

You'll select Close as the final action in the Position macro, and set its arguments by dragging the Position form from the Database window to the Object Name text box in the Action Arguments pane of the Macro window.

7. Click the right side of the third row's **Action** text box, click **Close**, press the **Tab** key, and then type **Close Position form** in the Comment text box.

8. Drag **Position** from the Forms list box in the Database window to the Object Name text box in the Action Arguments pane of the Macro window. When you release the mouse button in the Object Name text box, Access automatically sets the Object Type argument to Form and the Object Name argument to Position. See Figure 10-12.

**Figure 10-12** ▸ **Macro window with action arguments set by dragging**

The macro is now completed, so you'll run it to be sure it is correct.

## To run the Position macro:

1. Click the **Run** button ![Run icon] on the Macro Design toolbar, and then click the **Yes** button to save the modified macro. Access runs the first two macro actions by opening the message box after opening the Position form. See Figure 10-13.

First two mcrPosition macro actions

Figure 10-13

2. Click the **OK** button in the message box. Access closes the message box, and then runs the last macro action by closing the Position form.

3. Click the **Close** button ⊠ on the Macro window to close it. The Database window is now the active window.

   **Trouble?** If you accidentally clicked the Close button on the Database window and closed the Overseas database, simply reopen the Overseas database.

4. If necessary, reposition and resize the Database window. See Figure 10-14.

Database window repositioned and resized

Figure 10-14

**Trouble?** If your Database window's position differs from the position shown in figures later in this tutorial, this causes no problems. Just continue with the steps in the tutorial.

▶ **5.** If you are not continuing on to the next session, close the Overseas database, and then exit Access.

The Position form (see Figure 10-13) that Elsa created contains a command button that uses a macro. In the next session, you'll use this macro and the command button, and then you'll add a command button with an attached macro to the Employer form.

**Review**

## Session 10.1 Quick Check

1. Define a switchboard and provide two reasons for using one.
2. What is a hot key and how do you use it?
3. What is a macro?
4. What is an action argument? Give an example of an action argument.
5. What does the MsgBox action do?
6. What are you trying to accomplish when you single step through a macro?

# Session 10.2

## Using a Command Button with an Attached Macro

Elsa created a macro that she associated with, or attached to, a command button on the Position form that you opened in Session 10.1. In Session 10.1, you learned how to create a macro with actions that open and close forms, find records, and open message boxes. You can also add a command button to a form to execute a set of actions. To add a command button to a form, you open the form in Design view and use the Command Button tool on the toolbox. After adding the command button to the form and while still in Design view, you attach the macro with the desired actions to the command button. Then, when a user clicks the command button, the macro's actions are executed. Elsa asks you to use the View Employer command button on the Position form to see how the macro attaches to the command button, and then to view the macro.

### To use the View Employer command button:

▶ **1.** If you took a break after the previous session, make sure that Access is running, that the **Overseas** database in the Comp\Tutorial folder is open, and that **Forms** is selected in the Objects bar of the Database window.

▶ **2.** Open the **Position** form in Form view to display the Position form for the first position, with PositionID 2004 and EmployerID 10197.

▶ **3.** Click the **View Employer** command button. The Position form remains open, and the Employer form opens for EmployerID 10197. See Figure 10-15.

**After opening the Employer form with the View Employer command button**  **Figure 10-15**

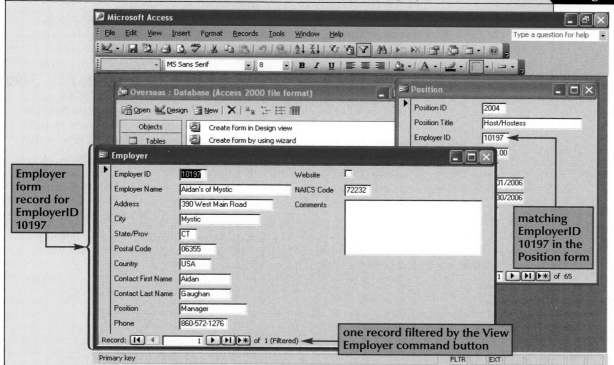

**Trouble?** If the Employer form blocks the Position form, drag the Employer form down and to the left as shown in Figure 10-15.

Clicking the View Employer command button triggered an attached macro that opened the Employer form. The record displayed in the Employer form is for the employer (EmployerID 10197) that offers the position displayed in the Position form. The text "Record 1 of 1 (Filtered)" that appears around the navigation buttons in the Employer form indicates that you can view only the record for EmployerID 10197 in the Employer form at this point.

As you navigate through the Position form, the contents of the Employer form do not change unless you click the View Employer command button again.

4. Click the Position form title bar, and then click the **Next Record** navigation button ▶ in the Position form. Record 2 for EmployerID 10146 is now the current record, but the Employer form is unchanged—it still shows the record for EmployerID 10197.

5. Click the **View Employer** command button. The record for EmployerID 10146 is now the current record in the Employer form. The Position form still displays record 2.

6. Close the Employer form. The Position form is now the active window.

Clicking the View Employer command button is an event, and the opening of the Employer form is controlled by setting an event property.

## Events

An **event** is a state, condition, or occurrence detectable by Access. For example, events occur when you click a command button on a form, when you use the mouse to position the pointer on a form, or when you press a key to choose an option. In your work with

Access, you've initiated hundreds of events on forms, controls, records, and reports without any special effort. For example, three form events are: Open, which occurs when you open a form; Activate, which occurs when the form becomes the active window; and Close, which occurs when you close a form and the form is removed from the screen. Each event has an associated event property. An **event property** specifies how an object responds when an event occurs. For example, each form has OnOpen, OnActivate, and OnClose event properties associated with Open, Activate, and Close events, respectively.

Event properties appear in the property sheet when you create forms and reports. Unlike most properties you've used previously in property sheets, event properties do not have an initial value. If an event property contains no value, it means the event property has not been set. In this case Access takes no *special action* when the associated event occurs. For example, if a form's OnOpen event property is not set and you open the form, then the Open event occurs (the form opens), and no *special action* occurs beyond the opening of the form. You can set an event property value to a macro name, and Access will execute the macro when the event occurs. For example, you could write a macro that automatically selects a particular field in a form when you open it. You can also create a group of statements using VBA code and set the event property value to the name of that group of statements. Access will then execute the group of statements, or **procedure**, when the event occurs. Such a procedure is called an **event procedure**.

When you clicked the View Employer command button on the Position form, the Click event occurred and triggered an attached macro. The View Employer command button contains an OnClick event property setting, which you will examine next.

### To view the OnClick event property setting for the View Employer command button:

▶ **1.** Switch to Design view, scroll down the form, right-click the **View Employer** command button, and then click **Properties** on the shortcut menu to open the property sheet.

You might notice that event properties, such as OnEnter and OnClick, do not contain a space, but the Event tab in the property sheet shows them as On Enter and On Click, with the spaces. In this case, OnClick and the On Click property in the property sheet are the same.

▶ **2.** Click the **Event** tab (if necessary), right-click the **On Click** text box, click **Zoom** on the shortcut menu to open the Zoom dialog box, and then click to the right of the selected text to deselect it. See Figure 10-16.

| Figure 10-16 | Macro attached to the OnClick event property |

The OnClick event property value shown in the Zoom dialog box is *mcrOverseasGroup.OpenEmployerForm*. This is an example of a reference to a macro in a macro group.

# Macro Groups

Instead of creating several separate macros, you can combine them into a macro group. A **macro group** is a macro that contains other macros. Macro groups allow you to consolidate related macros and to manage large numbers of macros. For the OnClick event property value shown in Figure 10-16, mcrOverseasGroup is the macro group name, and OpenEmployerForm is the macro name. A period separates the two names. When you click the View Employer command button on the Position form, Access processes the actions contained in the OpenEmployerForm macro, which is located in the mcrOverseasGroup macro group.

You'll now close the Zoom dialog box, and then open the Macro window from the property sheet.

### To open the mcrOverseasGroup macro in the Macro window:

▶ **1.** Click the **Cancel** button in the Zoom dialog box to close it. The OnClick event property value is selected in the property sheet for the selected View Employer command button (named cmdViewEmployer, where *cmd* is a prefix tag to identify a command button control), and the On Click text box contains a list arrow and Build button to its right. See Figure 10-17.

| OnClick event property value for the View Employer command button | Figure 10-17 |
| --- | --- |

You click the list arrow if you want to change the current macro to a different macro, and you click the Build button if you want to use the Macro window to view or change the existing macro. The Build button is also called the **Macro Builder** when you use it to work with macros.

▶ **2.** Click the **Build** button [...] to the right of the On Click text box. The Macro window opens and displays the mcrOverseasGroup macro. See Figure 10-18.

**Figure 10-18** ▶ **Macro window displaying the mcrOverseasGroup macro**

The **Macro Name column** in the Macro window lets you distinguish individual macros in a macro group. Each individual macro is identified by name in the Macro Name column. If a macro contains several actions, you leave the Macro Name column blank for actions added after the first one. To display or hide the Macro Name column, you click the Macro Names button on the Macro Design toolbar.

The OpenEmployerForm macro consists of a single action, OpenForm, which opens the Employer form (the Form Name argument value is Employer). The other OpenForm action arguments are as follows:

- The **View argument** specifies the window view in which to open the object. For forms, you can specify Datasheet, Design, Form, or Print Preview views.
- The **Filter Name argument** specifies the name of a query, or a filter that was saved as a query, that will be used to sort or filter the object's records.
- The **Where Condition argument** specifies an expression or SQL statement that will be used to select records to display in the form. You'll learn more about SQL statements later in this tutorial.
- The **Data Mode argument** specifies the form's data-entry options. Allowable settings for this argument are Add (users can add new records but can't change or delete existing records), Edit (users can change and delete existing records and can add new records), and Read Only (users can only view records). Edit is the default setting.
- The **Window Mode argument** specifies the form's window characteristics. Allowable settings for this argument are Dialog (the form opens as a dialog box), Hidden (the form opens but is not visible), Icon (the form opens minimized as a small title bar at the bottom of the screen), and Normal (the form opens as it normally would from the Database window).

The Where Condition argument value in Figure 10-18 specifies which Employer record appears in the form. You'll use the Zoom dialog box to view the entire Where Condition argument value.

**To view the Where Condition argument value in the Zoom dialog box:**

1. Right-click the **Where Condition** text box, click **Zoom** on the shortcut menu to open the Zoom dialog box, and then click to the right of the selected text to deselect it. See Figure 10-19.

**Where Condition expression for the OpenEmployerForm macro** ◀ **Figure 10-19**

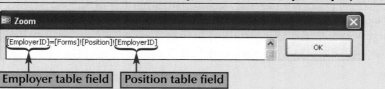

Employer table field     Position table field

The Where Condition argument value contains the expression *[EmployerID]=[Forms]! [Position]![EmployerID]*. In simple terms, the expression asks Access to find the record in the Employer form with the same EmployerID as the current record in the Position form. The expression, however, is complex. The OpenForm action in the macro opens the Employer form; the value *[EmployerID]* to the left of the equals sign determines which record will be displayed in the Employer form. What is this EmployerID value? It's the same as (equals sign) the EmployerID that appears in the current Position form record (*[Forms]![Position]![EmployerID]* to the right of the equals sign). On the right of the equals sign, *[Forms]* identifies the object collection, such as forms or queries. *[Position]* identifies the name of the specific object within the object collection—in this case, Position. Finally, *[EmployerID]* identifies the specific field within the specified object—in this case, the EmployerID field in the Position form.

Now that you've seen a macro that's attached to a command button, Elsa asks you to add a command button to the Employer form, and then attach a new macro to the command button. Elsa wants to be able to print the current record in the Employer form by clicking a command button on the form. Because Elsa doesn't want a large number of macros and because the Macro window is already open for the Overseas Group macro group, you'll add the new macro to it.

# Adding a Macro to a Macro Group

To print the contents of a form's current record, normally you have to click File on the menu bar, click Print, click Selected Record(s), and then click the OK button—a process that takes fours steps and several seconds. Instead of following this process, you can create a command button on the form and a macro that prints the contents of a form's current record, and then attach the macro to the command button on the form. To print the form's current record, you'd simply click the command button.

First, you'll add a macro to the Overseas Group macro group. You'll use the PrintOut action for the new macro. The **PrintOut action** prints the contents of an object; you can print the selected record (set the Print Range argument to Selection), a page range (set the Print Range argument to Pages), or the entire contents of the object (set the Print Range argument to All). You'll use a macro name of PrintCurrentRecord when you add it to the mcrOverseasGroup macro group, so that the macro's function is obvious.

| Reference Window | **Adding a Macro to a Macro Group** |
|---|---|

- Open the macro group in the Macro window. (For a macro group, the Macro Names button is already selected.)
- Type the macro name in the Macro Name column, select the action in the Action column, type an optional comment in the Comment column, and then set the arguments for the action.
- If the macro consists of more than one action, enter the remaining actions in the rows immediately following the first macro action. Leave the Macro Name column blank for each additional action.
- Click the Save button on the Macro Design toolbar.

You'll now add the PrintCurrentRecord macro to the Overseas Group macro group.

### To add the PrintCurrentRecord macro to the mcrOverseasGroup macro group:

1. Click the **Cancel** button in the Zoom dialog box to close it.

2. Click the second row's **Macro Name** text box, type **PrintCurrentRecord**, press the **Tab** key, click the **Action** list arrow, scroll down the list, click **PrintOut**, press the **Tab** key, and then type **Print current record** in the Comment column.

   You need to set only the Print Range argument; to print the current form record, you'll set its value to Selection.

3. Press the **F6** key, click the **Print Range** list arrow, and then click **Selection**. You've completed the action, which is the only action in the PrintCurrentRecord macro. The macro group now contains two macros. See Figure 10-20.

| Figure 10-20 | **Macro group containing two macros** |
|---|---|

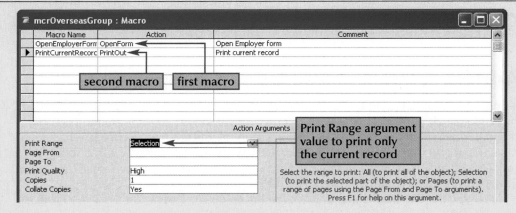

4. Save your macro design changes, and then close the macro. The Position form window is the active window.

   Because you're finished working with the Position form, you'll close the property sheet and the form.

5. Close the property sheet, close the form, and then click the **No** button if you're asked to save your form design changes.

   Next, you'll add a command button to the Employer form. After you attach the PrintCurrentRecord macro to the command button, you'll be able to click the command button to print the current Employer form record.

# Adding a Command Button to a Form

You use the Command Button tool on the toolbox to add a command button to a form. If the Control Wizards tool is selected when you click the Command Button tool, the Command Button Wizard guides you through the process of adding the command button. Instead, you'll add the command button directly to the Employer form without using the wizard. Then you'll set the command button's properties using its property sheet.

### To add a command button to the Employer form:

► 1. Open the **Employer** form in Design view.

   **Trouble?** If the field list is open, click its Close button 🗵 to close it.

► 2. Scroll down the Form Design window until you can see the middle of the Detail section.

► 3. If necessary, click the **Toolbox** button 🛠 on the Form Design toolbar to open the toolbox, and then if necessary dock the toolbox below the Formatting toolbar.

► 4. Make sure the **Control Wizards** tool 🗟 on the toolbox is not selected, and then click the **Command Button** tool ⌐ on the toolbox.

► 5. Move the pointer over the Detail section. The pointer changes to a ⁺☐ shape.

► 6. When the pointer's plus symbol (+) is positioned in the Detail section at the 3.5-inch mark on the horizontal ruler and the 2-inch mark on the vertical ruler, click the mouse button. Access adds a command button to the form. See Figure 10-21.

**After adding a command button to the Employer form** ◀ **Figure 10-21**

**Trouble?** If the Command Button Wizard dialog box opens, click the Cancel button to close it, and then click the Control Wizards button on the toolbox to deselect it.

**Trouble?** The command button on your screen might show a different number in its label, depending on how you completed the previous steps. This difference will not affect the command button or macro. Just continue with the tutorial.

You can now attach the PrintCurrentRecord macro to the command button.

# Attaching a Macro to a Command Button

You created the PrintCurrentRecord macro and added the command button to the Employer form. You'll attach the macro to the command button's OnClick property so that the macro is executed when the command button is clicked.

**To attach the PrintCurrentRecord macro to the command button:**

1. Right-click the command button, click **Properties** on the shortcut menu, and then if necessary click the **Event** tab.

2. Click the right side of the **On Click** text box to display the macros list, and then click **mcrOverseasGroup.PrintCurrentRecord**.

   **Trouble?** If the On Click list box is too narrow to see which macro is the correct one, drag the right border of the property sheet to the right, or the left border of the property sheet to the left, to increase the width of the property sheet, and then repeat Step 2.

   You can change the text that appears on the command button (also known as the command button's label or caption) by changing its Caption property, or you can replace the text with a picture by setting its Picture property. Elsa wants you to place a picture of a printer on the command button.

3. Click the **Format** tab, click the **Picture** text box, and then click the **Build** button [ ⋯ ] that appears next to the text box. The Picture Builder dialog box opens. See Figure 10-22.

| Figure 10-22 | Picture Builder dialog box |

The Picture Builder dialog box contains an alphabetical list of pictures supplied with Access. You can scroll the list and select one of the pictures, or you can click the Browse button to select your own picture. When you select a picture, a sample of the picture appears on the command button in the Sample box on the left.

4. Scroll down the Available Pictures list box, and then click **Printer**. A printer picture appears on the command button in the Sample box.

5. Click the **OK** button. The Picture Builder dialog box closes, and the printer picture appears on a resized command button.

6. Close the property sheet.

Next, you'll save the Employer form and test the command button.

### To save the form and test the command button:

▶ **1.** Save your form design changes, and then switch to Form view.

▶ **2.** Click the **Last Record** navigation button ▶| on the Employer form, and then click the **Print** command button on the form. The last record, for Lighthouse Tours, prints.

▶ **3.** Close the form.

You've now completed your initial work with macros. Next, you'll start to develop the user interface for the Overseas database. You'll create the dialog box to display the queries in the Overseas database, use an SQL statement to select the values for the list box, and then add command buttons and the list box to the dialog box.

## Creating the Queries Dialog Box Form

To create the user interface for the Overseas database, you need to create the Overseas Database and Reports switchboards and the Queries dialog box. First, you'll create the dialog box shown in Figure 10-23.

Queries DialogBox form ◀ **Figure 10-23**

The Queries dialog box is actually a form that you will create. You'll add a label, a list box, and three command buttons to the form, and you'll enter an SQL statement that will provide the contents of the list box. (SQL is a language used with relational databases.) NSJI staff members will use the dialog box as follows:

* Scroll the list box until the desired query name is visible.
* Click the query name, and then click the command button with the Print Preview icon to open the query in Print Preview. Alternatively, double-click the query name to open the query in Print Preview.
* Click the query name, and then click the command button with the Datasheet icon to display the query results.
* Click the Close button to close the dialog box and activate the Overseas Database switchboard. Alternatively, the underlined letter "C" in the Close command button identifies the button's hot key; pressing Alt+C will also close the dialog box.

To create the Queries dialog box, you'll begin by creating a blank form. Because none of the form controls need data from a table or query (an SQL statement will supply the list box with its values), you will create an unbound form, or one that does not use a table or query as its source.

### To create the QueriesDialogBox form:

▶ **1.** Make sure that **Forms** is selected in the Objects bar of the Database window, and then click the **New** button. The New Form dialog box opens.

▶ **2.** Make sure that **Design View** is selected, and then click the **OK** button. Access opens the Form window in Design view.

▶ **3.** Click the **Save** button 🔲 on the Form Design toolbar, type **QueriesDialogBox** in the Form Name text box, and then press the **Enter** key. The title bar displays the saved form's name.

Before adding any controls to the form, you need to set the overall form properties so that the form matches Elsa's design. You will set the Caption property to Queries, which is the value that will appear in the form's title bar. You will also set the Shortcut Menu, Record Selectors, Navigation Buttons, and Close Button properties to No, because Elsa doesn't want the form to include these features. You will set the Auto Resize property to No so that Access will not resize the form when it is opened, thereby maintaining a consistent form size for all users. Also, Elsa wants to disable other Access windows until the user closes the form, so you will set the Modal property to Yes. Finally, after you have completed the form's design, you will set the Border Style property to Dialog so that the form will look like a dialog box that a user cannot resize using the pointer. Figure 10-24 shows the form property settings you will use to create the QueriesDialogBox form for Elsa.

**Figure 10-24** ▶ **QueriesDialogBox form properties**

| Property | Setting | Function |
|---|---|---|
| Auto Resize | No | Opens a form using the last saved size |
| Border Style | Dialog | Prevents a user from resizing the form |
| Caption | Queries | Value that appears in the form's title bar |
| Close Button | No | Disables the display of the Close button on the form's title bar |
| Modal | Yes | Disables other Access windows until a user closes the form |
| Navigation Buttons | No | Disables the display of navigation buttons on the bottom of the form |
| Record Selectors | No | Disables the display of a record selector on the left side of the form |
| Shortcut Menu | No | Disables the display of the shortcut menu if a user right-clicks the form |

Working from this list, you can use the property sheet to set the form properties.

### To set the properties for the unbound form:

▶ **1.** Right-click the form selector, which is the gray box immediately to the left of the horizontal ruler in the Form window, and then click **Properties** on the shortcut menu to open the form's property sheet (as indicated by the word "Form" in the title bar).

▶ **2.** If necessary, click the **All** tab to display the All page of the property sheet.

You can now set the Caption property for the form. The Caption property value will appear in the title bar when the form is displayed.

▶ **3.** Scroll to the top of the property sheet (if necessary), click the **Caption** text box, and then type **Queries**.

Next, you'll set the Record Selectors property so that a record selector will not be displayed on the left side of the form. Because the form does not display any records, there's no need to include a record selector.

▶ **4.** Scroll down until the Record Selectors property is visible, and then double-click **Yes** in the Record Selectors text box to change the property setting from Yes to No.

You'll now set the remaining form properties.

▶ **5.** Continue scrolling as necessary, and set the **Navigation Buttons** property to **No**, set the **Auto Resize** property to **No**, set the **Modal** property to **Yes**, set the **Close Button** property to **No**, and then set the **Shortcut Menu** property to **No**.

▶ **6.** Close the property sheet, and then save your form design changes.

Now that you have set the form's properties, you can add a label and a list box to it. The label will identify the list box for the user, and the list box will display the list of queries in the Overseas database. You will not use the Control Wizards tool for the list box, because you'll be using an SQL statement to provide the query names for the list box.

# Adding a List Box to a Form

A **list box** is a control that displays a list of values. The list box in the QueriesDialogBox form will display the list of queries that the user can preview or view. Clicking the name of a query selects it, and then the user can click one of the command buttons to preview or view the query. Double-clicking a query name in the list box will open the query in the Print Preview window.

Reference Window

## Adding a List Box to a Form

- If necessary, click the Control Wizards tool on the toolbox so that it is appropriately selected or deselected.
- Click the List Box tool on the toolbox.
- Position the pointer where you want the list box to appear on the form, and then click the mouse button.
- If you used the List Box Wizard, complete the dialog boxes to choose the source of the list, select the fields to appear in the list box, size the columns, select the field that will provide the data for the field in the main form, choose to remember the value for later use or store it in a field, and then enter the value to appear in the list box label.

First, you'll add the label "Available Queries" to the form. Then you'll add the list box to display the list of queries from which to choose.

### To add the label to the form:

▶ **1.** Click the **Label** tool $Aa$ on the toolbox.

▶ **2.** Position the pointer in the Detail section; when the pointer's plus symbol is positioned at the 0.5-inch mark on the horizontal ruler and the 0.25-inch mark on the vertical ruler, click the mouse button. A small label box containing an insertion point opens on the form.

▶ **3.** Type **Available Queries** and then press the **Enter** key.

Elsa wants the label to stand out more, so you'll change the label's font size from the default of 8 to 10, make the label bold, and then resize the label box.

**4.** Click the **Font Size** list arrow on the Formatting toolbar, click **10**, and then click the **Bold** button **B** on the Formatting toolbar.

**5.** Click **Format** on the menu bar, point to **Size**, and then click **To Fit**.

Now you can add the list box to the form.

### To add the list box to the form:

**1.** Make sure that the **Control Wizards** tool on the toolbox is deselected.

**2.** Click the **List Box** tool on the toolbox, position the pointer's plus symbol in the row of grid dots below the left edge of the Available Queries label box, and then click the mouse button. Access adds a list box and attached label box to the form. See Figure 10-25.

| Figure 10-25 | Form design after adding the label and the list box |
| --- | --- |

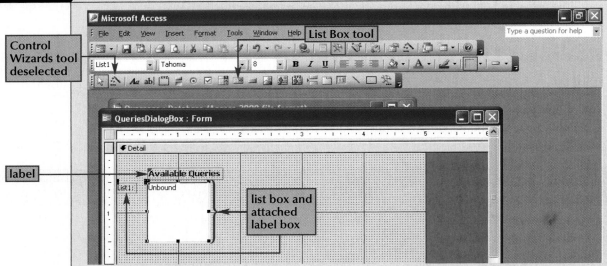

**Trouble?** If your list box is sized or positioned differently, resize it or move it until it matches the list box shown in Figure 10-25.

You can now save the form and then check your progress by switching to Form view.

**3.** Save your form design changes, and then switch to Form view. See Figure 10-26.

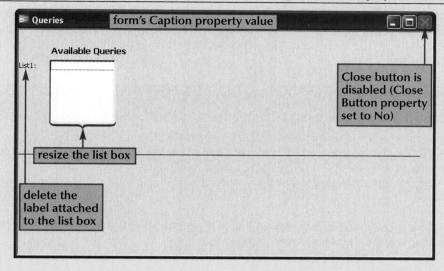

QueriesDialogBox form displayed in Form view | **Figure 10-26**

After viewing the form, Elsa asks you to make two changes to it. Because the form already includes the label "Available Queries," the label attached to the list box is unnecessary. Elsa asks you to delete this label. She'd also like you to resize the list box by making it wider so that it will accommodate the list of queries better.

### To delete the label attached to the list box and resize the list box:

1. Switch to Design view.

2. Right-click the label attached to the list box to open the shortcut menu, and then click **Cut** to delete it.

3. Click the list box to select it.

4. Use the middle-right sizing handle to drag the right border to the 2.75-inch mark on the horizontal ruler, and then save your form design changes.

You now can enter the SQL statement that will provide the query names for the list box.

# Using SQL

**SQL (Structured Query Language)** is a standard language used in querying, updating, and managing relational databases. Every full-featured relational DBMS has its own version of the current standard SQL, which is called SQL-99, although Access 2003 conforms more with the prior SQL-89 and SQL-92 standards. If you learn SQL for one relational DBMS, it's a relatively easy task to begin using SQL for other relational DBMSs. When you work with two or more relational DBMSs, which is the case in most companies, you'll learn that few differences exist among the various SQL versions.

Much of what Access accomplishes behind the scenes is done with SQL. Whenever you create a query in Design view, for example, Access automatically constructs an equivalent SQL statement. When you save a query, Access saves the SQL statement version of the query.

# Viewing an SQL Statement for a Query

When you are working in Design view or viewing the results of a query, you can see the SQL statement that is equivalent to your query by clicking the SQL View button or selecting SQL View from the View menu. In response, Access displays the SQL statement in the SQL window.

| Reference Window | **Viewing an SQL Statement for a Query** |
|---|---|

- Display the query in Design view or Datasheet view.
- Click the list arrow for the View button on the toolbar, and then click SQL View. Access opens the SQL window.
- Use the appropriate View button to return to either Design view or Datasheet view.

Next, you'll examine the SQL statements that are equivalent to two existing queries: SelectedEmployerInfo and EmployerPositions.

## To view the SQL statement for the SelectedEmployerInfo query:

1. Click the **Database Window** button 📠 on the Form Design toolbar to make the Database window the active window.

2. Open the **SelectedEmployerInfo** query in Datasheet view. Access opens the query recordset and displays the 45 records from the Employer table. The columns displayed are Employer ID, Employer Name, City, Contact First Name, Contact Last Name, and Website.

3. Click the list arrow for the **View** button 🔽 on the Query Datasheet toolbar, and then click **SQL View** to open the SQL window.

4. Make sure the SQL window is maximized, and that the SQL statement is deselected. See Figure 10-27.

| Figure 10-27 | **SQL window for the SelectedEmployerInfo query** |
|---|---|

SQL uses the **SELECT statement** to define what data it retrieves from a database and how it presents the data. For the work you've done so far, the Access menu commands and dialog box options have sufficed. If you learn SQL to the point where you can use it efficiently, you will be able to enter your own SELECT and other SQL statements in the SQL window. If you work with more complicated databases, you might find that you need the extra power of the SQL language to implement your database strategies fully.

The rules that SQL uses to construct a statement similar to the SELECT statement shown in Figure 10-27 are summarized as follows:

- The basic form of an SQL SELECT statement is: SELECT-FROM-WHERE-ORDER BY. After SELECT, list the fields you want to display. After FROM, list the tables used in the query. After WHERE, list the selection criteria. After ORDER BY, list the sort fields.
- If a field name includes a space or special symbol, enclose the field name in brackets. Because the Overseas database does not use field names with spaces or special symbols,

you don't have to enclose its field names in brackets. However, if you used a database that had field names such as Employer Name, then you would use [Employer Name] in an SQL statement.

- Precede a field name with the name of its table by connecting the table name to the field name with a period. For example, you would enter the EmployerName field in the Employer table as *Employer.EmployerName*.
- Separate field names and table names by commas, and end the statement with a semicolon.

The SQL statement shown in Figure 10-27 selects the EmployerID, EmployerName, City, ContactFirstName, ContactLastName, and Website fields from the Employer table. The SQL statement does not contain a WHERE clause or an ORDER BY clause, so all records are included in the recordset and listed in the default order, which is in ascending order by primary key.

You can enter or change SQL statements directly in the SQL window. If you enter an SQL statement and then switch to the Query window in Design view, you will see its equivalent in the design grid.

Next, you'll examine the SQL statement for the EmployerPositions query.

### To view the SQL statement for the EmployerPositions query:

1. Click the **Close** button ⊠ on the menu bar to close the SQL window and return to the Database window.

2. Open the **EmployerPositions** query in Design view. The query selects records from the joined Employer and Position tables, in ascending order by the PositionTitle field as the primary sort field and in descending order by the Openings field as the secondary sort field. The fields displayed are EmployerName, City, and StateProv from the Employer table, and PositionTitle, Openings, StartDate, and EndDate from the Position table.

3. Click the list arrow for the **View** button ▦ on the Query Design toolbar, and then click **SQL View** to open the SQL window.

4. Click the line below the SQL statement to deselect the statement. See Figure 10-28.

**SQL window for the EmployerPositions query** | Figure 10-28

The SELECT statement for this query is similar to the one shown in Figure 10-27, except for the following added features:

- The INNER JOIN clause selects records from the two tables only when the records have the same value in the common field that links the tables. The syntax for this clause is to type INNER JOIN between the two table names, followed by ON, and then followed by the names of the fields serving as the common field, connected by an equals sign. (Access uses the ON clause here instead of the standard SQL WHERE clause.)
- The ORDER BY clause specifies the sort order for the records.
- The notation DESC in the ORDER BY clause indicates a descending sort order. If DESC does not follow a sort key field, then SQL uses an ascending sort order.

The SQL SELECT statements mirror the query options you viewed in Design view. In effect, every choice you make in Design view is reflected as part of the SQL SELECT statement. Viewing the SQL statements generated from queries that you design is an effective way to begin learning SQL. Also, if you select an SQL keyword, such as SELECT or ORDER BY, in the SQL window and press the F1 key, Access displays context-sensitive Help for that keyword.

### To close the query and return to the QueriesDialogBox form:

▶ **1.** Close the SQL window, and then restore the Database window.

▶ **2.** Click the form title bar to make the QueriesDialogBox form the active window.

You now can enter the SQL statement that will provide the query names for the list box.

## Using an SQL Statement for a List Box

You'll use a SELECT statement to retrieve the list of query names from one of the Access system tables. **System tables** are special tables maintained by Access that store information about the characteristics of a database and about the structure of the objects in a database. Although system tables do not appear in the Database window's Tables list box, you can retrieve information from system tables using SELECT statements. One of the system tables, the **MSysObjects table**, keeps track of the names, types, and other characteristics of every object in a database. The Name and Type fields are the two MSysObjects table fields you'll use in the SELECT statement. The Name field contains a query name when the Type field value is 5, as shown in Figure 10-29.

| **Figure 10-29** ▶ | MSysObjects table Type field values |

| Object Type | Type Field Value in MSysObjects Table |
| --- | --- |
| Table | 1 |
| Query | 5 |
| Form | -32768 |
| Report | -32764 |
| Page | -32756 |
| Macro | -32766 |
| Module | -32761 |

Access creates its own queries to handle many tasks for you; each of these queries has a name that begins with the tilde (~) character. Because you want to exclude these special system queries from the list box, you'll also need to use the Left function in your SELECT statement. The **Left function** provides the first character(s) in a text string. The format of the Left function is *Left(text string, number of characters)*. You'll use *Left([Name], 1)* to retrieve the first character of the Name field. To include only those queries whose names do not begin with the ~ character, you'll use the expression *Left([Name], 1)<>"~"*. In this expression, the <> operator is the not equal operator. Access interprets this expression as "the first character of the Name field does not equal the ~ character." Figure 10-30 shows the Zoom dialog box, which contains the complete SELECT statement that you will use to select the list of query names.

**SELECT statement for the list box** | **Figure 10-30**

The **Row Source property** specifies the data source, such as a table, query, or SQL statement, to a list box and to other controls, so you'll enter the SELECT statement as the value for the list box's Row Source property.

### To set the Row Source property for the list box:

▶ **1.** Right-click the list box to open the shortcut menu, click **Properties** to open the property sheet, and then click the **All** tab (if necessary).

▶ **2.** Right-click the **Row Source** text box to open the shortcut menu, and then click **Zoom**. The Zoom dialog box opens.

▶ **3.** Type **SELECT [Name] FROM MSysObjects WHERE [Type]=5 And Left([Name],1)<>"~" ORDER BY [Name];** in the Zoom dialog box, and then click the OK button.

▶ **4.** Close the property sheet, save your form design changes, and then switch to Form view. See Figure 10-31.

**Completed list box** | **Figure 10-31**

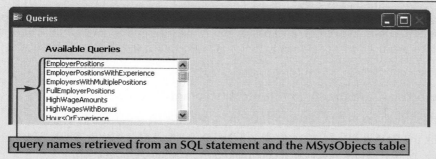

query names retrieved from an SQL statement and the MSysObjects table

**Trouble?** If a syntax-error message appears, click the OK button, switch to Design view, right-click the list box, click Properties, right-click the Row Source text box, and then click Zoom. Correct the SELECT statement until it's the same as the statement shown in Figure 10-30, click the OK button, and then repeat Step 4.

You can now add command buttons to the form.

## Adding Command Buttons to a Form

First, you will add the Print Preview command button to the form. You can add a command button to a form by placing the button directly on the form or by using the Control Wizards tool. If you use the Control Wizards tool, you can attach a standard Access action (such as opening a specific query or closing a window) or a macro to the button. You cannot use a standard Access action for this command button, because the query to be opened will depend on the query the user has selected in the list box. Instead, you will add the command button on the form now and attach VBA code to it in Tutorial 11.

## To add the Print Preview command button to the form:

1. Switch to Design view, make sure the **Control Wizards** tool on the toolbox is deselected, and then click the **Command Button** tool on the toolbox.

2. Position the pointer in the Detail section; when the pointer's plus symbol is positioned at the .75-inch mark on the horizontal ruler and the 1.75-inch mark on the vertical ruler, click the mouse button. Access adds a command button to the form.

3. Right-click the command button, and then click **Properties** on the shortcut menu to open the property sheet.

   **Trouble?** If the property sheet is covering the form, drag it out of the way.

   You can now change the text that appears on the command button to the Print Preview picture, which is the same picture that appears on the Print Preview button on the Form Design toolbar.

4. Click the **Format** tab, click the **Picture** text box, and then click the **Build** button that appears next to the Picture text box. The Picture Builder dialog box opens.

5. Scroll down the Available Pictures list box, and then click **Preview Document**. Access shows the picture on the command button in the Sample box.

6. Click the **OK** button. Access closes the Picture Builder dialog box, resizes the command button, places the picture on the command button, and increases the height of the form's Detail section.

Instead of repeating the steps to add the command button for viewing a query, you can copy the first command button and paste it in the Detail section. After moving the copied button into position, you can change the picture on it to show the Query Datasheet icon.

## To place the Datasheet command button on the form:

1. Right-click the command button, and then click **Copy** on the shortcut menu.

2. Click the **Paste** button on the Form Design toolbar. Access adds a copy of the command button below the original command button in the Detail section.

3. Move the new command button into position to the right of the original command button. See Figure 10-32.

**After adding a copy of the command button** ◀ **Figure 10-32**

4. Click the **Picture** text box in the property sheet, and then click the **Build** button ⟦⋯⟧.

5. Scroll through the Available Pictures list box, click **MS Access Query**, and then click the **OK** button. Access closes the Picture Builder dialog box and places the new picture on the command button.

6. Close the property sheet, and then save your form design changes.

You can now add the final command button using control wizards. The Close button will close the dialog box when the user clicks it.

## Adding a Command Button to a Form Using Control Wizards

- If necessary, click the Control Wizards tool on the toolbox so that it is selected.
- Click the Command Button tool on the toolbox.
- Position the pointer where you want the command button to appear, and then click the mouse button.
- Complete the Command Button Wizard dialog boxes to select the action category and the action for the command button, enter the text to display on the command button, define a hot key (or select a picture for the button), and then enter a name for the button.

To define the Close button, you'll use the Control Wizards tool, because the tool automatically attaches the correct VBA code (for closing the QueriesDialogBox form) to the command button. Standard operations, such as opening and closing forms, are good candidates for using the Control Wizards tool. Elsa also wants a user to be able to close the dialog box using a keyboard combination, so you will specify the letter "C" as the hot key for the Close button. To underline the letter C and make it the hot key, you need to enter &Close as the Caption property value for the command button control on the form. Placing an ampersand (&) to the left of a character in a caption underlines the character on the open form and makes it that control's hot key. Note that you can specify any character in a button's name, not just the first, as the hot key. However, each command button on a form must have a unique hot key.

## To add the Close command button to the form using the Control Wizards tool:

1. Click the **Control Wizards** tool on the toolbox to select it.

2. Click the **Command Button** tool on the toolbox, position the pointer's plus symbol at the 2-inch mark on the horizontal ruler and the 1.75-inch mark on the vertical ruler, and then click the mouse button. Access adds a command button to the form and, after a few seconds, opens the first Command Button Wizard dialog box. The Sample box shows how the command button will appear. See Figure 10-33.

**Figure 10-33** ▸ **First Command Button Wizard dialog box**

You'll now select the command that will be attached to the command button. The dialog box form must close when the user clicks the Close button, so you'll select the Close Form action in the Form Operations category for this button.

3. Click **Form Operations** in the Categories list box, click **Close Form** in the Actions list box, and then click the **Next** button. Access opens the next Command Button Wizard dialog box, in which you specify the text or picture you want to appear on the button. In this case, Elsa wants the button to display the word "Close," with the letter "C" identified as the hot key.

4. Click the **Text** option button, select **Close Form** in the text box, and then type **&Close**. Notice that the sample button changes to show the word "Close" with an underlined "C." See Figure 10-34.

**Figure 10-34** ▸ **Specifying the text on the command button**

**5.** Click the **Next** button to open the next Command Button Wizard dialog box, in which you enter a name for the button.

**6.** Type **cmdClose** in the text box, and then click the **Finish** button. Access closes the final Command Button Wizard dialog box and displays the new command button on the form.

In the next tutorial, you will create the VBA code for the Print Preview and Datasheet command buttons. This code will define what Access should do when a user clicks each button. The VBA code you will create must refer to the list box control. It is a good idea to give meaningful names to controls on your forms so you can identify them later, so you will enter the name lstQueryList for the list box control, where *lst* is a prefix tag to identify a list box control.

**To set the Name property for the list box:**

**1.** Open the property sheet for the list box control.

**2.** If necessary, click the **All** tab.

**3.** If necessary, scroll to the top of the property sheet, type **lstQueryList** in the Name text box, and then close the property sheet.

You've completed your work with the list box and command buttons for now, so you'll finish your initial work with the QueriesDialogBox form by modifying some of its properties.

# Modifying Form Properties

Next, you'll resize and position the form and set the form's Border Style property to Dialog, according to Elsa's design.

**To resize and position the form, and then set the form's Border Style property:**

**1.** Drag the right edge of the form's Detail section to the 3.25-inch mark on the horizontal ruler, and then drag the bottom edge of the form's Detail section to the 3-inch mark on the vertical ruler.

**2.** Switch to Form view, and then position and resize the form until it is in approximately the same position and it is approximately the same size as the form shown in Figure 10-35.

Figure 10-35 ▶ **Resized and repositioned form**

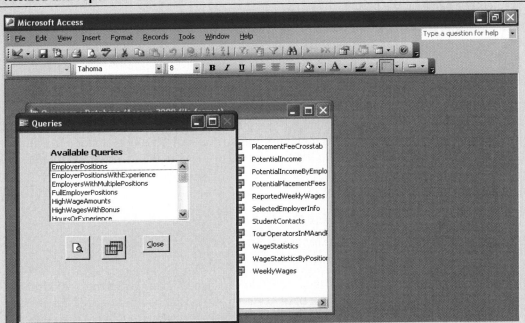

**Trouble?** If scroll bars appear on the form, slowly enlarge the form until they disappear.

▶ 3. Save your form layout changes, and then switch to Design view.

You'll now set the form's Border Style property to Dialog, which will prevent a user from resizing the form.

▶ 4. In the Form window, right-click the form selector to open the shortcut menu, click **Properties** to display the property sheet, and then click the **All** tab (if necessary).

▶ 5. Scroll down the property sheet, click the right side of the **Border Style** text box, and then click **Dialog**.

▶ 6. Close the property sheet, save your form design changes, and then switch to Form view.

**Trouble?** If the form is not the correct size or if scroll bars appear on the form, switch to Design view and set the form's Border Style property to Sizable. Switch back to Form view and resize the form. Save the form changes, switch to Design view, set the form's Border Style property to Dialog, and then save the form again and switch to Form view.

You'll now test the work you've completed for the QueriesDialogBox form.

# Testing the QueriesDialogBox Form

You can test the form in Form view. Clicking the Print Preview command button, clicking the Datasheet command button, or double-clicking a query name in the list box will have no effect, because you have not yet added the VBA code for these actions. However, you can click the Close button or press Alt+C to close the form.

## To test the form's design:

1. Click the **Close** button. The form closes and you return to the Database window.

2. Open the **QueriesDialogBox** form in Form view.

3. Double-click any query name in the list, click the **Print Preview** command button, and then click the **Datasheet** command button. You can select a query and click a command button, but doing so does not initiate any other action.

4. Press **Alt+C**. The form closes and you return to the Database window.

5. If you are not continuing on to the next session, close the Overseas database, and then exit Access.

You've completed the initial work with the QueriesDialogBox form. In the next session, you'll create the switchboard pages and their macros.

## Session 10.2 Quick Check

Review

1. What is an event property?
2. What is a macro group?
3. How do you determine the beginning and end of a macro in a macro group?
4. What is the purpose of the Where Condition argument for the OpenForm action?
5. What is the purpose of setting a form's Border Style property value to Dialog?
6. What is a list box control?
7. What are system tables?
8. How do you change the picture on a command button?
9. How do you make a copy of a form control in Design view?

# Session 10.3

## Reviewing the Overseas Database Switchboard Requirements

Recall that a switchboard is a form that provides controlled access to a database's tables, forms, queries, reports, and other objects. You need to create the switchboard form that will serve as the primary user interface for the Overseas database. Figure 10-36 shows the finished Overseas Database switchboard form that you will create.

**Figure 10-36** ▶ **Overseas Database switchboard form**

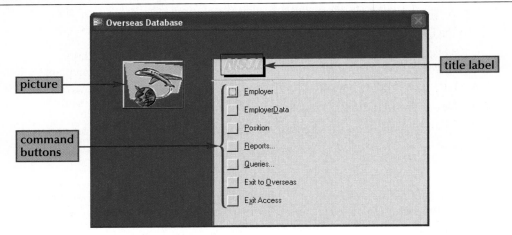

Elsa has the following design specifications for the Overseas Database switchboard:

- The form will not include Minimize, Restore, or Close buttons, scroll bars, navigation buttons, or a record selector.
- The form cannot be resized by the user.
- A picture of the plane and globe, with a raised special effect applied to it, will appear on the form.
- "Overseas Database" will appear in the form's title bar, and "NSJI" will be the form's title. The form title will have a shadowed special effect applied to it.
- The command buttons will have the same sizes.
- Macros will be attached to each command button to specify the actions that Access should take when the command button is clicked.

You'll also create the Reports switchboard, which will look similar to the Overseas Database switchboard. The Reports switchboard will have three command buttons: one to open the EmployersAndTheirPositions report, a second to open the PotentialIncome report, and a third to return to the Overseas Database switchboard.

Your first step in creating the switchboard forms is to create the macros you need to attach to the command buttons on the switchboard forms.

# Creating the Macro Group for the Switchboard

You'll create the macros for the switchboards in a macro group. The Macro Name column in the Macro window lets you distinguish macros in a macro group. Because a macro can contain many actions, the macro name tells Access where the macro begins. First, you'll name one macro and list the actions for it. Then you'll name the second macro, list the actions for it, and so on. You can define the macros in any order, and you can group as many macros as you want in the Macro window.

## Creating a Macro Group

- In the Database window, click Macros in the Objects bar to display the Macros list, and then click the New button.
- Click the Macro Names button on the Macro Design toolbar.
- Enter the macros in the macro group by entering each macro name in the Macro Name column and the corresponding action(s) in the Action column. Enter comments as needed in the Comment column, and set arguments as needed in the Action Arguments pane.
- Click the Save button on the Macro Design toolbar, enter the macro group name in the Macro Name text box, and then click the OK button.

You will use the name mcrSwitchboardMacros for the macro group, so it will be easy to locate the macro group containing the macros for the switchboard. Figure 10-37 shows the names and actions for the six macros in the macro group. Each macro is named the same as its associated command button on the switchboard. For example, the Employer macro will execute the OpenForm action to open the Employer form when a user clicks the Employer command button on the switchboard. Notice that both the ExitToOverseas and ExitAccess macros each contain two actions.

**Macros and actions in the mcrSwitchboardMacros macro group** | **Figure 10-37**

| Macro Name | Action(s) | Form Name |
| --- | --- | --- |
| Employer | OpenForm | Employer |
| EmployerData | OpenForm | EmployerData |
| Position | OpenForm | Position |
| QueriesDialogBox | OpenForm | QueriesDialogBox |
| ExitToOverseas | Close<br>SendKeys | Switchboard |
| ExitAccess | Close<br>Quit | Switchboard |

You will not use macros for the Reports command button on the Overseas Database switchboard or for any of the three buttons on the Reports switchboard. After you create the six macros, you'll use the Switchboard Manager to create the two switchboard forms and to handle the four buttons without macros.

You'll now create the mcrSwitchboardMacros macro group for the six command buttons on the switchboard form that use macros. First, you'll start a new macro. Because you can enter macros in any order in a macro group, you'll next enter two of the macros—ExitAccess and Employer—and then you'll save the macro group.

## To create the macro group:

1. If you took a break after the previous session, make sure that Access is running, that the **Overseas** database in the Comp\Tutorial folder is open, and that **Forms** is selected in the Objects bar of the Database window.

2. Click **Macros** in the Objects bar of the Database window, click the **New** button to open the Macro window, and then click the **Macro Names** button [icon] on the Macro Design toolbar. Access adds the Macro Name column to the left of the Action column.

Next, you'll enter the ExitAccess macro and its two actions: the Close action to close the switchboard form and the Quit action to exit Access.

▶ 3. Type **ExitAccess**, press the **Tab** key, click the **Action** list arrow, click **Close**, press the **Tab** key, and then type **Close Switchboard**.

You need to specify the arguments for the Close action. In the Object Type text box, you specify the type of object to close, in this case, a form. In the Object Name text box, you specify which object to close. Even though you haven't created the Switchboard form yet, you can specify it as the object to close.

▶ 4. In the Action Arguments pane, click the right side of the **Object Type** text box, and then click **Form**.

▶ 5. Click the **Object Name** text box, and then type **Switchboard**. You've completed the first action for the first macro.

Next, you'll define the second action for this macro, which will exit the Access program.

▶ 6. Click the right side of the second row's **Action** text box, scroll through the list, and then click **Quit**. You've completed the first macro, which contains two actions: the first to close the switchboard form and the second to exit Access. These two actions will occur in sequence when a user clicks the Exit Access command button on the switchboard.

Next, you'll define the second macro, Employer, which will open the Employer form.

▶ 7. Click the third row's **Macro Name** text box, type **Employer**, press the **Tab** key, click the list arrow, scroll through the list, click **OpenForm**, press the **Tab** key, and then type **Open Employer form**.

Next, you'll specify the name of the form to open.

▶ 8. In the Action Arguments pane, click the right side of the **Form Name** text box, and then click **Employer**. You've completed the second macro, which contains one action.

▶ 9. Save the macro as **mcrSwitchboardMacros**. See Figure 10-38.

| Figure 10-38 | Two macros in the macro group |

The macro name, which appears in the Macro window title bar, is mcrSwitchboardMacros. mcrSwitchboardMacros is also the name of the macro group, because the mcrSwitchboardMacros macro contains more than one macro. The first macro in the macro group is ExitAccess, and the second macro in the macro group is Employer. A macro in a macro group starts in the row containing the macro name and continues until the next macro name or a blank row.

When Access executes the ExitAccess macro, it runs the Close action, it runs the Quit action, and then the macro ends. The Employer macro begins with the OpenForm action and ends when it reaches the end of the macro group.

Next, you'll enter three more macros—the first to open the EmployerData form, the second to open the Position form, and the third to open the QueriesDialogBox form.

### To add three macros to the macro group:

▶ 1. Click the fourth row's **Macro Name** text box, type **EmployerData**, press the **Tab** key, click the **Action** list arrow, scroll through the list, click **OpenForm**, press the **Tab** key, and then type **Open EmployerData form**.

▶ 2. In the Action Arguments pane, click the **Form Name** text box, click the list arrow, and then click **EmployerData**. You've completed the third macro, which contains one action to open the EmployerData form.

▶ 3. Click the fifth row's **Macro Name** text box, type **Position**, press the **Tab** key, click the **Action** list arrow, click **OpenForm**, press the **Tab** key, and then type **Open Position form**.

▶ 4. In the Action Arguments pane, click the **Form Name** text box, click the list arrow, and then click **Position**. You've completed the fourth macro, which contains one action to open the Position form.

▶ 5. Click the sixth row's **Macro Name** text box, type **QueriesDialogBox**, press the **Tab** key, click the **Action** list arrow, click **OpenForm**, press the **Tab** key, and then type **Open QueriesDialogBox form**.

▶ 6. In the Action Arguments pane, click the **Form Name** text box, click the list arrow, and then click **QueriesDialogBox**. You've completed the fifth macro, which contains one action to open the QueriesDialogBox form.

The final macro you need to define is the ExitToOverseas macro, which will execute two actions: the Close action to close the switchboard and the **SendKeys action**, which sends keystrokes to Access or to another program. In this macro, you will use the SendKeys action to simulate pressing the F11 key, which activates the Database window, because Elsa wants users to return to the Database window after closing the switchboard.

### To finish creating the macro group:

▶ 1. Click the seventh row's **Macro Name** text box, type **ExitToOverseas**, press the **Tab** key, click the **Action** list arrow, click **Close**, press the **Tab** key, and then type **Close Switchboard**.

▶ 2. In the Action Arguments pane, click the **Object Type** text box, click the list arrow, click **Form**, click the **Object Name** text box, and then type **Switchboard**.

▶ 3. Click the right side of the eighth row's **Action** text box, scroll the list, click **SendKeys**, press the **Tab** key, and then type **Activate Database window**.

For the SendKeys action, you need to specify the Keystrokes argument value {F11}, which is the same as pressing the F11 key, so that the action will return to the Database window after the switchboard form closes.

▶ 4. In the Action Arguments pane, click the **Keystrokes** text box, and then type **{F11}**. Be sure to type the braces but not the period. You've completed the second of two actions for the final macro. See Figure 10-39.

**Figure 10-39** ▶ **Completed macro group containing six macros**

**Trouble?** Compare your macros to those shown in Figure 10-39. If any of your macros are not correct, click the appropriate text box and use the list arrow to select the correct option or edit the text to correct it.

5. Save your macro changes, and then close the Macro window.

Now that you've defined all the macros that will execute the necessary actions for the command buttons on the switchboard, you can create the form for the switchboard.

# Creating a Switchboard

To create the switchboard, you'll use the Access Switchboard Manager. The **Switchboard Manager** is a Microsoft Access tool that helps you create and customize a switchboard. When you use the Switchboard Manager, you specify the command buttons that will appear on the switchboard. For each button, you identify the command to execute when its button is clicked. The Switchboard Manager automatically attaches the command to the OnClick property for that command button; this property specifies the action to take when the command button is clicked. Some commands require one or more arguments, which you can specify as well. When you complete the switchboard design, the Switchboard Manager creates a form for your switchboard with the default name Switchboard. The Switchboard Manager also creates a table, named **Switchboard Items**, which contains records describing the command buttons on the switchboard.

The Switchboard Manager allows you to create only one switchboard form for a database, but the switchboard can contain many pages. You can designate only one of the switchboard pages as the default page. The **default page**, or **main page**, is the switchboard page that will appear when you open the switchboard form. You can place command buttons on the default page to open other switchboard pages.

You will use the Switchboard Manager to create the switchboard form for the Overseas database. Review the design of the form shown in Figure 10-36. Notice that each command button has an associated hot key, which is indicated by the underlined letter in the button's label. As you use the Switchboard Manager to create the form, you'll place the appropriate command buttons on the switchboard, define the hot keys, and associate the corresponding macros from the Switchboard Macros macro group with the buttons.

The Overseas Database switchboard shown in Figure 10-36 will be the default page. You'll create a second switchboard page for the Reports switchboard. As shown in Figure 10-40, this switchboard page will contain command buttons to print the EmployersAndTheirPositions report and the PotentialIncome report, and to return to the default page.

Reports switchboard as a second switchboard page ◄ **Figure 10-40**

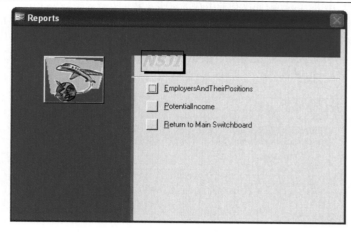

First, you'll create the switchboard form and two switchboard pages.

## To create the switchboard form with two pages:

▶ **1.** Click **Tools** on the menu bar, point to **Database Utilities**, and then click **Switchboard Manager**. Access opens a dialog box asking if you want to create a switchboard.

**Trouble?** If you do not see the Switchboard Manager command in the Database Utilities list, it might not be installed on your computer. See your instructor or technical support person for assistance.

▶ **2.** Click the **Yes** button. The Switchboard Manager dialog box opens. See Figure 10-41.

Switchboard Manager dialog box ◄ **Figure 10-41**

The Switchboard Manager has created the Main Switchboard page, which is the default page. You use the Switchboard Manager dialog box to add new pages, to edit and delete existing pages, or to change the default page. You will add a new page next.

▶ **3.** Click the **New** button. The Create New dialog box opens.

▶ **4.** Type **Reports** in the Switchboard Page Name text box, and then click the **OK** button. The Create New dialog box closes, and the Switchboard Pages list box now shows the original default page and the new Reports page.

Next, you'll edit the default page to change its name to Overseas Database.

5. Make sure the **Main Switchboard (Default)** page is selected, and then click the **Edit** button. The Edit Switchboard Page dialog box opens on top of the Switchboard Manager dialog box. This dialog box lets you edit the name of the selected switchboard page and add command buttons to the page.

6. Select the current entry in the Switchboard Name text box, and then type **Overseas Database**. See Figure 10-42.

**Figure 10-42** | **Edit Switchboard Page dialog box**

## Adding Command Buttons to a Switchboard Page

You can now add the command buttons for each macro in the Switchboard Macros macro group. Each command button will carry out the actions in its associated macro when the command button is clicked.

### To add the first command button to the switchboard page:

1. Click the **New** button in the Edit Switchboard Page dialog box. The Edit Switchboard Item dialog box opens.

   The first button you will add is the Employer button, which will open the Employer form. According to Elsa's design, the hot key for this button is E.

2. Type **&Employer** in the Text text box. This text will appear to the right of the command button on the form. Recall that the ampersand (&) creates the hot key.

   Next, you need to specify the command that will be executed when the user clicks the button. In this case, you want Access to run the Employer macro, which displays the Employer form. This macro is part of the mcrSwitchboardMacros group.

3. Click the **Command** list arrow, and then click **Run Macro**. The third text box in the Edit Switchboard Item dialog box now displays the label "Macro." In this text box, you need to specify the macro to run when the button is clicked. When you click the Macro list arrow, you will see a list of all the macros defined for the database. The names of macros that are part of the macro group you created are preceded with the text "mcrSwitchboardMacros" to identify them as belonging to that group.

4. Click the **Macro** list arrow, and then click **mcrSwitchboardMacros.Employer**. The first command button definition is now completed. See Figure 10-43.

**Edit Switchboard Item dialog box** ◀ **Figure 10-43**

name of button on the switchboard

macro to execute when the button is clicked

action to execute when the button is clicked

**5.** Click the **OK** button. The Switchboard Manager returns to the Edit Switchboard Page dialog box. Notice that the Items on this Switchboard list box now shows the Employer command button.

Five of the remaining six command buttons in the Overseas Database switchboard page have associated macros in the Switchboard Macros group; the Reports command button does not. Next, you'll add these five command buttons to the switchboard.

## To add five additional command buttons to the default page:

**1.** Click the **New** button in the Edit Switchboard Page dialog box. The Edit Switchboard Item dialog box opens.

**2.** Type **Employer&Data** in the Text text box.

**3.** Click the **Command** list arrow, and then click **Run Macro**.

**4.** Click the **Macro** list arrow, scroll down the list, and then click **mcrSwitchboardMacros.EmployerData**.

**5.** Click the **OK** button. The definition of the second command button, EmployerData, is now completed. When clicked, this button will run the EmployerData macro in the mcrSwitchboardMacros macro group, which opens the Employer Data form in Form view.

**6.** Repeat Steps 1 through 5 to define the **&Position** command button to run the macro named **mcrSwitchboardMacros.Position**.

The next command button you need to define is the button for opening the QueriesDialogBox form. According to Elsa's design, the name of this button includes the ellipsis after the word "Queries," indicating that a dialog box will open when the button is clicked.

**7.** Repeat Steps 1 through 5 to define the **&Queries...** command button (be sure to type the ellipsis in the button name) to run the macro named **mcrSwitchboardMacros.QueriesDialogBox**.

**8.** Repeat Steps 1 through 5 to define the **Exit to &Overseas** command button to run the macro named **mcrSwitchboardMacros.ExitToOverseas**.

**9.** Repeat Steps 1 through 5 to define the **E&xit Access** command button to run the macro named **mcrSwitchboardMacros.ExitAccess**. The switchboard's default page contains six command buttons. See Figure 10-44.

**command buttons added to the switchboard page will appear in this order**

**Trouble?** Compare your Edit Switchboard Page dialog box with the one shown in Figure 10-44. If any of your command buttons are incorrect, click the button name and then click the Edit button. Make the necessary changes and then click the OK button to return to the Edit Switchboard Page dialog box.

The Overseas Database switchboard page is completed, except for the Reports command button. You'll add this command button next.

### To add the last command button to the page:

▸ 1. Click the **New** button in the Edit Switchboard Page dialog box. The Edit Switchboard Item dialog box opens.

▸ 2. Type **&Reports...** in the Text text box. Be sure to type the ellipsis in the command button name.

Because you do not have a macro in the Switchboard Macros macro group for this command button, you will not select Run Macro in the Command text box. Instead, you'll accept the default command, Go to Switchboard, which allows you to change from one switchboard page to another.

▸ 3. Click the **Switchboard** list arrow, and then click **Reports**.

▸ 4. Click the **OK** button. The switchboard design for the Overseas Database switchboard page now contains all the necessary command buttons.

In Elsa's design for the Overseas Database switchboard page, the Reports command button precedes the Queries command button. You'll need to move the Reports command button to its correct position in the switchboard page.

## Moving Command Buttons in a Switchboard Page

You can delete and move command buttons in a switchboard page by selecting an entry in the Items on this Switchboard list box and then clicking the Delete, Move Up, or Move Down buttons. You'll use the Move Up button to reposition the Reports command button.

### To reposition the Reports command button:

▶ **1.** Click **&Reports...** in the Items on this Switchboard list box, and then click the **Move Up** button. The &Reports... entry moves up one position in the list box and remains selected. See Figure 10-45.

**Moving a command button** ◀ **Figure 10-45**

- deletes the selected button
- moves the selected button up one position
- moves the selected button down one position
- moved up one position

▶ **2.** Click the **Move Up** button two more times to correctly position the &Reports... entry above the &Queries... entry.

You've finished the Overseas Database switchboard page, so you can close the Edit Switchboard Page dialog box.

▶ **3.** Click the **Close** button to close the Edit Switchboard Page dialog box. You return to the Switchboard Manager dialog box.

Next, you'll add the command buttons to the Reports switchboard page.

## Adding Command Buttons to a Second Switchboard Page

You've already used the Run Macro and Go to Switchboard options in the Edit Switchboard Item dialog box. The other Command text box options in this dialog box that you can use are: Open Form in Add Mode, Open Form in Edit Mode, Open Report, Design Application, Exit Application, and Run Code. For the Reports switchboard page, you'll use the Open Report option for the first two command buttons (EmployersAndTheirPositions, PotentialIncome) and the Go to Switchboard option for the Return to Main Switchboard command button.

### To add command buttons to the Reports switchboard page:

▶ **1.** Click **Reports** in the Switchboard Pages list box, and then click the **Edit** button. The Edit Switchboard Page dialog box opens on top of the Switchboard Manager dialog box.

▶ **2.** Click the **New** button. The Edit Switchboard Item dialog box opens.

▶ **3.** Type **&EmployersAndTheirPositions** in the Text text box.

▶ **4.** Click the **Command** list arrow, and then click **Open Report**. The third text box in the Edit Switchboard Item dialog box now displays the label "Report." In this text box, you specify the report to open when the button is clicked. When you click the Report list arrow, you see a list of all the reports in the database.

▶ **5.** Click the **Report** list arrow, click **EmployersAndTheirPositions**, and then click the **OK** button.

6. Repeat Steps 2 through 5 to define the **&PotentialIncome** command button to open the report named **PotentialIncome**.

7. Click the **New** button, type **&Return to Main Switchboard**, click the **Switchboard** list arrow, click **Overseas Database**, and then click the **OK** button. The Reports switchboard page now contains all the necessary command buttons. See Figure 10-46.

**Figure 10-46** | **Completed Reports switchboard page**

three command buttons added

**Trouble?** Compare your Edit Switchboard Page dialog box with the one shown in Figure 10-46. If any of your command buttons are incorrect, click the button name and then click the Edit button. Make the necessary changes and then click the OK button to return to the Edit Switchboard Page dialog box.

## Viewing and Testing a Switchboard

You are finished using the Switchboard Manager, so you can now exit it and view the new switchboard.

### To exit the Switchboard Manager and view the Switchboard form:

1. Click the **Close** button to close the Edit Switchboard Page dialog box.

2. Click the **Close** button to close the Switchboard Manager dialog box and return to the Database window.

3. If necessary, click **Forms** in the Objects bar of the Database window to display the Forms list.

4. Right-click **Switchboard** to open the shortcut menu, and then click **Open**. Access opens the Switchboard form. See Figure 10-47.

name supplied by the Switchboard Manager

The Switchboard form contains the seven command buttons you defined for the Overseas Database switchboard page using the Switchboard Manager. Each command button has an attached label displaying the command button name. The underscore in the command button name indicates the hot key for that button. The title "Overseas" appears in white text in a label control above the command buttons; the Switchboard Manager automatically created this label on the form. Behind the Overseas label is another copy of the Overseas label displaying the text in gray letters, creating a shadowed effect. The Switchboard Manager also added the large green areas on the switchboard, which are green rectangle objects.

Overall, Elsa is pleased with the appearance of the Switchboard form, but there are some changes she would like you to make. Before you make these changes, you will test some of the command buttons to make sure that they work properly.

### To test the command buttons:

▶ **1.** Click the **Employer** command button. Access displays the record for Beantown Tours in the Employer form in Form view.

▶ **2.** Click the **Close** button ☒ on the Employer window title bar to close it and return to the switchboard.

▶ **3.** Press **Alt+P**. Access opens the Position form and displays the first Position record.

▶ **4.** Close the Position form to return to the switchboard.

▶ **5.** Click the **Reports** command button. Access replaces the Overseas Database switchboard page with the Reports switchboard page.

▶ **6.** Click the **PotentialIncome** command button. Access opens the Potential Income report in Print Preview.

▶ **7.** Close the PotentialIncome report to return to the Reports switchboard page.

▶ **8.** Click the **Return to Main Switchboard** command button to replace the Reports switchboard page with the Overseas Database switchboard page.

Elsa wants you to make some changes to the design of the switchboard. She likes the layout of the command buttons, but she wants you to make sure that the form always has the same size when it appears on the screen. She also wants you to remove the Overseas label control and add a new label with the text "NSJI." Finally, she asks you to include the picture of a plane and globe.

## Modifying a Switchboard

Because the switchboard is a form, you can make Elsa's changes in Design view. However, you need to be careful not to make any changes to the command buttons that would affect the actions and macros associated with them. You should only make these types of changes using the Switchboard Manager. If you were to change the definitions of any of the command buttons in Design view, the Switchboard Manager would not be able to make the necessary updates to its table, and the switchboard would not function correctly.

Next, you'll delete the Overseas label, place the new label "NSJI" on the form, and add the plane and globe picture.

### To delete the Overseas label:

1. Switch to Design view, right-click the **Overseas label** above the command buttons to open the shortcut menu, and then click **Cut**. The label is deleted. Notice that there is a second Overseas label now visible. This label appeared as the shadow of the first label on the switchboard.

2. Right-click the **Overseas label** above the command buttons to open the shortcut menu, and then click **Cut**. The second label is deleted.

You can now add the NSJI label in the area above the command buttons.

### To add the NSJI label to the switchboard:

1. If necessary, click the **Toolbox** button 🛠 on the Form Design toolbar to open the toolbox, and then make sure the toolbox is docked below the Formatting toolbar.

2. Click the **Label** tool 🄰 on the toolbox.

3. Position the pointer in the Detail section; when the pointer's plus symbol is positioned at the 2-inch mark on the horizontal ruler and the 0.375-inch mark on the vertical ruler, click the mouse button.

4. Type **NSJI**, and then press the **Enter** key.

   Elsa wants the title to stand out, so she asks you to format it in bold and italics, increase its font size, change its font color to yellow, and apply the shadowed special effect.

5. Click the **Bold** button 🅱 on the Formatting toolbar, click the **Italic** button 𝐼 on the Formatting toolbar, click the **Font Size** list arrow on the Formatting toolbar, and then click **18**.

6. Click the list arrow for the **Font/Fore Color** button 🅰 on the Formatting toolbar to display the palette of available colors.

7. Click the bright yellow color box (the third button in the fourth row). The NSJI label now appears bright yellow.

8. Click the list arrow for the **Special Effect** button ⊟ on the Formatting toolbar, and then click the **Shadowed** button ⊟.

9. Click **Format** on the menu bar, point to **Size**, and then click **To Fit**. Access resizes the label box to display the entire label.

Next, you'll add the picture of the plane and globe to the form, and then you'll apply the raised special effect to the picture to enhance it.

### To add the picture to the switchboard:

▶ **1.** Click the **Image** tool 🖼 on the toolbox, position the pointer's plus symbol at the 0.5-inch mark on the horizontal ruler and the 0.5-inch mark on the vertical ruler, and then click the mouse button to place the graphic image control. The Insert Picture dialog box opens.

▶ **2.** In the Look in list box, select the **Tutorial** folder on your Data Disk (if necessary), click **Airplane** in the file list, and then click the **OK** button. Access inserts the picture on the form.

▶ **3.** Click the list arrow for the **Special Effect** button 🔲 on the Formatting toolbar, and then click the **Raised** button 🔲. The raised effect is applied to the button. You've finished making the necessary changes to the layout of the Switchboard form. See Figure 10-48.

**Modified Switchboard form layout** ◀ **Figure 10-48**

Now you can change the form properties so that the form will be correctly sized and positioned on the screen.

### To change the Switchboard form properties:

▶ **1.** Right-click the form selector (see Figure 10-48) to open the shortcut menu, and then click **Properties** to display the property sheet for the form.

First, you'll set the Auto Resize property to No so that Access will not resize the form when it is opened.

▶ **2.** Click the **Format** tab, and then double-click **Yes** in the Auto Resize text box to change this property setting to No.

Now you'll set the Border Style property to Dialog to prevent users from resizing the form.

▶ **3.** Click the right side of the **Border Style** text box, and then click **Dialog**.

Setting the Close Button property to No disables the Close button on the form's title bar. You'll disable this button, because Elsa wants users to close the form by clicking the Exit to Overseas or Exit Access command buttons.

> **4.** Double-click **Yes** in the Close Button text box to change the property setting to No.
>
> **5.** Close the property sheet, save your form design changes, and then close the form.

Elsa wants to view the modified switchboard, so you'll open the switchboard in Form view.

### To view the switchboard:

> **1.** Open the **Switchboard** form in Form view. See Figure 10-49.

| Figure 10-49 | Modified switchboard in Form view |
| --- | --- |

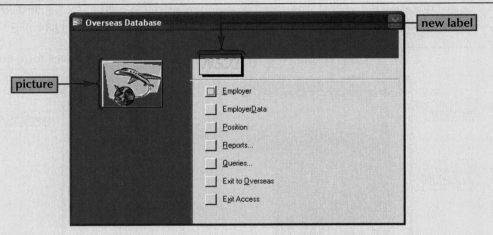

> **2.** Click the **Exit to Overseas** button. Access closes the switchboard and returns to the Database window.
>
> **3.** Exit Access.

Elsa's design for the Overseas database user interface also includes a restricted menu bar and a hidden toolbar. In Tutorial 12, you'll add these features to the switchboard, and in Tutorial 11 you'll create the necessary VBA code for the QueriesDialogBox form command buttons.

**Review**

## Session 10.3 Quick Check

1. What does the SendKeys action do?
2. What is the Switchboard Manager?
3. To which property does the Switchboard Manager automatically assign commands for each command button?
4. When using the Command Button Wizard, how do you define a hot key for a command button?
5. How do you specify that a form is a dialog box?
6. What are two special effects you can use for a control?

**Review**

# Tutorial Summary

In this tutorial, you worked with macros by running a macro, adding actions to a macro, single stepping a macro, creating a macro group, adding actions to a macro group, and attaching macros to command buttons. You also created a dialog box by adding a list box to a form, using an SQL statement to provide the source data for the list box, adding command buttons, and modifying form properties. Finally, you created a switchboard with two pages, attached macros to the command buttons on the switchboard, and modified the switchboard by adding a label and picture and by modifying the switchboard properties.

# Key Terms

| | | |
|---|---|---|
| action | Left function | SendKeys action |
| Action column | list box | shortcut keys |
| arguments | macro | single stepping |
| command button | Macro Builder | SQL (Structured Query |
| Comment column | macro group | Language) |
| custom dialog box | Macro Name column | switchboard |
| Data Mode argument | Macro window | Switchboard Items |
| default page | main page | Switchboard Manager |
| event | message box | system tables |
| event procedure | MsgBox action | user interface |
| event property | MSysObjects table | View argument |
| Filter Name argument | PrintOut action | Visual Basic for |
| FindRecord action | procedure | Applications (VBA) |
| graphical user interface (GUI) | Row Source property | Where Condition argument |
| hot keys | SELECT statement | Window Mode argument |

**Practice**

# Review Assignments

**Data Files needed for the Review Assignments: Globe.gif and Work.mdb (*cont. from Tutorial 9*)**

*Take time to practice the skills you learned in the tutorial using the same case scenario.*

Elsa wants you to create a switchboard interface for the Work database. To help with this request, complete the following steps:

1. Open the **Work** database in the Comp\Review folder provided with your Data Files.
2. Design and create a form named **ReportsDialogBox** that has the following components and characteristics:
   a. The text "Print Reports" appears in the form's title bar.
   b. A list box (with a Name property value of lstReportList) displays all the report names contained in the **Work** database. To place the report names in the list box, use an SQL SELECT statement to retrieve the report names from the **MSysObjects** table. Delete the label attached to the list box.
   c. The text "Reports Available," formatted with 10-point, bold font, appears as a heading above the list box.
   d. Two command buttons appear below the list box. The left command button displays the Preview Document icon, and the right command button displays the word "Close" with the letter "C" underlined. Double-clicking a report name has the same effect as selecting a report name in the list box and clicking the left command button. Both events cause Access to display the Print Preview window for the

selected report. (You will add the VBA code for these events in the next tutorial. For now, double-clicking or clicking should cause no action to occur.) Clicking the Close command button causes Access to close the dialog box. The letter "C" is the hot key.

    e. Resize the form's Detail section in Design view, resize the form in Form view, and then set form properties that are appropriate for a dialog box.

3. Create a macro group named **mcrSwitchboardMacros** that contains macros to be used with the command buttons on the switchboard you'll create in the next step. The macros perform these actions: open the **Territory** table datasheet, open the **Recruiter** form in Form view, open the **StudentInfo** form in Form view, open the **ReportsDialogBox** form in Form view, and close the switchboard and activate the Database window.

4. Design and create a switchboard form named **Switchboard**. Use Figure 10-50 and the following descriptions as a guide to create the switchboard.

**Figure 10-50**

    a. Use the Switchboard Manager to create the switchboard. Place the command buttons on the form; the command buttons should use the macros in the **mcrSwitchboardMacros** macro group. Define hot keys for each command button. Specify "Recruiting" as the main switchboard page name.

    b. Delete the default label and the shadow label on the form and place a label at the top of the switchboard. The label should read "NSJI Recruiting Center" and should appear as 14-point, underlined text in a font color of your choice.

    c. Add the **Globe** picture from the Comp\Review folder to the appropriate position on the switchboard.

**Explore**

    d. Set the background color for the switchboard, as shown in Figure 10-50, resize the switchboard in Form view, and then set form properties that are appropriate for a switchboard.

5. Save the **Switchboard** form, and then test the command buttons and the **ReportsDialogBox** form to make sure that your switchboard items work correctly. If necessary, return to the Switchboard Manager and make any corrections.

6. Click the Exit to Work command button to close the **Switchboard** form, and then exit Access.

## Apply

*Use the skills you learned in the tutorial to work with the data contained in a video photography database.*

# Case Problem 1

**Data Files needed for this Case Problem: Camera.bmp and Shoots.mdb (*cont. from Tutorial 9*)**

***Lim's Video Photography*** Youngho Lim wants the Shoots database to include an easy-to-use switchboard interface. To help Youngho with his request, complete the following steps:

1. Open the **Shoots** database in the Comp\Case1 folder provided with your Data Files.
2. Create a macro group named **mcrSwitchboardMacros** that contains macros to be used with the command buttons on the switchboard you'll create in the next step. The macros perform these actions: open the **ShootDesc** table datasheet, open the **Client** form in Form view, open the **ClientInfo** form in Form view, open the **TopContracts** query datasheet, open the **Clients** report in Print Preview, and close the switchboard and activate the Database window.
3. Design and create a switchboard form named **Switchboard**. Use Figure 10-51 and the following descriptions as a guide to create the switchboard.

**Figure 10-51**

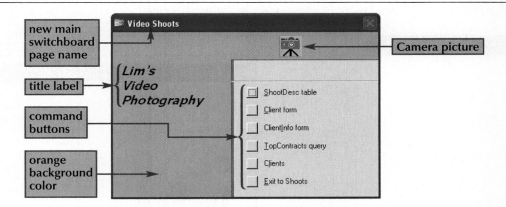

a. Use the Switchboard Manager to create the switchboard. Place the command buttons on the form; the command buttons should use the macros in the **mcrSwitchboardMacros** macro group. Define hot keys for each command button. Specify "Video Shoots" as the main switchboard page name.
b. Delete the default label and the shadow label on the form and place a label on the left side of the switchboard. The label should read "Lim's Video Photography" and should appear as 14-point, bold, italic text. (*Hint*: Press Shift + Enter after typing the first and second words in the label.)
c. Add the **Camera** picture from the Comp\Case1 folder to the appropriate position on the switchboard.
d. Set the background color for the switchboard, as shown in Figure 10-51, resize the switchboard in Form view, and then set form properties that are appropriate for a switchboard.
4. Save the **Switchboard** form, and then test the command buttons to make sure that your switchboard items work correctly. If necessary, return to the Switchboard Manager and make any corrections.
5. Click the Exit to Shoots command button to close the **Switchboard** form, and then exit Access.

# Case Problem 2

**Data Files needed for this Case Problem: AtHome.mdb (*cont. from Tutorial 9*) and ServeHot.gif**

***DineAtHome.course.com*** To make the AtHome database easier to use, Claire Picard wants you to create a switchboard interface for it. To help Claire with her request, complete the following steps:

1. Open the **AtHome** database in the Comp\Case2 folder provided with your Data Files.
2. Create a macro group named **mcrSwitchboardMacros** that contains macros to be used with the command buttons on the switchboard you'll create in the next step. The macros perform these actions: open the **Customer** table datasheet, open the **Restaurant** form in Form view, open the **LargeOrders** query datasheet, open the **OrdersByRestaurant** report in Print Preview, and close the switchboard and activate the Database window.
3. Design and create a switchboard form named **Switchboard**. Use Figure 10-52 and the following descriptions as a guide to create the switchboard.

**Figure 10-52**

a. Use the Switchboard Manager to create the switchboard. Place the command buttons on the form; the command buttons should use the macros in the **mcrSwitchboardMacros** macro group. Define hot keys for each command button. Specify "DineAtHome.course.com" as the main switchboard page name.
b. Delete the default label and the shadow label on the form and place a label at the top of the switchboard. The label should read "AtHome Main Control Center" and should appear as 14-point, italic, underlined, red text.
c. Add the **ServeHot** picture from the Comp\Case2 folder in the appropriate position on the switchboard.

**Explore**

d. Set the background color for the switchboard to white, as shown in Figure 10-52. (*Hint*: Delete the rectangle objects created by the Switchboard Manager on the **Switchboard** form before setting the Detail section Back Color property.)
e. Resize the switchboard in Form view, and then set form properties that are appropriate for a switchboard.
4. Save the **Switchboard** form, and then test the command buttons to make sure that your switchboard items work correctly. If necessary, return to the Switchboard Manager and make any corrections.
5. Click the Exit to AtHome command button to close the **Switchboard** form, and then exit Access.

## Apply

*Apply what you learned in the tutorial to work with a database that contains data about fund raising at a zoo.*

# Case Problem 3

**Data File needed for this Case Problem: ZooFunds.mdb** (*cont. from Tutorial 9*)

***Redwood Zoo*** Michael Rosenfeld wants the ZooFunds database to include an easy-to-use switchboard interface. To help Michael with his request, complete the following steps:

1. Open the **ZooFunds** database in the Comp\Case3 folder provided with your Data Files.
2. Design and create a form named **QueriesDialogBox** that has the following components and characteristics:
   a. The text "Queries" appears in the form's title bar.
   b. A list box (with a Name property value of lstQueryList) displays all the query names contained in the **ZooFunds** database. To place the query names in the list box, use an SQL SELECT statement to retrieve the query names from the **MSysObjects** table. Delete the label attached to the list box, and then widen the list box to approximately 2.25 inches.
   c. The text "Queries Available," formatted with 10-point, bold font, appears as a heading above the list box.
   d. Two command buttons appear below the list box. The left command button displays the MS Access Query icon, and the right command button displays the word "Close" with the letter "C" underlined. Double-clicking a query name has the same effect as selecting a query name in the list box and clicking the left command button. Both events cause Access to display the query datasheet for the selected query. (You will add the VBA code for these events in the next tutorial. For now, double-clicking or clicking should cause no action to occur.) Clicking the Close command button causes Access to close the dialog box. The letter "C" is the hot key.
   e. Resize the form's Detail section in Design view, resize the form in Form view, and then set form properties that are appropriate for a dialog box.
3. Create a macro group named **mcrSwitchboardMacros** that contains macros to be used with the command buttons on the switchboard you'll create in the next step. The macros perform these actions: open the **Reception** table datasheet, open the **Costs** form in Form view, open the **Funds** form in Form view, open the **QueriesDialogBox** form in Form view, and close the switchboard and activate the Database window.
4. Design and create a switchboard form named **Switchboard**. Use Figure 10-53 and the following descriptions as a guide to create the switchboard.

**Figure 10-53**

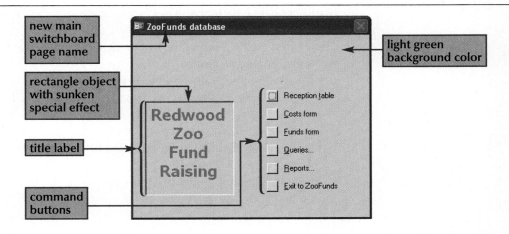

a. Use the Switchboard Manager to create the switchboard. The switchboard should have two pages. Specify "ZooFunds database" as the main switchboard page name, and "Reports" as the second switchboard page name.

b. Place the command buttons on the main switchboard page. Except for the "Reports..." command button, which should switch to the second switchboard page, the command buttons should use the macros in the **mcrSwitchboardMacros** macro group. Define hot keys for each command button.

c. Place three command buttons on the Reports switchboard page. The command buttons perform these actions: open the **Donor** report, open the **FundPledges** report, and return to the main switchboard. Define hot keys for each command button. Do not use macros for the Reports switchboard page.

d. Delete the default label and the shadow label on the form. On the left side of the form, enter the label shown in Figure 10-53 as 18-point, bold, red text; each word in the label should appear on a separate, centered line. (*Hint*: You can enter all words in the label as a single label control by pressing Shift + Enter after each word and then resizing the label box and centering the text after you're finished typing it.)

e. Draw a rectangle around the label box, and then apply the sunken special effect to the rectangle.

f. Set the background color of the form to light green, as shown in Figure 10-53. (*Hint*: Delete all rectangle and line objects created by the Switchboard Manager on the **Switchboard** form before setting the Detail section Back Color property.)

g. Resize the switchboard in Form view, and then set form properties that are appropriate for a switchboard.

5. Save the **Switchboard** form, and then test the command buttons to make sure that your switchboard items work correctly. If necessary, return to the Switchboard Manager and make any corrections.

6. Click the Exit to ZooFunds command button to close the **Switchboard** form, and then exit Access.

# Case Problem 4

**Data File needed for this Case Problem: Rivers.mdb (*cont. from Tutorial 9*)**

***Mountain River Adventures*** Connor and Siobhan Dempsey want you to create a user-friendly interface, including a switchboard and dialog boxes, for the Rivers database. To help them with their request, complete the following steps:

1. Start Access and then open the **Rivers** database in the Comp\Case4 folder provided with your Data Files.

2. Design and create a form named **QueriesDialogBox** that has the following components and characteristics:

a. The text "Queries" appears in the form's title bar.

b. A list box (with a Name property value of lstQueryList) displays all the query names contained in the **Rivers** database. To place the query names in the list box, use an SQL SELECT statement to retrieve the query names from the **MSysObjects** table. Delete the label attached to the list box, and then widen the list box to approximately 2.0 inches.

c. The text "Queries Available," formatted with 10-point, bold font, appears as a heading above the list box.

d. Two command buttons appear below the list box. The left command button displays the MS Access Query icon, and the right command button displays the word "Close" with the letter "C" underlined. Double-clicking a query name has the same effect as selecting a query name in the list box and clicking the left command button. Both events cause Access to display the query datasheet for the selected query. (You will add the VBA code for these events in the next tutorial. For now, double-clicking or clicking should cause no action to occur.) Clicking the Close command button causes Access to close the dialog box. The letter "C" is the hot key.

e. Resize the form's Detail section in Design view, resize the form in Form view, and then set form properties that are appropriate for a dialog box.

3. Create a copy of the **QueriesDialogBox** form and name it **ReportsDialogBox**. Make the following modifications to the **ReportsDialogBox** form:

a. Change the text that appears in the title bar to "Reports."

b. Change the SQL SELECT statement to retrieve the report names from the **MSysObjects** table.

c. Change the text that appears as a heading above the list box to "Reports Available."

d. Change the left command button to display the Preview Document icon.

e. Change the Name property value of the list box to "lstReportList."

f. Close the **ReportsDialogBox** form and save your changes.

4. Create one macro named **mcrExitSwitchboard** that will be used with a command button on the switchboard you'll create in the next step. The macro should close the switchboard and activate the Database window.

5. Design and create a switchboard form named **Switchboard**. Use Figure 10-54 and the following descriptions as a guide to create the switchboard.

**Figure 10-54**

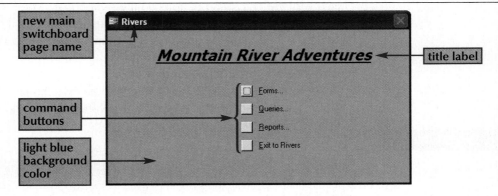

a. Use the Switchboard Manager to create the switchboard. The switchboard should have two pages. Specify "Rivers" as the main switchboard page name, and "Forms" as the second switchboard page name.

b. Place four command buttons on the first switchboard page. The command buttons perform these actions: switch to the second switchboard page; open the **QueriesDialogBox** form; open the **ReportsDialogBox** form; and close the switchboard and activate the Database window, using the **mcrExitSwitchboard** macro. Define hot keys for each command button.

c. Place three command buttons on the Forms switchboard page. The command buttons perform these actions: open the **Costs** form in edit mode, open the **Extra** form in edit mode, and return to the main switchboard. Define hot keys for each command button. Do not use macros for the Forms switchboard page.

d. Delete the default label and the shadow label on the form, and place a label at the top of the switchboard. The label should read "Mountain River Adventures" and should appear as 18-point bold, italic, and underlined text.

**Explore**

e. Set the background color of the form to light blue, as shown in Figure 10-54. (*Hint*: Delete all rectangle and line objects created by the Switchboard Manager on the **Switchboard** form before setting the Detail section Back Color property.)

f. Resize the switchboard in Form view, and then set form properties that are appropriate for a switchboard.

6. Save the **Switchboard** form, and then test the command buttons to make sure that your switchboard items work correctly. If necessary, return to the Switchboard Manager and make any corrections.

7. Click the Exit to Rivers command button to close the **Switchboard** form, and then exit Access.

**Apply**

*Apply what you learned in the tutorial to create additional objects for a database for an Internet auction site.*

# Case Problem 5

**Data File needed for this Case Problem: BuySell.mdb (*cont. from Tutorial 9*)**

**eACH Internet Auction Site** Chris and Pat Aquino want you to create a user-friendly switchboard interface for the BuySell database. To help them with their request, you'll complete the following steps.

1. Start Access and then open the **BuySell** database in the Comp\Case5 folder provided with your Data Files.

2. Create a macro group named **mcrSwitchboardMacros** that contains macros to be used with the command buttons on the switchboard you'll create in the next step. The macros perform these actions: open the **Subcategory** table datasheet, open the **Item** form in Form view, open the **Registrant** form in Form view, open the **ProjectedIncomeBasedOnMinimumBid** report in Print Preview, and close the switchboard and activate the Database window.

3. Design and create a switchboard form named **Switchboard**. Use Figure 10-55 and the following descriptions as a guide to create the switchboard.

**Figure 10-55**

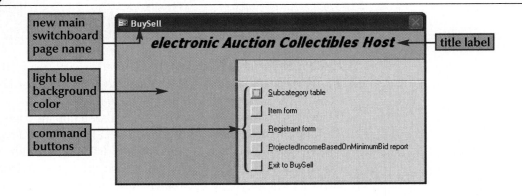

a. Use the Switchboard Manager to create the switchboard. Place the command buttons on the form; the command buttons should use the macros in the **mcrSwitchboardMacros** macro group. Define hot keys for each command button. Specify "BuySell" as the main switchboard page name.

b. Delete the default label and the shadow label on the form and place a label at the top of the switchboard. The label should read "electronic Auction Collectibles Host" and should appear as 16-point, bold, italic text.

c. Set the background color for the switchboard, as shown in Figure 10-55, resize the switchboard in Form view, and then set form properties that are appropriate for a switchboard.

4. Save the **Switchboard** form, and then test the command buttons to make sure that your switchboard items work correctly. If necessary, return to the Switchboard Manager and make any corrections.

5. Click the Exit to BuySell command button to close the **Switchboard** form, and then exit Access.

**Research**

# Internet Assignments

The purpose of the Internet Assignments is to challenge you to find information on the Internet that you can use to work effectively with this software. The actual assignments are updated and maintained on the Course Technology Web site. Log on to the Internet and use your Web browser to go to the Student Online Companion for New Perspectives Office 2003 at **www.course.com/np/office2003**. Click the Internet Assignments link, and then navigate to the assignments for this tutorial.

**Assess**

# SAM Assessment and Training

If you have a SAM user profile, you may have access to hands-on instruction, practice, and assessment of the skills covered in this tutorial. Log in to your SAM account and go to your assignments page to see what your instructor has assigned.

**Review**

# Quick Check Answers

### Session 10.1

1. A switchboard is a form that appears when you open a database and that provides controlled access to the database's tables, forms, queries, and reports. It lets you customize the organization of the user interface, and prevents users from changing the design of tables, forms, queries, reports, and other database objects.

2. A hot key is identified by an underlined letter in a command button, menu name, menu option, or toolbar button, and it provides a keyboard shortcut for the object's operation. You can use shortcut keys to make a selection by holding down the Alt key while typing the underlined letter.

3. A macro is an action, or a set of actions, that you want Access to perform automatically for you.

4. An action argument provides additional facts Access needs to execute an action. The action for opening a form, for example, needs the form name and the appropriate view in which to open the form as arguments.

5. The MsgBox action causes Access to open a message box that remains on the screen until you click the OK button.

6. Single stepping executes a macro one action at a time, pausing between actions. You use single stepping to make sure you have placed actions in the right order and with the right arguments, thereby ensuring that the macro works correctly.

## Session 10.2

1. An event property specifies how an object responds when an event occurs.

2. A macro group is a macro that contains other macros.

3. The beginning of each macro in a macro group has an entry in the Macro Name column of the Macro window; subsequent actions in the macro do not have entries in this column. The macro ends with the start of a new macro or at the end of the macro group, whichever comes first.

4. The Where Condition argument specifies which record to display in the form.

5. Users will not be able to resize the form using the pointer.

6. a control that displays a list of values

7. special tables maintained by Access that store information about the characteristics of a database and about the structure of its objects

8. In Design view, open the property sheet for the command button. Click the All tab in the property sheet, click the Picture text box, and then click the Build button. Select the picture using the Picture Builder dialog box, and then click the OK button.

9. Right-click the object, click Copy on the shortcut menu, and then click the Paste button on the toolbar.

## Session 10.3

1. The SendKeys action sends keystrokes to Access or to another program.

2. The Switchboard Manager is a Microsoft tool that helps you create and customize a switchboard.

3. OnClick

4. Type an ampersand (&) to the left of the hot key character in the command button name.

5. Open the form in Design view, open the form's property sheet, and then set the Border Style property to Dialog.

6. Shadowed and raised are two of the special effects.

## Objectives

**Session 11.1**
- Learn about Function procedures (functions), Sub procedures (subroutines), and modules
- Review and modify an existing subroutine in an event procedure
- Create a function in a standard module

**Session 11.2**
- Create event procedures
- Compile and test functions, subroutines, and event procedures

**Session 11.3**
- Hide text and change display colors
- Create event procedures for a dialog box

# Using and Writing Visual Basic for Applications Code

*Creating VBA Code for the Overseas Database User Interface*

## Case

## Northeast Seasonal Jobs International (NSJI)

Elsa Jensen reviews your progress in developing the graphical user interface for the Overseas database. So far, you have created the switchboard that contains command buttons for opening forms, opening a new switchboard page containing command buttons for opening reports, displaying a dialog box with a list of available queries, exiting the switchboard, and exiting the switchboard and Access. You also have created a macro group that contains the macros attached to the command buttons on the switchboard.

You'll continue developing the user interface by modifying the QueriesDialogBox form so that its command buttons carry out the appropriate operations. You'll also modify the Employer and Position forms to make data entry easier and to highlight important information on them. To make these modifications, you will write Visual Basic for Applications code to perform the necessary operations, and then you will attach the code to the appropriate event properties for the buttons and forms.

### Student Data Files

▼ **Comp**

▽ **Tutorial folder**
    Overseas.mdb (*cont.*)

▽ **Review folder**
    Work.mdb (*cont.*)

▽ **Case1 folder**
    Shoots.mdb (*cont.*)

▽ **Case2 folder**
    AtHome.mdb (*cont.*)

▽ **Case3 folder**
    ZooFunds.mdb (*cont.*)

▽ **Case4 folder**
    Rivers.mdb (*cont.*)

▽ **Case5 folder**
    BuySell.mdb (*cont.*)

# Session 11.1

## Introduction to Visual Basic for Applications

Your next task in the development of the graphical user interface for the Overseas database is to refine it further by adding a procedure to ensure proper capitalization of data entered using the Employer form. Elsa wants to make sure that all values entered in this form's StateProv field will be stored in the Employer table using uppercase letters. She asks you to modify the form so that it will automatically convert any lowercase letters entered in the StateProv field to uppercase. To accomplish this objective, you will use Visual Basic for Applications.

**Visual Basic for Applications (VBA)** is the programming language provided with Access and other Office programs. VBA is similar to **Visual Basic**, which is another Microsoft programming language, but VBA and Visual Basic each have features not found in the other programming language. When you use Access Help, you'll find Visual Basic references for many features shared by the two languages.

The process of writing instructions in a programming language, such as VBA, is called **coding**. You write each VBA instruction, which is called a **statement**, to respond to events that occur with the objects in a database. A language such as VBA is, therefore, called both an **event-driven language** and an **object-oriented language**. Your experience with macros, which are also event-driven and object-oriented, should facilitate your learning of VBA. You can do almost anything with VBA that you can do with macros, but VBA gives you more control over commands and objects than you have with macros. For example, with VBA you can create your own set of statements to perform special calculations. You can also change an object's properties dynamically; for example, VBA code can change the color in a form control when the user enters or views a specific field value.

### Events

Recall from Tutorial 10 that an **event** is a state, condition, or occurrence detectable by Access. For example, using the mouse to click a button and pressing a key to choose an option are events that users initiate. An **event property** specifies how an object responds when an event occurs. In Tutorial 10, you set event property values to macro names and Access executed the macros when those events occurred. You can also create a group of statements using VBA code and set an event property value to the name of that group of statements. Access will then execute the group of statements, or **procedure**, when the event occurs. Such a procedure is called an **event procedure**.

Access has over 60 events and associated event properties. Figure 11-1 describes several frequently used Access events.

| | Frequently used Access events | Figure 11-1 |

| Event | Description |
|---|---|
| AfterUpdate | Occurs after changed data in a control or a record is updated |
| BeforeUpdate | Occurs before changed data in a control or a record is updated |
| Click | Occurs when a user presses and then releases a mouse button over a control in a form |
| Current | Occurs when the focus moves to a record, making it the current record, or when a form is refreshed or requeried |
| DblClick | Occurs when a user presses and releases the left mouse button twice over a control in a form within the double-click time limit |
| Delete | Occurs when a user performs some action, such as pressing the Del key, to delete a record, but before the record is actually deleted |
| GotFocus | Occurs when a form or a form control receives the focus |
| Load | Occurs when a form is opened and its records are displayed |
| MouseDown | Occurs when a user presses a mouse button |
| NoData | Occurs after Access formats a report for printing that has no data (the report is bound to an empty recordset), but before the report is printed. Use this event to cancel the printing of a blank report. |
| Open | Occurs when a form is opened, but before the first record is displayed. For reports, the event occurs before a report is previewed or printed. |

As with the Access actions, you do not need to learn all Access events. You will gain experience with several events and event properties in this text, and if you need information on other events and event properties, you can use the Help system as a reference tool. Next, you'll use Help to review two topics about events.

## To use Help to learn about events:

1. Start Access, and then open the **Overseas** database located in the Comp\Tutorial folder provided with your Data Files.

   **Trouble?** If a dialog box opens with a message about installing the Microsoft Jet Service Pack, see your instructor or technical support person for assistance. You must have the appropriate Service Pack installed in order to open and work with Access databases safely.

   **Trouble?** If a dialog box opens, warning you that the Overseas database may not be safe, click the Open button. Your security level is set to Medium, which is the security setting that lets you choose whether or not to open a database that contains macros, VBA, or certain types of queries. The Overseas database does not contain objects that will harm your computer, so you can safely open the database.

   **Trouble?** If a dialog box opens, warning you that Access can't open the Overseas database due to security restrictions, click the OK button, click Tools on the menu bar, point to Macro, click Security, click the Medium option button, click the OK button, restart your computer if you're requested to do so, and then repeat Step 1. Your security level was set to High, which is the security setting that lets you open a database that contains macros, VBA, or certain types of queries only from trusted sources. Because the Overseas database does not contain objects that will harm your computer, you need to change the security setting to Medium and then safely open the Overseas database.

> **2.** Click the **Type a question for help** box on the menu bar, type **What are events?**, and then press the **Enter** key to display a list of relevant topics.

> **3.** Click **Example of setting the value of a property in response to an event** in the Search Results list to view the topic in the Microsoft Office Access Help window, and then if necessary maximize the Microsoft Office Access Help window. This topic provides examples using a macro and an event procedure to set the OnCurrent event property, which you'll use later in this tutorial. The OnCurrent event property specifies how an object responds when the Current event occurs.

> **4.** After reviewing the topic, close the Microsoft Office Access Help window, click **Order of events for database objects** in the Search Results list to view the topic in the Microsoft Office Access Help window, and then if necessary maximize the Microsoft Office Access Help window.

> **5.** Click the **Show All** link in the upper-right corner to expand all links, and then read the introductory paragraph of the displayed topic.

> **6.** Review the contents of the remainder of the displayed topic. Don't be concerned if you don't understand the topic, as long as you feel comfortable that you can find the topic if needed in the future.

> **7.** Close the Microsoft Access Help window to return to the Database window, and then close the Search Results task pane.

## Procedures

When you work with VBA, you code a group of statements that perform an operation or calculate a value, and then you attach the group of statements to the event property of an object. Access then executes, or **calls**, these statements every time the event occurs for that object. Each group of statements is called a procedure. The two types of procedures are Function procedures and Sub procedures.

A **Function procedure**, or **function**, performs operations, returns a value, accepts input values, and can be used in expressions (recall that an expression is a calculation resulting in a single value). For example, some of the Overseas database queries use built-in Access functions, such as Sum, Count, and Avg, to calculate a sum, a record count, or an average. To meet Elsa's request, you will create a function named CapAll by entering the appropriate VBA statements. The CapAll function will accept the value entered in a field text box—in this case, the StateProv field—as an input value, capitalize all characters of the field value, and then return the changed field value to be stored in the database and displayed in the field text box.

A **Sub procedure**, or **subroutine**, performs operations and accepts input values, but does not return a value and cannot be used in expressions. Later in this tutorial you will create a Sub procedure that displays a message in the Position form only when the data for a full-time position is displayed in the form.

## Modules

You store a group of related procedures together in an object called a **module**. Figure 11-2 shows the structure of a typical module.

Structure of a VBA module and its procedures ◀ **Figure 11-2**

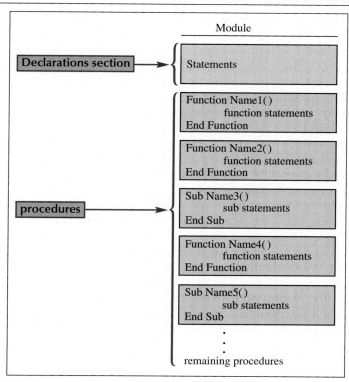

Each module starts with a **Declarations section**, which contains statements that apply to all procedures in the module. One or more procedures, which follow the Declarations section, constitute the rest of the module. The two basic types of modules are standard modules and class modules.

A **standard module** is a database object that is stored in memory with other database objects (queries, forms, and so on) when you open the database. You can use the procedures in a database's standard modules from anywhere in the database—even from procedures in other modules. A procedure that more than one object can use is called a **public procedure**. For example, the CapAll procedure that you will create capitalizes all letters in the value passed to it. Although you are creating this procedure specifically to work with StateProv field values, you will place it in a standard module and make it public. You could then use the CapAll procedure for any object in the database. All standard modules are listed on the Modules tab of the Database window.

A **class module** is usually associated with a particular form or report. When you create the first event procedure for a form or report, Access automatically creates an associated form or report class module. When you add additional event procedures to the form or report, Access adds them to the class module for that form or report. Each event procedure in a class module is a **local procedure**, or a **private procedure**, which means that only the form or report for which the class module was created can use the event procedure.

# Using Help and the Sample Northwind Database

The most difficult part of becoming proficient with Access is learning how to code effective VBA procedures. VBA is a powerful programming language containing hundreds of statements and built-in functions, along with hundreds of event properties, object properties, and built-in procedures. Deciding when and how to use each VBA feature can be intimidating to programming novices and even to experts. Fortunately, you can perform many fundamental operations without using VBA by setting control properties and by using macros, as you have done in previous tutorials.

When you use VBA to create new procedures, you can take advantage of the Access Help system as a reference tool. VBA Help is available in Access when you work with modules; you'll find additional VBA Help at Microsoft's Web site by searching for VBA. You can find Help for every VBA statement, function, event, and property; most of these topics even have a corresponding example that displays sample VBA code. If you find sample code similar to what you need, you can simply copy the statements to the Office Clipboard, paste them into a procedure in your own database, and modify the statements to work for your special case.

Another source for sample VBA code is the sample Northwind database that you can install with Access. When installed, you can open the Northwind database by clicking Help on the menu bar, pointing to Sample Databases, and then clicking Northwind Sample Database. The Northwind database contains a variety of simple and complex VBA procedures. You can view the effects of these procedures by using them in the sample database. Microsoft encourages you to copy and use the proven procedures in the Northwind database as a way to learn and use VBA more quickly. If you have time, you should explore the Northwind database on your own. Because Elsa has already studied the Northwind database, she doesn't need to open it to set up the VBA code for the Overseas database.

# Using an Existing Procedure

Before creating the CapAll procedure for Elsa, you'll use an existing procedure that Elsa created in the class module for the Employer form. This procedure displays the full province name in a text box to the right of the StateProv field value—Nova Scotia appears in red, Prince Edward Island in blue, and Quebec in magenta. Because all NSJI employees are familiar with the two-character state codes, state names do not appear in the text box.

You'll navigate the Employer form to observe the effects of the procedure.

### To navigate a form that uses a VBA procedure:

▶ **1.** Open the **Employer** form in Form view to display the first record for Beantown Tours. The state name of Massachusetts does not appear to the right of the StateProv field value of MA.

▶ **2.** Select the record number **1** in the Specific Record box between the navigation buttons, type **34**, and then press the **Enter** key. The Employer form displays record 34 for Gables & Golf Country Club. The province name of Prince Edward Island displays in blue to the right of the StateProv field value of PE. See Figure 11-3.

Using an existing VBA procedure | **Figure 11-3**

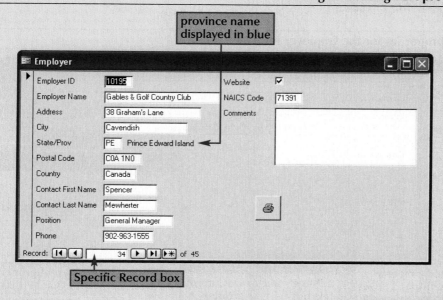

province name
displayed in blue

Specific Record box

3. Click the **Next Record** navigation button ▶ twice to display record 36 for Trudel Spa & Resort. The province name of Quebec displays in magenta to the right of the StateProv field value of QC.

4. Navigate to record 38 for Stonehurst Inn. The province name of Nova Scotia displays in red to the right of the StateProv field value of NS.

Elsa asks you to change the magenta color for Quebec to black to make it more readable.

## Displaying an Event Procedure

The VBA procedure that controls the display of the province name and its color for each record is in the class module for the Employer form. Access processes the statements in the procedure when you open the Employer form and also when the focus leaves one record and moves to another. (Recall that focus refers to the control that is currently active and awaiting user action; focus also refers to the object and record that are currently active.) Because the **Current event** occurs when a form opens and when the focus moves to another record, the VBA procedure is associated as an event procedure with the form's **OnCurrent property**.

To change the color of Quebec from magenta to black, you'll modify the event procedure for the form's OnCurrent property. First, you'll switch to Design view, and then you'll display the event procedure.

### To display the event procedure for the form's OnCurrent property:

1. Switch to Design view.

2. Right-click the form selector to display the shortcut menu, and then if necessary click **Properties** to open the property sheet for the form.

**3.** If necessary, click the **Event** tab to display the Event page of the property sheet. See Figure 11-4.

**Figure 11-4** | **Event properties for the Employer form**

The OnCurrent property is set to [Event Procedure], indicating that Access calls a VBA procedure when the Current event occurs. You'll click the Build button to display the procedure.

**4.** Click the **On Current** text box (if necessary), and then click the **Build** button ⋯ that appears to its right. The Code window opens in the Visual Basic window. See Figure 11-5.

**Figure 11-5** | **Code window in the Visual Basic window**

**Trouble?** If other windows appear in your Visual Basic window, click their Close buttons ✕ to close them.

**Trouble?** If your Code window opens in a restored window, maximize it.

The program you use to create and modify VBA code is called the **Visual Basic Editor** (**VBE**, or **editor** for short), and the **Visual Basic window** is the program window that opens when you use VBE. The **Code window** is the window in which you create, modify, and display specific VBA procedures. You can have as many Code windows open as you have modules in the database. In the Code window, the Object list box (the upper-left list box) indicates the current control (Form), and the Procedure list box (the upper-right list box) indicates the event name (Current) for the event procedure you are viewing.

All event procedures are subroutines. A horizontal line visually separates each procedure in the Code window. Each subroutine begins with a **Sub statement** and ends with an **End Sub statement**. The Sub statement includes the **scope** of the procedure (private or public), the name of the procedure (for example, Form_Current, which means the Current event for the form control), and an opening and closing parenthesis.

Notice the Option Compare statement in the Declarations section above the horizontal line. The **Option Compare statement** designates the technique Access uses to compare and sort text data. The default method "Database," as shown in Figure 11-5, means that Access compares and sorts letters in normal alphabetical order, using the language settings specified for Access running on your computer.

The remaining statements in the Form_Current procedure shown in Figure 11-5 use only two controls in the form: the StateProv field from the Employer table; and txtStateName, which is the text box control that displays the full province name. Based on the StateProv field value, the statements in the procedure do the following:

- If the StateProv field value is NS, then set txtStateName to Nova Scotia and set its font color to red.
- If the StateProv field value is PE, then set txtStateName to Prince Edward Island and set its font color to blue.
- If the StateProv field value is QC, then set txtStateName to Quebec and set its font color to magenta.
- If the StateProv field has any other value, then hide the txtStateName control.

The statements from the *Select Case [StateProv]* statement to the *End Select* statement are an example of a control structure. A **control structure** is a set of VBA statements that work together as a unit. The **Case control structure** is a conditional control structure; it evaluates an expression—the value of the StateProv field, in this case—and then performs one of several alternative actions based on the resulting value (or condition) of the evaluated expression. Each Case statement, such as *Case "NS"* and *Case Else*, designates the start of an alternative set of actions.

Statements such as *[txtStateName] = "Nova Scotia"* are assignment statements. An **assignment statement** assigns the value of an expression—Nova Scotia, in this case—to a field, control, or property—the txtStateName control, in this case.

Because a property is associated with a control, you use the general form of *ControlName.PropertyName* to specify a property for a control. An assignment statement such as *[txtStateName].ForeColor = RGB(255, 0, 0)*, for example, assigns a value to the txtStateName's ForeColor property. A control's **ForeColor property** determines the control's foreground, or font, color. The expression in this assignment statement uses a built-in VBA function named RGB. The **RGB function** returns an RGB (red, green, blue) color value, indicating the relative intensity of red (first value), green (second value), and blue (third value) in the color of a property for a control. Figure 11-6 displays a list of some common colors and the red, green, and blue values for the RGB function that produces those colors. Each color component value must be in the range 0 through 255.

**Figure 11-6** | **RGB function values for some common colors**

| Color | Red Value | Green Value | Blue Value |
| --- | --- | --- | --- |
| Black | 0 | 0 | 0 |
| Blue | 0 | 0 | 255 |
| Cyan | 0 | 255 | 255 |
| Green | 0 | 255 | 0 |
| Magenta | 255 | 0 | 255 |
| Red | 255 | 0 | 0 |
| White | 255 | 255 | 255 |
| Yellow | 255 | 255 | 0 |

The **Visible property** determines when Access displays a control. Access displays a control when its Visible property is True, and hides the control when its Visible property is False. The *[txtStateName].Visible = True* statement, which Access processes before the *Select Case [StateProv]* statement, displays the txtStateName control. Because Elsa doesn't want the txtStateName control to appear for states, the *[txtStateName].Visible = False* statement hides the txtStateName control if the StateProv field value doesn't equal one of the three Canadian provinces.

## Modifying an Event Procedure

Because Elsa wants you to change the magenta color for Quebec to black, you'll modify the last set of RGB function values in the event procedure. Also, because the txtStateName control will display only province names, Elsa asks you to change its name to txtProvinceName in the event procedure to make it more easily recognizable. Then you'll close the Visual Basic window, make the control name change in the form, and save and test your modifications.

### To modify, save, and test the event procedure:

▶ 1. Select **255, 0, 255** in the last RGB function, and then type **0,** (be sure you type the comma after the zero). A banner opens below the function and displays **syntax**, or valid format, information for the RGB function. See Figure 11-7.

**Modifying a built-in VBA function** ◀ **Figure 11-7**

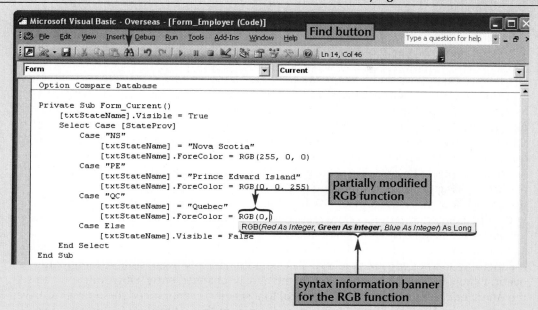

**Trouble?** If the banner does not open, click Tools on the menu bar, click Options, click the Editor tab, click the Auto Quick Info check box to select it, click the OK button, select "0," in the last RGB function, and then type "0," (without the quotation marks).

You'll now finish typing the RGB function.

2. Press the **spacebar**, and then type **0, 0** to complete the change to the RGB function.

Next, you'll replace all occurrences of txtStateName with txtProvinceName, by replacing the StateName portion of each occurrence with ProvinceName.

3. Click the **Find** button 🔍 on the Standard toolbar to open the Find dialog box, click the **Replace** button, type **StateName** in the Find What text box, press the **Tab** key, type **ProvinceName** in the Replace With text box, and then click the **Replace All** button. Access displays a message box informing you that eight replacements were made.

**Trouble?** If the toolbar is not displayed on your screen, click View on the menu bar, point to Toolbars, and then click Standard.

4. Click the **OK** button, and then close the Replace dialog box.

5. Click the **Save** button 🖫 on the Standard toolbar to save your changes, and then click the **Close** button ✕ on the Visual Basic window title bar to close it and return to the Form window in Design view.

You'll now change the name of the StateName text box to ProvinceName.

6. Click the **txtStateName** text box (the Unbound text box), click the **All** tab in the property sheet, type **txtProvinceName** in the property sheet's Name text box, and then close the property sheet.

7. Save your form design changes, and then switch to Form view.

8. Navigate to record 36 for Trudel Spa & Resort. The province name of Quebec displays in black to the right of the StateProv field value of QC. Your modification to the event procedure was completed successfully.

9. Close the **Employer** form.

You've completed your modifications to the event procedure. Next, you'll create the CapAll function.

# Creating Functions in a Standard Module

Elsa wants you to create a VBA procedure for the Employer form that will automatically convert the values entered in the StateProv field to uppercase. That is, if a user enters "ct" as the state, the procedure should automatically convert it to "CT". Elsa feels that this function will make data entry easier and reduce the number of data-entry errors. Users might not always be consistent about capitalizing entries in the StateProv field, and using this procedure to capitalize entries will ensure consistency.

To accomplish this change, you will first create a simple function, named CapAll, that accepts a **string** (text) input value and returns that string with all letters converted to uppercase. You create the function by typing the statements in the Module window. Then you will create an event procedure that calls the CapAll function whenever the user enters a value in the StateProv field using the Employer form.

Whenever a user enters or changes a field value in a control or in a form and changes the focus to another control or record, Access automatically triggers the **AfterUpdate event**, which, by default, simply accepts the new or changed entry. However, you can set the AfterUpdate event property of a control to a specific event procedure in order to have something else happen when a user enters or changes the field value. In this case, you need to set the StateProv field's AfterUpdate event property to [Event Procedure], and then code an event procedure to call the CapAll function. Calling the CapAll function will cause the entry in the StateProv field to be converted to uppercase letters before storing it in the database.

You will use the CapAll function with the Employer form, so you could add it to the class module for that form. Adding the function to the class module for the Employer form would make it a private function; that is, you could not use it in other forms or database objects. Because you might use the CapAll function in other forms in the Overseas database, you'll instead place the CapAll function in a new standard module named OverseasProcedures. Generally, when you enter a procedure in a standard module, it is public, and you can use it in event procedures for any object in the database.

To create a new standard module, you'll begin by opening the Code window.

Reference Window

**Creating a New Standard Module**

- In the Database window, click Modules in the Objects bar to display the Modules list.
- Click the New button. A new Code window, in which you create a new module, opens in the Visual Basic window.

You'll now create a new VBA standard module.

### To create a new standard module:

1. Click **Modules** in the Objects bar of the Database window, click the **New** button, and then maximize the Visual Basic window. A new Code window opens in the Visual Basic window. See Figure 11-8.

**Creating a new standard module** | **Figure 11-8**

In the Code window for the new standard module, the Procedure list box displays the Declarations section as the current procedure in the module. Access automatically includes the Option Compare statement in the Declarations section of a new module. The CapAll function is a simple function that does not require additional statements in the Declarations section.

## Creating a Function

Each function begins with a **Function statement** and ends with an **End Function statement**. Access visually separates each procedure in the Code window with a horizontal line. You can view a procedure's statements by selecting the procedure name from the Procedure list box.

The CapAll function begins with the statement *Function CapAll(FValue)*. CapAll is the function name and FValue is used as a placeholder for the input value in the function definition. When the user enters a value for the StateProv field in the Employer form, that value will be passed to the CapAll function and substituted for FValue in the function definition. A placeholder like FValue is called a **parameter**. The value passed to the function and used in place of the parameter when the function is executed is called an **argument**. In other words, the value passed to the function is the argument, which is assigned to the parameter named FValue.

All VBA function names, Sub procedure names, argument names, and other names you create must conform to the following rules:

- They must begin with a letter.
- They cannot exceed 255 characters.
- They can include letters, numbers, and the underscore character ( _ ). You cannot use a space or any punctuation characters.
- They cannot contain keywords, such as Function, Sub, Case, and Option, that VBA uses as part of its language.
- They must be unique; that is, you can't declare the same name twice within the same procedure.

You'll enter the CapAll function in the Code window and then test it. Then you'll attach it to an event procedure for the Employer form. As you enter the statements for the CapAll function in the Code window, remember that capitalization is important in all statements so that your code is readable and maintainable. You now can start entering the CapAll function.

## To start a new function:

**1.** With the insertion point two lines below the Option Compare statement, type **Function CapAll(FValue)** and then press the **Enter** key. The editor displays a horizontal line that visually separates the new function from the Declarations section. See Figure 11-9.

| Figure 11-9 | Starting a new function |
| --- | --- |

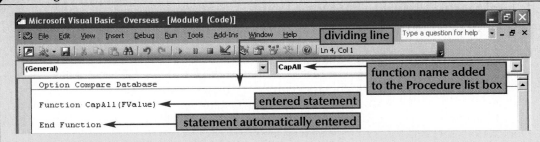

The function name CapAll now appears in the Procedure list box. The editor automatically added the End Function statement and moved the insertion point to the beginning of the blank line between the Function and End Function statements, where you will enter the procedure statements. The editor displays the reserved words Function and End Function in blue. The function name and the parameter name appear in black.

The CapAll function will consist of a single executable assignment statement that you will place between the Function and End Function statements. You'll enter the following assignment statement: *CapAll = UCase(FValue)*. The value of the expression, which is UCase(FValue), will be assigned to the function, which is CapAll.

The expression in the assignment statement uses a built-in Access function named UCase. The **UCase function** accepts a single string argument as input, converts the value of the argument to uppercase letters, and then returns the converted value. The assignment statement assigns the converted value to the CapAll function. Figure 11-10 illustrates this process.

| Figure 11-10 | Evaluation of the assignment statement |
| --- | --- |

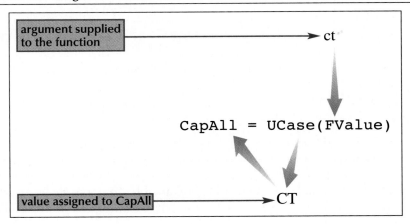

Before entering the assignment statement, you will add a comment line to explain the procedure's purpose. You can include comments anywhere in a VBA procedure to describe what the procedure or a statement does to make it easier for you and other programmers to identify the purpose of statements in your code. You begin a comment with the word Rem (for "Remark") or with a single quotation mark ('). VBA ignores anything following the word Rem or the single quotation mark on a single line. Because

VBA ignores comments, you can include spaces, special characters, and mixed-case letters in your comments. Also, you will indent these lines; indenting statements is a common practice that makes code easier to read.

### To add a comment and statement to the function:

1. Press the **Tab** key to indent the line.

2. Type **'Capitalize all letters of a field value** and then press the **Enter** key. Notice that the editor displays the comment in green and indents the new line. After entering the comment line, you can enter the assignment statement, which is the executable statement in the function that performs the actual conversion of the argument to uppercase.

3. Type **CapAll = UCase(FValue)**. See Figure 11-11. The editor provides assistance as you enter the statement. After you type UCase and the opening parenthesis, the editor displays a banner with a reminder that UCase accepts a single string argument. The editor displays a similar banner after you type CapAll and press the spacebar; you should ignore this banner because its reminder is incorrect.

CapAll function in the Code window  Figure 11-11

The editor scans each statement for errors when you press the Enter key or change the focus to another statement. Because the function is complete and you want the editor to scan the line you just entered for errors, you must move the insertion point to another line.

4. Press the ↓ key to move the insertion point to the next line. Because Access finds no errors, the insertion point continues to blink on the last line.

**Trouble?** If the editor finds an error in the assignment statement, it highlights the error in red and opens a dialog box with a message describing the nature of the error. Click the OK button and then change the highlighted error by comparing your entries with those shown in Steps 2 and 3. Then repeat Step 4 to scan the statement for errors again.

You have finished entering the function, so you'll save it before continuing with your work.

## Saving a Module

When you click the Save button in the Visual Basic window, the editor saves the module and its procedures. If you are entering a long procedure, it's a good idea to save your work periodically.

**To save the module:**

1. Click the **Save** button 🖫 on the Standard toolbar, type **OverseasProcedures** in the Module Name text box, and then press the **Enter** key. The editor saves the module and places the new module name in the title bar.

Before making the changes to the Employer form so that the CapAll function automatically acts on every entry in the StateProv field, you can test the function using the Immediate window.

# Testing a Procedure in the Immediate Window

When you finish entering a VBA statement, the editor checks the statement to make sure its syntax is correct. Although you may have entered all procedure statements with the correct syntax, the procedure may still contain logic errors. A **logic error** occurs when the procedure produces incorrect results. For example, the CapAll function would have a logic error if you typed ct and the function changed it to cT, Ct, or anything other than the correct result of CT. Even the simplest procedure can contain errors. Be sure to test each procedure thoroughly to ensure that it does exactly what you expect it to do in all situations.

When working in the Code window, you can use the **Immediate window** to test VBA procedures without changing any data in the database. In the Immediate window, you can enter different values to test the procedure you just entered. To test a procedure, type the keyword "Print" or a question mark (?), followed by the procedure name and the value you want to test in parentheses. For example, to test the CapAll function in the Immediate window using the test word ct, type *?CapAll ("ct")* and then press the Enter key. Access executes the function and prints the value returned by the function (you expect it to return CT). Note that you must enclose a string of characters within quotation marks in the test statement.

| Reference Window | **Testing a Procedure in the Immediate Window** |
| --- | --- |

- In the Code window, click View on the menu bar, and then click Immediate Window to open the Immediate window.
- Type a question mark (?), the procedure name, and the procedure's arguments in parentheses.
- Press the Enter key and verify the displayed answer.

Now you can use the Immediate window to test the CapAll function.

**To test the CapAll function in the Immediate window:**

1. Click **View** on the menu bar, and then click **Immediate Window**. The editor opens the Immediate window across the bottom of the screen and places the insertion point inside the window.

   The Immediate window allows you to run individual lines of VBA code for **debugging** (testing). You will use the Immediate window to test the CapAll function.

**2.** Type **?CapAll("ct")** and then press the **Enter** key. The editor executes the function and prints the function result, CT, on the next line. See Figure 11-12.

Immediate window

```
Immediate                                                                        ×
  ?CapAll("ct") ◀────────── function call statement
  CT
   ▲
   └── result of executing the function
```

**Trouble?** If Access displays a dialog box with an error message, click the OK button in the dialog box, correct the error in the Immediate window, and then press the Enter key. If the function does not produce the correct output (CT), correct the CapAll function statements in the Code window, save your changes, and then repeat Steps 1 and 2.

To test the CapAll function further, you could enter several other test values, retyping the entire statement each time. Instead, you'll select the current test value, type another value, and then press the Enter key.

**3.** Select the characters **ct** in the first line of the Immediate window.

**4.** Type **cT** and then press the **Enter** key. The editor executes the function and prints the function result, CT, on the next line.

**5.** Repeat Steps 3 and 4 two more times, using **Qc** and then **NH** as the test values. The editor prints the correct values, QC and NH.

**6.** Click the **Close** button ⊠ on the Immediate window title bar to close it, and then click the **Close** button ⊠ on the Visual Basic window title bar to return to the Database window.

**7.** If you are not continuing on to the next session, close the Overseas database, and then exit Access.

Your initial test of the CapAll function is successful. In the next session, you'll modify the Employer form to call the CapAll function for the StateProv field.

# Session 11.1 Quick Check

**Review**

1. Why is Visual Basic for Applications called an event-driven, object-oriented language?
2. What is an event procedure?
3. What are the differences between a Function procedure and a Sub procedure?
4. What are the two different types of modules?
5. The _____ of a procedure is either private or public.
6. What can you accomplish in the Immediate window?

# Session 11.2

## Creating an Event Procedure

Recall that when you add a procedure to a form or report, Access automatically creates a class module for that form or report. Each of these procedures is called an event procedure; Access runs a procedure when a specific event occurs.

Now that you have created the CapAll function as a public procedure in the standard module named OverseasProcedures, you can create an event procedure for the Employer form to call the CapAll function for the StateProv field's AfterUpdate event. Whenever a user enters or changes a StateProv field value, the AfterUpdate event occurs and Access will run your event procedure.

What exactly happens when Access calls a procedure? There is an interaction between the calling statement and the function statements as represented by a series of steps. Figure 11-13 shows the process for the CapAll procedure.

| Figure 11-13 | Process of executing a function |
| --- | --- |

The steps in Figure 11-13 are numbered in the order in which they occur as Access processes the statement and the function. Access goes through the following steps:

- Step 1. The call to the function CapAll passes the value of the argument [StateProv]. This is the value of the StateProv field that is entered or changed by the user.
- Step 2. The function CapAll begins, and the parameter FValue receives the value of [StateProv].
- Step 3. FValue is changed to uppercase.
- Step 4. The value of CapAll is set equal to the result of Step 3.
- Step 5. The function CapAll ends.
- Step 6. The value of CapAll is returned to the point of the call to the function.
- Step 7. The value of [StateProv] is set equal to the returned value of CapAll.

Although it looks complicated, the general function process is simple. The statement contains a function call. When the statement is executed, Access performs the function call, executes the function, returns a single value to the original statement, and completes that statement's execution. Study the steps in Figure 11-13 and trace their sequence until you understand the complete process.

## Designing an Event Procedure

Whenever a user enters a new value or modifies an existing value in the StateProv field in the Employer form, Elsa wants Access to execute the CapAll function to ensure that all StateProv field values appear in uppercase letters. After a user changes a StateProv field value, the AfterUpdate event automatically occurs. You can set the AfterUpdate event property to run a macro, call a built-in Access function, or execute an event procedure. Because you want to call your user-defined function from within the event procedure, you'll set the AfterUpdate event property to [Event Procedure], and then add the VBA statements needed to use the CapAll function.

All event procedures are subroutines. Access automatically adds the Sub and End Sub statements to an event procedure. All you need to do is place the statements between the Sub and End Sub statements. Figure 11-14 shows the completed event procedure. The following text describes the parts of the procedure.

**AfterUpdate event procedure for the StateProv field** ◀ **Figure 11-14**

Access names each event procedure in a standard way: the name of the control, an underscore ( _ ), and the event name. No parameters are passed to an event procedure, so Access places nothing in the parentheses following the name of the subroutine. If the name of the control contains spaces or special characters, Access substitutes underscores for them in the event procedure name.

A user might delete an existing StateProv field value, so that it contains no value, or becomes null. In this case, calling the function accomplishes nothing. The procedure is designed to call the CapAll function only when a user changes the StateProv field to a value that is not null. The If statement screens out the null values. In its simplest form, an **If statement** executes one of two groups of statements based on a condition, similar to common English usage. For example, consider the English statements, "If I work the night shift, then I'll earn extra spending money. Otherwise, I'll go to the movies, and I'll dip into my savings." In these sentences, the two groups of statements come before and after the "otherwise," depending on the condition, "if I work the night shift." The first group of statements consists of the clause "I'll earn extra spending money." This clause is called the **true-statement group** because it's what happens if the condition ("I work the night shift") is true. The second group of statements contains "I'll go to the movies, and I'll dip into my savings." This clause is called the **false-statement group** because it is what happens if the condition is false. VBA uses the keyword *If* to precede the condition. The keyword *Then* precedes the true-statement group and the keyword *Else* precedes the false-statement group. The general syntax of a VBA If statement is:

If condition Then
      true-statement group
[Else
      false-statement group]
End If

Access executes the true-statement group when the condition is true and the false-statement group when the condition is false. In this statement's syntax, the bracketed portions are optional. Therefore, you must omit the *Else* and its related false-statement group when you want Access to execute a group of statements only when the condition is true.

In Figure 11-14, the If statement uses the VBA **IsNull function**, which returns True when the StateProv field value is null and False when it is not null. The *Not* in the If statement is the same logical operator you've used previously to negate an expression. So, Access executes the statement *[StateProv] = CapAll([StateProv])* only when the StateProv field value is not null. Notice that the StateProv field name is enclosed in brackets, even though brackets are optional for field names and control names that do not contain spaces and special characters.

You are ready to make your changes to the Employer form.

## Adding an Event Procedure

To add an event procedure to the StateProv field's AfterUpdate event property, you need to open the Employer form in Design view.

### Adding an Event Procedure

- Open the form or report in Design view, select the control whose event property you want to set, and then open the property sheet for that control.
- Set the appropriate event property to [Event Procedure], and then click the Build button.
- Enter the subroutine statements in the Code window.
- Compile the procedure, fix any statement errors, and then save the event procedure.

You can now add the event procedure to the Employer form.

### To add the event procedure to the Employer form:

1. If you took a break after the previous session, make sure that Access is running, and that the **Overseas** database in the Comp\Tutorial folder is open.

2. Open the **Employer** form in Design view.

3. Right-click the **StateProv** text box (not the txtProvinceName text box, which is labeled "Unbound") to display the shortcut menu, and then click **Properties** to open the property sheet.

4. If necessary, click the **Event** tab. Access shows only the event properties in the property sheet. You need to set the AfterUpdate property.

5. Click the right side of the **After Update** text box, click **[Event Procedure]**, and then click the **Build** button [...] to the right of the After Update text box. The Code window opens in the Visual Basic window. See Figure 11-15.

**Starting a new event procedure in the Code window** | **Figure 11-15**

**Trouble?** If the Choose Builder dialog box opens, click Code Builder, and then click the OK button.

**Trouble?** If the Object list box displays the txtProvinceName control or any other control instead of the StateProv control, close the Visual Basic window, delete "[Event Procedure]" from the After Update text box on the property sheet, click the StateProv text box, and then repeat Step 5.

The new event procedure for the StateProv field's AfterUpdate event property contains the Private Sub and End Sub statements, and it follows the form's Current event procedure. You can now enter the statements to call the CapAll function.

6. Enter the statements shown in Figure 11-16. Use the **Tab** key to indent the lines as shown in the figure, press the **Enter** key at the end of each line, and press the **Backspace** key to move one tab stop to the left. Compare your screen with Figure 11-16, and make any necessary corrections.

**Completed event procedure** | **Figure 11-16**

```
Private Sub StateProv_AfterUpdate()
    'Capitalize the StateProv field value
    If Not IsNull([StateProv]) Then
        [StateProv] = CapAll([StateProv])
    End If
End Sub
```

**Trouble?** If your event procedure contains errors, correct them by highlighting the errors and typing the corrections. Use the Backspace or Delete keys to delete characters.

Before saving the event procedure, you'll compile it.

## Compiling Modules

The VBA programming language is not your native language, nor is it the computer's native language. Although you can learn VBA and become fluent in it, computers cannot understand or learn VBA. For a computer to understand the statements in your VBA modules, Access must translate the statements into a form that it can run. The process of translating modules from VBA to a form your computer understands is called **compilation**; you say that you **compile** the module when you translate it.

When you run a procedure for the first time, Access compiles it for you automatically and opens a dialog box only when it finds syntax errors in the procedure. If it finds an error, Access does not translate the procedure statements. If no errors are detected, Access translates the procedure and does not display a confirmation. You also can compile a procedure at any point as you enter it by clicking the Compile <database name> command on the Debug menu. In response, Access compiles the procedure and all other procedures in all modules in the database. It's best to compile and save your modules after you've made changes to them, to make sure they don't contain syntax errors.

You'll now compile the procedures in the Overseas database and save the class module for the Employer form.

**To compile the procedures in the Overseas database and save the class module:**

1. Click **Debug** on the menu bar, and then click **Compile Overseas**. Access compiles all the modules in the Overseas database. Because you have no syntax errors, Access translates the VBA statements and returns control to the Visual Basic window.

   **Trouble?** If Access identifies any errors in your code, correct the errors and repeat Step 1.

2. Save your module changes, close the Visual Basic window, and then close the property sheet.

You have created the function and the event procedure and have set the event property. Next, you'll test the event procedure to make sure it works correctly.

## Testing an Event Procedure

You need to display the Employer form in Form view and test the StateProv field's event procedure by entering a few different test StateProv field values in the first record of the form. Moving the focus to another control on the form or to another record triggers the AfterUpdate event for the StateProv field and executes your attached event procedure. Because the CapAll function is attached only to the Employer form, the automatic capitalization of StateProv field values is not in effect when you enter them in the Employer table or any other object in the Overseas database.

**To test the event procedure:**

▶ **1.** Switch to Form view.

▶ **2.** Select the **StateProv** field value (MA), type **ma** in the StateProv text box, and then press the **Enter** key. Access executes the AfterUpdate event procedure for the StateProv field and changes the StateProv field value to "MA". See Figure 11-17.

**Employer form after executing the event procedure** ◀ **Figure 11-17**

capitalized StateProv
field value

▶ **3.** Repeat Step 2 three more times, entering **Ma**, then **mA**, and finally **MA** in the StateProv text box. Access displays the correct value "MA" each time.

Elsa wants you to create a more complicated function for the PostalCode field in the Employer form.

# Adding a Second Procedure to a Class Module

Elsa has found that her staff makes frequent errors when entering Massachusetts zip codes, whose first three digits start 010 through 027, because they tend to transpose the first two digits. She asks you to create a procedure that will verify that Massachusetts zip codes are in the correct range when her staff updates the PostalCode field in the Employer form. For this procedure, you will use an event procedure attached to the BeforeUpdate event for the Employer form. The **BeforeUpdate event** occurs before changed data in a control or a record is updated. You'll use the form's BeforeUpdate event for this new procedure, because you want to find data-entry errors for Massachusetts zip codes and alert users to the errors before the database is updated.

## Designing the Field Validation Procedure

Figure 11-18 shows the procedure that you will create to verify Massachusetts zip codes. You've already seen several of the statements in this procedure in your work with the CapAll function and with the form's Current event.

**Figure 11-18** ▶ **PostalCode validation procedure**

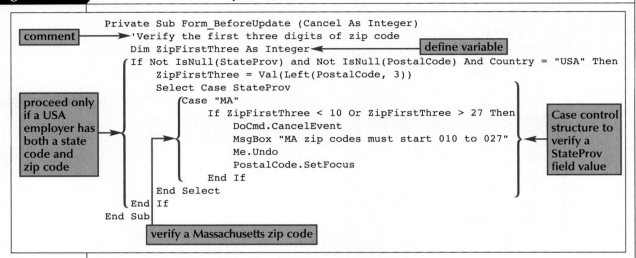

```
Private Sub Form_BeforeUpdate (Cancel As Integer)
    'Verify the first three digits of zip code
    Dim ZipFirstThree As Integer
    If Not IsNull(StateProv) and Not IsNull(PostalCode) And Country = "USA" Then
        ZipFirstThree = Val(Left(PostalCode, 3))
        Select Case StateProv
            Case "MA"
                If ZipFirstThree < 10 Or ZipFirstThree > 27 Then
                    DoCmd.CancelEvent
                    MsgBox "MA zip codes must start 010 to 027"
                    Me.Undo
                    PostalCode.SetFocus
                End If
        End Select
    End If
End Sub
```

- comment
- define variable
- proceed only if a USA employer has both a state code and zip code
- Case control structure to verify a StateProv field value
- verify a Massachusetts zip code

The Sub and End Sub statements begin and end the subroutine. As specified in the Sub statement, the subroutine executes when the form's BeforeUpdate event occurs. Within parentheses in the Sub statement, *Cancel As Integer* defines Cancel as a parameter with the integer data type. VBA has data types that are different from the Access data types you've used to define table fields, but each Access data type is equivalent to one of the VBA data types. For example, the Access number data type with an Integer field size is the same as the VBA integer data type, and the Access text data type is the same as the VBA string data type. Figure 11-19 shows the primary VBA data types.

**Figure 11-19** ▶ **Primary VBA data types**

| Data Type | Stores |
|-----------|--------|
| Boolean | True/False values |
| Byte | Integer values from 0 to 255 |
| Currency | Currency values from −922,337,203,685,477.5808 to 922,337,203,685,477.5807 |
| Date | Date and time values from 1 January 100 to 31 December 9999 |
| Decimal | Non-integer values with 0 to 28 decimal places |
| Double | Non-integer values from $-1.79769313486231*10^{308}$ to $-4.94065645841247*11^{-324}$ for negative values, from $4.94065645841247*11^{-324}$ to $1.79769313486232*10^{308}$ for positive values, and 0 |
| Integer | Integer values from −32,768 to 32,767 |
| Long | Integer values from −2,147,483,648 to 2,147,483,647 |
| Object | Any object reference |
| Single | Non-integer values from $-3.402823*10^{38}$ to $-1.401298*11^{-45}$ for negative values, from $1.401298*11^{-45}$ to $3.402823*10^{38}$ for positive values, and 0 |
| String | Text values up to 2 billion characters in length |
| Variant | Any numeric or string data type |

When an event occurs, Access performs the default behavior for the event. For some events, such as the BeforeUpdate event, Access executes the event procedure or macro before performing the default behavior. Thus, if you detect something is wrong and the default behavior should not occur, you can cancel the default behavior in the event procedure or macro. For this reason, Access automatically includes the Cancel parameter for the BeforeUpdate event.

The second procedure statement, which starts with a single quotation mark, is a comment. The third statement, *Dim ZipFirstThree As Integer*, declares the integer variable named ZipFirstThree that the subroutine uses. A **variable** is a named location in computer memory that can contain a value. If you use a variable in a module, you must explicitly declare it in the Declarations section or in the procedure where the variable is used. You use the **Dim statement** to declare variables and their associated data types in a procedure. The subroutine will assign the first three digits of USA zip codes (the PostalCode field) to the ZipFirstThree variable, and then will use the variable when verifying that a Massachusetts zip code begins in the correct range.

Although Elsa wants the procedure to verify the first three digits of only Massachusetts zip codes for now, she might want to expand the procedure in the future to verify the first three digits of other states, but never the first three characters of provinces. Therefore, the procedure should not attempt to verify Canadian postal codes. Further, the procedure should not attempt to verify records that contain null field values for the StateProv field and the PostalCode field. To screen out these conditions, the procedure uses the fourth procedure statement, *If Not IsNull(StateProv) And Not IsNull(PostalCode) And Country = "USA" Then*, which pairs with the last *End If* statement. The If statement determines whether both the StateProv and PostalCode fields are nonnull and the Country field equals "USA". If all three conditions are true, then Access executes the next statement in the procedure. If any condition is false, then Access executes the paired End If statement, and the following End Sub statement ends the procedure without the execution of any other statement.

The fifth procedure statement, *ZipFirstThree = Val(Left(PostalCode, 3))*, uses two built-in VBA functions, the Val function and the Left function, to assign the first three digits of the PostalCode field value to the ZipFirstThree variable. The **Left function** returns a string containing a specified number of characters from the left side of a specified string. In this case, the Left function returns the leftmost three characters of PostalCode. The **Val function** returns the numbers contained in a specified string as a numeric value. In this case, the Val function returns the leftmost three characters of PostalCode as an integer value.

You encountered the Case control structure previously in the Employer form's Current event procedure. For the BeforeUpdate event procedure, the *Select Case StateProv* statement evaluates the StateProv field value. For StateProv field values equal to MA (Massachusetts zip codes), the next If statement executes. For all other StateProv field values, nothing further in the procedure executes, Access performs the default behavior, and control returns back to the form for further processing.

Because valid Massachusetts zip codes start 010 through 027, invalid numeric values are less than 10 or are greater than 27. The next VBA statement, *If ZipFirstThree < 10 Or ZipFirstThree > 27 Then*, is true only for invalid Massachusetts zip codes. When the If statement is true, the next four statements execute. When the If statement is false, nothing further in the procedure executes, Access performs the default behavior, and control returns back to the form for further processing.

The first of the four VBA statements that execute for invalid Massachusetts zip codes is the DoCmd statement. The **DoCmd statement** executes an action in a procedure. The *DoCmd.CancelEvent* statement executes the CancelEvent action. The **CancelEvent action** cancels the event that caused the procedure or macro containing the action to execute. In this case, Access cancels the BeforeUpdate event and does not update the database with your changes to the current record. In addition, Access cancels subsequent events that would have occurred if the BeforeUpdate event had not been canceled. (These subsequent events are described in the "Order of events for database objects" Help topic that you reviewed earlier in this tutorial.) For example, because the form's BeforeUpdate event is triggered when you move to a different record, the following events are triggered when you move to a different record, in the order listed: BeforeUpdate event for the form, AfterUpdate event for the form, Exit event for the control with the focus, LostFocus event for the control with the focus, RecordExit event for the form, and Current event for the form. When the CancelEvent action executes, all these events are canceled and the focus remains with the record being edited.

The *MsgBox "MA zip codes must start 010 to 027"* statement displays its message in a message box that remains on the screen until the user clicks the OK button. The message box appears on top of the Employer form so the user can view the changed field values in the current record.

After the user clicks the OK button in the message box, the *Me.Undo* statement executes. The **Me keyword** refers to the current object, in this case the Employer form. **Undo** is a method that clears all changes made to the current record in the Employer form, so that the field values in the record are as they were before the user made current changes. A **method** is an action that operates on specific objects or controls.

Finally, the *PostalCode.SetFocus* statement executes. **SetFocus** is a method that moves the focus to the specified object or control. In this case, Access moves the focus to the PostalCode field in the current record in the Employer form.

## Adding a Second Event Procedure

After designing the procedure to verify Massachusetts zip codes, you add an event procedure for the Employer form's BeforeUpdate event property. Access will execute the event procedure whenever field values in a record are entered or updated.

### To add the event procedure for the Employer form's BeforeUpdate event:

1. Switch to Design view.

2. Right-click the form selector to display the shortcut menu, and then click **Properties** to open the property sheet for the form.

3. If necessary, click the **Event** tab in the property sheet.

4. Click the right side of the **Before Update** text box, click **[Event Procedure]**, and then click the **Build** button [ ... ] to the right of the Before Update text box. The Code window, which contains new Private Sub and End Sub statements, opens in the Visual Basic window. Notice that the Code window also contains the event procedure for the form's Current property, which you modified earlier. The Code window also displays the event procedure for the StateProv field's AfterUpdate property, which you entered earlier.

5. Press the **Tab** key, and then type the subroutine statements exactly as shown in Figure 11-20. Press the **Enter** key after you enter each statement, press the **Tab** key to indent lines as necessary, and press the **Backspace** key to move the insertion point one tab stop to the left. When you are finished, your screen should look like Figure 11-20.

**Event procedure for the Employer form's BeforeUpdate event** | **Figure 11-20**

new event procedure

```
Microsoft Visual Basic - Overseas - [Form_Employer (Code)]

File  Edit  View  Insert  Debug  Run  Tools  Add-Ins  Window  Help      Type a question for help

Ln 17, Col 11

Form                                    BeforeUpdate

    Option Compare Database

Private Sub Form_BeforeUpdate(Cancel As Integer)
    'Verify the first three digits of zip code
    Dim ZipFirstThree As Integer
    If Not IsNull(StateProv) And Not IsNull(PostalCode) And Country = "USA" Then
        ZipFirstThree = Val(Left(PostalCode, 3))
        Select Case StateProv
            Case "MA"
                If ZipFirstThree < 10 Or ZipFirstThree > 27 Then
                    DoCmd.CancelEvent
                    MsgBox "MA zip codes must start 010 to 027"
                    Me.Undo
                    PostalCode.SetFocus
                End If
        End Select
    End If
End Sub

Private Sub Form_Current()
    [txtProvinceName].Visible = True
    Select Case [StateProv]
        Case "NS"
            [txtProvinceName] = "Nova Scotia"
            [txtProvinceName].ForeColor = RGB(255, 0, 0)
        Case "PE"
            [txtProvinceName] = "Prince Edward Island"
```

type these 14 statements

existing event procedures for the form's Current property

▶ **6.** Click **Debug** on the menu bar, and then click **Compile Overseas**. Access compiles all the modules in the Overseas database.

**Trouble?** If the editor finds an error, it highlights the error and opens a dialog box with a message describing the nature of the error. Click the OK button and then change the highlighted error by comparing your entries with those shown in Figure 11-20. Then repeat Step 6 to scan the statements for errors again and to compile the modules.

▶ **7.** Save your class module changes.

▶ **8.** Close the Visual Basic window to return to the Form window, and then close the property sheet.

You can now test the event procedure. To do so, you'll switch to Form view for the Employer form and test the form's BeforeUpdate event procedure by entering valid and invalid PostalCode field values for a Massachusetts employer and for an employer from another state.

## To test the form's BeforeUpdate event procedure:

▶ **1.** Switch to Form view. Access displays record 1 for Beantown Tours. The first three digits of the PostalCode field value, 21 as an integer value, represent a valid Massachusetts zip code in the range of 10-27.

2. Select **02109** in the PostalCode text box, type **98765**, and then click the **Next Record** navigation button ▶ to move to the next record. Access executes the BeforeUpdate event procedure for the Employer form, determines that the Massachusetts zip code's first three digits are incorrect, and displays the message box you included in the procedure. See Figure 11-21.

**Figure 11-21**  **After the Employer form's BeforeUpdate event procedure detects an error**

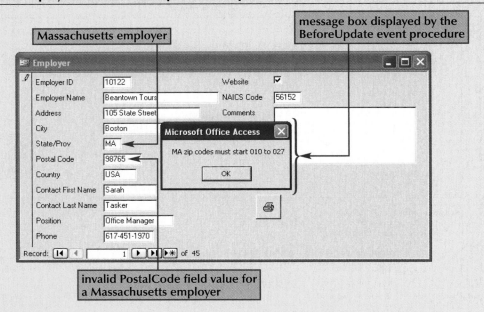

Massachusetts employer

message box displayed by the BeforeUpdate event procedure

invalid PostalCode field value for a Massachusetts employer

While the message box is open, the updated PostalCode field value of 98765 remains on screen for you to review.

3. Click the **OK** button. The message box closes, the Undo method changes the PostalCode field value to 02109, its original value, and the SetFocus method moves the focus to the PostalCode text box.

Next, you'll change the PostalCode field value to 01109, which is a valid Massachusetts zip code.

4. Change the PostalCode field value to **01109**, and then click the **Next Record** navigation button ▶ to move to the next record. The form's BeforeUpdate event procedure verifies that the zip code is a valid value for a Massachusetts employer, and the focus moves to the PostalCode text box in the next record.

5. Click the **Previous Record** navigation button ◀ to move to the first record, and then change the PostalCode field value to **02109**. The PostalCode field value for Beantown Tours now equals its original value.

You'll now test the BeforeUpdate event procedure for a non-Massachusetts zip code. Because the event procedure verifies only Massachusetts zip codes, you should be able to change a non-Massachusetts zip code to any valid or invalid value.

6. Click the **Last Record** navigation button ▶I to move to the last record for Lighthouse Tours, a Rhode Island employer, change the PostalCode field value to **98765**, and then click the **Previous Record** navigation button ◀. Access executes the form's BeforeUpdate event procedure, which does not verify the PostalCode field value for the non-Massachusetts employer, stores the updated PostalCode field value in the database, and moves the focus to the previous record.

Next, you'll change the PostalCode field value for the last record back to its original value.

▶ **7.** Click the **Last Record** navigation button ⏭, and then click the **Undo** button ↩ on the Form View toolbar. The PostalCode field value for Lighthouse Tours now equals its original value.

▶ **8.** If you are not continuing on to the next session, close the Overseas database, and then exit Access.

Elsa has one more procedure she wants you to create for the Employer form, and then she wants you to put the finishing touches on the Overseas database user interface. You'll fulfill Elsa's requests in the next session.

## Session 11.2 Quick Check

Review

1. The VBA _____ statement executes one of two groups of statements based on a condition.
2. What happens when you compile a module?
3. What is the purpose of the Dim statement?
4. The _____ function returns the numbers contained in a specified string as a numeric value.
5. What is the purpose of the DoCmd statement?
6. What is a method?

# Session 11.3

# Changing the Case of a Field Value

Elsa wants to make it easier for users to enter an employer's name when using the Employer form, so she asks you to create a procedure that will automatically convert the case of letters entered in the EmployerName field. This procedure will capitalize the first letter of each word in the field and change all other letters to lowercase. You'll use an event procedure attached to the AfterUpdate event for the EmployerName field to perform this automatic conversion. For example, if a user enters "beantOWn tours" as the EmployerName field value, the event procedure will correct the field value to "Beantown Tours."

You'll use the StrConv function in the event procedure to perform the conversion. The **StrConv function** converts the letters in a string to all uppercase letters or to all lowercase letters, or converts the first letter of every word in the string to uppercase letters and all other letters to lowercase letters. The statement you'll use in the event procedure is: *EmployerName = StrConv(EmployerName, vbProperCase)*. The StrConv function's second argument, the **vbProperCase constant**, is a VBA constant that specifies the conversion of the first letter in every word in a string to uppercase letters and the conversion of all other letters to lowercase letters. A **VBA constant** is a predefined memory location that is initialized to a value that doesn't change. Other VBA constants you can use with the StrConv function are the **vbUpperCase constant**, which specifies the conversion of the string to all uppercase letters, and the **vbLowerCase constant**, which specifies the conversion of the string to all lowercase letters. Recall that the CapAll function you created earlier in this tutorial used the statement *CapAll = UCase(FValue)* to capitalize every character in a string. Instead, you could have used the statement *CapAll = StrConv(FValue, vbUpperCase)* to accomplish the same result.

Next, you'll create the AfterUpdate event procedure for the EmployerName field in the Employer form to perform the automatic conversion of entered and updated EmployerName field values.

### To add the event procedure for the EmployerName field's AfterUpdate event:

1. If you took a break after the previous session, make sure that Access is running, that the **Overseas** database in the Comp\Tutorial folder is open, that **Forms** is selected in the Objects bar of the Database window, and that the Employer form is open in Form view.

2. Switch to Design view.

3. Right-click the EmployerName text box to display the shortcut menu, and then click **Properties** to open the property sheet for the field.

4. If necessary, click the **Event** tab in the property sheet.

5. Click the right side of the **After Update** text box, click **[Event Procedure]**, and then click the **Build** button ⋯ to the right of the After Update text box. The Code window, which contains new Private Sub and End Sub statements, opens in the Visual Basic window. The Code window also contains all the other event procedures defined in the form's class module.

6. Press the **Tab** key, and then type the subroutine statements exactly as shown in Figure 11-22.

**Figure 11-22** ▶ Event procedure for the EmployerName control's AfterUpdate event

7. Click **Debug** on the menu bar, click **Compile Overseas**, save your class module changes, close the Visual Basic window, and then close the property sheet.

You can now test the event procedure. To do so, you'll view the Employer form in Form view and test the EmployerName field's event procedure by entering different EmployerName field values.

### To test the new event procedure:

1. Switch to Form view. Access displays record 1 for Beantown Tours.

2. Select **Beantown Tours** in the EmployerName text box, type **test employer name**, and then press the **Enter** key. Access executes the AfterUpdate event procedure for the EmployerName field and changes the EmployerName field value to "Test Employer Name".

3. Press the ↑ key to highlight the EmployerName field value.

4. Repeat Steps 2 and 3 two more times, entering **sECond test namE** (correctly changed to "Second Test Name"), and then entering **beantown tours** (correctly changed to "Beantown Tours").

5. Close the Employer form.

# Hiding and Changing Display Color

Elsa wants you to add a message to the Position form that will remind users when a position is full-time (40 or more scheduled hours per week). Access will display the message, in red, only when the position is full-time. Also, she wants you to display the value in the Wage text box in red for full-time positions and in black for all other positions. The red font will help to draw attention to those positions that are full-time. See Figure 11-23.

**Position form with the full-time message and Wage field value in red**    **Figure 11-23**

In the Position form, you will add a label to the right of the HoursPerWeek text box that will display the text "Full-Time" in red. Because Elsa wants the text to appear only when the HoursPerWeek field has a value greater than or equal to 40, you will change the label's Visible property during execution. You will also change the foreground color of the value in the Wage text box to red for full-time positions and to black for all other positions.

Because the change to the Visible property takes place during execution, you will add code to the Current event procedure in the Position form. To set a property in a Visual Basic statement, you enter the object name followed by the property name, separating the two with a period. For example, if the label name for the message is FullTimeMsg, then the statement [FullTimeMsg].Visible = False hides the label on the form.

First, you'll add a label to the Position form that will display a message in red for full-time positions. For all other positions, the label will be hidden.

## To add the label to the Position form:

1. Open the **Position** form in Design view.

2. Click (if necessary) the **Toolbox** button [icon] on the Form Design toolbar to open the toolbox, and then click the **Label** tool [icon] on the toolbox.

3. Position the pointer in the Detail section; when the center of the pointer's plus symbol is positioned in the row of grid dots to the right of the HoursPerWeek text box and aligned with its top edge, click the mouse button.

4. Type **Full-Time** and then press the **Enter** key. The new label box appears in the form along with the Error Checking Options button. See Figure 11-24.

| Figure 11-24 | Position of the label box |
|---|---|

5. Position the pointer on the **Error Checking Options** button ⟨⧫⟩. The message, "This is a new label and is not associated with a control," appears. Because the new label should not be associated with a control, you'll choose to ignore this error.

6. Click the list arrow for the **Error Checking Options** button ⟨⧫⟩, and then click **Ignore Error**.

You'll now set the label's Name and ForeColor properties, and add the Current event procedure to the Position form.

## To set the label's properties, and add the Current event procedure to the Position form:

1. Right-click the **Full-Time** label to display the shortcut menu, and then click **Properties** to open the property sheet.

2. Click the **All** tab (if necessary), select the value in the **Name** text box (if necessary), and then type **lblFullTimeMsg**. (*lbl* is a prefix tag to identify a label control.)

   You can now set the ForeColor property for the label so that the message is displayed in red.

3. Scroll the property sheet, click the **Fore Color** text box, and then click the **Build** button [...] to the right of the Fore Color text box. Access opens the Color dialog box.

4. Click the **red color** box (the first color box in the second row of the Basic Colors section), click the **OK** button, and then press the **Enter** key. Access sets the ForeColor property value to the code for red (255). Notice that Access changes the foreground (text) color of the Full-Time label to red.

   **Trouble?** If the property sheet blocks your view of the form, drag it to an open area of the screen.

   You'll now enter the event procedure for the form's OnCurrent event. This event procedure will be executed whenever the Position form is opened or the focus moves from one record to another record.

5. Click the form selector, scroll down the property sheet to the OnCurrent property, click the right side of the **On Current** text box, click **[Event Procedure]**, and then click the **Build** button [...]. Access opens the Code window in the Visual Basic window, displaying the Sub and End Sub statements.

**6.** Press the **Tab** key, and then type the Sub procedure statements exactly as shown in Figure 11-25.

**Current event procedure for the Position form** ◄ **Figure 11-25**

The form's Current procedure uses an If statement to determine whether the current value of the HoursPerWeek field is greater than or equal to 40. If the current value of the HoursPerWeek field is greater than or equal to 40, the procedure sets the lblFullTimeMsg control's Visible property to True (which means the Full-Time message will appear in the Position form), and it sets the Wage control's ForeColor property to 255 (red). If the current value of the HoursPerWeek field is less than 40, the procedure sets the lblFullTimeMsg control's Visible property to False, hiding the Full-Time message on the form, and sets the Wage control's ForeColor property to 0 (black).

**7.** Click **Debug** on the menu bar, and then click **Compile Overseas**. Access compiles all the modules in the Overseas database.

**8.** Save your class module changes, close the Visual Basic window, and then close the property sheet.

You'll now test the Position form's Current event procedure.

## To test the Current event procedure for the Position form:

**1.** Switch to Form view. Access displays the first record for PositionID 2004, which is not a full-time position. The message "Full-Time" does not appear, and the Wage field value appears in black.

**Trouble?** If Access displays a dialog box indicating a run-time error, Access could not execute the event procedure. Click the Debug button in the dialog box. Access displays the event procedure in the Code window and highlights the line containing the error. Check the statements carefully and make sure that they are exactly like those shown in Figure 11-25. Make the necessary changes, compile the module, save the module, and then close the Code window. Then repeat Step 1.

**2.** Click the **Next Record** navigation button ▶ twice to display the third record for PositionID 2010, which is a full-time position. The message "Full-Time" appears in red, as does the Wage field value of 13.00.

3. Click the **Next Record** navigation button ▶ several times to make sure that each full-time position's message and Wage field value appear in red, and that each part-time position's Wage field value appears in black and the "Full-Time" message does not appear.

4. Close the form to return to the Database window.

You have finished your work on the Current event procedure for the Position form. Next, you'll create the necessary procedures for the command buttons on the QueriesDialogBox form.

# Creating the Procedures for the QueriesDialogBox Form

Your last programming task is to complete the procedures for the QueriesDialogBox form. Elsa wants Access to highlight the first item in the list box when the QueriesDialogBox form first opens, by placing the focus on it. Next, when a user double-clicks a query name in the list box or highlights a query name and then clicks the Print Preview command button, that query should open in the Print Preview window. Finally, when a user selects a query name in the list box and then clicks the Datasheet command button, the selected query should open in Datasheet view. You'll create the three procedures for the QueriesDialogBox form to perform these processes. Figure 11-26 shows the names for the three procedures.

| Figure 11-26 | QueriesDialogBox form's procedures |

## Coding the Load Event Procedure for the QueriesDialogBox Form

When a user opens the QueriesDialogBox form, Elsa wants Access to place the focus on the first query in the list box automatically. To accomplish this objective, you need to add VBA statements to the form's Load event. Figure 11-27 shows the code for the form's Load event.

**Load event procedure for the QueriesDialogBox form** ◄ Figure 11-27

new Load event procedure

```
Private Sub Form_Load()
    'Move the focus to the list box and then to the first query in the list box.
    lstQueryList.SetFocus
    SendKeys "{Down}"
End Sub
```

The **Load event** occurs when Access opens a form. Anything you specify for this event will happen each time the form is opened. The statement *[lstQueryList].SetFocus* moves the focus to lstQueryList, which is the name for the form's list box, but does not set the focus to any specific query name. The *SendKeys "{Down}"* statement sends the down arrow keystroke to the list box; Access responds to this statement by highlighting the first query in the list box. The end result of these statements is that when the user opens the dialog box, the first query is highlighted and has the focus.

You'll open the QueriesDialogBox form in Design view and create the Load event procedure.

### To create the Load event procedure for the QueriesDialogBox form:

1. Open the **QueriesDialogBox** form in Design view.

2. Right-click the form selector to display the shortcut menu, and then click **Properties** to open the form's property sheet.

3. Click the **Event** tab (if necessary), scroll the property sheet (if necessary), click the right side of the **On Load** text box, click **[Event Procedure]**, and then click the **Build** button ⌶. Access opens the Code window in the Visual Basic window, displaying the Sub and End Sub statements for the Load event procedure.

4. Press the **Tab** key, and then type the Sub procedure statements as shown in Figure 11-28.

**Load event procedure entered in the Code window** ◄ Figure 11-28

completed Load event procedure

```
Private Sub Form_Load()
    'Move the focus to the list box and then to the first query in the list box.
    lstQueryList.SetFocus
    SendKeys "{Down}"
End Sub
```

type these three statements

The word "Private" in the first line of the subroutine definition indicates that the procedure can be used only in the class module for this form. Form_Load indicates that this subroutine is the event procedure for the form's Load event. Make sure you type curly braces in the SendKeys statement.

5. Click **Debug** on the menu bar, click **Compile Overseas**, and then save your module changes.

> **6.** Close the Visual Basic window, and then close the property sheet.
>
> Next, you'll test the procedure by opening the QueriesDialogBox form in Form view and verifying that the first query in the list box is selected.
>
> **7.** Switch to Form view. Notice that the first query in the list box is selected.
>
> **Trouble?** If the first query in the list box is not highlighted, you probably did not type the curly braces { } in the SendKeys statement. Switch to Design view, and then open the form's property sheet. Click the On Load text box, click the Build button [ ··· ], and then correct the event procedure. Then repeat Steps 5 through 7.
>
> **8.** Close the form.

You have finished your work with the Load event procedure for the QueriesDialogBox form. Next, you need to create the form's PreviewQuery and DisplayQuery procedures.

## Coding the PreviewQuery and DisplayQuery Procedures for the QueriesDialogBox Form

In the QueriesDialogBox form, double-clicking a query name in the list box or selecting a query name and then clicking the Print Preview command button must open that query in the Print Preview window. Selecting a query name in the list box and then clicking the Datasheet command button must open that query in Datasheet view. Figure 11-29 shows the code you'll enter in procedures to perform these actions.

| Figure 11-29 | **PreviewQuery and DisplayQuery functions for the form** |

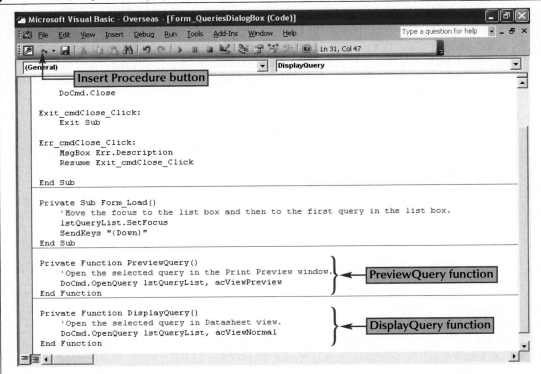

The DoCmd statements in these two procedures run the OpenQuery action. The parameter choices for the OpenQuery action are the selected query in the lstQueryList list box and the view you'll use when opening the selected query. The query view choices are selected from these VBA constants: acViewPreview to open the Print Preview window, acViewDesign to open the query in Design view, and acViewNormal to open the query in Datasheet view. Because the VBA constants (acViewPreview, acViewDesign, and acViewNormal) are standard features of Access, you do not have to define them in a Dim statement as you do for variables you create.

Next, you'll open the QueriesDialogBox form in Design view, create the two functions, and attach the functions to the appropriate control properties.

## To add the two functions to the QueriesDialogBox form:

1. Open the **QueriesDialogBox** form in Design view, and then click the **Code** button 🖾 on the Form Design toolbar to open the Code window for the form's class module in the Visual Basic window. (Note that you could also press the F7 key to open the Code window.)

2. Click the list arrow for the **Insert Module** button 🟫 on the Standard toolbar, and then click **Procedure**. The Add Procedure dialog box opens.

3. Type **PreviewQuery** in the Name text box, click the **Function** option button, click the **Private** option button, and then click the **OK** button. Access displays the Function and End Function statements for the new PreviewQuery procedure.

4. Press the **Tab** key, and then type the statements for the PreviewQuery function exactly as shown in Figure 11-30.

PreviewQuery function for the QueriesDialogBox form ◄ **Figure 11-30**

completed PreviewQuery function

```
Private Function PreviewQuery()
    'Open the selected query in the Print Preview window.
    DoCmd.OpenQuery lstQueryList, acViewPreview
End Function
```
← type these statements

Now you'll enter the second function, DisplayQuery, for opening the selected query in Datasheet view.

5. Click the **Insert Procedure** button 🔧 on the Standard toolbar, type **DisplayQuery** in the Name text box, click the **Function** option button, click the **Private** option button, and then click the **OK** button.

6. Press the **Tab** key, and then type the statements for the DisplayQuery function exactly as shown in Figure 11-31.

DisplayQuery function for the QueriesDialogBox form ◄ **Figure 11-31**

completed DisplayQuery function

```
Private Function DisplayQuery()
    'Open the selected query in Datasheet view.
    DoCmd.OpenQuery lstQueryList, acViewNormal
End Function
```
← type these statements

7. Click **Debug** on the menu bar, click **Compile Overseas**, and then save your module changes.

8. Close the Visual Basic window.

Next, you'll attach the appropriate procedure to the correct properties for the form objects.

### To specify the functions for the event properties:

1. Right-click the form's list box (the box containing the word "Unbound") to display the shortcut menu, and then click **Properties** to open the property sheet.

2. Make sure the **Event** tab is selected, scroll the property sheet as necessary, click the **On Dbl Click** text box, and then type **=PreviewQuery()**. This entry specifies that Access will execute the procedure for previewing a query whenever a user double-clicks a query name in the list box. See Figure 11-32.

| Figure 11-32 | Setting the list box's OnDblClick property |
| --- | --- |

OnDblClick property value

3. Click the form's **Print Preview** command button (the leftmost command button), click the property sheet's **On Click** text box, and then type **=PreviewQuery()**. This entry specifies that Access will execute the procedure for previewing a query whenever a user selects a query name and then clicks the Print Preview command button.

4. Click the form's **Datasheet** command button (the middle command button), click the property sheet's **On Click** text box, and then type **=DisplayQuery()**. This entry specifies that Access will execute the procedure for opening the query datasheet whenever a user selects a query name and then clicks the Datasheet command button.

5. Close the property sheet, and then save your form changes.

You'll now test the changes you made to the QueriesDialogBox form.

### To test the changes to the QueriesDialogBox form:

1. Switch to Form view.

2. Double-click a few of the query names, in turn, in the list box to verify that the correct query opens in Print Preview. Click the **Close** button ⊠ on the Print Preview window each time to return to the dialog box in Form view.

3. Click a query name in the list box, and then click the **Print Preview** command button to verify that the correct query opens in the Print Preview window. Click the **Close** button ⊠ on the Print Preview window to return to the dialog box in Form view.

4. Repeat Step 3 for several more query names in the form's list box.

5. Click a query name in the list box, and then click the **Datasheet** command button to verify that the correct query datasheet opens. Click the **Close** button ⊠ on the Query Datasheet window to return to the dialog box in Form view.

▸ **6.** Repeat Step 5 for several more query names in the form's list box.

▸ **7.** Click the **Close** command button on the dialog box to close it and return to the Database window.

▸ **8.** Exit Access.

Elsa stops by and views your results. She is very pleased with the modifications to the Employer, Position, and QueriesDialogBox forms. Next, she wants you to make access to the Overseas database more secure, and she wants you to make the final enhancements to the database and the user interface. In the next tutorial, you'll complete your work with the Overseas database.

## Session 11.3 Quick Check

**Review**

1. What is a VBA constant?
2. You can use the UCase function or the _____ function to convert a string to all uppercase letters.
3. What does the Visible property determine?
4. What does the ForeColor property determine?
5. When does the Current event occur?
6. When does the Load event occur for an object?

## Tutorial Summary

**Review**

In this tutorial, you worked with Visual Basic for Applications, the programming language for Microsoft Office programs. You executed, viewed, and modified an existing event procedure. You then created a new function to convert all characters in a field value to uppercase letters, tested it in the Immediate window, added an event procedure to a form to use the function, and then tested the event procedure after compiling the modules in the database. Next, you created three event procedures: one to validate a field value based on another field's value, a second to convert a field value to proper uppercase and lowercase letters, and a third to show/hide a control and to change font colors based on a condition. Finally, you completed the QueriesDialogBox form by adding one event procedure and two functions to coordinate a list box selection with two command buttons.

## Key Terms

| | | |
|---|---|---|
| AfterUpdate event | compile | event property |
| argument | control structure | event-driven language |
| assignment statement | Current event | false-statement group |
| BeforeUpdate event | debugging | ForeColor property |
| calls | Declarations section | function |
| CancelEvent action | Dim statement | Function procedure |
| Case control structure | DoCmd statement | Function statement |
| class module | End Function statement | If statement |
| Code window | End Sub statement | Immediate window |
| coding | event | IsNull function |
| compilation | event procedure | Left function |

Load event
local procedure
logic error
Me keyword
method
module
object-oriented language
OnCurrent property
Option Compare statement
parameter
private procedure
procedure
public procedure
RGB function

scope
SetFocus
standard module
statement
StrConv function
string
Sub procedure
Sub statement
subroutine
syntax
true-statement group
UCase function
Undo

Val function
variable
VBA constant
vbLowerCase constant
vbProperCase constant
vbUpperCase constant
Visible property
Visual Basic
Visual Basic Editor (VBE, editor)
Visual Basic for Applications (VBA)
Visual Basic window

## Practice

*Take time to practice the skills you learned in the tutorial using the same case scenario.*

# Review Assignments

**Data File needed for the Review Assignments: Work.mdb (*cont. from Tutorial 10*)**

Elsa asks you to continue your work with the user interface for the **Work** database. To help with this request, complete the following steps:

1. Open the **Work** database in the Comp\Review folder provided with your Data Files.
2. Create a procedure for the **StudentInfo** form to convert Nation field values to proper case—capitalize the first letter of each word, and convert all other letters to lowercase. Test the procedure, and then close the form.
3. Create a procedure to verify Salary field values in the **Recruiter** form by doing the following:
   a. For a BonusQuota field value of 40, the Salary field value must be less than or equal to $30,000. If the Salary field value is invalid, display an appropriate message, cancel the event, undo the change, and move the focus to the Salary field.
   b. For a BonusQuota field value of 60, the Salary field value must be greater than $40,000. If the Salary field value is invalid, display an appropriate message, cancel the event, undo the change, and move the focus to the Salary field.
   c. Test the procedure, and then save the form.
4. Create a procedure for the **Recruiter** form to do the following:
   a. Display the Salary field value in red when the value is greater than $35,000 and in black for other values.
   b. Display the message "High Salary" to the right of the Salary text box in bold, red text. Display the message only when the Salary field value is greater than $35,000.
   c. Test the procedure, and then save and close the form.
5. Complete the **ReportsDialogBox** form by doing the following:
   a. Create a Load event procedure that moves the focus to the first report name in the list box when the **ReportsDialogBox** form opens.
   b. Create a PreviewReport function to open a report in the Print Preview window.
   c. Attach the PreviewReport function to the OnDblClick property for the **ReportsDialogBox** form list box.

    d. Attach the PreviewReport function to the OnClick property for the Print Preview command button on the **ReportsDialogBox** form.

    e. Switch to Form view, and then test all the form options. Save and close the form.

6. Print all the procedures you created by doing the following:

    a. Start Word.

    b. In turn, open each form you changed in Design view, click the Code button on the Form Design toolbar, copy the procedure(s) you created, paste the procedure(s) in the Word document, close the Visual Basic window, and then close the form.

    c. After pasting all the procedures in the Word document, type your name in the document footer, save the document as Tutorial 11 Review Assignments in the Comp\Review folder, print the document, and then exit Word.

7. Exit Access.

# Case Problem 1

**Data File needed for this Case Problem: Shoots.mdb (*cont. from Tutorial 10*)**

*Lim's Video Photography*   Youngho Lim asks you to continue your work with the user interface for the Shoots database. To help Youngho with his request, complete the following steps:

1. Open the **Shoots** database in the Comp\Case1 folder provided with your Data Files.

2. Create a procedure for the **ClientInfo** form to convert City field values to proper case—capitalize the first letter of each word, and convert all other letters to lowercase. Test the procedure.

3. Create a procedure for the **ClientInfo** form to do the following:

    a. Display the City field value in normal, black text when the value is "San Francisco" and in bold, red text for all other cities. (*Hint*: Use the FontBold property, and make sure you enclose San Francisco in quotation marks in your VBA code.)

    b. Display the message "Not local" to the right of the City text box in bold, red text. Display the message only when the City field value is not "San Francisco".

    c. Test the procedure, and then save your form changes.

4. Print all the procedures you created by doing the following:

    a. Start Word.

    b. Make sure the **ClientInfo** form is open in Design view, click the Code button on the Form Design toolbar, copy the procedures you created, paste the procedures in the Word document, close the Visual Basic window, and then close the form.

    c. Type your name in the Word document footer, save the document as Tutorial 11 Case 1 in the Comp\Case1 folder, print the document, and then exit Word.

5. Exit Access.

---

**Apply**

*Use the skills you learned in the tutorial to work with the data contained in a video photography database.*

**Explore**

# Case Problem 2

**Data File needed for this Case Problem: AtHome.mdb (*cont. from Tutorial 10*)**

***DineAtHome.course.com*** Claire Picard asks you to continue your work with the user interface for the AtHome database. To help Claire with her request, complete the following steps:

1. Open the **AtHome** database in the Comp\Case2 folder provided with your Data Files.
2. Create a procedure for the **RestaurantInfo** form to convert City field values to proper case—capitalize the first letter of each word, and convert all other letters to lowercase. Test the procedure.
3. Create a procedure to verify DeliveryCharge field values in the **RestaurantInfo** form by doing the following:
    a. For a DeliveryCharge field value of $0.00, the MaxDistance field value must equal 0. If the DeliveryCharge field value is invalid, display an appropriate message, cancel the event, undo the change, and move the focus to the DeliveryCharge field.
    b. No special steps are taken for other DeliveryCharge field values.
    c. Test the procedure.

4. Create a procedure for the **RestaurantInfo** form to do the following:
    a. Display the message "No Delivery" to the right of the TakeoutOnly check box in bold, magenta text only when the TakeoutOnly check box is True. Otherwise, display the message "Delivers" in bold, blue text. (*Hint*: Use the Caption property in your VBA code, and make sure you enclose Caption property settings in quotation marks.)
    b. Test the modified form, and then save your form changes.
5. Print all the procedures you created by doing the following:
    a. Start Word.
    b. Make sure the **RestaurantInfo** form is open in Design view, click the Code button on the Form Design toolbar, copy the procedures you created, paste the procedures in the Word document, close the Visual Basic window, and then close the form.
    c. Type your name in the Word document footer, save the document as Tutorial 11 Case 2 in the Comp\Case2 folder, print the document, and then exit Word.
6. Exit Access.

# Case Problem 3

**Data File needed for this Case Problem: ZooFunds.mdb (*cont. from Tutorial 10*)**

***Redwood Zoo*** Michael Rosenfeld asks you to continue your work with the user interface for the ZooFunds database. To help Michael with his request, complete the following steps:

1. Open the **ZooFunds** database in the Comp\Case3 folder provided with your Data Files.
2. Create a procedure for the **Funds** form to convert all FundName field values to proper case—capitalize the first letter of each word, and convert all other letters to lowercase. Test the procedure, and then close the form.

3. Create a procedure for the **Pledges** form to do the following:

   a. Display the TotalPledged field value in bold, black text when the value is greater than 500 and in normal black text otherwise. (*Hint*: Use the FontBold property.)

   b. Display the message "Large Pledges" to the right of the TotalPledged text box in bold, black text. Display the message only when the TotalPledged field value is greater than 500.

   c. Resize and test the modified form, save the form in Form view, and then close the form.

4. Complete the **QueriesDialogBox** form by doing the following:

   a. Create a Load event procedure that moves the focus to the first query name in the list box when the **QueriesDialogBox** form opens.

   b. Create a DisplayQuery function to open the selected query in the list box in Datasheet view.

   c. Attach the DisplayQuery function to the OnDblClick property for the **QueriesDialogBox** form list box.

   d. Attach the DisplayQuery function to the OnClick property for the Datasheet command button on the **QueriesDialogBox** form.

   e. Switch to Form view, and then test all the form options. Save and close the form.

5. Print all the procedures you created by doing the following:

   a. Start Word.

   b. In turn, open each form you changed in Design view, click the Code button on the Form Design toolbar, copy the procedure(s) you created, paste the procedure(s) in the Word document, close the Visual Basic window, and then close the form.

   c. After pasting all the procedures in the Word document, type your name in the document footer, save the document as Tutorial 11 Case 3 in the Comp\Case3 folder, print the document, and then exit Word.

6. Exit Access.

# Case Problem 4

**Data File needed for this Case Problem: Rivers.mdb (*cont. from Tutorial 10*)**

***Mountain River Adventures***  Connor and Siobhan Dempsey ask you to continue your work with the user interface for the Rivers database. To help them with their request, complete the following steps:

1. Open the **Rivers** database in the Comp\Case4 folder provided with your Data Files.

2. Create a procedure for the **Client** form to convert Country field values to uppercase. Test the procedure.

3. You'll draw special attention to your client information and booked trips. Add the message "Trips of a Lifetime!" to the **Client** form. Display the message in 14-point, bold, orange text and position it in the upper-right corner of the Client Information tab on the tab control. Display the message only when the ClientName field value equals your name. (*Hint*: Make sure you enclose your name in quotation marks in your VBA code.) Save your form changes, switch to Form view, print your form record, and then close the form.

4. Complete the **ReportsDialogBox** form by doing the following:
   a. Create a Load event procedure that moves the focus to the first report name in the list box when the **ReportsDialogBox** form opens.
   b. Create a PreviewReport function to open a report in the Print Preview window.
   c. Attach the PreviewReport function to the OnDblClick property for the **ReportsDialogBox** form list box.
   d. Attach the PreviewReport function to the OnClick property for the Print Preview command button on the **ReportsDialogBox** form.
   e. Switch to Form view, and then test all the form options. Save and close the form.
5. Complete the **QueriesDialogBox** form by doing the following:
   a. Create a Load event procedure that moves the focus to the first query name in the list box when the **QueriesDialogBox** form opens.
   b. Create a DisplayQuery function to open a query in Datasheet view.
   c. Attach the DisplayQuery function to the OnDblClick property for the **QueriesDialogBox** form list box.
   d. Attach the DisplayQuery function to the OnClick property for the Datasheet command button on the **QueriesDialogBox** form.
   e. Switch to Form view, and then test all the form options. Save and close the form.
6. Print all the procedures you created by doing the following:
   a. Start Word.
   b. In turn, open each form you changed in Design view, click the Code button on the Form Design toolbar, copy the procedure(s) you created, paste the procedure(s) in the Word document, close the Visual Basic window, and then close the form.
   c. After pasting all the procedures in the Word document, type your name in the document footer, save the document as Tutorial 11 Case 4 in the Comp\Case4 folder, print the document, and then exit Word.
7. Exit Access.

**Challenge**

*Work with the skills you've learned, and explore some new skills, to create additional objects for a database for an Internet auction site.*

# Case Problem 5

**Data File needed for this Case Problem: BuySell.mdb (*cont. from Tutorial 10*)**

*eACH Internet Auction Site* Chris and Pat Aquino ask you to continue your work with the user interface for the BuySell database. To help them with their request, complete the following steps:

1. Open the **BuySell** database in the Comp\Case5 folder provided with your Data Files.
2. Modify the **Item** form by doing the following:
   a. Display the ReservePrice field value in bold, blue text when the value is greater than 1000 and in normal, black text for all other values. (*Hint*: Use the FontBold property.)
   b. Display the message "Very High Reserve" to the right of the ReservePrice text box in bold, blue text. Display the message only when the ReservePrice field value is greater than 1000.
   c. Test the modified form, and then save your form changes.

3. Modify the **Item** form by doing the following:
   a. To the right of the MinimumBid text box add a calculated field that calculates the difference between the ReservePrice and MinimumBid field values. Use a label caption of "Under Reserve Amount," and display both the label and calculated field value in bold, blue text.
   b. Perform the calculation and display the label and calculated field value only when the ReservePrice field value is not null.
   c. Test the modified form, and then save your form changes.
4. Print all the procedures you created by doing the following:
   a. Start Word.
   b. Make sure the **Item** form is open in Design view, click the Code button on the Form Design toolbar, copy the procedures you created, paste the procedures in the Word document, close the Visual Basic window, and then close the form.
   c. After pasting all the procedures in the Word document, type your name in the document footer, save the document as Tutorial 11 Case 5, print the document, and then exit Word.
5. Use the Combo Box Wizard to add a combo box to the Registrant form that lets you select from a list of registrant last and first names. Change the label to "Find Registrant by Name". Position the label and list box control to the right of the RegistrantID text box, resize the label to its best fit, and then resize the list box control's width so that all registrants' full names are visible. Sort the list box entries in ascending order by LastName field values, and then in ascending order by FirstName field values. Resize the form, and make sure the form does not auto resize. Find the record for your name, print the selected form record, and then save and close the form.
6. Exit Access.

# Internet Assignments

The purpose of the Internet Assignments is to challenge you to find information on the Internet that you can use to work effectively with this software. The actual assignments are updated and maintained on the Course Technology Web site. Log on to the Internet and use your Web browser to go to the Student Online Companion for New Perspectives Office 2003 at **www.course.com/np/office2003**. Click the Internet Assignments link, and then navigate to the assignments for this tutorial.

## SAM Assessment and Training

If you have a SAM user profile, you may have access to hands-on instruction, practice, and assessment of the skills covered in this tutorial. Log in to your SAM account and go to your assignments page to see what your instructor has assigned.

# Quick Check Answers

## Session 11.1

1. Visual Basic for Applications statements respond to events that occur with the objects in a database.
2. a procedure that runs when a specific event occurs
3. A Function procedure performs operations, returns a value, accepts input values, and can be used in expressions. A Sub procedure performs operations and can accept input values, but does not return a value and cannot be used in expressions.
4. A standard module is a database object that is stored in memory with other database objects when you open a database. A class module is associated with a specific database object, such as a form or report.
5. scope
6. You use the Immediate window to test VBA procedures when you are coding them, without changing any data in the database.

## Session 11.2

1. If
2. Access checks the modules in your database for syntax errors. If no syntax errors are found, Access translates the VBA code into a form that your computer understands.
3. A Dim statement is used to declare variables and their types.
4. Val
5. executes an action in a procedure
6. an action that operates on specific objects or controls

## Session 11.3

1. a predefined memory location that is initialized to a value that doesn't change
2. StrConv
3. whether Access displays a control
4. a control's foreground, or text, color
5. when the object opens and every time the focus moves to another record
6. when the object opens

## Objectives

**Session 12.1**
- Analyze a database's performance
- Link a database to a table in another database
- Use the Linked Table Manager
- Use replication to create a Design Master and replica of a database
- Synchronize the Design Master and replica databases

**Session 12.2**
- Split a database
- Set database startup options
- Encrypt and decrypt a database
- Set and unset a database password
- Use the User-Level Security Wizard to assign users, groups, and permissions to a database
- Create an MDE file

# Managing and Securing a Database

*Managing and Securing the Overseas Database*

## Case

## Northeast Seasonal Jobs International (NSJI)

Elsa Jensen has planned training sessions for NSJI staff members to learn how to use the Overseas database. These training sessions are scheduled to begin right after you finalize the Overseas database. Your remaining work will address Elsa's concerns about database management, database security, and the database's overall performance.

You will use Access analysis features, such as the Performance Analyzer, to analyze the Overseas database. You'll use the Linked Table Manager and the Database Splitter, create an MDE file, and set the startup options to protect the database design from user modification and to open the Switchboard form automatically when a user opens the Overseas database.

Elsa is leaving on a business trip to meet with potential employers. During her trip, she wants to have access to the Overseas database so that she can record information about new employers immediately if any potential employers decide to offer positions through NSJI. You'll create a replica of the Overseas database for Elsa to use on her trip.

Finally, you'll implement Access security features, such as passwords, encryption, and permissions, to protect the database from unauthorized use.

## Student Data Files

▼ **Comp**

▽ **Tutorial folder**
  Overseas.mdb (*cont.*)
  Schools.mdb

▽ **Review folder**
  Work.mdb (*cont.*)

▽ **Case1 folder**
  Payments.mdb
  Shoots.mdb (*cont.*)

▽ **Case2 folder**
  AtHome.mdb (*cont.*)
  Choices.mdb

▽ **Case3 folder**
  Donation.mdb
  ZooFunds.mdb (*cont.*)

▽ **Case4 folder**
  Rivers.mdb (*cont.*)

▽ **Case5 folder**
  BuySell.mdb (*cont.*)

# Session 12.1

## Analyzing Database Performance with the Performance Analyzer

Elsa wants the Overseas database to respond as quickly as possible to user requests, such as running queries and opening reports. You'll use the Performance Analyzer to check the performance of the Overseas database. The **Performance Analyzer** is an Access tool that you can use to optimize the performance of an Access database. You select the database objects you want to analyze for performance and run the Performance Analyzer, and then the Performance Analyzer lists three types of analysis results: recommendation, suggestion, and idea. Access can complete the recommendation and suggestion optimizations for you, but you must implement the idea optimizations. Analysis results include changes such as those related to the storage of fields and the creation of indexes and relationships.

| Reference Window | **Using the Performance Analyzer** |
| --- | --- |

- Start Access and open the database you want to analyze.
- Click Tools on the menu bar, point to Analyze, and then click Performance.
- Select the object(s) you want to analyze, and then click the OK button.
- Select the analysis result(s) you want the Performance Analyzer to complete for you, and then click the Optimize button.
- Click the Close button.

You'll use the Performance Analyzer to optimize the performance of the Overseas database.

### To use the Performance Analyzer to optimize the performance of the Overseas database:

▶ 1. Start Access, and then open the **Overseas** database located in the Comp\Tutorial folder provided with your Data Files.

**Trouble?** If a dialog box opens with a message about installing the Microsoft Jet Service Pack, see your instructor or technical support person for assistance. You must have the appropriate Service Pack installed in order to open and work with Access databases safely.

**Trouble?** If a dialog box opens, warning you that the Overseas database may not be safe, click the Open button. Your security level is set to Medium, which is the security setting that lets you choose whether or not to open a database that contains macros, VBA, or certain types of queries. The Overseas database does not contain objects that will harm your computer, so you can safely open the database.

**Trouble?** If a dialog box opens, warning you that Access can't open the Overseas database due to security restrictions, click the OK button, click Tools on the menu bar, point to Macro, click Security, click the Medium option button, click the OK button, restart your computer if you're requested to do so, and then repeat Step 1. Your security level was set to High, which is the security setting that lets you open a database that contains macros, VBA, or certain types of queries only from trusted sources. Because the Overseas database does not contain objects that will harm your computer, you need to change the security setting to Medium and then safely open the Overseas database.

**2.** Click **Forms** in the Objects bar of the Database window (if necessary), click **Tools** on the menu bar, point to **Analyze**, and then click **Performance**. The Performance Analyzer dialog box opens. See Figure 12-1.

Performance Analyzer dialog box | Figure 12-1

**Trouble?** If a dialog box opens and asks if you would like to install this feature, insert your Microsoft Office 2003 CD in the correct drive, and then click the Yes button. If you do not have the Office 2003 CD, see your instructor or technical support person for assistance.

Elsa wants you to analyze every object in the Overseas database.

**3.** Click the **All Object Types** tab, and then click the **Select All** button. All objects in the Overseas database appear in the list box, and all of them are now selected.

**4.** Click the **OK** button. The Performance Analyzer analyzes all the objects in the Overseas database and, after a few moments, displays its analysis results. See Figure 12-2.

Performance Analyzer analysis results | Figure 12-2

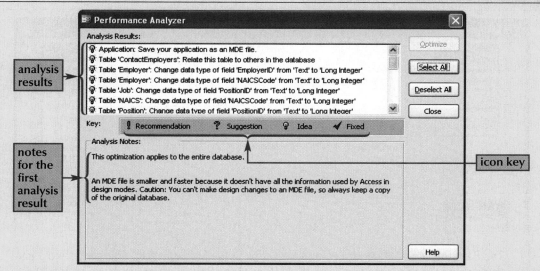

Most of the analysis results are in the idea category, which means that you have to implement them yourself. For example, the first analysis result ("Application: Save your application as an MDE file.") produces a smaller and faster database; you'll learn how to create an MDE file later in this tutorial. You should consider all idea analysis results later, but more important now are the recommendation and suggestion analysis results, which the Performance Analyzer can complete for you automatically.

▶ **5.** Click several of the entries in the Analysis Results list box, and read each entry and its analysis notes.

The Performance Analyzer can perform the one suggestion analysis result (relate the Student table to itself) for you automatically. You'll let the Performance Analyzer create a relationship between the Student table and itself because the table has a one-to-many relationship based on the StudentID field as the primary key and the Contact field as the foreign key. In Tutorial 8, you added the Contact field to the Student table and created a self-join query based on the Student query, but you did not add the one-to-many relationship in the Relationships window.

▶ **6.** Scroll the Analysis Results list box as necessary, click the **Table 'Student': Relate to table 'Student'** analysis result (its icon is a green question mark) to select it, and then click the **Optimize** button. Access creates a relationship between the Student table and itself, and the icon for the selected analysis result changes to a blue check mark to indicate a "Fixed" status.

▶ **7.** Click the **Close** button to close the dialog box and return to the Database window.

Next, you'll open the Relationships window to view the new relationship created by the Performance Analyzer.

### To view the relationship created by the Performance Analyzer:

▶ **1.** Click the **Relationships** button ⊞ on the Database toolbar to open the Relationships window, and then use the pointer to drag the bottom borders of the two Student field lists down until you can see all the fields in both lists. See Figure 12-3.

| Figure 12-3 | **Student table one-to-many relationship** |
|---|---|

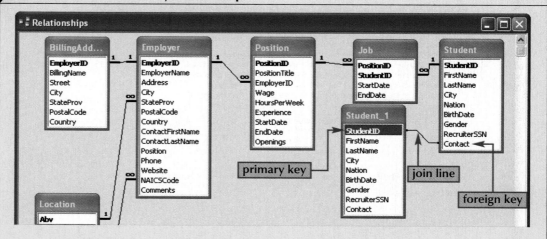

The Performance Analyzer added a second copy of the Student table (Student_1) and a join line between the Student and Student_1 tables to the Relationships window. The join line connects the primary table (Student_1) to the related table (Student) using the StudentID field as the primary key and the Contact field as the foreign key. You'll use the Edit Relationships dialog box to view the join properties for the relationship.

▶ **2.** Right-click the join line between the Student_1 and Student tables, and then click **Edit Relationship** on the shortcut menu to open the Edit Relationships dialog box. See Figure 12-4.

**Edit Relationships dialog box for the new relationship** ◀ **Figure 12-4**

The referential integrity options are not selected, so you'll select them now for the new one-to-many relationship.

▶ **3.** Click the **Enforce Referential Integrity** check box, click the **Cascade Update Related Fields** check box, and then click the **OK** button to close the dialog box.

Because you selected the referential integrity option, the "one" side of the relationship has the digit 1 at its end, the "many" side of the relationship has the infinity symbol at its end, and the join line is now thicker.

▶ **4.** Save your relationship changes, and then close the Relationships window.

Matt has the responsibility at NSJI for maintaining a separate database named Schools in which he stores information about overseas colleges and universities that NSJI recruiters visit to interview seasonal student workers. Elsa wants to retrieve the data in the School table in the Schools database from within the Overseas database. To provide Elsa with access to this table, you'll create a link to the School table in the Overseas database.

# Linking Tables and Using the Linked Table Manager

You'll provide Elsa and other users of the Overseas database with access to the School table by using a linked table in the Overseas database. A **linked table** is a table that is stored in a file outside the open database and that can be updated from the open database. You can retrieve and update (add, change, and delete) records in a linked table, but you can't change its structure. From the Overseas database, you'll be able to update the School table as a linked table, but you won't be able to change its structure. However, from the Schools database, Matt will be able to update the School table *and* change its structure. You can link a database to data stored in Excel worksheets, HTML documents, text files, other Access databases, and databases created by other DBMSs, such as SQL Server, Paradox, and dBASE. Although Access works faster with its own tables than it does with linked tables, you must use linked tables when you need access to data maintained in another Access database or by other programs.

Reference Window

## Linking to a Table in Another Access Database

- Click File on the menu bar, point to Get External Data, and then click Link Tables.
- Select the folder, file type, and file containing the linked data, and then click the Link button.
- Select the table(s) in the Tables list box, and then click the OK button.

You'll link to the School table in the Schools database from the Overseas database.

### To link to the School table in the Schools database:

1. Click **File** on the menu bar, point to **Get External Data**, and then click **Link Tables**. The Link dialog box opens.

2. In the Look in list box, make sure the **Tutorial** folder is selected, click **Schools** in the file list, and then click the **Link** button. Access opens the Link Tables dialog box. See Figure 12-5.

**Figure 12-5**  Link Tables dialog box

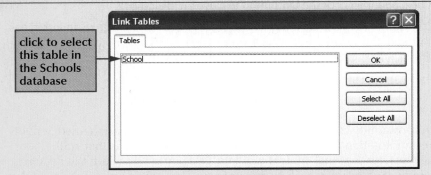

click to select this table in the Schools database

3. Click **School** in the Tables list box, and then click the **OK** button. The Link Tables dialog box closes, and you return to the Database window. A small blue arrow appears to the left of the School table icon in the Database window to identify the School table as a linked table.

Matt informs Elsa that he'll be reorganizing the NSJI network folders and might move the Schools database to a different folder. Elsa asks if moving the Schools database would cause a problem for the linked School table. You'll use the Linked Table Manager to show Elsa how to handle this situation. The **Linked Table Manager** is an Access tool you use to change the filename or disk location for linked tables in an Access database. When you use Access to link to data in another file, Access stores the file's location (drive, folder, and filename) in the database and uses the stored location to connect to the linked data. If you change the file's location, you can use the Linked Table Manager to change the stored file location, or **refresh the link**, in the Access database.

Reference Window

## Using the Linked Table Manager

- Click Tools on the menu bar, point to Database Utilities, and then click Linked Table Manager.
- Select the linked table(s), and then click the OK button.
- Select the linked table location, click the filename, and then click the Open button.
- Click the OK button, and then close the Linked Table Manager dialog box.

Next, you'll move the Schools database to a different folder, and then you'll use the Linked Table Manager to refresh the link to the School table in the Overseas database.

### To move the Schools database and refresh the link to the School table:

▶ **1.** Use Windows Explorer or My Computer to move the **Schools** database from the Tutorial folder to the root folder on the drive where you are storing your Data Files.

▶ **2.** In Access, click **Tools** on the menu bar, point to **Database Utilities**, and then click **Linked Table Manager**. The Linked Table Manager dialog box opens. See Figure 12-6.

Linked Table Manager dialog box ◀ **Figure 12-6**

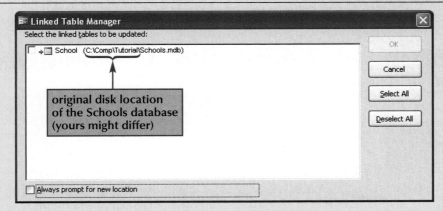

The School table is the only linked table, so it's the only table listed in the list box. The Comp\Tutorial folder provided with your Data Files, which is the original disk location of the Schools database, is listed as the current disk location for the School table.

▶ **3.** Click the **Select All** button, and then click the **OK** button. The Select New Location of School dialog box opens.

▶ **4.** Use the **Look in** list arrow to select the root folder on the drive where you are storing your Data Files, click **Schools** in the file list, and then click the **Open** button. A dialog box informs you that all selected linked tables were successfully refreshed.

▶ **5.** Click the **OK** button to close the dialog box. The Linked Table Manager dialog box now displays the root folder as the current disk location of the linked School table.

▶ **6.** Close the Linked Table Manager dialog box.

Next, you'll open the School table to show Elsa how she can update it as a linked table from the new disk location.

### To update the School table and change its design in the Overseas database:

▶ **1.** Open the **School** table in Datasheet view. The School table datasheet displays four fields and 39 records.

First, you'll add a new record to the School table.

▶ **2.** Click the **New Record** navigation button ▶✱, type **40** in the School ID column's text box, press the **Tab** key, type **Universidad de Colima** in the School Name column's text box, press the **Tab** key, type **Colima** in the City column's text box, press the **Tab** key, and then type **Mexico** in the Country column's text box.

Next, you'll switch to Design view to show Elsa that she can't change the design of the School table from the Overseas database.

▶ **3.** Switch to Design view. A message box informs you that the School table is a linked table and has some properties that you cannot modify.

▶ **4.** Click the **Yes** button to close the message box and switch to Design view. The SchoolID field is the current field, and the Help message in the Field Properties pane appears in red and indicates that you can't change the FieldName property for linked tables. See Figure 12-7.

---

**Figure 12-7** ▶ **Linked table in Design view**

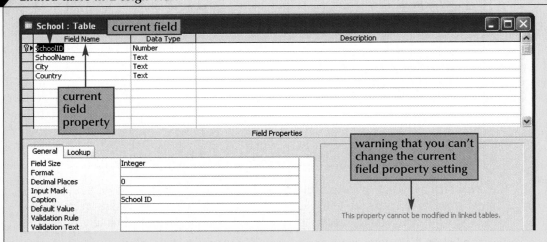

▶ **5.** Press the **F6** key to highlight the Field Size property in the Field Properties pane. The Help message indicates that you can't change the Field Size property.

▶ **6.** Press the **Tab** key, click the **Format** list arrow, and then click **General Number**. The Help message for the Format property appears in its normal blue, so you can change this field property. Because no objects in the Overseas database use the School table, you can ignore the Property Update Options button.

▶ **7.** Save and close the table.

Now you'll open the Schools database to show Elsa the new record in the School table. Then you'll delete that record and view the table in Design view.

### To update the School table and view its design in the Schools database:

▶ **1.** Open the **Schools** database located in the root folder on the drive where you are storing your Data Files, and then click **Tables** in the Objects bar of the Database window. A small blue arrow does not appear to the left of the School table icon, so this table is not a linked table in the Schools database.

▶ **2.** Open the **School** table datasheet, and then click the **Last Record** navigation button ▶❘. The record for Universidad de Colima, which you added to the School linked table in the Overseas database, appears as the last record in the School table in the Schools database.

3. Click the **Delete Record** button  on the Table Datasheet toolbar, and then click the **Yes** button to delete the last record in the table.

4. Switch to Design view. Because the School table is not a linked table in the Schools database, the Help message in the Field Properties pane appears in blue type, as do the Help messages for all field properties; you can make any design changes you want to the School table in the Schools database. The Format property setting is blank because the General Number setting you made is in effect only in the Overseas database.

5. Close the **School** table, and then open the **Overseas** database located in the Comp\Tutorial folder provided with your Data Files.

Elsa wants to know what happens if she deletes the linked School table in the Overseas database. You'll delete the linked School table in the Overseas database to show her that Access deletes the link to the School table but does not delete the School table in the Schools database.

### To delete the linked School table in the Overseas database:

1. Right-click **School** in the Tables list box to open the shortcut menu, and then click **Delete**. A message box asks if you want to remove the link to the School table. See Figure 12-8.

**Deleting a linked table message box** ◄ **Figure 12-8**

The message box confirms that you'll delete only the link to the School table, not the School table in the Schools database.

2. Click the **Yes** button. Access deletes the link to the School table, and the School table no longer appears in the Tables list box in the Overseas database.

Elsa now understands how to link to Matt's School table and to other data if she needs to do so in the future.

# Creating a Replica of a Database

Elsa wants to take a copy of the Overseas database with her on her upcoming business trip. She wants to be sure that while she is away, any updates that she makes to her copy of the database will not be lost.

If you simply created a copy of the Overseas database file and gave it to Elsa, her copy would not include any changes made by other NSJI employees while she is away, nor would the changes she makes to her copy of the database be included in the original database. Instead, you'll create a special copy of the Overseas database called a **replica**. When you create a replica of a database, the original copy of the database becomes the **Design Master**. The Design Master and all of its replicas are called the **replica set**. Access adds special tables and fields to the Design Master database to keep track of changes made to data and to the design of the database. Anyone using the Design Master can make changes to the design of database tables, queries, and other objects. Any changes in the data or design of database objects in the Design Master can then be automatically updated in a replica. Anyone using a replica of the database can make changes to the data in any of the database tables. A replica prevents the user from changing the structure or design of an existing table, query, or other database object. Any changes in the data in any replicas can be updated automatically in the Design Master. The process of updating the Design Master and the replicas is called **synchronization**.

Reference Window

## Creating a Replica of a Database

- Open the database you want to replicate.
- Click Tools on the menu bar, point to Replication, and then click Create Replica.
- Click the Yes button to close the database.
- Click the Yes button to make a backup copy of the database.
- Select the location where you want to store the new replica.
- Click the OK button.

You need to convert the Overseas database to a Design Master and create a replica of the database to give to Elsa.

### To convert the Overseas database to a Design Master and create a replica of it:

▶ **1.** Click **Tools** on the menu bar, point to **Replication**, and then click **Create Replica**. Access opens a message box asking if you want to close the database, convert it to a Design Master, and create a replica of the database.

▶ **2.** Click the **Yes** button. Access compacts and closes the Overseas database and, after a few moments, opens a message box asking if you want to make a backup copy of the Overseas database. See Figure 12-9.

Figure 12-9 ▶ **Creating a backup copy of the Overseas database**

Access can make a backup copy of your database in the folder provided with your Data Files. This backup can serve as an extra copy of the Overseas database in case anything goes wrong when Access creates the replica. You'll make a backup copy and, at the end of your replication work, you'll change the extension of the backup copy from .bak to .mdb, so you can use it instead of the Design Master for your remaining work in this tutorial.

**3.** Click the **Yes** button. A message box opens and shows the progress of converting the database to a Design Master, and then the Location of New Replica dialog box opens. See Figure 12-10.

**Location of New Replica dialog box** ◄ **Figure 12-10**

In the Location of New Replica dialog box, you choose the location and name for the replica. You also can set options for the **replica priority** (when multiple replicas update the same record, only the change for the replica with the highest priority is made), the **replica visibility** (specifies which members of the replica set the replica can synchronize with and which conflict resolution rules apply; choices are global, local, and anonymous), and **replica record deletion** (a check mark in the Prevent deletes check box prevents a user from deleting a record in the replica). The default settings are correct, so you can continue creating the replica.

**4.** Click the **OK** button. A message box opens and shows the status of creating the replica, and then Access names the replica "Replica of Overseas," converts the Overseas database to the Design Master, and opens a message box informing you of these actions. See Figure 12-11.

**After creating the Overseas Design Master and replica** ◄ **Figure 12-11**

**5.** Click the **OK** button. The message box closes, and the Design Master version of the Overseas database opens. See Figure 12-12.

| Figure 12-12 | Database window for the Overseas database Design Master |

The phrase "Design Master" in the Database window title bar indicates that this database is the Design Master of the Overseas database. A new symbol appears next to the table icons in the Tables list to indicate that these objects have been replicated.

You can now give Elsa a copy of the Overseas database replica on a disk to take with her on her trip.

# Synchronizing the Replica and the Design Master

While she is on her trip, Elsa visits several NSJI employer clients. Her visit to Harbourview Resort is successful, and the owner decides to offer an additional position with NSJI. Elsa adds a new record for Harbourview Resort in the Position table of the Overseas database replica.

### To add the new record to the Overseas database replica:

1. Close the Design Master of the Overseas database without exiting Access, open the **Replica of Overseas** database located in the Comp\Tutorial folder provided with your Data Files, and then click **Forms** in the Objects bar of the Database window.

   The word "Replica" in the Database window title bar indicates that this is a replica of the Overseas database.

   You can now enter Elsa's new record using the Position form.

2. Open the **Position** form in Form view, and then click the **New Record** button ▶ on the Form View toolbar to display a blank form.

3. Enter the data for the new record, as shown in Figure 12-13.

**New Position table record for Harbourview Resort** | Figure 12-13

▶ **4.** Close the form.

The replica of the Overseas database now contains a new record that is not recorded in the Design Master. When Elsa returns from her trip, you can update the Design Master by synchronizing the Design Master and the replica. The synchronization process compares the Design Master to the replica and checks for any differences. Access updates the Design Master with any changes that have been made to the data in the replica, and updates the replica with any changes that have been made to the data or the design of any database objects in the Design Master. This process ensures that the Design Master and the replica are consistent.

## Synchronizing the Design Master and a Replica

Reference Window

- Open the replica set database (either the Design Master or a replica) that you want to synchronize.
- Click Tools, point to Replication, and then click Synchronize Now.
- Enter the location and name of the replica set database you want to synchronize with the current database, and then click the OK button.
- Click the Yes button when asked if you want to close the database.
- Click the OK button when informed that the synchronization was completed successfully.

Elsa returned from her trip, so now you must synchronize the open replica of the Overseas database with the Design Master to enter the new Position record.

### To synchronize the replica and the Design Master:

▶ **1.** Click **Tools** on the menu bar, point to **Replication**, and then click **Synchronize Now**. The Synchronize Database dialog box opens.

▶ **2.** Make sure the **Directly with Replica** option button is selected. If the Directly with Replica list box does not display the name of the Design Master of the Overseas database, use the Browse button to select it. See Figure 12-14.

Figure 12-14 ▸ **Synchronize Database dialog box**

select this option

your path might differ

**Trouble?** The path statement in the Directly with Replica list box on your screen might not match the one in the figure. Be sure that it is accurate for your system and the location of your Data Files.

▸ 3. Click the **OK** button, and then click the **Yes** button when asked if you want to close the replica. After a few seconds, Access opens a message box indicating that the synchronization is complete.

▸ 4. Click the **OK** button to close the message box and to re-open the replica.

The Design Master and the replica are now synchronized. The new record that Elsa added to the replica copy of the Overseas database has been added to the Design Master. You can now view the Position table data using the Position form and display the new record in the Design Master.

### To find and display the new Position table record in the Position form in the Design Master:

▸ 1. Close the replica of the Overseas database without exiting Access.

▸ 2. Open the **Overseas** database located in the Comp\Tutorial folder, and then open the **Position** form in Form view.

▸ 3. Click the **Last Record** navigation button ▸I to display the new record that you added (see Figure 12-13).

▸ 4. Close the form.

Now that you have synchronized the databases, you can delete the replica of the Overseas database. You can easily create another replica whenever Elsa needs to take the database with her on future business trips. Even though you delete the replica of the Overseas database, the original Design Master of the database remains a Design Master. Because there can be many replicas of a database in a replica set, the Design Master keeps track of any changes you make to the database so that other replicas can be synchronized at any time.

In your remaining work for Elsa you won't use the Design Master of the Overseas database; you'll use the original version of the Overseas database (before you converted it to a Design Master and created the replica). Therefore, you'll also rename both versions of the Overseas database.

**To delete the replica of the Overseas database and rename databases:**

▶ 1. Close the Design Master of the Overseas database without exiting Access.

▶ 2. Use Windows Explorer or My Computer to open the **Comp\Tutorial** folder.

▶ 3. Right-click the **Replica of Overseas** database to open the shortcut menu, click **Delete**, and then click the **Yes** button (if necessary).

▶ 4. Right-click the **Overseas** database to open the shortcut menu, click **Rename**, press the **End** key, press the **spacebar**, type **Design Master**, and then press the **Enter** key. Overseas Design Master is the new database name.

   **Trouble?** If a message box opens and tells you that changing the filename extension might make the file unusable, click the No button, and then repeat Step 4 and type Design Master.mdb, with the filename extension, before pressing the Enter key.

▶ 5. Repeat Step 4 to rename the **Overseas.bak** database as **Overseas.mdb**.

▶ 6. Close the Windows Explorer or My Computer window to return to the Access window.

▶ 7. If you are not continuing on to the next session, exit Access.

   In the next session, you'll finish your work with the Overseas database by splitting the database, setting startup options, and making access to it more secure.

## Session 12.1 Quick Check

Review

   1. What is the Performance Analyzer?
   2. The Performance Analyzer lists three types of analysis results: recommendation, suggestion, and idea. Which type(s) of analysis results can Access complete for you automatically?
   3. When do you use the Linked Table Manager?
   4. What is a replica set?
   5. How does a Design Master differ from a replica?
   6. What does Access do when you synchronize a Design Master and a replica?

# Session 12.2

# Using the Database Splitter

Elsa wants to create several queries for the Overseas database, but she doesn't want the user interface for other users to be cluttered with queries they won't need to use. She asks if there's a way for her to have a special user interface to access the data in the Overseas database.

   Users might want to customize their own versions of the user interface, while accessing the same central table data. The **Database Splitter** is an Access tool that splits an Access database into two files: one file contains the tables, and the other file contains the queries, forms, and other database objects. Although a single master copy of the file containing the tables is stored and accessed, users can have their own copies of the other file and add their own queries, reports, and other objects to handle their processing needs. Each file created by the Database Splitter is an Access database. The database that contains the tables is called the **back-end database**; and the database that contains the other objects, including the user interface, is called the **front-end database**.

After you split a database, when users open a front-end database, the objects they open use data in the tables in the back-end database. Because the tables in the front-end database are linked tables that are stored in the back-end database, the front-end database contains the physical disk locations of the tables in the back-end database. You can move the front-end database to a different disk location without affecting the physical connections to the back-end database. However, if you move the back-end database to a different disk location, you'll need to use the Linked Table Manager to change the physical disk locations of the back-end database's tables in the front-end database.

People who develop databases and sell them to multiple companies usually split their databases. When a developer delivers a split database, the initial back-end database does not include the company's data, and the initial front-end database is complete as created by the developer. Companies use the front-end database to update their data in the back-end database, but they do not modify the front-end database in any way. Periodically, the database developer improves the front-end database by modifying and adding queries, reports, and other objects without changing the structure of the tables. In other words, the developer changes the front-end database, but does not change the back-end database. The developer gives its client companies replacement front-end databases, which continue to work with the back-end database that contains the company's data. This entire process is illustrated in Figure 12-15.

| Figure 12-15 | Split Access database |
| --- | --- |

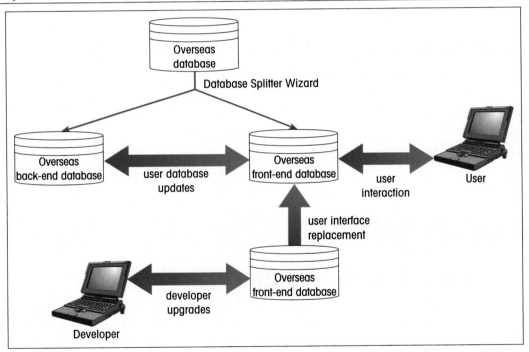

Splitting a database also lets you place the files on different computers. You can place the front-end database on each user's PC, and the back-end database on a network server that users access through their front-end databases; this arrangement distributes the workload across the network. Finally, as a company grows, it might need a more powerful database management system such as Oracle, Microsoft's SQL Server, or IBM's DB2. You could retain the original Access front-end database and replace the Access back-end database with a new non-Access back-end database, which is an easier task than replacing all database objects.

## Using the Database Splitter

- Make a backup copy of the database that you want to split.
- Start Access and open the database you want to split.
- Click Tools on the menu bar, point to Database Utilities, and then click Database Splitter.
- Click the Split Database button, select the drive and folder for the back-end database, type a name for the database in the File name text box, and then click the Split button.
- Click the OK button.

You'll use the Database Splitter to split the Overseas database into two files. As a precaution, you'll make a backup copy of the database before you split the database. You should always make regular backups of databases, but it's especially important to make a backup before you make a significant database change such as splitting the database.

### To use the Database Splitter:

1. Use Windows Explorer or My Computer to create a copy of the **Overseas** database in the Comp\Tutorial folder provided with your Data Files, and then rename the copy **NSJI**.

2. Start Access (if necessary), open the **Overseas** database located in the Comp\Tutorial folder, click **Tools** on the menu bar, point to **Database Utilities**, and then click **Database Splitter**. The Database Splitter dialog box opens. See Figure 12-16.

**Database Splitter dialog box**  ◄  **Figure 12-16**

**Trouble?** If a dialog box opens and asks if you would like to install this feature, insert your Office 2003 CD in the correct drive, and then click the Yes button. If you do not have the Office 2003 CD, see your instructor or technical support person for assistance.

3. Click the **Split Database** button. The Create Back-end Database dialog box opens. The back-end database will contain the tables from the Overseas database. You'll use the default filename (Overseas_be.mdb) for the back-end database.

4. Click the **Split** button. After several seconds, a message box informs you that the database was successfully split.

5. Click the **OK** button to close the message box and return to the Database window. See Figure 12-17.

| Figure 12-17 | Linked tables in the Overseas database |

Each table in the Overseas database has an icon next to its name indicating that there's a link to that table in another file. The tables are no longer stored in the Overseas database; they are stored in the Overseas_be database file you just created with the Database Splitter. You can use the tables as if they were stored in the Overseas database, except you cannot change a table's design from the Overseas database. You have to close the Overseas database and open the Overseas_be database to change a table's design.

6. Click **Queries** in the Objects bar of the Database window. The queries you've created appear in the Queries list box. The queries and objects other than tables are still stored in the Overseas database.

You'll close the Overseas database and then open the Overseas_be database to verify which objects are stored in the back-end database.

## To verify the contents of the back-end database:

1. Close the **Overseas** database without exiting Access, and then open the **Overseas_be** database located in the Comp\Tutorial folder. The tables from the Overseas database appear with their usual icons in the Tables list box. The tables are now stored in the Overseas_be database.

2. Open the **Employer** table in Design view. You can modify the design of the tables in the Overseas_be database because they are stored in that database; they are not linked as they are in the Overseas database.

3. Close the table, and then click **Queries** in the Objects bar of the Database window. No queries are listed because they are stored in the Overseas database.

4. Close the **Overseas_be** database without exiting Access, and then open the **Overseas** database located in the Comp\Tutorial folder.

Elsa is pleased with the changes you have made. As a final enhancement to the user interface, she asks you to set Access to open the Switchboard form automatically when a user opens the Overseas database.

# Setting the Database Startup Options

Access lets you specify certain actions, called **startup options**, that take place when a database opens. For example, you can specify the name that appears in the Access window title bar, prevent users from using the Database window, or specify a form that is automatically opened. If you want to bypass the startup options that you set, you can press and hold down the Shift key when you open the database.

Elsa wants users to be able to open the Overseas database and have the Switchboard form open automatically. This way, users won't need to use the Forms list box in the Database window to access the Switchboard form.

**Reference Window**

## Setting the Database Startup Options

- Click Tools on the menu bar, and then click Startup to open the Startup dialog box.
- Specify the startup options, and then click the OK button. The options will be in effect the next time the database is opened.

You need to set the Overseas database startup options so that the switchboard appears automatically when the database is opened, and so that the Database window is hidden from view. You'll also set startup options to provide users with restricted menus, to eliminate the toolbars, and to prevent users from making changes to toolbar and menu options.

### To change the Overseas database startup options:

1. Click **Tools** on the menu bar, and then click **Startup**. The Startup dialog box opens. See Figure 12-18.

Startup dialog box ◄ **Figure 12-18**

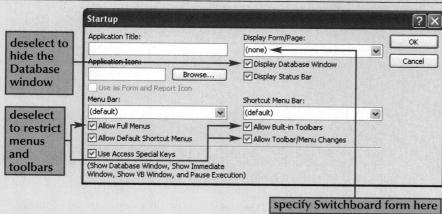

deselect to hide the Database window

deselect to restrict menus and toolbars

specify Switchboard form here

2. Click the **Display Form/Page** list arrow, and then click **Switchboard**. This setting specifies that the Switchboard form will be opened upon startup.

3. Click the **Display Database Window** check box to remove the check mark. This setting specifies that the Database window will not be opened upon startup.

4. Click the **Allow Full Menus** check box to remove the check mark. This setting eliminates menus and commands that enable users to change the design of the objects in the Overseas database. Only a subset of the built-in menus will be available.

5. Click the **Allow Built-in Toolbars** check box to remove the check mark. This setting elimi-nates the toolbars from all windows in the Overseas database.

6. Click the **Allow Toolbar/Menu Changes** check box to remove the check mark. This setting prevents users from customizing toolbars, menu bars, and shortcut menus.

7. Click the **OK** button to close the Startup dialog box.

To test the startup options, you need to close and then re-open the Overseas database.

## To test the startup options:

1. Close the **Overseas** database without exiting Access.

2. Click **File** on the menu bar, and then click **Overseas.mdb** to open the Overseas database. See Figure 12-19.

| Figure 12-19 | Overseas database user interface |
| --- | --- |

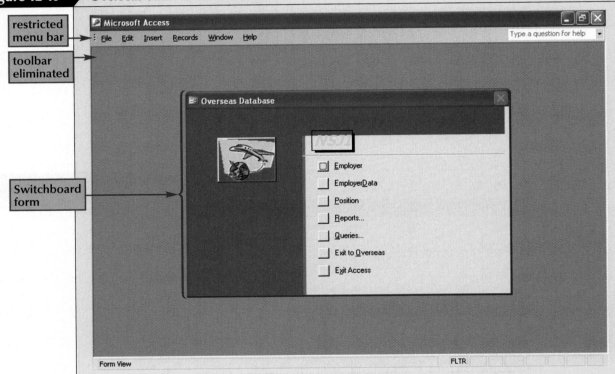

**Trouble?** The path to the Overseas.mdb database might be different on your File menu, depending on the location of your Data Files.

Access opens the Overseas database, opens the Switchboard form, hides the Database win-dow, displays a restricted menu bar, and eliminates the built-in Form View toolbar. Your test shows that the startup options are correctly set.

Now you can make one final test of the Overseas database user interface.

### To test the features of the Overseas database user interface:

▶ **1.** Make one final pass through all the command button options to verify that all features work properly on the Overseas database user interface.

▶ **2.** Click the **Exit to Overseas** command button on the Overseas Database switchboard as your last test to close the form and return to the Database window.

Elsa wants you to make access to the Overseas database more secure, which will require you to change the database design. Because the Overseas database now has a restricted menu bar and no toolbar, you won't be able to make further design changes to the database unless you bypass the startup options (by pressing and holding down the Shift key when you open the database) or modify the startup options to allow toolbars and full menus. It'll be easier for you to complete the remaining work for Elsa if you modify the startup options. To modify the startup options, you'll need to close the Overseas database and open it, bypassing the startup options.

### To modify the Overseas database startup options:

▶ **1.** Close the **Overseas** database without exiting Access.

▶ **2.** Click **File** on the menu bar, press and hold down the **Shift** key, click **Overseas.mdb** to open the Overseas database, continue holding down the Shift key until the Database window opens (click the appropriate button on any security dialog box that opens), and then release the **Shift** key. Access opens the Overseas database in the Database window, does not open the switchboard, and displays the Database toolbar and full menus; by pressing and holding down the Shift key you bypassed the startup options.

▶ **3.** Click **Tools** on the menu bar, and then click **Startup**. The Startup dialog box opens.

▶ **4.** Click the **Allow Full Menus** check box to add a check mark for that option, click the **Allow Built-in Toolbars** check box to add a check mark for that option, and then click the **OK** button.

▶ **5.** Close the **Overseas** database without exiting Access, open the **Overseas** database, and then click the **Exit to Overseas** command button to close the form and return to the Database window. Access displays the Database toolbar and full menu bar.

Next, Elsa wants you to make access to the Overseas database more secure.

# Securing an Access Database

**Security** refers to the protection of a database against unauthorized access, either intentional or accidental. Setting the database startup options to restrict the menu bar and to hide toolbars is one way you can prevent users from changing the database design. Access provides several additional security features, including encryption and passwords.

**Encryption** translates the data in a database to a format that's indecipherable to a word processor or other program and stores it in an encrypted format. If unauthorized users attempt to bypass Access and get to the data directly, they will see only the encrypted version of the data. However, users accessing the data using Access will have no problem working with the data. When a user stores or modifies data in an encrypted database, Access will encrypt the data before updating the database. **Decrypting** a database reverses the encryption. Once you've encrypted a database, you can use Access to decrypt it.

Before a user retrieves encrypted data using Access, the data will be decrypted and presented to the user in the normal format. If your encrypted database takes longer to respond to requests as it gets larger, you might consider decrypting it to improve its responsiveness.

To prevent access to a database by an unauthorized user through Access, you can assign a password to the database. A **password** is a string of characters assigned to a database that users must enter before they can open the database. As long as the password is known only to authorized users of the database, unauthorized access to the database is prevented. It's best if you use a password that's easily remembered by authorized users, but is not obvious and easily guessed by others.

Elsa wants to restrict access to the Overseas database to authorized NSJI employees and also wants to prevent people from using other programs to access the data in the Overseas database.

## Encrypting a Database

First, you'll encrypt the Overseas database for Elsa.

| Reference Window | **Encrypting or Decrypting a Database** |
| --- | --- |

- Start Access, but do not open the database you want to encrypt.
- In the Access window, click Tools on the menu bar, point to Security, and then click Encode/Decode Database.
- In the Encode/Decode Database dialog box, select the drive and folder that contains the database, select the database, and then click the OK button.
- In the Encode Database As or the Decode Database As dialog box, select the drive and folder for the modified database, type its name in the File name text box, and then click the Save button.

You'll encrypt the Overseas database. First, you need to close it without exiting Access.

### To encrypt the Overseas database:

1. Close the **Overseas** database without exiting Access.

2. Click **Tools** on the menu bar, point to **Security**, and then click **Encode/Decode Database**. The Encode/Decode Database dialog box opens.

3. If necessary, use the **Look in** list arrow to select the **Comp\Tutorial** folder provided with your Data Files.

4. Click **Overseas** in the list box, and then click the **OK** button. The Encode Database As dialog box opens.

   You can use the same name, drive, and folder for the original and encrypted versions of the database. If an error occurs during the encryption operation, Access doesn't delete the original file. If the operation is successful, Access replaces the original database with the encrypted version. If you use a different name, drive, or folder for the encrypted database, both the original and encrypted databases are retained.

   You'll replace the original database by using the same name, drive, and folder for the encrypted database.

5. Click **Overseas** in the list box, click the **Save** button, and then click the **Yes** button when asked if you want to replace the existing file. The dialog box closes, Access encrypts the Overseas database, and you return to the Access window.

Even though the Overseas database is encrypted, it won't look any different when you use Access to open it. However, if you attempt to open the Overseas database with another program, the data in the Overseas database would be indecipherable.

Next, you'll set a password for the Overseas database.

## Setting and Unsetting a Database Password

Encrypting a database does not prevent unauthorized users from using Access to open the Overseas database and viewing or changing its data. Elsa asks you to set a password for the Overseas database to prevent such unauthorized access.

### Setting a Database Password

Reference Window

- Start Access, click the Open button on the Database toolbar, select the drive and folder that contains the database, and then click the database.
- Click the Open list arrow, and then click Open Exclusive.
- Click Tools on the menu bar, point to Security, and then click Set Database Password.
- Type the password in the Password text box, type the same password in the Verify text box, and then press the Enter key.

The way you usually open an Access database allows **shared access** of the database with others; that is, two or more users can open and use the same database at the same time. When you set a password for the Overseas database, you need to open the database with exclusive access. When you open an Access database with **exclusive access**, you prevent other users from opening and using the database at the same time. You must open the database with exclusive access in order to set a password, so that you can guarantee that only one copy of the database is open when you set the password.

You'll now set the password for the Overseas database to Nereid.

### To set the password for the Overseas database:

1. Click the **Open** button 🖻 on the Database toolbar. The Open dialog box opens.

2. Click **Overseas** in the list box (if necessary), and then click the **Open** list arrow. See Figure 12-20.

| Figure 12-20 | Opening a database with exclusive access |
| --- | --- |

Clicking the Open option opens the selected database with shared access for both reading and updating, whereas clicking the Open Read-Only option opens the selected database with shared access for reading only. **Reading** includes any database action that does not involve updating the database, such as running queries (but not action queries) and viewing table records. Actions that are prohibited when you open a database as Read-Only (because they involve updating the database) include changing the database design and updating table records. The other two options in the Open list open the selected database with exclusive access for reading and updating (Open Exclusive) or for reading only (Open Exclusive Read-Only).

▶ **3.** Click **Open Exclusive**. The Overseas Database form opens in the Access window.

▶ **4.** Click the **Exit to Overseas** command button to close the form and return to the Database window, click **Tools** on the menu bar, point to **Security**, and then click **Set Database Password**. The Set Database Password dialog box opens. See Figure 12-21.

| Figure 12-21 | Set Database Password dialog box |
| --- | --- |

You must type the password twice: once in the Password text box, and again in the Verify text box. Passwords are case-sensitive, so you must type the same password in both text boxes. Because the password is stored in the database, you cannot open the database if you forget the password.

**5.** Type **Nereid** in the Password text box, press the **Tab** key, type **Nereid** in the Verify text box, and then press the **Enter** key. The dialog box closes, and Access sets the Overseas database password to Nereid.

**Trouble?** If a message box opens, asking you to verify the new password by retyping it in the Verify text box, click the OK button, type Nereid in the Verify text box, and then press the Enter key.

Next, you'll close and re-open the Overseas database to verify that the password has been set. Then you'll unset, or remove, the password.

Reference Window

## Unsetting a Database Password

- Start Access, click the Open button on the Database toolbar, select the drive and folder that contains the database, and then click the database.
- Click the Open list arrow, and then click Open Exclusive.
- Click Tools on the menu bar, point to Security, and then click Unset Database Password.
- Type the password in the Password text box, and then press the Enter key.

Unsetting a password cancels the password protection for the database. It also permits you to modify the password; after unsetting the password, you can set a new password.

### To test and unset the password for the Overseas database:

**1.** Close the **Overseas** database without exiting Access.

**Trouble?** If the Password Required dialog box opens, type Nereid, and then press the Enter key.

Because you'll be unsetting the password, you need to open the Overseas database with exclusive access.

**2.** Open the **Overseas** database with exclusive access. The Password Required dialog box opens. See Figure 12-22.

Password Required dialog box | Figure 12-22

type password here

**3.** Type **nereid** (all lowercase) in the text box, and then press the **Enter** key. A message box opens, warning you that you did not enter a valid password.

**4.** Click the **OK** button, type **Nereid** in the text box, and then press the **Enter** key. The Overseas Database form opens in the Access window.

You'll now unset the password.

**5.** Click **Exit to Overseas** to close the form and return to the Database window, click **Tools** on the menu bar, point to **Security**, and then click **Unset Database Password**. The Unset Database Password dialog box opens. See Figure 12-23.

**Figure 12-23** ▶ **Unset Database Password dialog box**

▶ **6.** Type **Nereid** in the Password text box, and then press the **Enter** key.

The next time you open the Overseas database, you won't be asked to enter a password because you've unset it.

Elsa asks if she can restrict access to the Overseas database for selected NSJI employees.

# Establishing User-Level Security

Setting a database's startup options to restrict the menu bar and hide toolbars, encrypting a database, and setting a database password are security measures that apply to all users of the database. The security needs for a database might be more individualized. For example, you might need to set the database so that some users can only update or view objects, and so that other users can only view selected objects. In this situation, you can use **user-level security**, which lets you grant users or groups of users specific permissions to tables, queries, forms, reports, and macros. A user's **permissions** specify what type of access the user has to the objects in a database. Examples of permissions are Modify Design (view, add, change, and delete the design of database objects), Read Data (view data in tables and queries), and Delete Data (view and delete, but not modify or insert, data in tables and queries). You can assign permissions to individual objects (specific queries and reports, for example), to object types (all tables and queries, for example), or to combinations of individual objects and object types. Companies such as NSJI assign the responsibility for database security to an individual, often called the **database administrator**, or to a group, often called **database administration (DBA)**. The database administrator or DBA, in consultation with company management, controls the permissions assigned to database users.

When you establish user-level security, you usually first create groups and assign permissions to the groups. A **group** is a collection of users identified by a group name and ID. Next, you assign each user a name and password, and then assign each user to one or more groups, depending on the permissions that user needs. Group names and IDs, user names and passwords, and group membership information are stored in an Access **workgroup information file** that is read at startup, as shown in Figure 12-24. The permissions that you assign to groups for the database's objects are stored in hidden system tables in the database.

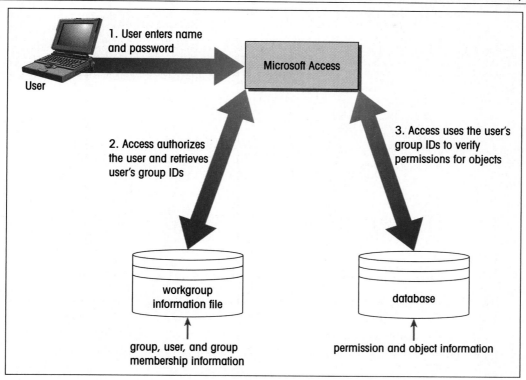

1. User enters name and password

Microsoft Access

User

2. Access authorizes the user and retrieves user's group IDs

3. Access uses the user's group IDs to verify permissions for objects

workgroup information file

database

group, user, and group membership information

permission and object information

## Using the User-Level Security Wizard

You'll use the **User-Level Security Wizard**, also called the **Security Wizard**, to create the workgroup information file and establish groups, users, and their permissions.

### To start the User-Level Security Wizard and create the workgroup information file:

▶ **1.** Click **Tools** on the menu bar, point to **Security**, and then click **User-Level Security Wizard**. A message box opens, informing you that you can't use the Security Wizard with the Overseas database opened in exclusive mode; the database must be opened in shared mode.

▶ **2.** Click the **Yes** button. Access closes the Overseas database, re-opens it in shared mode, and then opens the first Security Wizard dialog box. See Figure 12-25.

| Figure 12-25 | Creating a new workgroup information file |

overview description of the Security Wizard's objectives

make sure this option is selected

The Security Wizard will create a backup copy of the Overseas database without user-level security and add user-level security to the Overseas database. Most businesses would save the unsecured backup copy to a CD or other portable medium and store it in a safe or other secured, protected place. Your first step is to create a new workgroup information file.

3. Make sure the **Create a new workgroup information file** option button is selected, and then click the **Next** button to display the next Security Wizard dialog box.

In this Security Wizard dialog box, you enter the name and workgroup ID for the workgroup information file, and optionally a user name and a company name. The **workgroup ID (WID)** is a unique, case-sensitive, 4- to 20-character string that uniquely identifies the workgroup. Only those users who know the WID will be able to create a copy of the workgroup information file. You'll accept the default filename and folder (Security.mdw located in the Comp\Tutorial folder provided with your Data Files) for the workgroup information file, create a new WID, and add Elsa's information.

4. Select the value in the WID text box, type **ZYxOverseasCBA7**, press the **Tab** key, type **Elsa Jensen** in the Your name (optional) text box, press the **Tab** key, and then type **NSJI** in the Company (optional) text box. See Figure 12-26.

Naming the workgroup information file ◄ **Figure 12-26**

You want to use this workgroup information only for the Overseas database, so you'll select the option for creating a shortcut to the secured Overseas database.

5. Make sure the **I want to create a shortcut to open my security-enhanced database** option button is selected, and then click the **Next** button to display the next Security Wizard dialog box. See Figure 12-27.

Securing database objects ◄ **Figure 12-27**

By default, running the Security Wizard secures all existing database objects and all new objects created in the database. You can select objects that will not be secured, which means that all users will have full permissions for those objects. You don't usually want to bypass security for any object, so you'll accept the default security settings.

6. Click the **Next** button to display the next Security Wizard dialog box, in which you select optional groups for the workgroup information file.

7. Click each group (but don't click the group check box), and then read the description in the Group permissions section.

Elsa wants Matt Griffin to be assigned to the Full Permissions group and Kelley Kellogg assigned to the Read-Only Users group, so you'll select these two groups and change their Group IDs.

8. Click the **Full Permissions** check box, select the value in the Group ID text box, and then type **OverseasFP**. See Figure 12-28.

**Figure 12-28** ▶ **Selecting optional groups**

9. Click the **Read-Only Users** check box, select the value in the Group ID text box, type **OverseasRP**, and then click the **Next** button to display the next Security Wizard dialog box.

In this Security Wizard dialog box and the remaining dialog boxes, you'll add Matt and Kelley as users, assign them to groups, and set permissions for the Users group. The **Users group** is one of two groups created by default when you create a new workgroup information file. Access adds each user to the User group automatically as you add a new user. The Admins group is the second group created by default. Users assigned to the **Admins group** have full permissions and are the only users who can create users and groups. A new workgroup information file also contains one default user, the **Admin user**, which is assigned to the Admins group.

You'll now complete the remaining Security Wizard steps. First, you'll accept the default setting of granting no permissions to the Users group.

## To complete the Security Wizard:

1. Make sure the **No, the Users group should not have any permissions** option button is selected, and then click the **Next** button to display the next Security Wizard dialog box, in which you add users to the workgroup information file.

Before adding Matt and Kelley as users, you'll enter a password for the Administrator user and change its **personal ID (PID)**, which serves the same purpose and has the same format rules for users as the WID does for workgroups. The Security Wizard automatically adds the Administrator user and assigns it to the Admins group.

2. Click **Administrator** in the list box, click the **Password** text box, type **Triton** in the Password text box, press the **Tab** key, and then type **BR73elsa**.

   **Trouble?** If your dialog box displays a different user name for the Administrator user, select that user name in Step 2.

   Next, you'll add Matt and Kelley as users.

3. Click the **Add a New User** button, type **Mgriffin** in the User name text box, press the **Tab** key, type **Poseidon** in the Password text box, press the **Tab** key, and then type **Matt44G** in the PID text box. See Figure 12-29.

---

Adding a user to the workgroup information file ◄ **Figure 12-29**

4. Click the **Add This User to the List** button to add Mgriffin (Matt Griffin) as a user to the workgroup information file.

5. Type **Kkellogg** in the User name text box, press the **Tab** key, type **Thetis** in the Password text box, press the **Tab** key, type **Kelley5K** in the PID text box, click the **Add This User to the List** button to add Kkellogg (Kelley Kellogg) as a user to the workgroup information file, and then click the **Next** button to display the next Security Wizard dialog box.

   You now will assign users Mgriffin and Kkellogg to groups and accept the default Admins group for the Administrator user.

6. Make sure the **Select a user and assign the user to groups** option button is selected, click the **Group or user name** list arrow, click **Mgriffin**, and then click the **Full Permissions** check box. See Figure 12-30.

**Figure 12-30**   **Assigning a user to a group**

**7.** Click the **Group or user name** list arrow, click **Kkellogg**, click the **Read-Only Users** check box, and then click the **Next** button to display the next Security Wizard dialog box, in which you enter the filename and location of the backup copy of the unsecured database. You'll place the backup copy in the Comp\Tutorial folder with the name OverseasUnsecured.mdb.

**8.** Position the insertion point before **.bak** in the text box, type **Unsecured**, and then click the **Finish** button. The Security Wizard creates the workgroup information file, the secured Overseas database, an unsecured backup copy of the database, and the report named One-step Security Wizard Report.

The report named One-step Security Wizard Report lists the names of the unsecured and secured databases, the name and properties of the workgroup information file, the names of all secured objects in the Overseas database, group names and properties, and user names and properties. You'll print the report, because you'll need its information if you need to re-create the workgroup information file.

**9.** Print the report, close the Security Wizard window, and then click the **No** button when asked if you want to save the report. A message box opens. See Figure 12-31.

**Figure 12-31**   **Security Wizard message box**

The Security Wizard message box informs you that it encrypted the secured Overseas database, and that you must exit Access and open the Overseas database in the future by using the shortcut on the Windows desktop to the Overseas database's workgroup information file.

**10.** Click the **OK** button, and then exit Access.

Elsa wants to see how to work with a secured database.

# Testing User-Level Security

First, you'll use the new workgroup information file to test user-level security by logging on as Kkellogg, who is assigned to the Read-Only Users group. You'll use the Overseas.mdb icon, which is a shortcut to the Overseas database's workgroup information file, on the Windows desktop to start Access and open the Overseas database.

## To test user-level security:

▶ **1.** Make sure the Windows desktop is visible, then double-click the **Overseas.mdb** shortcut icon. Access starts and opens the Logon dialog box. See Figure 12-32.

First, you'll enter an incorrect password. As you type a password, asterisks appear in the Password text box as a security feature.

▶ **2.** Select the entry in the Name text box and type **Kkellogg** (if necessary), press the **Tab** key, type **thetis** in the Password text box, and then press the **Enter** key. A message box opens to inform you that you entered an incorrect name or password—remember, passwords are case-sensitive.

▶ **3.** Click the **OK** button, type **Thetis** in the Password text box, and then press the **Enter** key. The Overseas Database form opens in the Access window.

The Read-Only User group does not have the permissions needed for the Kkellogg user to update data in the Overseas database. You'll open the EmployerData form and try to change a value.

▶ **4.** Click the **EmployerData** command button to open the EmployerData form. The Kkellogg user can read, or view, data, which is why you could open the EmployerData form. The Employer field value is selected, so you'll try to update its value.

▶ **5.** Type **8**. The Employer field value remains highlighted and unchanged.

Next, you'll exit Access and log on as the Mgriffin user. The Mgriffin user is assigned to the Full Permissions group, which lets you view and update all objects in a database.

▶ **6.** Close the form, click the **Exit Access** command button, and then double-click the **Overseas.mdb** icon on the Windows desktop.

▶ **7.** Select **Kkellogg** in the Name text box to highlight it, type **Mgriffin**, press the **Tab** key, type **Poseidon** in the Password text box, and then press the **Enter** key to open the Overseas Database form in the Access window.

▶ **8.** Click the **EmployerData** command button to open the EmployerData form, and then type **8** in the Employer text box. The digit 8 replaces the original Employer field value, indicating that the Mgriffin user can update data in the Overseas database.

Elsa now understands how user-level security works, so you'll undo the Employer field value change and exit Access.

▶ **9.** Click the **Undo typing** button 🔄 on the Form View toolbar, close the form, and then click the **Exit Access** command button to return to the Windows desktop.

▶ **10.** Use Windows Explorer or My Computer to move the **Overseas.mdb** shortcut from the desktop to the Comp\Tutorial folder.

Before completing your work with the Overseas database, Elsa asks you to research another Access security feature—creating an MDE file.

## Saving a Database as an MDE File

If a database contains VBA code, you can save an MDE file version of the database to prevent people from viewing or changing the VBA code. Saving an Access database as an **MDE file**, which has the .mde extension instead of the .mdb extension for a normal Access database, compiles all VBA modules, removes all editable VBA source code, and compacts the resulting database. The database and its VBA code continue to run as normal, but the VBA code can't be viewed or edited. Also, you can't view, modify, or create forms, reports, or modules in Design view, and you can't import or export forms, reports, or modules. Because an MDE file limits your database design changes to tables, queries, and data access pages, saving a database as an MDE file is best suited to a front-end database. You should keep a backup copy of the complete front-end database in case you need to modify the database design. To save a database as an MDE file, follow these steps:

1. If necessary, convert the database to the Access 2002 file format. You can save an Access database as an MDE file only if you have converted it to the Access 2002 file format.
2. Close the database, click Tools on the menu bar, point to Database Utilities, and then click Make MDE File.
3. In the Database to Save as MDE dialog box, select the name of the database you want to save, and then click the Make MDE button.
4. In the Save MDE As dialog box, enter a new name for the new MDE file, and then click the Save button.

   Because the Overseas database has very few VBA modules and because Elsa believes user-level security provides an acceptable level of security, you won't save the Overseas database as an MDE file.

   Your work with the Overseas database is now completed. Elsa reviews the final user interface, security measures, and database management tools with Matt and Zack, and they agree that the database will fully satisfy NSJI's requirements.

**Review**

## Session 12.2 Quick Check

1. What does the Database Splitter accomplish?
2. What is a startup option?
3. How do you display a form automatically when a database opens?
4. _____ refers to the protection of a database against unauthorized access, either intentional or accidental.
5. If an encrypted database takes longer to respond to your requests as it gets larger, you might consider _____ it to improve its responsiveness.

**6.** What are permissions?

**7.** Which two groups are created by default when you create a new workgroup information file?

**8.** Saving an Access database as a(n) _____ compiles all VBA modules, removes all editable VBA source code, and compacts the resulting database.

**Review**

# Tutorial Summary

In this tutorial, you finished your work with the Overseas database by completing tasks related to its management, security, and overall performance. You used the Performance Analyzer to analyze the database's performance, and you linked to a table in another database and then used the Linked Table Manager to re-link to the table after you changed its location. Next, you created a replica and synchronized the replica and the Design Master, used the Database Splitter, and set the startup options for the database. Finally, you secured the database by encrypting it, setting a database password, establishing user-level security, and learning about saving the database as an MDE file.

## Key Terms

| | | |
|---|---|---|
| Admin user | linked table | replica set |
| Admins group | Linked Table Manager | replica visibility |
| back-end database | MDE file | security |
| database | password | Security Wizard |
|     administration (DBA) | Performance Analyzer | shared access |
| database administrator | permissions | startup options |
| Database Splitter | personal ID (PID) | synchronization |
| decrypting | reading | user-level security |
| Design Master | refresh the link | User-Level Security Wizard |
| encryption | replica | Users group |
| exclusive access | replica priority | workgroup ID (WID) |
| front-end database | replica record deletion | workgroup information file |
| group | | |

**Practice**

*Take time to practice the skills you learned in the tutorial using the same case scenario.*

# Review Assignments

**Data File needed for the Review Assignments: Work.mdb (*cont. from Tutorial 11*)**

Elsa asks you to implement management and security features for the Work database. To fulfill her request, complete the following steps:

1. Open the **Work** database in the Comp\Review folder provided with your Data Files.

2. Use the Performance Analyzer to analyze the entire **Work** database, excluding the **ReportsDialogBox** form, but do not implement any of the analysis results. How many analysis results of the recommendation type did the Performance Analyzer find? Of the suggestion type? Of the idea type? Close the Performance Analyzer dialog box.

3. Create a replica of the **Work** database in the Comp\Review folder, making a backup of the database in the same folder. Accept the default settings in the Location of New Replica dialog box, and then complete the following steps:

   a. Close the Design Master, and then open the replica. Open the **Country** table, add a record with Canada as the Nation field value, and then close the **Country** table.

    b. Synchronize the replica with the Design Master. Close the replica, open the Design Master, verify that the new record was added to the **Country** table, and then close the Design Master.

    c. Use Windows Explorer or My Computer to rename the **Work** database as **Work Design Master**, and then rename the **Work.bak** database as **Work.mdb**.

4. Use Windows Explorer or My Computer to create a copy of the **Work** database in the Comp\Review folder, and then rename the copy as **Employer**. Open the **Work** database in the Comp\Review folder, and then use the Database Splitter to split the **Work** database. Use the default name for the back-end database and store it in the Comp\Review folder.

5. Set the database startup options to hide the Database window and open the **Switchboard** form when the **Work** database is opened. Close the **Work** database.

6. Encrypt the **Work_be** database by overwriting the existing **Work_be** database in the Comp\Review folder.

7. Convert the **Work** database to Access 2002 file format, saving the converted file as **Work2002** in the Comp\Review folder. Then save the **Work2002** database as an MDE file with the name **Work2002 MDE**.

8. Exit Access.

# Case Problem 1

**Data Files needed for this Case Problem: Payments.mdb and Shoots.mdb (*cont. from Tutorial 11*)**

***Lim's Video Photography*** Youngho Lim asks you to implement management and security features for the Shoots database. To help Youngho with his request, complete the following steps:

1. Open the **Shoots** database in the Comp\Case1 folder provided with your Data Files.

2. Use the Performance Analyzer to analyze the entire **Shoots** database. How many analysis results of the recommendation type did the Performance Analyzer find? Of the suggestion type? Of the idea type? Close the Performance Analyzer dialog box.

3. Link to the **Payment** table in the **Payments** database located in the Comp\Case1 folder. Use Windows Explorer or My Computer to move the **Payments** database to the root folder, and then use the Linked Table Manager to refresh the link to the **Payment** table. Open the **Payment** table in Datasheet view, and then print and close the table.

4. Close the **Shoots** database, use Windows Explorer or My Computer to create a copy of the **Shoots** database in the Comp\Case1 folder, and then rename the copy as **Lim**. Open the **Shoots** database, delete the link to the **Payment** table, and then use the Database Splitter to split the **Shoots** database. Use the default name for the back-end database and store it in the Comp\Case1 folder.

5. Set the database startup options to hide the Database window and open the **Switchboard** form when the **Shoots** database is opened. Close the **Shoots** database.

6. Encrypt the **Shoots_be** database by overwriting the existing **Shoots_be** database in the Comp\Case1 folder.

7. Convert the **Shoots** database to Access 2002 file format, saving the converted file as **Shoots2002** in the Comp\Case1 folder. Then save the **Shoots2002** database as an MDE file with the name **Shoots2002 MDE**.

8. Exit Access.

# Case Problem 2

**Data Files needed for this Case Problem: AtHome.mdb (*cont. from Tutorial 11*) and Choices.mdb**

*DineAtHome.course.com*   Claire Picard asks you to implement management and security features for the AtHome database. To help Claire with her request, complete the following steps:

1. Open the **AtHome** database in the Comp\Case2 folder provided with your Data Files.
2. Use the Performance Analyzer to analyze the entire **AtHome** database. How many analysis results of the recommendation type did the Performance Analyzer find? Of the suggestion type? Of the idea type? Close the Performance Analyzer dialog box.
3. Link to the **Selection** table in the **Choices** database located in the Comp\Case2 folder. Use Windows Explorer or My Computer to move the **Choices** database to the root folder, and then use the Linked Table Manager to refresh the link to the **Selection** table. Open the **Selection** table in Datasheet view, print only the first page, close the table, and then delete the link to the **Selection** table.
4. Set the database startup options to hide the Database window and open the **Switchboard** form when the **AtHome** database is opened. Close the **AtHome** database.
5. Encrypt the **AtHome** database by overwriting the existing **AtHome** database in the Comp\Case2 folder, and then set the database password to bronco. Close the **AtHome** database, use Windows Explorer or My Computer to create a copy of the **AtHome** database in the Comp\Case2 folder, and then rename the copy as **ToGo**. Open the **AtHome** database, unset the database password, and then close the **AtHome** database.
6. Convert the **AtHome** database to Access 2002 file format, saving the converted file as **AtHome2002** in the Comp\Case2 folder. Then save the **AtHome2002** database as an MDE file with the name **AtHome2002 MDE**.
7. Exit Access.

# Case Problem 3

**Data Files needed for this Case Problem: Donation.mdb and ZooFunds.mdb (*cont. from Tutorial 11*)**

*Redwood Zoo*   Michael Rosenfeld asks you to implement management and security features for the ZooFunds database. To help Michael with his request, complete the following steps:

1. Open the **ZooFunds** database in the Comp\Case3 folder provided with your Data Files.
2. Use the Performance Analyzer to analyze the entire **ZooFunds** database. How many analysis results of the recommendation type did the Performance Analyzer find? Of the suggestion type? Of the idea type? Close the Performance Analyzer dialog box.
3. Link to the **Donation** table in the **Donation** database located in the Comp\Case3 folder. Use Windows Explorer or My Computer to move the **Donation** database to the root folder, and then use the Linked Table Manager to refresh the link to the **Donation** table. Open the **Donation** table in Datasheet view, print and close the table, and then delete the link to the **Donation** table.
4. Create a replica of the **ZooFunds** database in the Comp\Case3 folder, making a backup of the database in the same folder. Accept the default settings in the Location of New Replica dialog box, and then complete the following steps:
   a. Close the Design Master, and then open the replica. Open the **Reception** table, add a record with field values of 56 for Reception ID, Holiday ball for Purpose, and 12/10/2006 for Date Held. Close the **Reception** table.

   b. Synchronize the replica with the Design Master. Close the replica, open the Design Master, verify that the new record was added to the **Reception** table, and then close the Design Master.

   c. Use Windows Explorer or My Computer to rename the **ZooFunds** database as **ZooFunds Design Master**, rename the **ZooFunds.bak** database as **ZooFunds.mdb**, and then close Windows Explorer or My Computer.

5. Open the **ZooFunds** database, and then set the database startup options to hide the Database window and open the **Switchboard** form when the **ZooFunds** database is opened. Close the **ZooFunds** database.

6. Encrypt the **ZooFunds** database by overwriting the existing **ZooFunds** database in the Comp\Case3 folder.

7. Convert the **ZooFunds** database to Access 2002 file format, saving the converted file as **ZooFunds2002** in the Comp\Case3 folder. Then save the **ZooFunds2002** database as an MDE file with the name **ZooFunds2002 MDE**.

8. Exit Access.

## Case Problem 4

**Apply**

*Apply what you learned in the tutorial to work with the data for an outdoor adventure company.*

**Data File needed for this Case Problem: Rivers.mdb (*cont. from Tutorial 11*)**

***Mountain River Adventures*** Connor and Siobhan Dempsey ask you to implement management and security features for the Rivers database. To help them with their request, complete the following steps:

1. Open the **Rivers** database in the Comp\Case4 folder provided with your Data Files.

2. Use the Performance Analyzer to analyze the entire **Rivers** database. How many analysis results of the recommendation type did the Performance Analyzer find? Of the suggestion type? Of the idea type? Implement any suggestion-type analysis results, and then close the Performance Analyzer dialog box. Open, print, and then close the Relationships window without saving the report.

3. Create a replica of the **Rivers** database in the Comp\Case4 folder, making a backup of the database in the same folder. Accept the default settings in the Location of New Replica dialog box, and then complete the following steps:

   a. Close the Design Master, and then open the replica. Open the **Guide** table, add a record with field values of Les for Guide ID, Leslie for First Name, Duncan for Last Name, and Libby for Lead Guide. Close the **Guide** table.

   b. Synchronize the replica with the Design Master. Close the replica, open the Design Master, verify that the new record was added to the **Guide** table, and then close the Design Master.

   c. Use Windows Explorer or My Computer to rename the **Rivers** database as **Rivers Design Master**, rename the **Rivers.bak** database as **Rivers.mdb**, and then close Windows Explorer or My Computer.

4. Open the **Rivers** database, and then use the User-Level Security Wizard to create a workgroup information file by completing the following steps:

   a. Type Dempsey99 in the WID text box, type your name in the Your name (optional) text box, type Mountain River Adventures in the Company (optional) text box, and select the option to create a shortcut to open the security-enhanced database.

   b. Make sure all objects are secure.

   c. Include Read-Only Users, and type Rivers88 in the Group ID text box.

   d. Make sure the Users group has no permissions.

   e. For the Administrator user, type a password of WhiteWater, and type a PID of Rivers77.

f.  Add a new user with a user name of ConnorD, a password of RaftTrip, and a PID of Rivers44.

g.  Make sure the Administrator user is assigned to the Admins group, and assign the ConnorD user to the Read-Only Users group.

h.  Accept the default name for the backup copy of the unsecured database.

i.  Print the Security Wizard report, do not save the snapshot report, and then exit Access.

j.  Use Windows Explorer or My Computer to move the **Rivers.mdb** shortcut from the Windows desktop to the Comp\Case4 folder.

k.  Open the **Rivers.mdb** shortcut, and then log on as the Administrator user.

l.  Open the **Rafting Trip** table, and then print and close the table.

5.  Exit Access.

# Case Problem 5

**Data File needed for this Case Problem: BuySell.mdb (*cont. from Tutorial 11*)**

***eACH Internet Auction Site***   Chris and Pat Aquino ask you to implement management and security features for the BuySell database. To help them with their request, complete the following steps:

1.  Open the **BuySell** database in the Comp\Case5 folder provided with your Data Files.

2.  Use the Performance Analyzer to analyze the entire **BuySell** database. How many analysis results of the recommendation type did the Performance Analyzer find? Of the suggestion type? Of the idea type? Close the Performance Analyzer dialog box.

3.  Create a replica of the **BuySell** database in the Comp\Case5 folder, making a backup of the database in the same folder. Accept the default settings in the Location of New Replica dialog box, and then complete the following steps:

a.  Close the Design Master, and then open the replica. Open the **Category** table, and then add a record with a value of Other for the Category field. (*Note:* If the Category ID field value for the record you add is not equal to 13, simply continue with the case.) Close the **Category** table.

b.  Synchronize the replica with the Design Master. Close the replica, open the Design Master, and then verify that the new record was added to the **Category** table. Switch to Design view for the **Category** table, and then review the properties for the CategoryID field. Using Access Help as necessary, prepare a written report explaining why Access doesn't assign consecutive values for the CategoryID field. Close the Design Master.

c.  Use Windows Explorer or My Computer to rename the **BuySell** database as **BuySell Design Master**, rename the **BuySell.bak** database as **BuySell.mdb**, and then close Windows Explorer or My Computer.

4.  Open the **BuySell** database, and then set the database startup options to hide the Database window and open the **Switchboard** form when the **BuySell** database is opened. Close the **BuySell** database.

5.  Convert the **BuySell** database to Access 2002 file format, saving the converted file as **BuySell2002** in the Comp\Case5 folder. Then save the **BuySell2002** database as an MDE file with the name **BuySell2002 MDE**.

6.  Exit Access.

**Research**

# Internet Assignments

The purpose of the Internet Assignments is to challenge you to find information on the Internet that you can use to work effectively with this software. The actual assignments are updated and maintained on the Course Technology Web site. Log on to the Internet and use your Web browser to go to the Student Online Companion for New Perspectives Office 2003 at **www.course.com/np/office2003**. Click the Internet Assignments link, and then navigate to the assignments for this tutorial.

**Assess**

# SAM Assessment and Training

If you have a SAM user profile, you may have access to hands-on instruction, practice, and assessment of the skills covered in this tutorial. Log in to your SAM account and go to your assignments page to see what your instructor has assigned.

**Review**

# Quick Check Answers

### Session 12.1

1. The Performance Analyzer is an Access tool that you can use to optimize the performance of an Access database.
2. Access can complete the recommendation and suggestion optimizations for you, but you must implement the idea optimizations.
3. Use the Linked Table Manager to change the filename or disk location for linked tables in an Access database.
4. When you create a replica of a database, the Design Master and all of its replicas are called the replica set.
5. Anyone using the Design Master can make changes to the design of the database tables, queries, and other objects. A replica prevents a user from changing the structure or design of an existing table, query, or other database object.
6. The synchronization process compares the Design Master to the replica and checks for any differences. Access updates the Design Master with any changes that have been made to the data in the replica, and updates the replica with any changes that have been made to the data or to the design of any database objects in the Design Master.

### Session 12.2

1. The Database Splitter is an Access tool that splits an Access database into two files: one file contains the tables, and the other contains the other database objects.
2. an action that takes place when a database opens
3. In the Startup dialog box, click the Display Form/Page list arrow, and then select the form.
4. security
5. decrypting
6. A user's permissions specify what kind of access the user has to objects in a database.
7. Users group and Admins group
8. MDE file

## Objectives

- Change field properties
- Add fields to a table
- Enter data in a table
- Create table relationships
- Create select, parameter, and crosstab queries
- Create a form using the Form Wizard
- Create calculated controls in a form
- Create a custom report
- Create macros
- Create a switchboard

In this case you will use skills you learned in the following tutorials:
- Tutorials 1–7, 9–10, and 12 (startup options only)

# Enhancing an Investment Club Database

## Case

## Nest Egg Investment Club

Barbara and Neal Hennessey and some friends recently formed an investment club. Researching investment clubs on the Web, Barbara found the National Association of Investors Corporation (NAIC) site. Established in 1951, NAIC is a nonprofit organization founded to educate investment clubs and individual investors. Following guidelines recommended by NAIC, the club members chose Nest Egg as their club name, prepared and approved a partnership agreement and a set of bylaws, registered their club, obtained the club's tax ID, and established an online brokerage account to handle the club's investments.

The club decided to meet monthly and to set monthly dues at $200. The 15 permanent club members, each having one vote for all club matters, include 13 individuals and two couples for a total of 17 individuals. Each of the 15 members can contribute $200 monthly, a participation level of 1, or $400 monthly, a participation level of 2, but the participation level does not affect the voting rule of one vote per member.

The online brokerage account will track the club's investments, but Felicia Rodriquez, the club treasurer, has created a database to handle club accounting for monthly dues and for any future withdrawals. Felicia's database consists of two tables, Member and Contribution. Figure 1 shows the structure of the Member table, which stores data about each club member. Each Member table record contains a member ID number and each member's first name, last name, address, phone, join date, and participation level (the Level field).

## Student Data Files

▽ AddCase1 folder
    Dollars.jpg
    NestEgg.mdb

Figure 1

**Structure of the Member table**

| Field Name | Data Type | Properties |
|---|---|---|
| MemberID | AutoNumber | Description—Primary key<br>Caption—Member ID |
| FirstName | Text | Field Size—15<br>Caption—First Name |
| LastName | Text | Field Size—15<br>Caption—Last Name |
| Address | Text | Field Size—32 |
| Phone | Text | Field Size—12 |
| JoinDate | Date/Time | Format—mm/dd/yyyy<br>Caption—Join Date |
| Level | Number | Description—Participation level used to determine the member's<br>monthly dues<br>Field Size—Byte<br>Decimal Places—0 |

Figure 2 shows the structure of the Contribution table, which contains one record for each monthly dues payment. PaymentID is the table's primary key. MemberID is a foreign key in the Contribution table, and the Member table will have a one-to-many relationship with the Contribution table. The other fields in the Contribution table are PaidDate and InvestmentAmt.

Figure 2

**Structure of the Contribution table**

| Field Name | Data Type | Properties |
|---|---|---|
| PaymentID | AutoNumber | Description—Primary key<br>Caption—Payment ID |
| MemberID | Number | Description—Foreign key<br>Field Size—Long Integer<br>Decimal Places—0<br>Caption—Member ID |
| PaidDate | Date/Time | Format—mm/dd/yyyy<br>Caption—Paid Date |
| InvestmentAmt | Currency | Decimal Places—2<br>Caption—Investment Amt |

Felicia wants to create special queries, forms, and reports in the database to help her manage club accounting. To help Felicia finish her work with the database, complete the following steps:

1. Make sure you have created your copy of the Access Data Files, and that your computer can access them. Start Access, and then open the **NestEgg** database located in the AddCase1 folder.
2. Review the **Member** and **Contribution** tables to become familiar with their structures and data. If you are unfamiliar with any property setting, use the Access Help system for an explanation of that property.

3. For the **Contribution** table, specify PaymentID as the primary key and resize all datasheet columns to their best fit. For the **Member** table, add a validation rule for the Level field to store only values equal to 1 or 2, add an appropriate validation text message, and then add these three new text fields between the Address and Phone fields: City (Field Size 24), StateProv (Field Size 2 and Caption of State/Prov), and PostalCode (Field Size 10 and Caption of Postal Code).

4. Modify the first record in the **Member** table datasheet by entering your name, city, state or province (two-character postal abbreviation), postal code (zip code), and phone number; enter phone numbers in 987-654-3210 format. For the last four records, enter the same city, state or province, postal code, and phone area code but enter different phone numbers. Select a second city, state or province, postal code, and phone area code, and then enter these values in records 2-6, using five different phone numbers. Finally, select a third city, state or province, postal code, and phone area code, and then enter these values in records 7-11, using five different phone numbers. Resize all datasheet columns to their best fit.

5. Define a one-to-many relationship between the primary **Member** table and the related **Contribution** table, using MemberID as the common field, enforcing referential integrity, and selecting the Cascade Update Related Fields option. Resize the Member field list so that all fields are visible, and then print the Relationships window without saving the created report.

6. Create and save a query named **DistantMembers** that displays the FirstName, LastName, Address, City, StateProv, PostalCode, and Phone fields for all members not living in the same city where you live in ascending order by LastName. Print the query recordset in landscape orientation after testing and saving the query.

7. Create and save a query named **April21Contributions** that displays the FirstName, LastName, Phone, and InvestmentAmt fields for all contributions made on 4/21/2006 in ascending order by LastName. Print the query recordset after testing and saving the query.

8. Create and save a query named **InvestmentTotalsByMember** that displays each member's first name, last name, and total investment amount. For the total field, use a name of TotalInvested and a Caption value of Total Invested. Sort in ascending order by LastName. Print the query recordset after testing and saving the query. Modify the query by deleting the FirstName and LastName fields, adding the PaidDate field as the first field in the query, and then saving the query as **InvestmentTotalsByDate**. Print the query recordset.

9. Create and save a parameter query named **LevelParameter** that displays the FirstName, LastName, Phone, JoinDate, and Level fields in ascending order by LastName for a Level field value that the user enters. If the user doesn't enter a field value, select and display all records. After creating and saving the query, run the query and enter 2 as the Level field value. Print the query results.

**Explore**

10. Create a crosstab query that uses PaidDate field values for the row headings, Level field values for the column headings, and the sum of the InvestmentAmt field as the summarized value. (*Hint*: Create a query named **InvestmentAmounts** that contains the three fields you need for the crosstab query.) Save the query as **InvestmentAmountsCrosstab**, resize the columns in the query recordset to their best fit, and then save and print the query recordset.

11. Use the Form Wizard to create a form containing a main form and a subform. Select all the fields from the **Member** table for the main form, and select all fields except MemberID from the **Contribution** table for the subform. Use the Tabular layout and the Standard style. Specify the title **ContributionsByMember** for the main form and the title **ContributionSubform** for the subform. Print only the first main form record and its subform records.

12. Create a copy of the **ContributionsByMember** form, and use **ContributionsByMemberModified** as the new form's name. Modify the new form by adding a calculated control, as shown in Figure 3, that displays the sum of the InvestmentAmt field values that appear in the subform. Set the calculated control's Format property to Currency, set its ControlTip Text property to "Calculated total investment amount," set its Back Color property to the same value as the form's background color, and set its Tab Stop property to No. Print only the first main form record and its subform records. (*Hint*: If the Form Footer section appears in the subform in your finished form, set its Visible property to No.)

| Figure 3 | Modified form |
| --- | --- |

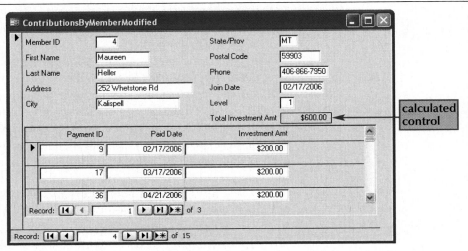

13. Create the Contributions by Date report shown in Figure 4. The report contains Page Header, Detail, PaidDate Footer, and Report Footer sections. Sort the detail records in ascending order by the PaidDate field, and then in ascending order by the LastName field. Hide duplicate values for the PaidDate field. Calculate and print totals of the InvestmentAmt field for each PaidDate field value and in grand total. Save the report as **ContributionsByDate**. Print the report.

| Figure 4 | ContributionsByDate report |

### Contributions by Date

Page 2 of 2

| Paid Date | First Name | Last Name | Phone | Level | Investment Amt |
|-----------|------------|-----------|-------|-------|----------------|
| 04/21/2006 | Kathy & Bob | Bakanas | 509-776-0099 | 1 | $200.00 |
| | Francine | Barnes | 403-851-6247 | 2 | $400.00 |
| | Kevin | Bioski | 406-245-8557 | 1 | $200.00 |
| | Nancy | Ciriello | 406-784-4827 | 1 | $200.00 |
| | Shawn | Erickson | 403-418-9376 | 1 | $200.00 |
| | Thomas | Evensen | 406-243-0219 | 2 | $400.00 |
| | Maureen | Heller | 406-866-7950 | 1 | $200.00 |
| | Barbara & Neal | Hennessey | 509-241-2655 | 2 | $400.00 |
| | Student First | Last | 403-224-5634 | 2 | $400.00 |
| | Lee | Nguyen | 403-216-5719 | 1 | $200.00 |
| | Peter | O'Rourke | 509-698-9400 | 1 | $200.00 |
| | Naomi | Ramos | 406-785-1311 | 1 | $200.00 |
| | Felicia | Rodriguez | 403-431-4409 | 1 | $200.00 |
| | Yonglei | Tao | 509-878-1555 | 1 | $200.00 |
| | Marsha | Van Ry | 509-364-8320 | 2 | $400.00 |
| | | | | | $4,000.00 |
| | | | | | $11,000.00 |

14. Create a macro group named **mcrSwitchboardMacros** that contains macros to be used with the command buttons on the switchboard you'll create in the next step. The macros perform these actions:
    - Open the **InvestmentAmounts** query
    - Open the **InvestmentTotalsByDate** query
    - Open the **InvestmentTotalsByMember** query
    - Close the switchboard and activate the Database window
15. Design and create a switchboard form named **Switchboard**. Use Figure 5 and the following descriptions as a guide to create the switchboard.
    a. Use the Switchboard Manager to create the switchboard. Place the command buttons on the form; the command buttons should use the macros in the **mcrSwitchboardMacros** macro group as appropriate. Define hot keys for each command button. Specify "Nest Egg Investment Club" as the main switchboard page name.
    b. Delete the default label and the shadow label on the form. Use an appropriate background color for the switchboard, and add the **Dollars.jpg** picture located in the AddCase1 folder to the locations shown on the switchboard in Figure 5.
    c. Resize the switchboard in Form view, and then set form properties that are appropriate for a switchboard.

**Figure 5** | NestEgg database switchboard

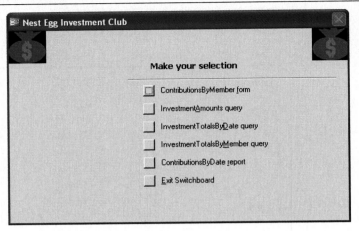

16. Set the startup options to hide the Database window and open the **Switchboard** form whenever the **NestEgg** database is opened.
17. Test the switchboard and all objects, and then exit Access.

## Objectives

- Change field properties
- Create a new table
- Enter data in a table
- Create table relationships
- Create select, query wizard, parameter, and crosstab queries
- Create forms using wizards, and customize forms
- Create calculated controls in a form
- Create a custom report
- Create a dialog box
- Create macros
- Create a switchboard

In this case you will use skills you learned in the following tutorials:
- Tutorials 1–7, 9–11, and 12 (startup options only)

# Tracking Parking Permits and Violations

## Case

## Tophill College

Sandy Tatoian is the office manager in the Public Safety department at Tophill College. Among her responsibilities, Sandy coordinates issuing parking permits to staff, faculty, and students, and processing citations for on-campus parking violations. Reductions in the college budget have forced her department to reduce the number of part-time student workers. As a result, the department is experiencing an increase in the backlog for processing citations and parking permit requests. After discussing the problem with her supervisor, Sandy meets with Pat Davis, a database analyst in the college computer center.

Pat questions Sandy about her requirements and agrees to design a database to reduce her workload and to help her gain better control over her coordination responsibilities. Sandy explains that parking permits are issued to students, faculty, and staff for their vehicles. The permit is affixed to the windshield in the lower corner on the driver's side. Each parking permit request form includes the parking permit number, the vehicle license plate number, and the person's name. With each issued permit, a person receives a brochure that describes the campus parking regulations and the fines for parking violations.

The Public Safety department includes a patrol force that enforces the campus parking regulations. The patrol force issues citations for parking violations. Each citation includes the citation number, the date and time of the violation, and a description of the violation. For vehicles with permits, the citation includes the permit number and the license plate number. For vehicles without permits, the citation includes the license plate number but not the permit number. Sandy's staff also tracks payments for the fines levied with the citations.

Pat's initial database contains three tables: Permit, Citation, and Payment. Figure 6 shows the structure of the Permit table, which stores data about each parking permit issued to students, faculty, and staff. Each Permit table record contains a permit number, the vehicle license plate number, and the permit requester's name.

## Student Data Files

▽ AddCase2 folder
  NoPark.bmp
  Tophill.mdb

**Figure 6** **Structure of the Permit table**

| Field Name | Data Type | Description |
| --- | --- | --- |
| PermitNum | Text | Primary key: unique number issued to an individual's vehicle |
| LicensePlateNum | Text | License plate number of the vehicle issued the permit |
| OwnerFirst | Text | Vehicle owner's first name |
| OwnerLast | Text | Vehicle owner's last name |

Figure 7 shows the structure of the Citation table, which contains one record for each issued citation. Each Citation record contains the citation number, date, and time; the vehicle license plate number; the violation code; and the permit number, if a permit is visible on the front windshield.

**Figure 7** **Structure of the Citation table**

| Field Name | Data Type | Description |
| --- | --- | --- |
| CitationNum | Text | Primary key: unique number assigned to a citation for a parking violation |
| CitationDate | Date/Time | Issue date for the citation |
| CitationTime | Date/Time | Issue time for the citation |
| PermitNum | Text | Null if the vehicle has no visible permit |
| LicensePlateNum | Text | Vehicle license plate number |
| ViolationCode | Text | Violation code for the parking infraction |

Figure 8 shows the structure of the Payment table, which contains one record for each parking violation payment. Each Payment record contains a unique payment ID, the payment amount and date, and the number of the citation to which the payment applies.

**Figure 8** **Structure of the Payment table**

| Field Name | Data Type | Description |
| --- | --- | --- |
| PaymentID | AutoNumber | Primary key: unique number assigned to a payment for a parking violation |
| PaymentAmt | Currency | Amount paid |
| PaymentDate | Date/Time | Payment date |
| CitationNum | Text | Citation to which the payment applies |

Pat turns the completed database design over to Sandy, who wants to create special queries, forms, and reports in the database to help her manage parking permits and violations. To help Sandy finish her work with the database, complete the following steps:

1. Make sure you have created your copy of the Access Data Files, and that your computer can access them. Start Access, and then open the **Tophill** database located in the AddCase2 folder.
2. Review the **Permit**, **Citation**, and **Payment** tables to become familiar with their structures and data. If you are unfamiliar with any property setting, use the Access Help system for an explanation of that property.

3. The **Citation** table contains a two-character ViolationCode field. Design and create a new table to store the violation codes, descriptions, and fine amounts, using the names ViolationCode, ViolationDesc, and FineAmt, making ViolationCode the primary key, and setting the Caption property and other field properties to appropriate values. Name this table **Violation**, add the eight records shown in Figure 9 to the table, resize all datasheet columns to their best fit, and then print the Violation table recordset.

| Figure 9 | Payment table records |

| ViolationCode | ViolationDesc | FineAmt |
| --- | --- | --- |
| BE | Improper Parking Building Entrance | $10 |
| EM | Expired Meter | $5 |
| HA | Improper Parking Handicapped Area | $25 |
| OA | Improper Parking Other Areas | $7 |
| RA | Improper Parking Reserved Area | $15 |
| RD | Improper Parking Roadway | $10 |
| SD | Improper Parking Service Drive | $12 |
| WL | Improper Parking Walk/Lawn | $10 |

4. Modify the first record in the **Permit** table datasheet by entering your name in the Owner First and Owner Last columns.
5. Add all four tables to the Relationships window, make sure all fields are visible in the field lists, and then define the three one-to-many relationships. Enforce referential integrity, and select the Cascade Update Related Fields option for each relationship. Rearrange the field lists as appropriate so that join lines don't cross field lists, save your design, and then print the Relationships window without saving the created report.
6. Create and save a query named **CollegeCitations** that displays, in order, all fields from the **Citation** table, and the OwnerFirst and OwnerLast fields from the **Permit** table. Sort in ascending order by OwnerLast as the first sort field, OwnerFirst as the second sort field, CitationDate as the third sort field, and CitationTime as the fourth sort field. Print the query recordset in landscape orientation after testing and saving the query, but don't close the query.
7. Save the **CollegeCitations** query as **AllCitations**, and then modify the new query to an outer join to include all records from the **Citation** table and the matching records from the **Permit** table. Print the query recordset in landscape orientation after testing and saving the query, and then close the query.
8. Create and save a query named **TotalPaymentsByDate** that displays the PaymentDate field and the sum of the PaymentAmt field from the **Payment** table. For the total field, use a Caption value of Total Payments. Sort the query in ascending order by PaymentDate. Resize all datasheet columns to their best fit, and then print the query recordset after testing and saving the query.
9. Create a find duplicates query based on the **Citation** table. Select LicensePlateNum as the field that might contain duplicates, and select all the other fields in the table as additional fields in the query recordset. Save the query as **VehiclesWithMultipleCitations**, and then view and print the query recordset.

10. Make a copy of the **AllCitations** query, save the copy as **AllCitationsParameter**, and then modify the new query to display records for a ViolationCode field value that the user enters. If the user doesn't enter a field value, select and display all records. After modifying and saving the query, run the query and enter OA as the ViolationCode field value. Print the query recordset in landscape orientation.

**Explore**

11. Make a copy of the **AllCitations** query, save the copy as **AllCitationsWithoutPermits**, and then modify the new query to display only those records that have a null PermitNum field value. After modifying and saving the query, run the query and print the query results in landscape orientation.

12. Create a crosstab query that uses the **Citation** table. Select the CitationDate field values for the row headings, ViolationCode field values for the column headings, and the count of the CitationNum field as the summarized value. Save the query as **CitationCrosstab**, use a Caption value of Total Citations for the Count Row Heading column, resize the columns in the query recordset to their best fit, print the query results, and then save and close the query.

13. Create and save a query named **CitationsAndPayments** that displays, in order, all fields from the Citation table, and the PaymentID, PaymentAmt, and PaymentDate fields from the Payment table. Sort in ascending order by CitationNum. Print the query recordset in landscape orientation after testing and saving the query.

14. Use the Form Wizard to create a form containing the main form and subform shown in Figure 10. Select all the fields from the **Permit** table for the main form, and select the appropriate fields from the **CitationsAndPayments** query for the subform. Use the Tabular layout and the Standard style. Specify the title **PermitAndCitations** for the main form and the title **CitationsAndPaymentsSubform** for the subform. Modify the form by adding the Total Payments calculated control that displays the total PaymentAmt field values from the subform. Print only main form record 29 and its subform records.

**Figure 10** | **Form created using the Form Wizard**

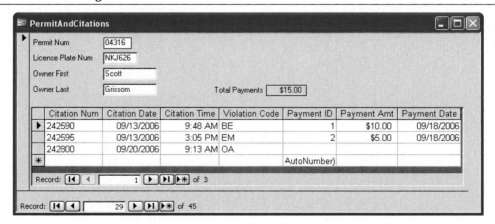

15. Use the AutoForm: Columnar Wizard to create the **Citation** form based on the **Citation** table. Modify the form by replacing the ViolationCode text box and its associated label with a combo box that displays all three fields from the Violation table. Resize text boxes as appropriate for the displayed values. Print only the last form record.

16. Create a custom report named **CitationsAndPayments** based on the **CitationsAndPayments** query. Use landscape orientation, and increase the report width to at least 8.5". Add an appropriate title centered in the Page Header section. In the Detail section, add all the fields from the query that are based on the Citation table in a row across the page, resizing and repositioning controls as necessary. In a row below these controls, add the three fields that are based on the Payment table, and resize and reposition controls as necessary. Draw a horizontal line across the width of the report and below the second row of controls in the Detail section. Print the first page of the report.

**Explore**

17. Make a copy of the **CitationsAndPayments** report, and save the copy as **CitationsAndPaymentsModified**. Modify the new report to suppress the printing of the three controls that are based on the Payment table when the PaymentID control value is null. (*Hint*: Use the Detail section's Format event, and use assignment statements similar to *Me![control name].Visible = True/False*, where *Me* refers to the open form, and *True/False* means to select the appropriate property setting.) After modifying and saving the report, print the first page of the report.

18. Design and create a form named **QueriesDialogBox** that has the following components and characteristics:

   a. The text "Queries" appears in the form's title bar.

   b. A list box (with a Name property value of lstQueryList) displays all the query names contained in the **Tophill** database. To place the query names in the list box, use an SQL SELECT statement to retrieve the query names from the **MSysObjects** table. Delete the label attached to the list box, and then widen the list box to approximately 2.25".

   c. The text "Queries Available," formatted with 10-point, bold font, appears as a heading above the list box.

   d. Two command buttons appear below the list box. The left command button displays the MS Access Query icon, and the right command button displays the word "Close" with the letter "C" underlined. Double-clicking a query name has the same effect as selecting a query name in the list box and clicking the left command button. Both events cause Access to display the query datasheet for the selected query. Clicking the Close command button causes Access to close the dialog box. The letter "C" is the hot key.

   e. Create a Load event procedure that moves the focus to the first query name in the list box when the **QueriesDialogBox** form opens.

   f. Create a DisplayQuery function to open the selected query in the list box in Datasheet view.

   g. Attach the DisplayQuery function to the OnDblClick property for the **QueriesDialogBox** form list box.

   h. Attach the DisplayQuery function to the OnClick property for the Datasheet command button on the **QueriesDialogBox** form.

   i. Resize the form's Detail section in Design view, resize the form in Form view, and then set form properties that are appropriate for a dialog box.

   j. Switch to Form view, and then test all the form options. Save and close the form.

19. Create a macro group named **mcrSwitchboardMacros** that contains macros to be used with the command buttons on the switchboard you'll create in the next step. The macros can perform these actions: open the **QueriesDialogBox** form in Form view, open the **Citation** form in Form view, open the **PermitAndCitations** form in Form view, and close the switchboard and activate the Database window.

20. Design and create a switchboard form named **Switchboard**. Use Figure 11 and the following descriptions as a guide to create the switchboard:
    a. Use the Switchboard Manager to create the switchboard. Place the command buttons on the form; the command buttons should use the macros in the **mcrSwitchboardMacros** macro group as appropriate. Define hot keys for each command button. Specify "Tophill Database" as the main switchboard page name.
    b. Delete the default label and the shadow label on the form. Add a label above the command buttons, and add the **NoPark.bmp** picture located in the AddCase2 folder to the locations shown on the switchboard in Figure 11.
    c. Resize the switchboard in Form view, and then set form properties that are appropriate for a switchboard.

| Figure 11 | Tophill database switchboard |

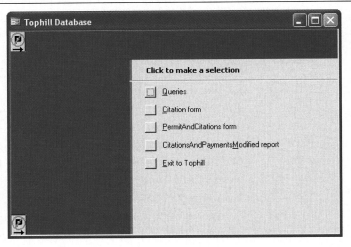

21. Set the startup options to hide the Database window and open the **Switchboard** form whenever the **Tophill** database is opened.
22. Test the switchboard and all objects, and then exit Access.

## Objectives

- Design a database and draw its entity-relationship diagram
- Create the tables and relationships for the database
- Create forms to maintain the database
- Design and enter test data for the database
- Create queries and reports from the database
- Design and create a switchboard

In this case you will use skills you learned in the following tutorials:

- Tutorials 1–7, 9, and the "Relational Databases and Database Design" appendix

# Internship Program for Pontiac College

## Case

## Pontiac College

Pontiac College provides students with opportunities for professional development and field study through its internship program, which is administered by the Office of Internships and Field Experience. Students complement their courses with a structured training experience provided by qualified professionals in selected fields. Internships are offered in many different areas, including law, counseling, government, administration, public relations, communications, health care, software engineering, and marketing.

Anjali Bhavnani has just been hired as Pontiac College's new Internship Coordinator. She is eager to make information about the sponsoring agencies, potential internships, and current student interns more readily available to her office and to the students who qualify for the program. Anjali's most ambitious project is to develop a computerized database for the internship program to help meet these goals.

Instead of visually scanning all internship possibilities, Anjali, her staff, and interested students will be able to select internships of specific interest to them. The new database will allow potential interns to view only the internships that meet the criteria they specify. Anjali asks Roula Mendes, an information systems major working in the Office of Internships and Field Experience, to help the office develop a computerized database system for the internship program.

Anjali first outlines the steps in the internship program process for Roula:

- Identify and document the available internships.
- Arrange for student intern placements.
- Assign and track student interns.

As the first step in the internship program process, Anjali receives a letter or phone call from a potential sponsoring agency. After some discussions, a sponsoring agency proposes an internship possibility and fills out the Agency/Internship Information form shown in Figure 12.

## Student Data Files

▽ AddCase3 folder
    Intmatch.bmp
    Inttrack.bmp

Figure 12 Agency/Internship Information form

AGENCY/INTERNSHIP INFORMATION

AGENCY INFORMATION

NAME OF AGENCY _____

DEPARTMENT _____

ADDRESS _____
　　　　　Street

　　　　　_____
　　　　　City　　　　　　　　　　State　　Zip

CONTACT _____ PHONE _____

INTERNSHIP INFORMATION

TITLE _____

DESCRIPTION OF _____
DUTIES _____
　　　　　_____

ORIENTATION & _____
TRAINING _____
　　　　　_____

ACADEMIC _____
BACKGROUND _____
REQUIRED _____

SUPERVISOR _____ PHONE _____

Office Use

Agency ID _____
Internship ID _____
Category _____

Many agencies offer more than one type of internship possibility. For each possible internship, the agency fills out a separate form and assigns one person as the contact for all internship questions and problems. In addition, each internship lists a supervisor who will work with the student intern. The internship remains active until the agency notifies the Office of Internships and Field Experience that the internship is filled or no longer available.

Anjali assigns a four-digit Agency ID to each new agency and a three-digit Internship ID to each new internship using sequential numbers. She also classifies each internship into a category that helps students identify internships that are related to their academic major or interests. For example, a student might be interested in health care, accounting, social service, or advertising.

A copy of each Agency/Internship Information form is placed in reference books in the Office of Internships and Field Experience. Students browse through these books to find internships that interest them. If an internship interests a student, the student copies the information about the internship and contacts the sponsoring agency directly to request an interview.

When a student gets an internship, the student and agency establish a Learning Contract, outlining the goals to be accomplished during the internship. The student then fills out the Student Internship form, shown in Figure 13, to provide basic personal information for the office files.

| Figure 13 | **Student Internship form** |

**STUDENT INTERNSHIP**

NAME _____ SS# _____

ADDRESS _____
Street

_____
City                                      State            ZIP

PHONE _____        CLASS _____ Junior _____ Senior

MAJOR _____GPA _____

Office Use

Internship ID        _____
Internship Term      _____ Fall _____ Spring _____ Summer
Internship Year      _____

Anjali enters the Internship ID and year on the Student Internship form and checks the term for the internship. Next, a clerk enters information from the form into a word processor to prepare lists of current interns and internships, and then places the form in a binder.

Anjali and Roula determine that getting these two forms into an Access database is their first priority, and then they will work on creating several new reports. The first report, the design of which is shown in Figure 14, lists all student interns alphabetically by last name for a selected term. In order to identify the student interns who should be included in the report, the system prompts the user for the term and year.

| Figure 14 | **Student Interns report design** |

<today's date>                 **Student Interns**                 Page x
                            As of <term><year>

**Last Name**          **First Name**     **Agency Name**                  **Internship Title**
x_____x     x_____x     x_____x     x_____x
x_____x     x_____x     x_____x     x_____x
x_____x     x_____x     x_____x     x_____x
x_____x     x_____x     x_____x     x_____x

**End of Report**

A second new report lists all agencies in the database alphabetically by agency name. Figure 15 shows the design of this report.

**Figure 15** **Internship Agencies report design**

<today's date>                  **Internship Agencies**                        Page x


**Agency Name**          **Department**           **Contact**              **Phone**

x------------x      x------------x      x------------x      x------------x
x------------x      x------------x      x------------x      x------------x
x------------x      x------------x      x------------x      x------------x
x------------x      x------------x      x------------x      x------------x


**End of Report**

The Internship by Category report, the design of which is shown in Figure 16, lists internships grouped by category. The staff will use this report when talking with students about the internship program.

**Figure 16** **Internship by Category report design**

<today's date>                **Internship by Category**                      Page x


Category x------------ x
**Internship ID**       **Internship Title**        **Internship Description**
  xxx                x------------x      x------------------------------ x
                                         x------------------------------ x
                                         x------------------------------ x
  xxx                x------------x      x------------------------------ x
  xxx                x------------x      x------------------------------ x
                                         x------------------------------ x


Category x------------ x
**Internship ID**       **Internship Title**        **Internship Description**
  xxx                x------------x      x------------------------------ x
  xxx                x------------x      x------------------------------ x
                                         x------------------------------ x
                                         x------------------------------ x


**End of Report**

At the end of an internship, the intern's supervisor evaluates the intern's work experience, using an evaluation form mailed from the Office of Internships and Field Experience. Anjali needs mailing labels addressed to the supervisor of each intern for the current term and year. The mailing labels should contain the supervisor's name on the first line; the agency name on the second line; the agency's street on the third line; and the agency's city, state, and zip code on the fourth line.

To create the database system, complete the following steps:

1. Read the appendix titled "Relational Databases and Database Design," which appears at the end of this book.
2. Identify each entity (table) in the database for the internship system.
3. Draw an entity-relationship diagram showing the entities and the relationships between the entities.
4. Design the database for the internship system. For each table, list the fields and their attributes, such as data types, field sizes, and validation rules. Place the set of tables in third normal form and identify all primary, alternate, and foreign keys.
5. Create the database structure using Access and name the database **Intern**. Be sure to define relationships between appropriate tables.
6. Create and save forms to maintain data on agencies, internships, student interns, and any other table in your database structure. The forms should be used to view, add, edit, and delete records in the database.
7. Create test data for each table in the database and add the test data, using the forms you created in Step 6.
8. Create and save the **StudentInterns** report, the **InternshipAgencies** report, and the **InternshipByCategory** report. The layouts shown in Figures 14 through 16 are guides—improve them as you see fit. Then create the **MailingLabels** report to create mailing labels for agencies using a label of your choice.
9. Design, create, and save a form that a student can use to view internships for a selected category. Display one internship at a time on the screen. For each internship, display the category, internship ID, title, description of duties, orientation and training, academic background, agency name, department, agency address, contact name, and contact phone. Provide an option to print the internship displayed on the screen. (*Note*: The AddCase3 folder contains two picture files, **Intmatch.bmp** and **Inttrack.bmp**, which you can include on this form.)
10. Design, create, and save a switchboard to coordinate the running of the internship system. (*Note*: The AddCase3 folder contains two picture files, named **Intmatch.bmp** and **Inttrack.bmp**, which you can include on the switchboard if you want.)
11. Test all features of the internship system.

## Objectives

- Learn the characteristics of a table
- Learn about primary, candidate, alternate, foreign, composite, and surrogate keys
- Study one-to-one, one-to-many, and many-to-many relationships
- Learn to describe tables and relationships with entity-relationship diagrams and with a shorthand method
- Study database integrity constraints for primary keys, referential integrity, and domains
- Learn about determinants, functional dependencies, anomalies, and normalization
- Understand the differences among natural, artificial, and surrogate keys
- Learn about naming conventions

# Relational Databases and Database Design

This appendix introduces you to the basics of database design. Before trying to master this material, be sure you understand the following concepts: data, information, field, field value, record, table, relational database, common field, database management system (DBMS), and relational database management system (RDBMS).

## Student Data Files

There are no Student Data Files needed for this appendix.

# Tables

A relational database stores its data in tables. A **table** is a two-dimensional structure made up of rows and columns. The terms table, **record** (row), and **field** (column) are the popular names for the more formal terms **relation** (table), **tuple** (row), and **attribute** (column), as shown in Figure A-1.

▶ **A table (relation) consisting of records and fields**

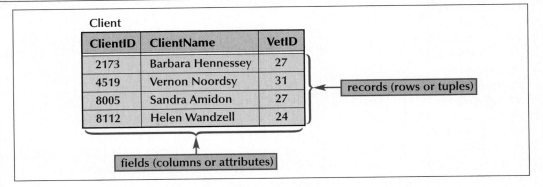

The Client table shown in Figure A-1 is an example of a relational database table, a two-dimensional structure with the following characteristics:

- Each row is unique. Because no two rows are the same, you can easily locate and update specific data. For example, you can locate the row for ClientID 8005 and change the ClientName value, Sandra Amidon, or the VetID value, 27.
- The order of the rows is unimportant. You can add or view rows in any order. For example, you can view the rows in ClientName order instead of ClientID order.
- Each table entry contains a single value. At the intersection of each row and column, you cannot have more than one value. For example, each row in Figure A-1 contains one ClientID, one ClientName, and one VetID.
- The order of the columns is unimportant. You can add or view columns in any order.
- Each column has a unique name called the **field name**. The field name allows you to access a specific column without needing to know its position within the table.
- The entries in a column are from the same domain. A **domain** is a set of values from which one or more columns (fields) draw their actual values. A domain can be broad, such as "all legitimate names of people" for the ClientName column, or narrow, such as "24, 27, or 31" for the VetID column. The domain of "all legitimate dates" could be shared by the BirthDate, StartDate, and LastPayDate columns in a company's employee table.
- Each row in a table describes, or shows the characteristics of, an entity. An **entity** is a person, place, object, event, or idea for which you want to store and process data. For example, ClientID, ClientName, and VetID are characteristics of the clients of a pet-sitting company. The Client table represents all the client entities and their characteristics. That is, each row of the Client table describes a different client of the company using the characteristics of ClientID, ClientName, and VetID. The Client table includes only characteristics of a client. Other tables would exist for the company's other entities. For example, a Pet table might describe the clients' pets and an Employee table might describe the company's employees.

Knowing the characteristics of a table leads directly to a definition of a relational database. A **relational database** is a collection of tables (relations).

Note that this book uses singular table names, but many people use plural table names. You can use either singular table names or plural table names, as long as you consistently use the style you choose.

## Keys

Primary keys ensure that each row in a table is unique. A **primary key** is a field, or a collection of fields, whose values uniquely identify each row in a table. In addition to being *unique*, a primary key must be *minimal* (that is, contain no unnecessary extra fields) and must not change in value. For example, in Figure A-2 the State table contains one record per state and uses the StateAbbrev field as its primary key.

A table and its keys    **Figure A-2**

primary key     alternate keys

State

| StateAbbrev | StateName | EnteredUnionOrder | StateBird | StatePopulation |
|---|---|---|---|---|
| CT | Connecticut | 5 | American robin | 3,405,565 |
| MI | Michigan | 26 | robin | 9,938,444 |
| SD | South Dakota | 40 | pheasant | 754,844 |
| TN | Tennessee | 16 | mockingbird | 5,689,283 |
| TX | Texas | 28 | mockingbird | 20,851,820 |

Could any other field, or collection of fields, be the primary key of the State table?

- Could the StateBird field serve as the primary key? No, because the field does not have unique values (for example, the mockingbird is the state bird of more than one state).
- Could the StatePopulation field serve as the primary key? No, because the field values change periodically and are not guaranteed to be unique.
- Could the StateAbbrev and StateName fields together serve as the primary key? No, because the combination is not minimal. Something less, the StateAbbrev field by itself, can serve as the primary key.
- Could the StateName field serve as the primary key? Yes, because the field has unique values. In a similar way, you could select the EnteredUnionOrder field as the primary key for the State table. One field, or a collection of fields, that can serve as a primary key is called a **candidate key**. The candidate keys for the State table are the StateAbbrev field, the StateName field, and the EnteredUnionOrder field. You choose one of the candidate keys to be the primary key, and each remaining candidate key is called an **alternate key**. The StateAbbrev field is the State table's primary key in Figure A-2, so the StateName and EnteredUnionOrder fields become alternate keys in the table.

Figure A-3 shows a City table containing the fields StateAbbrev, CityName, and CityPopulation.

**A table with a composite key**

| StateAbbrev | CityName | CityPopulation |
|---|---|---|
| CT | Hartford | 121,578 |
| CT | Madison | 17,858 |
| CT | Portland | 8,732 |
| MI | Lansing | 119,128 |
| SD | Madison | 6,540 |
| SD | Pierre | 13,876 |
| TN | Nashville | 569,891 |
| TX | Austin | 656,562 |
| TX | Portland | 14,827 |

What is the primary key for the City table? The values for the CityPopulation field periodically change and are not guaranteed to be unique, so the CityPopulation field cannot be the primary key. Because the values for each of the other two fields are not unique, the StateAbbrev field alone cannot be the primary key and neither can the CityName field (for example, there are two cities named Madison and two named Portland). The primary key is the combination of the StateAbbrev and CityName fields. Both fields together are needed to identify, uniquely and minimally, each row in the City table. A multiple-field primary key is called a **composite key** or a **concatenated key**.

The StateAbbrev field in the City table is also a foreign key. A **foreign key** is a field, or a collection of fields, in one table whose values must match the values of the primary key of some table or must be null. As shown in Figure A-4, the values in the City table's StateAbbrev column match the values in the State table's StateAbbrev column. Thus, the StateAbbrev field, the primary key of the State table, is a foreign key in the City table. Although the field name StateAbbrev is the same in both tables, the names could be different. Most people give the same name to a field stored in two or more tables to broadcast clearly that they are really the same field.

**StateAbbrev as a primary key (State table) and a foreign key (City table)** | **Figure A-4**

primary key

State

| StateAbbrev | StateName | EnteredUnionOrder | StateBird | StatePopulation |
|---|---|---|---|---|
| CT | Connecticut | 5 | American robin | 3,405,565 |
| MI | Michigan | 26 | robin | 9,938,444 |
| SD | South Dakota | 40 | pheasant | 754,844 |
| TN | Tennessee | 16 | mockingbird | 5,689,283 |
| TX | Texas | 28 | mockingbird | 20,851,820 |

primary key

City

foreign key

| StateAbbrev | CityName | CityPopulation |
|---|---|---|
| CT | Hartford | 121,578 |
| CT | Madison | 17,858 |
| CT | Portland | 8,732 |
| MI | Lansing | 119,128 |
| SD | Madison | 6,540 |
| SD | Pierre | 13,876 |
| TN | Nashville | 569,891 |
| TX | Austin | 656,562 |
| TX | Portland | 14,827 |

A **nonkey field** is a field that is not part of the primary key. In the two tables shown in Figure A-4, all fields are nonkey fields except the StateAbbrev field in the State and City tables and the CityName field in the City table. *Key* is an ambiguous word because it can refer to a primary, candidate, alternate, or foreign key. When the word key appears alone, however, it means primary key and the definition for a nonkey field consequently makes sense.

# Relationships

The Capital table, shown in Figure A-5, has one row for each state capital. The CapitalName and StateAbbrev fields are candidate keys; selecting the CapitalName field as the primary key makes the StateAbbrev field an alternate key. The StateAbbrev field in the Capital table is also a foreign key because its values match the values in the State table's StateAbbrev column.

primary key

State

| StateAbbrev | StateName | EnteredUnionOrder | StateBird | StatePopulation |
|---|---|---|---|---|
| CT | Connecticut | 5 | American robin | 3,405,565 |
| MI | Michigan | 26 | robin | 9,938,444 |
| SD | South Dakota | 40 | pheasant | 754,844 |
| TN | Tennessee | 16 | mockingbird | 5,689,283 |
| TX | Texas | 28 | mockingbird | 20,851,820 |

primary key          foreign key

Capital

| CapitalName | StateAbbrev | YearDesignated | PhoneAreaCode | CapitalPopulation |
|---|---|---|---|---|
| Austin | TX | 1845 | 512 | 656,562 |
| Hartford | CT | 1662 | 860 | 121,578 |
| Lansing | MI | 1847 | 517 | 119,128 |
| Nashville | TN | 1843 | 615 | 569,891 |
| Pierre | SD | 1889 | 605 | 13,876 |

## One-to-One

The State and Capital tables, shown in Figure A-5, have a one-to-one relationship. A **one-to-one relationship** (abbreviated 1:1) exists between two tables when each row in each table has at most one matching row in the other table. The StateAbbrev field, which is a foreign key in the Capital table and the primary key in the State table, is the common field that ties together the rows of each table.

Should the State and Capital tables be combined into one table? Although the two tables in any one-to-one relationship can be combined into one table, when each table describes different entities, as they do in this case, they should usually be kept separate.

## One-to-Many

The State and City tables, shown once again in Figure A-6, have a one-to-many relationship. A **one-to-many relationship** (abbreviated 1:M) exists between two tables when each row in the first table matches many rows in the second table and each row in the second table matches at most one row in the first table. "Many" can mean zero rows, one row, or two or more rows. The StateAbbrev field, which is a foreign key in the City table and the primary key in the State table, is the common field that ties together the rows of the two tables.

primary key

State

| StateAbbrev | StateName | EnteredUnionOrder | StateBird | StatePopulation |
|---|---|---|---|---|
| CT | Connecticut | 5 | American robin | 3,405,565 |
| MI | Michigan | 26 | robin | 9,938,444 |
| SD | South Dakota | 40 | pheasant | 754,844 |
| TN | Tennessee | 16 | mockingbird | 5,689,283 |
| TX | Texas | 28 | mockingbird | 20,851,820 |

City     primary key

foreign key

| StateAbbrev | CityName | CityPopulation |
|---|---|---|
| CT | Hartford | 121,578 |
| CT | Madison | 17,858 |
| CT | Portland | 8,732 |
| MI | Lansing | 119,128 |
| SD | Madison | 6,540 |
| SD | Pierre | 13,876 |
| TN | Nashville | 569,891 |
| TX | Austin | 656,562 |
| TX | Portland | 14,827 |

## Many-to-Many

In Figure A-7, the State table (with the StateAbbrev field as its primary key) and the Crop table (with the CropName field as its primary key) have a many-to-many relationship. A **many-to-many relationship** (abbreviated as M:N) exists between two tables when each row in the first table matches many rows in the second table and each row in the second table matches many rows in the first table. In a relational database, you must use a third table to serve as a bridge between the two many-to-many tables; the third table has the primary keys of the many-to-many tables as its primary key. The original tables now each have a one-to-many relationship with the new table. The StateAbbrev and CropName fields represent the primary key of the Production table that is shown in Figure A-7. The StateAbbrev field, which is a foreign key in the Production table and the primary key in the State table, is the common field that ties together the rows of the State and Production tables. Likewise, the CropName field is the common field for the Crop and Production tables.

**Figure A-7** | A many-to-many relationship

primary key

**State**

| StateAbbrev | StateName | EnteredUnionOrder | StateBird | StatePopulation |
|---|---|---|---|---|
| CT | Connecticut | 5 | American robin | 3,405,565 |
| MI | Michigan | 26 | robin | 9,938,444 |
| SD | South Dakota | 40 | pheasant | 754,844 |
| TN | Tennessee | 16 | mockingbird | 5,689,283 |
| TX | Texas | 28 | mockingbird | 20,851,820 |

**Crop**

| CropName | Exports | Imports |
|---|---|---|
| corn | $4,965.8 | $68.5 |
| cotton | $2,014.6 | $11.4 |
| soybeans | $4,462.8 | $15.8 |
| wheat | $4,503.2 | $191.1 |

primary key

**Production**

foreign keys

| StateAbbrev | CropName | Quantity |
|---|---|---|
| MI | corn | 241,500 |
| MI | soybeans | 47,520 |
| MI | wheat | 35,280 |
| SD | corn | 377,200 |
| SD | soybeans | 63,000 |
| SD | wheat | 119,590 |
| TN | corn | 79,360 |
| TN | soybeans | 33,250 |
| TN | wheat | 13,440 |
| TX | corn | 202,500 |
| TX | cotton | 3,322 |
| TX | soybeans | 12,870 |
| TX | wheat | 129,200 |

## Entity Subtype

Figure A-8 shows a special type of one-to-one relationship. The Shipping table's primary key is the StateAbbrev field, and the table contains one row for each state having an ocean shoreline. Because not all states have an ocean shoreline, the Shipping table has fewer rows than the State table. However, each row in the Shipping table has a matching row in the State table, with the StateAbbrev field serving as the common field; the StateAbbrev field is the primary key in the State relation and is a foreign key in the Shipping relation.

State

primary key

| StateAbbrev | State Name | EnteredUnionOrder | StateBird | StatePopulation |
|---|---|---|---|---|
| CT | Connecticut | 5 | American robin | 3,405,565 |
| MI | Michigan | 26 | robin | 9,938,444 |
| SD | South Dakota | 40 | pheasant | 754,844 |
| TN | Tennessee | 16 | mockingbird | 5,689,283 |
| TX | Texas | 28 | mockingbird | 20,851,820 |

foreign key

primary key

Shipping

| StateAbbrev | OceanShoreline | ExportTonnage | ImportTonnage |
|---|---|---|---|
| CT | 618 | 3,377,466 | 2,118,494 |
| TX | 3,359 | 45,980,912 | 109,400,314 |

The Shipping table, in this situation, is called an **entity subtype**, a table whose primary key is a foreign key to a second table and whose fields are additional fields for the second table. You can create an entity subtype when a table has fields that could have null values. A **null value** is the absence of a value for a field. (A null value is not blank, nor zero, nor any other value.) You give a null value to a field when you do not know its value or when a value does not apply. For example, instead of using the Shipping table, you could store the OceanShoreline, ExportTonnage, and ImportTonnage fields in the State relation and allow them to be null for states not having an ocean shoreline. You should be aware that database experts are currently debating the validity of the use of nulls in relational databases, and many experts insist that you should never use nulls. This warning against nulls is partly based on the inconsistent way different RDBMSs treat nulls and partly due to the lack of a firm theoretical foundation for how to use nulls. In any case, entity subtypes are an alternative to the use of nulls.

# Entity-Relationship Diagrams

A common shorthand method for describing tables is to write the table name followed by its fields in parentheses, underlining the fields that represent the primary key and identifying the foreign keys for a table immediately after the table. Using this method, the tables that appear in Figures A-5 through A-8 are described in the following way:

State (<u>StateAbbrev</u>, StateName, EnteredUnionOrder, StateBird, StatePopulation)
Capital (<u>CapitalName</u>, StateAbbrev, YearDesignated, PhoneAreaCode,
    CapitalPopulation)
    Foreign key: StateAbbrev to State table
City (<u>StateAbbrev</u>, <u>CityName</u>, CityPopulation)
    Foreign key: StateAbbrev to State table
Crop (<u>CropName</u>, Exports, Imports)

Production (<u>StateAbbrev</u>, <u>CropName</u>, Quantity)
    Foreign key: StateAbbrev to State table
    Foreign key: CropName to Crop table
Shipping (<u>StateAbbrev</u>, OceanShoreline, ExportTonnage, ImportTonnage)
    Foreign key: StateAbbrev to State table

    Another popular way to describe tables *and their relationships* is with entity-relationship diagrams. An **entity-relationship diagram (ERD)** shows a database's entities and the relationships among the entities in a symbolic, visual way. In an entity-relationship diagram, an entity and a table are equivalent. Figure A-9 shows an entity-relationship diagram for the tables that appear in Figures A-5 through A-8.

| Figure A-9 | An entity-relationship diagram |
| --- | --- |

    Entity-relationship diagrams have the following characteristics:

- Entities, or tables, appear in rectangles, and relationships appear in diamonds. The entity name appears inside the rectangle, and a verb describing the relationship appears inside the diamond. For example, the City rectangle is connected to the State rectangle by the Found in diamond and is read: "a city is found in a state."
- The 1 by the State entity and the M by the City entity identify a one-to-many relationship between these two entities. In a similar manner, a many-to-many relationship exists between the State and Crop entities and one-to-one relationships exist between the State and Capital entities and between the State and Shipping entities.
- A diamond inside a rectangle defines a composite entity. A **composite entity** is a relationship that has the characteristics of an entity. For example, Production connects the State and Crop entities in an M:N relationship and acts as an entity by containing the Quantity field, along with the composite key of the StateAbbrev and CropName fields.

- An entity subtype, for example, Shipping, appears in a double rectangle and is connected without an intervening diamond directly to its related entity, for example, State.
- You can also show fields in an ERD by placing each individual field in a bubble connected to its entity or relationship. However, typical ERDs have large numbers of entities and relationships, so including the fields might confuse rather than clarify the ERD.

# Integrity Constraints

A database has **integrity** if its data follows certain rules; each rule is called an **integrity constraint**. The ideal is to have the DBMS enforce all integrity constraints. If a DBMS can enforce some integrity constraints but not others, the other integrity constraints must be enforced by other programs or by the people who use the DBMS. Integrity constraints can be divided into three groups: primary key constraints, foreign key constraints, and domain integrity constraints.

- One primary key constraint is inherent in the definition of a primary key, which says that the primary key must be unique. The **entity integrity constraint** says that the primary key cannot be null. For a composite key, none of the individual fields can be null. The uniqueness and nonnull properties of a primary key ensure that you can reference any data value in a database by supplying its table name, field name, and primary key value.
- Foreign keys provide the mechanism for forming a relationship between two tables, and referential integrity ensures that only valid relationships exist. **Referential integrity** is the constraint specifying that each nonnull foreign key value must match a primary key value in the related table. Specifically, referential integrity means that you cannot add a row with an unmatched foreign key value. Referential integrity also means that you cannot change or delete the related primary key value and leave the foreign key orphaned. In some RDBMSs, if you try to change or delete a primary key value, you can specify one of these options: restricted, cascades, or nullifies. If you specify **restricted**, the DBMS updates or deletes the value only if there are no matching foreign key values. If you choose **cascades** and then change a primary key value, the DBMS changes the matching foreign key values to the new primary key value, or, if you delete a primary key value, the DBMS also deletes the matching foreign key rows. If you choose **nullifies** and then change or delete a primary key value, the DBMS sets all matching foreign key values to null.
- Recall that a domain is a set of values from which one or more fields draw their actual values. A **domain integrity constraint** is a rule you specify for a field. By choosing a data type for a field, you impose a constraint on the set of values allowed for the field. You can create specific validation rules for a field to limit its domain further. As you make a field's domain definition more precise, you exclude more and more unacceptable values for the field. For example, in the State table you could define the domain for the EnteredUnionOrder field to be a unique integer between 1 and 50 and the domain for the StateBird field to be any name containing 25 or fewer characters.

# Dependencies and Determinants

Tables are related to other tables. Fields are also related to other fields. Consider the StateCrop table shown in Figure A-10. Its description is:

StateCrop (<u>StateAbbrev</u>, <u>CropName</u>, StateBird, BirdScientificName, StatePopulation, Exports, Quantity)

| StateAbbrev | CropName | StateBird | BirdScientificName | StatePopulation | Exports | Quantity |
|---|---|---|---|---|---|---|
| CT | corn | American robin | Planesticus migratorius | 3,405,565 | $4,965.8 | |
| MI | corn | robin | Planesticus migratorius | 9,938,444 | $4,965.8 | 241,500 |
| MI | soybeans | robin | Planesticus migratorius | 9,938,444 | $4,462.8 | 47,520 |
| MI | wheat | robin | Planesticus migratorius | 9,938,444 | $4,503.2 | 35,280 |
| SD | corn | pheasant | Phasianus colchicus | 754,844 | $4,965.8 | 377,200 |
| SD | soybeans | pheasant | Phasianus colchicus | 754,844 | $4,462.8 | 63,000 |
| SD | wheat | pheasant | Phasianus colchicus | 754,844 | $4,503.2 | 119,590 |
| TN | corn | mockingbird | Mimus polyglottos | 5,689,283 | $4,965.8 | 79,360 |
| TN | soybeans | mockingbird | Mimus polyglottos | 5,689,283 | $4,462.8 | 33,250 |
| TN | wheat | mockingbird | Mimus polyglottos | 5,689,283 | $4,503.2 | 13,440 |
| TX | corn | mockingbird | Mimus polyglottos | 20,851,820 | $4,965.8 | 202,500 |
| TX | cotton | mockingbird | Mimus polyglottos | 20,851,820 | $2,014.6 | 3,322 |
| TX | soybeans | mockingbird | Mimus polyglottos | 20,851,820 | $4,462.8 | 12,870 |
| TX | wheat | mockingbird | Mimus polyglottos | 20,851,820 | $4,503.2 | 129,200 |

(StateCrop table. "primary key" points to CropName; "null value" points to the empty Quantity cell for CT.)

The StateCrop table combines several fields from the State, Crop, and Production tables that appeared in Figure A-7. The StateAbbrev, StateBird, and StatePopulation fields are from the State table. The CropName and Exports fields are from the Crop table. The StateAbbrev, CropName, and Quantity fields are from the Production table. The BirdScientificName field is a new field for the StateCrop relation, whose primary key is the combination of the StateAbbrev and CropName fields.

Notice the null value in the Quantity field for the state of Connecticut (StateAbbrev CT). If you look back to Figure A-7, you can see that there were no entries for Quantity for the state of Connecticut, which is why its Quantity field is null in the StateCrop relation. However, note that the CropName field requires an entry because it is part of the composite key for the table. If you want the state of CT to be in the StateCrop table, you need to assign a dummy CropName value for the CT entry, in this case, Corn.

In the StateCrop table, each field is related to other fields. To determine field relationships, you ask "Does a value for a particular field give me a single value for another field?" If the answer is Yes, then the two fields are related. For example, a value for the StateAbbrev field determines a single value for the StatePopulation field, and a value for the StatePopulation field depends on the value of the StateAbbrev field. In database discussions, the word functionally is used, as in: "StateAbbrev functionally determines StatePopulation" and "StatePopulation is functionally dependent on StateAbbrev." In this case, StateAbbrev is called a determinant. A **determinant** is a field, or a collection of fields, whose values determine the values of another field. A field is functionally dependent on another field (or a collection of fields) if that other field is a determinant for it.

You can graphically show a table's functional dependencies and determinants in a **bubble diagram**; a bubble diagram is also called a **data model diagram** and a **functional dependency diagram**. Figure A-11 shows the bubble diagram for the StateCrop table.

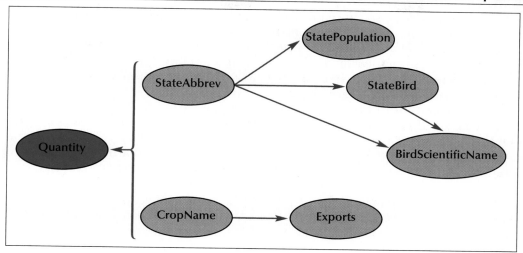

- The StateAbbrev field is a determinant for the StatePopulation, StateBird, and BirdScientificName fields.
- The CropName field is a determinant for the Exports field.
- The Quantity field is functionally dependent on the StateAbbrev and CropName fields together.
- The StateBird field is a determinant for the BirdScientificName field.

Note that StateAbbrev and CropName together is a determinant for the Quantity field and for all fields that depend on the StateAbbrev field alone and the CropName field alone. Some experts include these additional fields and some don't. The previous list of determinants does not include these additional fields.

An alternative way to show determinants is to list the determinant, a right arrow, and then the dependent fields, separated by commas. Using this alternative, the determinants shown in Figure A-11 are:

StateAbbrev → StatePopulation, StateBird, BirdScientificName
CropName → Exports
StateAbbrev, CropName → Quantity
StateBird → BirdScientificName

Only the Quantity field is functionally dependent on the table's full primary key, the StateAbbrev and CropName fields. The StatePopulation, StateBird, and BirdScientificName fields have partial dependencies because they are functionally dependent on the StateAbbrev field, which is part of the primary key. A **partial dependency** is a functional dependency on part of the primary key, instead of the entire primary key. Does another partial dependency exist in the StateCrop table? Yes, the Exports field has a partial dependency on the CropName field.

Because the StateAbbrev field is a determinant of both the StateBird and BirdScientificName fields, and the StateBird field is a determinant of the BirdScientificName field, the StateBird and BirdScientificName fields have a transitive dependency. A **transitive dependency** is a functional dependency between two nonkey fields, which are both dependent on a third field.

How do you know which functional dependencies exist among a collection of fields, and how do you recognize partial and transitive dependencies? The answers lie with the questions you ask as you gather the requirements for a database application. For each field and entity, you must gain an accurate understanding of its meaning and relationships in the context of the application. **Semantic object modeling** is an entire area of study within the database field devoted to the meanings and relationships of data.

# Anomalies

When you use a DBMS, you are more likely to get results you can trust if you create your relations carefully. For example, problems might occur with tables that have partial and transitive dependencies, whereas you won't have as much trouble if you ensure that your tables include only fields that are directly related to each other. Also, when you remove data redundancy from a table, you improve that table. **Data redundancy** occurs when you store the same data in more than one place.

The problems caused by data redundancy and by partial and transitive dependencies are called **anomalies** because they are undesirable irregularities of tables. Anomalies are of three types: insertion, deletion, and update.

To examine the effects of these anomalies, consider the Client table that is shown in Figure A-12. The Client table represents part of the database for Pet Sitters Unlimited, which is a company providing pet-sitting services for homeowners while they are on vacation. Pet Sitters Unlimited keeps track of the data about its clients and the clients' children, pets, and vets. The fields for the Client table include the composite key ClientID and ChildName, along with the ClientName, VetID, and VetName fields.

| Figure A-12 | The Client table with insertion, deletion, and update anomalies |

Client

| ClientID | ChildName | ClientName | VetID | VetName |
|----------|-----------|------------|-------|---------|
| 2173 | Ryan | Barbara Hennessey | 27 | Pet Vet |
| 4519 | Pat | Vernon Noordsy | 31 | Pet Care |
| 4519 | Dana | Vernon Noordsy | 31 | Pet Care |
| 8005 | Dana | Sandra Amidon | 27 | Pet Vet |
| 8005 | Dani | Sandra Amidon | 27 | Pet Vet |
| 8112 | Pat | Helen Wandzell | 24 | Pets R Us |

- An **insertion anomaly** occurs when you cannot add a record to a table because you do not know the entire primary key value. For example, you cannot add the new client Cathy Corbett with a ClientID of 3322 to the Client table when you do not know her children's names. Entity integrity prevents you from leaving any part of a primary key null. Because the ChildName field is part of the primary key, you cannot leave it null. To add the new client, your only option is to make up a ChildName field value, even if the client does not have children. This solution misrepresents the facts and is unacceptable, if a better approach is available.
- A **deletion anomaly** occurs when you delete data from a table and unintentionally lose other critical data. For example, if you delete ClientID 8112 because Helen Wandzell is no longer a client, you also lose the only instance of VetID 24 in the database. Thus, you no longer know that VetID 24 is Pets R Us.
- An **update anomaly** occurs when you change one field value and either the DBMS must make more than one change to the database or else the database ends up containing inconsistent data. For example, if you change a ClientName, VetID, or VetName field value for ClientID 4519, the DBMS must change multiple rows of the Client table. If the DBMS fails to change all the rows, the ClientName, VetID, or VetName field now has two different values in the database and is inconsistent.

# Normalization

**Database design** is the process of determining the content and structure of data in a database in order to support some activity on behalf of a user or group of users. After you have determined the collection of fields users need to support an activity, you need to determine the precise tables needed for the collection of fields and then place those fields into the correct tables. Crucial to good database design is understanding the functional dependencies of all fields; recognizing the anomalies caused by data redundancy, partial dependencies, and transitive dependencies when they exist; and knowing how to eliminate the anomalies. Failure to eliminate anomalies leads to data redundancy and can cause data integrity and other problems as your database grows in size.

The process of identifying and eliminating anomalies is called **normalization**. Using normalization, you start with a collection of tables, apply sets of rules to eliminate anomalies, and produce a new collection of problem-free tables. The sets of rules are called **normal forms**. Of special interest for our purposes are the first three normal forms: first normal form, second normal form, and third normal form. First normal form improves the design of your tables, second normal form improves the first normal form design, and third normal form applies even more stringent rules to produce an even better design. Note that normal forms beyond third normal form exist; these higher normal forms can improve a database design in some situations but won't be covered in this section.

## First Normal Form

Consider the Client table shown in Figure A-13. For each client, the table contains ClientID, which is the primary key; the client's name and children's names; the ID and name of the client's vet; and the ID, name, and type of each client's pets. For example, Barbara Hennessey has no children and three pets, Vernon Noordsy has two children and one pet, Sandra Amidon has two children and two pets, and Helen Wandzell has one child and one pet. Because each entry in a table must contain a single value, the structure shown in Figure A-13 does not meet the requirements for a table; therefore, it is called an **unnormalized relation**. The ChildName field, which can have more than one value, is called a **repeating group**. The set of fields that includes the PetID, PetName, and PetType fields is a second repeating group in the structure.

**Repeating groups of data in an unnormalized Client relation** ◄ **Figure A-13**

Client

| ClientID | ClientName | ChildName | VetID | VetName | PetID | PetName | PetType |
|---|---|---|---|---|---|---|---|
| 2173 | Barbara Hennessey | | 27 | Pet Vet | 1<br>2<br>4 | Sam<br>Hoober<br>Sam | bird<br>dog<br>hamster |
| 4519 | Vernon Noordsy | Pat<br>Dana | 31 | Pet Care | 2 | Charlie | cat |
| 8005 | Sandra Amidon | Dana<br>Dani | 27 | Pet Vet | 1<br>2 | Beefer<br>Kirby | dog<br>cat |
| 8112 | Helen Wandzell | Pat | 24 | Pets R Us | 3 | Kirby | dog |

First normal form addresses this repeating-group situation. A table is in **first normal form** (**1NF**) if it does not contain repeating groups. To remove a repeating group and convert to first normal form, you expand the primary key to include the primary key of the repeating group. You must perform this step carefully, however. If the unnormalized relation has independent repeating groups, you must perform the conversion step separately for each.

The repeating group that consists of the ChildName field is independent from the repeating group that consists of the PetID, PetName, and PetType fields. That is, the number and names of a client's children are independent of the number, names, and types of a client's pets. Performing the conversion step to each independent repeating group produces the two 1NF tables shown in Figure A-14.

**Figure A-14** ▶ **After conversion to 1NF**

Child

primary key

| ClientID | ChildName | ClientName | VetID | VetName |
|----------|-----------|------------|-------|---------|
| 4519 | Pat | Vernon Noordsy | 31 | Pet Care |
| 4519 | Dana | Vernon Noordsy | 31 | Pet Care |
| 8005 | Dana | Sandra Amidon | 27 | Pet Vet |
| 8005 | Dani | Sandra Amidon | 27 | Pet Vet |
| 8112 | Pat | Helen Wandzell | 24 | Pets R Us |

Client

primary key

| ClientID | PetID | ClientName | VetID | VetName | PetName | PetType |
|----------|-------|------------|-------|---------|---------|---------|
| 2173 | 1 | Barbara Hennessey | 27 | Pet Vet | Sam | bird |
| 2173 | 2 | Barbara Hennessey | 27 | Pet Vet | Hoober | dog |
| 2173 | 4 | Barbara Hennessey | 27 | Pet Vet | Sam | hamster |
| 4519 | 2 | Vernon Noordsy | 31 | Pet Care | Charlie | cat |
| 8005 | 1 | Sandra Amidon | 27 | Pet Vet | Beefer | dog |
| 8005 | 2 | Sandra Amidon | 27 | Pet Vet | Kirby | cat |
| 8112 | 3 | Helen Wandzell | 24 | Pets R Us | Kirby | dog |

The alternative way to describe the 1NF tables is:

Child (<u>ClientID</u>, <u>ChildName</u>, ClientName, VetID, VetName)
Client (<u>ClientID</u>, <u>PetID</u>, ClientName, VetID, VetName, PetName, PetType)

Notice that the ClientName, VetID, and VetName fields appear in both 1NF relations, but the placement of these three fields in both relations is not necessary. A second acceptable conversion of the original unnormalized relation to 1NF is:

Child (<u>ClientID</u>, <u>ChildName</u>, ClientName, VetID, VetName)
Client (<u>ClientID</u>, <u>PetID</u>, PetName, PetType)

For either pair of tables in 1NF, Child and Client are now true tables and both have composite keys. Both tables, however, suffer from insertion, deletion, and update anomalies. (Find examples of the three anomalies in both tables.) In the first pair of Child and Client tables, the

ClientID field is a determinant for the ClientName, VetID, and VetName fields, so partial dependencies exist in both tables. It is these partial dependencies that cause the anomalies in the two tables, and second normal form addresses the partial-dependency problem.

## Second Normal Form

A table in 1NF is in **second normal form (2NF)** if it does not contain any partial dependencies. To remove partial dependencies from a table and convert it to second normal form, you perform two steps. First, identify the functional dependencies for every field in the table. Second, if necessary, create new tables and place each field in a relation, so that the field is functionally dependent on the entire primary key. If you need to create new tables, restrict them to ones with a primary key that is a subset of the original composite key. Note that partial dependencies occur only when you have a composite key; a table in first normal form with a single-field primary key is automatically in second normal form.

Figure A-15 shows the functional dependencies for the first pair of 1NF Child and Client tables.

**A bubble diagram for the 1NF Child and Client tables** — **Figure A-15**

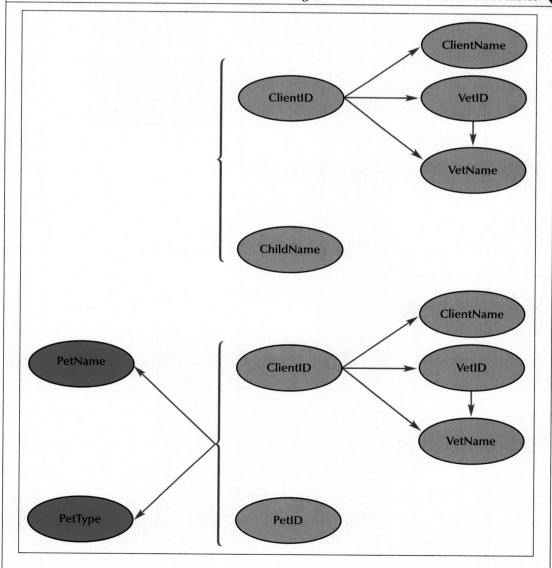

The ClientID field is a determinant for the ClientName, VetID, and VetName fields in both tables. The composite key ClientID and PetID is a determinant for the PetName and PetType fields. The ChildName field is not a determinant, nor is the PetID field. Is the composite key of ClientID and ChildName a determinant? Yes, it is a determinant because this composite key contains the ClientID field, which is a determinant by itself. In the conversion of the tables from 1NF to 2NF, you place fields into new tables so that each nonkey field is functionally dependent on the entire primary key, not just a part of the primary key. However, because all nonkey fields that are functionally dependent on the ClientID and ChildName fields together are also functionally dependent on the ClientID field alone, converting to 2NF doesn't require a table with the ClientID and ChildName fields as a composite key. What happens, however, if you do not have a table with this composite key? You lose the names of the children of each client. You need to retain this composite key in a table to preserve the important 1:M relationship between the ClientID and ChildName fields. Performing the second conversion step produces the three 2NF tables shown in Figure A-16.

**Figure A-16** After conversion to 2NF

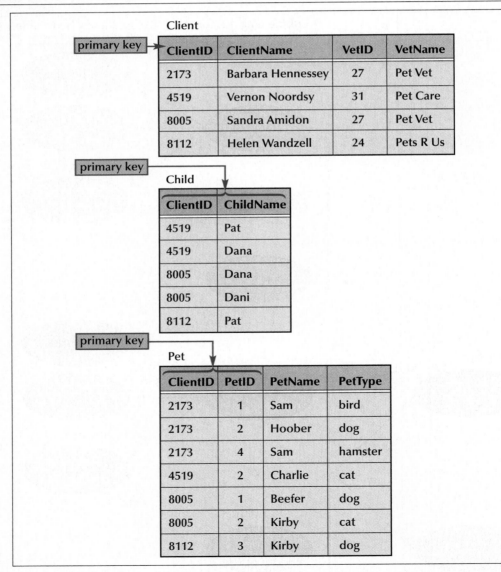

Client

| primary key → | | | | |
|---|---|---|---|---|
| **ClientID** | **ClientName** | | **VetID** | **VetName** |
| 2173 | Barbara Hennessey | | 27 | Pet Vet |
| 4519 | Vernon Noordsy | | 31 | Pet Care |
| 8005 | Sandra Amidon | | 27 | Pet Vet |
| 8112 | Helen Wandzell | | 24 | Pets R Us |

Child

| **ClientID** | **ChildName** |
|---|---|
| 4519 | Pat |
| 4519 | Dana |
| 8005 | Dana |
| 8005 | Dani |
| 8112 | Pat |

Pet

| **ClientID** | **PetID** | **PetName** | **PetType** |
|---|---|---|---|
| 2173 | 1 | Sam | bird |
| 2173 | 2 | Hoober | dog |
| 2173 | 4 | Sam | hamster |
| 4519 | 2 | Charlie | cat |
| 8005 | 1 | Beefer | dog |
| 8005 | 2 | Kirby | cat |
| 8112 | 3 | Kirby | dog |

The alternative way to describe the 2NF relations is:

Client (<u>ClientID</u>, ClientName, VetID, VetName)
Child (<u>ClientID</u>, <u>ChildName</u>)
    Foreign key: ClientID to Client table
Pet (<u>ClientID</u>, <u>PetID</u>, PetName, PetType)
    Foreign key: ClientID to Client table

All three tables are in second normal form. Do anomalies still exist? The Child and Pet tables show no anomalies, but the Client table suffers from anomalies caused by the transitive dependency between the VetID and VetName fields. (Find examples of the three anomalies caused by the transitive dependency.) You can see the transitive dependency in the bubble diagram shown in Figure A-15; the VetID field is a determinant for the VetName field, and the ClientID field is a determinant for the VetID and VetName fields. Third normal form addresses the transitive-dependency problem.

## Third Normal Form

A table in 2NF is in **third normal form (3NF)** if every determinant is a candidate key. This definition for 3NF is referred to as **Boyce-Codd normal form (BCNF)** and is an improvement over the original version of 3NF.

To convert a table to third normal form, remove the fields that depend on the non-candidate-key determinant and place them into a new table with the determinant as the primary key. For the Client table, the VetName field depends on the VetID field, which is a non-candidate-key determinant. Thus, you remove the VetName field from the table, create a new Vet table, place the VetName field in the Vet table, and then make the VetID field the primary key of the Vet table. Note that only the VetName field is removed from the Client relation; the VetID field remains as a foreign key in the Client relation. Figure A-17 shows the database design for the four 3NF tables.

**Figure A-17** ▶ **After conversion to 3NF**

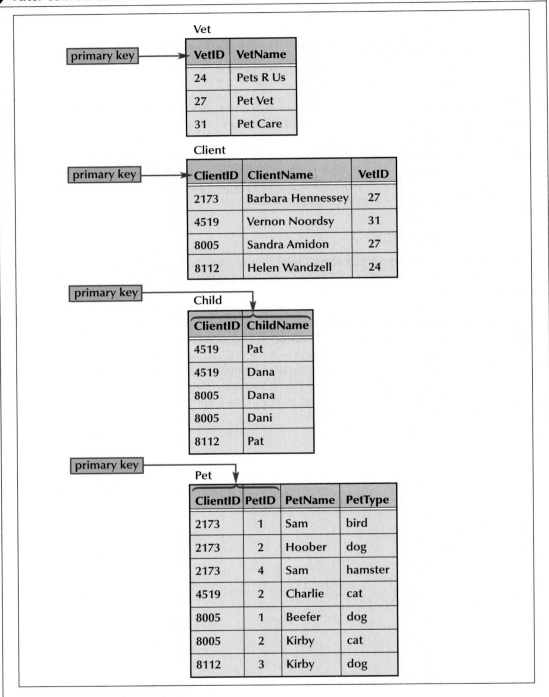

The alternative way to describe the 3NF relations is:

Vet (<u>VetID</u>, VetName)
Client (<u>ClientID</u>, ClientName, VetID)
    Foreign key: VetID to Vet table
Child (<u>ClientID</u>, <u>ChildName</u>)
    Foreign key: ClientID to Client table

Pet (<u>ClientID</u>, <u>PetID</u>, PetName, PetType)
    Foreign key: ClientID to Client table

The four tables have no anomalies because you have eliminated all the data redundancy, partial dependencies, and transitive dependencies. Normalization provides the framework for eliminating anomalies and delivering an optimal database design, which you should always strive to achieve. You should be aware, however, that experts sometimes denormalize tables to improve database performance—specifically, to decrease the time it takes the database to respond to a user's commands and requests. When you denormalize a table, you reintroduce redundancy to the table. At the same time, you reintroduce anomalies. Thus, improving performance exposes a database to potential integrity problems. Only database experts should denormalize tables, but even experts first complete the normalization of their tables.

# Natural, Artificial, and Surrogate Keys

When you complete the design of a database, your tables should be in third normal form, free of anomalies and redundancy. Some tables, such as the State relation (see Figure A-2), have obvious third normal form designs with obvious primary keys. The State table's description is:

State (<u>StateAbbrev</u>, StateName, EnteredUnionOrder, StateBird, StatePopulation)

Recall that the candidate keys for the State table are StateAbbrev, StateName, and EnteredUnionOrder. Choosing the StateAbbrev field as the State table's primary key makes the StateName and EnteredUnionOrder fields alternate keys. Primary keys such as the StateAbbrev field are sometimes called natural keys. A **natural key** (also called a **logical key** or an **intelligent key**) is a primary key that consists of a field, or a collection of fields, that is an inherent characteristic of the entity described by the table and that is visible to users. Other examples of natural keys are the ISBN (International Standard Book Number) for a book, the SSN (Social Security number) for a U.S. individual, the UPC (Universal Product Code) for a product, and the VIN (vehicle identification number) for a vehicle.

Is the ClientID field, which is the primary key for the Client table (see Figure A-17), a natural key? Because a typical Client table would contain many additional fields and many additional records, before answering the question first add two fields and two records to the table. Figure A-18 shows the expanded Client table.

**The Client table with additional fields and records** ◀ **Figure A-18**

| ClientID | ClientName | Street | FirstContactDate | VetID |
|----------|------------|--------|------------------|-------|
| 2173 | Barbara Hennessey | 810 Brent Blvd | 05/14/2006 | 27 |
| 4519 | Vernon Noordsy | 3552 Crystal Ct | 07/22/2006 | 31 |
| 8005 | Sandra Amidon | 2200 River Rd | 10/04/2006 | 27 |
| 8071 | Barbara Hennessey | 300 Agate Ave | 10/04/2006 | 31 |
| 8112 | Helen Wandzell | 66 Sage St | 10/04/2006 | 24 |
| 8130 | Robert Sanchez | 2200 River Rd | 11/11/2006 | 24 |

Suppose that the ClientID field is not a field in the Client table. Is there a natural key in the remaining fields? No single field is unique and, thus, can't be the natural key. You could choose a pair of fields—for example, the ClientName and Street fields—to be the natural key. However, there are several problems with this choice of a composite key. First, because neither key field can be null, you can't add a record if you don't know the client's street. Second, the composite key is lengthy. Because this composite key is a foreign key in the Child and Pet tables (see Figure A-17), the length issue propagates to related tables. Finally, you have no guarantee that the composite key will remain unique. If duplicate natural key values are possible, you need to add a third field to the composite key, the FirstContactDate field for example, to guarantee uniqueness.

Although each record in the Client table is unique, these problems with a composite key surfaced when Pet Sitters Unlimited switched to a database system. Consequently, the users at Pet Sitters Unlimited added the ClientID field to the Client table as a way to identify each client uniquely. So, is the ClientID field is a natural key? The ClientID field is not a natural key because it's not an inherent characteristic of a client. Instead, the ClientID field is an **artificial key**, which is a field that you add to a table to serve solely as the primary key and that is visible to users. Using the ClientID field as the Client table's primary key, you can add a record even if you don't know the client's address. The ClientID field is not lengthy as a primary key and as a foreign key. Finally, the ClientID field is guaranteed to be unique.

Another reason for using an artificial key arises in tables that allow duplicate records. Although relational database theory and most experts do not allow duplicate records in a table, consider a database that tracks donors and their donations. Figure A-19 shows a Donor table with an artificial key of DonorID and with the FirstName and LastName fields. Some cash donations are anonymous, which accounts for the fourth record in the Donor table. Figure A-19 also shows the Donation table with the DonorID field, a foreign key to the Donor table, and the DonationDate and DonationAmt fields.

**Figure A-19** | **The Donor and Donation tables**

primary key

Donor

| DonorID | DonorFirstName | DonorLastName |
|---------|----------------|---------------|
| 1 | Christian | Chang |
| 2 | Franco | Diaz |
| 3 | Angie | Diaz |
| 4 | | Anonymous |
| 5 | Tracy | Burns |

Donation

| DonorID | DonationDate | DonationAmt |
|---------|--------------|-------------|
| 1 | 10/12/2005 | $50.00 |
| 1 | 09/30/2006 | $50.00 |
| 2 | 10/03/2006 | $75.00 |
| 4 | 10/10/2006 | $50.00 |
| 4 | 10/10/2006 | $50.00 |
| 4 | 10/11/2006 | $25.00 |
| 5 | 10/13/2006 | $50.00 |

duplicate records

What is the primary key of the Donation table? No single field is unique, and neither is any combination of fields. For example, on 10/10/2006 two anonymous donors (DonorID value of 4) donated $50. You need to add an artificial key, DonationID for example, to the Donation table. The addition of the artificial key makes every record in the Donation table unique, and the descriptions of the Donor and Donation tables become:

Donor (<u>DonorID</u>, DonorFirstName, DonorLastName)
Donation (<u>DonationID</u>, DonorID, DonationDate, DonationAmt)
  Foreign key: DonorID to Donor table

For another common situation, consider the 3NF tables you developed in the previous section (see Figure A-17) that have the following descriptions:

Vet (<u>VetID</u>, VetName)
Client (<u>ClientID</u>, ClientName, VetID)
  Foreign key: VetID to Vet table
Child (<u>ClientID</u>, <u>ChildName</u>)
  Foreign key: ClientID to Client table
Pet (<u>ClientID</u>, <u>PetID</u>, PetName, PetType)
  Foreign key: ClientID to Client table

Recall that a primary key must be unique, must be minimal, and must not change in value. In theory, primary keys don't change in value. However, in practice, you might have to correct a misspelled ChildName field value, or you might have to change ClientID field values that you incorrectly entered in the Child and Pet tables. Further, if you need to change a ClientID field value in the Client table, the change must cascade to the ClientID field values in the Child and Pet tables. Also, changes to a VetID field value in the Vet table must cascade to the Client table. For these and other reasons, many experts add surrogate keys to tables such as the Vet, Client, and Child tables. A **surrogate key** (also called a **synthetic key**) is a system-generated primary key that is hidden from users. Usually you can use an automatic numbering data type, such as the Access AutoNumber data type, for a surrogate key. Figure A-20 shows the four tables with surrogate keys added to the Vet, Client, and Child tables.

**Figure A-20** ▶ **Using surrogate keys**

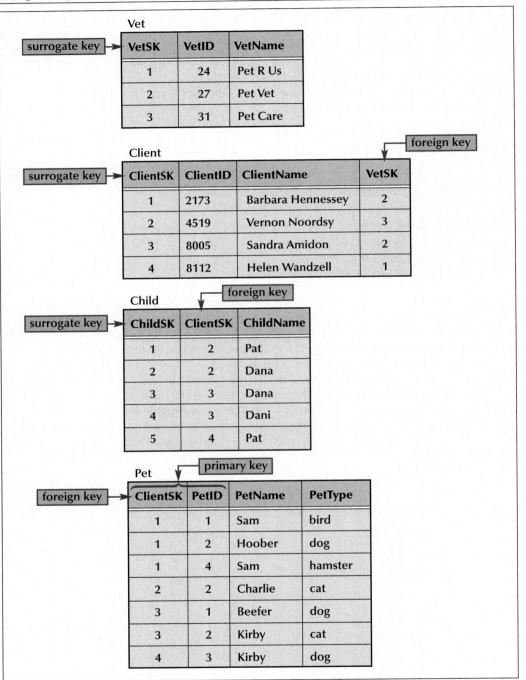

The ClientSK field replaces the ClientID field as a foreign key in the Child and Pet tables, and the VetSK field replaces the VetID field as a foreign key in the Client table. When you change an incorrectly entered ClientID field value in the Client table, you don't need to cascade the change to the Child and Pet tables. When you change an incorrectly entered VetID field value, you don't have to cascade the change to the Client table.

As you design a database, you should *not* consider the use of surrogate keys, and you should use an artificial key only for the rare table that has duplicate records. At the point when you implement a database, you might choose to use artificial and surrogate keys, but be aware that database experts debate their use and effectiveness. Some of the trade-offs between natural and surrogate keys that you need to consider are:

- You use surrogate keys to avoid cascading updates to foreign key values. Surrogate keys can also replace lengthier foreign keys when those foreign keys reference composite fields.
- You don't need a surrogate key for a table whose primary key is not used as a foreign key in another relation, because cascading updates is not an issue.
- Tables with surrogate keys require more joins than do tables with natural keys. For example, if you need to know all clients for the vet with a VetID field value of 27, the surrogate key in Figure A-20 requires that you join the Vet and Client tables to answer the question. Using natural keys as shown in Figure A-17, the VetID field appears in the Client table, so no join is necessary.
- Although surrogate keys are meant to be hidden from users, they cannot be hidden from users who create SQL statements and use other ad hoc tools.
- Because you need a unique index for the natural key and a unique index for the surrogate key, your database size is larger and index maintenance takes more time when you use a surrogate key. On the other hand, a foreign key using a surrogate key is usually smaller than a foreign key using a natural key, especially when the natural key is a composite key, so those indexes are smaller and faster to access for lookups and joins.

## Microsoft Access Naming Conventions

In the early 1980s, Microsoft's Charles Simonyi introduced an identifier naming convention that became known as Hungarian notation. Microsoft and other companies use this naming convention for variable, control, and other object naming in Basic, Visual Basic, and other programming languages. When Access was introduced in the early 1990s, Stan Leszynski and Greg Reddick adapted Hungarian notation for Microsoft Access databases; their guidelines became known as the Leszynski/Reddick naming conventions. In recent years, the Leszynski naming conventions, the Reddick naming conventions, and other naming conventions have been published. Individuals and companies have created their own Access naming conventions, but many are based on the Leszynski/Reddick naming conventions, as are the naming conventions covered in this section.

An Access database can contain thousands of objects, fields, controls, and other items, and keeping track of their names and what they represent is a difficult task. Consequently, you should use naming conventions that identify the type and purpose of each item in an Access database. You can use naming conventions that identify items generally or very specifically.

For objects, include a prefix tag to identify the type of object, as shown in Figure A-21. In each example in Figure A-21, the final object name consists of a three-character tag prefixed to the base object name. For example, the form name of frmClientsAndPets consists of the frm tag and the ClientsAndPets base form name.

**Figure A-21** ▶ Object naming tags

| Object type | Tag | PetType |
|---|---|---|
| Form | frm | frmClientsAndPets |
| Macro | mcr | mcrSwitchboard |
| Module | bas | basCalculations |
| Query | qry | qryClient |
| Report | rpt | rptClientsAndPet |
| Table | tbl | tblClient |

The tags in Figure A-21 identify each object type in general. If you want to identify object types more specifically, you could expand Figure A-21 to include tags such as fsub for a subform, qxtb for a crosstab query, tlkp for a lookup table, rsub for a subreport, and so on.

For controls in forms and reports, a general naming convention uses lbl as a prefix tag for labels and ctl as a prefix tag for other types of controls. For more specific naming conventions for controls, you'd use a specific prefix tag for each type of control. Figure A-22 shows the prefix tag for some common controls in forms and reports.

**Figure A-22** ▶ Control naming tags

| Control type | Tag |
|---|---|
| Check box | chk |
| Combo box | cbo |
| Command button | cmd |
| Image | img |
| Label | lbl |
| Line | lin |
| List box | lst |
| Option button | opt |
| PivotTable | pvt |
| Rectangle | shp |
| Subform/Subreport | sub |
| Text box | txt |

Some database developers use a prefix tag for each field name to identify the field's data type (for example, dtm for date/time, num for numeric, and chr for text or character), others use a prefix tag for each field name to identify in which table the field is located (for example, cli for the Client table and vet for the Vet table), and still others don't use a prefix tag for field names.

You might use suffix tags for controls that might otherwise have identical names. For example, if you have two text boxes in a form for calculated controls that display the average and the sum of the OrderAmt field, both could legitimately be named txtOrderAmt unless you used suffix tags to name them txtOrderAmtAvg and txtOrderAmtSum.

You should ensure that any name you use does not duplicate a property name or any keyword Access reserves for special purposes. In general, you can avoid property and keyword name conflicts by using two-word field, control, and object names. For example, use ClientName instead of Name, and use OrderDate instead of Date to avoid name conflicts.

All database developers avoid spaces in names, mainly because spaces are not allowed in server database management systems (DBMSs), such as SQL Server, Oracle, and DB2. If you are prototyping a Microsoft Access database that you'll migrate to one of these server DBMSs, or if future requirements might force a migration, you should restrict your Access identifier names so that they conform to the rules common to them all. Figure A-23 shows the identifier naming rules for Access, SQL Server, Oracle, and DB2.

**Identifier naming rules for common database management systems** ◄ **Figure A-23**

| Identifier naming rule | Access | SQL Server | Oracle | DB2 |
|---|---|---|---|---|
| Maximum character length | 64 | 30 | 30 | 30 |
| Allowable characters | Letters, digits, space, and special characters, except for period (.), exclamation point (!), accent grave (`), and square brackets ([]) | Letters, digits, dollar sign ($), underscore (_), number symbol (#), at symbol (@) | Letters, digits, dollar sign ($), underscore (_), number symbol (#) | Letters, digits, at symbol (@), dollar sign ($), underscore (_), number symbol (#) |
| Special rules | | No spaces; first character must be a letter, or at symbol (@) | No space; first character must be a letter; stored in the database in uppercase | No space; first character must be a letter; at symbol (@), dollar sign ($), or number symbol (#) stored in the database in uppercase |

The Microsoft Access Naming Conventions section of the Student Online Companion page for this appendix, located at *www.course.com/np/office2003/access*, contains links that you can follow to learn more about naming conventions for Microsoft Access databases.

# Summary

In this appendix, you learned about tables and their characteristics, keys (primary, candidate, alternate, composite, and foreign), relationships (one-to-one, one-to-many, many-to-many, and entity subtypes), entity-relationship diagrams, integrity constraints (entity, referential, and domain), dependencies and determinants, and anomalies. You also learned how to design a database using normalization to place all tables in third normal form. Finally, you learned about natural, artificial, and surrogate keys, and you examined naming conventions.

## Key Terms

alternate key
anomalies
artificial key
attribute
Boyce-Codd normal
   form (BCNF)
bubble diagram
candidate key
cascades
composite entity
composite key
concatenated key
data model diagram
data redundancy
database design
deletion anomaly
determinant
domain
domain integrity constraint
entity
entity integrity constraint
entity subtype

entity-relationship
   diagram (ERD)
field
field name
first normal form (1NF)
foreign key
functional dependency
   diagram
insertion anomaly
integrity
integrity constraint
intelligent key
logical key
many-to-many
   relationship (M:N)
natural key
nonkey field
normal forms
normalization
null value
nullifies

one-to-many
   relationship (1:M)
one-to-one relationship (1:1)
partial dependency
primary key
record
referential integrity
relation
relational database
repeating group
restricted
second normal form (2NF)
semantic object modeling
surrogate key
synthetic key
table
third normal form (3NF)
transitive dependency
tuple
unnormalized relation
update anomaly

# Review Questions

1. What are the formal names for a table, for a row, and for a column? What are the popular names for a row and for a column?
2. What is a domain?
3. What is an entity?
4. What is the relationship between a primary key and a candidate key?
5. What is a composite key?
6. What is a foreign key?
7. Look for an example of a one-to-one relationship, an example of a one-to-many relationship, and an example of a many-to-many relationship in a newspaper, magazine, book, or everyday situation you encounter. For each one, name the entities and select the primary and foreign keys.
8. When do you use an entity subtype?
9. What is a composite entity in an entity-relationship diagram?

10. What is the entity integrity constraint?
11. What is referential integrity?
12. What does the cascades option, which is used with referential integrity, accomplish?
13. What are partial and transitive dependencies?
14. What three types of anomalies can be exhibited by a table, and what problems do they cause?
15. Figure A-24 shows the Vet, Client, and Child tables with primary keys VetID, ClientID, and both ClientID and ChildName, respectively. Which two integrity constraints do these tables violate and why?

**Figure A-24**

Vet

| VetID | VetName |
|-------|---------|
| 24 | Pets R Us |
| 27 | Pet Vet |
| 31 | Pet Care |

Client

| ClientID | ClientName | VetID |
|----------|------------------|-------|
| 2173 | Barbara Hennessey | 27 |
| 4519 | Vernon Noordsy | 31 |
| 8005 | Sandra Amidon | 37 |
| 8112 | Helen Wandzell | 24 |

Child

| ClientID | ChildName |
|----------|-----------|
| 4519 | Pat |
| 4519 | Dana |
| 8005 | |
| 8005 | Dani |
| 8112 | Pat |

16. The State and Capital tables, shown in Figure A-5, are described as follows:
    State (<u>StateAbbrev</u>, StateName, EnteredUnionOrder, StateBird, StatePopulation)
    Capital (<u>CapitalName</u>, StateAbbrev, YearDesignated, PhoneAreaCode, CapitalPopulation)
    Foreign key: StateAbbrev to State table
    Add the field named CountyName for the county or counties containing the state capital to this database, justify where you placed it (that is, in an existing table or in a new one), and draw the entity-relationship diagram for all the entities. The counties for the state capitals shown in Figure A-5 are Travis and Williamson counties for Austin TX; Hartford county for Hartford CT; Clinton, Eaton, and Ingham counties for Lansing MI; Davidson county for Nashville TN; Hughes county for Pierre SD.

17. Suppose you have a table for a dance studio. The fields are dancer's identification number, dancer's name, dancer's address, dancer's telephone number, class identification number, day that the class meets, time that the class meets, instructor name, and instructor identification number. Assume that each dancer takes one class, each class meets only once a week and has one instructor, and each instructor can teach more than one class. In what normal form is the table currently, given the following shorthand description?
    Dancer (<u>DancerID</u>, DancerName, DancerAddr, DancerPhone, ClassID, ClassDay, ClassTime, InstrName, InstrID)
    Convert this relation to 3NF and represent the design using the shorthand description method.

18. Store the following fields for a library database: AuthorCode, AuthorName, BookTitle, BorrowerAddress, BorrowerName, BorrowerCardNumber, CopiesOfBook, ISBN (International Standard Book Number), LoanDate, PublisherCode, PublisherName, and PublisherAddress. A one-to-many relationship exists between publishers and books. Many-to-many relationships exist between authors and books and between borrowers and books.
    a. Name the entities for the library database.
    b. Create the tables for the library database and describe them using the shorthand method. Be sure the tables are in third normal form.
    c. Draw an entity-relationship diagram for the library database.

19. In the following database, which consists of the Department and Employee tables, add one record to the end of the Employee table that violates both the entity integrity constraint and the referential integrity constraint.

**Figure A-25**

Department

| DeptID | DeptName | Location |
|--------|----------|----------|
| M | Marketing | New York |
| R | Research | Houston |
| S | Sales | Chicago |

Employee

| EmployeeID | EmployeeName | DeptID |
|------------|--------------|--------|
| 1111 | Sue | R |
| 2222 | Pam | M |
| 3333 | Bob | S |
| 4444 | Chris | S |
| 5555 | Pat | R |
| 6666 | Meg | R |

20. Consider the following table:

Patient (PatientID, PatientName, BalanceOwed, DoctorID, DoctorName, ServiceCode, ServiceDesc, ServiceFee, ServiceDate)

This is a table concerning data about patients of doctors at a clinic and the services the doctors perform for their patients. The following dependencies exist in the Patient table:

PatientID → PatientName, BalanceOwed

DoctorID → DoctorName

ServiceCode → ServiceDesc, ServiceFee

PatientID, DoctorID, ServiceCode → PatientName, BalanceOwed, DoctorName, ServiceDesc, ServiceFee, ServiceDate

a. Based on the dependencies, convert the Patient table to first normal form.

b. Next, convert the Patient table to third normal form.

21. What is the difference among natural, artificial, and surrogate keys?

22. Why should you use naming conventions for the identifiers in a database?

# Glossary/Index

Note: Boldface entries include definitions.

## Special Characters

> (greater than symbol), AC 102

< (less than symbol), AC 102

<> (not equal to symbol), AC 102

! (exclamation mark), AC 137

# (number symbol), AC 188

# (pound sign), AC 137

& (ampersand), AC 196

* (asterisk), AC 137, AC 188

+ (equal sign), AC 102

- (hyphen), AC 137

>= (greater than or equal to symbol), AC 102

<= (less than or equal to symbol), AC 102

? (question mark), AC 137, AC 188

[] (square brackets), AC 137

## A

**absolute path(s)** A string, or text, expression that identifies a specific file on a specific disk drive. AC 378

**Access.** *See* Microsoft Access 2003

**Access window** The program window that appears when you start the Access program. AC 7, AC 9

**action(s)** An instruction to Access to perform an operation. AC 492, AC 493

    adding to macros, AC 495–498, AC 500–504

**Action column** A column in the Macro window in which you enter the actions you want Access to perform. AC 496

**action query(ies)** A query that adds, changes, or deletes multiple table records at a time. AC 444–457

    append, AC 444, AC 448–450

    delete, AC 444, AC 451–452

    make-table, AC 444–448

    update, AC 444, AC 453–457

Address bar, FM 8

**Admin user** The one default user, which is assigned to the Admins group, that the User-Level Security Wizard creates automatically in a new workgroup information file. AC 628

**Admins group** One of the two groups created by default when you create a new workgroup information file. Users assigned to the Admins group have full permissions and are the only users who can create users and groups. AC 628

**Advanced Filter/Sort** A form and datasheet tool that lets you specify multiple selection criteria and specify a sort order for selected records in the Filter window, in the same way you specify record selection criteria and sort orders for a query in Design view. AC 267, AC 273–275

**AfterUpdate event** An event that occurs after changed data in a control or a record is updated. AC 564

**aggregate function(s)** A function that performs an arithmetic operation on selected records in a database. AC 117–119, AC 198

**Align command** A Format menu and shortcut menu command that provides options for aligning controls in a form or report. Align options include Left, Right, Top, Bottom, and To Grid. AC 313

aligning labels in reports, AC 313–314

**alternate key(s)** A candidate key that was not chosen to be the primary key. AC A3

**ampersand (&)** A concatenation operator that joins expressions. AC 196

**And logical operator** The logical operator you use in a query when you want a record selected only if two or more conditions are met. AC 107–109, AC 193–194

**anomalies** Undesirable irregularities of tables caused by data redundancy and by partial and transitive dependencies. Anomalies are of three types: insertion, deletion, and update. AC A14

**append query(ies)** A query that adds records from existing tables or queries to the end of another table. AC 444, AC 448–450

**argument(s)** A value passed to a procedure and used in place of a parameter when the procedure is executed. Also, additional facts Access needs to execute an action. AC 496, AC 565

**artificial key(s)** A field that you add to a table to serve solely as the primary key and that is visible to users. AC A22–23

**assignment statement(s)** A statement that assigns the value of an expression to a field, control, or property. AC 561

asterisk (*), wildcard character, AC 137, AC 188

**attribute(s)** The formal term for a column in a relation (table). AC A2

**AutoForm Wizard** A Form Wizard that places all the fields from a selected table (or query) on a form automatically, and then displays the form on the screen, making it the quickest way to create a form. AC 18–19, AC 130

**AutoFormat(s)** A predefined style that you can apply to a form or report.

    changing, AC 133–135

AutoNumber data type, AC 39

**AutoReport Wizard(s)** A Report Wizard that places all the fields from a selected table (or query) on a report automatically, and then displays the report on the screen, making it the quickest way to create a report. AC 21–22

Avg function, AC 118, AC 198

## B

**Back Color property** A property that specifies the background color for a control or a section on a form or report. AC 265

**back-end database** A database that contains the tables that are needed for an application. AC 613–614

**backing up** The process of making a copy of a database file to protect your database against loss or damage. AC 24–25

backup copies, FM 7

BCNF (Boyce-Codd normal form), AC A19–21

Beep action, AC 493

**BeforeUpdate event** An event that occurs before changed data in a control or a record is updated. AC 575

Boolean data type, AC 576

**Border Style property** A property that controls the type of border to use for a control or a form. For controls you can choose settings of solid (default), transparent, dashes, short dashes, dots, sparse dots, dash dot, and dash dot dot. For forms you can choose settings of none, thin, sizable (default), and dialog. AC 317

**bound control(s)** A control that is connected, or bound, to a field in the underlying table or query and that is used to display and maintain a table field value. AC 230

    adding to grid, AC 232

    adding to reports, AC 309–310

**bound form(s)** A form that has a table or query as its record source and is used for maintaining and displaying table data. AC 229

Bound Object Frame button, AC 231

**Boyce-Codd normal form (BCNF)** A second normal form table is in Boyce-Codd normal form if every determinant is a candidate key. BCNF is also called third normal form in this book, although BCNF is an improvement over the original version of third normal form. AC A19–21

**bubble diagram(s)** A diagram that graphically shows a table's functional dependencies and determinants. Also known as a data model diagram and a functional dependency diagram. AC A12

Byte data type, AC 576

# C

**calculated control(s)** A control that displays a value that is the result of an expression. The expression usually contains one or more fields, and the calculated control is recalculated each time any value in the expression changes. AC 230, AC 259–264

adding to main form, AC 261–264

adding to subform Footer section, AC 260–261

group totals, AC 322–325

testing, AC 265

**calculated field(s)** A field that displays the results of an expression in a query datasheet or a form or report, but does not exist as a field in the database. AC 112–117

assigning conditional values, AC 303

creating, AC 113–117

calculations, AC 112–120

aggregate functions, AC 117–119

calculated fields. *See* calculated fields

grand totals, AC 295–298

group, AC 119–120

group totals, AC 322–325

**call(s)** When a procedure is executed. AC 556

**Can Grow property** A property that controls the appearance of a control or section in a form or report when printed or previewed. When you set the property to Yes, the control or section expands vertically to print or preview all the data within the control or section. When you set the property to No, the data that doesn't fit within the fixed size of the control or section doesn't print or preview. AC 312, AC 341

**Can Shrink property** A property that controls the appearance of a control or section in a form or report when printed or previewed. When you set the property to Yes, the control or section shrinks vertically so that the data it contains is printed or previewed without leaving blank lines. When you set the property to No, the control or section doesn't shrink. AC 316–317, AC 341

**CancelEvent action** An action that cancels the event that caused the procedure or macro containing the action to execute. AC 577–578

**candidate key(s)** A field, or a collection of fields, whose values are non-changing and uniquely and minimally identify each row of a table, but has not necessarily been chosen as the primary key. AC A3

**Caption property** A property that specifies the text that appears in a label in a form, report, or data access page, or that appears in the column heading in a datasheet. AC 40

labels, changing, AC 235–237

**cascade(s)** A referential integrity option in which the DBMS, when you change a primary key value, automatically changes the matching foreign key values to the new primary key value, and when you delete a record, automatically deletes the matching foreign key rows. AC A11

**cascade deletes option** A referential integrity rule that permits a record in the primary table to be deleted and also deletes all records in related tables that have matching foreign key values. AC 89

**cascade updates option** A referential integrity rule that permits a change in value to the primary key and changes the appropriate foreign key values in related tables. AC 89

**Case control structure** A conditional control structure that evaluates an expression, and then performs one of several alternative actions based on the resulting value (or condition) of the evaluated expression. AC 561

**category axis label(s)** A label that identifies an individual data marker in a PivotChart.

PivotCharts, AC 405

**category field(s)** A field in a PivotChart that identifies which values are displayed as category axis labels.

PivotCharts, AC 405

Check Box button, AC 231

**class module(s)** A module that is usually associated with a particular form or report. AC 567

Close action, AC 493

closing

files, OFF 21–22

forms, AC 20

tables, AC 13

**Code window** The window in which you create, modify, and display specific VBA procedures. AC 561

**coding** The process of writing instructions in a programming language such as VBA. AC 554

procedures, AC 586–591

collapse icon, FM 7

color(s)

background, of form controls, AC 245–246

display, hiding and changing, AC 583–586

report label fonts, AC 319

column(s), newspaper-style (snaking), AC 349

**column area** The portion of a PivotTable, consisting of a column field and column field items, that provides column groupings.

PivotTables, AC 393

**column field(s)** A field in a PivotTable's column area that provides column groupings.

PivotTables, AC 393

**column field item(s)** The values in a PivotTable's column area that identify the contents of each column.

PivotTables, AC 393

**column selector(s)** In a datasheet, the column heading (also called the field selector), which you click to select the entire column. AC 11

Columns option, Page Setup dialog box, AC 349–350

**combo box(es)** A control that provides the features of a test box and a list box; you can choose a value from the list or type an entry. AC 224

adding to forms, AC 252–255

Combo Box button, AC 231

**Combo box tool** A toolbox tool that you use to add a combo box to a form or data access page. AC 252

**command button(s)** A control on a form that starts an action, or a set of actions, when you click it. AC 492

adding to switchboard pages, AC 534–536, AC 537–538

with attached macros. *See* command buttons with attached macros

moving in switchboard pages, AC 536–537

switchboards, AC 491

Command Button button, AC 231

command buttons with attached macros, AC 504–506, AC 511

adding to forms, AC 521–523

attaching macros, AC 512–513

events, AC 505–506

Commands and Options dialog box, AC 401

comment(s), adding to functions, AC 567

**Comment column** A column in the Macro window in which you enter optional comments to document the specific actions selected for the macro. AC 496

**common field(s)** A field that appears in more than one table, allowing you to connect the records in the separate tables. AC 5, AC 37

common window elements, OFF 9

compact disc(s) (CDs), FM 4

**compacting** A process that rearranges the data and objects in a database to decrease its file size, thereby making more space available on your disk and letting you open and close the database more quickly. AC 25–27

automatically, AC 25–27

**comparison operator(s)** In a query, an operator that asks Access to compare the value in a database field to the condition value and to select all the records for which the relationship is true. AC 102, AC 188, AC 191

matching ranges of values, AC 106–107

**compilation** The process of translating modules from VBA to a translated form that a computer can understand. AC 574

**compiling** Translating a module from VBA to a translated form that a computer can understand. AC 574

**composite entity(ies)** A relationship in an entity-relationship diagram that has the characteristics of an entity; used to implement a many-to-many relationship. AC A10

# Task Reference

| TASK | PAGE # | RECOMMENDED METHOD |
|------|--------|--------------------|
| **Access, start** | AC 7 | Click Start, point to All Programs, point to Microsoft Office, click Microsoft Office Access 2003 |
| **Action, add by dragging** | AC 501 | *See* Reference Window: Creating an Action by Dragging |
| **Action, add to macro** | AC 501 | In the Macro window, click the Action list arrow, click the action |
| **Advanced filter, apply** | AC 273 | *See* Reference Window: Applying an Advanced Filter/Sort |
| **Aggregate functions, use in a query** | AC 118 | Display the query in Design view, click Σ |
| **And operator, enter selection criteria for** | AC 193 | Enter selection criteria in the same Criteria row in the design grid |
| **Append query, create** | AC 448 | *See* Reference Window: Creating an Append Query |
| **AutoFormat, change** | AC 133 | *See* Reference Window: Changing a Form's AutoFormat |
| **Calculated field, add to a query** | AC 113 | *See* Reference Window: Using Expression Builder |
| **Caption, change for a form label** | AC 235 | *See* Reference Window: Changing a Label's Caption |
| **Color, change a control's background** | AC 245 | *See* Reference Window: Changing the Background Color of a Control |
| **Column, resize width in a datasheet** | AC 64 | Double-click ↔ on the right border of the column heading |
| **Combo box, add to a form** | AC 253 | Make sure ⬚ is selected, click ⬚, click in the grid at the upper-left corner for the combo box, specify your choices in the Combo Box Wizard dialog boxes |
| **Command button, add to a form** | AC 504–505 | Click ⬚ on the toolbox, position the pointer in the form, click the left mouse button |
| **Command button, add to a form using Control Wizards** | AC 523 | *See* Reference Window: Adding a Command Button to a Form Using Control Wizards |
| **Conditional formatting rules, define** | AC 325 | *See* Reference Window: Defining Conditional Formatting for a Control |
| **Control, align** | AC 250 | *See* Reference Window: Aligning Controls in a Form |
| **Control, apply special effect** | AC 388 | Select the control, click the list arrow for ⬚, click the special effect |
| **Control, change to another control type** | AC 251 | Click the control in Design view, click Format, point to Change To, click the new control type |
| **Control, delete** | AC 386 | Right-click the control, click Cut |
| **Control, hide** | AC 319 | Set Visible property to No |
| **Control, move in a form** | AC 233 | *See* Reference Window: Selecting and Moving Controls |
| **Control, move in a report** | AC 292 | *See* Reference Window: Moving and Resizing Controls |
| **Control, resize in a form** | AC 238 | *See* Reference Window: Resizing a Control |
| **Control, resize in a report** | AC 292 | *See* Reference Window: Moving and Resizing Controls |
| **Control, select** | AC 233 | *See* Reference Window: Selecting and Moving Controls |
| **Crosstab query, create** | AC 200 | *See* Reference Window: Using the Crosstab Query Wizard |
| **Data access page, create a custom** | AC 381 | *See* Reference Window: Creating a Data Access Page in Design View |
| **Data access page, display related records** | AC 391 | Click ⊞ |
| **Data access page, filter records** | AC 380 | Click filter field text box, click ⬚ |
| **Data access page, hide related records** | AC 392 | Click ⊟ |
| **Data access page, select theme** | AC 389 | In Design view, click Format, click Theme, select desired theme, click OK |
| **Data access page, sort records** | AC 380 | Click sort field text box, click either ⬚ or ⬚ |
| **Data access page, update with a browser** | AC 379 | *See* Reference Window: Viewing and Updating Data in a Page Using Internet Explorer |
| **Data access page, use Page Wizard to create** | AC 376 | Click Pages in the Objects bar, click New, click Page Wizard, choose the table or query to use, click OK, choose wizard options |
| **Data access page, view with a browser** | AC 379 | *See* Reference Window: Viewing and Updating Data in a Page Using Internet Explorer |

| TASK | PAGE # | RECOMMENDED METHOD |
|---|---|---|
| **Data, find** | AC 135 | *See* Reference Window: Finding Data in a Form or Datasheet |
| **Data, group in a report** | AC 307 | *See* Reference Window: Sorting and Grouping Data in a Report |
| **Data, sort in a report** | AC 307 | *See* Reference Window: Sorting and Grouping Data in a Report |
| **Database startup options, set** | AC 617 | *See* Reference Window: Setting the Database Startup Options |
| **Database, compact and repair** | AC 26 | Click Tools, point to Database Utilities, click Compact and Repair Database |
| **Database, compact on close** | AC 26 | *See* Reference Window: Compacting a Database Automatically |
| **Database, compile** | AC 574 | Click Debug, click Compile database name |
| **Database, convert to another Access version** | AC 28 | Click Tools, point to Database Utilities, point to Convert Database, click the format to convert to |
| **Database, create a blank** | AC 41 | Click Create a new file in the task pane, click Blank database, type the database name, select the drive and folder, click Create |
| **Database, create using a wizard** | AC 41 | Click ▢ on the Database toolbar, click On my computer in the task pane, click the Databases tab, select a template, click OK, type the database name, select the drive and folder, click Create, follow the instructions in the wizard |
| **Database, decrypt** | AC 620 | *See* Reference Window: Encrypting or Decrypting a Database |
| **Database, encrypt** | AC 620 | *See* Reference Window: Encrypting or Decrypting a Database |
| **Database, open** | AC 8 | Click Open (or More) in the task pane, select the database to open |
| **Database, split** | AC 615 | *See* Reference Window: Using the Database Splitter |
| **Datasheet view, switch to** | AC 53 | Click ▦ |
| **Datasheet, print** | AC 12 | Click ⎙ |
| **Date, add to a report** | AC 333 | *See* Reference Window: Adding the Date to a Report |
| **Delete query, create** | AC 451 | *See* Reference Window: Creating a Delete Query |
| **Design Master and replica, synchronize** | AC 611 | *See* Reference Window: Synchronizing the Design Master and a Replica |
| **Design view, switch to** | AC 57 | Click ⬒ |
| **Documenter, use** | AC 226 | *See* Reference Window: Using the Documenter |
| **Domain aggregate function, add** | AC 330 | *See* Reference Window: Using a Domain Aggregate Function in a Report |
| **Duplicate values, hide** | AC 294 | *See* Reference Window: Hiding Duplicate Values in a Report |
| **Event procedure, add** | AC 572 | *See* Reference Window: Adding an Event Procedure |
| **Event procedure, display an existing** | AC 560 | Open the property sheet for the control, click the event property text box, click ▣ |
| **Field property change, update** | AC 61 | Click the list arrow for ⚡, select option for updating field property |
| **Field, add to a form or report** | AC 309 | *See* Reference Window: Adding Fields to a Form or Report |
| **Field, add to a table** | AC 59 | *See* Reference Window: Adding a Field Between Two Existing Fields |
| **Field, define in a table** | AC 43 | *See* Reference Window: Defining a Field in a Table |
| **Field, delete from a table** | AC 57 | *See* Reference Window: Deleting a Field from a Table Structure |
| **Field, move to a new location in a table** | AC 58 | Display the table in Design view, click the field's row selector, drag the field with the pointer |
| **Filter By Form, activate** | AC 269 | Click ▦ |
| **Filter By Form, using** | AC 269 | *See* Reference Window: Selecting Records Using Filter By Form |
| **Filter By Selection, activate** | AC 100 | *See* Reference Window: Using Filter By Selection |
| **Filter, save as a query** | AC 271 | *See* Reference Window: Saving a Filter as a Query |
| **Filter, saved as a query, apply** | AC 272 | *See* Reference Window: Applying a Filter Saved as a Query |
| **Find duplicates query, create** | AC 203 | *See* Reference Window: Using the Find Duplicates Query Wizard |
| **Find unmatched query, create** | AC 205 | *See* Reference Window: Using the Find Unmatched Query Wizard |
| **Form Footer, add** | AC 240 | *See* Reference Window: Adding and Removing Form Header and Form Footer Sections |

| TASK | PAGE # | RECOMMENDED METHOD |
|---|---|---|
| **Form Footer, remove** | AC 240 | *See* Reference Window: Adding and Removing Form Header and Form Footer Sections |
| **Form Header, add** | AC 240 | *See* Reference Window: Adding and Removing Form Header and Form Footer Sections |
| **Form Header, remove** | AC 240 | *See* Reference Window: Adding and Removing Form Header and Form Footer Sections |
| **Form Wizard, activate** | AC 130 | Click Forms in the Objects bar, click New, click Form Wizard, choose the table or query for the form, click OK |
| **Form, create a custom** | AC 229 | *See* Reference Window: Creating a Form in Design View |
| **Freeze columns** | AC 176 | Select a column or adjacent columns, click Format, click Freeze Columns |
| **Function, create** | AC 566 | Enter function statements in the Code window |
| **Group totals, calculating in a report** | AC 295 | *See* Reference Window: Calculating Totals in a Report |
| **Hot key, create** | AC 524 | Type an ampersand (&) to the left of the hot key letter in the object's name |
| **HTML document, export an Access object as** | AC 371 | *See* Reference Window: Exporting an Access Object to an HTML Document |
| **HTML document, view** | AC 373 | *See* Reference Window: Viewing an HTML Document in a Web Browser |
| **Hyperlink field value, enter** | AC 424 | *See* Reference Window: Entering a Hyperlink Field Value in a Table |
| **Hyperlink field, create** | AC 423 | *See* Reference Window: Creating a Hyperlink Field in a Table |
| **Hyperlink, use** | AC 427 | Click the hyperlink field value |
| **Index, create** | AC 468 | *See* Reference Window: Creating an Index |
| **Indexes, view a table's existing** | AC 466 | *See* Reference Window: Viewing a Table's Existing Indexes |
| **Input Mask Wizard, activate** | AC 180 | Click the field's Input Mask text box, click ⬚, specify your choices in the Input Mask Wizard dialog boxes1 |
| **Label, add to a form or report** | AC 242 | *See* Reference Window: Adding a Label to a Form |
| **Line, add to a form or report** | AC 320 | *See* Reference Window: Adding a Line to a Form or Report |
| **Linked Table Manager, use** | AC 604 | *See* Reference Window: Using the Linked Table Manager |
| **List box, add to a form** | AC 515 | *See* Reference Window: Adding a List Box to a Form |
| **Lookup feature, remove a field's** | AC 224 | Select the field in Table Design view, click the Lookup tab, set the Display Control property to Text Box |
| **Lookup field, create** | AC 173 | Click the Data Type list arrow, click Lookup Wizard, specify your choices in the Lookup Wizard dialog boxes |
| **Macro group, create** | AC 529 | *See* Reference Window: Creating a Macro Group |
| **Macro, add to a macro group** | AC 510 | *See* Reference Window: Adding a Macro to a Macro Group |
| **Macro, attach to a command button** | AC 512 | Open the property sheet for the command button, click the right edge of the event property text box, click the macro name |
| **Macro, create** | AC 499 | *See* Reference Window: Creating a Macro |
| **Macro, run from the Database window** | AC 494 | Click Macros in the Objects bar, right-click the macro name, click Run; or click Tools, point to Run Macro, click the macro name from the list, click OK |
| **Macro, run from the Macro window** | AC 498 | Click ⬚ on the Macro Design toolbar |
| **Macro, single step** | AC 498 | *See* Reference Window: Single Stepping a Macro |
| **Mailing labels, create** | AC 345 | *See* Reference Window: Creating Mailing Labels and Other Labels |
| **Make-table query, create** | AC 445 | *See* Reference Window: Creating a Make-Table Query |
| **MDE file, save a database as** | AC 632 | Close the Access 2002 file-formatted database, click Tools, point to Database Utilities, click Make MDE File, select the database, click Make MDE |
| **Module, create** | AC 564 | *See* Reference Window: Creating a New Standard Module |
| **Module, save** | AC 568 | Click ⬚ on the VBA Standard toolbar, enter the module name, press Enter |

| TASK | PAGE # | RECOMMENDED METHOD |
|------|--------|--------------------|
| **Multiple-column report, modify** | AC 349 | In Design view, click File, click Page Setup, click Columns, set multiple-column options |
| **Object Dependencies task pane, open** | AC 183 | Right-click an object name, click Object Dependencies |
| **Object, export as an Excel worksheet** | AC 420 | *See* Reference Window: Exporting an Access Object to an Excel Worksheet |
| **Object, open** | AC 10 | Click the object's type in the Objects bar, click the object's name, click Open |
| **Object, save** | AC 12 | Click 🖫, type the object name, click OK |
| **Overall totals, calculating in a report** | AC 295 | *See* Reference Window: Calculating Totals in a Report |
| **Page numbers, add to a report** | AC 334 | *See* Reference Window: Adding Page Numbers to a Report |
| **Parameter query, create** | AC 195 | *See* Reference Window: Creating a Parameter Query |
| **Password, set a database** | AC 621 | *See* Reference Window: Setting a Database Password |
| **Password, unset a database** | AC 623 | *See* Reference Window: Unsetting a Database Password |
| **Performance Analyzer, use** | AC 600 | *See* Reference Window: Using the Performance Analyzer |
| **Picture, add to a form** | AC 244 | *See* Reference Window: Adding a Picture to a Form |
| **Picture, change on a command button** | AC 512 | Open the property sheet for the command button, click the Picture text box, click ⋯, select the picture, click OK |
| **Picture, insert in a report** | AC 158 | In Design view, select the report section in which to insert the picture, click Insert, click Picture, select the picture file, click OK |
| **PivotChart, add to data access page** | AC 406 | *See* Reference Window: Adding a PivotChart to a Data Access Page |
| **PivotTable, add a total field** | AC 402 | Click a detail field's column heading, right-click it a second time, point to AutoCalc, click an aggregate option |
| **PivotTable, add to data access page** | AC 394 | *See* Reference Window: Adding a PivotTable to a Data Access Page |
| **Primary key, specify** | AC 51 | *See* Reference Window: Specifying a Primary Key for a Table |
| **Procedure, test in the Immediate Window** | AC 568 | *See* Reference Window: Testing a Procedure in the Immediate Window |
| **Property sheet, open** | AC 116 | Right-click the object or control, click Properties |
| **Query results, sort** | AC 97 | *See* Reference Window: Sorting a Query Datasheet |
| **Query, define** | AC 82 | Click Queries in the Objects bar, click New, click Design View, click OK |
| **Query, run** | AC 86 | Click ❗ |
| **Record, add a new one** | AC 63 | Click ▶* |
| **Record, delete** | AC 69 | *See* Reference Window: Deleting a Record |
| **Record, move to a specific one** | AC 11 | Type the record number in the record number box, press Enter |
| **Record, move to first** | AC 12 | Click ⏮ |
| **Record, move to last** | AC 12 | Click ⏭ |
| **Record, move to next** | AC 12 | Click ▶ |
| **Record, move to previous** | AC 12 | Click ◀ |
| **Records, print selected in a form** | AC 141 | Click File, click Print, click Selected Record(s), click OK |
| **Records, redisplay all after filter** | AC 101 | Click ▽ |
| **Redo command, use to redo multiple operations in a database object** | AC 110 | Click the list arrow for ↻, click the action(s) to redo |
| **Relationship, define between database tables** | AC 90 | Click 🖼 |
| **Relationships window, print** | AC 226 | Click File, click Print Relationships, click 🖨 |
| **Replica and Design Master, synchronize** | AC 611 | *See* Reference Window: Synchronizing the Design Master and a Replica |
| **Replica, create** | AC 608 | *See* Reference Window: Creating a Replica of a Database |
| **Report Footer, add** | AC 328 | *See* Reference Window: Adding and Removing Report Header and Report Footer Sections |
| **Report Footer, remove** | AC 328 | *See* Reference Window: Adding and Removing Report Header and Report Footer Sections |

| TASK | PAGE # | RECOMMENDED METHOD |
|---|---|---|
| **Report Header, add** | AC 328 | *See* Reference Window: Adding and Removing Report Header and Report Footer Sections |
| **Report Header, remove** | AC 328 | *See* Reference Window: Adding and Removing Report Header and Report Footer Sections |
| **Report Wizard, activate** | AC 148 | Click Reports in the Objects bar, click New, click Report Wizard, choose the table or query for the report, click OK |
| **Report, check errors in Design view** | AC 155 | Click the list arrow for ⬦, choose to correct or ignore errors |
| **Report, create a custom** | AC 306 | *See* Reference Window: Creating a Report in Design View |
| **Report, print specific pages of** | AC 23 | Click File, click Print, click Pages, enter number of pages to print in the From and To boxes, click OK |
| **Self-join, create** | AC 476 | *See* Reference Window: Creating a Self-Join |
| **Sort, specify ascending in datasheet** | AC 96 | Click ⬥ |
| **Sort, specify descending in datasheet** | AC 96 | Click ⬥ |
| **SQL statement, use for a list box** | AC 521 | Open the property sheet for the list box, right-click the Row Source text box, click Zoom, enter the SQL statement, click OK |
| **SQL statement, view** | AC 518 | *See* Reference Window: Viewing an SQL Statement for a Query |
| **Subdatasheet, display related records** | AC 178 | Click ⊞ |
| **Subdatasheet, hide related records** | AC 179 | Click ⊟ |
| **Subform/Subreport Wizard, activate** | AC 256 | Make sure ⬥ is selected, click 🔲, click in the grid at the upper-left corner for the subform/subreport |
| **Subreport, open in a new window** | AC 317 | Right-click the subreport, click Subreport in New Window |
| **Switchboard Manager, activate** | AC 533 | Click Tools, point to Database Utilities, click Switchboard Manager |
| **Tab Control, add to a form** | AC 247 | Click ⬚, click in the grid at the upper-left corner for the tab control |
| **Tab order, change in a form** | AC 265 | Click View in Design view, click Tab Order, change the control tab order |
| **Table structure, save in a database** | AC 52 | *See* Reference Window: Saving a Table Structure |
| **Table, create in a database** | AC 42 | Click Tables in the Objects bar, click New, click Design View, click OK |
| **Table, import from another Access database** | AC 67 | Click File, point to Get External Data, click Import, select the folder, click Import, select the table, click OK |
| **Table, link in another Access database** | AC 604 | *See* Reference Window: Linking to a Table in Another Access Database |
| **Table, open in a database** | AC 10 | Click Tables in the Objects bar, click the table name, click Open |
| **Template, use an HTML** | AC 372 | Click the Save formatted check box in the Export dialog box, click Export, select template, click OK |
| **Title, add to a form or report** | AC 242 | Click **Aa**, click in the grid at the upper-left corner for the title, type the title, click anywhere outside the label box |
| **Top values query, create** | AC 207 | *See* Reference Window: Creating a Top Values Query |
| **Totals, calculating in a report** | AC 295 | *See* Reference Window: Calculating Totals in a Report |
| **Undo command, use to undo multiple operations in a database object** | AC 110 | Click the list arrow for ↺, click the action(s) to undo |
| **Update query, create** | AC 453 | *See* Reference Window: Creating an Update Query |
| **User-Level Security Wizard, use** | AC 625 | Click Tools, point to Security, click User-Level Security Wizard, complete the entries in the dialog boxes |
| **Validation Rule property, set** | AC 185 | Display the table in Design view, select the field or click 🗗, enter the rule in the Validation Rule text box |
| **Validation Text property, set** | AC 187 | Display the table in Design view, select the field or click 🗗, enter the text in the Validation Text text box |
| **XML file, export an Access object to an** | AC 417 | *See* Reference Window: Exporting an Access Object as an XML File |
| **XML file, import as a table** | AC 414 | *See* Reference Window: Importing an XML File as an Access Table |

# Microsoft Office Specialist Certification Grid

| Standardized Coding Number | Certification Skill Activity | Courseware Requirements | Tutorial: Pages |
|---|---|---|---|
| **AC03S-1** | **Structuring Databases** | | |
| AC03S-1-1 | Create Access databases | Creating databases using Database Wizard | Tutorial 2: 41 |
| | | Creating blank databases | Tutorial 2: 41 |
| AC03S-1-2 | Create and modify tables | Creating tables using Table Wizard | Tutorial 2: 42 |
| | | Modifying table properties or structure | Tutorial 2: 43–52, 56–60 |
| AC03S-1-3 | Define and modify field types | Creating Lookup fields | Tutorial 2: 39<br>Tutorial 5: 172–177 |
| | | Changing field types | Tutorial 2: 38–39<br>Tutorial 5: 172 |
| AC03S-1-4 | Modify field properties | Changing field properties to display input masks | Tutorial 5: 179–182 |
| | | Modifying field properties for tables in Table Design view | Tutorial 2: 43–52, 60–62<br>Tutorial 5: 180–182, 185–187 |
| AC03S-1-5 | Create and modify one-to-many relationships | Creating and modifying one-to-many relationship | Tutorial 3: 87–93 |
| AC03S-1-6 | Enforce referential integrity | Enforcing referential integrity in a one-to-many relationship | Tutorial 3: 93 |
| AC03S-1-7 | Create and modify queries | Creating and modifying Select queries using the Simple Query Wizard | Tutorial 1: 15–17<br>Tutorial 3: 103–104 |
| | | Creating and modifying Crosstab, unmatched and duplicates queries | Tutorial 5: 198–206 |
| AC03S-1-8 | Create forms | Creating forms using the Form Wizard | Tutorial 1: 18–19<br>Tutorial 4: 130–132 |
| | | Creating auto forms | Tutorial 1: 18–19<br>Tutorial 4: 133–134 |
| AC03S-1-9 | Add and modify form controls and properties | Modifying form properties | Tutorial 4: 145–146<br>Tutorial 6: 245–246 |
| | | Modifying specific form controls (e.g., text boxes, labels, bound controls) | Tutorial 4: 145<br>Tutorial 6: 235, 238, 243 |
| AC03S-1-10 | Create reports | Creating reports | Tutorial 1: 20–22<br>Tutorial 4: 147–151<br>Tutorial 7: 288–291, 306–312 |
| AC03S-1-11 | Add and modify report control properties | Adding calculated controls to a report section | Tutorial 7: 295–296, 322–323 |
| AC03S-1-12 | Create a data access page | Creating data access pages using the Page Wizard | Tutorial 8: 376–377 |
| **AC03S-2** | **Entering Data** | | |
| AC03S-2-1 | Enter, edit and delete records | Entering records into a datasheet | Tutorial 2: 63 |
| AC03S-2-2 | Find and move among records | Using navigation controls to move among records | Tutorial 2: 70<br>Tutorial 6: 237, 259 |
| AC03S-2-3 | Import data to Access | Importing structured data into tables | Tutorial 2: 65–68<br>Tutorial 8: 414–416 |

# Microsoft Office Specialist Certification Grid

| Standardized Coding Number | Certification Skill Activity | Courseware Requirements | Tutorial: Pages |
|---|---|---|---|
| **AC03S-3** | **Organizing Data** | | |
| AC03S-3-1 | Create and modify calculated fields and aggregate functions | Adding calculated fields to queries in Query Design view | Tutorial 3: 113–120<br>Tutorial 5: 208 |
| | | Using aggregate functions in queries (e.g., AVG, COUNT) | Tutorial 3: 117–118<br>Tutorial 5: 198–202 |
| AC03S-3-2 | Modify form layout | Aligning and spacing controls | Tutorial 6: 238–239 |
| | | Showing and hiding headers and footers | Tutorial 6: 240–241 |
| AC03S-3-3 | Modify report layout and page setup | Aligning, resizing and spacing controls | Tutorial 4: 154–157 |
| | | Changing margins and page orientation | Tutorial 4: 151 |
| AC03S-3-4 | Format datasheets | Formatting a table or query for display | Tutorial 2: 64<br>Tutorial 5: 176 |
| AC03S-3-5 | Sort records | Sorting records in tables, queries, forms and reports | Tutorial 3: 95–100<br>Tutorial 7: 307–309<br>Tutorial 8: 376, 380 |
| AC03S-3-6 | Filter records | Filtering datasheets by form | Tutorial 3: 100<br>Tutorial 6: 266–271 |
| | | Filtering datasheets by selection | Tutorial 3: 100–101<br>Tutorial 6: 266–267 |
| **AC03S-4** | **Managing Databases** | | |
| AC03S-4-1 | Identify object dependencies | Identifying object dependencies | Tutorial 5: 183–184 |
| AC03S-4-2 | View objects and object data in other views | Previewing for print | Tutorial 1: 22<br>Tutorial 6: 226 |
| | | Using datasheet, PivotChart, Web page and layout view | Tutorial 4: 131, 143<br>Tutorial 8: 404–413 |
| AC03S-4-3 | Print database objects and data | Printing database objects and data | Tutorial 6: 225–228 |
| AC03S-4-4 | Export data from Access | Exporting data from Access (e.g., Excel) | Tutorial 8: 417–422 |
| AC03S-4-5 | Back up a database | Backing up a database | Tutorial 1: 24–25 |
| AC03S-4-6 | Compact and repair databases | Using Compact and Repair | Tutorial 1: 26–27 |